EUROPE, 1555-1848

EUROPE, 1555-1848

EDITORS:
Theo van Wijk   M.C. van Zyl

CONTRIBUTORS:
*M.S. Appelgryn   M. Boucher   P.G. Eidelberg   A.J. Fick   Andrew Harington
J.W. Kew   S.F. Malan   Fransjohan Pretorius   L.E. van Niekerk*

ACADEMICA
Pretoria   Cape Town

Cover illustration: Napoleon crossing the Alps. Painting by David.

First edition 1985
Second, illustrated edition 1986

The series, *History of Europe,* general editor: Theo van Wijk, consists of the following:
Theo van Wijk and S. B. Spies (eds): *Western Europe from the decline of Rome to the Reformation*
Theo van Wijk and M. C. van Zyl (eds): *Europe, 1555-1848*
Theo van Wijk and Maurice Boucher (eds): *Europe, 1848-1980*

Copyright © in text 1985 by the respective authors
Published by Academica,
a division of Human & Rousseau (Pty) Ltd
Atrium Building, 60 Glenwood Road, Pretoria
State House, 3-9 Rose Street, Cape Town
Cover Design by Sharon Bock
Typeset in 10 on 11 pt Times Roman and
printed by National Book Printers, Goodwood

ISBN 0 86874 277 5

No part of this book may be reproduced or
transmitted in any form or by any means,
electronic or mechanical, or by photocopying,
recording or microfilming, or stored in any retrieval
system, without the written permission of the publisher

FOREWORD

Europe, 1555-1848 is intended to serve as a text-book for students at South African universities and colleges. It is hoped that it will also appeal to anyone interested in knowing more about the history of Europe. For a clear image of our own past and of the complex present a study of European history is indeed essential. It is true, of course, that we are not all of European descent, but western civilization has had such an important influence on all the inhabitants of southern Africa and is still of such significance that it cannot be lightly ignored.

The years 1555-1848, which may be regarded as the transitional period between the Middle Ages and modern times, span almost three eventful centuries. So much occurred in this period that it is clearly impossible to cover it all in one volume. This book therefore does not lay claim to completeness. We did attempt to see the years concerned in their totality, but we do realize that this, too, was not entirely possible. This book should therefore be regarded rather as a series of chapters selected from the general history of Europe. It should also be taken into account that this book is the result of the labours of nine authors. Although there was close co-operation between editors and authors and amongst the authors themselves, there was no attempt to enforce uniformity, particularly in regard to content and approach – each contributor is individually responsible for his chapter. Chapters 2, 6, 7 (pp. 218-231), 9, 10, 11 and 12 are translations from the original Afrikaans texts.

This work is a team effort by a number of lecturers in the Department of History of the University of South Africa. One of them, Professor A. J. Fick, has subsequently left and is currently at the Vista University. We also enjoyed the competent assistance of three willing ladies, Joey Willemse, Tinkie Theron and Lorraine Schönfeldt, who typed several of the chapters. Finally, we could at all times rely on the years of experience and wide knowledge of a former colleague, Professor Theo van Wijk, who acted as general editor. Professor van Wijk is now Principal of Unisa. My cordial thanks and appreciation go to all those who collaborated in this venture.

M.C. van Zyl
Pretoria
1984

CONTENTS

LIST OF MAPS (xi)

J.W. Kew
1. THE THIRTY YEARS WAR: PRELUDE AND COURSE, 1555-1648   1
   - Background to the war   1
   - Prelude to war   9
   - The Bohemian revolt   11
   - The Bohemian War and the conquest of the Palatinate, 1618-1623   13
   - The Danish War, 1625-1629   17
   - The climax of imperial power, 1629   20
   - The Swedish War, 1630-1635   23
   - The Franco/Swedish-Austrian/Spanish conflict, 1635-1648   28
   - The Peace of Westphalia   35

S.F. Malan
2. SPAIN: RISE AND DECLINE, 1556-1713   39
   - Founding of the Spanish empire   39
   - The Spanish golden era   42
   - The decline of Spain   53

M. Boucher
3. FRANCE: TURMOIL AND ASCENDANCY, 1556-1715   62
   - Civil and religious anarchy, 1556-1589   62
   - Henry IV and religious compromise, 1589-1610   72
   - The establishment of royal authority, 1610-1642   75
   - The era of Mazarin, 1642-1661   80
   - Louis XIV and Colbert, 1661-1683   83
   - The revocation of the Edict of Nantes, 1685   86
   - Louis XIV's foreign policy up to 1697   88
   - The War of the Spanish Succession, 1701-1714   92

Andrew Harington
4. THE BRITISH ISLES: CONFLICT AND CHANGE, 1558-1714   97
   - The Elizabethan Settlement, 1558-1603   97
   - James I, 1603-1625: prelude to revolution   107
   - Charles I, 1625-1649, and civil war   112
   - Cromwell and the English republic, 1649-1660   126
   - Charles II, 1660-1685, and the triumph of the Anglicans   127
   - James II, 1685-1688, and the "Glorious Revolution"   130
   - William, Mary and Anne, 1689-1714: a crowned republic   133

L.E. van Niekerk
5. THE NORTHERN ALLIANCES, 1648-1721 — 140
The emergence of the Swedish empire, Brandenburg-Prussia and Russia — 140
The Great Northern War: the first phase, 1700-1715 — 154
The Great Northern War: the second phase, 1715-1721 — 166

A.J. Fick
6. THE ECONOMIC, SOCIAL AND INTELLECTUAL STRUCTURE OF EUROPE IN THE 17th CENTURY — 173
Introduction — 173
Population — 175
Capitalism — 177
Mercantilism — 180
The trading companies — 184
Agriculture and industry — 186
Expansion of trade and commericial competition — 189
The social structure — 195
Science and thought — 203
The influence of the scientific movement — 214

A.J. Fick and M. Boucher
7. EUROPE: BALANCE OF POWER AND COLONIAL EXPANSION — 218
The idea of a balance of power — 218
Influence of the expansion of Europe — 220
Balance of power after the Peace of Utrecht: a peaceful era — 221
The War of the Polish Succession — 226
The War of the Austrian Succession and the struggle for trade and colonies — 228
Europe after Aix-la-Chapelle — 231
Colonial rivalry — 234
The Diplomatic Revolution and the Seven Years War — 236
Colonial problems and American independence — 244
Europe after 1763 — 247

P.G. Eidelberg
8. THE FIRST INDUSTRIAL REVOLUTION: IRON AND COAL — 253
The steam engine — 253
Iron and coal — 258
The heritage of the countryside: convertible husbandry and enclosure — 261
Wool and cotton — 269
Population and standard of living — 272
On the eve of the railway age: Britain in 1830 — 276
The steam engine railway — 278
Britain and France — 282
Conclusion — 289

A.J. Fick
9. ENLIGHTENMENT AND ENLIGHTENED DESPOTS IN THE 18th CENTURY — 290
- The origins of the Enlightenment — 290
- The early Enlightenment — 294
- France — 297
- The mature Enlightenment — 302
- Influence of the *philosophes* — 310
- Enlightened despotism — 313
- Frederick II — 319
- Joseph II — 323
- Catherine II — 327

Fransjohan Pretorius
10. THE FRENCH REVOLUTION — 331
- The *ancien régime* in France — 331
- The reform movement under the *ancien régime* — 337
- The National Assembly, 1789-1791 — 348
- The failure of the constitutional monarchy, 1791-1792 — 355
- The Convention, 1792-1795 — 359
- The Directory, 1795-1799 — 365

Fransjohan Pretorius
11. NAPOLEON BONAPARTE — 372
- The Constitution of 1799 and the war against the Second Coalition — 372
- The reconstruction of France and the extension of Napoleon's power, 1799-1815 — 375
- The reorganization of Europe, 1803-1807 — 386
- Reaction and the fall of Napoleon, 1807-1815 — 394

M.S. Appelgryn
12. REVOLUTION AND COUNTER-REVOLUTION, 1815-1848 — 406
- Introduction — 406
- The Treaty of Paris and the Congress of Vienna — 408
- The congress system — 411
- The restoration of the Bourbon monarchy in France, 1815-1830 — 414
- The July Monarchy in France, 1830-1848 — 417
- The German states, 1815-1848 — 419
- Austro-Hungary, 1815-1848 — 421
- The Italian states, 1815-1848 — 423
- Great Britain, 1815-1848 — 426
- The failure and the meaning of the revolutions of 1848 — 428

NOTES AND SUGGESTIONS FOR SUPPLEMENTARY READING 430

INDEX 441

MAPS

1. Spanish lines of communication: Milan to Brussels — 3
2. Sweden and the Baltic up to 1660 — 6
3. Europe after the Peace of Westphalia, 1648 — 33
4. Spain and Portugal in 1555 — 40
5. Europe in 1581 — 46
6. France in 1630, with later territorial gains — 76
7. The territories of Brandenburg-Prussia, 1660 — 142
8. The Swedish empire — 147
9. The Great Northern War, 1700-1721 — 159
10. Central Europe in the Seven Years War — 239
11. India in the 18th century — 241
12. North America and the Seven Years War — 242
13. Europe in 1810 at the height of the Napoleonic empire — 396
14. Europe in 1815 — 407

CHAPTER 1

THE THIRTY YEARS WAR: PRELUDE AND COURSE, 1555-1648

The first half of the 17th century in Europe was an eventful period marked by successive armed conflicts, revolts against established authority, the assassination of one monarch and the execution of another. The idea of a "Europe in crisis", as this period has been aptly characterized by numerous historians,[1] is strengthened by evidence of economic decline, demographic contraction and social instability. Yet historians favouring the crisis thesis have failed to reach agreement on the exact causes, nature, consequences or span of these phenomena. They have, however, raised serious reservations regarding the historical justifiability of demarcating the series of wars from the Bohemian revolt in 1618 to the Peace of Westphalia in 1648 as a distinct historical event under the title of "The Thirty Years War". It has been pointed out that for Spain and the Netherlands, for instance, the period from 1618 to 1648 represents only part of their Eighty Years War, while for France the struggle with Spain continued for a further eleven years after the Peace of Westphalia.

S. H. Steinberg ridicules the term "Thirty Years War" as a "figment of retrospective imagination", yet admits that its undeniable convenience will probably defy all attempts to eradicate it as a means of identifying the series of conflicts in the early 17th century.[2] Historians continue to use the term, yet with greater circumspection. Moreover, whether the Thirty Years War is treated as part of a general European crisis or as a distinct topic of study, the events traditionally associated with it can only be understood in the light of problems which germinated during the latter half of the 16th century within the confines of the Holy Roman empire, the unresolved nature of western and northern European interstate relations at the beginning of the 17th century, and the fact that events in Germany and the aspirations and rivalries of the leading European states were inextricably interwoven on religious, political, economic and dynastic levels.

BACKGROUND TO THE WAR

Superficially, the 17th century began on a promising note for a general European peace. Certain of the rulers of the time, James I of England and the Archduke Albert in the southern Netherlands, for instance, were men of peace, while others such as Philip III of Spain and Henry IV of France accepted peace negotiations as a matter of practical necessity. Consequently, in 1598 the war between France and

Spain was brought to an end by the Peace of Vervins, and that between England and Spain in 1604. In 1606 a truce was negotiated between the empire and the Osmanli Turks, while a twelve year truce between Spain and the United Provinces (the northern Netherlands) was signed in 1609. Despite the fact that peace treaties were signed and truces negotiated, however, the major underlying rivalries in European international affairs were left unresolved.

In western Europe the most important and the oldest feud was that between France and the Habsburg powers of Spain and Austria. Despite internal problems in both the Austrian and the Spanish territories, the loss of the Spanish Armada, and Spain's inability to crush the revolt in the United Netherlands, the Habsburg dynasty was still the greatest power in Europe at the beginning of the 17th century. The Austrian Habsburgs occupied the German imperial throne, owned the territories of Austria, Tyrol, Styria, Carinthia and Carniola and had subsequently added to their possessions a quasi-hereditary title to the thrones of Bohemia and Hungary. The Spanish Habsburgs reigned over a vast empire in the New World, while in Europe their possessions included Portugal, the kingdoms of Naples, Sicily and Sardinia, the duchy of Milan in northern Italy, Franche-Comté in the Rhineland and the southern Netherlands. Spain's European possessions, together with those of her Austrian Habsburg cousins in Germany, virtually encircled France.

Threatened on all her landward borders by Spanish armies from as far back as the late 15th century, successive French kings had been compelled to engage in periodic defensive wars to avoid Habsburg strangulation of their state. From 1562 to 1596 France was racked by a series of political and religious civil wars during which the monarchy could barely counter direct Spanish involvement in their internal affairs. France was in danger of becoming a mere Habsburg satellite, but in 1596 the situation changed dramatically. Out of the chaos of the civil wars there arose a new French dynasty – the house of Bourbon. Henry IV, the first Bourbon king of France, resolved the immediate political and religious problems and consolidated monarchical authority.

The revival of France under the new Bourbon dynasty was of great importance. Despite the Peace of Vervins and a brief period of pro-Spanish sentiment under the weak regency government of Maria de Medici, Henry IV and, from 1624, Cardinal Richelieu were able to launch an active anti-Habsburg policy that enabled France to intervene in the affairs of Europe whenever French interests were believed to be at stake, to exploit local disturbances in the states bordering France in order to reduce the threat of Habsburg encirclement, and eventually to challenge the Habsburg dynasty for the hegemony of Europe.

French involvement in local disputes along her borders brought about a conjuncture between the Bourbon-Habsburg conflict and Spain's attempt to suppress the revolt in the United Provinces. The twelve year truce of 1609 was considered by neither the Spanish nor the Dutch as a prelude to peace, but as an opportunity to strengthen their respective positions before the resumption of hostilities in 1621. For Spain this meant securing her lines of communication, along which men, materials and money could be safely transmitted to the theatre of war. From the late

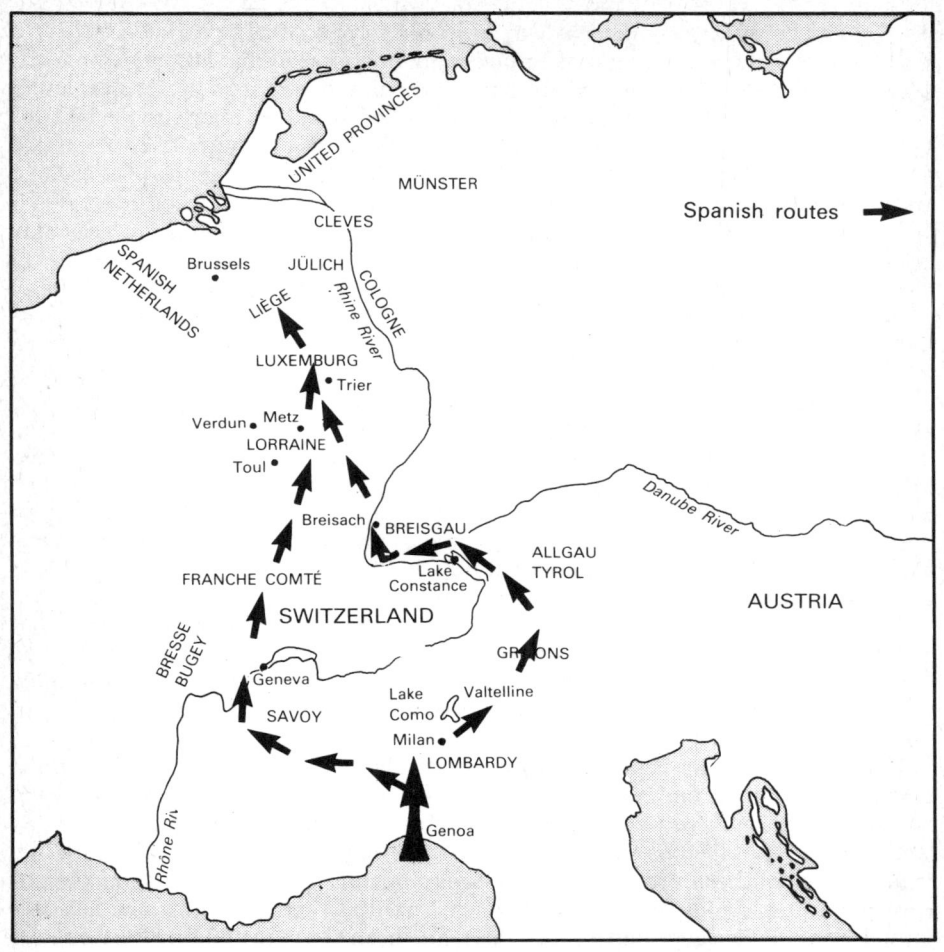

Spanish lines of communication: Milan to Brussels

16th century the direct route from Spain, via the English Channel, to the southern (or Spanish) Netherlands was virtually inoperative during wartime owing to the growth of English and Dutch sea power. Spain was compelled to rely increasingly on alternative land-routes from Spanish-owned Milan in northern Italy. There were two major land-routes from Milan to Brussels: the one via Savoy and Franche-Comté, and the other through the Valtelline pass, Austrian Tyrol and Alsace in southern Germany. The Savoyard route (the so-called "Spanish Road") was subject to the vacillating policy of the duke of Savoy and, from the early 17th century, threatened by French expansion into the district west of the river Rhône. The Valtelline (or Rhineland route) consequently became the "essential pivot" of the Spanish empire; to protect it was a primary concern of Spanish policy – to enforce its closure, a major aim of France, and, of course, of the Dutch. Moreover, a reunited France under a powerful Bourbon monarchy provided local rulers along the length of the route, especially the Grisons in the Valtelline valley and the bishops and princes along the Rhine in southern Germany, with an alternative to Spanish power. Local difficulties in the Valtelline and the Rhineland tended to become microcosms of the greater Bourbon-Habsburg and Spanish-Dutch conflict, involving the three major powers of Spain, France and the United Provinces increasingly in German and northern Italian political and religious disagreements.

Interstate relations in northern Europe and the Baltic countries were equally volatile and were also linked, directly or indirectly, to events and circumstances within the Holy Roman empire. For centuries Baltic trade and shipping had been dominated by the Hansa towns of northern Europe, but by the turn of the 16th century the Hanseatic League was virtually moribund. Its progressive decline had allowed the Dutch and English to substantially increase their trade and shipping in the Baltic. The Baltic region provided western Europe with essential commodities – fish, salt, German linen, copper, iron, Polish and east German grain and naval materials such as timber, hemp and tar. The importance of these goods and the growing volume of trade at the beginning of the 17th century was of considerable economic value for the states bordering the Baltic. It also constituted a major cause of conflict, the principal issue of which centred around the political and economic control of the Baltic. The United Kingdom of Denmark-Norway, Sweden, Poland and Russia were all involved in the struggle in the Baltic, while the United Provinces tried to prevent any one of these states from gaining complete supremacy – a situation which could adversely affect Dutch trade and shipping in the region.

The major rivalry in the Baltic, however, was that between the two Scandinavian kingdoms, Denmark and Sweden. Denmark had long been the most powerful of the two, originally occupying the whole of Scandinavia. In the 1520s Sweden gained its independence, but Denmark still maintained a strong position in the western Baltic, retained the southern provinces of the Scandinavian peninsula and a number of strategic Baltic islands, by means of which it virtually encircled the new Swedish state. Denmark also acquired a foothold in northern Germany and a direct interest in imperial affairs by virtue of its monarch's position as duke of Holstein. In addition, control of the Sound (the major navigable strait between the Baltic and the North Sea) provided the Danish crown with a substantial source of income from dues imposed on passing ships, and also enabled Denmark to inhibit Swedish trade with the North Sea and western Europe. The conflict between Denmark and Sweden revolved around political and economic considerations; religion played no role, as both the Scandinavian kingdoms had adopted Lutheranism early in the 16th century. Since its independence Sweden was constantly threatened by Danish attempts to restore their sovereignty. To secure her position against Denmark, and to benefit from the revived Baltic trade, Sweden embarked on a policy of expansion around the Gulf of Finland and in the eastern Baltic – a move which brought her into conflict with Russia and Poland.

The conflict with Russia centred around the eastern Baltic provinces, from Swedish Finland in the north to Polish Livonia in the south. By 1582 Sweden had acquired Estonia, bordering on Livonia, and in 1617 (by the Peace of Stolbova) Sweden forced Russia to cede to her the provinces of Karelia and Ingria, linking Swedish Finland and Estonia. This gave Sweden control of the Gulf of Finland and barred Russia from access to the Baltic – a situation that was to remain unchanged until the expansionist policy of Tsar Peter the Great at the beginning of the 18th century.

After the Peace of Stolbova Sweden could concentrate on her war with Poland for control of Livonia and of the Baltic ports and river estuaries from Riga to Danzig. The latter were particularly important, as they yielded a valuable source of income from tolls and customs duties. In 1629, after a protracted war, Sweden acquired from Poland temporary possession of Livonia, the ports of Riga, Memel and Pillau, and with them the river mouths of the Duna, the Niemen and the Pregel. The conflict with Poland, however, involved far more than economic considerations. Poland was Roman Catholic and its monarch, Sigismund III, a member of the Vasa royal house, had a hereditary right to the Swedish throne, a position which he had briefly occupied in the 1590s prior to being deposed by the Swedish nobility and the Lutheran clergy. Sigismund's claim to the throne constituted a recurring threat to Swedish Lutheranism and to the security of members of the Lutheran branch of the Vasa dynasty, who had acquired the throne after Sigismund's deposition. Moreover, as Sigismund was related by marriage to the house of Habsburg, an extension of imperial Catholic power into Protestant northern Germany would, by strengthening Catholic Poland, seriously threaten the economic, religious and dynastic security of Sweden. Similarly, Danish dominance in the western Baltic, their monarch's position as duke of Holstein and the occupation of secularized Catholic territory within the empire by members of his family would be jeopardized. Northern Germany, with its important Baltic ports, naval fortresses and river estuaries, increasingly became the pivot of Baltic rivalries, vital to the conflicting ambitions of Sweden, Denmark and Poland, and a direct link between Baltic politics and circumstances within the Holy Roman empire.

In the Baltic and in western Europe, as Wedgwood strikingly observes, "the arch of European politics rested on the keystone of Germany", and "the part that Germany played would be decisive".[3] – But what was the position in Germany?

Around the turn of the 16th century the prospect for continued peace within the Holy Roman empire of the German people (or Germany) was rapidly diminishing. The empire had, since the decline in power of the medieval Hohenstaufen emperors, become no more than a loose confederation of some 300 states, free imperial cities and imperial knights under the nominal authority of the emperor. The states were infinitely varied, being either secular or ecclesiastical, and ranging in size and importance, from a dozen or so principalities sufficiently powerful to play a low-key role in European politics, to the numerous petty estates and abbacies no more than a few acres in size. Each state, whether secular or ecclesiastical, and whatever its size or relative strength, had its own ruler. Many of these rulers aspired to increase their power and territory in relation to other rulers and, either individually or collec-

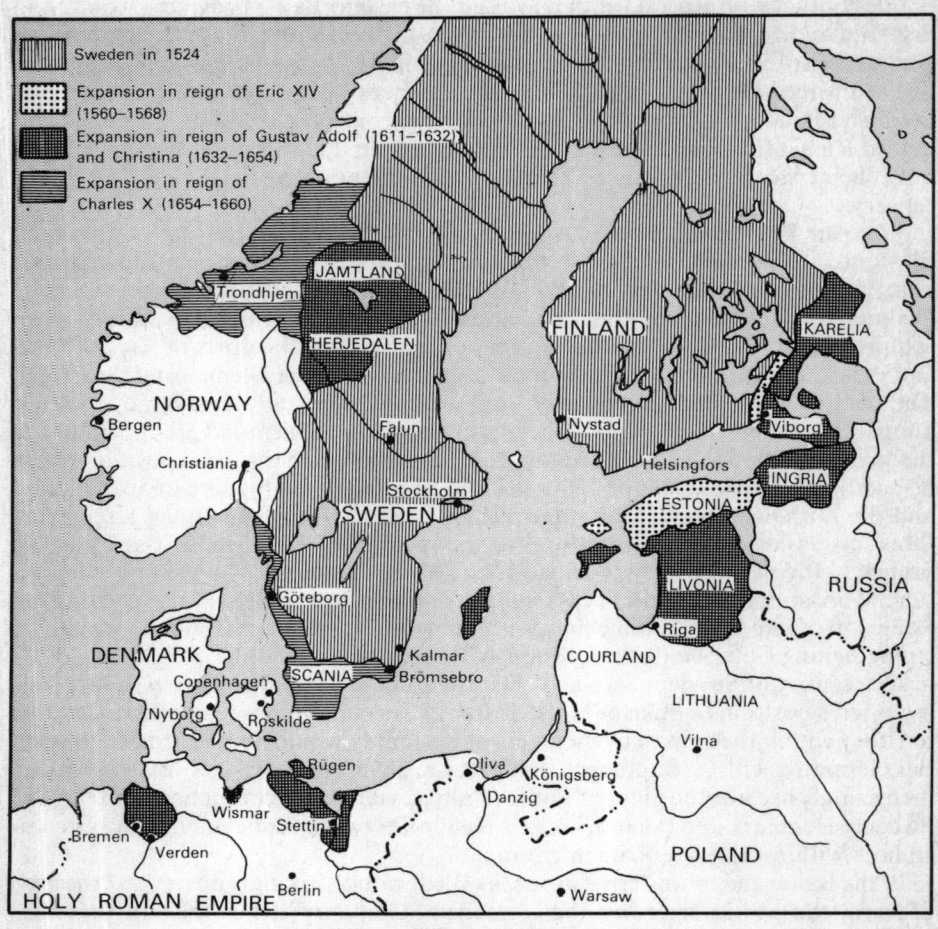

Sweden and the Baltic up to 1660

tively, to enhance their independence *vis-à-vis* the emperor by opposing all efforts to extend and centralize imperial power. The age-old antagonism between the separatist and independent ambitions of the German princes and the centralizing and absolutist designs of the emperors posed a serious threat to peace.

Since 1437 the emperor had been chosen, almost uninterruptedly, from the Austrian Habsburgs, a position that conferred on the house the prestige attached to the imperial throne and a theoretical claim, as feudal overlords, to authority over all other princes and rulers within the empire. In practice, however, the emperor could exercise his authority only by virtue of the strength of his personality or by utilizing the resources of his own territories. The house of Habsburg had acquired extensive patrimonial lands in southern Germany and, in addition, could often rely on the assistance of their Spanish cousins; attempts to impose their policies throughout the empire were, however, constantly obstructed. This was in no small measure due to the almost total ineffectiveness of the machinery of government within the empire.

The Imperial Diet, or the constitutional assembly of the empire, "was rarely able to arrive at, let alone enforce, major decisions, and was little more than a convention of independent princes".[4] Moreover, as the Diet did not function according to the procedure of majority decision-making, each prince had the right to obstruct any issue that he disliked. This defect, in the opinion of Wedgwood, "made the Diet as a legislative body for the whole Empire wholly useless".[5]

For administrative purposes, particularly with regard to fiscal and military matters, the empire had been divided into ten large territorial regions, or circles, each with its own president. The president, although nominally an official of the emperor, was always the most powerful local ruler and as such usually acted in his own, rather than in imperial, interests. The maintenance of peace and the practical efficacy of resolutions regarding taxation for the empire or the imposition of military requisitions for the imperial army depended on the goodwill of the presidents of the various circles and the support of individual rulers who had to carry out these tasks in their own territories. The division into circles was consequently not very effective: it failed to solve the organizational problems within the empire and further weakened the central power. Similarly, imperial justice, administered since 1486 by the Imperial Chamber, was ineffective unless its decisions were enforced by the rulers of each state.

The aim of the German princes to resist any further increase in the real power of the emperor was strengthened by the fact that succession to the imperial throne was not a hereditary right vested in the house of Habsburg, but was subject to an election by an Electoral College comprising seven electoral princes. Three of the electors were ecclesiastical princes – the archbishops of Mainz, Cologne and Trier; the remaining four were lay princes – the king of Bohemia, the duke of Saxony, the margrave of Brandenburg and the count palatine of the Rhine. While it had become customary to elect a Habsburg as emperor, it could never be taken for granted. The Electoral College, since acquiring legal status by the Golden Bull in 1356, had insisted on exercising their right to elect the emperor and demanded from each emperor-designate an "imperial capitulation" confirming the privileges and powers of the princes. The weaker the emperor-designate, the greater the demands made by the Electoral College. This was precisely the Habsburgs' problem during the latter 16th century and the early 17th century. Emperor Ferdinand I (1558-1564) divided the provinces over which the Habsburgs exercised direct control between three branches of the family, thereby reducing the private resources directly available to the emperor. Moreover, the three emperors Maximilian II (1564-1576), Rudolf II (1576-1611) and Matthias (1611-1619) were men of weak character and were therefore inept. Despite these problems, the dynasty never lost sight of its aim to dominate the princes, and this ambition would resurface should the Habsburg territories be reunited under a strong and capable leader.

While the German princes involved themselves in a conflict with the emperor in order to prevent imperial absolutism, they claimed to be absolute rulers in their own states. This claim brought each of the princes into conflict with the local Diets or representative estates. In fact, a revolt by the Bohemian estate against the absolutist designs of their monarch, who was incidentally also the emperor, is generally regarded as the occasion for the outbreak of the Thirty Years War. Political life in Germany became increasingly volatile as the two conflicts – the one between the emperor and the princes, and the other between the princes (including the emperor in his capacity as a German prince) and the representative estates within their territories – disrupted the fabric of German society.

At the end of the 16th century, political discord within the empire was further exacerbated by religious division. Prior to the 16th century Protestant Reformation a common faith, Roman Catholicism, had preserved a measure of imperial unity, but the rapid spread of Lutheranism in Germany during the first half of the 16th century added religious division to the existing political discord. In fact, religious and political discord became almost inseparable, as many German princes seized on Protestantism to enhance their independence from the emperor. After decades of largely inconclusive armed conflict between German Catholics, including the emperor, and Lutheran princes, the war-weary parties realized that a position of stalemate had been reached. As neither could dictate terms, they agreed in 1555 to a practical compromise known as the Peace of Augsburg.

The major clause of the Peace of Augsburg, based on the principle *"cuius regio, eius religio"* recognized the right of the ruler of each principality within the empire to enforce either Catholicism or Lutheranism in his own state. The Peace of Augsburg also recognized the secularization of church (Catholic) land that had taken place prior to 1552 – the year in which the Augsburg negotiations had commenced – but forbade all future secularization. Related to the issue of secularization was a clause known as the "ecclesiastical reservation". This clause had been added to the peace agreement on the exclusive authority of the emperor and was aimed at preventing a prince of the church, bishop or abbot from retaining the administration of his lands if he converted to Protestantism. In the event of such a conversion the church lands had to be handed over to a Catholic successor.

In the short term the Peace of Augsburg brought about a cessation of hostilities, but it failed to provide a permanent solution for religious dissension within the empire. After 1555 the Lutherans, exploiting the many ambiguities in the peace settlement, continued to extend their influence, especially in northern Germany. Within a decade after the Peace of Augsburg, however, Lutheranism gradually began to lose the initiative to Calvinism, a new revolutionary form of Protestantism. The spread of Calvinism posed a major threat to the peace settlement. Only the confessions of Catholicism and Lutheranism had been recognized by the Peace of Augsburg, and while the exclusion of Calvinism had seemed reasonable in 1555 as there were no Calvinist princes in the empire at that time, this was no longer the case by the turn of the century. Calvinism made rapid strides in Germany and was even adopted by some of the German princes, most notably by the elector palatine directly after the peace settlement, and by the elector of Brandenburg in 1613. Excluded from the protection of the Peace of Augsburg, Calvinism could extend its influence only by rejecting the terms of the "ecclesiastical reservation" and those of the peace settlement itself.

Almost entirely excluded from northern Germany by the Lutherans and threatened in their stronghold of southern Germany by the spread there of Calvinism, the Catholics believed that, if left unchecked, Protestantism would, in time, supplant Catholicism throughout the entire empire. The Catholics had, from the outset, regarded the Peace of Augsburg as no more than a truce to be interpreted, or even discarded, in their favour as soon as circumstances permitted. This situation was achieved by the success of the Catholic Counter-Reformation. Led by the Capuchin and Jesuit religious orders, and provided with a doctrinal unity and a firm commitment to oppose all Protestant innovations by the Council of Trent in 1563, the Church of Rome launched a new offensive to regain territory and souls lost to the Protestants.

The Peace of Augsburg remained in force, but its attempt to maintain religious peace was consistently undermined by the consolidation of Lutheranism in northern Germany, aggressive Calvinist proselytizing, and the progress of the Catholic Counter-Reformation. The conflicting interests, which were almost as serious between Lutherans and Calvinists as they were between Catholics and Protestants, resulted in a series of political and religious crises which revealed what was perhaps the major weakness of the Peace of Augsburg: in its attempt to freeze the position as it obtained in 1555, the peace settlement failed to create the mechanisms to adjust its terms to meet changed circumstances or to settle, in an orderly and legal manner, possible future disputes between the various confessions.

The Imperial Diet had negotiated the settlement and was its only guarantor. As the 16th century progressed, however, the Diet and most of the other imperial institutions became increasingly ineffective. This was a serious threat to peace, as it convinced the emperor, the German princes and the adherents of opposing confessions that disputes within the empire could be resolved only by recourse to arms.

PRELUDE TO WAR

Around the turn of the 16th century there was no shortage of crises, each further inflaming the strained political and religious relations within the empire, and each capable of escalating into armed conflict. The issues at stake varied, but in most instances involved a trial of strength between the Catholics and the Protestants.

In 1573 the abbot of Dernbach forced the Protestant knights in his domains to become Roman Catholics. The following year a similar success was achieved by the elector of Mainz, while in 1582 an attempt by the elector of Cologne to retain his office and lands after becoming a Calvinist was thwarted. These Catholic successes caused growing concern amongst German Protestants, especially amongst the Calvinists (excluded from the protection of the Peace of Augsburg) and the Lutheran princes in the Catholic-dominated southern Germany. Their fear of Catholic domination seemed to be confirmed when yet another crisis, this time in the predominantly Protestant imperial city of Donauwörth, once again ended in a Catholic victory. In 1606 a religious procession by the Catholic minority through the streets of Donauwörth ended in a riot, a situation which was exploited by the emperor to place the city under the imperial ban. Maximilian of Bavaria, an ardent Catholic and the most important of the non-electoral princes in Germany, was authorized by the emperor to enforce the ban. Maximilian occupied the city, arranged for its transfer to the Bavarian administrative circle and, contrary to the Augsburg settlement, suppressed Protestant worship in it. The loss of Donauwörth persuaded many Lutheran and Calvinist princes that the need for Protestant unity outweighed the doctrinal differences that separated them, and in 1608 they combined to form the Evangelical Union under the leadership of the Calvinist, Frederick V, elector palatine. Within twelve months the Catholics responded by forming the Ecclesiastical League, with Maximilian of Bavaria at its head.

The formation of opposing, armed leagues had ominous implications for continued peace, as it reaffirmed the conviction that force, rather than the imperial constitution, had to be relied on to resolve problems within the empire. More important, however, was the fact that both the Evangelical Union and the Ecclesiastical League had connections with foreign powers. England and the United Provinces were members of the Evangelical Union, and the Catholic, but anti-Habsburg Henry IV of France was the patron of this union. The Habsburg king of Spain was the patron of the Catholic League. These foreign entanglements in German affairs would make it increasingly difficult to localize any future crises within the empire.

How tenuous the threads of peace were was revealed in 1609 when a dispute over the succession to the provinces of the duke of Jülich-Cleves brought both Germany and Europe to the brink of war. On the 25th March 1609 the Roman Catholic duke, John William of Jülich-Cleves, died without leaving any direct heirs. His lands, comprising the duchies of Jülich and Cleves and the counties of Mark, Berg and Ravensberg, were of great economic and strategic importance; they included the fertile lower Rhine and the Ruhr valley and controlled the Rhine crossing – a vital link in the Spanish lines of communication between Milan and Brussels. The chief claimants (John Sigismund, elector of Brandenburg, and Wolfgang William of Neuburg) were both Lutherans.

The emperor, whose position had been weakened by family feuds and by his exclusion from the Ecclesiastical League, tried to reassert imperial authority by commissioning the use of imperial troops to occupy the fortress of Jülich and to hold it pending his arbitration. John Sigismund and Wolfgang William interpreted the emperor's action as an attempt to retain the territories for Catholicism and, in order to strengthen their position, immediately agreed on the joint occupancy of the inheritance. Their agreement was guaranteed by the Protestant Union. The dispute then crystallized into yet another Catholic-Protestant trial of strength, but on this occasion the opposing faiths were represented by armed leagues (the Evangelical Union and the Ecclesiastical League), each with their own foreign protectors who, needless to say, were also directly concerned with the issue of who controlled these strategically situated territories.

Thereafter events moved rapidly: the Protestant Union, with the assistance of

Dutch and English contingents, drove the imperial army out of Jülich and occupied the fortress themselves; Spain offered to subsidize the Catholic League for a period of three years and brought her troops in the southern Netherlands onto a war footing; Henry IV of France, intent on frustrating Spain's attempt to maintain her lines of communication, pledged his support to the Protestant Union and began to mobilize an army of 30 000 men. The dispute was on the point of escalating into a major war when two fortuitous incidents – the assassination of Henry IV in May 1610, as he left Paris to take command of the army, and the death of the Emperor Rudolf in January 1612 – eased the tension and opened the way for a negotiated settlement. The regency government in France sought a *rapprochement* with Spain, while the new emperor, Matthias, advocated prudence.

The controversy dragged on from negotiation to negotiation until eventually a compromise solution became possible when Wolfgang William married the sister of Maximilian of Bavaria and announced his conversion to Roman Catholicism. The threat of the entire inheritance falling into Protestant hands was removed, and in 1614, by the Treaty of Xanten, both claimants agreed to a division of the disputed lands. Catholic Neuberg was given the county of Berg and the duchy of Jülich, together with its control of the Rhine crossing, while Brandenburg received the county of Mark and that of Ravensberg and the duchy of Cleves which was situated adjacent to the Protestant United Provinces.

Peace had been restored, and for a few years after 1614 there was a lull in German affairs. European diplomats, however, recognized the fact that a renewal of hostilities was drawing inexorably closer. All eyes focused on Madrid and The Hague in the confident belief that the end of the Spanish-Dutch truce in 1621 would be the signal for the outbreak of war – both the predicted date and the locality were, however, inaccurate. The event that precipitated what has become known as the Thirty Years War was a revolt, in 1618, of the predominantly Protestant Bohemian estates against the pro-Catholic and centralizing policy of their Austrian Habsburg monarch. Limited to Bohemian and imperial issues at the outset, the conflict soon escalated to include, either directly or indirectly, most of the major western and northern European states. The Thirty Years War was indeed both a civil war within the Holy Roman empire and a general European war.

THE BOHEMIAN REVOLT

The Austrian Habsburgs, in addition to their position as emperors of the Holy Roman empire, acquired the throne of Bohemia and the adjoining associated territories of Moravia, Silesia and Lusatia in 1526. Although the four territories formed a single kingdom under one monarch (the king of Bohemia), there was no central administration and each territory enjoyed complete autonomy, with its own capital and Diet. The Habsburgs nevertheless considered Bohemia in particular as the essential part of the composite kingdom and established their court in Prague, the Bohemian capital. But Bohemia was not an easy state to rule. Its people differed from their Catholic German monarch in respect of race, language and religion.

Most Bohemians were Czech-speaking Slavs, and although many of the top posts in the state were occupied by Catholics, the Bohemians were predominantly Protestant. Bohemia also had a long history of revolt, dating back to the time of John Hus when it became one of the first states to break with the authority of Rome. Moreover, the Bohemian estates and their Habsburg rulers disagreed on the issue of whether the Bohemian kingship was a hereditary right of the Habsburgs or whether it was dependent on an election by the Diet.

Although Bohemia was difficult to rule, it was imperative for the Habsburgs to retain control of the kingdom. Bohemian taxes made a substantial contribution to the imperial treasury – more than half, according to Wedgwood[6] – a fact of which the Habsburgs were acutely aware, especially at a time when effective imperial power depended largely on the patrimonial resources of the emperor. Politically, however, Bohemia was of even greater importance for the Habsburgs. The king of Bohemia was one of the seven electoral princes who elected the emperor of the Holy Roman empire. As the remaining electors were, since the Reformation, equally divided between Catholics (electors of Trier, Mainz and Cologne) and Protestants (electors of Saxony, Brandenburg and the Palatinate), the king of Bohemia possessed the casting vote necessary to ensure for the Habsburgs the continued acquisition of the imperial throne.

From the close of the 16th century the Catholic and pro-Austrian chancellor of Bohemia, Count Lobkowitz, began to push for the realization of the Habsburg aims of bureaucratic centralization and political absolutism – a policy that gradualy eroded the prerogatives of the Bohemian nobility and Diet. At the same time Bohemian Protestantism, tolerated but not officially recognized, was threatened by the Catholic Habsburgs' aim at religious uniformity and by the headway made by the Counter-Reformation. In 1609, however, the Bohemian Protestants exploited divisions and dissensions within the house of Habsburg in order to secure concessions from the ruling king-emperor, Rudolf II. He was forced to grant to Bohemia a "letter of majesty" or formal statute, by means of which Bohemian Protestantism was officially recognized. In addition, the letter of majesty guaranteed to the Protestants the right to build a church on royal land in those areas where they had no place of worship, and to appoint Protestant defensors to safeguard their interests.

The letter of majesty, however, offered no more than a temporary respite for the Bohemian Protestants. It was reluctantly accepted by the Catholics – in fact, some Bohemian Catholics such as Lobkowitz, the chancellor, and Martinitz and Slavata, two members of the upper administrative hierarchy, refused to sign the letter of majesty – and would constantly be under pressure from that quarter. Moreover, as it had been granted at a time when the imperial power was at a low ebb, it could be revoked in the future should the fortunes of the house of Habsburg be reunited and strengthened under a dynamic ruler.

In 1617 the first step in that direction was taken. The ruling king-emperor at the time was the old and childless Matthias. He had succeeded his brother, Rudolf II, as king of Bohemia in 1611, and as emperor in 1612. By early 1617, however, Matthias's health had deteriorated to such an extent that the issue of his successor became most pressing. Ferdinand, archduke of Styria and a cousin of Matthias, was chosen by the Habsburg princes as heir to all the Austrian Habsburg territories, including the Bohemian and the imperial thrones. Young, energetic and above all an ardent pupil of the Jesuits, Ferdinand would eventually reunite the Austrian Habsburg territories under the rule of one man. Moreover, as clearly revealed by his extirpation of heresy and suppression of the estates within his native province of Styria, he was the embodiment of Habsburg absolutist and Catholic ideals.

Matthias and his advisors realized that to ensure Ferdinand's election as emperor it was necessary to have him recognized in advance as king-designate of Bohemia – a step that could prove most difficult as the Bohemians were well aware of Ferdinand's actions in defence of his authority and his faith. When the issue was raised, however, the Bohemians failed to grasp the opportunity of asserting their claim to elect their own monarch. Adroitly handled by Lobkowitz and unable to agree amongst themselves on an alternative candidate, the Bohemian Diet recognized Ferdinand as king-designate in June 1617.

With the succession issue out of the way, Lobkowitz stepped up his policy of political centralization and interpreted the letter of majesty with an increasingly anti-Protestant bias. Consequently, when Matthias and the chancellor left Prague to arrange Ferdinand's succession to the throne of Hungary, they appointed a council of ten regents, of whom seven were Catholics, to rule Bohemia in their absence. Protestant rights, as guaranteed by the letter of majesty, were progressively undermined, and eventually a crisis was precipitated when permission to build Protestant churches on royal land in the two towns of Klostergrab and Braunau was refused. The Protestant defensors called a meeting of delegates from the entire country, but failed to get satisfaction from the regents and were forbidden to meet again. The order was ignored, and during subsequent meetings the defensors decided, under the direction of Count Matthias von Thurn, to "bring the Protestant Estates of Bohemia into the revolt and to make the breach irreparable by the judicial murder of the most hated of the regents".[7]

This decision was carried out on the 23rd May 1618 when two members of the council of regency, Slavata and Martinitz, and their secretary were hurled out of an upstairs window of the Hradschin palace by a deputation of Bohemian Protestants. All three escaped with their lives. Yet this act, known as "the Defenestration of Prague", marked the beginning of the Bohemian revolt and the occasion for the outbreak of the Thirty Years War. Although an almost continuous struggle, it is customary to divide the Thirty Years War into four sections: the Bohemian War and the conquest of the Palatinate, 1618-1623; the Danish War, 1625-1629; the Swedish War, 1630-1635 and the Franco/Swedish-Austrian/Spanish conflict, 1635-1648.

THE BOHEMIAN WAR AND THE CONQUEST OF THE PALATINATE, 1618-1623

After the Defenestration of Prague the Protestant assembly chose a directory of thirty members to administer the country in the place of the regents. They appointed Thurn as commander-in-chief of the army. Having thus countered the Habsburg policy of centralization and anti-Protestantism and having provided for the continuation of civil government, the Protestant assembly dissolved.

Initially the Habsburg response was restrained. Matthias, old and sickly at the time, advised caution and conciliation and tried to negotiate with the rebels. Despite Matthias's attitude and the rebels' claim that their argument was with the regents of the crown and not the crown itself, the two parties failed to reach an agreement. By July 1618 attitudes were hardening on both sides and the possibility of a compromise settlement became increasingly remote. In Prague steps were taken to sequester the property of the Catholic church; the Jesuits were expelled, and the remaining provinces of Moravia, Lusatia and Silesia were urged to join the revolt, while the Bohemian army under Thurn began military operations to clear Bohemia of any pockets of resistance against the rebellion. In Vienna Matthias was relegated to the background and, for all practical purposes, Archduke Ferdinand, although still only king-designate of Bohemia, began to dictate Habsburg policy. Unlike Matthias, Ferdinand was not prepared to negotiate with the rebels and advocated the use of force to crush the revolt.

The Bohemians received support from the duke of Savoy, an old enemy of the Habsburgs in northern Italy, who provided them with an experienced mercenary army under the command of a professional soldier, Count Ernst von Mansfeld, and from Gabriel Bethlen, a prince of Transylvania. Ferdinand received financial aid together with a small contingent of troops from his Spanish cousins. Both the Bohemians and the Austrian Habsburgs were strengthened, but neither sufficiently so as to enable them to strike a decisive blow. The next few months were characterized by a number of largely inconclusive campaigns. What was important, however, was the fact that the Bohemian revolt was slowly being drawn into the vortex of imperial and international affairs – a process that reached its climax four months after the death of Matthias in March 1619 with the refusal by Ferdinand to recognize the Act of Confederation between Bohemia, Lusatia, Moravia and Silesia. It was then that the Bohemians decided to carry their revolt to its logical conclusion by deposing Ferdinand and electing Frederick V, elector palatine, as king of Bohemia.

Frederick's decision to accept the Bohemian throne was of crucial importance – it disrupted the delicate political and religious equilibrium in Germany. In the opinion of E. A. Beller it was instrumental in transforming "a rebellion in Bohemia into a German, and inevitably, into an international war."[8] The successful substitution of a Protestant for a Catholic Habsburg as king of Bohemia would change the balance of electoral votes in the imperial Electoral College in favour of the Protestants and, although Ferdinand managed to ensure his election as emperor two days after the Bohemian throne was offered to Frederick, could in future lead to the election of a Protestant emperor. This possibility was obviously of grave concern to the Austrian Habsburgs, but would also be inimical to the interests of Spain. With the end of the Dutch truce in sight, it was imperative for Spain that the imperial title should remain in Habsburg hands. Equally important was the fact that Frederick's acceptance of the throne of Bohemia would involve his strategically situated German territories in the dispute. This was of particular significance for Spain, as Frederick's Lower Palatinate occupied a vital position on the Rhine from where

Spanish lines of communication between Milan and Brussels could easily be disrupted. While acting on behalf of her Austrian cousins, Spain was determined to invade and occupy the Lower (or Rhenish) Palatinate. It was purely Spanish interests, rather than family considerations or a commitment to a Catholic crusade, that were the prime motive for Spanish involvement in the Thirty Years War.

Frederick's action also facilitated Ferdinand's procurement of support from within the empire. John George, the Lutheran elector of Saxony, and Maximilian, the Catholic duke of Bavaria, sided with the emperor, and in both cases Frederick's acceptance of the Bohemian throne was an important catalyst. Maximilian was intent on acquiring the Palatine electoral title which, it could be argued, Frederick had forfeited by his sedition against the emperor. Consequently, after securing from the emperor a guarantee that the Upper Palatinate, and more particularly the Palatine electoral dignity, would be transferred to the Bavarian Wittelsbachs should Frederick be defeated and should the Bohemian rebellion be crushed, Maximilian pledged his support and that of the Catholic League to Ferdinand's cause. John George's decision to support Ferdinand rather than his Lutheran co-religionists in Bohemia can be ascribed partly to the elector's abhorrence of Frederick's Calvinism, and partly to the fact that Ferdinand offered the Bohemian province of Lusatia to Saxony in exchange for her support.

For Bohemia the choice of Frederick V as their king proved disastrous. In addition to creating circumstances favourable for Ferdinand, Frederick fell far short of the expectations of the Bohemians. They had relied on him to provide the unity of action and leadership previously lacking in the revolt, and, more important, they believed that his German and foreign connections would constitute the pivot for a formidable anti-Habsburg alliance. In both instances the Bohemians were disappointed. Dismissed by S. H. Steinberg as "a pleasure-loving nonentity",[9] Frederick with his immature idealism, inexperience and timidity was an uninspiring choice as a leader of a rebellion, while his extreme Calvinist views antagonized his predominantly Lutheran subjects soon after his arrival in Prague.

Within Germany Frederick was the leader of the Evangelical Union; in western Europe he was linked by bonds of kinship to the two most powerful Protestant states – England (as the son-in-law of James I), and the United Provinces (as the grandson of William the Silent). In the war with Ferdinand, however, no aid of any real substance was forthcoming from any of these sources.

The Evangelical Union agreed to protect Frederick's German territories – a task which they performed only briefly and with little success – but refused to support his Bohemian ambitions. James I of England was disinclined by both his personality and his policy from assisting his son-in-law. James was peace-loving and had a strong antipathy towards rebellions. Since 1604 he had been at peace with Spain and was at the time of the Bohemian revolt involved in negotiating a marriage alliance between his son and heir and the Spanish Infanta. More important, however, was the constant struggle between the Stuart kings and their parliaments, which prevented England from embarking on a decisive and united foreign policy and ensured that her involvement in imperial and international affairs throughout most of the Thirty Years War was largely peripheral.

Of all Frederick's foreign connections the United Provinces seemed the least likely to refuse to come to his aid, as their own interests, in terms of the impending renewal of the Spanish-Dutch conflict, were involved. Yet it was precisely this fact, together with the debilitating civil conflict between Maurice of Nassau and Oldenbarneveldt, that forced the Dutch rather to concentrate on building up their own defences. France, the traditional Habsburg opponent, was the only other western European power that might have intervened on Frederick's behalf. But France still suffered from the internal unrest of the regency period while Richelieu, the true heir to Henry IV's aggressive anti-Habsburg policy, had not yet established control over French foreign policy. By the time military campaigns began in the autumn of 1620 the anti-Habsburg alliance anticipated by Frederick and his advisors had failed to materialize; Gabriel Bethlen withdrew soon afterwards to suppress a revolt in Hungary, while the duke of Savoy refused to continue his subsidy of Mansfeld, thereby immobilizing his army until a new paymaster could be found. The Bohemians were consequently virtually isolated when Ferdinand and his allies launched their offensive. Saxony's army marched into Lusatia, Spanish troops from the southern Netherlands invaded the Lower Palatinate, while the imperial army under Bucquoy and the army of the Catholic League commanded by Maximilian's general, Count Tilley, after first suppressing uprisings in Lower and Upper Austria, crossed into Bohemia and confronted the Bohemian army on a low chalkhill a few kilometres outside Prague. In the ensuing battle of the White Mountain (on the 8th November 1620) the Bohemian army was routed. When news of the disaster reached him, Frederick hurriedly left Prague and fled, first to Germany, and later to The Hague where he spent the remainder of his life in exile. With Frederick's flight, the revolt in Bohemia came to an end. Ferdinand reimposed his authority and over the next few years extirpated all creeds except for Catholicism and reduced Bohemia to the status of an Austrian province by revoking the letter of majesty and making the Bohemian throne hereditary in the house of Habsburg.

After the revolt in Bohemia ended in November 1620, the conquest of Frederick's German territories was taken in hand. Spanish troops had been campaigning in the Lower Palatinate since the start of the Bohemian War, and they were now joined by the army of the Catholic League, under Tilley, which invaded the Upper Palatinate. In Frederick's hereditary lands Ferdinand and his allies were opposed by Mansfeld and some minor German Protestant princes who were fighting under Dutch patronage, especially after the end of the Dutch-Spanish twelve year truce in 1621. Even James I of England, pressed by his Protestant subjects and angered by the humiliating failure of his proposed Spanish marriage alliance, made a financial contribution to the cost of the campaigns. For Frederick, however, the support came too late and was too little, and the forces trying to prevent his disinheritance were too disunited to secure a victory; they only managed to prolong the struggle for three years. By the end of 1623 the conquest of the Palatinate was completed and its electoral title transferred to Maximilian. Spain, with her control of the strategic Lower Palatinate, and Maximilian of Bavaria, with his possession of the Upper Palatinate and Frederick's electoral title, were obviously major beneficiaries of the Bohemian-Palatinate War. In addition, Ferdinand emerged from the war with his control over his hereditary lands strengthened, his imperial power enhanced and his faith strongly in the ascendant.

THE DANISH WAR, 1625-1629

With the exception of the Dutch-Spanish War which had been resumed in 1621, all armed opposition to the Habsburg and Catholic ascendancy was at a standstill at the beginning of 1624; this was, however, no more than a lull, as the successes of the emperor, the Catholic League and Spain could not fail to evoke a reaction – both within the empire and in Europe.

In Europe the Dutch, initially hard pressed to maintain their defences against Spain, received support from England and France, as both these powers jettisoned their former pro-Spanish policies. In France this was largely the work of Cardinal Richelieu who became first minister in 1624. Richelieu realized that France was not yet powerful enough to challenge Spain outright, but he was determined to break the Spanish encirclement of France, to support the enemies of Spain, in particular the Protestant Grisons in the Valtelline and the Dutch, and to initiate a diplomatic assault within the empire to counter the growing absolute power of the Austrian Habsburgs. Although he was a pious Catholic, religious considerations played no role in his anti-Habsburg foreign policy. Any allies, Catholic or Protestant, were welcome if they enabled him to achieve his ends. It is therefore somewhat ironical that it was internal unrest in France, brought about by a Huguenot revolt in January 1625, that forced Richelieu to terminate the French campaign in the Valtelline, allowing Spain to reimpose her authority over this vital Alpine pass, and to withdraw from negotiations between the United Provinces, England, Denmark, Sweden, Savoy and Venice for the formation of a giant anti-Habsburg coalition. The negotiations foundered, but agreement was reached by England, the United Provinces and Denmark for a Danish invasion of Germany, to which England and the Dutch would contribute by means of an annual subsidy.

For England and the United Provinces the object of the invasion was to remove Bavaria and Spain from the Palatinate, to restore Frederick in his hereditary lands and to counter the spread of Catholicism in Bohemia and northern Germany. The Lutheran king of Denmark and duke of Holstein, Christian IV, obviously had sympathy with these aims, but he also had his own reasons for entering the war. In his capacity as king of Denmark, Christian IV wanted to establish a Danish enclave on the north German coast to the south of Holstein, including control of the estuaries of the Elbe and Weser rivers. This would confirm Denmark's dominant position in the western Baltic, consolidate her control of the Sound and substantially increase her revenue. More important, it would forestall the feared expansionist designs of Gustavus Adolphus II of Sweden, Denmark's major rival for Baltic supremacy.

In addition to his Baltic ambitions as king of Denmark, Christian IV also had, as duke of Holstein and as such a prince of the Holy Roman empire, purely German motives for entering the war. As a Protestant German prince Christian had extended his territory, wealth and power by the outright secularization of Catholic property or by arranging for the election of members of his family as administrators of dioceses – a position that gave them control of the revenues of the diocese. Christian's son had, for instance, been elected bishop-administrator of Verden, while he claimed succession to Halberstadt and was in the process of arranging his election to the bishoprics of Bremen and Osnabrück. Previous emperors had objected to this practice, but did not have the power to prevent or reverse it. By the end of the Palatinate War, however, the possibility of imperial action to reverse the practice of secularization or the election of Protestant administrators in Catholic bishoprics was feared throughout north-western and northern Germany. By disinheriting Frederick and transferring the Palatinate electoral title to Maxmilian without consulting the Electoral Union, Ferdinand had successfully challenged the imperial constitution and indicated his intention of making imperial authority a reality throughout the empire. Moreover, the quartering of the army of the Catholic League in the lower Saxon circle by Tilley after he had pursued and defeated the last remnants of Frederick's supporters, would provide Ferdinand with the instrument of power with which he could intervene in north-western and northern Germany. It was principally to prevent just such a possibility that decided Christian to enter into the war.

Christian IV's involvement in the war as king of Denmark and as duke of Holstein clearly underlines the dual character of the Thirty Years War, a feature which had emerged almost from the beginning and was to remain a characteristic of the war for most of its course. In a sense the Thirty Years War consisted of two wars being waged concurrently and constantly interacting with each other – the one between the emperor and the German princes, the other a series of European and Baltic conflicts. The former was a German civil war, the latter a struggle for Baltic or western European hegemony.

Although Christian's intervention did not alter the character of the war, it did extend the area of conflict. It shifted the theatre of war from Bohemia and the Palatinate northwards to the Baltic and focused attention on the emerging political and economic struggle for control of the bishoprics, especially those in Protestant northern Germany. Imperial and Catholic successes in the struggle for the bishoprics would obviously adversely affect most of the north German Protestant princes, yet they were reluctant to become involved in a war which they believed would be fought primarily to further the claims of Christian IV and his family. In this respect David Maland aptly observes that "they too wanted bishoprics for their sons, and Christian, with his sharp appetite for Catholic plunder, could not expect to be received with any enthusiasm".[10] Especially damaging to Christian's cause was the fact that the two major north German Protestant princes, the electors of Saxony and Brandenburg, refused to take up arms against the emperor. Consequently, when Christian crossed the Elbe river in mid-1625 he could count on the support of only the dukes of Brunswick and Mecklenburg and on that of the mercenary commander, Ernst von Mansfeld, who, once again, was in need of a new paymaster.

Initially, however, the Danish threat seemed serious enough to make Ferdinand

and his advisors doubt the ability of Tilley and the army of the Catholic League to contain it. Ferdinand was urged to raise an army of his own. Without sufficient financial resources, he resolved the problem by commissioning an imperial army to be recruited, maintained and commanded by a man who was to become the most successful mercenary commander of the Thirty Years War – Albrecht von Waldstein, or Wallenstein as he is more commonly known. Wallenstein was the son of an impoverished Protestant Bohemian noble. Orphaned at an early age, he was educated by the Jesuits, converted to Catholicism, and entered the service of Ferdinand while the latter was still archduke of Styria. Wallenstein made his fortune by exploiting every opportunity offered to Ferdinand's supporters during the suppression of the Bohemian revolt. He purchased large tracts of land, used the debasement of the Bohemian coinage to consolidate his fortune and by 1625 was in a position to offer to raise a private army of 20 000 men, which soon grew to 50 000. By 1628 Wallenstein had over 100 000 men under his command. Wallenstein organized this huge force along the lines of a business enterprise, maintaining it by means of compulsory contributions from the states and cities in the districts where his men were campaigning or, in emergencies, from his own vast private resources. Strict discipline and regular pay ensured that his recruits soon developed into a formidable army which not only served as an effective counter to the Danish invasion but also – and this is perhaps more important – provided Ferdinand with the means for independent action. Imperial successes would, in the future, not be compromised by the emperor's dependence on the military support of the Catholic princes of the Ecclesiastical League.

When the Danish War began in earnest with the campaigns of early 1626 it soon became obvious that Christian's intervention was a most hazardous undertaking: he had gambled on the support of all the north German Protestant princes and had relied heavily on financial aid from England and the United Provinces. Both sources proved to be wholly inadequate. At the battle of Dessau bridge in April 1626 Wallenstein defeated Mansfeld, while four months later Tilley, strengthened by 8 000 of Wallenstein's men, routed Christian at the battle of Lutter. Moreover, both the duke of Brunswick and count Mansfeld died in 1626, and when a combined offensive by Tilley and Wallenstein advanced into Denmark in 1627, Christian was forced to seek refuge on the island of Funen. In 1628 a last, desperate effort by Christian to re-enter the war ended in the total destruction of his army, and he was compelled to sue for peace, which was finally signed at Lübeck in June 1629. Christian retained his hereditary lands (Denmark and Holstein), but was forced to renounce all his family's claims to north German bishoprics. For all practical purposes, however, the Danish threat had been neutralized by the offensive of 1627, immediately after which Wallenstein turned his attention to a scheme – first suggested some years earlier by Spain – of conquering the northern seas.

As early as 1624 Spain had recognized that trade in the North Sea and the Baltic was the life-blood of the United Provinces' resistance to Spanish reconquest. When the intervention of Denmark shifted the centre of hostilities northwards, Spain, in her own interests, extended her activity in the German War in the hope of acquiring control of the naval bases along the German shore of the North Sea and the Baltic –

a prerequisite for the successful establishment of a Spanish North Sea and Baltic war fleet which would enable Spain to terminate Dutch trade in those waters.

Wallenstein wasted no time in launching his plan to establish imperial control over the German coastline. Turning eastwards late in 1627 he occupied the duchies of Mecklenburg and Pomerania before the end of that year. The Baltic ports in the two duchies – Wismar and Rostock in Mecklenburg and Stralsund in Pomerania – each had their own defences, however, and would have to be individually subdued and occupied. Wismar fell rapidly, opening its gates to an imperial garrison by the end of 1627, but it took Wallenstein until October 1628 to achieve the same success with Rostock. These were important acquisitions, but it was Stralsund, the key to the control of the Baltic, that was Wallenstein's major objective. In July 1628 the city was besieged by imperial troops. Stralsund, however, was surrounded by the sea on three sides and although Wallenstein had been appointed "general of the North and Baltic seas" he had, as yet, no imperial fleet to command. Without a fleet, Wallenstein was unable to prevent foreign aid from reaching the city by sea, and this was precisely what the Swedish king, Gustavus Adolphus, intended. Although still at war with Poland, Gustavus Adolphus was so alarmed by the spread of imperial and Catholic power in northern Germany and by the attempt to occupy Stralsund, that he supplied the besieged city with provisions and troops to enable it to withstand the siege. In August Wallenstein was forced to admit failure, and the siege was lifted.

THE CLIMAX OF IMPERIAL POWER, 1629

Despite the setback to his Baltic scheme, Wallenstein had by 1629 secured for the emperor a formidable army independent of the Catholic princes and the prospect of making imperial power a practical reality throughout the entire Holy Roman empire. Much of Germany had already been occupied, while the remainder was subject to intimidation by Wallenstein's troops.

Imperial power was indeed at a peak in 1629, but instead of consolidating his position after his victory over Denmark, Ferdinand revealed a lack of restraint and caution in his relationship with the German princes and in his decision to support his Spanish cousins in the Netherlands and in northern Italy.

As early as January 1628, while the submission of northern Germany was still in progress, Ferdinand had already shown his hand within the empire by deposing the duke of Mecklenburg for rebellion (by his support of the king of Denmark), and transferred his duchy and title to Wallenstein. As was the case with Maximilian's investiture as elector palatine, Ferdinand once again acted as though he was not bound by the traditional division of power within the empire. The German princes were appalled: Maximilian had at least been a prince of the empire; Wallenstein they considered to be no more than an "upstart Bohemian noble", and moreover one whose growing power, independence and influence on the emperor they envied and feared.

Three months before the Peace of Lübeck the fears of the princes were confirmed.

Philip II of Spain.

Gustavus Adolphus of Sweden. Portrait by Van Dyck.

Louis XIV of France. Life-size wax medallion by Antoine Benoist.

On the 6th March 1629, with Wallenstein's troops to guarantee its implementation, Ferdinand unilaterally and by imperial decree issued the Edict of Restitution – a document aimed at radically altering the map of Germany in favour of Catholicism and, wherever possible, to the advantage of the emperor. The edict reaffirmed the ban on Calvinism, and Catholic rulers were authorized to expel their dissenting subjects. In addition, and more serious for the existing territorial and religious balance within the empire, the edict decreed that all ecclesiastical property that had been in the hands of the church in 1555, and had subsequently been secularized, purchased, or "lost" to the church by the election of Protestant administrators, had to be returned to its original owners. Moreover, imperial commissioners were to be appointed to investigate disputed cases and they were empowered to use force (Wallenstein's army) to ensure acceptance of their decisions.

For the Protestant princes the loss of their secularized lands was a bitter blow, and many were reduced to positions of insignificance. Their opposition towards the emperor would in future centre around their demands for the withdrawal, or at least a major revision, of the edict. The Catholic princes, however, supported the principle of restitution, but they objected to the fact that in the scramble for re-Catholicized land the emperor ensured that he acquired the most valuable of the spoils. Ferdinand's son, for instance, was installed as bishop of Magdeburg, Halberstadt and Bremen. But it was the legal and constitutional implications of the edict and the manner in which it was implemented that brought out more bitterly than before the conflict between the princes and the emperor. Protestant and Catholic princes found common cause in their anxiety that the edict had been issued on no more authority than an imperial writ and that it was executed, ruthlessly and efficiently, by the sword of Wallenstein.

While Ferdinand's policy within the empire engendered hostility and dissension, the foreign situation became increasingly threatening, particularly as Ferdinand allowed Spanish Habsburg setbacks in the Netherlands and northern Italy to weigh more heavily for him than his own interests in Germany. "He might have achieved a renewed power alone," claims Wedgwood, "he could not drag the carcass of Spain with him."[11] There was certainly more life left in Spain than Wedgwood implies, but there can be no doubt that Ferdinand subordinated the interests of Germany to those of Spain and in the process thrust the empire more deeply into the maelstrom of European rivalries.

As the Danish War came to an end in mid-1629, Ferdinand sent 20 000 of Wallenstein's men to assist the Spanish army in Flanders, but it was his intervention in northern Italy in support of Spanish opposition to the duchy of Mantua and Montferrat – with its control of the strategic line of communication between Genoa and Milan – from falling into French hands that truly revealed the folly of Ferdinand's attachment to Spain. The transfer of imperial troops from Flanders to northern Italy in September 1629 caused a breach between the papacy and the emperor, as Pope Urban VIII feared that Ferdinand's involvement in Mantua would serve as a stepping stone for the re-emergence of imperial power in Italy. More serious, however, was the presence of imperial troops in Italy in support of Spain, which brought down on Ferdinand the hostility of France.

In France the Huguenot revolt that had forced Richelieu to withdraw from the Valtelline in 1625 was resolved with the surrender of the Huguenot stronghold, La Rochelle, in 1628 and by the Huguenots' final submission to royal authority by the Peace of Alais in October 1629. As the Huguenot threat subsided, and particularly after the fall of La Rochelle, Richelieu was once again in a position to pursue his declared aim to arrest the progress of Spain; the disputed inheritance to the duchy of Mantua and Montferrat provided the opportunity. The arrival of imperial troops in northern Italy, however, convinced Richelieu that while Ferdinand maintained his recently acquired position of power within the empire, the outcome of Franco-Spanish conflicts would depend as much on the emperor as on the king of Spain. As France was not yet capable of direct military involvement in the empire, French enmity towards the Austrian Habsburgs was, for some years, confined to the support of foreign enemies of the emperor and to the encouragement of opposition to imperial absolutism from within the empire. Since the defeat of Denmark and the relief of Stralsund, Sweden had emerged as the most probable future foreign aggressor in Germany. Richelieu recognized this, and to expedite a possible Swedish invasion of the empire, he mediated the Truce of Altmark between Sweden and Poland in September 1629 and opened negotiations with Gustavus Adolphus for a Franco-Swedish alliance. The negotiations were protracted, but meanwhile, within the empire, Richelieu's agents, while trying to win over Maximilian to an anti-Habsburg alliance, were actively encouraging the German princes to oppose the growing power of the emperor. Not that the princes needed much encouragement: "While Wallenstein marched and counter-marched across northern Germany," Maland astutely observes, "they (the German princes) needed no prompting in the matter of 'German liberties'."[12]

The revolt of the German electoral princes against the emperor came to a head at the Diet of Regensburg (June to August 1630). While Ferdinand remained obdurate regarding a revision of the Edict of Restitution, and the two Protestant electors (of Saxony and Brandenburg) refused to attend the Diet in person, the Catholic electors were nevertheless determined to use the meeting to curb the emperor's power. To achieve this, they launched an attack on Wallenstein – the financial and military cornerstone of Ferdinand's power – demanding his dismissal and a reduction of the imperial army. The Diet was vitally important for the princes, but it was no less so for Ferdinand. To consolidate his position within the empire he required from the Electoral College recognition of his son as heir apparent to the imperial throne while, in line with his desire to assist his Spanish cousins, he also hoped to gain their support for campaigns in northern Italy and in the Netherlands. The electors refused to even consider Ferdinand's requests until the issue of Wallenstein was resolved; and to force his hand they hinted at a united front in alliance with the Protestant electors while no attempt was made to conceal the Franco-Bavarian negotiations. Ferdinand bowed to their demands. In fact, he had himself begun to mistrust Wallenstein's personal ambitions and disapproved of his commander-in-chief's cynical view of the Edict of Restitution and his reluctance to support Spain. Wallenstein was dismissed, the imperial army reduced by one-third and placed under the command of Tilley. However, with Wallenstein retired to his Bohemian estates and Tilley in command of the imperial army, the electors refused to support either of the emperor's proposals; they postponed the election of his son as king of the Romans and flatly refused to become involved in any conflicts from which only Spain could benefit. The Diet of Regensburg was a major setback for the emperor; the first, in fact, since his victory over the Bohemian rebels at the outset of the Thirty Years War. Moreover, it could not have come at a more inopportune time for Ferdinand – while the Diet was still in progress, Gustavus Adolphus landed on the Pomeranian coast with an army of 40 000 men.

THE SWEDISH WAR, 1630-1635

Regarding his intervention in Germany, Gustavus II has been represented as a Protestant crusader, a practical statesman acting under the pressure of events, a pawn in the hands of Richelieu, a foreign aggressor with imperialist aims, or simply as a "military adventurer fighting for the sake of fighting and ready to chase the horizon on whatever pretext would best serve".[13] With the exception of the view that Gustavus Adolphus was a mere agent of French foreign policy, which has no substance whatsoever, all the remaining characteristics are discernible, in varying degrees and at various stages, in his involvement in Germany.

Since his ascension to the Swedish throne in 1611 Gustavus had almost constantly been involved in wars with Denmark, Russia and Poland, during which he established Swedish control over the Baltic littoral from Finland to Polish Prussia. Moreover, Sweden also gained command of the ports, naval fortresses and river estuaries along that stretch of the Baltic coast. This was of particular importance: the ports and naval fortresses provided Sweden with defensive outposts by means of which her opponents could be constrained to peace, while control of the river estuaries, including the right to levy tolls and custom dues on all river-borne trade passing through them, provided the royal treasury with substantial financial resources.

Gustavus realized that in order to consolidate Sweden's gains along the eastern and south-eastern Baltic coast, to further her encirclement of the Baltic (to transform it into a "Swedish lake") and to secure unhindered access to the North Sea by means of the Sound, Sweden would have to control the southern Baltic coast and, in particular, the naval fortresses in Pomerania. With these aims in mind, it seems likely that Sweden would have invaded Pomerania irrespective of the situation in Germany. By 1630, however, Sweden's involvement in northern Germany became imperative, as with the defeat of Denmark, the emperor and Wallenstein seemed intent on establishing imperial and Catholic control over the entire north German coast and launching the Austrian Habsburgs as a Baltic power. Sweden's involvement in the Thirty Years War was consequently partly a continuation of her monarch's ambition to achieve Swedish security and prosperity by dominating the Baltic politically and economically, and partly a consequence of the political and religious situation within northern Germany, brought about by the imperial victory over Denmark and by the Edict of Restitution.

The extension of imperial power and the Edict of Restitution carried the

Counter-Reformation to the Baltic shore. Gustavus, a devout Lutheran, was obviously concerned about the threat to his co-religionists in northern Germany, but he was not a religious fanatic nor even primarily a Protestant crusader. For economic and political reasons, Gustavus was more interested in establishing an informal north German Protestant confederation under the leadership of Sweden, than in disinterestedly aiding German Protestants – a fact that was recognized by the north German Protestant princes who consequently initially refused to side with Sweden against the Catholic Habsburgs. Gustavus's religious motive had further political undertones, as he feared that an unchecked Catholic Habsburg victory in northern Germany could facilitate the restoration in Sweden of his Catholic Polish cousin. Moreover, by the Treaty of Bärwalda in January 1631 Catholic France and Protestant Sweden agreed to act together against the Austrian Habsburgs. Richelieu would provide a subsidy of 200 000 *Reichstaler* twice yearly, while Gustavus agreed to continue the war in Germany which he had begun in June 1630, to guarantee freedom of worship in the Roman Catholic districts he occupied and to respect the neutrality of Bavaria. The Treaty of Bärwalda confirmed the trend away from religious towards dynastic and economic considerations as the main motivating factors in European interstate relations.

Richelieu hoped to dictate Swedish war aims by means of his subsidy agreement, but he underestimated Gustavus's independent spirit and his financial and material resources. Income from copper exports, Baltic tolls and custom dues, the production of iron and, with the aid of Dutch enterprise, the development of a Swedish armaments industry enabled Gustavus to finance his army. The French subsidy was welcome, but its withdrawal would not adversely affect Sweden's military operations.

When Gustavus landed in Pomerania in July 1630, a contingent of 20 000 Swedes and Finns – Europe's first national army recruited on the basis of virtually universal conscription – constituted the nucleus of his invading force. The majority were battle-hardened veterans from the Polish campaigns during which they had mastered the many tactical innovations introduced by Gustavus and had developed a strong *esprit de corps* and sense of devotion to their charismatic leader. In addition, they were disciplined and well armed – a lighter, more mobile cannon proving particularly effective during the German War.

During the latter half of 1630 Gustavus rapidly and successfully established a secure military base in the duchy of Pomerania, which included control of the important naval fortress of Stralsund. Further advances, however, would depend on how he was received by the north German princes. By the end of 1630 the exiled dukes of Mecklenburg, the deposed Protestant administrator of Magdeburg and the landgrave of Hesse-Cassel declared their support for the Swedish king, but without the support of the Protestant electors of Saxony and Brandenburg, whose territories virtually straddled Gustavus's route from Pomerania, he could not risk an engagement with the imperial forces besieging Magdeburg. Both Saxony and Brandenburg, although alienated from the emperor by the Edict of Restitution, feared being subjected to Swedish domination and objected to the intervention of a foreign power in the affairs of Germany. They wanted to preserve their neutrality or, alternatively, use the presence of Gustavus in Pomerania to extract from Ferdinand concessions regarding the Edict of Restitution in exchange for their support in driving Gustavus out of Germany. This, in essence, was the message conveyed to the emperor after a meeting of Protestant princes held at Leipzig from February to April 1631. Ferdinand, however, refused to compromise on the issue of the Edict of Restitution and lost perhaps one of the best chances of ending the Swedish War and of bringing peace to the increasingly war-torn empire.

Caught between Ferdinand's obduracy and Gustavus's ambitions, the two electors continued to waver. Unable to make up their minds, the decision was eventually taken out of their hands. By mid-June George William of Brandenburg was forced, under the threat of Swedish cannons trained on Berlin, to sign a treaty of alliance with Gustavus. The decision by John George of Saxony to join forces with the Swedes was dictated by the actions of the imperial army. While besieging Magdeburg the imperial army, without Wallenstein's financial and material resources, was in great difficulties lacking virtually all the provisions required to keep it in the field. To remedy this, a final assault on the walls of the city was launched on the 20th May. Magdeburg was taken, but the officers lost control over their exhausted and deprived troops, and it resulted in one of the worst episodes of the entire German War: 20 000 men, women and children were massacred, and almost the entire city, including all the supplies Tilley had hoped for, was destroyed by fire. The news of the sack of Magdeburg sent shock waves throughout the entire Protestant world, and when, three months later, Tilley was forced to cross the border of Saxony in search of provisions, John George had no alternative but to agree to an alliance with Gustavus. This was signed on the 11th September 1631.

Six days later a combined Saxon-Swedish army under the personal command of Gustavus met and decisively defeated Tilley's imperial army at Breitenfeld, a small village just north of Leipzig. One of the crucial battles of the Thirty Years War, Breitenfeld ended the threat of both the Counter-Reformation and of Habsburg domination in northern Germany. Richelieu hoped that after the imperial defeat at Breitenfeld Gustavus would thrust directly southwards to Vienna. This would serve the French cardinal's aim of weakening the power of the Austrian Habsburgs, but Gustavus preferred a campaign to the south-west, aimed at the rich Catholic lands of the middle Rhine, off which his armies could live and from where he could more effectively protect his northern conquests.

After sending John George to invade Bohemia, Gustavus headed for the Rhineland. In an astonishing series of victories he advanced across Thuringia and Franconia to Frankfurt-on-Main and then southwards into Bavaria, capturing its capital, Munich, on the 5th May 1632. This was the high-water mark of Swedish successes: northern Germany had been saved for Protestantism; southern Germany was virtually at Gustavus's feet, and Vienna seemed to be within his grasp. Initially Gustavus's motives for becoming involved in the German War had included nothing so quixotic as an aspiration toward the imperial title; at most Gustavus had hoped to bring about an informal confederation of north German Protestant states recognizing Sweden as their natural leader. By May 1632, however, his dramatic military successes so fuelled his ambition that he began to talk about restructuring the entire empire and perhaps even of acquiring the imperial throne.

These grandiose schemes, about which there is some doubt in any case as to whether they were ever seriously entertained, were not realized. The Swedish victories not only made Gustavus increasingly arrogant towards his own allies, but they also evoked a resurgence of imperial power. Bavaria, whose neutrality had initially been assured by Maximilian's agreement with Richelieu (by the Treaty of Fontainebleu, May 1631) was forced back into the imperial camp by Gustavus's successful occupation of the Rhineland and his invasion of Bavaria. More importantly, however, Ferdinand finally realized that unless the Swedish advances were checked, Austrian Habsburg crown lands, the Habsburg position within the empire and perhaps even German Catholicism could be in the balance. Ferdinand also realized that his only hope of reversing the situation was by calling upon Wallenstein, with whom he had been negotiating for some months. Consequently, in April 1632, a month before Gustavus captured Munich and shortly after Tilley had been mortally wounded at the battle of Lech, Wallenstein was reappointed as commander-in-chief of the imperial army – but this time with greatly increased powers. Wallenstein was treated almost as a sovereign ally with the right to raise his own troops and an almost free hand to negotiate with allies and enemies.

Wallenstein's first action was to drive all Saxon troops from Bohemia, after which he joined forces with Maximilian. Instead of launching a direct attack on Gustavus, Wallenstein then placed the Swedish king on the defensive by invading Saxony and threatening the Swedish army's line of communication with their Pomeranian base. Gustavus was forced to withdraw from Bavaria, and finally, in November 1632, the two commanders met in battle at Lützen. The Swedish army carried the day, but victory was achieved at a crippling cost, as Gustavus was killed in action.

With the death of Gustavus Adolphus, the Swedish-Protestant German camp was thrown into a state of confusion and uncertainty. In Sweden control passed into the hands of the royal council, acting as regent for Gustavus's six year old daughter Christina, while Axel Oxenstierna, Gustavus's life-long friend and chancellor of Sweden, was entrusted with the conduct of the war in Germany. Practical and cautious in character, Oxenstierna jettisoned the more fantastic of the king's plans while remaining determined to stay in Germany until Sweden's Baltic aims had been secured. Oxenstierna had matched Gustavus in many respects, but he was no military leader, nor did he have the charismatic qualities or driving force of his erstwhile monarch to hold together the anti-imperial alliance. Sweden's Protestant German allies began to reconsider their position, and some of them, in particular the elector of Saxony, seemed inclined, either individually or collectively, to negotiate a peace with the emperor on whatever terms they could get. Oxenstierna, much to his consternation, recognized the fact that without Gustavus's leadership or German allies Sweden could be driven out of Germany empty-handed.

Richelieu's reaction to the death of Gustavus was ambivalent: he was relieved that the Swedish king's rampant ambition had been stilled, but was apprehensive that an end to hostilities under such circumstances would leave the Austrian Habsburgs in too powerful a position.

Neither Richelieu nor Oxenstierna wanted peace, but each hoped to dominate any revival of an anti-imperial coalition. Oxenstierna was the first to move; in March he called a meeting of delegates from the Franconian, Swabian, Upper Rhenish and Lower Rhenish circles and Brandenburg and with them formed the Heilbronn League. Saxony, isolated from the Protestant party and unwilling to negotiate with the emperor without their backing, was forced to join the league. Oxenstierna, however, was not only unable to dictate to the German Protestants as Gustavus had, but was also eventually forced to share the active decisions with France. By astute diplomacy Richelieu's agents acquired for Louis XIII the role of patron of the Heilbronn League, while the cardinal's decision, when renewing the Treaty of Bärwalda, to pay the French subsidy to the league, rather than direct to Sweden, enhanced France's position in the alliance.

Ironically, the death of Gustavus also brought to the fore an underlying fractiousness within the imperial camp. Wallenstein's presence, so necessary in Ferdinand's hour of need, became a devisive factor once the danger had been removed. The old antagonism between Wallenstein and Maximilian, concealed for a time by the threat of Gustavus's extensive military successes, resurfaced soon after the battle of Lützen and was exacerbated by Wallenstein's unwillingness to commit the imperial army to the liberation of war-torn Bavaria. Meanwhile in Vienna Wallenstein's position was undermined at every opportunity by the pro-Spanish faction, particularly when it became evident that he had no intention of supplying troops for the reconquest of Spain's Rhineland route. Moreover, since the death of Gustavus, Wallenstein was no longer considered as indispensable, while his negotiations with Saxony, Sweden and France were construed as treasonable. Ferdinand's break with Wallenstein came early in 1634. Dismissed as commander-in-chief of the imperial army on the 24th January, Wallenstein and four of his closest accomplices were assassinated a month later – probably with the connivance of the emperor.

With the private intrigues and dilatarianism of Wallenstein at an end, the imperial camp once again presented a united and purposeful front marked by close co-operation with Spain. Wallenstein's troops were placed under the command of the emperor's son and heir, Archduke Ferdinand, while Spanish support was provided by the Cardinal-infante Ferdinand, governor-designate of the southern Netherlands and brother of Philip IV of Spain. The two Ferdinands combined their forces and in September 1634 inflicted a crushing defeat on the Swedes at the battle of Nördlingen, forcing Oxenstierna and his German allies to evacuate southern Germany altogether. In addition to its military consequences, the Swedish defeat at Nördlingen also had important political repercussions. It brought about the disintegration of the Heilbronn League, and encouraged the north German Protestant princes to renew negotiations with the emperor, which eventually, in May 1635, culminated in the Peace of Prague.

After seventeen years of almost continuous and destructive warfare both the emperor and the German princes wanted peace and the removal of foreign armies from German soil. To achieve this they were prepared to compromise – the emperor on the issue of the Edict of Restitution and the princes on that of their autonomy vis-à-vis the emperor. Consequently, in the Peace of Prague, Ferdinand agreed to an adjustment of the Edict of Restitution to the effect that all church land secularized prior to 1627, rather than the original date of 1555, could be retained by their new owners. In return, the princes agreed to relinquish their autonomous military commands, place their troops in imperial service and assist the emperor in his conflict with foreign powers within the Holy Roman empire.

Both the emperor and the princes had made concessions, but it was Ferdinand who emerged from the Peace of Prague as the victor – his authority within Germany was equal, in most respects, to what it had been in 1629. The adjustment to the Edict of Restitution had confirmed the gains made by the north German Protestant princes, but it did so without threatening imperial and Bavarian Catholic acquisitions in Bohemia and the Palatinate. Calvinists, in line with the emperor's policy, were once again denied recognition. Moreover, with the exception of Bernard of Saxe-Weimar and the landgrave of Hesse-Cassel, all the major German princes, Catholic and Protestant, signed the Peace of Prague, thereby enhancing Ferdinand's supremacy within the empire. This situation Ferdinand II exploited in order further to consolidate the position of the Austrian Habsburgs within the empire. In September 1636, at a Diet of electoral princes at Regensburg, he secured the election of his eldest son, Ferdinand, king of Hungary, as king of the Romans, a step that guaranteed his succession to the imperial throne (as Ferdinand III) on the death of Ferdinand II in February 1637.

But we are looking too far ahead. Despite its obvious advantages for the emperor, the Peace of Prague failed in its major objective to bring about an end to the war. Hostilities, in which European issues dominated, were resumed almost immediately and lasted for a further thirteen years. The Peace of Prague failed partly because the emperor's power had, once again, been disproportionately increased and, more importantly, because the settlement failed to address itself to the European interstate rivalry which had been an integral component of the conflict almost since the beginning of the Thirty Years War in 1618. The war between Spain and the United Provinces continued unabated; Sweden was not prepared to accept any settlement that ignored her claims for territorial satisfaction in Pomerania and other strategic areas along the southern Baltic coast, while France, fearing the effect of a revived imperial power on the outcome of the Bourbon-Habsburg conflict for European hegemony, was finally compelled to enter the war as an overt belligerent.

THE FRANCO/SWEDISH-AUSTRIAN/SPANISH CONFLICT, 1635-1648

The defeat of Sweden and of the Heilbronn League at the battle of Nördlingen in September 1634 and, shortly thereafter, the first steps towards a negotiated settlement between the emperor and the German princes forced Richelieu to realize that direct French involvement in the war was rapidly becoming a matter of necessity, rather than being a matter of choice. Richelieu, however, was also aware that despite France's impressive national resources in population and wealth, the country was ill-prepared for war – the government was in debt, there was no reserve of trained soldiers nor were there any competent and experienced military commanders to lead them. Consequently, from late 1634, the French cardinal explored all possible avenues of reconstructing the crumbling anti-Habsburg alliance short of committing France to an open declaration of war.

To this end an agreement between France and the United Provinces was signed on the 8th February 1635. Its purpose was the conquest and partition of the southern Netherlands; yet, on a technical point at least, Richelieu ensured that this action could not be construed as an open breach between France and Spain. In addition, France and Sweden struggled to find an equitable basis for a renewal of their former co-operation. The result was the Treaty of Paris (November 1634) and the Treaty of Compiègne (April 1635), but neither of these treaties were ratified. Since Nördlingen Richelieu had also tried to entice Bernard of Saxe-Weimar to place his army under France in return for a French subsidy.

None of these measures, however, offered a secure basis for an effective anti-Habsburg alliance. The Dutch, for instance, were concerned only with the conflict in the Netherlands and their growing commercial interests. Sweden's position was even more complex. Not only was Sweden's efficacy in the German War curtailed by the termination of the Truce of Altmark with Poland and the consequent threat of renewed hostilities in that theatre, but the Swedish council of regency, alarmed by the demands of continued warfare on the kingdom's limited resources, urged Oxenstierna to make peace on almost any terms. Moreover, Oxenstierna himself, at least until the death of the last duke of Pomerania in March 1637, entertained the hope of acquiring that strategic north German duchy by means of a unilateral treaty with the emperor. Sweden was consequently reluctant to bind herself too closely to France in the period immediately following the battle of Nördlingen. Bernard was also in no hurry to subordinate his army to French interests unless he was promised both financial assistance and territorial compensation within the empire to offset the loss of his original duchy. The latter demand France could meet only at the expense of the Habsburgs.

The anti-Habsburg cause was leaderless, and by May 1635 Richelieu realized that direct French involvement was imperative. Rather an immediate French declaration of war in the hope that this step would serve as the focus for a revived and effective anti-Habsburg alliance, than for France to delay and run the risk of eventually having to face the combined power of Spain and Austria alone. Consequently, on the 19th May, less than two weeks before the signing of the Peace of Prague, France declared war on the king of Spain and the cardinal-infante, the Spanish governor of the southern Netherlands. With the direct and active participation of France, the war lost all semblance of a religious struggle; power politics and secular dynastic issues became dominant as Catholic France (supported by Protestant Sweden) challenged the Catholic Habsburgs for supremacy in Europe during the final phase of the Thirty Years War, from 1635 to the Peace of Westphalia in 1648.

Still not nearly adequately prepared for war, Richelieu nevertheless planned to attack Spain on three fronts simultaneously: in alliance with the Dutch in the southern Netherlands, in the Valtelline with a force under command of the French Huguenot duke of Rohan, and, in alliance with Savoy and Parma, in northern Italy.

Success, albeit short-lived, was achieved in the Valtelline where the local population, mainly Protestant Grisons, initially identified with and supported the Huguenot duke of Rohan, but the campaigns in northern Italy and in the southern Netherlands were unmitigated failures. Although the French military initiative in 1635 was a failure, Richelieu's decision in favour of that step nevertheless facilitated cooperation between France and the other anti-Habsburg powers. In September 1635, partly owing to French mediation, the Swedish-Polish conflict was settled by the Treaty of Stuhmsdorf. The end of hostilities with Poland released Swedish troops urgently required in Germany and encouraged Oxenstierna and his commanders to resume the war against the emperor. In addition, Bernard of Saxe-Weimar and Louis XIII finally reached an agreement in October 1635, whereby France would pay for the maintenance of Bernard's army "on condition that he commanded them 'under authority of the king' and employed them wherever the king considered it necessary".[14] These diplomatic successes, however, required time to filter down to the practical level while, in France, Richelieu still had to tackle the daunting task of raising a French army with the necessary manpower, leadership and resources for a large-scale offensive war.

While this process of realignment and reorganization was underway, France was faced by its worst crisis of the entire war: Spain and the emperor took the initiative and in the summer of 1636 launched a two-pronged offensive against France. From the southern Netherlands a Spanish force, under the command of the cardinal-infante, and supported by Bavarian cavalry, invaded Picardy, while an imperial army advanced into eastern France from Franche-Comté. The cardinal-infante, meeting little effective resistance, advanced rapidly and by August 1636 captured the town of Corbie, only 80 km from Paris, and from there the vanguard of the Bavarian cavalry pressed on to the outskirts of the French capital. Paris was in danger of being taken – an event that would have constituted a psychological blow so severe that it could have changed the course of the war. Fortunately for France, she was saved the ignominy of her capital falling into the hands of the Habsburgs. The imperial army, approaching through eastern France to join with the cardinal-infante in the assault of Paris, was checked by the courageous defence of the garrison of Saint-Jean-de-Losne (renamed Saint-Jean-Belle-Défense in recognition of this action); and finally, threatened by Bernard of Saxe-Weimar in its left flank, the imperial army retreated to its Austrian base. The cardinal-infante was reluctant to attack on his own, and when Richelieu, and in particular Louis XIII, rose to the occasion, organized the defence of Paris and drove back the vanguard of the Bavarian cavalry, the Habsburg offensive lost its momentum. Gradually throughout the year of 1637 the Spanish and Bavarian force dispersed and withdrew from French soil.

The year 1637 was one of mixed fortunes for the Habsburgs. Although forced to withdraw from France, they nevertheless were successful in the Valtelline and against Sweden in northern Germany. When a local uprising in March 1637 drove the French duke of Rohan out of the Valtelline, Spain reopened its lines of communication from Milan to Brussels by negotiating an agreement with the Grisons that guaranteed to Spanish troops the use of that vital trans-Alpine pass. Meanwhile the emperor and those German princes bound to the imperial cause by the Peace of Prague recovered from the Swedish victory at the battle of Wittstock (October 1636) and by the end of 1637 had forced the Swedish army to retreat to a precarious foothold in Pomerania.

Despite the loss of the Valtelline and the vulnerable position of Sweden in northern Germany, the year 1637 saw the beginning of an anti-Habsburg revival. The United Provinces, exploiting Spain's involvement in the offensive against France, recaptured Breda in October 1637. In France, Richelieu began to reap the benefits of his indefatigable efforts to reorganize the country's army and finances. Adequately manned, provisioned and financed, the French army became an effective war machine, while the rise of young and dynamic commanders such as the vicomte de Turenne and the duc d'Enghien (better known as the prince de Condé) provided France with military leaders of undoubted genius. In fact, by the end of 1637 Richelieu was in a position to launch an invasion of Artois – an essential step in the protection of France's north-eastern frontier.

The war was turning in favour of the anti-Habsburg alliance and this trend was increasingly confirmed by the events taking place from 1638 onwards. On the 15th March 1638, by the Treaty of Hamburg, France and Sweden finally arrived at a firm alliance. Oxenstierna agreed to withdraw Swedish claims to territory in the Rhineland (a point of dispute between France and Sweden since the Rhineland campaign of Gustavus Adolphus), while, in return, France undertook to formally declare war on the emperor and to pay Sweden an annual subsidy of 400 000 *Reichstaler*. The treaty also provided for the rejection by both France and Sweden of any separate peace or truce with the enemy. The Treaty of Hamburg undoubtedly enhanced the efficacy of the anti-Habsburg camp; the French subsidy enabled Sweden to re-emerge as an effective military force in northern Germany, while the spirit of co-operation engendered by the treaty encouraged France and Sweden to co-ordinate their future military campaigns.

Of even greater consequence for the growing anti-Habsburg ascendancy than the French-Swedish accord was the capture of Breisach – "the key to the Rhine and the gateway to Germany"[15] – by Bernard of Saxe-Weimar, supported by French auxiliaries under Turenne, in December 1638, and, in October of the following year, the destruction of a Spanish armada by the Dutch Admiral Tromp in the battle of the Downs. These two events virtually excluded Spain from imperial affairs. Breisach, and with it, control of the Upper Rhine and Alsace, enabled the anti-Habsburg camp to block Spain's land-route from Milan to Brussels, while the inability of Spain to readily replace the fleet lost in the battle of the Downs precluded the use of the alternative sea-route to transport men, money and provisions to the southern Netherlands. Spain's fundamental weakness was increasingly revealed[16] and was further compounded by revolts breaking out within the Spanish empire during 1640 (in Catalonia in July, and in Portugal in December) and in the Spanish territories of Naples and Palermo in Italy in 1647. Any chance that Spain had of reversing her exclusion from the empire had, in any case, been finally shattered by May 1643, when a French army, under the prince de Condé, inflicted a crushing defeat on the flower of the Spanish infantry at the battle of Rocroy.

The emperor had, however, realized as early as 1640 that he could no longer rely on military and financial aid from his Spanish cousins. Moreover, with French control of Alsace enabling France to invade southern Germany at will, and with Swedish pressure in northern Germany growing in intensity and regularity, the emperor was made acutely aware of his dependence on the support of the German princes. In an attempt to get them to reaffirm their commitment to the imperial cause made in the Peace of Prague, and to induce them to increase their military and financial aid, the emperor called an Imperial Diet (the first since 1608). The Diet opened on the 13th September 1640, and initially it seemed as though the emperor's plan would be successful. In December 1640, however, Elector George William of Brandenburg died, and his son and heir, Frederick William (later known as the Great Elector), immediately indicated his refusal to accept the Peace of Prague as the basis for a settlement of relationships within the empire. In July 1641 the new elector of Brandenburg took his rejection of the Peace of Prague to its locigal conclusion and signed a truce with Sweden. Although none of the other major German princes immediately followed Frederick William's example, they became less sympathetic to the emperor's requests, and when the Diet ended in October 1641, it had failed in its primary objective.

After the unsatisfactory conclusion of the Imperial Diet at Ratisbon, and faced with increasing military and financial demands, the emperor considered it expedient to instruct his ambassadors, who had been engaged in sporadic meetings with French and Swedish representatives since as early as 1638, to negotiate a preliminary treaty. The preliminary treaty, signed on the 25th December 1641 and ratified by all parties by July 1642, provided for two simultaneous peace conferences – one at Münster between the emperor, France and the Catholic princes, and the other at Osnabrück between the emperor, Sweden and the Protestant princes. Both these towns are in the German province of Westphalia, hence the collective term "the Peace of Westphalia" for the settlements finally arrived at by 1648.

By 1642 the predominant sentiment amongst most of the belligerents was in favour of peace, and this was especially so in the case of the German princes whose territories had been used as the battlefield for almost the entire course of the Thirty Years War. Yet it took a further six years before a general peace settlement was concluded – and even then France and Spain still continued their war for an additional eleven years until the Peace of the Pyrenees was signed in 1659.

There were many reasons for the slow and protracted negotiations, the most important being the fact that the preliminary treaty of 1641 made no provision for a cease-fire or truce while the peace congresses were in session. The war continued without interruption, as each side waited for the moment that would be most advantageous for its proposals. In fact, the negotiators constantly employed delaying tactics whenever they believed that an imminent military victory would improve their bargaining power. This was, for instance, the case in 1643 when the outbreak of war between Sweden and Denmark (on the issue of Sound dues) raised the hopes of the emperor that a Swedish defeat would force the anti-Habsburg camp to be more amenable at the conference table. Nothing came of this, however, as Sweden crushed Denmark, enhanced her dominant position in the Baltic by the Treaty of

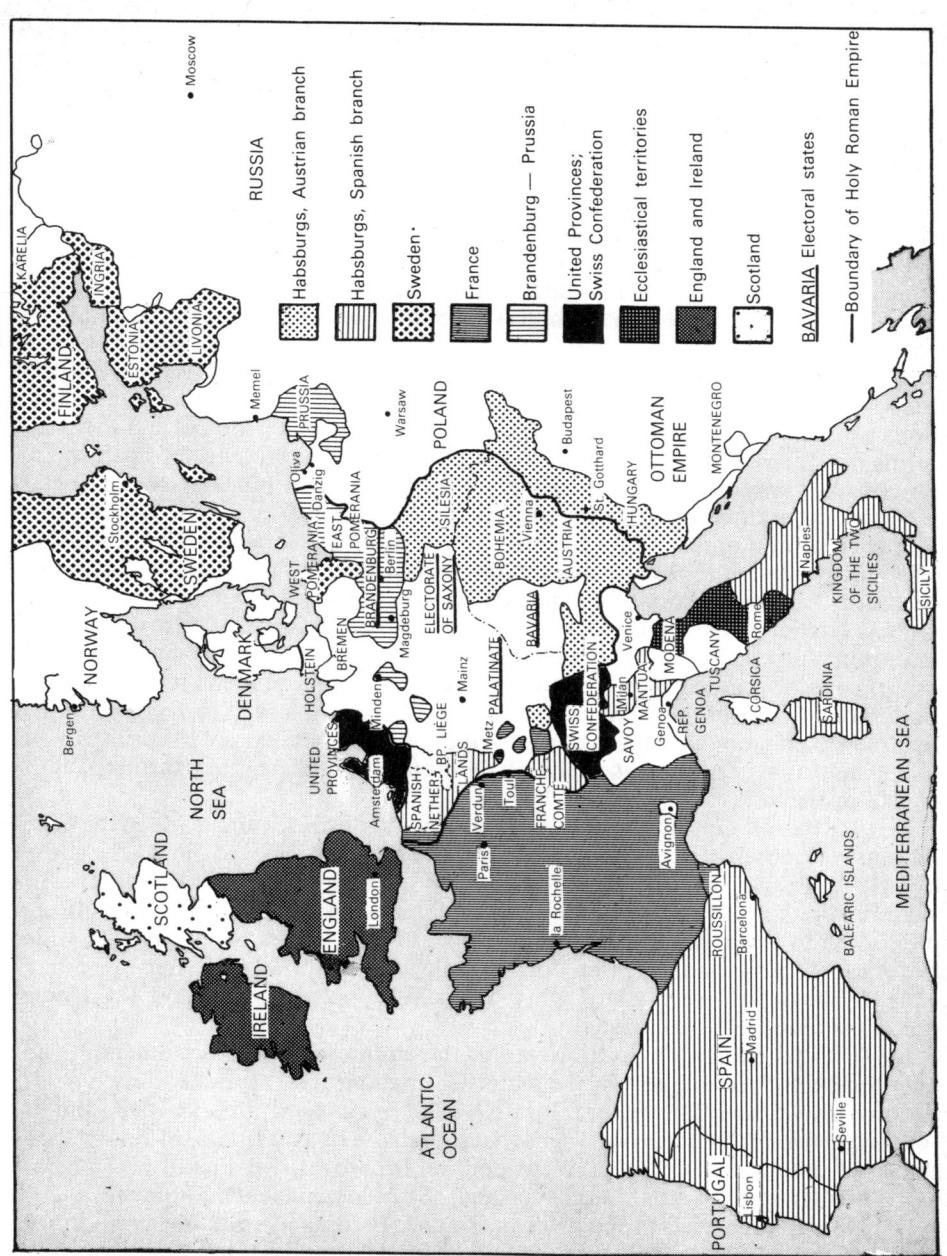

Europe after the Peace of Westphalia, 1648

Brömsebro in 1645 and, immediately thereafter, successfully resumed her campaigns within the empire.

In addition, the drawn-out nature of the negotiations can also be ascribed to the inability of either side to achieve a final military solution. Devastation of large tracts of the countryside, which prevented the armies from living off the land, dwindling resources and smaller, more mobile armies made it virtually impossible for an invading force to maintain an offensive of sufficient duration or intensity to ensure the complete subjugation of its opponent. Of less importance, but nevertheless time-consuming, was the fact that the two towns Münster and Osnabrück at which negotiations were simultaneously conducted were at least 40 km apart, necessitating an elaborate and tedious system of couriers on all issues of joint concern. Finally, although the protagonists were in favour of peace, the question of who should be invited to send representatives to the proposed peace conference and the status of these representatives had to be resolved before meaningful negotiations could be commenced. On one level the disputes about protocol and the status of the delegates, especially those concerning the possible presence of Spanish ambassadors at the conference, were simply a manoeuvre by France to cloak its determination to exclude Spain from the negotiations. Mazarin, who had succeeded Richelieu as first minister of France on the death of the latter in December 1642, was quite prepared to discuss peace terms within the empire as long as Spain was excluded from the negotiations and left isolated in her war with France and the United Provinces. On another level, protocol and status disputes were intrinsically important, especially as the German princes, supported by the anti-Habsburg camp, each demanded the right to send their own independent representatives. Ferdinand III was initially reluctant to ascede to this demand as he recognized that to do so would amount to the tacit acceptance of the sovereignty of the princes – one of the important issues at stake between the emperor and the princes throughout the course of the war.

Despite the difficult circumstances, intrigues and obstacles under which the negotiations were conducted, some concrete results had been achieved during the course of 1646 and early 1647. By the middle of 1648, however, some of the negotiators were finally dictated to by military and diplomatic considerations within the empire, some by difficulties within their own states and others by events with wider European connotations such as, for example, the Treaty of Münster in January 1648, by means of which the Eighty Years War beween Spain and the United Provinces was finally concluded.

By 1648 the emperor's position within the empire had become untenable: not only had he lost the support of the major German princes – Brandenburg in 1641, Saxony in 1645, and Bavaria, briefly in 1647 and permanently in May 1648 – but the combined French-Swedish onslaught that caused the final defection of Bavaria also shattered the western defences of the empire. Moreover, Ferdinand was increasingly threatened in his Austrian crown lands: Sweden had invaded Bohemia and by July 1648 had advanced to the gates of Prague. Ferdinand could delay no longer and urged his delegates to finalize the settlement. He could not have chosen a more propitious time. In France the government was faced with civil disturbances (the first Fronde) and pressing financial problems. Mazarin consequently realized that "if France were to wage war successfully with Spain, and without the aid of the Dutch, who had made their own peace, she had to extricate herself without delay from the German war".[17] By 1648 Sweden, under the young queen Christina – an assiduous worker for peace – was also in favour of bringing the war in Germany to an end. Sweden had, in any case, so depleted her resources during more than half a century of wars, that it would not have been able to remain at war in Germany without French subsidies.

Between August and October 1648 all outstanding problems were speedily resolved, the two treaties negotiated separately at Münster and Osnabrück were co-ordinated, and on the 24th October 1648 the Peace of Westphalia was signed.

THE PEACE OF WESTPHALIA

The Thirty Years War was both a civil war within the Holy Roman empire and a "Europe-wide" war, and this duality is clearly reflected in the Peace of Westphalia. Unlike previous peace initiatives – the Peace of Prague, for instance, that had tried to bring the war to an end in 1635 by resolving only the German or imperial issues involved in the conflict – the terms adopted by the negotiating parties in 1648 constituted both a German and a European peace. In the former context the Peace of Westphalia, although not an Imperial Diet, established the basis for the religious and political constitution of the empire which was to last until the empire came to an end in 1806. In the latter context the Peace of Westphalia was the first in a long line of European congresses – such as the congresses held in Utrecht in 1713 and in Vienna in 1815 – and, from the 17th to the beginning of the 19th century, was considered as one of the cornerstones of European state relations and international law.

The terms of the Peace of Westphalia were arrived at after many years of negotiations in which European and German interests and considerations interacted and overlapped. For the sake of clarity, however, it is best to separate the two components. Regarding the internal German settlement, two categories can be identified: religious and constitutional issues and the question of restitution, amnesty and compensation for those German princes and states who took up arms either for or against the emperor during the course of the war.

The religious settlement was an amplification and clarification of the Peace of Augsburg which was, like the constitutional clauses of the Peace of Westphalia, largely a formal recognition of an existing situation. Both the conflict between the emperor and the German princes, and the religious disputes within the empire had, for all practical purposes, resolved themselves some years before the end of the war.

The religious and constitutional terms of the treaty and their consequences can best be summarized as follows:

1. The Augsburg settlement, previously restricted to Catholics and Lutherans, was extended to include Calvinists.

2. The principle of *"cuius regio, eius religio"* was confirmed, but with some important reservations. The principle would in future apply only to public worship, and dissident subjects were to be allowed private worship of their own choice or, if they so desired, the right to emigrate under reasonably advantageous conditions. In addition, a prince's subjects would no longer automatically be obliged to follow the prince's example should he at some stage change his religion. With minor exceptions, these reservations did not apply in the territories that formed the private patrimony of the emperor.

3. The Edict of Restitution was repealed, but the principle of the "ecclesiastical reservation" was accepted by all parties. The date 1624 as the "standard" year for the retention of secularized church property, was agreed to as a compromise between the Protestant demand for 1618 and the Catholic insistence that 1627 – the date adopted by the Peace of Prague – be retained.

4. Protestant administrators of secularized church property were admitted to the Imperial Diet with full voting rights.

5. To ensure that the religious settlement would not be subverted in the future it was agreed that the composition of the major imperial institutions, including some of the imperial courts, would be based on the principle of equal representation by Catholics and Protestants. By its very nature, however, and despite the admittance of Protestant administrators, equality of representation on religious grounds could not be guaranteed in the Imperial Diet. This problem was resolved by the clause that religious disputes brought before the Imperial Diet would no longer be decided by majority vote, but would be settled by compromise.

6. In addition to their independence in religious matters, the German princes were also granted "territorial supremacy" or sovereignty within their own states.

7. In their relationship with other countries or states the German princes were granted the right to negotiate alliances, subject only to a vaguely worded restriction that such alliances should not be directed against the emperor or the empire. The centrifugal forces and the growing independence of the princes *vis-à-vis* the emperor, processes which had been at work in the empire since the 15th century, were now confirmed and guaranteed by an international treaty.

8. The emperor's absolutist designs were further curtailed by the transference to the Imperial Diet of his right to act independently, on behalf of the empire, on issues such as the declaration of war, the conclusion of peace, the levying and quartering of troops and the building and garrisoning of fortresses.

The second group of problems settled by the Peace of Westphalia relate to the question of restitution, amnesty and compensation for those states within the empire whose circumstances had been altered either by the war or during the peace negotiations. For the sake of uniform treatment and of separating the terms relating to the German states from the terms involving European considerations, the territorial claims of those states within the empire although not always directly related to the issues of restitution, amnesty or compensation, are also included in this section. Briefly summarized, the relevant terms are as follows:

1. The year 1618 was fixed as the date of restitution of estates and amnesty for all subjects who had taken up arms against the emperor. The dukes of Brunswick and Württenberg, the landgravine of Hesse-Cassel, the margrave of Baden-Durbach and the archbishop of Trier, to mention the most important, were all restored to their estates. Regarding, however, the emperor's partrimonial lands, particularly Bohemia and Austria, the year 1630 was adopted as the effective date, thereby confirming the emperor in his possession of property confiscated in those states after the battle of the White Mountain.

2. In the Palatinate a special adaptation of the clause regarding restitution had to be negotiated in order to satisfy the conflicting claims of Maximilian of Bavaria and of Charles Louis, the son and heir of the former elector palatine, Frederick V. It was finally agreed that Maximilian would retain the Upper Palatinate, adjacent to Bavaria, as well as the electoral title initially granted to him in 1623 for his support of the emperor in the Bohemian and Palatinate War. Charles Louis was restored to the Lower Palatinate, and an additional electoral title was created for him.

3. The elector of Brandenburg was confirmed in his possession of Cleves, Mark and Ravensburg which he had originally acquired by the Treaty of Xanten in 1614. In addition, he acquired eastern Pomerania, the adjacent bishopric of Cammin and, as compensation for the loss of the more valuable and strategic western Pomerania (granted to Sweden), the bishoprics of Minden, Halberstadt and Magdeburg (to which he would succeed on the death of the ruling Saxon administrator).

4. John George of Saxony was confirmed in his acquisition of Lusatia, which he had originally received as payment for his support of the emperor against Frederick V and the Bohemians.

5. The emperor and archduke of Austria, Ferdinand III, acquired recognition of the Austrian Habsburgs' claim to hereditary succession to the throne of Bohemia and its associated territories of Moravia and Silesia.

In its European component the Peace of Westphalia was concerned with the settlement of the demands for territorial adjustments and satisfaction by the foreign powers, principally France and Sweden, involved in the conflict. Briefly summarized, the terms involving the demands and interests of the European powers comprise the following:

1. Of the foreign powers involved in the war, France emerged from the peace with the major benefits. France was granted the bishoprics of Metz, Toul and Verdun in Lorraine, the towns of Breisach, Philippsburg, Zabern and Benfield on the right bank of the Rhine and sovereignty over Alsace (excluding Strasburg). These acquisitions represented the first permanent step towards securing France's exposed north-eastern frontier and towards breaching the stranglehold of Habsburg encirclement. Moreover, the stationing of French garrisons in the Rhenish towns laid southern Germany open to future French intervention, while the vague and legally complex wording of the Alsace clause could, as anticipated by Mazarin, be interpreted to justify French involvement in the affairs of the empire. In addition to these acquisitions along the imperial frontier, France was also granted the fortress

of Pinerolo in Savoy – a gateway into Italy. Finally, the emperor and other members of the empire were forced to agree to remain neutral in France's current war with Spain – a significant diplomatic success, especially in light of the independence of the United Provinces and the consequent loss of the Dutch alliance in the Spanish War.

2. Sweden was granted the naval fortresses of Stralsund and Stettin, western Pomerania and control of the mouth of the Oder, the Pomeranian islands of Rügen, Usedom and Wollin and, as compensation for the loss of eastern Pomerania to Brandenburg, the port of Wismar in the duchy of Mecklenburg and, on the North Sea coast, the secularized bishoprics of Bremen and Verden, together with these territories' control of the mouths of the Elbe and Weser rivers. Sweden was also paid an indemnity of 5 000 000 *Reichstaler*. These acquisitions, together with those granted to Sweden by the Treaty of Brömsebro (1645) virtually brought to consummation the policy initiated by Gustavus Adolphus of making the Baltic a "Swedish lake". To achieve this goal, however, Sweden had overtaxed her limited resources – that country's meteoric rise to dominance in northern Europe and the Baltic was followed, within seventy years, by an equally rapid decline.

3. The independence of Switzerland and the United Provinces from the empire of which they were nominally member-states was recognized, and the Treaty of Münster of January 1648, which granted the United Provinces its independence from Spain, was confirmed.

4. The French duke of Nevers was confirmed in his inheritance of Mantua, Montferrat and Casale.

The significance of the Thirty Years War and the Peace of Westphalia for the individual states involved in the conflict, referred to in passing in some instances, is best assessed in subsequent chapters dealing with these states and their relationships with each other: here it is appropriate to conclude by reiterating that in its German and European aspects the Thirty Years War and the Peace of Westphalia destroyed the last vestiges of medieval universalism in both the church and the empire, heralded a new era of secular, independent states and confirmed the rise of power politics in interstate relations.

CHAPTER 2

SPAIN: RISE AND DECLINE, 1556-1713

FOUNDING OF THE SPANISH EMPIRE

At the beginning of the 16th century, Spain was no more than a purely geographic expression. It consisted of two large regional areas, Aragon (comprised of Aragon, Catalonia and Valencia) and Castile (Castile, Andalusia and Leon), which were joined in 1479 through the marriage between Ferdinand II of Aragon and Isabella I of Castile.

The united kingdom was far from being a political entity. It was only a personal union, conjoined by the royal couple. There was no question of any firm unity, even less of any vital overall Spanish nationalism. The forms of government of the two territories also differed widely. In the Aragon of Ferdinand authority vested in the king, and the parliament (*Cortes*) lost more and more of its power. In Castile, on the other hand, the queen's power was largely circumscribed by prerogatives of the nobles and the authority of the *Cortes*. Yet Ferdinand and Isabella strove to extend the authority of the crown in Castile.

Castile was an extensive territory with a relatively dense population and with far greater potential than Aragon. This area was to play a central role in the unification and rise of Spain. It was also chiefly owing to the support Ferdinand had from Castile that he succeeded in capturing the last Moorish stronghold in western Europe, namely Granada, in 1492. The Moors were given the choice of going into exile or converting to Christianity. Although large numbers chose the latter, these Moriscos, as the converts became known, were Christians only in name. In practice they continued in the Muslim faith.

Aragon, fronting on the Mediterranean, controlled the Balearic Islands as well as Sardinia and Sicily at the time of Ferdinand's accession to the throne. In 1503 Ferdinand also succeeded in capturing the kingdom of Naples from the French. This was the first show of power by the united kingdom of Aragon-Castile, and Spain now replaced France as the strongest power in western Europe. Its control of Italian territories provided Spain not only with an important source of military replenishment, but gradually provided it with a controlling interest in the lively trade of the Mediterranean. In 1512 Ferdinand further increased his territories by incorporating Navarre into Spain.

With its large numbers of Moorish and Jewish inhabitants, Spain was a truly heterogenous state. Much of the development of a typically Spanish culture and point of view is due to these two population groups. Both contributed significantly

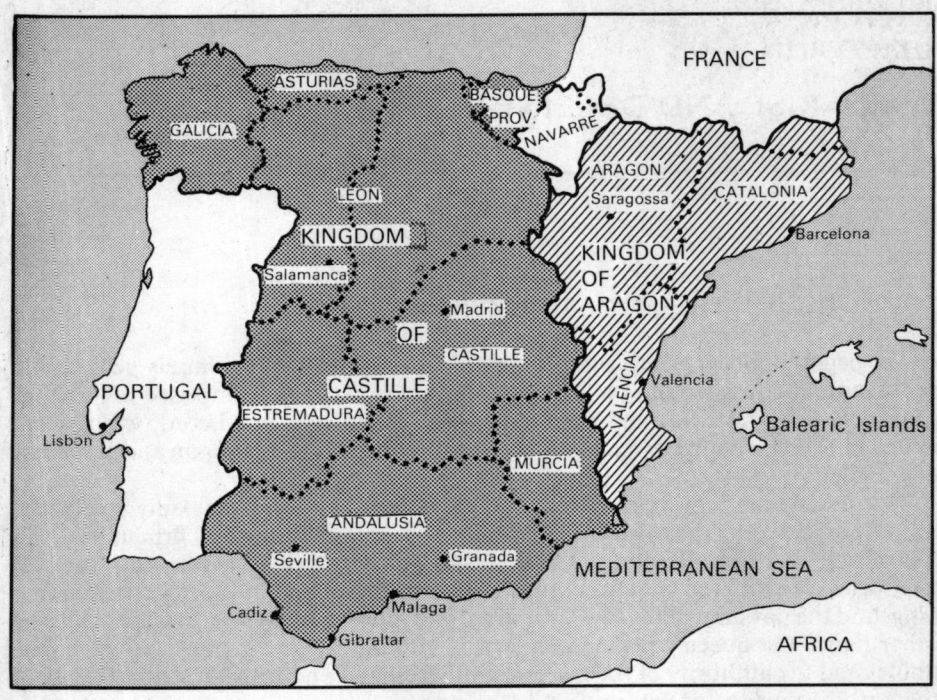
Spain and Portugal in 1555

to the rise of Spain and were known in particular for their economic activities. The latter factor ultimately became a cause for jealousy amongst the Spaniards and would eventually degenerate into strong anti-Moorish and anti-Jewish sentiments. This feeling was so powerful that it must be held directly responsible for the institution of the Spanish Inquisition (1478). The Inquisition initially busied itself with secondary heresies: matters such as witchcraft, bigamy and the like. After the appearance of Protestantism in Spain the Inquisition gained a new lease of life, also in territories under Spain's control. Over the years the bonds between the state and the Inquisition intensified, and in due course the latter took its orders not from Rome, but directly from the Spanish ruler. This fused the political and religious ideals of the Spanish throne even further. The Inquisition also helped to ensure the independence of the Roman Catholic church of Spain from that of Rome.

Without an understanding of the role which the Roman Catholic church played in Spain, Spanish history is incomprehensible. The struggle against Islam in particular was the cornerstone of the religious tradition in Spain, and this, together with the vast treasures of the church, gave it its prestige. The Catholic church was, however, of utmost national importance because it was initially a unifying factor in a country devoid of a true national consciousness.

One key to Spain's domination of the European scene at the beginning of the 16th century was the Spanish army. Temperamentally the Spaniards were among the best soldiers in the world. A military career in Spain was initially regarded as a highly honourable profession, and men of quality could therefore be recruited into the army. Its morale was boosted because of the conviction that military operations against all heretical beliefs (in particular Islam and Protestantism) were undertaken in the name of Roman Catholicism. The basis for the Spanish army was created by the famous Gonzalo de Córdoba. The tactics of warfare which he developed were so successful that they were imitated throughout Europe. The development of the Spanish fleet did, however, not lag far behind. Spain had excellent harbours such as Cadiz and Barcelona, and Italian seafarers also made an important contribution in this respect.

Spanish navigators were soon criss-crossing the oceans, and with the opening up of the riches of the Americas and the New World, Castile could come into its own as the exponent of a Spanish imperialism. All imports from the Americas were controlled by Cadiz, later replaced by Seville. The *Casa de Contratacion* or ministry of trade, which controlled this trade, for years took the lead in the seagoing business of Europe. Spain also made its influence thoroughly felt in the east.

Despite outward appearances, Spain remained a relatively poor country. The superficial wealth did not filter down to create a common purpose and to unify the population politically, but the various territories reacted with jealousy and rebelliousness against Castile's attempts to monopolize the riches of the New World. What national consciousness there now developed was consequently chiefly restricted to the Castilian élite (the *quistadores*), and in many parts of Spain local interests would continue to enjoy priority over the national interest. It is small wonder therefore that the Castilian royal house so frequently had to employ force and violence to convince certain parts of the country that they had to make a contribution towards the protection and development of the broader Spanish interest.

Ferdinand died in 1516, and his and Isabella's heir, Juana, married a member of the Habsburg royal family (Austria). This meant that Spain now became concerned with the politics of central Europe. Juana's son, Charles V, became heir to the Spanish possessions as well as to the Netherlands and certain German states. In 1519 Charles V was also designated emperor of the Holy Roman empire. Charles V controlled a powerful and extensive kingdom, but simultaneously faced a dilemma which would, for many years, directly influence the weal and woe of Spain. According to its geographical position, the country's true interests were centred on the Mediterranean and in the New World, but for political reasons its resources and energies were increasingly devoted to disputes in central Europe.

Charles V acted as patron of the interests of the Holy Roman empire and accordingly clashed with the supporters of the Reformation. Spain was called upon as a leader to protect Catholic interests against the Turks, Islam and the Protestantism which was flourishing in France and the Netherlands. In addition, France was trying to break the stranglehold which Spain had on its borders. Spain bore a heavy burden. It had simultaneously to colonize the Americas, keep the Turks in check, effectively surround France, maintain the Habsburg empire and challenge British supremacy at sea. It is hardly surprising that this brought to the fore differences and divisiveness in Spain's history. Charles had to cope with insurrections even in Castile (the so-called *communero* movement).

The most important contribution Charles made at national level was that he succeeded, despite all this, to shatter the narrow, localized view of many of his subjects and to make them conscious of a greater Spain and its role in world affairs. In the Spaniards this created pride in Spanish achievements and in the graciousness of Spain's royalty. Charles was the founder of Spain as a world power with an extended empire. Another significant development in the course of his government was the rise of the minor nobility (the *hidalgos*). They were strong royalists and aided the establishment of royal power in the country.

On the other hand, the *hidalgos'* influential position in the *Cortes* had a deleterious effect on the country's development. They mulishly opposed measures which could have aided industrial development, and their short-sightedness eventually also seriously hampered agricultural production; one of Spain's few flourishing operations. Thus an unhealthy situation was created which would lead to stagnation in industry as well as trade. Spain did, indeed, experience a brief industrial revolution, but by 1560 it had already begun to decline. Income from the wealth of the New World was not applied towards the establishment of local industries. Castile could therefore not supply its colonial empire with manufactured goods; virtually everything had to be imported from elsewhere and foreigners came to have a firm grip on the Spanish economy. Consequently, the country continued desperately to do battle with the imbalance between its imports and exports.

To make matters worse, Charles's European obligations were such a liability to the economy that the monarchy itself ran up an alarmingly large debt. Huge local and international loans had to be raised to finance Charles's military campaigns. Every possible source of revenue therefore had to be tapped to the utmost. This led to an onerous tax system in which a sales tax (*alcabala*) was the most important feature. (It was 10 per cent, subsequently rising to 14 per cent.) This situation further depressed trade and industry. Spain's subsistence economy became increasingly dependent on the supplies of silver which its fleets annually brought from the Americas to Seville.

THE SPANISH GOLDEN ERA

After a reign of 40 years Charles V abdicated and divided his empire. His brother Ferdinand I was given the Holy Roman empire, and his son, Philip II, inherited Spain with its possessions in America, the Netherlands, Naples, Sicily and Milan. The reign of Philip II is one of the most interesting in the history of Spain and the personality of the monarch has been the subject of widely differing interpretations. While some historians agreed that he was "the demon of the noonday", others lauded him in most favourable terms.[1] Although Philip II was not an inspiring military leader in the tradition of an Alexander the Great, he compensated for this with his dedication and industriousness. He entered the political arena at the age of sixteen by participating in the administration of his father's extensive kingdom. He married Maria of Portugal at the same age, hoping thus to create political unity on the Iberian peninsula. Two years later, however, she died at the birth of the mentally disturbed Don Carlos.

The kingdom of Philip II was still a loose conglomerate of semi-independent states, and the new king did not possess the personality to create mutual unity; his nature was simply too cold, distrustful and aloof. His own background, coupled with his fiery Castilian patriotism, ensured that the policy of turning Spain into a larger model of Castile would be continued. Although Philip II was not the founder of Spanish supremacy in Europe, he gave it a new purpose and direction. His reign therefore represents a new dawn in Spanish history, namely one in which the Spanish kingdom would be totally independent of the Holy Roman empire. Like his predecessor, Philip II would none the less dominate the European scene for almost half a century to a greater or lesser degree, so that this period has become known as the golden era in the history of Spain.

Philip II set himself a threefold task: to establish royal authority over Spain on a firm basis, to maintain his country's position of leadership in Europe and to protect the interest of Roman Catholicism in Europe against the rising tide of Protestantism. Where royal authority was concerned, Philip II believed in the divine right of kings to govern in terms of absolutist principles. He therefore extended the authority of the state over the church in Spain and also adapted the rest of his governmental system to this end. His hostility towards Protestantism should also be seen as an attempt to safeguard the divine right of kings.

To establish royal authority in Spain, Philip increased the number of royal councils to twelve. These councils dealt with aspects of government such as justice, finance, administration of overseas possessions and the like. Members of royal councils were totally subservient to the king and reacted solely to his decisions. The most important was the Council of State (or *Junta Grande*) which only advised the king. This body collected and evaluated data, but the final decision remained the monarch's. Administration of state matters was undertaken by two royal secretaries of state, who were also the link with the royal councils. Philip's mistrustful attitude was probably inculcated by his father, Charles V, for he impressed on him: "Depend on none but yourself."[2] One of Philip's aims was to ensure that the Council of State would represent opposing points of view in equal strength. This was done in the hope that all aspects of a matter would be considered and that he would never be outvoted by his advisers. The administrative system of Philip II should also be seen in the light of his convictions about absolutism. He was perfectly convinced that he, as reigning monarch, was responsible to God for the prosperity and interests of his subjects. This is why he approached and administered his task in such earnest.

Only the king himself had access to all the information concerning matters of state, which enabled him to ensure that only he could take all decisions. Philip II centralized all power in his own hands in an attempt to counteract corruption. He distrusted the more illustrious members of the nobility and kept them out of key posts, or appointed them in distant parts to diminish their influence. The great weakness of the system was that it consumed so much time. Everything, down to the most trivial matter once the councils had made their recommendations, had to await the king's final decision. Important issues in the national and imperial interest were therefore frequently pushed into the background by matters of purely local nature. These delays were, in the long term, detrimental to the extension and maintenance of the interests of the Spanish empire.

While under Philip II Roman Catholic nepotism was replaced by its royal counterpart, it would not be entirely accurate to describe Philip's government as absolutely autocratic. There were too many curbs on his power for this, inside and outside Castile, and the Spanish Inquisition was too independent of royal authority. Another feature of Philip's government was its pursuit of social justice, and protection of the rights of the poor enjoyed his active attention.

As outlined above, the unification of Spain was the personal achievement of the king rather than the outcome of a strongly developed national consciousness. The relationship between the two old kingdoms of Aragon and Castile continued to create problems. Aragon was hostile to Philip's attempts at innovation, and the king had to rely chiefly on Castile to realize his plans. This in turn irritated the Castilians. Philip attempted to save the situation by putting a tighter rein on Aragon, but this ultimately led to an uprising in this territory in 1591. The Castilian army suppressed the Aragonese insurrection, but this engendered a passive resistance to royal authority, which was to have detrimental consequences for the whole of Spain.

Similarly, Philip II experienced varying success in his attempts to extend his authority over the Moors in Spain. To the strictly Catholic Philip these Arabs, settled mainly in Granada, and firm believers in Islam, were a thorn in the flesh. The Moriscos paid lip service to Catholic customs, but simultaneously remained loyal to their traditional faith. From 1567 onwards Philip forbade all Muslim customs by royal decree, while the use of Arabic was forbidden from 1570 onwards. The Moriscos rebelled against this suppression and it took Philip's army under Don Juan of Austria three years to break the resistance in Granada. This war cost a great deal of money, and the king had to keep an army stationed in the territory to ensure order and obedience.

Philip II was a devoted Catholic who was meticulous in his religious observances. He therefore constantly kept in mind the interests of the Catholic church in his government. It would be a mistake, however, as has happened in the past, to assert that his political actions were purely religiously motivated. It is true that the achievement of his religious aims and the extension of the Spanish empire were almost synonymous to him, but in his political decisions he was ultimately influenced by the purely political considerations and the political situation in Europe. Where religious fervour was in conflict with political interest, the latter was always given priority. Thus, for example, Philip II preferred Elizabeth I to Mary Stuart, queen of Scotland, on the British throne, although the former had adopted a policy of secession from the Roman Catholic church while the latter was a loyal Catholic – but an equally loyal ally of France.

In his relationship with the papacy Philip gave evidence of an equally independent and sometimes inflexible attitude. He accepted no papal decree unless it had previously been approved by the Council of Castile, or if it was in conflict with Spanish law. His position was so independent that Pope Pius IV upbraided the Spaniards with: "You in Spain wish to act as Pope and refer all matters to the king." He did not hesitate to take up arms against the papacy to protect Spanish interests and his own rights. In the years 1556-1559, for example, Philip was embroiled in a struggle against an alliance between France and the papacy. Although he was finally victorious, the Peace of Cateau-Cambrésis (1559) was beneficial to all parties concerned, mainly because Philip's treasury was exhausted and because it was expedient, from a political point of view, to stop the war with Rome.

Political decrees reduced the influence of the papacy in Spain to a minimum. It would therefore be a complete misrepresentation to describe Philip II as the secular arm of the Roman Catholic Counter-Reformation. The Spanish king, however, and the Jesuit order of Ignatius de Loyola, were to contribute a great deal to its financial and military support.

The fact of the matter is of course also that Philip II and the papacy needed each other's aid. For Philip, the church was a useful end towards promoting his political objectives. Support of the church increased his standing, and frequently the slogan that the ends justify the means was applicable here. The papacy, on the other hand, had to rely on the Spanish monarch to protect Rome against the attacks of the Turks.[3]

The Turks under Suleiman II were a great impediment to the Spaniards in the Mediterranean. After the Peace of Cateau-Cambrésis Philip II devoted his full attention to this problem. His plan was to obtain control of the narrowest part of the Mediterranean and thus stem the westward spreading of Mohammedanism. In 1561, however, the Spaniards experienced serious setbacks at Tripoli, Djerba and Málaga. The Turks captured 10 000 Spaniards, and the Spanish fleet was diminished to such an extent that Philip had to announce a new fleet construction programme. The Turkish fleet was virtually the cock of the walk in the Mediterranean and a serious threat to Spain as well as to the Papal States. In addition the Turks took the offensive and between 1565 and 1566 repeatedly attacked the Spanish fleet and besieged the island of Malta. The Spanish war effort cost the country enormous sums of money. Furthermore, Philip's inability to deal the Turks a death-blow was harming his image in Europe. The rebellious Dutch exploited the situation to the hilt and forced Spain to divide its attention on two fronts. The policy of Philip II to act as protector of Roman Catholicism in Europe was also tarnished by the Turks, in particular after they conquered Cyprus in 1570 and represented a direct threat to the Papal States. This situation resulted, in 1571, in the formation of the Holy Alliance between Spain, Venice and the Papal States. The joint fleets of the alliance, under Don Juan of Austria, won a decisive battle against the Turks at Lepanto in the same year. It did not finally drive them out of the Mediterranean, but the victory had important moral implications. In the eyes of Europe, the Spaniards had established themselves as the champions of Christian interests. In Spain itself this view was accepted equally readily, and this explains to a large extent why an important part of the population willingly supported their monarch's religious and imperial campaigns during difficult times.

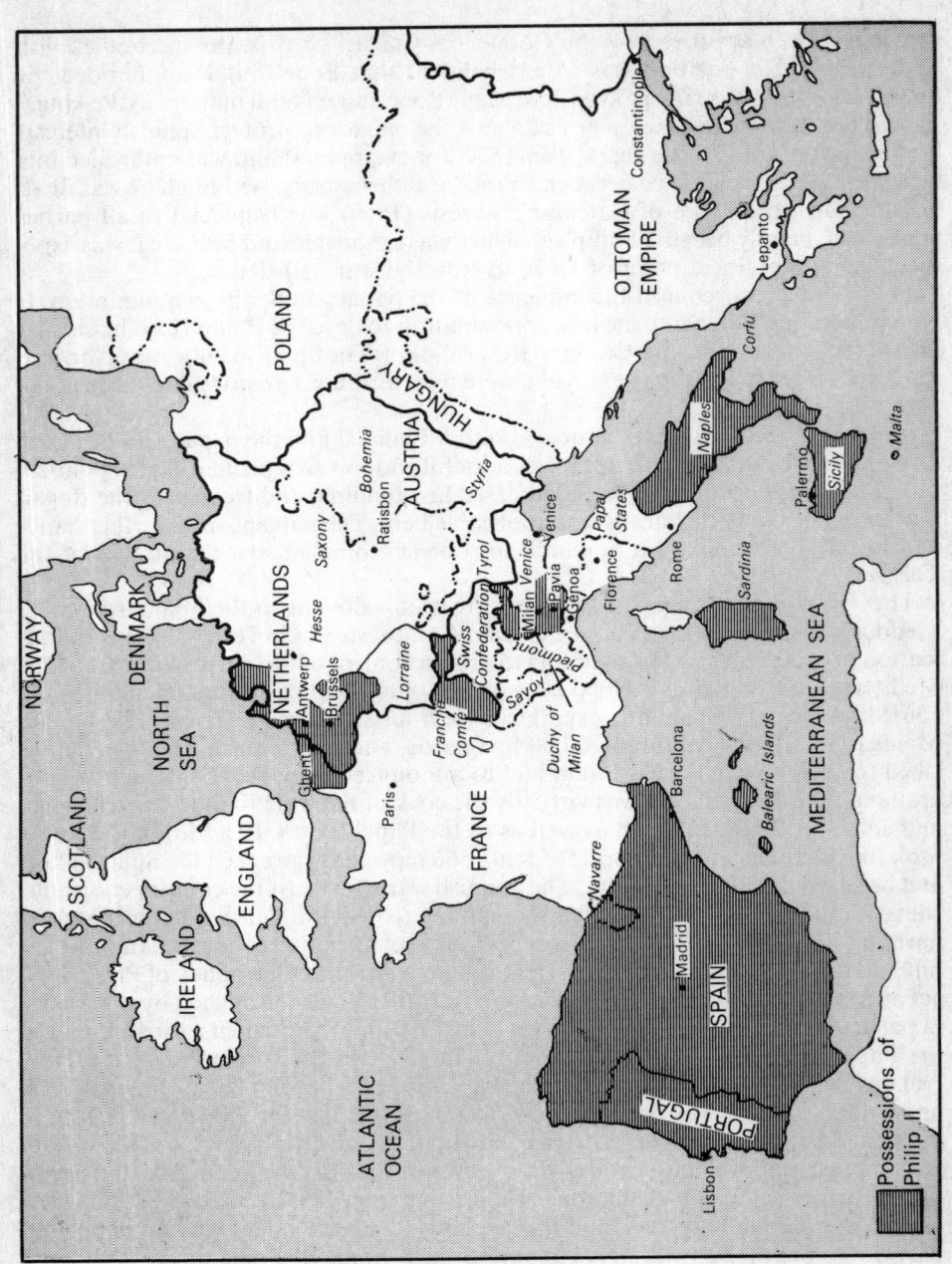

Europe in 1581

Where the protection and development of his imperial interests were concerned, Philip II was to act in the main on four fronts. He concerned himself with Mediterranean matters, became involved in Portugal, was embroiled in the uprising of the Netherlands where he ultimately came into conflict with England and France, and he also took action in northern Italy. Philip's affairs were complicated by the fact that his involvements on the various fronts were often closely connected. Not only did it divide his attention, but it sapped the Spanish economy.

Philip's battles with the Turks in the Mediterranean have been discussed above. After Lepanto the position in this area was a stalemate. Only in 1580 did the Spaniards and Turks sign a truce which allowed Philip to devote his attentions elsewhere.

The second foreign front to engage Philip was Portugal.[4] The Spanish king had long fostered the secret ideal of uniting the whole Iberian peninsula under his authority. In addition he was, by heredity, a pretender to the Portuguese throne. An opportunity presented itself in 1578, when the Portuguese throne was left vacant by Dom Sebastian. In 1580 the Portuguese army suffered a severe setback in North Africa, and Philip exploited the opportunity by sending crack troops to Portugal. By employing bribery and collusion Philip considerably strengthened the pro-Spanish party in Portugal and, in the same year, after a brief campaign, he was able to accept the Portuguese crown. The occupation of Portugal was of great potential benefit to Spain. It meant control not only of their eastern, American and African possessions, but the Spanish could also add the highly strategic port of Lisbon to their territory. Lisbon was already an established trading centre in western Europe, and in addition Spain, from the military viewpoint, had now eliminated any threat from the west, having gained a further base from which to disrupt English and French shipping.

The alliance between Spain and Portugal never, however, fulfilled Philip's expectations. Although it entailed certain trading advantages and the Portuguese were also forced to supply Philip, the final result was an ever-increasing anti-Spanish (and particularly anti-Castilian) sentiment amongst the Portuguese. They regarded the Spanish rulers in their country with impatience and viewed the campaigns of the Spanish empire as matters which did not concern them. The traditional hostility between Portuguese and Castilians was therefore nurtured rather than ended by the political alliance.

The last two fronts on which Philip II intervened were connected with the Spanish occupation of the seventeen provinces of the Netherlands. The Netherlands had come into the possession of the Habsburgs in the 15th century. Charles V realized how important the Netherlands were to Spain and governed them with great forbearance. He also understood and respected the traditional differences between the Walloons of the south and the Flemish and Dutch of the north. Even after the rise of Protestantism in the northern parts of the Netherlands, Charles did not allow his actions to influence the trade between the two countries. Philip II did not display the skilful circumspection with which his father had treated the Dutch. His autocracy aside, his religious intolerance was to set the scene for a bloody clash in the Netherlands.

Continued control of the territory was important to Spain from both a religious and a political point of view. Calvinism had found a strong foothold in the Netherlands and was also making headway in France. As has been shown, the possibility that a Protestant could ascend to the French throne was a real danger. From the Roman Catholic point of view, Spain had to keep the area firmly in its grasp. The Netherlands were, however, also important in the political area. Their occupation coincided with the Spanish policy of encircling France and keeping it weak. Flanders was regarded as an industrial area which should on no account be lost to Spain, and Antwerp had become the economic centre of Europe. In addition the Dutch were increasingly competing with Spain in the east.

The Dutch Catholics in the south as well as their Protestant countrymen in the north rose against the Spanish overlordship. The Dutch nobility in particular felt wronged because Philip had denied them virtually all their privileges and influence. He had appointed his half-sister, Marguerite of Parma, as regent of the Netherlands and also saw to it that no Dutchman served on her advisory council. Highly centralized government authority was instituted. The fact that this lost them their voice in local affairs went against the Dutchmen's grain. In addition, the Spanish Inquisition was brutal towards non-Catholics. This political and religious situation polarized matters between the years 1560 and 1564. The Netherlands States-General, headed by the nobility, was thoroughly aware of the dilemma in which the Spaniards found themselves regarding the Moors in the Mediterranean and fully exploited the situation. In 1566 Marguerite of Parma was approached with a petition which requested a greater role in matters of state for the States-General. In the course of this interview, the dissidents were slightingly referred to as *"geuse"* (beggars), a name which the rebels readily made their own and invested with great honour. Marguerite of Parma was favourably disposed towards them, but a turn of the tide on the Turkish front to Spain's advantage made Philip repudiate any possibility of change. Public rebelliousness amongst the citizenry subsequently forced Marguerite to make certain concessions which Philip, in the light of a worsening situation on the Turkish front, tacitly had to accept. In 1566, however, the famous iconoclastic riots (destruction of statues) occurred, in the course of which Roman Catholic churches were destroyed and plundered.

Philip II realized that a conciliatory policy would now be fruitless and decided to suppress the rioting with force, particularly as there was once again less pressure on the Turkish front. In 1567 Marguerite of Parma was replaced by the callous count of Alva, and 10 000 of the finest Spanish soldiers were transferred from the Mediterranean to the Netherlands. Their march took them along the Valtelline route from Milan via Piedmont and the Franche-Comté to Brussels. Alva scattered the Dutch rebels under William of Orange, also known as William the Silent, and the counts of Egmont and Hoorn. This was followed by oppressive religious, political and economic measures aimed at stifling all signs of unrest. An extraordinary court of justice, called the Council of Blood, became infamous in this period for its excessive persecution of the rebels.

Matters did not, however, take the course Philip and Alva had expected. Alva's government created so much bitterness that the Dutch began a new uprising. This struggle, which began in 1568, was aimed at forcing recognition of their religious and political independence and is known in history as the Netherlands (or Dutch) revolt or the Eighty Years War. The Dutch tackled an apparently hopeless task, as the Spaniards could rely on the reserves of a world empire. In their favour, however, they were fighting on home ground and had the clandestine support of the French and English. At sea the Dutch proved to be more than a match for the Spanish, but on land the course of the war was less successful. In 1573 William of Orange became a Protestant, thus ending the crippling divisiveness in the northern parts. Plundering of the southern Netherlands by the Spanish soldiers caused a gradual *rapprochement* between north and south. In 1576 the seven northern Protestant provinces and the ten Catholic ones in the south reached an accord, the Pacification of Ghent, making common cause of the attempt to drive the Spaniards out of the country. The Spaniards now faced a united front and the sea-route to the Netherlands was closed to them. The Valtelline route was the only one by which supplies and reinforcements could reach the Netherlands.

The position of the Spaniards was further complicated by the drawn-out struggle against the Turks in the Mediterranean. It meant war on two fronts, which placed an awesome burden on the Spanish economy.[5] According to calculations, the Netherlands campaign at its height cost the Spaniards about four billion rand in current terms over a period of eleven years. But Philip did not see his way clear to forsaking either front. The Spanish position deteriorated steadily, and soldiers even refused service because they were not receiving their pay. The new Spanish regent, Don Juan of Austria, was forced to sign the Eternal Edict, withdrawing Spanish troops and restoring the old political rights. Philip's attitude remained implacable and he ignored the treaty. He continued borrowing ever larger sums of money for the Netherlands campaign; the interest rates on these loans ran from 15 to 30 per cent. In 1575 the Italian, German and Flemish money-lenders finally refused to advance any further loans. Philip thereupon simply wrote off his debts by royal decree. Although he was now again in control of his finances, the Spanish found themselves in an untenable position as far as their campaigns in the Netherlands and the Mediterranean were concerned, for international bankers now refused to handle monetary transactions on behalf of Spain. Although Philip II resolved his dispute with the bankers in 1578, the Spanish position remained critical.

While the Dutch revolt was throttling the Spanish economy, it had precisely the opposite effect on the economic activities of the northern Netherlands. The war caused many inhabitants of the south to flee northwards, and Antwerp, once a great port and centre of trade, bled to death. The same happened in the previously flourishing province of Flanders. In addition, the war stimulated shipping and its related industries in the northern parts, which experienced unprecedented economic growth. Amsterdam replaced Antwerp as the most important harbour in western Europe, while the southern parts went into economic decline. This position was exacerbated because the southern states broke away from the Pacification of Ghent and cast their lot in with the Spaniards. Their economies were therefore coupled to the shaky Spanish economy. This decision by the southerners was based chiefly on religious considerations, aided and abetted by Alexander Farnese, the new Spanish regent. In 1579 the ten southern provinces – more or less the present Belgium and

Luxemburg – signed the Treaty of Arras and began supporting the Spaniards against the north. These territories became known as the Spanish Netherlands and later as the Austrian Netherlands. The seven northern, Protestant, provinces – Holland, Friesland, Utrecht, Zeeland, Gelderland, Groningen and Overijssel – thereupon formed the Union of Utrecht. In 1581 the members of the union declared themselves independent of Spain and proclaimed themselves the United Netherlands Provinces. From 1584 onwards they were to continue their struggle against the Spaniards under Maurice of Orange.

Developments in the Netherlands determined Philip to crush the revolt once and for all. Before this attempt could be launched, the Spanish monarch's attention was once again diverted from the Netherlands, this time by his Portuguese adventure. In 1582, once the Portuguese campaign had been concluded, the struggle in the Netherlands was tackled with renewed energy and the Spaniards achieved fair success. In 1585, however, something happened which Philip had always quietly feared – intervention in the Dutch revolt by a foreign power. Elizabeth I of England finally decided in that year to range herself on the side of the United Netherlands against Spain. This decision was to some extent brought about by Philip II himself, a result of his scores of intrigues.

To Spain the Dutch revolt was a challenge of its international leadership. This Philip wanted to protect at all costs. To safeguard his position in western Europe, and in the Netherlands in particular, Philip initially devoted himself to ensuring that France would remain friendly, waiting for an opportunity to settle his accounts with England.

In the first years of Philip's reign the relationship with England was very healthy. Even before his father's death, Philip had been married to the English Mary Tudor. During this period Spain therefore had England's full support for the strategy of preventing France from becoming a strong power. Mary was succeeded by the Protestant sympathizer Elizabeth. Elizabeth I refused to marry Philip, and relationships between the two countries deteriorated rapidly, particularly as a result of the activities of British freebooters who attacked the Spanish silver fleets sailing from South America. The sea-route to the Netherlands became equally unsafe. Philip none the less bore with the situation as he feared *rapprochement* between England and France.

In 1599 Spain agreed to the Peace of Cateau-Cambrésis with France, in which they pledged mutual support and co-operation on the religious front. The peace was brought about because the French king feared that the Guise family in France might realize its ideal of an empire consisting of England, Scotland, Ireland and France if they should be able to get rid of Elizabeth I and place Mary Stuart, queen of Scots, on the throne. This development induced Philip to remain sympathetic towards Elizabeth I. This attitude in turn enabled Elizabeth to consolidate her position and to prepare herself for the ensuing struggle against Spain. Philip II found his inability to take any constructive hostile action against Elizabeth a bitter pill to swallow and he therefore relied on half-hearted plots to have her assassinated. All of the plots failed.

In France, meanwhile, the Guise family under Henry of Navarre began supporting Roman Catholicism and became more favourably disposed towards Spain. Elizabeth I realized too late that she had made a mistake in alienating the Spanish, and her attempts at *rapprochement* were ignored by Philip. As a result, Elizabeth had Mary Stuart, queen of Scots, beheaded to safeguard her own position. Because of financial considerations, Philip II remained hesitant to begin a war with England and provisionally put his faith in the success of one of the plots against Elizabeth, or in the possibility of a Roman Catholic uprising in England. The last straw was the treaty in 1585 between England and the rebellious Netherlands. The Spanish king decided that the day of reckoning was at hand. His plan was that a combined Spanish-Portuguese fleet would take reinforcements to the Netherlands, from where an army under Alexander Farnese would be transported for an incursion into England. When the English got wind of the plan, Drake attacked Spanish shipping in Cadiz and Lisbon in 1587 and Philip had to postpone his plans for a year. In 1588 the Spanish armada of 130 ships and more than 30 000 men set sail for England.[6]

The armada was doomed from the outset. Unlike the antiquated Spanish ships, the English vessels were better equipped and designed, while English tactics were also superior to the Spanish. Dissension was rife amongst the leaders of the armada, the heterogenous force acted much too independently and there were frequent misunderstandings because of a confusion of languages. Gales and foul winds further sealed the fate of the fleet and enabled the English to wreak havoc in the Spanish lines. The result was a serious blow to Spain's military power and international standing, an early indication that Spain's leading military position was now endangered. The Spanish fleet could subsequently never hold a candle to the British fleet.

To maintain Spain's position in western Europe following his failure to subjugate England, Philip devoted all his attention to France and the safeguarding of the Valtelline route. In France, torn as it was by civil war, he found a firm ally in the Roman Catholic party known as the Catholic League. The league, supported by the influential house of Guise, was determined that the French monarchy – in the hands of the weakling Henry III – should not fall to the Protestant Henry of Navarre.

Philip therefore gave the league all the diplomatic and financial support he could muster and militarily intervened in the French civil war on several occasions. After 1590 his most capable general, the duke of Parma, with his veteran Spanish battalions, achieved several tactical victories over the French. Despite all his intrigues, however, Philip failed to have himself or a regent of his choice elevated to the French throne. He was frustrated chiefly by English support for Henry of Navarre, papal opposition and by Henry of Navarre himself, who with political acumen succeeded in inciting the French nobility against the undesirable and uncalled-for Spanish intervention in their domestic matters. In 1593 Philip's dreams involving France finally faded away when Henry of Navarre converted to Catholicism and thereby gained the support of the league.

Spain's large-scale gamble to establish its leadership in western Europe, in the course of which the empire's wealth and best troops were unhesitatingly put at stake, had come to nought. Philip could not maintain hostilities against a united France, supported by England and the Netherlands rebels. This diplomatic defeat

51

meant that Philip had also failed in his attempt to establish Roman Catholicism in a dominant position in western Europe. He could take credit, however, for indirectly ensuring that France was not lost for Catholicism, which in turn hampered the expansion of Protestantism.

This Pyrrhic victory cost Philip an exorbitant price. In 1598 he had to conclude the Peace of Vervins with France, which confirmed the stalemate position reached by the Peace of Cateau-Cambrésis (1559). The war with France also took its internal toll. In 1591 the Aragonese hostility towards Castilian ideals led to an open revolt. In the ensuing year Philip had to suppress the rebellion by military force and to consolidate his grip on Aragon. But this did not mean that the Aragonese accepted the political ideas of Philip II, against which they were to continue their stubborn resistance.

Seen superficially, Spain had succeeded in maintaining her leading position in Europe. The Spanish military machine was still a respected organization, and in other areas as well Spain seemed to be on the crest of the wave. New universities such as those in Toledo and Granada arose everywhere and Spain was a leader in intellectual circles. In the areas of astronomy, medicine, navigation and mineral technology the Spaniards were the acknowledged masters. In literature, writers such as Cervantes (with his *Don Quixote de la Mancha*), De Vega and De la Barca gave the world the novel and the Spanish drama, while artists such as Velasquez and Murillo achieved undying fame in the fine arts. In addition, Spain could rely on the riches of South America and, in particular, on the Mexican silver mines, to maintain her position in Europe.

It was, however, precisely in the economic sphere where the danger signs for the Spanish empire began to make their irrefutable appearance. The campaigns against England, France and the Dutch rebels tried the Spanish treasury to the utmost, and ultimately it also became impossible to tax the population any further. Moreover, most taxes were leased in attempts to raise further credit. Massive loans, guaranteed by silver imports, were raised, and soon the state's obligations for these loans became the single largest item in the Spanish budget. When financial institutions refused Philip further loans because of the arrears in payment, he was obliged to force them to do so by royal decree. In the last decade of his reign he even had to resort to writing off state debts by decree to obtain new loans at higher rates of interest, guaranteed once again by the American silver mines.

Other alarming symptoms also began to appear. Up to about 1650 Spain could count on a regular supply of silver from the New World to fuel its shaky economy, but the supply began to vary sharply after 1650. Some of the most profitable mines were exhausted and the American colonists increasingly turned to other states for manufactured goods, goods which Spain was unable to supply. In addition, British freebooters and Barbary pirates of North Africa, as well as smugglers, were disrupting communications between Spain and the New World and undermining the Spanish economy. Equally alarming was the loss of manpower Spain was suffering and could hardly afford. Impoverished Spaniards were leaving the land to make their way to the cities where unemployment figures rose sharply. Some of Spain's most progressive and entrepreneurial citizens were driven to fresh expectations in

Maria Theresa of Austria.

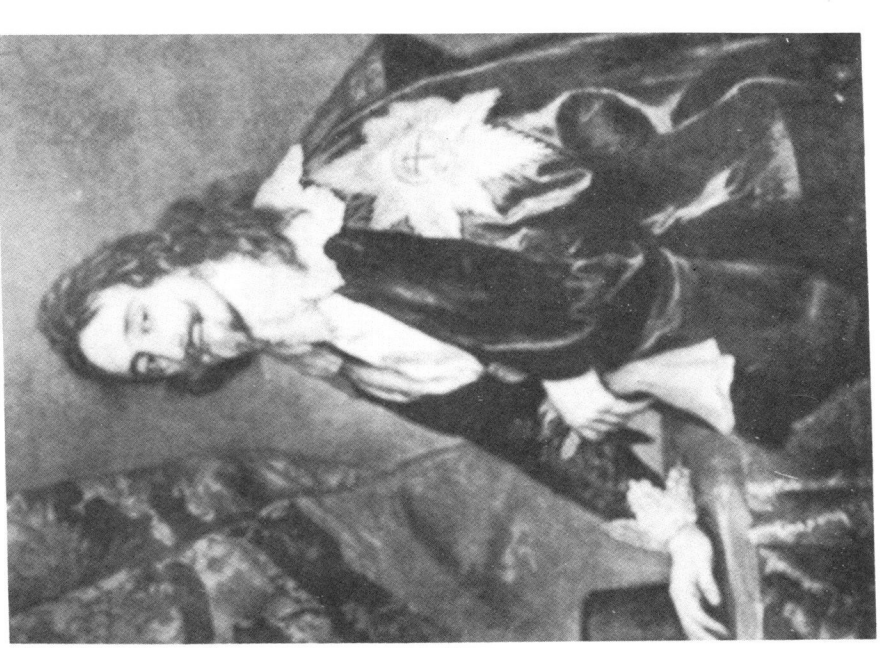

Charles I of England. Painting by Van Dyck.

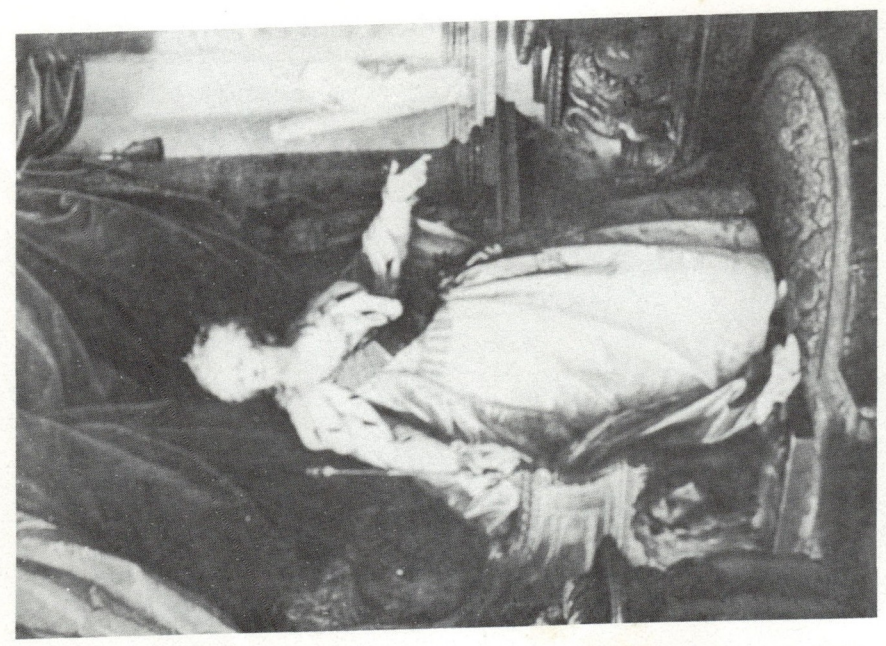

Frederick II, the Great, of Prussia.

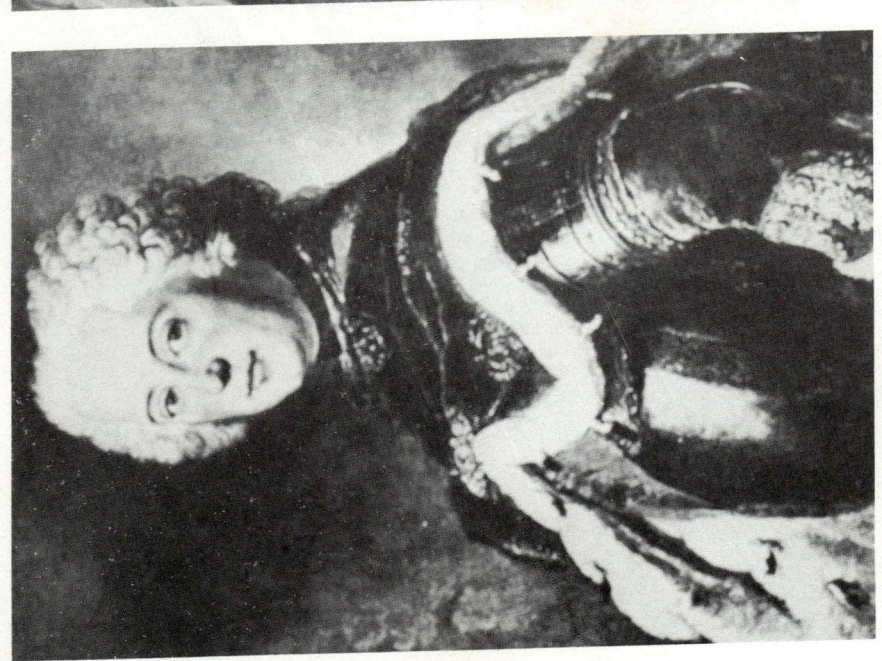

Catherine II, the Great, of Russia.

the New World by the weakening of economic prospects in Spain. The continually diminishing production capability of the country resulted in a doubling of prices for household articles in the last half of the 16th century.

As long as Philip II reigned he was successful in propping up the economy and conceal the Spanish dilemma from the rest of Europe. At his death in 1598, however, the government was taken over by less able successors who were at their wits' end concerning the enormous state debt.

THE DECLINE OF SPAIN

Philip II was succeeded by his son, Philip III. The latter had no interest whatsoever in matters of state, and for the next twenty years power was, for all practical purposes, concentrated in the hands of his favourite minister, the duke of Lerma.

Lerma initially tried to gloss over the necessity for Spain to conclude international peace and continued the struggle against England and the United Provinces with renewed vigour. However, he soon realized that Spain could not continue the exhausting war any longer and therefore subtly attempted to reach an understanding with both parties.

The English under Elizabeth I were, following their success against the Spanish armada, not remotely inclined towards favourable terms of peace. Lerma therefore tried conniving with the Irish to bring about the downfall of Elizabeth. The attempt was unsuccessful, and it was only after James I succeeded to the English throne that matters began to look more favourable for Spain. Although James supported a peace treaty, he was inexorably committed to the English claim to free trade with Spanish possessions and the right to support the Dutch rebels. The Peace of London was none the less signed in 1604 after tough negotiations. Lerma had temporarily safeguarded Spain against one of its most dangerous enemies.

Lerma now turned his attention to the rebellious Netherlands. All the efforts made by Philip II to regain control of the northern provinces had failed. Attempts to reach a settlement were bedevilled by the Roman Catholic Spaniards' unwillingness to recognize the heretic Protestants, while the Dutch in turn were benefiting financially by the state of war. Finally Spain, with the help of the Spinola brothers of Italy, reinforced the Spanish access routes, broke through the Netherlands lines and achieved one success after the other. At sea it was a different matter, however, and the Dutch inflicted heavy losses on the fleets of obsolescent Spanish galleons.

The ruthless and lengthy struggle had now reached a phase in which both parties desired peace. The Netherlands rebels feared Spinola's advance and Spain's economic position had deteriorated into further lows. But a true peace could not be achieved because of Spain's obstinate refusal to recognize the independence of the northern Netherlands and to accord them trading rights in India. Ultimately the Peace of Antwerp in 1609 only provided for a twelve year truce. Thus Lerma temporarily ended Spanish involvement in an extremely expensive war in northern Europe.

The situation in southern Europe now engaged Lerma's attentions. Here the

Venetians were developing into formidable trading competitors, threatening to take over the whole of the Mediterranean and to cut off the strategic Valtelline route at its Alpine passes. Moreover, the Turks and the Barbary states of North Africa were adding to the problems which were rendering the southern trading territories unsafe. Lerma tried to paralyse the Turks and Berbers by concluding alliances behind their lines, for instance with the shah of Persia and the kings of the Atlas mountains, but the Venetian Republic remained a thorn in the flesh of Spain, which it could never quite remove. Spain had no choice but to maintain a significant military force in the Mediterranean region.

Although Lerma's policies in the international field were reasonably successful, his interior policy left much to be desired. Despite the large debts of state, the royal household was allowed to continue its extravagances. The minister believed that all costs would be paid for by the American silver supplies. Lerma appointed relatives and favourites to state posts, and nepotism was rife. Above all he allowed the *Cortes*, motivated by jealousy, to virtually destroy the *mesta* (the guild which controlled sheep farming) and thus robbed Spain of its most flourishing industry. As if all this was not sufficient, Castile was struck by a terrible plague which, according to some calculations, killed about a tenth of the population. This saw the beginning of a population decrease which would only be stemmed half a century later.

The step which created more dissatisfaction in Spain than any other and which was probably Lerma's biggest single contribution to the country's decline was his decision to tamper with Spain's currency. In the years 1599, 1602, 1603 and 1618 the silver coins in circulation were withdrawn and gradually replaced by copper coins minted at double the previous value. Lerma had hoped to amortize the state debt in this way and to pay for the interminable wars. Instead, the measure caused an unheard-of rate of inflation, and in due course nobody was able to estimate costs or determine expenses. The monetary system became so weak and clumsy that many territories in Spain fell back on the barter system. Imports from the New World were mortgaged to such an extent that almost all of them ended in foreign hands to pay interest and amortize state loans. The small remaining amount had to pay for imports, and Lerma and his favourites lived on the rest. There was no prospect of an improvement in the financial position.

The decline of the Spanish economy was further accelerated by a decision to act against the Moriscos. These descendants of the Moors were a progressive part of the population and, unlike the Spaniards, did not look down their noses at manual labour. They had therefore become an important factor in the Spanish economy, pre-eminent as its tradesmen, agriculturalists and labourers. The Moriscos were, however, from a religious and national point of view, difficult to assimilate as a group and some of them were in collusion with the Berbers of North Africa and the French, English and Dutch, and organized raids into Spain. Finally Philip III, on the advice of Lerma, decided to solve the problem permanently by exiling the Moriscos to North Africa. This decision, which was not an uncommon one in European history, had been implemented by 1614, and between 200 000 and 300 000 Moriscos were removed from Spain.

Although the issue of the Moriscos in the decline of Spain has often been overemphasized in the past, their loss undoubtedly represented a disadvantage to the Spanish economy, the more so as their exile coincided with the depression referred to above.

By the second decade of the 17th century dissatisfaction with Lerma's government was noticeable everywhere. The Castilians were tired of bearing the burdens of the whole of the empire and insisted that other territories should accept their fair share of obligations. Plots to unseat Lerma were the order of the day. The Portuguese exacerbated matters by making it abundantly clear that they would no longer bear the yoke of Spain. To crown it all, Spain became involved in the Thirty Years War from 1618 onwards. The reasons for this were the safeguarding of the Valtelline route through the Swiss Alps against France and Savoy, and the family ties between the Spanish monarchy and the Austrian house of Habsburg. An attempt was to be made, in concert with Austria, to confirm the Habsburgs' leading position in Europe and to develop Roman Catholic interests. However, events turned against Lerma who was forced to resign in 1618. Shortly afterwards Philip III died, to be succeeded by his son, Philip IV.[7]

Philip IV, on acceding to the throne in 1621, appointed the power-hungry Viscount Olivares as his principal minister and temporarily withdrew from politics. Olivares ruled Spain for twenty one years, during which the disintegration of the once mighty Spanish empire could no longer be checked. The aim Olivares set himself was to restore Spain to the greatness she had enjoyed under Charles V. Unfortunately he did not always appreciate the restrictions of the available economic and military capabilities in the process and consequently hopelessly overstrained the country.

Keeping in mind his ideal of European leadership he launched a tripartite internal plan of action. To begin with, corruption had to be ended, administration improved and extravagant expenses combated. Next, the power of the *Cortes* was to be curtailed and, finally, he wanted to centralize authority so that he himself would be in full control of affairs.

Olivares achieved only partial success in respect of these aims. The clumsy administration was overhauled to some extent and the excessive number of state officials reduced, the expenses of the royal household were checked and luxury items were excluded from the country. But these measures fell short of solving Spain's economic dilemma, treating the symptoms rather than the malady. Olivares's attempts to centralize authority were equally unsuccessful. He regarded the *Cortes* as a stumbling block to efficient central control and therefore attempted to circumvent it by instituting councils (*juntas*). He wanted to break down provincialism and create a firmer base for royal authority. Although he succeeded to some extent in obtaining a firmer royal grip on Valencia and Aragon, Catalonia in particular remained stubborn and succeeded in evading its obligations to the crown. Internal dissension and stubbornness continued to paralyse Spain's external actions and Olivares's attempts to centralize authority were regarded with suspicion. Valencia, Aragon and Catalonia pointed out that state expenditure on foreign campaigns was undertaken purely in the interests of Castile and it was therefore only fair that this state should bear all costs (financing, supplies and troops) itself. Olivares failed to overcome the narrow-mindedness of local interest and there was still no united Spanish attempt at maintaining and safeguarding the interests of the empire. This task fell squarely and with increasing weight on the shaky economic and manpower potential of Castile.

As far as foreign affairs were concerned, Olivares continued the policy of Lerma and involved Spain in the Thirty Years War against France. The truce with the Netherlands expired in 1621 and Spain took the important decision to resume this war, too. Thus the struggle between Spain and the United Netherlands became part of the Thirty Years War. Within a short period Spain was once again embattled on all her fronts.

Olivares now had to deal with the cunning cardinal of France, Richelieu. Unlike Richelieu, Olivares did not first assure himself of his internal support before taking action outside his country. Moreover, he had the disadvantage against Richelieu in that his external policies were hamstrung to a much greater degree by local and provincial structures of authority. The optimistic Olivares also made the mistake of over-estimating his country's capabilities, under the delusion that circumstances were improving. Spain was therefore carelessly and irresponsibly thrown into the maelstrom of the international struggle for the balance of power in Europe.

Richelieu, like Olivares, fully realized the strategic value of the Valtelline route to Spain. Consequently, he had it occupied, aiming at scuttling Spain's trade with Europe, cutting its military passage to the Netherlands and wearing the mantle of European leadership. Richelieu's case was strengthened by the revolt of Nice and Savoy against Spain, but the cardinal did somewhat underestimate Spain's powers. He was forced to acknowledge this in 1626 when the war was ended and the neutrality of the Valtelline route recognized. Richelieu's plans had been temporarily thwarted.

Olivares's entry into the Thirty Years War also shows his attempt to deploy a new strategy against the Dutch rebels. He was trying to obtain control of the strategic Palatinate under Frederick of Bohemia, thus safeguarding his access routes and furthermore attempting to threaten Dutch trading activities in the North Sea and Baltic. With an eye to the latter, Olivares needed to obtain harbour facilities on the German north coast. He was successful when, during the Danish phase of the Thirty Years War (1625-1629) he pressurized the Austrian emperor to take possession of these parts. Matters improved, but in the subsequent Swedish phase of the same war (1630-1635) Olivares saw his plans collapse. The Swedes captured not only the German north coast, but also the Rhine territory, cutting Spain off from the North Sea and threatening its route through central Europe. The Dutch moreover, supported by the English, achieved a series of successes against the Spaniards. Piet Hein captured the Spanish silver fleet returning from America, while territories such as Limburg, Brabant and Flanders were occupied. Richelieu in the interim availed himself of the opportunity to acquire a hold on the strategic Italian duchy of Mantua. Richelieu aided the duke of Nevers (a French prince) to maintain his claim to the dukedom. The duke of Mantua controlled the important border towns of Casale and Montferrat between Milan and Savoy. Once the French prince had staked his claim to Mantua, Ferdinand II, emperor of the Holy Roman empire, occupied the territory in the name of his Spanish nephew, Philip IV, as French control of the dukedom could disrupt the route of communication between Milan and the Spanish Netherlands. Because the Diet of Regensburg was unwilling to become involved in the quarrel of succession concerning Mantua, Richelieu captured the dukedom and, as a result of the Treaty of Cherasco of 1631, the French prince kept Mantua.

The loss of Mantua meant a threat to Spain's routes in Europe on all sides. Militarily and economically, Spain was hovering on the brink of collapse. Castile could no longer bear the whole burden of empire, but the impetuous Olivares refused to admit that peace above all was in the paramount interest of Spain. Conscious as he was that Spain alone could no longer fend for itself, he took the humiliating step of requesting aid from the Austrian emperor – a monarchy which, for almost a century, had relied on Spain for her protection. The joint Spanish-Austrian force recaptured the Rhine territory in 1634 with the battle of Nördlingen, but success quickly waned. The following year France, the Northern Netherlands, northern Italy and Sweden declared war on Spain and Austria with a view to finally eliminating Habsburg domination of Europe. In contrast to the divided Spain, France entered the war united. This phase of the Thirty Years War, known as the French phase, dealt Spain a ruinous military blow. While Spain initially succeeded in resisting the French and their allies on land, the Spanish fleet as a military factor was wiped out in 1639. This situation was aggravated in 1643 and 1648, when the once powerful and inimitable glory of the Spanish foot soldier was ground into the dust during the battles of Rocroi and Lens. Spain's economic and political decline had now spread to its military force as well.

Olivares's political failures meanwhile had led to his dismissal, and the temperamental Philip IV personally took over the reins of state. His favourite minister, Luis de Haro, as incompetent as his predecessor, took the place of Olivares. The glorious era of a proud and assertive Spain had passed, giving way to an attitude of peace at all costs. Thus the country reaped the bitter harvest of Olivares's rash administration. Financially and morally, Spain was on its knees. The country had no alternative but to end the long drawn-out Eighty Years War in 1648 and to recognize the independence of the northern Netherlands at the Peace of Münster.

Spain was virtually defenceless against France, and conquest by this country was prevented only by the outbreak of a French civil war (the *Fronde*). France therefore had to end her war against Spain at the Peace of Westphalia (1648). Where Spain in her heyday maintained her position in Europe by military means, she now had to fall back on the diplomatic ingenuity of her leaders to save what was left. This is clearly proved by the peace negotiations of 1648. Philip IV, powerless to suppress the Portuguese rebellion militarily, managed to persuade the pope not to support Portugal's claim to independence during the negotiations preceding the treaties of 1648, and consequently, the country could not participate. Philip further revealed his impotence in dealing with Portugal by encouraging the United Provinces of the Netherlands to occupy as much as they could of the Portuguese empire.

The French phase of the Thirty Years War once again emphasized Spain's internal dissent which seriously hampered the Spanish war effort. De Haro, desperate to obtain the funds required for the war chest, taxed the few remaining untaxed articles, for example fruit. These were the only goods the impoverished people could still afford and, with nothing to lose, it is small wonder that they turned to anarchy. The first revolts broke out in Naples and Sicily, to be followed shortly thereafter by riots in the Basque provinces and separatist movements in Catalonia and Andalusia. Although these revolts were all finally suppressed, they were symptomatic of the Spanish decline and further impaired the country's already waning prestige and self-confidence.

In this respect the Portuguese insurrection had an equally serious influence. Despite the political alliance after her subjugation by Spain, Portugal had remained a semi-independent state. Like the other Spanish territories and provinces the Portuguese also rebelled against attempts to centralize authority in Castile. They objected equally to supplying Spain with soldiers and supplies for her military campaigns in Europe by refusing conscription and taxes. In their opinion Castile was acting only for its own benefit, neglecting to protect Portugal against its enemies. After 1657 several expeditions were undertaken against the Portuguese. The French and British, however, supported Portugal, which became a running sore in Spain's body politic. In 1665, for example, Spain put 23 000 men in the field against Portugal, only to see this huge army virtually destroyed. In 1668 Spain capitulated, recognized Portugal's independence and thus bade farewell to her dream of a united Iberian peninsula.

The Peace of Westphalia officially ended the war between Spain and France, but De Haro decided that the French civil war was an opportunity to regain some of the lost glory of Spain. The war against France was therefore continued, but all Spanish hopes were dashed when England unexpectedly joined the French side. One military setback after another proved that Spanish military might had perished and that the country simply did not possess the financial resources to counter the Anglo-French attack. Ultimately the important Spanish communications point, Dunkirk, fell into Anglo-French hands, which was such a strategic and economic blow that the Spaniards were forced to sign the humiliating Peace of the Pyrenees. Major towns in the Spanish Netherlands had to be handed over and France obtained a considerable amount of territory in central, southern and south-eastern Europe. These peace terms closed the Valtelline route and cut through the connection with Austria. After the peace France was the indisputable leader in Europe and its position was so predominant that there could be no hope of restoring Spain to its former glory.

In fact, it was only a diplomatic manoeuvre which prevented France from attacking and conquering Spain. A marriage was arranged between Louis XIV of France and the Spanish princess, Mary Theresa. For Spain the marriage was an act of desperation in an attempt to ensure her future independence, but for Louis XIV it contained the possibility of taking over the Spanish throne without a military campaign.

Philip IV died in 1665, and the sickly Charles II, who was a minor, succeeded him. He was the last direct Habsburg descendant who could lay claim to the Spanish throne. His mother, Mariana of Austria, acted as his regent. Being a thoroughbred Austrian, she made every effort to strengthen the links between Spain and Austria, and did not hesitate to sacrifice Spanish interests in the process. Mariana was aware that her son's condition would open the way for a number of pretenders to lay claim to the throne, and she and her chief minister, Nithard, continually worked at consolidating Charles's position. With such selfish aims it is no wonder that matters went from bad to worse. The fermenting restlessness in the interior frequently threatened to boil over and conspiracies against the government were penny-a-piece. Mariana and Nithard managed to resist them, but had none of the expertise required to set matters in Spain to rights, and the state of depression continued. The once powerful Spanish army had by now deteriorated to such an extent that it was dependent on its enemies for its weaponry.

At the international level there was no respite for Spain and it was challenged particularly by the imperialism of Louis XIV. In 1667 a new Franco-Spanish war broke out after Louis claimed the Spanish Netherlands as part of the dowry of his wife, Mary Theresa, the half-sister of Charles II. Spain was powerless, but catastrophe was averted by the formation of the tripartite alliance between England, Sweden and the United Northern Provinces of the Netherlands, countries which all feared French domination of Europe. This forced France to conclude the Peace of Aix-la-Chapelle in 1668, but none the less she obtained a number of border posts in Flanders. Spain was clearly no more than a political football amongst European nations in their attempts to manipulate the balance of power on the continent.

In 1673 a further war broke out between Spain and France after England had left the tripartite alliance and had begun supporting France. To make matters worse, there was an uprising in Sicily, and soon the Spaniards were once again fighting an exhausting war on two fronts. In 1678 the Spaniards had to capitulate and sign the Peace of Nijmegen, losing Franche-Comté and thus being finally cut off from the Spanish Netherlands. A fair amount of territory in the Spanish Netherlands was also lost.

The war-weary Spaniards joyfully welcomed the peace despite its humiliating terms. Internal dissatisfaction with Nithard grew to such proportions, however, that Charles took matters into his own hands and appointed the war hero and illegitimate son of Philip IV, Don Juan, as his most important minister. Much was expected of Don Juan, but disenchantment soon followed. From 1680 onwards the Spanish depression eased slightly, chiefly as a result of the flow of gold from Brazil to Europe. The institution of an economic policy based on the ideas of the French minister Colbert was an attempt to straighten out the Spanish economy, but met with no success, and its failure led to new fluctuations in the monetary system and further doubts about the stability of the economy.

In the midst of all this yet another Franco-Spanish war broke out, but fortunately for Spain, this so-called War of the Augsburg League was ended in 1697 by the Peace of Rijswick. Louis XIV had rather decided to try and appropriate the Spanish throne by peaceful means. The fact that Spain up to this time had succeeded in remaining intact against the French despite their numerous wars is something of a miracle. France chose to devote all its attentions to the Spanish Netherlands and therefore a territory such as Flanders in effect became a shield which deflected assaults on Spain. Moreover, French aggression in central Europe roused the suspicions of various nations who desisted from hostilities against Spain to counter the new French threat. The issue of a Spanish successor, however, once again directed French attention to Spain herself.

The marriages of Charles II to Mary of Orléans and, after her death, to Mary Anne of Neuburg, brought him no successor. The whole of Europe was conjecturing about a possible successor on Charles's death. There were three claimants: the eldest son of Louis XIV and French crown prince, Philip, duke of Anjou, was in terms of heredity the legal pretender. His mother had, however, when she married Louis XIV, renounced all claims to the Spanish throne. As her dowry had not been fully paid, Louis maintained that the renunciation had lapsed. The electress of Bavaria was another claimant, but her mother had also renounced her rights. Emperor Leopold I of Austria was the third and strongest candidate, particularly if the renunciations were to be upheld.

The Spaniards themselves were divided about the matter. One group, in particular Aragon, Valencia and Catalonia, wanted to maintain the connection with the Austrian house of Habsburg, while others such as Castile and Naples favoured the French Bourbons. Charles realized that matters were heading for a civil war and that the European nations would not simply stand by and watch. He was aware that attempts had already been made to reach an agreement on dividing the Spanish empire amongst the European powers on his death, and in an effort to avert a catastrophe and to preserve the unity of the empire, Charles left his empire to Philip of Anjou a month before his death in 1700.

When Anjou succeeded to the Spanish throne as Philip V, the fat was in the fire. France was accused of violating the agreement about division and England, the United Netherlands and Austria declared war on the French. The so-called War of the Spanish Succession broke out in 1701 and the aim of the allies was to put Archduke Charles, the son of Leopold I, on the Spanish throne, preventing France from achieving a monopoly over European trade by acquiring the Spanish empire.

Spain was invested by the allies, and by 1706 Aragon, Valencia and Catalonia were put under the control of Charles. Castile and Andalusia had, however, made a remarkable about-turn, and mainly as a result of Philip's heroic conduct and his queen's equally courageous example, they whole-heartedly supported the king against the allied enemy. This reaction prevented Spain from falling to the allies altogether, in particular after France, in 1709, was forced to withdraw her troops in Spain because of pressure on her own borders.

Ultimately developments elsewhere in Europe again came to the rescue of Spain. Repeated efforts by the allies to occupy Paris failed and thoroughly weakened their war effort. Philip V also renounced all his claims to the French throne and indicated that he would create a Spanish court which would be independent of France. This removed the threat of French domination over Europe. Of equal importance to the allies was the fact that Charles succeeded to the throne of Austria on the death of the emperor and the danger of Habsburg domination now replaced the fear of the Bourbons. The allied coalition disintegrated and the war was ended in 1713 with the Peace of Utrecht.

Although Spain was superficially the victor in the struggle, it was a bitter peace. The treaty cruelly divided the Spanish empire: Austria got the Spanish Netherlands, Milan, Naples and Sardinia; Sicily was added to Savoy and formed a separate kingdom; Britain was given possession of Gibraltar and Minorca. Of the once extensive empire only the Hispanic-American possessions remained in Spanish hands. But the peace also had its positive side, as Spain was freed of the European preoccupations which, over so many years, had been bleeding the country to death. After 1713 Spain would finally enter a period of peace, enabling her to deal with her internal problems.

CHAPTER 3

FRANCE: TURMOIL AND ASCENDANCY, 1556-1715

CIVIL AND RELIGIOUS ANARCHY, 1556-1589

By 1492, with the termination of the regency of Anne de Beaujeu and the assumption of full power by her brother, Charles VIII, the Valois dynasty had sufficiently asserted its authority over the feudal nobility to make of France a nation-state.

There ensued more than sixty years of intermittent warfare, during which the French sought to replace Spain as the major foreign influence in the Italian peninsula. The long struggle failed in its objective, but demonstrated the considerable defensive strength of the new nation, assailed not only along the Pyrenean frontier, but also in Provence and from Flanders and Artois. The contest, however, gave the French kings little opportunity to come to terms with a potential new threat to internal stability and at the same time to emulate Spanish policy in the Americas by building a colonial empire.

The movement for church reform had taken root in France before the close of the 15th century and after 1536 assumed a Calvinistic form based on the Genevan model. Francis I (1515-1547) took measures from 1529 to extirpate Protestantism, and his successor, Henry II, influenced by the decisions of the Council of Trent in 1545 to combat reform, intensified the persecution. The Huguenots, however, as the French adherents to Calvinism came to be called, displayed a remarkable resilience and continued to gain converts from all social classes.

While Spain was carving out an American empire from Mexico to the river Plate, French expeditions across the Atlantic were largely exploratory. Jacques Cartier's voyages of 1534 and 1535-1536 led to an abortive colonizing attempt on the St Lawrence river by Cartier and Roberval in 1541-1543. Ephemeral colonial bases were established between 1555 and 1565 in Brazil and Florida, but it was not until Champlain founded Quebec in 1608 that the history of New France in America began.

The abdication of the emperor Charles V in 1556 seemed to promise an end to the protracted struggle for supremacy in Italy, but a brief truce was broken in the following year when the violently anti-Spanish pope, Paul IV, induced the French to revive their claim to Naples. François de Guise, however, met with little success and was soon recalled to France to meet the challenge of the emperor's successor in Spain, Philip II, and his second wife, Mary Tudor of England. The French were defeated at Saint-Quentin in August 1557 and their invasion of the Spanish Netherlands was halted at Gravelines in July 1558. The duke of Guise, on the other hand, compelled the English to surrender Calais in January 1558.

Financial exhaustion on both sides and the changed political situation resulting from the accession of Elizabeth I to the English throne in November 1558 led to the signing of the Treaty of Cateau-Cambrésis in April 1559. France retained Calais and the overlordship of the three bishoprics of Metz, Toul and Verdun in Lorraine which she had gained in 1551. An independent Savoy provided a check to French aggression in northern Italy; Henry II's daughter Elisabeth de Valois was to marry Philip II, and both monarchs promised to work for the restoration of religious unity and the eradication of heresy. The treaty, as has been well said, "marks the end of an epoch more clear than most of the alleged epochs of history".[1] Philip II clearly emerged as head of the most powerful state in Europe; French interest was deflected from Italy towards the internal problem of religious confrontation, and thus the onward march of Protestantism on the Continent was checked. Within a few weeks of Cateau-Cambrésis Elizabeth of England was to find her *via media* in matters ecclesiastical through the creation of the Anglican Church; France, however, was to follow no such easy road to religious peace.

Before discussing the years of civil strife which engulfed France from 1562 to 1598, we would do well to examine the strengths and weaknesses of the French state in that year of Cateau-Cambrésis, which also saw the death of Henry II and the promulgation of the Discipline and the Confession of Faith of the Calvinistic Reformed Church, meeting in Paris for the first time in national synod.

In a geographic sense, Lorraine apart, France was an integral state, and the handful of small enclaves within her boundaries would, in time, inevitably lose their autonomy: the Charolais, a Habsburg domain in south-western Burgundy, was ceded in 1684; the Orange principality of the house of Nassau was finally incorporated in 1713; and the adjoining Comtat Venaissin and its capital Avignon, was removed from papal control in 1791. There was still room for expansion, particularly towards the Rhine, and for the annexation of such French-speaking regions as Franche-Comté and Artois beyond the existing frontiers, but the France of 1559 was roughly enclosed within natural borders: the English Channel, the Bay of Biscay and the Mediterranean Sea to the north, west and south respectively; the Pyrenees to the south-west; the Alps, the Jura and the river Meuse to the east, with an approximate linguistic frontier separating Picardy from the lands of Flemish speech to the north-east. The Habsburgs were France's closest neighbours and natural foes, with Philip II in Spain, the Netherlands and Franche-Comté, as well as in Milan, the Two Sicilies and Sardinia, and his uncle Ferdinand I as Holy Roman emperor. However, a common interest in promoting the Catholic cause throughout Europe, and revolt in the Netherlands combined with the internal strife in France to prevent any complete rupture until after the Valois dynasty had expired in 1589.

But if the French state was a geographic unit, it was by no means homogeneous in composition. It has been described as "a federation, given unity and coherence by the crown, but composed of distinct, if sometimes overlapping groups, whose members saw no reason to cede their rights and privileges and thus lose their separate identity".[2] Central, then, to the political, social and economic organization of the nation was the monarchy. The king was, in theory, absolute, but there existed checks upon the unbridled abuse of power. The main organ of government, for example, the royal council, was an advisory body representative of the princes of the blood, the great aristocratic families and the chief officers of church and state, amongst them the chancellor, the constable and the cardinals. Conciliar government, the norm in most European states of the period, enshrined the tradition of prior consultation in decision-making. At the same time, however, the increasing complexity of administration had by 1559 already led to the emergence of a professional bureaucracy which foreshadowed the centralized absolutism of the later 17th century. The work of the royal council was undertaken by specialized committees, state secretaries moved in the direction of ministerial rank with specific spheres of interest, and masters of requests *(maîtres des requêtes)*, ancestors of the intendants of the following century, assisted the council in the supervision of judicial affairs in the provinces.

A more significant check on royal absolutism was provided by the jurists of the supreme courts of appeal, the *parlements*, who had the function of scrutinizing legislation before registering it as the law of the land. Seven of these courts had been established in the provinces between 1443 and 1554: at Toulouse, Grenoble, Bordeaux, Dijon, Rouen, Aix-en-Provence and Rennes. These regional courts could, and often did, defend provincial interests against royal power, but it was the *parlement* of Paris, in view of its seniority, the extent of its territorial jurisdiction and its special privileges, which provided the major constitutional curb on royal absolutism at national level. The king could, however, refuse to listen to the remonstrances of the *parlement* and override its objections by the issue of *lettres de jussion*, or in the last resort, by appearing before it in person in a ceremony known as a *lit de justice*.

What was conspicuously lacking amongst the restraints on the king's power was anything approaching the emergent English parliamentary system. Neither the Estates-General of the realm nor the surviving provincial estates of France enjoyed legislative rights, but served rather as a means of consultation between the royal administration and the people, with particular regard to fiscal matters. In addition, they provided an avenue for the presentation to the king of grievances listed in *cahiers de doléances* which might then be redressed by edict. The Estates-General met irregularly, and sectional and regional differences greatly diminished its effectiveness. The fact that each order – the clergy, the nobility and the commonalty – voted separately also inhibited action.

Much of France consisted of *pays d'élections* under direct royal control, in which the king's officers were alone responsible for administration, including the collection of taxes. Despite a continuing tendency to eliminate provincial assemblies, there remained a number of *pays d'états*, particularly on the periphery of the kingdom, amongst them Brittany, Burgundy, Languedoc and Provence. In these, provincial estates jealously guarded local privileges. The Languedoc assembly, for example, which met annually and in which the towns were well represented and even some of the peasantry were eligible for election, exercised wide control over provincial finances and was able to moderate royal tax demands. Recognition of such regional autonomy represented yet another check to autocracy. Taxation was not the only method used by the king to fill the treasury. The sale of offices brought in considerable revenue. Many new posts were created, often alongside existing ones, adding to that administrative confusion which was so marked a feature of France under the *ancien régime*.

Royal absolutism was also tempered by the inherited traditions attaching to the royal office, the so-called "fundamental laws". The king's right to exercise sovereign power in the state was founded upon his obligation to dispense justice to his subjects. This duty was closely associated with the quasi-spiritual nature of the monarchy. The king was God's lieutenant on earth, and his secular legislation was expected to reflect Christian standards of social morality. This close link with the church contributed greatly to the prestige of the monarchy, and the king's authority in matters spiritual was reinforced by the Concordat of Bologna which Francis I signed with Pope Leo X in 1516. This agreement remained the basis of relations with the papacy and gave the Catholic church in France (the Gallican Church) a degree of independence from Rome. The pope merely confirmed royal nominations to major benefices, receiving in return the annates, or first year's revenue accruing. The royal hold on the Gallican Church made the king the guarantor of religious orthodoxy in the kingdom, and any accommodation with the Calvinist minority could only weaken the authority of the monarchy.

Calvinism had made great strides in France, but its adherents numbered probably no more than 15 per cent of a total population of something in the neighbourhood of 19 000 000. Its spread had been facilitated by the main arteries of trade, in particular the valleys of the Rhône and the Loire, and by 1559 Calvinists were to be found in all parts of the kingdom. They were, however, numerically strongest in a wide arc of territory extending from Poitou in the west to Dauphiné in the south-east, embracing Aunis, Saintonge, Guyenne and Languedoc, with an outlying concentration in coastal Normandy. This distribution was to remain constant throughout a century and more of confrontation between Catholics and Protestants in France.

The peasantry and the lower orders in the towns were as well represented in the Calvinist ranks as they were in the Catholic, but in the general unrest and bankruptcy which followed the Italian wars it was the gains Calvinism made amongst the nobility which gave the religious movement its militant political arm. Calvinism stood apart from the French tradition and its alliance with aspiring pressure groups in an era of monarchical incapacity made it a dangerous threat to stability. The turmoil into which France was about to be plunged can therefore not be seen in terms of religion alone. "The preconditions of civil conflict were contained in the coincidence of religious passion, financial crisis, and factional division."[3]

Leaders of the Huguenot faction whose influence determined many of the lesser nobility to enlist under the Calvinist banner were the Bourbon princes Antoine de Vendôme, king of Navarre, and his younger brother, Louis de Condé. Both were moved by ambition, rather than by depth of religious conviction, and Antoine was soon to defect to the Catholic cause. The Bourbons, however, were a cadet branch of the Valois family and stood next to the sons of Henry II in the line of succession to the throne. This circumstance lent an air of respectability to the Huguenot challenge. The Châtillon family also produced outstanding Huguenot leaders, of whom Gaspard de Coligny, admiral of France and nephew of the Catholic constable, Anne Pierre Adrien de Montmorency, was the most energetic, with a strong following in Normandy. Head of the Catholic faction was François de Guise, supported by his brother, Charles, cardinal of Lorraine.

The death of Henry II in 1559 inaugurated a long and disastrous period of weak monarchy in France, initially, but briefly, under Guise dominance. Henry was succeeded by his young son, Francis II, who was married to the Scottish queen, Mary Stuart, whose mother Marie de Guise exercised the regency in Edinburgh with French military support. Calvinism, however, had also taken root in Scotland, and its militant supporters, with English help, forced a French withdrawal in the Treaty of Edinburgh of July 1560. Mary was to return to a troubled homeland in the following year and within a decade had abdicated and fallen into English hands.

Mary Stuart's uncles, the ultra-Catholic Guise brothers, retained their power at the French court, despite the failure of their sister in Scotland, although their zeal to extirpate Calvinism was to some extent modified after the appointment of the liberal chancellor, Michel de l'Hôpital. He allied himself with moderate elements in the royal council to tone down an intended act of repression in 1560, the Edict of Romorantin, so that it differentiated between religious and political Calvinism. Nevertheless, dislike of the Guise faction resulted in an unsuccessful attempt by the Huguenots to rescue the king from Guise clutches in the conspiracy of Amboise in the same year. Condé was at length arrested and sentenced to death for his complicity in this affair, but was saved by the decease of Francis II in December 1560 and the loss of Guise influence in high places.

Charles IX, Francis II's brother, was only ten years of age when he ascended the throne, and the queen-mother, Catherine de Medici, assumed the regency. Catherine's policy was to support moderation by conciliating the Huguenots and holding the Guise party at bay. Condé was released, Navarre was appointed lieutenant-general of France, and Michel de l'Hôpital remained chancellor. The Estates-General met at Orléans and Pontoise (1560-1561), where the nobility and the third estate, with a disproportionately high representation of Huguenots, preached anti-clericalism and spoke out for religious toleration. L'Hôpital convened a conference of Catholic and Calvinist theologians at Poissy in September 1561 in a vain endeavour to reach a doctrinal compromise. Finally, in January 1562, the chancellor issued an Edict of Toleration, permitting Calvinist worship outside town walls and the holding of synods with prior royal approval. "The January edict was to remain the charter of Huguenot emancipation."[4] Meanwhile, the Catholic party had not been inactive, and in April 1561 François de Guise, Montmorency and the marshal Jean d'Albon de Saint-André formed a triumvirate to offer armed resistance to the Huguenots. They were joined by Navarre in the following year.

The signal for the outbreak of the first of the nine brutal civil wars which were to ravage France until 1598 was the massacre by Catholics under François de Guise of a Calvinist congregation at Wassy in Champagne in March 1562. This display of savagery was, however, no more than the latest in a long series of outrages committed by both sides in the course of the previous two years. Widespread Calvinist rioting and desecration of churches engendered Catholic reprisals, while Huguenot terrorist activity in Provence soon had its imitators. In the general breakdown of law and order old scores were sometimes paid off without reference to religious belief.

The first war lasted less than a year. Both sides initiated the policy of using German mercenaries who joined forces to pillage Champagne as they withdrew; both, too, received foreign aid: Spanish and papal aid for the Catholics, and English aid for the Huguenots. English troops, however, merely occupied Havre-de-Grâce (Le Havre) as a surety for the restoration of Calais and had to be dislodged by a joint Catholic and Huguenot army when peace returned. On balance, the Catholic, or royalist, party had the better of the exchanges, despite such early Huguenot successes as the capture of Lyons. By the end of 1562, however, the Huguenots had lost Blois and Tours on the Loire, Poitiers, Angoulême and Bourges to the south, and Rouen in Normandy. Their troops had also been defeated at Vergt in the southwest. Coligny was able to withdraw in safety after the indecisive action at Dreux on the confines of Normandy in December 1562, but François de Guise besieged the Huguenot capital Orléans, where he was assassinated in February 1563. Navarre had died of wounds which he received at Rouen, and Saint-André had been killed at Dreux, a battle in which both Montmorency and Condé were captured.

The losses in the leadership of the Catholic party enabled Catherine de Medici to regain the initiative and on the 19th March 1563 the edict known as the Pacification of Amboise was promulgated. Its terms strongly favoured the militant Huguenot nobility, permitting them, according to their varying degrees, complete religious freedom on their estates, or the right to hold private services in their households. Pastors and their flocks generally were disappointed in these concessions to the aristocracy, since Calvinist worship outside the great estates was restricted to Huguenot garrison towns and one additional locality in each bailiwick. Paris was excluded from these arrangements, and Catholic property was to be restored, but these were small gains for the Catholics, and it was only with the greatest difficulty that Catherine was able to ensure the registration of the edict by the *parlement* of Paris and those of the provinces.

Catherine endeavoured to restore the authority of the king by conducting him on an extensive tour of his dominions (1564-1566), and L'Hôpital contributed to this planned rehabilitation by drawing up the reforming Edict of Moulins in 1566. In the course of the grand tour, a meeting with the Spanish court took place at Bayonne, at which the duke of Alva, who was soon to be sent to quell the revolt in the Netherlands, was present. This diplomatic move sowed the seeds of the brief second civil war. An attempt to capture the French court was foiled at Meaux in September 1567, but a number of important towns, amongst them Valence and Montpellier, fell into Huguenot hands in simultaneous uprisings. Condé invested Paris, but was driven off after the battle of Saint-Denis on the 10th November 1567, in which the aged Montmorency was mortally wounded. The Huguenot leader effected a junction with German troops from the Palatinate near Troyes and moved westward to besiege Chartres. In the meantime, Huguenot forces made important gains in the Loire valley. The royalists were compelled to seek peace.

The Peace of Longjumeau, signed on the 23rd March 1568, restored the status quo, but provided no lasting solution to internal differences. Both sides remained under arms, and local Catholic leagues were formed to combat Calvinism. Events in the Netherlands became closely linked with the struggle in France. Huguenot ships from La Rochelle and the ports of Normandy assisted the Dutch in revolt, a Calvinist force entered Artois, but was crushed by Alva, and William of Orange signed a treaty of alliance with Condé and Coligny. Catherine de Medici, influenced by the abortive coup at Meaux and the Dutch threat, turned away from moderation. L'Hôpital was forced to resign in May 1568, and a plot to seize the Huguenot leaders was hatched. Condé and Coligny, however, escaped to La Rochelle, henceforth to be the main Huguenot base, and took the offensive in September 1568, in conjunction with an advancing Bavarian army from the east. Royal edicts proclaimed in September and December 1568 gave the struggle added point. While liberty of conscience was accorded, the practice of any religion but the Catholic was forbidden. The conditions of the time, however, made this act of intolerance virtually a dead letter.

Although the Germans took La Charité on the upper Loire before joining Coligny, the Huguenot offensive in the west met with little success. Condé was defeated and killed at Jarnac in March 1569 by forces under the future king, Henri de Valois, Duke of Anjou. With German and Swiss mercenaries of his own, Anjou then turned on Coligny, inflicting a heavy defeat on him at Moncontour, north of Poitiers, in October. Coligny, however, withdrew to Languedoc before moving to the north-east, where he was victorious over a royalist army at Arnay-le-Duc in Burgundy in June 1670. Catherine de Medici, fearing perhaps a conjunction of Huguenot forces with the Dutch, opened peace negotiations and on the 8th August 1570 the third civil war was ended by the Peace of Saint-Germain. All Calvinist privileges were restored and a new policy inaugurated, that of permitting Huguenot troops to garrison for two years the fortress towns of La Rochelle, La Charité, Montauban and Cognac.

With the restoration of peace, Coligny and the Huguenot nobility gained an unexpected ascendancy at court and their influence inclined Charles IX to follow, rather hesitantly, a foreign policy more favourable to England and the Dutch patriots, and greatly to the disadvantage of the Guisards. In April 1572, England and France signed the defensive Treaty of Blois and in the following month, contrary to the assurances the king had given Spain, Huguenot troops were permitted to cross the north-eastern frontier and capture Valenciennes and Mons. In Paris, the marriage of the queen-mother's daughter, Marguerite de Valois, to the Calvinist prince of the Bourbon family, Henri de Navarre, took place on the 18th August. Four days later Coligny was shot and wounded in an assassination attempt. The Huguenots cried out for revenge, but there occurred a sudden change in policy when Charles IX was persuaded that the Huguenots were plotting to overthrow the monarchy and gave orders for the execution of all their leaders, many of whom had come to Paris for the royal wedding.

There ensued the St Bartholomew's Day Massacre which began on the 24th August 1572 and lasted for six days in the capital and for a further two weeks in the provinces. Mob violence took command and the killings went far beyond the removal of such Huguenot leaders as Coligny, whose mutilated body was publicly exhibited on the orders of the Paris *parlement*. It seems possible that as many as 15 000 people perished, and the great majority of these outside the capital.

There is no evidence to suggest that the crime was premeditated, nor was it intended that it become a general blood-bath. Catherine de Medici and her advisers must shoulder some of the blame. She disliked Coligny personally and also for his influence on her son, the king. She had no wish to antagonize Spain and was also aware that her own internal policy of reconciliation, even to the royal marriage, enjoyed no wide support. Catherine doubtless felt that the Huguenot fury after the failure of the first attempt to murder Coligny would lead to her downfall and saw a golden opportunity of ridding herself of those who were sure to turn against her. We would, however, agree with J. H. M. Salmon that Charles IX's actions cannot be excused: "His conduct of foreign policy in the two years after the peace of Saint-Germain largely provoked the internal crisis, and constituted the only set of decisions taken on his own initiative. The extraordinary vacillations which this policy involved clearly demonstrate the incapacity of the morose and unstable king."[5]

The massacre inevitably engendered a fourth civil war, in which the Huguenots, now lacking effective leadership, fell back upon their fortress towns. La Rochelle and Sancerre were invested by royalist troops, but neither was taken. The Edict of Boulogne in July 1573 ended the war in the west. Calvinists were granted liberty of conscience, and worship was permitted at La Rochelle, Nîmes, Montauban and in the homes of certain of the nobility. Sancerre subsequently obtained its freedom on the same conditions. The Huguenots had in part been saved in this defensive war through the sympathy expressed by many moderate Catholics who were repelled by the massacre. Many of the Catholic nobility had little taste for continued fighting along religious lines and formed the *Politique* party under François de Valois, duke of Anjou and heir to the throne, as titular head. The *Politiques* were committed to toleration as the only means of establishing a lasting peace. Amongst this number were the Bourbon princes, Henri de Navarre and Henri de Condé, who had escaped death in August 1572 by accepting Catholicism. In Languedoc, however, militant Calvinism was moving towards federal republicanism, or the creation of a state within the state. In July 1574 the Huguenots there formed an alliance with Henri de Montmorency-Damville, governor of the province and real leader of the *Politique* group, under which they accepted royal authority, but without disbanding their federal organization. Charles IX, however, had already decided to attack the Huguenots and was taking steps to crush the opposition of the *Politiques* when he died on the 30th May 1574. His brother, Anjou, who had been elected king of Poland in the previous year, hastened back to his war-torn homeland where, as Henry III of France, he was to display none of that ability which had characterized his earlier military career. His reign was unworthy of a man of his undoubted intelligence.

The fifth civil war of 1574-1576 was by no means a clear-cut struggle between Catholics and Calvinists, although complete religious toleration was the goal of both the Huguenots and their allies, the *Politiques*. Damville led the combined forces in the south, while the future duke of Bouillon, not yet a Calvinist, headed the Huguenot forces in the south-west. Although Henri de Guise scored a notable victory for the royalists at Dormans on the Marne in October 1575, the alliance had generally the better in much confused fighting, with the help of an English subsidy and marauding German mercenaries from the Palatinate threatening Paris. Both Condé and Navarre were able to rejoin the allied ranks.

The *Paix de Monsieur*, ratified by the Edict of Beaulieu in May 1576, showed the weakness of royal power. Complete freedom of worship was accorded to the Calvinists, except in Paris and towns with royal palaces, and eight towns could be garrisoned by the Huguenots, who were also permitted to hold office under the crown. *Chambres mi-parties* were created in the *parlements*, with Protestant and Catholic judges in equal numbers to hear cases involving Calvinists. The leaders of the Huguenots and the *Politiques* were rewarded. Condé was restored to the governorship of Picardy, Navarre was given Guyenne and Damville confirmed as governor of Languedoc.

Scandals at court and the excesses of Henry III's favourites, the *mignons*, contributed to the rise of Henri de Guise, popular and respected, as the champion of the Catholic cause. In 1576 he organized a Catholic league which was committed to the eradication of Calvinism and the protection of Catholicism. It was a shrewd move, since the *Politiques* had deserted their former allies in favour of an alliance with the crown to prevent the Guisards from becoming too powerful in the state. A short civil war ensued in 1577, during which the Huguenots lost La Charité on the Loire to Anjou. Peace was signed at Bergerac and confirmed by the Edict of Poitiers in October 1577. The Huguenots were at a disadvantage and their gains under the *Paix de Monsieur* were reduced. Their rights in the *chambres mi-parties* were curtailed, and outside their fortified towns Calvinist worship was again restricted to a single locality in each bailiwick.

The year 1578 saw a change in French foreign policy, when Anjou occupied Mons on the invitation of William of Orange and with the tacit consent of the French monarchy. At the same time, Catherine de Medici, still active in the interests of the state, travelled to Guyenne and at length secured the support of the Huguenots of the south-west in the Peace of Nérac (signed on the 28th February 1579), by which the Calvinists obtained fifteen garrison towns. Despite this achievement, however, and Catherine's further efforts as peacemaker in Languedoc, Provence and Dauphiné, a seventh civil war broke out in November 1579, although its causes had more to do with personal ambitions than with religious problems. It was inaugurated by Condé who sought redress for his failure to make good his right to the governorship of Picardy awarded to him. He took La Fère in that province and held it for almost a year against the royalists. This was an independent action, but in Guyenne, Navarre was persuaded to renounce the Peace of Nérac in order to acquire the lands he had been promised as his wife's dowry. This *Guerre des Amoureux* ("Lovers' War") was unsupported by Condé and, except in Provence, by the Huguenots of the south and west. Navarre scored a notable success at Cahors in May 1580, but the Peace of Fleix (the 26th November 1580) brought the fighting to an end and restored the status quo.

There ensued a confused period which illustrates further monarchical weakness and indecision. The Guisards conspired against the crown, Henry III tried to make himself independent of both factions and Anjou's ambitions in the Netherlands were thwarted in 1583, the year of the marriage of William of Orange to Louise de Coligny, daughter of the French admiral. There was growing friendship between the Guise faction and Philip II of Spain, when it became clear that the Scottish protégée of the Guisards, Mary Stuart, then detained in England, would pursue a pro-Spanish policy if her abdication were set aside. The French king's attitude towards Spain hardened and Philip II's incorporation of Portugal in 1580 gave Henry III a chance to assert himself. A considerable fleet was sent to assist the Portuguese pretender, Dom António, in the Azores, but was routed by the Spanish in 1582.

At home, peasant revolts in Provence, the Vivarais and Dauphiné between 1578 and 1580 were a foretaste of the savage uprisings in Normandy and Brittany after 1589 and of the rebellion of the Croquants of the south-west in 1594. Escalating food prices, widespread famine and outbreaks of the plague were the tragic consequences of civil war, and the price paid by the peasantry was a population decline which probably exceeded 20 per cent.

The death of Anjou on the 10th June 1584 introduced a new element into the power struggle, since the heir to the French throne was now the Bourbon leader, Henri de Navarre, a Calvinist and, indeed, to Catholics a lapsed member of the faith. His eventual succession could well strike at the ancient traditions of the French monarchy and posed a serious problem in a predominantly Catholic society. The immediate result was a revival of the Catholic League by the Guise faction. The league's manifesto of March 1585 was dedicated to the restoration of good government in a Catholic France, and it lent its support to the pretensions to the throne of the Catholic Bourbon, the cardinal Charles, on the death of Henry III. Philip II of Spain had already promised the league financial help in the Treaty of Joinville (December 1584); Henry III accepted the Guise programme in the Treaty of Nemours (July 1585) which outlawed Calvinism in France, and Pope Sixtus V excommunicated Navarre and Condé two months later, depriving the former of his right of succession.

The stage was set for the eighth civil war, the War of the Three Henrys, the king, Navarre and Guise, which was to merge after 1589 into the ninth and final conflict, fought on a larger, international scale. The Huguenot position in 1587, when hostilities began, was grave and was rendered no easier by the wave of popular support for the Guisards and the league after the execution of Mary Stuart by Elizabeth I of England in February of that year, an act dictated in part by the *rapprochement* between the Guise faction and Philip II of Spain. The English queen, it is true, had provided resources to raise a German and Swiss mercenary army to invade France in the Huguenot interest, but Guise defeated the mercenaries at Vimory and Auneau towards the end of 1587, thus compensating for Navarre's victory over royalist forces at Coutras in the south-west in October. Navarre was also to lose another ally in March 1588, when Condé died, although close co-operation between the two had not been a marked feature of recent years.

Disunity in the ranks of the royalist-league alliance was, however, actual, not potential, and the problems of waging successful war against the Huguenots compounded by Philip II's preoccupation with the invasion of England, averted by the defeat of the Spanish Armada in July 1588 and its subsequent dispersal. Savoy, too, took the opportunity of French discomfiture by invading Saluces (Saluzzo). Moreover, the popularity of Guise aroused the jealousy of the king. Guise, in defiance of a royal ban, entered Paris and on the 12th May 1588, the Day of the Barricades, forged an alliance with radical revolutionary elements within the capital. This urban movement was to spread throughout France and was to colour league politics for the next six years. The king was forced to leave Paris and temporized by signing the Edict of Union with the leaguers. He was, however, determined to destroy Guise influence, finding his opportunity when the Estates-General met in Blois. Guise was murdered on the king's orders on the 23rd December 1588 and his cardinal brother, Louis, met the same fate on the following day. A third brother, Charles, duke of Mayenne, took over the league leadership, which henceforth had to work in close conjunction with urban radicalism. Catherine de Medici's death in January 1589 ended the sporadic Valois attempts at conciliation, Henry III joined forces in an unholy alliance with Navarre, and their combined armies advanced on Paris, where at Saint-Cloud on the western outskirts, Henry III was stabbed by Jacques Clément, a young Dominican friar obsessed by the king's apparent change of heart on the religious issue. Henry died on the 1st August 1589 and the Calvinist Navarre inaugurated the Bourbon dynasty.

HENRY IV AND RELIGIOUS COMPROMISE, 1589-1610

Henry IV had to contend with the defection of some of his Catholic supporters, the active intervention of Spain and even an incursion into Provence by a Savoyard army. Papal troops also helped the league, while German mercenaries proved less valuable to the king than they had in the past. On the credit side, apart from a general desire for the restoration of peace under a strong monarchy, Henry IV enjoyed certain advantages: he had English support in the field and considerable Dutch Protestant sympathy, while divided counsels prevailed in the league ranks, and their only generally accepted claimant to the throne, the aged Charles de Bourbon, died in 1590 at Chinon, where Henry IV had held him in captivity.

The new king raised the siege of Paris and defeated Mayenne in Normandy at Arques (September 1589) and Ivry (March 1590). Although Spanish reinforcements were now reaching the leaguers, the Bourbon forces were successful in Auvergne and Dauphiné, and held their own in Languedoc and Provence. Paris was again invested by Henry IV, but in August 1590 Parma led a Spanish army out of the Netherlands and in collaboration with Mayenne forced the royalists to raise the siege. Henry IV now turned for help to England whose troops landed in Brittany and at Dieppe. The siege of Rouen was begun in 1591 with English assistance, but in January 1592 Parma again invaded France and succeeded in relieving the Norman capital. In the previous year Mayenne had gained the upper hand in Paris over the radical controlling group known as the Sixteen, but their association with the Spanish who maintained a garrison in the capital, made him tread warily. The league was in disarray, and only the choice of a generally acceptable pretender to the throne could bring back a semblance of unity. Accordingly, in 1593, with the Bourbon cause everywhere in the ascendant and Henry IV just outside the capital at Chartres, Mayenne convened in Paris a meeting of the Estates-General of the league faction. In the absence of a suitable candidate the leaguers introduced the novel concept of the elective factor for kingship, while the Spanish party's claims for Philip II's daughter Isabel Clara Eugenia were rejected by the *parlement* as contrary to the Salic law debarring women from the succession.

The failure of the Estates-General to reach agreement resulted in no small measure from a momentous decision taken by Henry IV. In May 1593 he decided to seek instruction in the Catholic faith and on the 25th July attended mass at Saint-Denis. On the 27th February 1594 he was crowned king at Chartres according to ancient custom and on the 22nd March Paris received him with acclamation; a capitulation followed by many of the provincial towns and cities in the following two months. Papal approval of the abjuration at Saint-Denis was longer delayed and it was not until the 17th September 1595 that Henry IV was finally received into the Catholic church. Henry IV was not a man of intense religious principles, but the saying attributed to him that "Paris is well worth a mass", should not be regarded as the flippant observation of a self-seeking opportunist. The maintenance of the hereditary principle of monarchical succession in the age-old tradition of Catholicity was essential to the restoration of peace in an overwhelmingly Catholic country in which the fortunes of church and state had always been closely intertwined. Henry IV could afford to be generous to his former co-religionists, and, indeed, the continuing influence of their leaders in arms dictated this as a wise course. Calvinism had, however, not been gaining during the long years of civil strife. Abjuration, emigration and extermination had, in fact, further reduced the numbers of its adherents, who probably represented no more than 10 per cent of the total population at the accession of Henry IV.

The war did not end in 1594. Spain and the leaguers were still active on the borders of Picardy and the Ile de France, and in August of that year Laon fell to the king's troops. In January 1595 Henry IV declared war on Spain. He gained a brilliant victory over the Spanish at Fontaine-Française in Burgundy in June of that year, and by 1596 the whole of the south-east to the Mediterranean had been pacified. Mayenne, deserted by most of his leaguers, made peace and secured generous terms in the Edict of Folembray (December 1595), including six garrison towns and the governorship of the Ile de France. Spain's main thrust was in the north-east, where her troops defeated Bouillon and Villars at Doullens in July 1595 before taking Cambrai, and in April 1596 entered Calais. Amiens fell in the following year, but was recaptured in September 1597. The Peace of Vervins of the 2nd May 1598 brought the Spanish War to a close on the basis of the settlement of Cateau-Cambrésis of almost 40 years before. The pacification of Brittany was completed in the same year.

There remained the Huguenot problem. The king had rescinded the violently anti-Calvinist legislation of 1585 and 1588 by the Declaration of Mantes (July 1591), but the Huguenot leadership was growing restive in the absence of a firm settlement. This was provided by the Edict of Nantes which, in its various sections, was completed between the 13th April and the 2nd May 1598. A measure of the general lack of enthusiasm in Catholic circles for Henry IV's solution to the problem of peaceful co-existence is the fact that the Paris *parlement* only ratified the

Edict of Nantes in February 1599 after receiving assurances that Calvinist worship would be barred from episcopal and archiepiscopal cities and that the *parlement* of Rouen delayed registration until 1609. It must be remembered, too, that the warrants which, in guaranteeing the royal edict, gave bite to the legislation, depended entirely on the king's favour. Moreover, the preamble to the main clauses makes it clear that Henry IV did not lose sight of the possibility of achieving religious unity in the future. Nor did the Edict of Nantes place both religions on an equal footing, since Catholicism was everywhere re-established, and the revenues of which it had been despoiled were restored.

The edict had a religious side and a political aspect and was largely based upon the various attempts made during the late wars to achieve a workable *modus vivendi* in the public interest. The Edict of Nantes recognized three categories of Calvinist worship: on the estates of the nobility, open to all in the case of the great landowners, but only at household level for the lesser nobility; in all places where services had been held between January 1596 and August 1597; and elsewhere in two localities in each bailiwick outside municipal boundaries, with certain restrictions which, initially only, included Paris. Commissioners, Calvinist and Catholic, were to be appointed to apply these rules. The *chambres mi-parties* were resuscitated and Calvinists were to enjoy full civil liberties. Secret articles dealt with reformed church government by consistory, colloquy and synod, provincial and national, while the warrant of the 13th April and a later one issued in August 1598 made financial provision for local churches and educational establishments, together with a lump sum in compensation for Catholic revenues surrendered.

There was a partial silence on the political organization of Calvinism, but the strength of militant reform could not be ignored. Political assemblies were tolerated and Henry IV conceded a large number of garrison towns to the Huguenots and control over certain other localities, amongst them the *places de mariage*, to be guarded by detachments of troops. The king was to appoint the governors of garrison towns on Huguenot advice, and the guarantee of military autonomy was underwritten by an annual subsidy.

The Huguenots therefore entered the 17th century possessed of organs of government, ecclesiastical and lay, which were opposed to the principles of absolute monarchy. Yet under Henry IV, the Edict of Nantes was generally upheld in that system of balanced concessions which characterized the king's approach to those of both religions. His task of pleasing all men was, in part, facilitated by the continuing influence of the *Politiques* who saw in the protection of Calvinism a move away from Romanism within the Gallican Church. Moreover, the Edict of Nantes allowed Calvinists to submit gracefully to royal authority, and with this submission went a renewed and sometimes exaggerated loyalty to the king's person. This was to prove a chink in the Calvinist armour, but it accorded well with the reassertion of absolutism after the civil wars by the first of the Bourbons.

Henry IV's absolutist tendencies were clearly in evidence when he summoned the notables of France to assemble at Rouen in November 1596. There was a crying need for firm guidance at the top in order to counter widespread economic distress, to check separatism and to improve the nation's standing in European affairs.

Aided by Maximilien de Béthune, created duke of Sully in 1606, Henry IV set about his task with determination. Sully's contribution as administrator "was to produce order out of chaos, to defeat corruption, to govern justly",[6] and as a corollary, to extend royal power in the provinces. His major success lay in fiscal reform, in which he did much to remedy the injustices of tax assessment and collection, with particular reference to the *taille*, a direct tax, variously levied on persons or land, which caused great hardship to the peasantry. This brought him into conflict with provincial administrators, and the advance towards absolutism may be seen in Sully's extension of direct royal control in Guyenne, despite local opposition. France made a rapid recovery from her economic decline. A commercial council was established in 1602 under Barthélemy Laffemas; industry was stimulated and foreign trade encouraged by the negotiation of commercial treaties with the Ottoman empire, Spain and England.

In the international field Henry IV followed an anti-Habsburg policy. Savoy, the gateway to northern Italy, was brought back into the French system of alliances after a brief campaign in 1600. By the Peace of Lyons (1601) Charles Emmanuel of Savoy was allowed to retain the Saluzzo territory he had long coveted, but ceded Valromey, Bresse and Bugey to France, regions lying close to imperial Franche-Comté. Lower Navarre on the Pyrenean frontier, Henry's own kingdom, was fully integrated into the French state in 1607. Two years later the French king placed himself at the head of the Protestant Union of German states designed to prevent the duchy of Cleves-Jülich on the Rhine from falling into imperial hands. Henry IV planned to attack Spain and the empire on three fronts, but his death at the hands of the assassin François Ravaillac on the 14th May 1610 ended the Grand Design, although Maurice of Nassau, with English help, took Jülich.

THE ESTABLISHMENT OF ROYAL AUTHORITY, 1610-1642

Henry's son was a minor at the time of his succession as Louis XIII, and power was in the hands of the regent, Marie de Medici, whom Henry IV had married in 1600 after the annulment of his earlier Valois marriage. The result was a complete reversal of French foreign policy, with arranged marriages binding France to Spain and the empire, including that of the young king to Anne of Austria. Moreover, "the death of Henry IV resurrected all the forces of incipient feudal disorder and showed on what slender foundations royal authority rested. France in the next few years slipped back into feudal anarchy and chaos".[7] It was a period of court intrigue, of insubordination amongst the nobility whose pretensions were bought off by the queen-mother, and of growing financial instability. The Estates-General, summoned in 1614 for the last time before the French Revolution, displayed its usual lack of solidarity, but at least remonstrated on the parlous condition of the state. The *parlement* of Paris, too, attacked abuses and defied the monarchy. Nor was the situation improved when Louis XIII assumed control of the government in 1617, banished his mother to intrigue behind his back in the provinces and turned for advice to his favourite, the future duke of Luynes.

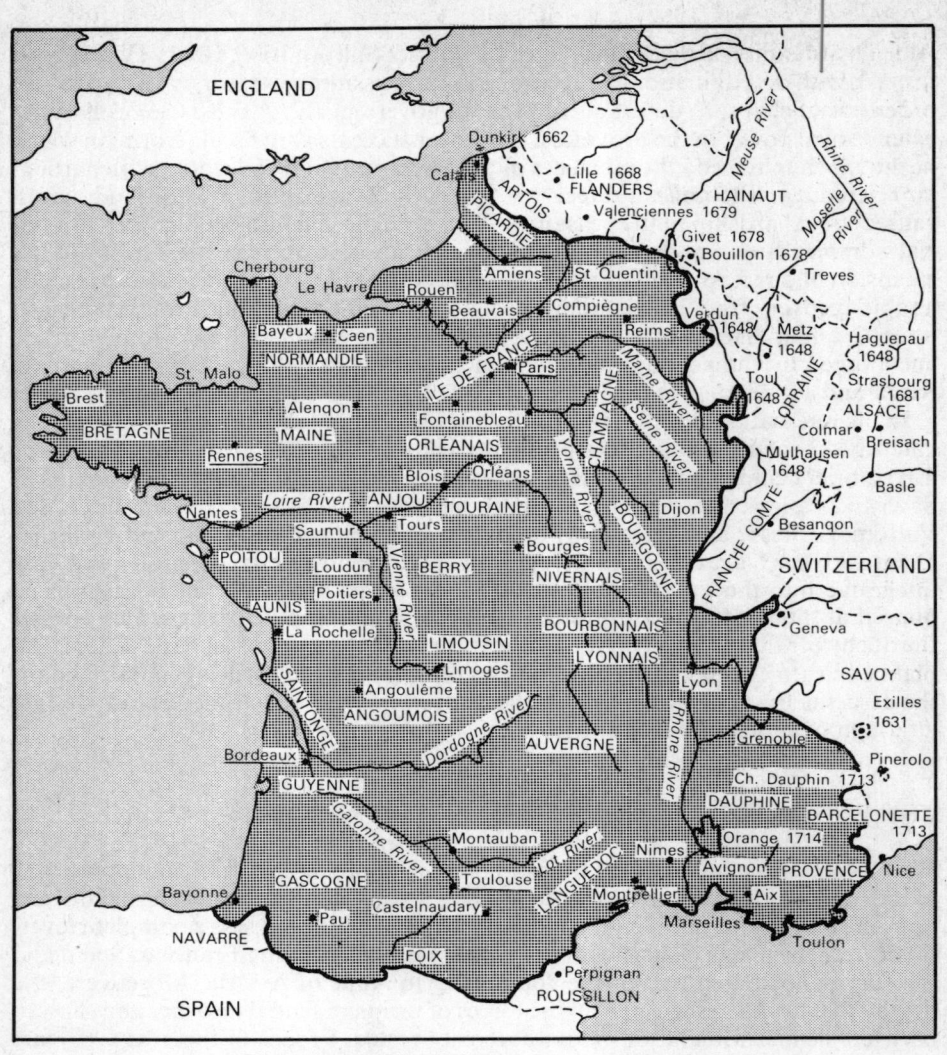

France in 1630, with later territorial gains

The assumption of power by Louis XIII, confirmed by his defeat of forces supporting Marie de Medici at Les Ponts-de-Cé on the Loire in 1620, brought the young king into conflict with the Huguenots. The new civil war was sparked off by the incorporation of autonomous Béarn on the Spanish frontier into the French kingdom in 1617. Béarn was strongly Calvinistic, but in 1620 royalist troops were sent there to restore Catholic supremacy, taking the opportunity of capturing several Huguenot strongholds in Poitou and Guyenne in their advance on the Pyrenean province. The Huguenots, meeting at La Rochelle, called for war, and Henri de Rohan and his brother, the prince of Soubise, raised the standard of revolt.

The campaigns of 1621 and 1622 were a considerable royalist success. Many towns in the south and west fell to the king's forces, and only Montauban and Montpellier held out, joining La Rochelle as centres of Huguenot resistance. The troubled state of Europe in the Thirty Years War, however, led to an early peace in the Treaty of Montpellier (1622), by which the king confirmed the Edict of Nantes, made Rohan Governor of the Cévennes, but insisted on the razing of Montpellier's defences and permitted only the retention of La Rochelle and Montauban as fortified garrison towns. The lack of enthusiasm for military adventure outside the war zones, the defection and, indeed, the abjuration of many of the Calvinist nobility as well as the hostility displayed in Paris to a renewal of religious strife, particularly after the death of the popular Mayenne at the siege of Montauban, boded ill for the Huguenot cause.

The death of Luynes in 1621 during the first phase of the campaign against the Huguenots led to the appointment in 1624 of a rising politician, Cardinal Richelieu, as first minister of state, a position he was to hold until his death in 1642. Richelieu had effected a temporary reconciliation between Louis XIII and his mother and was destined to save the tottering monarchy and to set the Bourbon dynasty on the course of absolutism it was not to relinquish until 1789, when a new political dispensation was in the making. Richelieu's drive to make France the paramount state in Europe was initially hampered by the threat of Huguenot autonomy and by the closely allied obstacle of aristocratic privilege. Until these internal problems were solved, France could not hope for greatness, and it is a measure of Richelieu's political courage that he was able to do so against the ever-present Habsburg menace and an escalating European conflict.

Richelieu was quick to see that retention of La Rochelle was vital to the Huguenot war effort. Already blockaded by royal forces, its difficult position sparked off a second conflict with the Bourbon monarchy in 1625. Richelieu was able to obtain ships from both England and the United Provinces to attack the port; Soubise was defeated on the Ile de Ré and royal troops occupied the Ile d'Oléron. La Rochelle held out, however, although in the south and south-west Rohan found it difficult to arouse any enthusiasm for the war in the Calvinist municipalities. He retained the Cévennes, and the king's armies suffered defeats at Sainte-Affrique and Le Mas-d'Azil, but a royal "scorched-earth" policy caused great hardship in the countryside. As in 1622, however, the international situation made Richelieu reluctant to press home his advantage. The Treaty of Paris, signed in February 1626, generally restored the status quo, although Catholic worship was to be permitted in La Rochelle and the property of the Catholic church was to be returned.

La Rochelle's days as the bastion of political Calvinism were, however, numbered; so, too, was the militant state within a state which, as Richelieu pointed out to the king in May 1625, not only limited Louis's authority at home, but also stood between him and European greatness. The final solution was achieved in a war which broke out as a reaction to English help for the Huguenots. England's war with France (1627-1629) was a reversal of the policy which had in 1625 led to the marriage of the Stuart prince, the future Charles I of England and Scotland, to Henrietta Maria, sister of Louis XIII. Now, however, England's claim to the right of search on the high seas in her continuing war with Spain combined with Charles I's championship of the Huguenots and his minister Buckingham's astonishing lack of finesse to bring about a complete break in relations.

English help could, perhaps, have saved the Huguenots of La Rochelle had it been better organized and directed. Buckingham, however, was pinned down on the Ile de Ré in 1627 and forced to evacuate the island; after his murder in the following year, two more attempts to relieve the besieged garrison failed, and in October 1628 the city surrendered to the royalists. Rohan held on until the summer of 1629 in the south and south-west, but after the loss of Privas and Alès was forced to capitulate. The Peace of Alès was signed on the 28th June 1629 and was followed by the *Edit de Grâce*, drawn up at Nîmes in the following month. The Edict of Nantes was confirmed in its religious clauses but the age of Huguenot garrison towns and political assemblies was over, and the last vestiges of a federal, pluralistic France thus gave way to the full development of the unitary state.

To the majority of French Catholics, Calvinism had come to be equated with revolution, treason and the overthrow of social order. It would not, therefore, have been surprising if the Edict of Nantes had been abrogated in its entirety in 1629, particularly as Richelieu did not regard it as sacrosanct. Apart from a general feeling that Calvinism was a dying force which might well be absorbed into an all-embracing Gallicanism, there were, however, good reasons of state for taking less drastic action.

Men such as Rohan and Soubise were not merely Huguenot leaders, they were also representatives of a nobility still capable of challenging royal authority without reference to religious considerations. Richelieu was not unaware of the danger. Already in 1626 he had decreed the destruction of all privately fortified places, except those on the frontier. In the same year, too, he had been forced to strike ruthlessly at the plot hatched by César, duke of Vendôme, the marquis of Chalais and other conspirators to place the king's brother, Gaston d'Orléans, on the throne. Gaston, heir apparent until 1638, was to be the centre of further intrigues against Richelieu and Louis XIII: the Day of the Dupes in November 1630, engineered by Marie de Medici on behalf of her favourite son, which led to her permanent exile; Gaston's attempted revenge with Spanish help in 1632, which merely gave Louis XIII *de facto* control of Lorraine; and in the south, Montmorency's rising in sympathy, crushed at Castelnaudary in September of that year. Even as late as 1642 Gaston was involved in the Cinq-Mars conspiracy to oust Richelieu, the failure of which gave Sedan to France.

Richelieu's answer to opposition within the state was not confined to relentless counter-measures. Its main thrust was directed at the strengthening of the nation under royal authority. The nucleus of a professional army was formed, and in an age which saw the expansion of French colonialism in North America, in the West Indies, the Indian Ocean and Senegal, the foundations of naval strength were laid and trading companies established in emulation of those of England and the northern Netherlands. Royal government was advanced in the provinces, and more effective use was made of those agents of central power at local level, the intendants. Nevertheless it must be conceded that the king's minister made little impact on the structure of administration. "If Richelieu made no really important changes in the government machinery of France, this was simply because he had no new conception of government to offer."[8] He did nothing to rid the nation of its multiplicity of administrative bodies, and although he abolished such feudal survivals as the offices of admiral and constable, his constant need for money to finance an active foreign policy caused him to create new and often unnecessary posts for purchase by the highest bidder. For the same reason, there was no relaxation in the burden of taxation, nor was any attempt made to remove inequalities or to cut back the sums pocketed by tax farmers. Richelieu's prodigality also resulted in a massive increase in the public debt. The cardinal was therefore in no sense the architect of a later, more centralized, despotism, although his arbitrary dictates produced a climate which allowed a greater autocracy to flourish.

Richelieu was a master diplomatist, and it was in the field of foreign affairs that he was most at home. Here again, any attempt to proscribe Calvinism must have impeded his plans. Already he had crossed swords with Spain over the Valtelline, the valuable Alpine link between the Spanish duchy of Milan and the Austrian Habsburg dominions, claimed by the Swiss Grisons leagues. Spain had obtained transit rights in 1623, with papal troops occupying the forts dominating the valley, but Richelieu intervened, and by 1625 France had gained complete control over the Valtelline. By the Treaty of Monzón in 1626, however, the region was returned to the Grisons, thus facilitating eventual reoccupation by Spanish and imperial troops.

A satisfactory settlement of the Valtelline question had been hampered by the Huguenot problem at home, but after the fall of La Rochelle, Richelieu could again take the initiative against Spain in northern Italy. The opportunity had arisen over the claim to the Mantuan succession of a French subject, Charles de Gonzaga, the duke of Nevers. This was opposed by Spain and Savoy, and in January 1629 a French army was set in motion to secure Richelieu's interests. The campaign was delayed by the internal intrigues of Gaston d'Orléans and the queen-mother, but a settlement with Spain and Savoy was finally reached at Cherasco in March 1631, which was highly advantageous to France. Nevers was confirmed as ruler, although acknowledging imperial suzerainty, since Mantua was a fief of the Holy Roman empire. Savoy was compensated for renewing her friendship with France by territorial gains in Montferrat, but France acquired the important Alpine fortress of Pinerolo.

Richelieu was now free to do more than subsidize the Dutch and Swedes in the Thirty Years War, thus turning that conflict more into a struggle between France and the Habsburgs than a war of religion. The French officially declared war on Spain in May 1635. Three years later open warfare on the empire was proclaimed, although France already held advance positions at imperial expense through gains from Spain and the protection it had extended to such ecclesiastical fiefs as Basle and Trier. It was Spain's capture of Trier that provided the pretext for the French declaration of war in 1635, and although repulsed in Lorraine, the French fought with some success in that year, defeating the Spanish near Namur, invading Franche-Comté, and, under Richelieu's old antagonist Rohan, regaining control of the Valtelline. The year 1636, however, saw the loss of Franche-Comté, the expulsion of Rohan from the Valtelline and, more serious, a Spanish invasion from the north-east which reached Compiègne and caused consternation in Paris. Richelieu's fortunes were at a low ebb, and his position was rendered more desperate by sporadic tax riots in many parts of France. Fortunately a Swedish advance in Brandenburg compelled the Spanish invaders to retreat from France.

The tide was to turn even more decisively in favour of France. Bernhard of Saxe-Weimar, with troops in French pay and with military assistance from that country, captured the fortress of Breisach in December 1638, and in the following year, after Bernhard's death, the French government took over the administration of conquered Alsace. Savoy fell under French domination, and by 1640 Louis XIII's troops were in Turin, while on the Spanish frontier France occupied Roussillon in 1639. Worse was to befall Spain in 1640. The revolt in Catalonia inaugurated a period of French occupation of much of that province, which lasted for more than a decade and also enabled France's invading troops to penetrate Aragon. Portugal took the opportunity afforded by the Catalan rebellion to throw off the Spanish yoke, an independence which enjoyed some limited assistance from France.

THE ERA OF MAZARIN, 1642-1661

Richelieu died in December 1642, with France in the ascendancy in the still continuing war, her frontier secure on the Pyrenees, in full command of the approaches to Italy and with a firm foothold on the Rhine. Power in the state descended to Richelieu's Italian-born protégé, Cardinal Mazarin, whose friendship with Anne of Austria, regent for the young king Louis XIV after the death of his father in May 1643, enabled him to maintain his dominant position against a court plot to oust him.

The war was pursued with increasing vigour, and within days of Louis XIII's death, Louis, duke of Enghien and from 1646 the prince of Condé, gained an overwhelming victory over the Spanish at Rocroy near the Meuse. On the imperial front across the Rhine, Enghien and Turenne, the future marshal, won only Pyrrhic victories at Freiburg (1644) and Nördlingen (1645) over the Bavarians, but between 1646 and 1648 Turenne joined his Swedish allies to ravage Bavaria itself. In the north-east, Gravelines and Dunkirk fell to the French, but Archduke Leopold reconquered several towns in French hands, amongst them Armentières and Landrecies, before he was defeated by Condé at Lens in August 1648. In 1646 the new French fleet succeeded in checking the Spanish at Orbetello on the Tuscan coast, allowing France to take the island of Elba and Piombino on the mainland. Spain's Italian allies began to waver in their allegiance; Tuscany sought neutrality and Modena went over to the French.

In the meantime, peace negotiations had been in progress at Münster and Osnabrück, at which the Spanish delegates offered France generous terms in 1646, but without reaching agreement. Thereafter the Spanish position improved, both diplomatically and in the field. Lérida in Catalonia had been recaptured in 1644, and there were hopes of further advances in the province, a French-inspired revolt in Naples was quashed, and, more significant, Spain came to terms with the Dutch, now growing increasingly fearful of French intentions in the Low Countries. The result was a continuation of the conflict with France and the exclusion of Spain from the decisions of the Peace of Westphalia of October 1648, which ended the Thirty Years War. By the terms of the treaty France was awarded much of Alsace, although without imperial Strasburg. This went far towards giving the country an unbroken Rhine frontier from Switzerland to the Palatinate. As a further protection, France obtained the fortresses of Breisach and Philippsburg across the river. The long French occupation of the three bishoprics, Metz, Toul and Verdun, was confirmed, while Pinerolo in the Alps also remained in French hands. The treaty gave France an important say in imperial affairs, while the somewhat vague provisions regarding Alsace were to provide Louis XIV with a pretext for further action.

Failure to end the Spanish War caused much bitterness in France at Mazarin's expense, and the Peace of Westphalia was not ratified by that country until 1651. While war with Spain did not, in itself, cause the unrest which was to plague France until 1653, its effects, both in the divided counsels of the nobility and in the economic distress of the nation as a whole, cannot be divorced from it. The Fronde, as the movement which began in 1648 came to be called, was in all its aspects a revolt against the absolutism with which Mazarin was associated. For the *frondeurs* of low estate, the distressing results of grinding taxation were uppermost, as they had always done and would continue to do throughout the period of the *ancien régime*. This was, however, not another in the long series of peasant revolts, despite its support in the third estate. The Fronde began well enough, inspired in some measure by the contemporary constitutional struggle in Stuart England, but it soon lost its progressive, reforming character to become a fight for the restoration of ancient and now anachronistic privilege. Despite Richelieu's efforts to curb its power, the landed nobility still retained enough independence and armed strength to challenge royal authority, as expressed by the queen regent and Mazarin. Moreover, even in the first and more glorious phase of the Fronde, the reforming body had little power of its own and found itself in alliance with a self-seeking bourgeoisie, a handful of disaffected aristocrats, and a mob easily swayed by changing circumstances.

The Fronde began in Paris in the aftermath of tax demands calculated to increase the cost of living. In July 1648 the Paris *parlement*, dismayed by the sad condition of the nation, formulated a number of demands, including the abolition of the office of intendant, a 25 per cent reduction in the *taille*, a measure of protection from arbitrary arrest by *lettres de cachet* and control by its own members of taxation. Mazarin tried to halt agitation by ordering the arrest of a leading councillor in the *parlement*, Pierre Broussel. A violent street reaction compelled him to release Broussel, and the court deemed it prudent to retire briefly from the capital. Bowing before the storm, the court party issued an edict, registered on the 24th October 1648, accepting the *parlement's* demands. The court returned to Paris at the end of that month, but early in January 1649, Mazarin, Anne of Austria and the boy-king left for Saint-Germain, leaving Condé in charge of a royal army charged with the task of starving the capital into surrender. In the course of its activities a number of villages were sacked and burnt, but the *frondeurs* managed to get some supplies through the blockade. Finally, on the 1st April 1649, the Peace of Rueil was arranged, restoring the status quo.

The second stage of the Fronde – the Fronde of the Princes – followed the arrest by Mazarin in January 1650 of Condé, his brother Armand, the prince of Conti, and his brother-in-law, the duke of Longueville. All three had flirted with the *frondeurs*, but the arrests were rather a reaction to personal ambitions. This action against princes of the blood was undiplomatic. Other nobles rose in sympathy and made common cause with the *frondeurs*, but for different motives. Normandy, Burgundy and Guyenne sided with the princes, the arch-conspirator Gaston d'Orléans joined the movement, and Turenne placed himself at the head of an invading Spanish army. The dismissal of Mazarin and the restitution of the rights of the nobility were now the main objects of the revolt. Although Normandy and Burgundy were soon subjugated and Turenne defeated at Rethel on the Aisne in December 1650, Mazarin deemed it prudent to retire to Brühl in the electorate of Cologne in February 1651, first releasing the princely hostages.

Condé raised the standard of revolt in Anjou, Poitou and Guyenne, but Turenne returned to the royalist fold, and before the end of the year Mazarin was back in France. In March 1652 Turenne gained control at Angers for the king, and although Condé, hastening back to Paris, won a qualified victory at Bléneau to the south, he was defeated by Turenne in July 1652 at the battle of Saint-Antoine in the suburbs of the capital. As a gesture of conciliation, Mazarin retired to Sedan in August, and in October Louis XIV re-entered Paris. Continuing unrest in Bordeaux was suppressed and Condé, after skirmishing on the borders of Champagne, accepted service in the armies of Spain. Mazarin returned to Paris on the 3rd February 1653 and the Fronde was at an end.

Mazarin had achieved one of his objectives, the virtually complete subjugation of a militant nobility and the ruin of all hopes of constitutional reform in the interests of the absolute monarchy. His success must be seen against the background of regicide in England and the triumph of the protector, Cromwell. There remained for Mazarin the Spanish threat.

Spain had taken full advantage of the Fronde, driving the French from Catalonia, recapturing Elba and Piombino in Tuscany, Casale in the duchy of Milan and Gravelines and Dunkirk in Flanders. After the Fronde, Condé served his new Spanish masters well, winning victories at Arras, Valenciennes and Cambrai between 1654 and 1657. Mazarin, however, enlisted Cromwell's aid. An English fleet blockaded Dunkirk, and Turenne, assisted by veterans of the New Model Army, won the battle of the Dunes in June 1658. The price was cession of Dunkirk to England, but France purchased it back in 1662, after the restoration of the Stuart monarchy. "Poor, but prodigal," wrote Voltaire later, "Charles II had the shame of selling what had been bought at the price of English blood."[9]

The Peace of the Pyrenees in 1659 brought the long war with Spain to a close. France retained Roussillon, together with Conflans and Cerdagne, thus providing the country with a complete natural frontier against the threat of Spanish invasion. Pinerolo in the Alps remained in French hands, the frontier in the north-east was advanced into Artois, and several defensive positions from Flanders to Lorraine were annexed or retained by France, amongst them Gravelines, Thionville, Landrecies, Avesnes, Clermont and Stenay. The fortifications of Nancy were to be dismantled, and Lorraine proper was returned to the duke, Charles IV. Spain also accepted the settlement of Westphalia regarding Alsace. The marriage of Louis XIV to the Spanish infanta, Maria Theresa, was arranged and celebrated in June 1660. She was to renounce all claim to the Spanish throne for herself and her descendants, but was to bring with her a substantial dowry. Failure to pay this was to give France a pretext for a dynastic claim. Finally, at the instance of Philip IV, Condé was pardoned, his estates restored and the governorship of Burgundy bestowed on him. Henceforth he was to remain a loyal subject of Louis XIV.

LOUIS XIV AND COLBERT, 1661-1683

The year 1659 marks the eclipse of Spain by France as the leading power in Europe. It was Mazarin's final triumph and an important part of his legacy to Louis XIV, for on the 10th March 1661, immediately after the cardinal's death, the king made himself solely responsible for government.

The absolutism which has come to be associated with the personal rule of the Sun King is summed up in the youthful boast attributed to him: "l'état c'est moi" ("I am the state"). It did not make France a unified state, for there remained widespread privilege, ancient institutions perpetuating in various ways a feudal past and jealously guarded provincial rights, all prejudicial to the attainment of real unity. What, however, was needed in France, as the turbulent background, from the wars of religion to the Fronde, makes clear, was the strong leadership which only the king seemed able to provide. "In the monarchy" therefore "rested the hope of Frenchmen to escape the multiplied tyrannies of anachronistic localisms".[10] Just as the Fronde had almost destroyed the independence of the nobility – and Louis XIV was to crush the last stirrings of their anti-social activity in such remote corners of the kingdom as Auvergne after 1656 – so too did the new monarch's centralizing policies clip the wings of those who might challenge royal dictates. From 1673, the *parlements* could no longer delay legislation, but were compelled to register edicts first, before making known their objections. Municipal autonomy was eroded, and provincial governors and surviving estates were made subservient to royal officials. Nobility was no longer a passport to a share in policy-making. Louis XIV turned increasingly to commoners for advice, advancing them on occasion for services rendered to the *noblesse de robe*, while the old aristocracy of birth, the *noblesse d'épée*, became increasingly mere hangers-on at court. And the peripatetic court of the early years, which finally came to rest in the new palace of Versailles in 1682, was the social centre of the greatest monarchy in Europe: "Louis XIV's great house was . . . the outward and visible sign of that ascendancy."[11] The elaborate ceremonial of the French court under Louis XIV was not in the French tradition, but was modelled on Habsburg practices.

Louis XIV retained the system of advisory royal councils of which the *Conseil d'Etat*, dealing with all major issues, including foreign affairs, was the most important. It became a more intimate body after 1661, with a membership never exceeding five, all of whom were chief ministers of state. The main subordinate governmental councils were the *conseil des dépêches*, prototype of the ministry of the interior, the *conseil des finances* and the *conseil privé*, this last being at once an appeal court and an administrative tribunal. The king, in theory, presided over all these councils, but in practice usually delegated his authority in the *conseil privé* to the highest legal officer in the realm, the chancellor. No single adviser dominated the scene as Richelieu and Mazarin had done, but two posts took precedence: the secretaryships of finance and of military affairs.

For provincial administration, the intendants were transformed into permanent regionally based officials with extensive powers in the *généralités* allocated to them. These *généralités*, not necessarily coterminous with the provincial boundaries, became the chief units of local government in France. The delegated authority of the intendants grew steadily throughout the reign and, with the inclusion of Brittany in the system after 1689, extended throughout the kingdom. An important innovation in the maintenance of law and order in Paris was the creation in 1667 of a police force under La Reynie. This organization was also responsible for such other functions of municipal administration as street cleaning and lighting. The Paris venture proved so successful that it formed the model for the police of provincial towns after 1699.

These new administrative approaches owed their introduction to Jean Baptiste Colbert whose policies dominated the financial, economic and maritime life of France from 1661 until his death in 1683. Colbert, in true mercantilist style, sought to increase the power of the state by increasing its gold and silver reserves and by harnessing to its service the entire resources of the nation. Although excessive government control, royal extravagance, vested interests and the sheer magnitude of the task frustrated his efforts, his achievements were nevertheless remarkable.

Colbert inherited from his predecessor Fouquet a corrupt financial system and immediately turned his attention to possible remedies. The assessment and collection of the *taille* were overhauled, public expenditure was drastically reduced and accounts were subjected to efficient auditing. The result was a substantial surplus as early as 1662. While Colbert strongly supported tariffs to protect France from foreign commercial competition, he disapproved of the multiplicity of internal customs duties impeding trade between the provinces. Although he was unable to abolish these entirely, he managed to bring order out of chaos in the northern third of the country. Colbert also did much to stimulate internal trade by improving communications by road and along inland waterways. His greatest achievement in this field was the construction between 1666 and 1681 of the Languedoc canal which provided an effective link between the Atlantic Ocean and the Mediterranean Sea.

In the agricultural sphere Colbert endeavoured to improve production, particularly of grain crops. The great famine of 1661-1662, when many peasants were reduced to eating roots and the bark of trees, suggested to him the need to build up grain stocks in case of future poor harvests. This led to a ban on wheat exports on several occasions between 1675 and 1681, a policy which caused a lowering of prices and consequent hardship.

Although France was predominantly an agricultural country, Colbert's main interest lay in the promotion of industry. For this purpose he was anxious to encourage foreign entrepreneurs and artisans to settle in France, bringing with them new skills and techniques. Many industries were either placed under direct government control, such as the Gobelin tapestry works, or given generous state subsidies, like the woollen manufactories of the Dutchman, Josse van Robais, at Abbeville in Picardy, and those of a similar company at Villeneuvette in Languedoc. Although many of the new enterprises were in the luxury trade, including the manufacture of fine lace, glassware and mirrors, Colbert by no means neglected basic industries, as his promotion of sugar refining, the casting of iron and the manufacture of textiles indicates. His first steps in the codification of French law have been of enduring significance in the commercial field, while his industrial legislation, backed by government inspection, increasingly placed the ancient guilds under state control.

French expansion overseas attracted Colbert's attention. The merchant marine was built up and a new start was made in emulation of the English and the Dutch in the creation of great trading companies, amongst them the East India Company and the West India Company of 1664, the Senegal Company of 1673 for the slave trade, the Company of the North of 1669 to trade with the Baltic, and the Levant Company of 1670. Although these companies were undercapitalized and not uniformly successful, they testified to the wider interests of the French state. For it was under Louis XIV that the drive for empire, allied with missionary zeal and a desire for commercial advantage, really began. It was the age of expansion in the sugar-producing islands of the Caribbean, of the development of New France in North America and the exploration of the American hinterland by men such as La Salle and Father Marquette, of the founding of Pondichéry in India and of relations with Persia, Siam and China.

In defence of these world-wide interests, Colbert revitalized the navy. By 1677 the fleet had been increased more than tenfold, a shipbuilding industry created at Brest, and a system of compulsory service instituted for sailors on the Atlantic seaboard. Brest, Rochefort, Toulon and Dunkirk became fortified naval bases. The creation of a professional army between 1661 and 1690 was the work of Le Tellier and his son, Louvois. A disciplined, well-armed force with an efficient commissariat and a technical staff of outstanding ability, which included the great engineer, Vauban, the French army under such generals as Turenne and Condé was the finest military machine in Europe. It was to see action in many campaigns and also provided an effective check to insurrection at home. For peasant revolt remained endemic, the result of economic distress in general, and taxation in particular. Poorly led, badly organized and largely local, it was suppressed by the soldiery, as in the Vivarais in 1670, Guyenne in 1674 and Brittany in 1675, with great brutality. It was the king's vengeance, yet the rebels made no attack on the monarchy or, indeed, on the social order. "The one enemy all men could see, the sole scapegoat, was not the king, ever beloved ('If only the King knew'), but Power, abstract and distant; and especially the administration of the national finances."[12]

THE REVOCATION OF THE EDICT OF NANTES, 1685

It was this loyalty to the king, combined with the loss of its militant arm and its continuing decline in popular support, which contributed to the downfall of Calvinism in France. For the king, to many, could do no wrong; it was his advisers who were misguided. The period from 1661 to 1685 was marked by a series of attacks on the Reformed Church, alternating with years of relative calm, often coinciding with new priorities in the field of foreign policy. Alongside the attacks on Calvinism went attempts to find a common theological ground with the Catholics, the establishment of a national conversion fund to provide Calvinists with a financial inducement to abjure and the organization of missionary drives to gain converts to the Catholic church. More direct hostility was shown in the closing of temples, often on the flimsiest of pretexts, a growing interference with church government, finances and educational work, the systematic exclusion of Calvinists from trades and professions, the abrogation of their legal rights and such interference in their personal lives as the freedom given Calvinist children of seven years of age and upwards in 1681 to abjure their parents' religion.

These various approaches certainly made inroads into the strength and numbers of Calvinists in France, but did not destroy the faith. There remained another road to conversion: the use of force, already proved effective in dealing with a recalcitrant peasantry. Marillac's dragonnade of 1681 in Poitou, echoed also at Rochefort in Saintonge, gained more than 30 000 unwilling Catholic converts, but Catholic public opinion, foreign dismay and papal hostility caused Louis XIV to call it off. Armed Calvinist resistance in the Vivarais, Dauphiné and the Cévennes in 1683, however, gave legitimacy to the military reprisals taken, and two years later general dragonnades, beginning in Béarn, were instigated in all Calvinist regions south of the Loire and west of the Rhône, as well as in Dauphiné, resulting in the forcible conversion of more than 300 000 Calvinists in their regions of greatest strength. The way was clear for Louis XIV to revoke the Edict of Nantes by that of Fontainebleau. The legislation outlawing the Reformed Church was registered on the 22nd October 1685, and another series of dragonnades from Normandy to Picardy and in Burgundy and Provence crushed any further resistance.

The Edict of Fontainebleau commanded the demolition of surviving temples, prohibited all Calvinist religious ceremonies and assemblies and ordered the expulsion of pastors who refused to abjure. Those Protestants who did not wish to conform were allowed in theory, if not always in practice, freedom of conscience, as long as they did not attempt to worship in public. Calvinism was kept alive through the efforts of preachers labouring clandestinely, and a last flicker of armed resistance occurred in the revolt of the Camisards of the Cévennes between 1702 and 1704. An attempt to rouse Calvinists in the Vivarais in conjunction with a British landing at Sète failed in 1710. The mystic propheticism of the Camisards did nothing to further the Huguenot cause.

The immediate result of the revocation of the Edict of Nantes was a sudden surge in the numbers of Calvinists fleeing the country, despite stringent measures to stem the flow. Perhaps as many as 200 000 people left France in the last quarter of the 17th century, rather more than 20 per cent of all French Calvinists, but no more than 1 per cent of the total population, made good in part by the influx of Catholic refugees from Ireland and Scotland after 1688. The exodus certainly caused a temporary recession in some local industries, but the effects of the revocation are better gauged in the export of capital, skills and labour which enriched the economies of countries which gave the Calvinists a refuge. Most settled in the United Provinces, England and Brandenburg, some moving yet again to regions as far afield as the British North American colonies and the Dutch settlement at the Cape of Good Hope.

Louis XIV's action was not universally approved amongst his closest advisers and inevitably caused bitterness abroad. The reasons impelling him to outlaw Calvinism remain a matter of guesswork. Freedom from taxation had been offered members of the Reformed Church who abjured; the revocation would obviate the need for special and expensive concessions of this kind. The king had no need in 1685 of Protestant alliances abroad, and Catholic churchmen at home remained deeply suspicious of Calvinism. Louis, too, had become a better Catholic and he doubtless saw the opportunity of posing as the champion of Catholicism in Europe. Yet, in the final analysis, national unity was probably the real goal. Louis XIV regarded religious separatism in the light in which the monarchy had always seen it: as a weakening of the power of the state. As king by divine right it would be his triumph to achieve uniformity of belief.

Moreover, the Catholic church in France was a politico-religious force requiring tactful handling, particularly as the clergy met in assembly once in every five years to grant the King a "free gift". In quarrels between the Gallicans and the Rome-orientated Ultramontanists, Louis XIV had to tread a careful path. The issue came to the fore in 1673, when the king extended the *droit de régale*, the right he enjoyed to the revenues of certain vacant bishoprics. Opposition came from the bishops of Aleth and Pamiers in western Languedoc, Pavillon and Caulet, who appealed to Rome. Troops were used against the Ultramontanists of Pamiers in 1680, and Gallicanism reached its apogee in 1682 with the publication of the anti-papal Four Articles. Meanwhile the papacy refused to confirm royal nominations to vacant benefices and the breach was not healed until a settlement was reached with Pope Innocent XII in 1693, when the French church retreated from extreme Gallicanism.

Currents of Catholic reform continued to flow in late 17th century France, having their source in the earlier influence of men such as François de Sales and Vincent de Paul. The stream, however, sometimes forced its way into heterodox channels. One was the doctrine of Quietism, preaching the intimate union of man and God; another was Jansenism, whose adherents "found a doctrine of predestination that closed the gates of heaven to all save God's elect".[13] Both compromised the unity of the Catholic church; both were quelled, although not destroyed, by the forces of orthodoxy in the interests of church and state. Jeanne Guyon, the apostle of Quietism, was silenced in 1699 and her supporter, Fénelon, bishop of Cambrai, forced to recant. The Jansenists of Port-Royal-des-Champs near Versailles fought a longer battle, and such leaders of the movement as the theologians Antoine Arnauld and Pasquier Quesnel, and the writers Blaise Pascal and Pierre Nicole extended its spiritual influence from Normandy to the south of France. The Jesuits spearheaded the attack on Jansenism and succeeded in having Pascal's famous *Lettres provinciales* burned. The sect, however, had influential friends and was not dispersed until 1709. Pope Clement XI's bull of 1713, *Unigenitus Dei Filius*, condemned Jansenist teachings, but the movement long survived the attack, fusing with Gallicanism and revitalizing it. "In the long run Jansenism came to be, not so much a doctrine as a spirit; a spirit harsh, forbidding, austere, sternly opposing the progressive dulcification of faith and morals."[14]

LOUIS XIV'S FOREIGN POLICY UP TO 1697

In any consideration of Louis XIV's foreign policy there is much to said for the view that his main quest was glory and the prestige of the French monarchy. The picture of Louis as a latter-day Charlemagne, championing the cause of orthodox Christendom, does much to render comprehensible some of the more frivolous pretexts for war which mark this turbulent period of European history. There were, however, other facets of the international scene which at various times took prominence in determining French policy, other considerations of immediate concern to France which directed the course of French diplomacy. In all these there was one constant: the defence of the eastern and north-eastern frontiers, so close to Paris, containing one region with no natural border and another, with a natural border on the Rhine, as yet incompletely assimilated into the French state. The emphasis therefore must fall upon the defensive nature of French objectives. When Louis XIV took personal control of the fortunes of France, the modern natural frontiers had almost been attained. Offensive action in this direction was therefore not paramount in his thinking, and it is evident that he was often prepared to sacrifice a gain in one eastern frontier area for a stronger position elsewhere which might strengthen his defences.

The desire for economic advantage also played a significant part in Louis XIV's foreign policy. The Dutch and the English were serious rivals in the commercial sphere and economics coloured his relations with Spain, particularly in the southern Netherlands and Italy. He had his dynastic ambitions at the expense of the Habsburgs and regarded himself as the defender both of the monarchical tradition and of political legitimacy. In this, he found himself out of step with England after the revolution of 1688 which toppled James II from the throne, and with the United Provinces, whose republicanism could scarcely meet with his approval. The wide sweep of his ambitions resulted in shifting alliances, and the hostility his policies aroused was largely engendered by the fear that an all-powerful France would ultimately reduce western Europe to ignominious servitude. French policy was therefore also dictated by the objectives of Louis XIV's near neighbours.

Louis XIV showed in the first years of his personal rule that he was prepared to stand up for his rights by extracting apologies from Philip IV of Spain in 1661 and Pope Alexander VII in 1662 for slighting French ambassadors. French troops helped the emperor, Leopold I, to defeat the Turks in 1664, and in the following year levies under Schomberg contributed to a Portuguese victory over the Spanish. In 1666 France declared war on England after fulfilling a treaty obligation to assist the Dutch when they were attacked by England's ally, Münster. Prolongation of the Anglo-Dutch War in his own interests was Louis XIV's only motive and while still nominally at war with England, he signed a secret treaty in 1667 with the Stuart king, Charles II, promising compensation for that country in the West Indies if England kept clear of anti-French alliances for a year.

The real objective for France was the Spanish Netherlands. Philip IV had died in 1665 and had been succeeded by Charles II, the sickly child of his second marriage. Louis XIV claimed the Spanish Netherlands by virtue of a law of devolution which was applicable in Brabant, but extended by the French king to the entire territory. By this law, female children of a first marriage – and here Louis XIV's wife Maria Theresa comes into the picture – had precedence over male children of a second marriage. Maria Theresa had renounced her claim to the Spanish dominions, but in French eyes, failure to pay her dowry rendered this null and void. Turenne marched into the Spanish Netherlands in May 1667 and Condé occupied Franche-Comté in February 1668. Louis XIV had the tacit support of the emperor, but England, the United Provinces and Sweden formed a triple alliance to combat the French threat, compelling Louis to come to terms with Spain at Aix-la-Chapelle on the 29th May 1668. France returned Franche-Comte, but received a number of defensive fortresses along the Netherlands border, including Charleroi, Tournai, Lille, Armentières and Courtrai.

Louis XIV now determined to humble the Dutch, architects of the alliance against him in 1668 as well as major commercial rivals. A diplomatic campaign bribed or coerced the emperor and most of the German states to remain neutral, the English king signed the secret Treaty of Dover in June 1670, undertaking to support France and to return England to Catholicism with French help in exchange for the neutrality of the Spanish Netherlands, and in April 1672 Sweden was also detached from the Triple Alliance. The attack on the United Provinces was launched in May 1672 under the personal direction of Louis XIV. Support for the Dutch by Lorraine was countered by the occupation of that duchy, while the French armies under Turenne, Condé and the duke of Luxemburg advanced along the valley of the Rhine, crossed the Dutch border and by June had reached the outskirts of Amsterdam. The United Provinces were saved by the emergence of William III of Orange as Stadtholder, the opening of the dykes and Brandenburg's hostility to France which caused the French to protect their allies Münster and Cologne by halting the attack in the north in order to take Maastricht in June 1673. Meanwhile the Dutch had secured their coasts by defeating an Anglo-French fleet off Southwold, Suffolk, on the 7th June 1672 and were able to hold their own in three subsequent naval battles against the combined enemy in June of the following year.

By 1674 the whole diplomatic and military situation had changed in favour of the

Dutch. In the previous year the nucleus of the Grand Alliance against Louis XIV had been formed by the association of the emperor, Spain and Lorraine with the Dutch cause. Brandenburg and other German states joined the alliance, together with Denmark. Münster and Cologne were detached from the French, and in February 1674 England made peace with the United Provinces, although France secured England's friendly neutrality in another secret treaty in 1676. Nevertheless, English sympathy veered towards the Dutch, and it was an Anglo-Dutch alliance which brought the war to a close in 1678.

France now faced a formidable coalition, with Sweden alone to support her. France succeeded in reoccupying Franche-Comté in 1674 and drove the imperial troops out of Alsace in the next year, but lost Turenne at Salzbach in July 1675 during a follow-up operation beyond the Rhine. The French armies enjoyed considerable success on the Netherlands front, taking Valenciennes in 1677 and Ghent and Ypres in 1678. Duquesne won three naval battles in 1676 against combined Spanish and Dutch fleets off Sicily and in the West Indies, Jean d'Estrées attacked Dutch colonies, taking Cayenne in 1676 and recapturing Tobago in 1677. The Dutch, however, retained the mastery at sea in northern waters. Serious disturbances at home and general war-weariness induced France to seek peace. The treaties which brought the war to an end, begun at Nijmegen in August 1678 and concluded at Saint-Germain in June 1679, placed Louis XIV in a strong position with regard to Spain, but represented a check to his ambitions against the Dutch. France retained Franche-Comté and *de facto* control of Lorraine. Only Freiburg remained to France as a Rhine bridgehead, but although France surrendered several towns on the Netherlands border, amongst them Charleroi and Courtrai, she kept Ypres, Valenciennes, Cambrai, Maubeuge, Saint-Omer and several others. Her ally, Sweden, although defeated by Brandenburg, had most of Pomerania restored.

After Nijmegen, Louis XIV sought to exploit the ambiguous status of many regions on the eastern and north-eastern borders in order to incorporate them into his territories. French tribunals, the so-called *chambres de réunion*, were established to examine all claims. As a result, a number of localities came under French jurisdiction, including the imperial city of Strasburg, occupied in 1681, Montbéliard and the Duchy of Zweibrücken, whose duke was Charles XI of Sweden. It was an anxious period for the empire. At the same time, France began to supplant Spain as the chief naval power in the Mediterranean by attacking pirate bases in Algiers and Tripoli. France also became master of the strategically important town of Casale in northern Italy, and thereby threatened Milan. Spain, alarmed by these advances and by territorial claims in the Netherlands, declared war on France in October 1683. French troops took Courtrai and Dixmude in early 1684, Luxemburg fell in June of that year, Catalonia was invaded and Spain's ally, Genoa, forced into submission. The emperor, acting for Spain, agreed to a truce of twenty years at the Peace of Ratisbon (Regensburg), signed on the 15th August 1684. Courtrai and Dixmude were returned to Spanish control, but France retained Luxemburg, and her possessions in Alsace were confirmed.

The truce of 1684 was short-lived. Relations between Spain and France remained cool, and Louis XIV continued to follow an anti-imperial policy, maintaining an alliance with Brandenburg and standing aside from Pope Innocent XI's Holy League of 1684 to drive the Turks from Hungary after their defeat before Vienna in the previous year. Louis entertained dynastic ambitions in the Holy Roman empire, and it is not without significance that he controlled a majority of votes in the Electoral College between 1683 and 1688.

But French dominance in Europe was weakening. The revocation of the Edict of Nantes in 1685 hardened opinion against France in Protestant states, and Brandenburg moved towards the emperor, Leopold I. Spain still smouldered over the imposed peace of 1684, and the Swedish king over the loss of Zweibrücken. Innocent XI suffered the indignity of seeing French troops in Rome during his dispute with France over the Gallican church issue, and although the Turkish war dragged on until 1699 for Leopold, his star was always in the ascendant. In 1686 the League of Augsburg was formed between the empror, Spain, Sweden, the United Provinces and many of the German princes. The league aimed at opposing France and also gained the adherence of Bavaria and Savoy, as well as enjoying papal support. For Louis XIV there remained only England amongst the major powers, but James II had troubles enough, and there was already a plan afoot to bring William of Orange to the throne as co-ruler with James's daughter, Mary, William's wife.

Louis XIV, already determined to invade the empire, gambled that a Dutch invasion of England would lead to civil war, paralysing both countries. He sadly misjudged English hostility to the Catholic James II. William was welcomed with open arms when he landed at Torbay in November 1688, England's adherence to the League of Augsburg was assured and James retired to Saint-Germain to become the French-supported claimant to the English and Scottish thrones. He was to land in Ireland in 1689 with French support, but his forces were defeated at the battle of the Boyne in July 1690 and he returned to France, leaving the Irish War to peter out at Limerick in the following year.

Meanwhile Louis XIV, with succession problems in the Palatinate and Cologne as a pretext for action, had invaded the Rhineland in September 1688, and the War of the League of Augsburg had begun. It was to develop into the first major global conflict. In 1693 the Dutch took Pondichéry, the French factory on the Coromandel coast, and held it until the end of the war. There was action off the African coast and in the Antilles, but the most serious clashes occurred between England and France in North America, in what was described there by the English colonials as King William's War. The balance of success lay with the French under Le Moyne d'Iberville and Frontenac, but, as in most of the colonial regions, peace ultimately restored the status quo. In the West Indies, however, France gained a part of Hispaniola from Spain. The war at sea initially favoured France. Tourville's victory off Beachy Head in July 1690 against a combined Anglo-Dutch fleet was followed by a French landing at Teignmouth in Devonshire and command of the Channel. His defeat at La Hougue in May 1692, however, tilted the balance in favour of England and the United Provinces. The main threat from France thereafter came from commerce raiding by privateers, warfare in which Jean Bart made his name famous.

The War of the League of Augsburg was essentially a Continental land clash.

Imperial troops neutralized Louis's initial successes in 1689 by recapturing Mainz and Bonn, but Luxemburg's victory at Fleurus in 1690 blocked any plans for an allied invasion of France. Between 1691 and 1693 Mons, Namur and Charleroi fell to the French, and Luxemburg gained victories at Steenkerke and Neerwinden. William III, however, recaptured Namur in 1695. In the south, Noailles invaded Spain, but by 1694 was on the defensive. Catinat won a series of victories against Savoy between 1690 and 1693, although he was unable to hold Casale or to prevent an attack on Dauphiné.

The defection of Savoy from the alliance against France by the Treaty of Turin in 1696 led directly to the Treaty of Rijswijk, finalized in October 1697. The terms were a blow to French aspirations. An independent Savoy gained Pinerolo, Casale and Nice. All French acquisitions since 1678, except Strasburg, including those awarded to France by the *chambres de réunion*, were to be surrendered. The Dutch obtained rights in some of the barrier fortresses of the Spanish Netherlands and France retained no bridgeheads over the Rhine. Louis XIV was forced to modify his support for the exiled James II, and even in the succession issues in Cologne and the Palatinate which had precipitated the war, his candidates were rejected. "Europe was astonished and France ill-pleased to see Louis XIV making peace as though he had been vanquished."[15] France was to suffer another diplomatic defeat in the year of Rijswijk. Louis François, the prince of Conti, was elected king of Poland, but the elector of Saxony successfully challenged the decision and ascended the Polish throne as Augustus II. A French show of strength in the Baltic failed to make good Conti's claim.

THE WAR OF THE SPANISH SUCCESSION, 1701-1714

France, however, was by no means at the end of her resources. The seeds of another conflict lay in the ultimate destination of the vast empire of the ailing king of Spain, Charles II. Charles was childless, and there were fears that the inheritance might go intact to either the French Bourbons or the Austrian Habsburgs, thus seriously disturbing the European balance of power. Moreover, England and the United Provinces had a vested interest in keeping France out of the Spanish Netherlands. A secret partition treaty of October 1698 between England, Louis and the Dutch suggested a useful compromise: a wholly acceptable and neutral claimant, the Wittelsbach prince, Joseph Ferdinand of Bavaria, should inherit the bulk of this global estate, with small compensations to be made to France and Austria. Charles II agreed in principle, but without accepting the compensations, and in the following month made a will, leaving all his possessions to the Bavarian claimant. Unfortunately, however, Joseph Ferdinand, a small boy, died in February 1699, and the only remaining candidates were the Bourbons and the Habsburgs.

The result was a second secret partition treaty signed by France, England and the United Provinces, awarding Spain, the Spanish Netherlands and the colonies to the Austrian archduke, Charles, with compensation to France in Italy and the likelihood of the exchange of one territory there, Milan, for Lorraine, already partly in French hands. For the emperor, Leopold I, it was a question of all or nothing;

Spain, too, wanted no division of the spoils, but realized that an Austrian succession would inevitably mean a French invasion. Charles II was therefore prevailed upon to make another will which accepted the French view that non-payment of the dowry had left Maria Theresa, the sister of the Spanish king and wife of Louis XIV who had died in 1683, a legitimate claimant to the Spanish throne in her own right and for her descendants. The will, however, rejected a direct union of the French and Spanish crowns and stipulated that the grand dauphin's second son, the duke of Anjou, should succeed to the undivided Spanish dominions.

A month later, on the 1st November 1700, Charles II died, and Anjou ascended the throne as Philip V, the first Bourbon king of Spain. The emperor rejected the succession, but England and the United Provinces accorded Philip their recognition. Louis XIV, however, immediately acted as though the Pyrenees had ceased to exist. In February 1701 he took over the Dutch barrier fortresses and began negotiations for the cession to him of the Spanish Netherlands. He gained commercial advantage for France in the Spanish colonial empire and in June 1701 concluded a treaty of alliance with Spain and with a reluctant Portugal. Leopold I had early begun to prepare for war and on the 7th September 1701 formed the Grand Alliance with England and the Dutch, designed to give the Austrian Habsburgs a share of the Spanish empire in Europe, the other two signatories similar gains in the Spanish colonies and the United Provinces safeguards in the southern Netherlands. Louis XIV's recognition of the royal status of James Stuart on the death of his father, James II, on the 16th September 1701, while not explicitly a contravention of the Rijswijk agreement, added fuel to the fires of war across the English Channel.

The War of the Spanish Succession had already begun in Italy in the spring of 1701, and the Grand Alliance was soon strengthened by the adherence of Brandenburg, Hanover, the Palatinate and other German states, although Bavaria and Cologne supported France. Mantua sided with France and Spain, but Savoy deserted Louis in 1703, and Spain declared war on Portugal in 1704 after the Methuen Treaty of the previous year had brought the Portuguese into the Grand Alliance.

The war was again a world-wide conflict. Known to the English-speaking colonists in North America as Queen Anne's War, its early colonial phase was limited to border clashes between the French and the English, with Indian participation. In 1710, the French garrison at Port Royal in Acadia (Nova Scotia) was forced to surrender, but an attack on the heart of New France failed. Further south there were skirmishes between South Carolina and the Spanish in Florida and with the French, now established in Louisiana. In 1702, the island of St Kitts in the West Indies came under full English control, but France resisted an attack on Guadeloupe. French and Spanish privateers were active in the Caribbean, and in 1711 the French captain, Duguay-Trouin, scored a notable success on the Brazilian coast. In conventional naval operations the French and Spanish navies made little impression. An Anglo-Dutch fleet reaped a rich harvest at Vigo in 1702, Rooke captured Gibraltar in 1704, and Port Mahon on Minorca fell in 1708. However, the War of the Spanish Succession was primarily a land struggle in Europe, coinciding with the first years of another conflict, the Great Northern War, in which Russia, with intermittent Polish, Saxon and Danish support, faced Sweden and, later, the Turks.

The war in Italy began well for France, when Catinat occupied the Milanese in 1701. The imperial forces, however, found a worthy leader in Prince Eugene, and with the defection of Savoy and superior allied naval strength in the Mediterranean, the tide began to turn. Eugene's victory at Turin in 1706 led to the recovery of the Milanese, and in the next year the French abandoned northern Italy. Eugene penetrated Provence in 1707 and laid unsuccessful siege to Toulon before retiring, but Austrian troops took Naples in that year, and in 1708 Sardinia was lost to an allied fleet and Mantua was incorporated into the imperial domains.

In the north, apart from the capture of Ghent and Bruges by Louis Joseph, the Duke of Vendôme, in 1708 and the late successes of Villars against Eugene at Denain and at Freiburg in 1712 and 1713, when peace was in the air, the allies generally held the whip-hand. They owed their dominance in large measure to the brilliance of the English general, Marlborough, whose first major achievement was the capture of Bonn in 1703, thus forcing the electorate of Cologne out of the war. In the following year he foiled a Franco-Bavarian attempt to attack Vienna by crushing them at Blenheim on the Danube and causing the Bavarians, too, to abandon the French. Marlborough's further successes, before intrigue at home lost him his command in 1711, occurred in the Spanish Netherlands. His victory over Villeroi at Ramillies, north of Namur, drove the French back to their borders. They recovered from the blow, but Marlborough's defeat of Vendôme at Audenaarde (Oudenarde) on the Scheldt in 1708 restored the allied advantage and led to the capture of Lille, gallantly defended by Boufflers, in October of that year. The French made a last effort under Villars in 1709, but he was defeated by Eugene and Marlborough at Malplaquet during a savage battle which opened the way to the allied occupation of Mons. The French were henceforth to concentrate on a defensive war to protect their north-eastern frontier. The Act of Union of 1707, which abolished a separate Scottish parliament, offered Louis XIV the opportunity of striking at Britain through the Catholic Stuart pretender. The invasion force mounted at Dunkirk in March 1708 turned back from the Scottish coast, however, without having risked a landing.

The campaigns in Spain centred upon the attempts by the allies to foist the imperial archduke, Charles, upon the nation in place of Philip V. Only in separatist Catalonia was there prolonged and enthusiastic support for the archduke; and despite initial successes in 1705, the war in Spain virtually ended in Philip's favour in 1710. French troops contributed to his victory, and French generals, Berwick and Vendôme, at various times led his armies. Berwick, French-born, but the illegitimate son of James II and Arabella Churchill, Marlborough's sister, gained Valencia for Philip V by defeating allied troops under the French Calvinist exile, Ruvigny, then the earl of Galway, at Almanza in April 1707.

While throughout the war Louis XIV sought to sow dissension in the allied ranks opposing him and to find support for his policies in nations such as Sweden which were not directly involved in the western struggle, France also, from 1706 onwards, put out peace feelers. These led to inconclusive negotiations at The Hague and Gertruidenberg in 1709 and 1710. What finally brought the war to an end was a threatened upsurge in imperial power, in nobody's interests but the emperor's.

Leopold I had died in 1705 and had been succeeded by his son, Joseph I, who retained the imperial throne until his death in 1711. His brother, the archduke whom the allies had sponsored as a possible king of Spain, now became emperor as Charles VI. Here was a threatened Habsburg domination which bid fair to destroy the European balance of power completely.

Britain and France had already begun secret negotiations for peace designed to cut through the conflicting demands of the other members of the Grand Alliance; the imperial election hastened agreement and an armistice was arranged between the two powers in 1712. The decisions taken at the Peace of Utrecht, signed on the 13th July 1713, were based upon the Anglo-French preliminaries. The emperor, however, refused to take part. Torcy, Colbert's nephew, had seen to it that the terms for France were in no way humiliating. This was understandable since despite set-backs, the nation, as Pierre Gaxotte has said, "for the third time had proven to be invincible".[16] The frontiers were intact, and on the vulnerable north-eastern border the capture of Le Quesnoy, Bouchain and Douai in 1712 after the great victory of Villars at Denain showed that France was still capable of defending them. Louis XIV therefore lost no considerable territory, apart from his conquests during the war. The Dutch were awarded barrier fortresses against French aggression in what was now to become the Austrian Netherlands, while a strengthened Savoy gained some Dauphiné border regions in the Alps, including Fenestrelle, but gave France compensation in the Alpine valley of Barcelonnette to the south. In North America, Hudson Bay, Newfoundland and Nova Scotia – the last with ill-defined boundaries – went to Britain, and the far west was opened to the fur traders of both nations. St Kitts in the West Indies remained British.

Other terms concerning France reflected British supremacy, and the desire of that nation to retain it. Gibraltar and Minorca gave Britain valuable bases in the Mediterranean, where France had earlier supplanted Spain as the leading European naval power. The proposed Hanoverian succession in Britain on the death of Queen Anne, who had succeeded Wiliam III in 1702, was to be recognized. The pretender James Stuart was banished from France. He fled to Lorraine, but this did not prevent Louis XIV from providing him with financial assistance for his abortive rising in Scotland in 1715, after George I's accession in the previous year. Dunkirk, haunt of privateers and port of departure for the pretender's earlier invasion attempt, was a threat to British security. The port was to be filled in, the citadel razed and the seaward defences dismantled. Britain also supplanted France as the main foreign participant in Spanish commerce.

The Spanish succession question was solved by the general recognition of Philip V. Spain was therefore abandoned and the dissident Catalans were forced into submission at Barcelona in the autumn of 1714 by Berwick's Franco-Spanish besiegers, with a British fleet blockading the port. "English opinion was shocked and shamed."[17] Philip V was compelled to renounce the French succession, and the Bourbon kingdoms were never to unite. The problem was a very real one, since by the early months of 1712 only the delicate future Louis XV stood between Philip and the French throne. The emperor fought on after Utrecht, but with Villars driving towards the Danube, his lack of allies made peace imperative. Terms were agreed on at Rastatt on the 6th March 1714 between France and Charles VI, and a few months later French differences with the German princes were resolved at Baden. At Rastatt, France retained Alsace, including Strasburg, but surrendered all conquests east of the Rhine and confirmed the agreement reached at Utrecht.

Louis XIV died on the 1st September 1715. His death opened up the possibility that external and internal affairs, long disturbed by his wars, could at last be stabilized.[18] The Spanish succession struggle had ruined commerce, and moreover, the nation was financially bankrupt. Chamillart and Colbert's nephew, Desmarets, had been unable to prevent a growing annual deficit. Loans, currency manipulation and the sale of offices and patents of nobility proved insufficient to meet expenditure. Ministers of finance had recourse to increased taxation. Chamillart reintroduced the *capitation* in 1701, a poll-tax devised by his predecessor, Pontchartrain, and in 1710 Desmarets instituted the *dixième*, a tax levied on incomes and profits. These supplements to the *taille* contributed to that general *malaise* which was ultimately to lead to the overthrow of the monarchical system.

Louis XIV had made the name of France great and had built upon a long tradition to glorify the monarchy, but the cost had been excessive: in financial instability, in grinding and inequitable taxation, in the progressive weakening of checks upon the exercise of power, in the quest for a vague spiritual unity under the crown, while perpetuating outworn institutions, ancient privilege and an infinite variety of administrative practices.

Yet France remained a powerful force in the Europe of 1715, although other nations would soon challenge her hegemony. Greatness is not to be measured only in terms of military and economic strength: French thought and French fashions were in the ascendant, in short, "French civilization, illustrated by the brilliance and learning of its authors, ruled supreme and gave the law to every social group which aspired to the faintest tincture of culture, from the Russian border to the Atlantic Ocean."[19] The French language, too, had become the medium of expression in polite society and in international diplomacy throughout Europe. The true measure of French greatness is therefore to be found elsewhere than in the glorification of monarchy and in strength of arms. In the literary field it lies in the work of the playwrights, Corneille, Racine and Molière, in the social satire of La Bruyère and the moral judgement of Fénelon, in the philosophies of Descartes and Pascal, in the fables of La Fontaine and the literary criticism of Boileau, and in the many-sided genius of Fontenelle. In other intellectual fields, too, France made outstanding contributions in the 17th century: Le Vau and the Mansards in architecture, Le Brun and Rigaud in painting, Girardon in sculpture, Lully in music, Le Nôtre in landscape gardening, and Desargues, Fermat, Picard, La Hire, the elder Cassini and Papin in the sciences and mathematics. Nor was the state behindhand in fostering French culture. Richelieu sponsored the *Académie française* in 1635, and Colbert, the *Académie des Sciences* in 1666. Other institutions devoted to the fine arts and the study of antiquity were founded between 1648 and 1671.

Kings die and dynasties fall, but the greatness of an age is best measured by the living products of its civilization. In this sense, the France of the 17th century stands high in the scale of European values.

CHAPTER 4

THE BRITISH ISLES: CONFLICT AND CHANGE, 1558-1714

THE ELIZABETHAN SETTLEMENT, 1558-1603

There are few more pathetic events in English history than the death of Queen Mary (on the 17th November 1558), "the most honest and ill-advised of the Tudors".[1] She believed it her God-given duty to return her country to Rome, and to found a Catholic dynasty which would keep it there. To realize these objectives she had married Philip II, had reduced her country to a dependency of Spain and had involved it in a disastrous and eventually humiliating war with France. She had burnt 300 of her countrymen at the stake, and aroused a hatred of herself and her church, and of her husband and his country. The accession on Mary's death of her half-sister Elizabeth, wholly English and Protestant, was hailed with joy and relief, especially amongst the new middle class in the south: the squires, merchants, sailors and parliamentarians. In the north, where conditions were still semi-feudal, and amongst many of the clergy, there was less or no enthusiasm.

Dominating an off-shore island, England had long been the most nationalistic state of Europe, and during the 16th century it became still more so. The weakening of the great nobility during the 15th century "Wars of the Roses" had facilitated the establishment of an effective and strongly centralized Tudor despotism by Henry VII (1485-1509). This completed the ruin of divisive feudalism, and furthered the growth of united nationalism, through institutions such as the common law, the king's peace, royal courts, Parliament, where the representatives of the whole country gathered together, a national literature and a national language. Nationalism was also promoted by increasing prosperity, in itself the outcome of new, national industries, especially cloth manufacture and trade. Next King Henry VIII (1509-1547) severed the religious link with Rome, making himself so-called "Head of the Church" in England. Despite this, Henry, who was no Protestant, died certain of his Catholicism, but by his politically motivated action he cleared the way for separatist Protestantism at the expense of the international church of Rome. The voyages of discovery, the opening of the ocean trade routes, together with the country's geographical position, completed the transformation process; England, despite Catholic Mary's every effort, entered a new stage of the country's history, insular, outward-looking, Protestant, and nationalist. This was the country which Elizabeth was now called upon to rule.

It was the greatest and most successful reign in the history of England, indeed there is little to compare with it in the history of all Europe. Elizabeth I has become something of a legend, so that the accession of Elizabeth II (1952) was hailed, with more optimism than realism, as the dawn of a new Elizabethan age. History, however, is not so easily induced to repeat itself! Reacting against the adulation of Elizabeth I some contemporary historians have suggested that it was her ministers who made the reign great, rather than she herself. Certainly William Cecil (1520-1598), later Lord Burghley, was a very great statesman who served his sovereign mistress faithfully and brilliantly from her accession until his death, and there were others like him. None the less it should be remembered that the final decisions and responsibility were the queen's, and that it was in any case she who chose her council.

Her choice showed her awareness of the need for some form of religious settlement, and the need to turn away from Rome, for she did not reappoint the Catholics who had formed the majority of Mary's council. She retained the moderates who wished to follow a middle course between Rome and Geneva, and added seven staunch Protestants. This should not be regarded as a sure indication of where Elizabeth's own religious inclinations tended; she was of the High church rather than the Low church, and disliked religious as much as political enthusiasm. It is quite probable that she was not particularly religious temperamentally, and in a more tranquil period she might have accepted Catholicism itself, but as far as the English were concerned Pope Paul IV had equated Protestantism with patriotism by his foolish pronouncement that, being illegitimate, Elizabeth had no right to the throne, which he would dispose of as a fief of the Holy See! In England the result had been great anger and great mirth. So it was that in 1559, during the first year of the queen's reign, two major acts of Parliament restored the Anglican church, a compromise church, in which Roman Catholic and Protestant elements were blended. The Act of Supremacy of the 8th May 1559 denied the authority of the pope in England, and made the sovereign, not "Head of the Church", which had been Henry VIII's title by the first Act of Supremacy (of 1534), but "Supreme Governor". Shortly afterwards the Act of Uniformity laid down the only permissible liturgy as the one set out in the *Book of Common Prayer*, i.e. Cranmer's book of 1552, modified to give a more Protestant slant, while still maintaining a recognizably Catholic position. Elizabeth and her government knew that, confronted as they were by the Catholic church and the Spanish empire, they were going to need the support of every Englishman possible, from those who still yearned for "the old religion" to those who regarded Rome as the latter-day Babylon.

Its foundations having been firmly laid, what has become known as "the Elizabethan Settlement" was effectively completed in the course of the next few years. Most of the lower clergy accepted it, but the Marian (and therefore Roman Catholic) bishops could not. By 1560 all but one of them had been replaced by men who had gone into exile when Mary had come to the throne in 1553, or who had at least themselves been deprived. The settlement was finalized in 1563, by the parliamentary promulgation of the Thirty-nine Articles which dogmatically defined the Church of England's theological position. These articles were included in the prayer book, and are so framed as to make it possible for the church's members to subscribe to either free will, which was associated with Catholicism, or predestination, a Calvinist concept!

Apart from its purposefully and (in view of the circumstance that it came at the end of a reform movement which had been political in deliberate inception rather than religious in involuntary inspiration) understandably ambiguous dogma, the Anglican church resembled the Catholic church in both the form and conduct of its services and in its organization, which was episcopalian. As such it was broad enough to accommodate wavering Catholics whose loyalty to their country was stronger than their loyalty to their church, and also those many conservatives who, while they entirely repudiated the Roman connection, would have been disconcerted by an utterly and overtly Protestant service.

However, several groups remained beyond the limits of compromise. To "the right" were unyielding Roman Catholics who believed that England should be forced back into the Catholic fold, either because of or despite their patriotism. To "the left", vociferous and influential, were those who wished to "purify" the Church of England, i.e. to conduct a religiously inspired reformation rather than a politically motivated adjustment. Generally known as "Puritans", they ranged from those who were still in the Church of England but who attached little significance to episcopacy, the priesthood and the sacraments, and amongst whom the origins of the present "Low church" party within Anglicanism may be found, to extremists, the Brownists, or early Congregationalists, who insisted that each local congregation should be free, independent and autonomous, in accordance, they claimed, with the practice of the primitive church. Between these limits were the Presbyterians who wished to replace church government by bishops with presbyters and synods, in accordance, they argued, with the apostolic practice as described in the New Testament; the Baptists, who, unlike Presbyterians and Congregationalists, did not accept predestination; the Particular Baptists, who did; the Family of Love, who believed that the resurrection of the dead had already come about, in themselves; and the Seekers, who later became the Quakers. All these movements tended to shade into one another; though all held that priests and ceremonies came between the individual soul and its maker. The Elizabethan settlement could, with an effort, contain them all, except the Congregationalists and, of course, the Catholics, at the other end of the spectrum. They were both accordingly persecuted, with a severity that varied according to circumstances.

Though essentially a domestic issue, and none the less urgent for that, the religious problem was closely bound up with foreign policy and politics. It could not have been otherwise in as religious an age as the late 16th century. All through her reign Elizabeth's first concern was to maintain the independence of her country against the two great powers of the day, France and Spain, both immeasurably more powerful than England, both Catholic, but, fortunately for the heretical islanders, ardent political rivals. Had it not been for that, it is difficult to see how England could have survived, for all Elizabeth and Cecil's genius, the skill and insight with which they encouraged and supported the Protestant rebels of the Netherlands against Spain and the Huguenots against the government of France, and for all her sailors' skill and daring.

Elizabeth had not reigned six months before the Treaty of Cateau-Cambrésis (signed on the 2nd April 1559) ended the war between England and France. Henry

II, the formidable French king, recognized Elizabeth as queen of England, while for her part Elizabeth had finally and formally to give up Calais, England's last mainland possession. A few months later Henry II died (on the 10th July 1559) and was succeeded by his son, Francis II (1544-1560). This was an unfavourable development for England, for although Francis was weak and insignificant, he was already king of Scotland, by virtue of his having married (in 1558) Mary Stuart, the daughter of the late James V of Scotland and his wife, Mary of Guise. The Guises were a powerful, ambitious and pro-Spanish French ducal family, and during Francis II's brief reign (1559-1560) the duke of Guise and his brother, the cardinal of Lorraine, were in effective control of France, while their sister, Mary of Guise, was ruling Scotland as regent during the minority of her daughter, Mary Stuart.

However, from the English point of view the situation was by no means as bad as it at first appeared. The pro-French and Catholic party in Scotland were only maintaining themselves, if at all, with great difficulty against a strong movement for religious reform, led and inspired by the great Calvinist, John Knox (*c.* 1513-1572). By the Treaty of Berwick (signed on the 27th February 1560) Elizabeth gave the reformers her cautious but real support, the first example of the strategy she would use, with great effect, against the French and Spanish in Europe. The French troops in Scotland were besieged at Leith, and eventually withdrawn from the country (in terms of the Treaty of Edinburgh of the 6th July 1560). Mary of Guise had already died (on the 10th June 1560), and Scotland was, temporarily, left in the hands of the reformers' Council of Regents.

The great politico-religious issues had, however, by no means been finally settled in Scotland; on the 5th December 1560 Francis II of France died, and eight months later his widow, Mary Stuart, returned to the country of her birth, and which she had been free to rule, as queen, since her mother's death over a year before. Mary, queen of Scots, as she is known, was a Catholic (had she not been, she could never have been married to the dauphin of France), which promised complications, for the Protestant cause was gaining the upper hand in Scotland. None the less, despite an eventual and probably unavoidable clash with John Knox and the Presbyterian church, whose general assembly had taken the place left vacant by the moribund Parliament, her reign began well. Mary was ambitious, and as the great-granddaughter of Henry VII, founder of the Tudor dynasty in England, her ambitions were by no means confined to poor Scotland. Indeed, in England she was the hope of those Catholics who agreed with the pope that Elizabeth was illegitimate and therefore an usurper. But Mary seems to have been quite unable to control her private passions: after a sordid series of amorous intrigues and quarrels, involving two murders, in one of which she was suspected of having played a part, she was forced to abdicate on the 24th July 1567. James VI, the son of her marriage to her cousin, Darnley, succeeded her, and after further confusion and struggle Mary took refuge in England in May 1568, to the considerable embarrassment of Elizabeth.

Just why Mary should have chosen to surrender her freedom is not clear, for as she was a standing menace to Elizabeth's throne, she had to be imprisoned at once, with little hope of release. It may have been sheer desperation; her situation in early 1568 was indeed desperate and she may have felt that there was no other refuge. It is also possible that she was sufficiently infatuated to hope that her mere presence in England would bring Elizabeth down. When it did not, she was foolish enough to lend herself to the schemes and plots of Philip II's agents, and let herself become the focal point of potential rebellions. Since a substantial body of English Catholics did, indeed, look to her to save England for Rome, this was as much as Elizabeth could bear, and too much for her advisers. But it was only when Mary was found involved in a plot to assassinate Elizabeth, that they had their way, after nineteen years, and were able to persuade their mistress, very unwillingly, to execute her dangerous, treacherous cousin on the 8th February 1587. Elizabeth's hesitation is quite understandable. The execution of an anointed queen regnant, even one who had abdicated, was an awful deed, besides which it drew down upon England the full fury of Spain, as Elizabeth had known it must.

Apart from doing what she could to promote the rivalry between England's two great enemies, France and Spain, Elizabeth had tried to exacerbate their internal problems, which, in both instances, were religious in origin. She had given help and encouragement to the Huguenots in France, and had seen that country breaking down in civil war and chaos, even before the Peace of Troyes on the 11th April 1564 had ended the renewed fighting between England and France, rather ingloriously for England. By then, however, and for years after, France had ceased to be a great danger to England.

Spain was another matter. Elizabeth employed similar tactics against Spain as soon as she was given the opportunity. This was in 1572, when the Dutch revolt began. As usual, Elizabeth was too cautious to become completely involved, and in 1575 prudently declined the proffered throne of the Netherlands. However, English assistance to the Dutch did not cease but, rather, increased, especially after the assassination of William of Orange on the 10th July 1584, and after the fall of Antwerp to Alexander of Parma on the 17th August 1585. In December 1585 an English expedition under the command of Elizabeth's favourite, the Earl of Leicester, landed in the northern Netherlands, to support the rebels, though Elizabeth, typically, insisted that she should not be compelled to formally declare war on Spain, and left herself in a position to negotiate, if possible, between the Dutch and the Spaniards. Despite the victory of Zutphen in September 1586, the expedition was a failure, and in August 1587 Leicester returned to England in disgrace.

Failure or not, Leicester's expedition had been the culmination of a long series of incidents and provocation, infuriating to the Spaniards. The activities of English privateers had been especially annoying. Aided and abetted by their government, they had for years traded, robbed and plundered, at the cannon's point, all along the coasts of Spanish America, in the Caribbean, the North Atlantic and even in the Pacific, an ocean which the Spaniards chose to regard as peculiarly their own, for had not the Holy Father in Rome granted the whole western hemisphere to them, and the eastern to Portugal, in 1494? The line between privateer and pirate was scarcely discernible, but the English gave nothing for a papal decree, nor had they the slightest intention of being shut out of every continent except parts of Europe. So Spanish trade restrictions were ignored, colonial towns were burnt, Spanish ships were seized and sunk, and Spanish treasure was carried off to England. There

Elizabeth assured the Spanish ambassador that she would hang men such as Francis Drake, but instead, she knighted him as a reward for his audacious voyage around the world (1577-1580), and for the huge (plundered) wealth which he had prudently presented and was to continue to present to her.

Trevelyan calls it the most important knighthood ever conferred by an English sovereign, for it was a direct challenge to Spain, and an appeal to the English people to look to the sea as the source of their strength.[2] Elizabeth's action also shows that she could act boldly and independently, for Cecil disapproved, while Philip was predictably angry. What made it worse was that Drake was not alone: He was only the greatest of many – the greatest of heroes to the English, the greatest of thieves to the Spaniards. So it was that in 1587, as the result of great provocation, in the Americas, on the high seas, in the Netherlands, culminating in what he saw as the judicial and sacrilegious murder of the rightful sovereign of England, Mary, queen of Scots, a Catholic and a martyr, Philip determined on the invasion of England. A great fleet or "armada" would sail up the Channel to the Netherlands, where the duke of Parma's army would embark, for conveyance to England. Once ashore, the renowned Spanish infantry, the finest in Europe, would soon put paid to the heretic islanders and the bastard usurper who ruled them. England would be brought back into the true faith, Spain's greatest enemy would be destroyed, and a blow struck against Protestantism, from which, hopefully, it would never recover!

The danger was very great. Spain was then the greatest military and, it was thought, naval power in the world. Accordingly, in April 1587 Drake descended upon Cadiz, took his fleet into the very harbour where the armada was being built, and largely destroyed it, with gun and fireship, "singeing the King of Spain's beard", as he himself put it. He thus gained vital time for his threatened country. The danger, though considerable, was, however, not quite as great as some feared. Mary's execution had finally roused Philip, but it had largely united the English behind Elizabeth. Moderate Catholics whom she had not persecuted (apart from 12d fines, frequently though irregularly imposed on those who did not attend Anglican services), might have fought for Mary, in their eyes the legitimate queen, but Mary being dead, they would fight for Elizabeth, an Englishwoman, against the Spanish Philip, Catholic or not.[3]

The damage done by Drake was eventually repaired and in mid-1588 "the invincible Armada" set sail, some 130 ships, 11 000 sailors and 19 000 soldiers. England had never been in such peril although the country, or Great Britain, would face similarly fearful threats twice again. There is little doubt that, once ashore in strength, Parma's army would have conquered the island, just as would Napoleon's or Hitler's, once ashore in strength. But that was the would-be invaders' problem. In this case "the invincible Armada" proved a sad misnomer. The Royal Navy had been effectively founded by Henry VIII (1491-1547) and had been more or less consistently developed and maintained ever since. The ships which sallied out under the supreme command of Lord Howard of Effingham were little smaller in size or numbers than the Spanish, under the duke of Medina Sidonia, but with their lower hulls they were faster and more manoeuvreable than the Spanish galleons which were especially unwieldy on a lee shore. Nor were the Spaniards much helped by their monstrous cannon firing 60 lb shot, mounted high upon deck where they tended to make the ship top-heavy; the English again had the advantage, with larger numbers of much smaller guns, 17-pounders, firing through portholes, and, most important, with a higher rate of fire and a greater range (up to 1,8 kilometres) than the Spanish guns.

It was the Spanish tactics, decided mainly by the military officers, who took precedence over the naval, to come alongside and board, hence the large number of soldiers already in their ships. Once they had won what would have resembled a land battle, though fought at sea, they intended proceeding to the Netherlands, whence Parma's army would be ferried across the Channel. This was just what Howard, himself a competent seaman, and whose immediate subordinates, excellent sailors, included the incomparable Drake, would not allow. Two days after the Spaniards had entered the Channel (on the 19th July 1588) they encountered the English, and one of the decisive battles of history commenced. It raged until the evening of the 29th July, when Medina Sidonia decided to abandon the invasion attempt and escape back to Spain around the Orkneys. Pursued and harassed by Howard as far as the Firth of Forth, and shattered by storms, the fifty three surviving ships did not reach Spain until September. Catholic morale and Spanish prestige were severely damaged, and England's prestige and the morale of all Protestant Europe rose accordingly. *"Deus flavit, et dissipati sunt"* ("God blew, and they were scattered") was the inscription on the medal struck by Elizabeth, whose fleet had lost not a single ship.

The main significance of this battle, for Europe generally, was that it checked the triumphant course of the Counter-Revolution; for England it meant that political and economic development could proceed for many years to come, secure from the threat of invasion; for Spain, although that country long continued a major European power, it was the beginning of decline.

Apart from its being an island, one of the main factors which had enabled England to maintain itself against the militarily far greater power of Spain was the country's prosperity. Southern England especially was rich, and London with its 100 000 inhabitants was the greatest port in Europe, far larger in proportion to other English cities than it is today. The then second largest, Norwich, was only one-twentieth the size. The internal consequences of this wealth were as profound as the external. In poor Scotland the Parliament had withered away in the 1560s, and the general assembly of the Presbyterian church had become the centre of opposition to Mary, with her Catholic beliefs and absolutist ideas. In wealthy England, Parliament was a well-established institution, quite able to carry out that function for which such bodies had originally been called into existence in late medieval times, namely to provide for the financial needs of princes. Its members also had a proper appreciation of their own importance, and of the potentialities of their position.

Although its origins are obscure, by the time Elizabeth came to the throne, Parliament, as an institution with an element of popular representation, was already some 300 years old. During the 14th century and the early 15th century the expenses of an apparently interminable war with France had forced the kings of England to pay a fair amount of attention to Parliament. By *c.* 1430, therefore, the position was that the king called Parliament frequently, and would give serious attention, quite possibly assent, to its petitions. It had been established that the king was part of Parliament; his participation was essential to its functioning, he attended its opening and closing, and if he wished, its other meetings. The king was not obliged to act in accordance with its wishes and usually made law by issuing *ordinances* through his council. However, *statutes, i.e.* acts of Parliament, were coming to be regarded as superior to ordinances by the end of the 14th century. Ordinances made by the king through his council, could be revoked by him, but not statutes. The extent of the suspending power by which the king could suspend the statutes, and the dispensing power by which he could grant immunity to a particular person was uncertain, and would later become major issues. A little later, in the early 15th century, the Commons, the lower of the two houses of which Parliament was composed, began to initiate legislation, and to claim a measure of control over taxation. This was most significant, for the House of Commons was, however inadequately, a representative body, unlike the Upper House, or the House of Lords, the members of which owed their positions to inheritance or, in the case of the lords spiritual, the upper clergy, to their appointments.

This advance was not maintained. During the Wars of the Roses Parliament's position deteriorated. The lords temporal who dominated the Upper House, who had encouraged the Commons to demand and criticize, and who had given them a measure of protection, practically destroyed themselves, under circumstances which rendered the Commons particularly dependent upon the king for the maintenance of some vestiges of law and order. Not surprisingly, the first king to reign after the wars, Elizabeth's shrewd and miserly grandfather, Henry VII, was in as strong a position as any monarch had ever been.

Under him and his son, Henry VIII, an obedient and respectful House of Commons and House of Lords, both of them filled with the king's creatures, were little more than the collective instrument of the crown; Parliament was accepted as part of the constitutional scene, but it was not regarded as a regular and necessary part. It was for the use of the sovereign, to fulfil particular needs in times of emergency. It might be said that there was not "a Parliament", but only Parliaments in the plural, which were called whenever the crown needed them and dismissed when it was satisfied. Normally the business of the Tudor state was run through the Privy Council, the direct descendant of the *curia regis*, the king's council of Norman times.

For all that the Tudor sovereigns, by directing Parliament in a programme of important legislation, caused it to gain prestige as much as it lost influence. This applied to the House of Commons more than to that of Lords; the Upper House which was being filled with a new aristocracy, men with a vested interest in the Tudor settlement, began to decline in importance, a process which has continued to this day. There is no gainsaying that during the 16th century and especially during the reign of Elizabeth the ground was being prepared for the great constitutional conflict which was to dominate English history throughout the 17th century.

Although Parliaments did not meet very often and sessions were short (during the whole of Elizabeth's forty five year reign the total sessions amounted to only thirty five months), the actual life of an elected House of Commons became longer. This helped members to get to know one another, and the mutual recognition process was further promoted by a change in the collective character of the House of Commons. This was due to the non-observance by the Tudors of the custom which had required members to be actually resident in the areas they represented. That was possible because growing prosperity led to an increase in the number of country gentry, lawyers and businessmen who were willing and even eager to serve, without pay. This phenomenon and also the burgeoning size of the Lower House, to 467 members by the end of Elizabeth's reign (1603), testify to the increasing status of the body as well as to growing prosperity. By then MPs were beginning to act in concert, and social distinctions between town and country were becoming blurred. The blurring process and the development of common interests apart from politics was accelerated by the lawyers, merchants and sea captains buying land, one of the few existing forms of investment. Parliamentarians were therefore men of standing, substance and some prominence in national affairs; they knew each other or knew of each other, often they were related, frequently they had gone to one or other of the universities, and/or the Inns of Court. It was not a chance collection of strangers but a vital well-to-do middle-class organism, with links, ties, common views and interests. Steeped as it was in the classics, the education of the parliamentarians inclined them to think highly of government by an assembly of notables, such as themselves! It is therefore scarcely surprising that as the Spanish danger receded, and as the queen grew older, they began trying to assert themselves, and to extend their power and influence.

It was probably the great part that it played in the Tudor religious revolution, culminating in the passing of the Act of Supremacy and the Act of Uniformity, that first made Parliament an institution of permanent political significance, though the monarchs were too close to the event to realize what had happened. As late as 1610 James I was still reminding Parliament that it had been summoned to supply his wants, which, in his eyes (though not its members') was its primary purpose. What its purpose actually was, in the last years of Elizabeth's reign, can be quite simply summarized: it had to grant taxes, legislate (statutes), and, on occasion, act as a court of law. There was an element of urgency or of the special need about the performance of these tasks. Therefore, as regards taxes, the sovereign had numerous other sources of income: rents, fines, fees, forfeitures, feudal dues, the proceeds of traditional customs duties and the tonnage and poundage which Parliament customarily granted to him at the beginning of his reign.

Similarly, for legislation, the king was not entirely dependent on Parliament, for the competence of the king-in-council was accepted by the judges. Whatever the trend two centuries earlier, royal proclamations and statutes carried equal weight at the end of the Tudor period. Individual members were, however, beginning to raise a question, the implications and possible consequences of which were unlimited: what was the relation of the monarch himself to parliamentary legislation? They asserted (*c.* 1595), as loudly as they dared, that the monarch himself was subject to law and should govern in accordance with it. Although at this time it was no more than a straw showing which way 17th century "winds of change" might blow, the matter was fundamental; should Parliament gain its point it would become the ultimate source of power.

Finally in its judicial capacity Parliament was also there for emergencies. Such occasions might be to try peers charged with treason or felony, to hear impeachments and to declare or revoke attainders. The Commons were concerned with the latter, as they required acts of Parliament; in the other cases it was the Lords that sat as a court.

As its prestige and sense of importance grew, Parliament claimed certain privileges: its members should not be arrested during sessions other than on charges of treason and felony, and it should have the right to summon and punish persons, including its own members, who made slanderous or abusive statements about Parliament. MPs claimed freedom of access to the sovereign through their speaker, and, finally, they claimed the right freely to discuss not only the subjects put before them by the monarch, but anything else as well. In other words, they claimed freedom of initiation as well as of speech.

As regards the first three claims, they had more or less succeeded by the end of the queen's reign, but on the last and most important Elizabeth never really gave way. She wanted it understood that certain subjects, such as religion and the succession, were barred, and it is worth noting that one of the most extreme of Parliament's spokesmen, Peter Wentworth, died in prison!

That, however, was exceptional. On the whole, Elizabeth governed with the support and affection of Parliament. She or her ministers frequently addressed Parliament and strove to win its co-operation, many of the ministers were MPs, who took part in debates and elections. Out of concern for her sex and, later, her age, to say nothing of a distaste for the Tower, MPs generally refrained from "pushing" controversial matters, especially fundamental issues such as the relation of the monarch to statutes and freedom of speech and initiation. Besides, the queen was growing old, and many an ambitious politician would have resolved that while certain issues could wait they would be brought up under her successor, whoever that might be.

Nevertheless at the beginning of the 17th century, Parliament did not govern and was not even essential to government. The monarch did not have to call it; he could govern by proclamation through his Privy Council, enforce his will through prerogative courts such as the Star Chamber, and raise funds by means already mentioned.

Parliament's only real weapon was its control of taxation, which was not meant to provide for the regular and financial needs of government. A thrifty and fortunate monarch might manage without ever having to ask Parliament for money. But that would require internal and external peace and prudent management. Although Elizabeth had been positively miserly, and her ministers had been efficient, she had always been short of cash! The position, when she died on the 24th March 1603, was both delicate and open. Much would depend on the characters and understanding of her successors. If they were cautious and thrifty, subtle and wise, flexible and tolerant, they had a chance of gaining the co-operation of Parliament, even though they might lose their financial independence.

JAMES I, 1603-1625: PRELUDE TO REVOLUTION

Elizabeth's successor was Mary, queen of Scots's son (1566-1625) by her second husband, Lord Darnley. As James VI he had been king, in name, since his mother's enforced abdication (1567), but his real rule had only begun in 1583, and had been characterized by constant struggle against the turbulent nobility and obstinate Presbyterians of Scotland. Unlike his mother, James was not a Roman Catholic, but he was a fervent episcopalian. His experiences in Scotland had convinced him that bishops were essential for the support and maintenance of the king's absolute power and divine right to rule. His intention to practise those theories in his new, fatter and fairer kingdom of England would certainly have led to a confrontation with Parliament, but the large and influential Puritan presence in that body made the clash come very soon. The king was convinced that the Puritans, the left wing of the (episcopalian) Anglican church, were intent upon the introduction of Presbyterianism into England. Early in his reign, at the unfortunate Hampton Court conference of the 12th-18th January 1604, he threatened to "harry them out of the land". The Arminians were delighted at this. They were the High church party amongst the Anglicans, named after the Dutch theologian, Jacobus Arminius, who stressed free will in reaction to Calvinism. The Puritans, however, and therefore many a potential parliamentarian, were infuriated.

A foolish though intelligent man, King James I understood neither Parliament, nor the Church of England, nor England itself. His years of ruling Scotland were a handicap rather than a help; certainly he knew and understood nothing of the centralized bureaucracy that had developed in England, as in the other advanced countries of western Europe, during the previous century. He merely regarded it as a field for patronage, for the advancement of his worthless favourites. A really disastrous ending to his reign was only prevented because Parliament was not yet ready to push its claims to the limit, and because, where principles were concerned, James was always ready to compromise, unlike his son Charles I who ended on the scaffold. But given James's background, personality and opinions, and the political climate of the time, clashes with Parliament were certain, just as it was certain that he would have to summon Parliament.

Despite every possible care, Elizabeth had left her successor with a load of debt. He could not hope to meet it as well as the normal expenses of government just when an influx of gold and silver from Spanish America was causing general inflation. To make matters worse, the normal sources of royal revenue were more or less fixed, and, unlike the great queen, he was extravagant, and had a large family.

The clash at Hampton Court ensured that the Parliament which assembled on the 19th March 1604 was not in the most favourable mood, nor were matters improved by his speech from the throne, which contained a hostile reference to the Puritans. But the king's plight is revealed by his retention of this Parliament, despite several adjournments, until the 9th February 1611.

Before it would advance the funds which the king expected, the House of Commons brought up two cases of privilege. The less important was Shirley's Case, where Parliament successfully asserted and secured the freedom of an MP from arrest while Parliament was in session, other than on charges of treason, felony or breach of the peace. This was a slight but real parliamentary gain. The importance of the second dispute was enhanced by the king being involved. Goodwin v. Fortescue concerned the alleged right of the Lord Chancellor to nullify election results in terms of a proclamation issued by James before the election, which commanded, *inter alia*, that bankrupts and outlaws should not be "chosen". Goodwin, who had defeated Fortescue, was an outlaw, and the court of chancery therefore declared the election void. The Commons nevertheless ordered Goodwin to take his place in the Lower House, insisting that he was not an outlaw, and that anyway there were precedents for outlaws sitting in the House. James replied that they could not judge returns, that all their privileges came from him anyway, and that the legal opinion of the judges regarding outlaws in the House should be obtained. Eventually there was a compromise. The king acknowledged Parliament's competence to judge returns, while the Commons agreed to a fresh election in Buckinghamshire, the county concerned.

Parliament next turned to two remnants of feudalism, from which the crown derived a considerable income. These were "purveyance", of doubtful legality, and "wardship", which was definitely legal, so much so that the Commons offered James an alternative and larger source of revenue, for which they got only a humiliating reprimand. They retorted with what was the first major document of the constitutional struggle with the Stuarts. "The Form of Apology and Satisfaction to be Presented to His Majesty" was a respectful lecture to a foreign-born king on the constitutional position and outlook in his new realm, as seen by Parliament. In it the Commons took up the largely mistaken position that they were defending an established position against the encroachment of the crown. They pointed out, as respectfully as possible, that their privileges were matters of right, and could not be withheld without endangering the liberty of the whole country. Having established their position, which involved a rather distorted view of English constitutional history, the Commons passed on to specific grievances. The "rights and liberties of the Commons of England" were bound up with freedom of election, freedom of MPs from arrest, and freedom of speech (i.e. in the House), and included freedom of initiation. All of these had been encroached upon.

Finally, as regards religion, they thought religious uniformity essential for the security of the state (here James was ahead of them), but the uniformity which they approved would favour the Puritans, weaken the bishops, and infuriate the king. The latter consideration did not deter the Commons at all, for they no more considered the king supreme in matters spiritual than they did in matters temporal!

These were the questions over which the king and Parliament eventually fought a great civil war, but James appeared unaware of their significance. His response was the first revelation of a characteristic Stuart weakness: that of regarding expressions of major political grievances as personal insults.

In November 1606 the verdict in Bates's Case, concerning the king's right to alter (i.e. raise) import duties, raised the possibility of the monarch obtaining an adequate source of revenue, independent of Parliament. However, Cecil, first earl of Salisbury, who had become treasurer in 1608, was so cautious in his application of new levies that the additional revenue was not very large. In 1610 the position was that some £700 000 of debt had been paid off, but £300 000 was still owing, while revenue was falling short of expenditure by about £50 000 per annum, without considering extraordinary expenses. So that same year Parliament was recalled, in the hope of voting additional taxes. But when they only offered £100 000 instead of the £200 000 required, before proceeding to discuss Bates's Case, James reiterated his right to impose import and export duties.

Parliament's response, two days later, was a petition claiming the right "to debate freely all matters which do properly concern the subject". The king, possibly because of his need for money, let them continue with a great debate on impositions, in which sweeping assertions were made concerning two alleged types of royal power, those of the king out of Parliament and the king in Parliament. The second, i.e. the king acting with the assent of his Lords and Commons, was "the most sovereign and supreme power above all and controllable by none". In 1510 such a claim would have brought its makers to the Tower; in 1610 it was only a sign of things to come. It was also a consequence of the Tudors' constant use of Parliament as the convenient instrument of their will, which had nevertheless given that body an enhanced idea of its own importance.

While this was going on, Salisbury was attempting to arrive at a "great contract" whereby, in return for considerable concessions, Parliament would make an annual grant of £200 000. Negotiations were still in train when the king, furious at attacks upon his Scottish favourites and his court's waste of money, dissolved his first Parliament on the 9th February 1611, after it had sat, with some long intervals, for seven years.

There was no disguising the fact that the Tudor system of government had been found wanting, for it was too dependent on the sovereign's personal character. James had also allowed the dominant position which privy councillors had enjoyed in Elizabeth's parliaments to wither away, by failing to ensure that enough of them had seats. As a result, his interests were neglected while ambitious private members came to the fore. Many of them were lawyers who understood procedure and were well equipped to advance Parliament's claims. They were especially good as chairmen of committees, of which there were an increasing number. They grew to include the whole house, when the speaker would be excluded, conveniently, for he was still the servant of the king.

Finally, James had kept Parliament in being far too long. It had gained more of a sense of cohesive purpose than ever.

Fundamentally his whole view of the institution was distorted. He regarded it as a tiresome necessity, to be bullied or wheedled into providing funds when needed. There was no idea of giving it a share in the responsibilities of government, or of paying serious attention to its members' opinions. The consequent deterioration in relations was accelerated and exacerbated by the continuing rise of Puritanism and the diminution of the Spanish threat abroad. Although James I had made few if any formal concessions, by 1611 the whole position of the crown had begun to be insidiously undermined.

When Salisbury and Archbishop Bancroft died in 1612, the rot really set in, as the king fell increasingly under the influence of his worthless favourites, a process which culminated in the disgraceful "reign" of Villiers, duke of Buckingham.

For the rest of his reign James and his incapable advisers floundered along, with the two institutions which could have done much to strengthen the monarchy, the Privy Council and the Bench of Bishops, being sadly neglected.

Financial problems forced James to call a Parliament in 1614, and he did his best to arrange for the return of a House of Commons that would favour him, a "parliament of love". There was nothing unusual in that, but the obtrusive nature of James's efforts aroused alarm. His favoured candidates were rejected, and a lot of inexperienced young men elected, all under the influence of experienced leaders such as Wentworth, Eliot and Pym.

The "Addled Parliament" passed no acts, received no concessions, and voted no supplies. Its most significant feature was its members' increasingly hostile and critical attitude. The Parliament and James's patience lasted two months only.

For the next seven years the king struggled on without a Parliament, raising money by unpopular financial devices of dubious legality, such as "benevolences", "impositions" and the sale of commercial and industrial "monopolies" to wealthy favourites. They aroused far more discontent than money, and that at a time when Chief Justice Sir Edward Coke's efforts to establish the Bench as an independent arbitrator between sovereign and subject were approaching a climax.

The law was by no means clear on any of the points at issue between the crown and Parliament, and precedents could be cited either way. Hence the importance of judicial decisions, and the possible utility of the Bench to make law by establishing favourable precedents. In other words, the courts could be used to legalize what Parliament disapproved of. The first two Stuarts, James I, and his son and successor, Charles I, frankly expected support from the judges, whom they appointed. Such an attitude was bound to lead to a clash with Coke, who had stressed the legislative supremacy of Parliament as early as 1605. Only that body could change the law; certainly the king could not, for he himself was subject to it! The only surprising thing about Coke's dismissal in November 1617 over the Commendams case, was that it had been so long coming. None the less, it did great damage to the idea of an independent judiciary, his eleven colleagues on the King's Bench having acceded to James's demand that they consult him before delivering their verdict.

One of the first acts of James's reign had been to conclude peace with Spain (in 1604), thereby giving England a feeling of security which had increased Parliament's intransigence! But peace had enabled James to avoid expenses which would have made him utterly dependent upon Parliament. Despite many difficulties, by 1620 the king's monetary position had so improved, thanks to the financial genius of Lionel Cranfield, earl of Middlesex, that some observers concluded that he might never have to summon Parliament again. It would have been as well if he had not, for Cranfield's methods had made a bitter struggle certain if ever another one did meet. The crown's security, in short, depended on the avoidance of foreign complications.

Unluckily for James, the very next year the disastrous defeat of his son-in-law, Frederick, the elector palatine, in the opening campaigns of the Thirty Years War necessitated calling a Parliament on the 30th January 1621. Frederick was regarded as a Protestant hero in England; assisting him, however, would be expensive. Parliament had no sooner assembled than the usual dissension arose, made worse by James's haughty refusal to explain his position, intentions and needs. He felt that the conduct of foreign affairs was beyond the competence of Parliament, and adhered to his conviction that Parliament's function was simply to provide the money he required. Parliament, for its part, was suspicious of his attempts to marry Prince Charles to the Spanish infanta, and felt that his idea of recovering the Palatinate by diplomatic representations at Madrid was humiliating, even dangerous, and was convinced that the best way to combat Catholicism was by seizing a Spanish treasure fleet.

Frederick's popularity and James's conciliatory opening address were sufficient to produce two modest subsidies, after which, led by Coke, the former Chief Justice, Parliament turned eagerly to their latest grievance, monopolies. These had been found to be illegal, in both statute and common law, as long ago as 1603, in the case of Darcy v. Allen, but the judges' finding had been simply ignored by the government, despite repeated Parliamentary protests, in 1606, 1610 and 1614. It was against two monopolists, Mompesson and Mitchell, that Parliament now revived a half-forgotten constitutional weapon, namely impeachment. Though neglected since the mid-15th century it was used with great effect against Mompesson, Mitchell and others who were fined and banished, until Parliament was sufficiently emboldened to proceed against one of the king's ministers, no less a person than the Lord Chancellor Sir Francis Bacon (1561-1626) himself. He was impeached by the Commons, for corruption, and tried and found guilty by the Lords, who fined him £40 000 (later remitted) and banned him from future office. The case was of the greatest political and historical importance because a pillar of autocracy had been brought down; impeachment would be used again, with similar effectiveness, against Middlesex in 1624 and, later, devastatingly, against Strafford and Laud. It was also of great constitutional significance because a minister had been impeached; all these impeachments amount to successful assertion of ministerial responsibility to Parliament, while for the existence of any form of royalist supremacy it was essential that they be responsible to the sovereign only.

By June 1621 the king had had enough, and he prorogued Parliament, which had only granted him the original two small subsidies, until November. When they reassembled it was to present him with a petition expressing their concern at the advance of Catholicism in central Europe and at home. It also contained Parliament's view regarding counter-measures: a war against Spain, renewed measures against English Roman Catholics, and a Protestant wife for Prince Charles. Although this infringed the royal prerogative, and James had every right to remonstrate with them as he did, the only result was that Parliament presented him with the so-called "Great Protestation", insisting, incorrectly, that they were entitled to discuss foreign affairs with complete freedom, like anything else concerning sovereign, state and church. The enraged king tore the "Great Protestation" out of the journals of the Commons, dissolved the parliament and sent its most prominent leaders, Coke, Southampton, Pym and Seldon, to the Tower. It was an effective denial of free speech and a moral victory for the crown.

For the next two years and more James managed without Parliament, but eventually called his fourth, which assembled on the 19th February 1624, was prorogued on the 29th May 1624, and finally dissolved by the king's death, on the 27th March 1625. His relations with it were better than with any of the others, partly because he gave up much of what he had struggled to retain in 1621. This change of attitude was partly owing to the breakdown of the Spanish marriage negotiations; Parliament had been right, it appeared, where the king had been wrong. Delighted as it was to hear that the treaties with Spain had been dissolved, and to find its opinions on foreign policy being seriously considered, Parliament passed a subsidy bill, though even then they included unheard-of provisions to make sure that the money was actually used against Spain. Partly because James was in a state of shock, and partly because the direction of affairs had largely fallen into the hands of Buckingham, who was anxious to retain the popularity which his return from Spain had aroused, these were accepted. The first tentative step towards the allocation of funds for specific purposes, the "appropriation of supply", had been taken.

This Parliament also confirmed the right to impeach ministers, by overthrowing Middlesex, and also managed to get the royal assent to a bill outlawing monopolies! When the king died, this remained the solitary important concrete gain Parliament had made by legislation. None the less there had been a great change in the relations between the crown and Parliament. Impeachment had been revived, and it had been established that it could be used against ministers of the crown, so laying the foundation of ministerial responsibility. The right to debate all matters concerning the church and the state had been claimed, and as far as foreign policy was concerned James had given way. Parliament had also protested against impositions and had asserted that proclamations did not have the force of law; they had obtained acknowledgement of their right to judge their own returns, and they had laid the foundations of the modern doctrine of supply. James had made mistakes which had helped to weaken his position: his autocratic attitude and messages had provoked the Commons, his attempts to influence them himself had undermined his privy councillors in Parliament, while trying to use the speaker as his representative had initiated the practice whereby the whole House goes into committee, so that the Speaker left the chair. Parliament had made real advances, even if they were not formal and final, and the task of maintaining the royal prerogative would be all the more difficult for the new king.

CHARLES I, 1625-1649, AND CIVIL WAR

The likelihood of a really serious clash between the king and Parliament increased with the accession of Charles I. The new king (1601-1649) was a most attractive person, a cultured man and an affectionate husband and father. His public life, however, was a disaster which culminated in tragedy. Like his father he lacked Elizabeth's flexibility and political understanding, and again like James I, he upheld absolute monarchy. With the obstinacy and fervour of a slightly stupid man, Charles believed in the "divine right of kings", in other words, that kings, appointed by God, were responsible for the welfare of their peoples to God alone. Unlike James, whose desire to retain his English throne could in the last resort be relied upon to triumph over his principles, Charles was absolutely unyielding. At the same time he did resemble his father in being easily influenced by badly chosen advisers. By nature he was inclined to intrigue and to insincerity, but he regarded his willingness to do anything to defend his position as perfectly justifiable, for as an anointed king he was above the law, and could do no wrong. Consequently, he could not be trusted; agreements with him were impossible; and eventually nothing could be done save kill him. On the very scaffold he remained true to his principles, declaring that the people had no claim whatsoever to share in government. A sovereign and a subject, he insisted, were clean different things.

As if all this was not enough, he was suspected of being too favourable to Catholicism. Although he lived and died an Anglican and his children were all baptized in that church, he had married a Catholic princess, Henrietta Maria of France, and under him the Catholic Mass was celebrated openly. Well it might be, for while at the time of the marriage Charles had promised Parliament that there would be no relaxation regarding Catholicism in England, the marriage treaty had contained a secret clause promising that very thing! Quite apart from such deceitfulness Charles's acknowledged religious views came between him and the increasingly influential Puritans, so making it difficult for him to strengthen the Anglican episcopal system which itself supported the monarchy.

Charles's foreign policy, which greatly affected constitutional and internal political developments in the early years of his reign, was that of his father's favourite, the vain and incompetent Buckingham.

All in all, the new king's prospects depended upon two unknowns: how well the crown would succeed in governing with its ordinary revenue only, and to what extent the Lords would support the Commons. Should Charles and Buckingham involve the country in a war, Parliament would have to be called, and would begin to demand what Charles regarded as none of its business, namely a greater say in government. And owing to the offence James had given by his lavish bestowal of peerages upon English favourites and Scotsmen, and the much resented influence of the jumped-up Buckingham and the "court-lords", it was likely that the majority of the Upper House, the "country lords", would give the Commons every support.

In the Lower House the landed gentry predominated, only about one-tenth of its members being representatives of the increasingly important commercial class. Under-represented and wealthy, the business community was a possible alternative source of revenue. Obtaining their support was the more urgent in view of the complete hostility of the landed gentry to what they saw as the crown's unjustifiable and unhistorical pretensions.

Despite the crucial importance of maintaining peace, Charles was hardly on the throne before ambitious preparations were begun for war with Spain, Buckingham having been offended by the failure of the negotiations for the hand of the infanta in Madrid. These preparations included summoning Parliament which assembled on the 18th June 1625. To Charles's disappointment they were in no hurry to advance large sums for the coming conflict. He had failed to realize that the sort of war with

Spain favoured by most Englishmen was merely seizing treasure ships and looting Central and South American colonial ports. Parliament dismissed the idea of attacking metropolitan Spain, merely because Buckingham was piqued, as absurd and wasteful. Advising the king to replace his worthless favourites with a well-selected council, they voted him the utterly inadequate sum of £140 000 and turned to their grievances.

The Commons' first move was to refuse Charles the life grant of tonnage and poundage (customs and excise) which had for centuries been customarily granted to a new monarch by his first Parliament. They made the grant for one year only, so gaining an opportunity to reconsider the whole question of indirect taxation. When the Lords refused to support them, the king was not granted tonnage and poundage at all, but, nothing daunted, he proceeded to levy it himself! Naturally this further damaged his relations with Parliament, relations which were already strained by his tolerant attitude to the Catholics, and his support for Arminianism which, as far as the Calvinistic Puritans of the Commons were concerned, was a very long stride along the road to Rome. But Charles saw Arminianism as important for the maintenance of episcopalianism, which was important for the maintenance of absolute monarchy.

Relations deteriorated still further when the terms of the marriage treaty and the king's deceitfulness were revealed, but when it was learned that the obnoxious Buckingham had promised Cardinal Richelieu help in reducing the Huguenot stronghold of La Rochelle, Parliament was enraged as well as alarmed. They insisted that they would never vote supplies to be spent by a man in whom they had no confidence, so taking another step towards a responsible executive. When it looked as though the duke might be impeached, Charles hurriedly dissolved his first Parliament, on the 12th August 1625.

Within six months the expenses of the Spanish War, begun on the 8th September 1625, and growing tension between England and France had compelled Charles to summon another Parliament which assembled in time to hear of Buckingham's disgraceful and wasteful mishandling of the war. They were further roused by the king's futile attempt to cripple them by appointing their leaders, including Coke and Wentworth (who later, as earl of Strafford, became a pillar of autocracy), sheriffs in their respective counties. All that this did was to reveal the extent of Charles and his advisers' misunderstanding of the nature and depth of Parliament's opposition. New leaders at once came forward, including one of the very greatest, Sir John Eliot. The Commons especially were also much disturbed by a provocative sermon by that prominent Arminian William Laud, later (in 1633) archbishop of Canterbury, who told them that the king's commands reflected the glory of God, and that as subjects it was not only their duty, but also an honour, to obey!

Encouraged by the independent attitude of the Lords, the Commons insisted that full redress of grievances should precede supply, and attacked Buckingham as vigorously as ever. When Eliot and another prominent member, Sir Dudley Digges, were imprisoned in the Tower for alleged insolence, they forced the king to climb down by simply refusing to conduct any further business until the prisoners were released. And when business was resumed, it was to prepare to impeach Buckingham for high treason. Charles saved him by a hasty dissolution of Parliament on the 15th June 1626, but he was left without funds, at war with Spain, and soon to be at war with France. This fresh complication was no more than a cynical attempt by Buckingham to gain popularity by seizing French shipping and going to the aid of the Huguenots. The resulting conflict lasted almost four years. In a desperate situation desperate measures had to be taken. Tonnage and poundage were exacted without sanction, coastal towns and counties were compelled to pay "ship money" to raise a fleet, and finally, and most bitterly resented of all, a "forced loan" was imposed. There the government was taking advantage of a loophole in the law (though in the last resort the king regarded himself as above the law). Whatever the legal position, there were a fair number of refusals to pay, by Eliot, Wentworth and Sir John Hampden amongst others. The most prominent resisters were gaoled until they gave way; lesser men found themselves pressed into the army, or had soldiers billeted upon them. By these means Charles raised much bitter enmity, but also much money. Worse still, from the parliamentary point of view the outcome of the Case of the Five Knights of 1627 indicated that, *habeas corpus* or not, the king was able to detain people at his pleasure, without charge.

Meanwhile the French War had brought nothing but ignominious defeats and ruinous expenses, so that there was nothing left but to call another Parliament, Charles's third. Strenuous efforts to influence the elections in favour of royalist candidates failed totally; the House of Commons that was finally returned was so hostile that it seemed unlikely to last a week.

Charles adopted a threatening tone from the beginning; for its part, Parliament refused to pass any form of money bill until there had been a satisfactory response to their complaints. The Commons formed themselves into a committee of grievances to consider forced loans and the arbitrary treatment of those who had refused to make them. They also initiated a constitutional development of real significance, conferences between the two Houses to secure agreement on a line of action. The earliest conferences resulted in the drawing up of the Petition of Right; its eventual acceptance by the king in 1628 was a major historical and constitutional event. The authors of the petition claimed to represent the people of England, and they did not merely ask for the benefit of the law, but actually dared to declare what the law was. Briefly, what they demanded, and what Charles reluctantly conceded, was the prohibition of all forms of taxation without parliamentary consent, a cessation of both billeting and the application of martial law to ordinary citizens in peace time, and that imprisonment should only follow a definite charge. None of these things were requested as favours, they were demanded as rights, ". . . according to the laws and statutes of this realm". Because the majority in the Lords were against him and beause he was desperate, Charles gave way, and what may be regarded as a compact between the crown and the nation became an act of Parliament. As such it had apparently destroyed the two major instruments of autocracy, namely the king's right (in practice) to tax as he pleased, and his right (in practice) to imprison his subjects at pleasure.

Relief and gratitude moved the Commons to grant five subsidies worth £300 000. They were also preparing a bill which would have granted Charles tonnage and poundage for life when they were prorogued on the 26th June 1628, the king having been angered by a remonstrance demanding Buckingham's removal from office and the proposal that another be drawn up, protesting against the continued illegal imposition of tonnage and poundage. They held that the last was contrary to the Petition of Right, and were much disconcerted by the attorney-general's argument that the petition had done no more than confirm ". . . the ancient liberties and rights of the subject". From this Charles brazenly concluded that the position was just the same as it had been before the petition. The king, not surprisingly, took the same attitude. Time, however, would soon show that the prerogative power had suffered a major defeat.

During the interval between sessions the assassination of Buckingham on the 23rd August 1628 removed a major cause of dissension between the king and Parliament, although the king was outraged by his opponents' obvious pleasure. As has been indicated, their attacks upon the favourite were the early manifestations of the doctrine of ministerial responsibility. In the early 17th century the executive and legislative powers had been separate. The fact that many of the king's ministers or councillors, whom he picked as he pleased, were in the Lords was not due to constitutional policy, but to their being peers. The idea of a union between the executive and legislature began in the Commons, when they criticized James I's and Charles I's ministers and tried to back up their criticisms through impeachment, the only method they had.

Parliament reassembled on the 20th January 1629 in a bitter frame of mind. It was obvious that, collecting tonnage and poundage as he was, Charles was simply ignoring the petition, while the Puritans, rapidly growing in numbers, were concerned, even incensed, at the trend of religious affairs, which appeared to them to be all in favour of "popery and Arminianism", and to the detriment of Calvinism.

During the interval between sessions one Rolle, an MP and a merchant, had protested against the tonnage and poundage, whereupon the customs officers had seized his goods. Parliament now summoned those officers to appear before it, only to be adjourned by the king who insisted, correctly, that his executive officers were responsible to him alone. The Commons refused to obey, and proceeded to pass resolutions moved by Eliot, while the Speaker, still the servant of the monarch, rather than of the House, was forcibly prevented from leaving his chair. It was resolved that whoever introduced religious innovations disagreeing with the true church, and whoever advised the imposition of tonnage and poundage, or voluntarily paid it, without parliamentary sanction, should be regarded as enemies of the country, liable, in the two former instances, to capital punishment.

That done, the Commons adjourned; and the inevitable dissolution came on the 10th March 1629. It was the beginning of what has became known as "the eleven years' tyranny", for the king had decided on a determined effort to rule without parliament. He remained convinced that he was only accountable for his actions to God, and the Petition of Right would have no practical effect, for the king and his complaisant judges would decide what constituted "just liberties and rights". Charles made his view of the position clear when he asserted, quite reasonably, that precedents were mostly on his side, and that it was Parliament which was encroaching on matters that had never been its concern. And as for religion, he wished merely to preserve the Anglican church against innovations, schisms and Roman Catholicism.

As regards Charles's assertions that it was Parliament which was actually the aggressor, there is no doubt that they were making some new claims, not all of which were supported by precedent, despite the strained arguments of parliamentary leaders such as Coke. On the other hand, the 17th century was one of growing autocracy, during which the efficiency and power of some European central governments was steadily increasing, the first example being that of France, under the cardinals Richelieu and Mazarin. The same tendency was present in England; where England was "different" was that its Parliament, an institution which was not unique to that country, was peculiarly well placed to resist, even to counter-attack. Indeed it may not have been a counter-attack, but simply a collision between two opposing political tendencies. Whatever the real nature of the situation, we must not see it in terms of democracy v. dictatorship; that would be profoundly unhistorical. It was a struggle for power and concerning the nature and source of power, and it was a 17th century, not a 20th century quarrel.

From 1629 to 1641 Charles, true to his word, and assisted by his great minister, Thomas Wentworth, the first earl of Strafford, formerly a leading parliamentarian, and by Archbishop Laud, his Arminian ally, governed without Parliament, busying himself with the maintenance of "true religion" and "just rights", with himself as the judge of what was true and just. The label "the eleven years' tyranny" comes from 19th century liberal historians; actually it was never as tyrannical as Charles's opponents declared, nor as disinterested and free from corruption as his supporters maintained. One of Charles's first acts was to arrest and bring to trial Eliot and seven other prominent members of the House of Commons, whom he regarded as having incited the House to resist his lawful command to adjourn. They were sent to prison during His Majesty's pleasure, the judges of the King's Bench denying their claim that only Parliament was competent to try an offence which had allegedly been committed within its precincts.

In order to maintain his government Charles had to both save and find money. The wars with France and Spain were terminated on the 14th April 1629 and the 5th November 1630 respectively. Charles's brother-in-law, Frederick, the elector palatine, and the Protestant cause in Europe, were abandoned, further humiliating England, but a great drain upon the exchequer was stopped. Every effort was made to economize; tonnage and poundage were enforced on the king's sole authority, while monopolies were revived and applied to practically everything in daily use, advantage being taken of an ambiguity in the Monopolies Act of 1624. Simultaneously, various forms of medieval taxation, long out of use, were revived and ruthlessly (and probably illegally) applied. Finally ship money was collected with such vigour that the king was able to maintain and even enlarge the fleet without getting deeper into debt. From 1630 to 1635 the royal revenue averaged £600 000 per annum, the deficit being only £20 000. The books almost balanced, if an initial debt of £1 000 000 was ignored! That it was, although some creditors got compensation in various forms, such as pensions, offices or shares in monopolies.

Such compensation may have done something to diminish discontent, but if the savage punishment imposed by the prerogative Courts of Star Chamber and High Commission are any guide, Charles must have infuriated and embittered many of his subjects, both prominent and obscure. The collection of ship money aroused especially determined opposition, and most judges of the King's Bench gave the royal prerogative every support. This was starkly revealed in a test case (1637-1638) brought by John Hampden, who was later to become a prominent parliamentary leader. Five of the twelve judges found for him, but only two of them actually maintained that in defying statutes the king had gone beyond his rights. Worse still, the seven who found for the king found him to be omnipotent. The law could not confine the king, and contrarily it was the instrument which he employed to govern his people. *Lex* was not *rex*, but *rex* certainly was *lex*. The king could do no wrong. And just as the law was for the king to use as he thought fit, so was Parliament, if he saw fit to use it at all!

Though concerned, the king's opponents were not dismayed. The judges were written off as mere political creatures, and resistance, if anything, increased. It was increased still further by Strafford and Laud's support for the king. The former wished to set up a benevolent despotism in England, his earlier support for Parliament having really only been opposition to Buckingham. The death of the favourite had enabled him to move over to the crown, where he believed the real initiative in government ought to lie, rather than with an elected council. Strafford's intense dislike of Puritanism also influenced him, as did enormous personal ambition. Though a loyal and able minister, Strafford was not able to play the part of a Richelieu in England.

Archbishop William Laud's High church episcopalianism fitted Strafford's political theories like a hand a glove. Through the Court of High Commission he endeavoured to impose a formal and elaborate liturgy, to prop up the episcopal system and to diminish Calvinism. Nevertheless, Laud was no Catholic. There were real doctrinal differences between Canterbury and Rome, though his policies obscured them. In 1633, in the very week that he became archbishop of Canterbury, he was twice offered a cardinal's hat (!), to the alarm and rage of the Puritans. Finally, Laud aroused opposition amongst the great city merchants, bankers and entrepreneurs, those of them who were Puritans, by his religious policies, and all of them, by his material demands, i.e. increased tithes and the restoration of church lands. From the king's point of view this was unfortunate, for his resolution to govern without Parliament had amounted to a decision to rely upon the commercial rather than the landed interest. That would have been feasible, for, as ever, "big business" was inclined to support what it saw as strong orderly government, personal or not. So Laud may have done the royal cause as much harm as good. However, it is also possible that his policies were irrelevant as far as support for the king in the city was concerned, and that the real reason why the money magnates refused to assist Charles in the crisis of 1640 was that his administration had been so inefficient that they were afraid they would never see their money again. Still more simply, they may have decided that the king was a likely loser, and therefore an unacceptable risk.

Whatever the effect of Laud's policy in England, there is not the slightest doubt where Scotland was concerned. The attempt to enforce High church episcopalianism and the use of the Anglican *Book of Common Prayer* north of the Tweed led directly to a revolt in 1637 and, eventually, to Charles's destruction. There was, of course, more to it than that; both Charles and his father had neglected their northern kingdom, so that frustrated nationalism was compounded with outraged religious sentiment, but the latter was paramount.

By the time (on the 27th February 1638) the so-called "Scottish National Covenant" announced the adherence of the country to "the word of God and the Kirk of Scotland", as opposed to the "Roman Antichrist", Charles had lost all control; he was also quite unaware of the full significance of what had happened. Half-hearted attempts at conciliation having failed, both sides began preparations for war, which were interrupted by the Treaty of Berwick (signed on the 18th June 1639) before shots had been exchanged. It was as well for Charles who simply did not have the resources to raise an effective army. But it was only a temporary respite; in terms of the treaty, Charles had to submit the religious dispute to a new assembly of the kirk, and political issues to the Scottish parliament. When he did so (though it is quite certain that he would not have felt bound by whatever they decided), the assembly endorsed all its predecessor's acts, while the once servile parliament came out in defiance of all crown control (so, as it happened, smoothing the way to the Anglo-Scottish Union of 1701).

Such defiance, unchecked, meant the end of Charles's rule in Scotland, and, eventually, in England also. Action was essential, but without funds it was impossible. There was nothing left but to summon the English parliament. Charles hoped that patriotism, traditional Anglo-Scottish rivalry, even enmity, Scottish dalliance with France, and some modest concessions would incline the Commons to pass the grants he so desperately needed, and the Parliament which assembled on the 13th April 1640 was actually surprisingly moderate in its attitude. It was only with difficulty that Pym, the most prominent of the anti-royalists, was able to persuade them that consideration of a long list of grievances should precede that of supply. Angry and disappointed, Charles dissolved "the Short Parliament" on the 5th May 1640, much to the relief of Pym and others of the king's most outspoken opponents. They were confident, however, that the next Parliament would be less moderate. Nor, thanks in part to the continuing provocative actions of Laud, were they disappointed. In the midst of crisis, and with the approval of the king, the clergy were ordered to preach the divine right of kings, while Charles himself proceeded to exact forced loans, create new monopolies and beg, unsuccessfully, for loans from the City, from Spain, from France and from Rome. Without funds, and with his army mutinous and humiliated in its attempts to eject an invading Scottish force, Charles called a Great Council, a council of the peers of the realm, on the 7th September 1640. This body concluded the Treaty of Ripon, leaving the Scots in possession of Northumberland and County Durham, and £850 a day, until final settlement of their grievances which, they carefully stressed, were those of many Englishmen, too. Charles was at last compelled to call a Parliament, which assembled on the 3rd November 1640, after an election which had shown practically the whole of rich and populous southern England to be against the king. The new Parliament, "the Long Parliament", was determined that this time all grievances were going to be finally redressed and the king was at their mercy, for without their aid he would be unable to pay the Scots, who might then march on London and overthrow him.

Parliament had three primary goals. The first was speedily obtained with the release of those who had been imprisoned by the Courts of Star Chamber and High Commission; the second with the impeachment and confinement to the Tower of Strafford and Laud, on the 11th November and the 19th December 1640 respectively. Strafford was charged with high treason; when it became obvious that the charge would fail, Parliament simply passed a bill of attainder sentencing him to death. Strafford urged Charles to sign it, which he finally did on the 10th May 1641, with the London mob around his Whitehall palace, and his queen and children in physical danger. The fallen minister was executed two days later. Laud, also the victim of an attainder, followed him, but only after four years' imprisonment. Bishops, judges and ministers who had supported Arminianism and the doctrine of divine right were imprisoned or fled abroad as what was becoming a revolution gathered momentum.

The third of Parliament's great objectives, the preclusion of the possibility of a revival of the royal prerogative, was achieved by the passing of six acts of the utmost constitutional importance. At the same time Parliament showed its consciousness of its debt to the Scots by granting them £300 000 for their "brotherly assistance".

The "Triennial Act" of the 15th February 1641 laid down that Parliament had to be summoned at least once every three years. And once summoned, it could not be dismissed for at least fifty days. This was followed by an act making it impossible to dissolve "the Long Parliament" other than with its own consent. The "Tonnage and Poundage Act" of the 22nd June 1641 terminated the crown's long disputed right to impose customs on merchandise; that would in future be the prerogative of Parliament. Two further acts abolished the Courts of Star Chamber and High Commission, while yet another did away with ship money. Parliament then adjourned in September 1641 for a six weeks' recess. The position later to be accepted at the Restoration had been reached; the monarchy, though still intact, had lost those powers which, as Parliament saw it, the Tudors had wrongly appropriated and bequeathed to their Stuart successors. Henceforth owing to the work of "the Long Parliament", the establishment of absolute monarchy would be difficult, perhaps impossible, and certainly illegal. A monarchical revolution had been defeated by a parliamentary counter-revolution.

The struggle had, however, by no means ended, the counter-revolution was itself destined to turn into revolution. An extreme group of MPs, the so-called "Root and Branch" party, was growing in numbers, in influence, and in their determination to carry matters much further, despite the opposition of the moderate majority in the House of Commons, and of nearly all the Lords. As with so much in the politics of the time, religious differences lay at the root of continuing political tension. Apart from reducing the power of the Lords the radicals wished to destroy the episcopalian system "root and branch" and set up a Presbyterian-type church organization. The moderates would have none of that; on the whole they desired a limited episcopacy in which the bishops would share their authority with the diocesan clergy.

For his part the king was also disinclined to let matters rest. Answerable, as he saw it, only to God, it followed that acts of Parliament could not bind him, and there was nothing to prevent his attempting to regain his lost supremacy. In fact, it was his duty to do so, and in addition, he was encouraged by the sight of his enemies quarrelling and by the realization that he was not entirely without supporters. During 1641 both moderates and extremists attempted to get bills expressing their points of view passed and there is no doubt that had Charles made his acceptance of the status quo clear, things would have gone the moderates' way, for the "Root and Branch" group were distrusted by many Englishmen and feared by some. There was a growing feeling in the country that Parliament, having curbed the power of the king, had completed what it had been elected to do, and was becoming presumptuous. A more realistic and discerning ruler than Charles might have saved his throne, and spared his people much suffering. But then, a realistic and discerning king would not have come to such a pass; obsessed as he was with his divine right, and utterly determined to recover all that he had lost, Charles removed himself to Scotland, in a hopeless attempt to find support there. With him went a parliamentary committee, to watch his every move.

Even at this juncture the situation might have been saved, but for an unfortunate occurrence. For neither the first nor the last time events in Ireland influenced developments in Britain. The outbreak of a revolution there, on the 23rd October 1641, followed by the massacre of several thousand Protestant Scottish and English settlers, caused an eruption of anti-Catholic fears and prejudices, probably still the major obstacles to an understanding between Charles and the majority of his subjects. Not only did the news strengthen the position of the extremists in Parliament, in that it simultaneously raised the difficult and dangerous question as to who would control the forces of revenge and retribution; it also precipitated the civil war. It was impossible for Parliament to give Charles command of an effective army. He would certainly have tried to turn it on them first, and on the Irish second. For Parliament itself to take command of the army would, however, be outright revolution. Pym found a possible way out of the dilemma when he persuaded the Commons to ask the king to only employ such counsellors and ministers that Parliament felt it could trust.

It was the first appearance in English constitutional history of a clear-cut demand that the executive be approved by and be answerable to the legislature. Contentious, even revolutionary, it was not accepted easily or by a large majority. The Commons divided 151 to 110, and from this time on those who were satisfied with the status quo tended to look increasingly like an opposition party, confronting a radical majority intent on change without limit. The depth of the division in Parliament and the nearly even balance of the two parties was revealed even more clearly in the debate concerning the Grand Remonstrance, which was presented to the king on the 1st December 1641, after having been carried by only 159 votes to 148. The minority had contested it clause by clause in a manner worthy of what would later be called "His Majesty's Opposition".

The Grand Remonstrance is one of the most important documents in the constitutional history of England, being an exhaustive statement of the extreme Puritan and parliamentary point of view. According to it, all England's troubles were due to attempts to subvert the "fundamental laws and principles of government" by "Jesuited Papists", "the Bishops and the corrupt part of the Clergy", and certain "Councillors and Courtiers", who were more concerned for their own and foreign rulers' interests than they were for those of their country. There was, as yet, no hostility to the institution of monarchy itself; the only direct reference to the king was an allegation representing that evilly disposed persons were trying to mislead him and arouse enmity between him and Parliament, representing the people. That was the preamble; a long list of all the monarch's policies and actions which were regarded as contrary to the letter and spirit of the law followed, and an outline of those acts of the Long Parliament which were intended to restore the rule of law. Parliament insisted that it had acted in a spirit of loyalty to the king throughout.

Probably many MPs really believed that, but the extremists who were intent on taking matters further saw the Grand Remonstrance as an appeal to the nation, which was becoming convinced that they had gone far enough. The last parts of the Grand Remonstrance, which followed these defensive and placatory assertions, amounted to an outline of "Root and Branch" policy and intentions. There was to be a uniform religious settlement for the whole nation; no individual persons or congregations would be allowed to worship as they pleased. Here we find one of the first portents of the conflict between the Presbyterians, who came to dominate Parliament, and the Independents, who eventually formed the bulk of the New Model Army, which was to wreck the Commonwealth. Then came the political aims, in which the idea of a responsible executive can again be seen. Parliament should have some control over it, while the appointment of the king's "Councillors, Ambassadors and other Ministers" should be subject to its approval.

The Grand Remonstrance, together with a petition asking Charles to co-operate in carrying out the programme set out in it, was presented to the king on the 1st December 1641. It was scarcely possible for Charles to accept it, for in claiming control of religious policy and the executive Parliament was making major incursions upon what had always been the sovereign's prerogative, despite its claims to be merely defending an established position. Their claims were such that if granted, they would go a long way towards reducing the king to a mere constitutional figurehead.

The king's eagerly awaited reply came on the 23rd December 1641. As far as religion was concerned, Charles temporized and avoided committing himself. He asserted that he always had and always would "concur with all the just desires of our people", and he reminded the petitioners that the episcopal system and the Anglican liturgy were established "upon the fundamental law of the kingdom and constitution of Parliament". As regards the executive, he refused Parliament any sort of general control. Insisting that it was his right to choose whomever he thought fit, he only promised to choose able men of integrity. The nearest that he came to a concession was to agree that ministers and councillors should not be privileged with respect to the laws of the land.

At the end of 1641 two possible courses remained to the king. He could exercise discretion, govern as constitutionally as possible, and so take advantage of the general and growing feeling in his favour, or he could resort to force in a desperate bid to overthrow Parliament. Nothing, of course, could excuse the latter, except total success which was unlikely, but given Charles's convictions it was practically certain that he would move in that direction. By the end of that year it was generally supposed that the king was planning some act of violence, so much so that he felt it incumbent upon himself to promise the Commons that they need not fear for their physical safety. Simultaneously, articles impeaching five of them for high treason were delivered to the Lords! This bold attempt to seize the initiative found the Lords uncertain how to react. The Commons simply declared the attempted impeachment a breach of privilege, and refused to surrender the five members, not even when Charles marched into the House of Commons on the 4th January 1642 with an armed troop. He found, as he himself expressed it, "that the birds had flown", and had to retire, disconcerted and discredited.

Apart from putting himself in the wrong, revealing that the rule of law meant nothing to him, and so making the civil war almost inevitable, this appeal to force had two major consequences: It caused a revolution in the nature of the Speaker's office, for Mr Lenthall took the opportunity to make it clear that he regarded himself as the servant of the Commons, not the agent of the crown; and it dissipated much of the goodwill which had been accruing to the king. The effect of this was at once apparent in the House of Lords, where Charles's majority dwindled and vanished, so that the Bishops' Exclusion Bill was passed on the 5th February 1642. Eight days later it was signed by the king, who had left London, taking with him the great seal, to marshal his forces preparatory to regaining control of his kingdom by force. At York he was joined by thirty two peers and sixty five members of the Commons. From that date on the assembly at Westminster (strictly speaking it should no longer be called "Parliament" since the king is part of Parliament) was obliged to pass ordinances, which, since they were not submitted to the king and did not appear under the great seal, were no more than the instructions of what had became a revolutionary gathering.

The final break came in mid-1642. On the 5th March the Militia Ordinance was adopted, according to which various fortresses and the militia were entrusted to Lords-Lieutenant appointed by Parliament. On the 27th May the king replied with a proclamation forbidding the militia to obey any ordinance of Parliament without his consent. The war had started, though the royal standard was not raised until the 22nd August 1642.

The ensuing conflict (1642-1646), like so many civil wars, was fought with great bitterness and obstinacy. Similarly, the revolution, of which it was a part, resembled many other revolutions in that it got out of control, and finally ended in a state of affairs unlike that which had been envisaged by the original revolutionaries, one which was in many ways considerably less desirable than that which had given rise to it! The war was won for Parliament by one of the greatest of English soldiers and, indeed, one of the greatest of Englishmen, Oliver Cromwell, a tragic figure, but one who towers over the Stuart kings as well as over all his contemporaries.

At the beginning of the struggle the king could rely on northern and western-central England, on the whole the poorer parts of the country, and certainly the most conservative as regards both faith and politics. Richer, radical East Anglia and the south, including London, were for Parliament. It is impossible to generalize about the social composition of either the Cavalier (royalist) or Roundhead (parliamentary) armies, other than that all High Anglican clergy supported the king, and practically all Puritans the Parliament. Most of the peasantry, more instinctively than for any other reason, were for the king, most of the great nobility supported the Parliament, and some of the middle class, the gentry and the well-to-do merchants followed the royal standard. The religious quarrel, between High church and Low church Anglicans, the Arminians and the Puritans, was inextricably linked with the political. Religious convictions generally but not invariably overrode political loyalties. Their Catholic origins were still discernible amongst the Arminians, while Calvinist influence was increasingly influential amongst their opponents. Eventually religion was to divide the victors, and the triumphant Puritans split between the Presbyterians, who dominated the Parliament, and the Independents, who controlled the army. Until the end of 1643 the war was mainly an affair of skirmishes and raids, of which the royalists generally had the better. In November 1642 the king's march on London was only halted at Brentford, on the outskirts of the capital. None the less Parliament continued to sit, without interruption, until 1649! During 1643 much of its time and attention was taken up by religious issues, culminating in the conclusion, with the Scots, of the Solemn League and Covenant (on the 25th September 1643), in which parties agreed to introduce uniformity of religion and worship, according to the Scriptures and the examples of "the best reformed Churches", in England, Scotland and Ireland. While the Catholic Irish could be relied upon to resist any such thing with their utmost strength, and the majority of the English people were extremely dubious, the Covenant led directly to Scottish intervention in the war on behalf of Parliament in January 1644 when Charles had just gained control of three-quarters of England. The king then made the mistake of seeking help from the Irish, so alienating many of his own English supporters.

These things, together with the development of "the Ironsides", cavalry raised by the East Anglian Association (the counties of Norfolk, Suffolk, Essex, Cambridge, Hertfordshire and Huntingdonshire) and commanded by Oliver Cromwell (1599-1658), into the best mounted force on either side, better even than those commanded by the king's dashing nephew, Prince Rupert, gradually inclined events Parliament's way. The defeat of Rupert by Cromwell at Marston Moor on the 2nd July 1644 was an especially serious setback for the Cavaliers, though they continued to win victories. During the early part of 1645 the king even held most of Scotland, thanks to the Highlanders taking up arms for him against the Lowland Covenanters. But Parliament had the greater resources and the greater staying power; eventually the Roundheads wore the Cavaliers down. Their eventual success was made the more sure by the reorganization of the whole army into the "New Model", on the same lines as the "Ironsides", and motivated by a similar religious fervour. Within that enthusiasm, however, lay the seeds of eventual disaster for the republican cause, for while the Puritans of Westminister were mostly becoming Presbyterian, as was the established church, the New Model Army was dominated by the Independents, with their totally different views regarding church organization, of which they wanted as little as possible. The Self-Denying Ordinance of the 3rd April 1645, which excluded members of both houses, except Cromwell, from the armed forces, may have been very necessary, but it had the effect of further widening a growing and ominous gap. Meanwhile the loss of the crucial battle of Naseby on the 14th June 1645 spelt the end for Charles, but his supporters struggled on until the final collapse in March of the following year. Two months later, on the 5th May 1646, Charles gave himself up to the Scots. He had still not abandoned hope, for a clash between the Independents/army and the Presbyterians/Parliament appeared imminent. He therefore refused to consider the terms submitted to him in July as the "Newcastle Proposals".

On the 30th January 1647, when they had received their back pay (£400 000), the Scots gave up Charles to Parliament, from whose custody he was forcibly removed by the army four months later as the quarrel between the winners opened wide. Coincidentally, Cromwell chose the same day (the 4th June 1647) to remove himself from Westminster to Triptow Heath. There the army was assembled, having sworn not to disband until Parliament had granted a measure of religious toleration. Charles spent much of the second half of 1647 negotiating with the soldiers, although his intentions were not really serious, for he was convinced that things were going his way. In November he escaped and fled to the Isle of Wight, where he expected to be given refuge by the governor of Carisbrooke Castle, but was, instead, placed in protective custody. That, however, did not prevent him from entering into an "engagement" with the Scots, whereby he would abolish episcopacy in return for their restoration of him to the thrones of England and Scotland. Consequently, during early 1648, while England sank into growing chaos, a second civil war began; it was simultaneously a war between Roundheads and Cavaliers, England and Scotland, Independents and Presbyterians. But under Cromwell's inspired leadership the New Model Army beat down all its enemies, and by late August 1648 the war was over, and order had been restored. On the 1st December Charles was arrested by the army, where feeling in favour of a republic was running high. A week later Colonel Pride, acting at the behest of the army council, drove ninety six Presbyterian members from the parliament, a move known as "Pride's Purge", so reducing it to a "Rump Parliament" of about sixty.

During the greater part of the year (1648) Cromwell had been in favour of retaining the monarchy in some truncated form, but he had eventually concluded that to further deal with the king, "that man of blood", would be futile as well as wrong. In that, Cromwell was correct; at his trial on the 20th-27th January 1649 Charles I denied the jurisdiction of the court, and also that subjects could bind a king in any way whatsoever. Obviously no agreements could be entered into with a person holding such views; while he lived, he was a standing threat to the stability of England and the safety of his political opponents. Nothing remained save to kill him, and he was duly executed outside his own palace of Whitehall on the 30th January 1649. The awful deed was watched by a vast and silent crowd.

CROMWELL AND THE ENGLISH REPUBLIC, 1649-1660

From 1649 to 1660 England was part of a republic, the Commonwealth of England, Scotland and Ireland. The monarchy and the House of Lords having been abolished, the legislative power was exercised by the sixty or so survivors of Pride's Purge, and the executive by a council of state of forty one. This was made up of thirty MPs, five ex-peers, three senior army officers and three judges. Since the real source of power was the New Model Army, Cromwell, to whom the troops gave complete support, was a virtual dictator. That was all the more true after he had defeated both the Scots, who had proclaimed Charles II in 1649, and the Irish, who had also risen in support of the new king. Following upon those triumphs, the second of which had left Ireland a conquered and embittered country, where thousands of Catholics had been either killed or driven off their lands, or left at the mercy of usurping Protestant landlords, a series of victories in the naval war of 1652 against the Dutch had restored England's naval renown. They had also made Oliver Cromwell's name as much respected abroad as it was admired and dreaded at home.

Within the ranks of the Rump Parliament Cromwell's name was mostly dreaded. The relationship between Parliament and the army had been becoming increasingly tense, and eventually, on the 20th April 1653 Cromwell, accompanied by soldiers, turned them out of the places they had occupied since November 1640 ("You have too long sat here"). They were replaced by the "Little Parliament", with 129 English members, five Scottish and six Irish, choosen by senior army officers from candidates nominated by Independent congregations. This curious assembly, generally known as "Barebone's Parliament", and so named after one of its more prominent members, Praise-God Barebone, lasted from the 4th July to the 11th December 1653. On the latter date its more moderate members, concerned by attacks on ecclesiastical patronage and tithing, resigned their powers to Cromwell. He promptly took the opportunity to establish the Protectorate, on the 16th December 1653, with himself as Lord Protector of the Commonwealth of England, Scotland and Ireland. The constitution of this new form of state was known as the Instrument of Government. According to it, the legislature would consist of the Lord Protector and a House of Commons of 460, representing reformed constituencies. Parliaments were triennial, and could not be dismissed within five months of being summoned. The executive was the Lord Protector (whose office, it was later decided, should be elective, not hereditary), assisted by his twenty one member Council of State. When Parliament was not sitting, the council could issue ordinances, but not appropriate supplies or levy taxes. As might be expected of a constitution drawn up by Independents, there was provision for religious toleration, only excepting Catholics and Episcopalians.

From the beginning, despite a spectacular and successful foreign policy, the Protectorate was unpopular with most Englishmen, and the constraints of rigid Puritan rule made the situation worse. Cromwell quarrelled with his Parliament and did not hesitate to exclude members in the midst of a gradually deteriorating situation, which was not noticeably improved by alterations to the constitution (viz. the

"Humble Petition and Advice" drawn up in March-May 1657). One alteration which was not put into effect was a proposal to make the Lord Protector a king; Cromwell himself refused it.

The following year, on the 3rd September 1658, Cromwell died and was succeeded by his son, Richard Cromwell, but the Commonwealth did not long survive the man who had dominated and maintained it from the beginning. Richard did not have his father's status, character and charisma, and in May 1659 he resigned, in the face of renewed dissension between the army and Parliament, and amid growing anarchy and frustration.

As the year went on, it became increasingly obvious that the question was not whether the monarchy would be restored, but when. One of the people who did not understand this was General John Lambert. He had always seen himself as Oliver Cromwell's political heir, and many of the soldiers shared that view, a view, however, that was not shared by General George Monk, commander of the forces in Scotland. Himself without political ambition, he enjoyed the complete loyalty of his troops; he did not hesitate to make it known that while he could accept the personal rule of a great man such as Oliver Cromwell, that of John Lambert was out of the question! On the 3rd February 1660 Monk led his army across the border at Coldstream, and marched on London, gathering support as he went.

Monk's sole goal was political stability, and he had decided that that could best be obtained by securing the willing consent of the Long Parliament, which had recommenced sitting on the 26th December 1659, to its supersession by a freely chosen Convention Parliament. Monk was fully aware that that would mean the return of the king, for the Presbyterians, unlike the Independents of the army, had never been republicans, but had always wanted some form of constitutional monarchy. Meanwhile, on the 4th April 1660, exiled Charles II had facilitated matters with his Declaration of Breda, in which he promised freedom of conscience, and also that the punishment of any who were excluded from a general pardon would be left to Parliament, as would the settlement of property disputes. On the 1st May 1660 the 556 strong Convention Parliament returned a favourable answer and seven days later proclaimed him king. On the 29th King Charles II entered London in triumph, amid general if not universal rejoicing.

CHARLES II, 1660-1685, AND THE TRIUMPH OF THE ANGLICANS

There could hardly have been a greater contrast than that between martyred Charles I and his son. The new king was quite the most intelligent of the Stuarts (not a very difficult thing), as well as lazy, selfish, amoral, unprincipled, cynical, witty and likeable. He differed most from his father in that he could give way, and from his grandfather, in that he could do so gracefully. In only one respect was he completely unyielding: he was determined never to "go on his travels again", as he himself put it. The restoration settlement provided for a constitutional monarchy, and he did not hesitate to accept it. Every act of Parliament which Charles I had accepted before leaving London remained in force, so that even the Tudor monarchy, to say nothing of the absolute pretensions of James I and Charles I, had become a dead letter. The prerogative courts and the criminal jurisdiction of the Privy Council had been abolished, nor could the king arrest MPs without showing due cause. Most significant of all, it had finally been settled that it was legally impossible for the king to raise money in any way whatsoever, whether by taxation, forced loans or revived medieval devices, without parliamentary sanction.

Parliament itself was restored as it had been before the civil wars; Cromwell's delimitation and franchise experiments were ignored. So prejudice caused much-needed reform to be delayed until the 19th century. Again, Cromwell had tried to govern the whole of the British Isles as one state; but blind eyes were turned to that reality, too.

There was as yet no cabinet; the executive was the Privy Council, over which the king usually presided. Eventually all business was first considered by an appropriate committee of that council. A case has been made for the cabinet's having grown out of the committee for foreign affairs, but be that as it may (and the more usual explanation, that its origins lay in the growing importance of the treasury, is set out below), while there was no cabinet, there could, of course, be no prime minister. The king's chief minister, the chancellor, was Charles I's one-time opponent, Edward Hyde, who had been created earl of Clarendon, and whose son-in-law was none other than the king's younger brother, James.

The Convention Parliament, which had recalled Charles, continued in being until the 29th December 1660, and was, in fact, responsible for the details of the Restoration Settlement. An act of indemnity, from which less than thirty people, including the regicide judges, were exempt, wiped out all political offences committed between the 1st January 1637 and the 24th June 1660. This prudent and merciful act facilitated the disbandment of the army on the 2nd October 1660 and did much to assure the future of the restored monarchy and the tranquillity of the kingdom.

One of Charles II's first acts, on the 25th October 1660, was to declare temporary freedom for all Christians, but despite that and a genuine desire in sections of both the Anglican church and the Presbyterian church for some form of comprehension, the thorny problem of religion was not dealt with as wisely and tolerantly as was the political. There were many Presbyterians in the Convention Parliament, and on the 5th April 1661 leading members of that church and the Anglican met at the Savoy palace to discuss problems of dogma and liturgy. They were still in conference when Charles II's first Parliament assembled in May 1661. Coming in on a flood of royalist and anti-Puritan reaction it was aptly labelled the "Cavalier Parliament", and it was responsible, between November 1661 and October 1665, for four major acts dealing with religion. Generally known as "the Clarendon Code", they imposed severe disabilities on all whose conscience and convictions made it impossible for them to comply.

The first of the acts in question was the Corporation Act of November 1661, which compelled all magistrates to take communion in the Church of England. Next came the Act of Uniformity in August 1662, which required all clergymen, university lecturers and school teachers to accept the *Book of Common Prayer*, i.e. the official Anglican service book. Those who would not, became known as "nonconformists"; prominent amongst them were Presbyterians and Independents. The third, the Conventicle Act of May 1664 forbade nonconformist religious gatherings of more than five people, except in private houses, and the even more absurd Five-Mile Act of October 1665 demanded that all who had not submitted to the Act of Uniformity swear an oath of non-resistance, failing which they were barred from coming within five miles of any incorporated town or of any place where they had formerly been clergymen. Clarendon himself neither approved nor opposed many of the provisions of these acts, which did not cause the less bitterness for being nearly impossible to enforce.

An equally difficult problem, which was also not satisfactorily handled, was that of property, especially real estate, forfeited and seized, lost and won, during a time of revolutionary upheaval and civil war. Property belonging to the crown and the church, which had been seized by the Commonwealth, was restored by statute, but in general royalists received no special treatment or compensation, although many had been beggared by their loyalty to an exiled king. They were, of course, entitled to go to court in attempts to recover whatever they had lost; some made the attempt, and succeeded, but most failed, and many were left bitter and resentful. By the same token, some parliamentarians who had acquired valuable property for little or nothing managed to retain it. In general these seems to have been little overall change, especially as regards the greatest landed families; the general tendency, as ever, was for the rich to get richer, frequently at the expense of the poor.

As regards public finance, the Convention Parliament did remarkably little, although that little was portentous. It is no exaggeration to say that the effect of such changes as were made was to further enrich and strengthen the political influence of the great landowners, so setting the pattern for 18th century England. Taking a longer view, they constituted the final elimination of the last traces of feudal practice in the financing of government, which now entered the modern era. An almost immediate, unforeseen and unfortunate consequence of making parsimonious and inadequate provision for the king's income was to make him too easily reliant on subsidies from Louis XIV, in return for inclining the foreign policy of England in favour of France!

The first half of the reign of King Charles II, up to 1674, was characterized by the uniform immorality and frivolity of the court, its increasingly Catholic leanings, and a disastrous and humiliating foreign policy. Attempts to enforce and later to prop up the Clarendon Code, the latter by means of the Test Acts of 1673 and 1678, were equally unfortunate. These were aimed most particularly at Roman Catholics, and had the effect of excluding them, whose numbers included many patriotic and intelligent men, from public office and from Parliament until these acts were at last repealed in 1828-1829. In addition, the acts greatly offended the king's brother, James, heir to the throne and himself a Roman Catholic. Obtaining their repeal was to become almost an obsession with him.

Dominating the second half of the reign, up to 1685, when the king died and was succeeded by James, were continued and serious unrest in Scotland, and a steady deterioration of the politico-religious situation in England, until another civil war and the king's probable return to exile were only narrowly avoided. It was during this period that the first real political parties began to emerge. There is, indeed, a real link between the court party, which supported the king's government, and the later Tories, eventually the Conservatives, while the opposition, styled the Country Party, became the Whigs and finally the Liberals.

JAMES II, 1685-1688, AND THE "GLORIOUS REVOLUTION"

Superficially, it is a matter for astonishment that the brief and unhappy reign of James II, from February 1685 to December 1688, commenced as calmly as it did, for, besides being haughty and autocratic by temperament, James II was an avowed and outspoken Roman Catholic by conviction. Once again, the king was out of step as far as religion was concerned. Charles I, a High church Anglican, had confronted an increasingly Puritan Parliament; now, the excesses of their revolution had discredited the Puritans, but the triumphant High church men had to deal with a Catholic king! For the time being, however, they were content to wait upon developments. That seemed sound policy, for the Princesses Mary and Anne, the children of James's first wife, Clarendon's daughter, Anne Hyde, were both Anglicans, and it was thought unlikely that James's second wife, Mary of Modena, would ever produce a child. Parliament was moreover aware that it had a difficult and obstinate man to deal with, while all thoughtful Englishmen dreaded another civil war, with everything that it might entail.

For this part the king seems to have seen nothing strange in relying upon the passive loyalty of men whose beliefs he did not share and whose rights he viewed with scepticism and hostility. James, like his father, did not believe that the royal prerogative should be burdened with constitutional fetters. But the emphasis had shifted since Charles I's time. He had tried to strengthen episcopalianism because he had thought, correctly, that it reinforced his absolutism. James II was determined to make every possible use of what remained of the prerogative, on principle, but also in order to obtain toleration for Catholicism, hopefully as a preliminary to the return of his heretic subjects (High Anglican bishops and all!) to Rome. The predictable outcome of his rash and impetuous actions was to embarrass his Catholic subjects and greatly weaken their position, besides bringing about the final and complete destruction of every trace of divine right in England.

The continuing significance of the religious factor in political affairs was made manifest as the Whigs and Tories temporarily desisted from their abrasive rivalry and closed ranks to bring the king down in that final assertion of parliamentary supremacy known as the "Glorious Revolution" (1688), all the more so in that the Tories had not been really hostile to a reviving prerogative! Certainly in 1685 the crown was stronger than it had been at any time since 1660. But James II entirely failed to realize that that was due to the effective partnership which had been established with the Lords and Commons, a partnership which was utterly dependent on the retention of the supremacy of the Church of England and the avoidance of any real dependence on France. James's Jesuit advisors, with their cosmopolitan background and training, were no better placed to appreciate the situation. The outcome of a pooling of ignorance and prejudice was the king's grotesque plan to substitute the old alliance between the Anglicans and the Stuarts by one with the Dissenters, bribing the latter with a policy of toleration which would extend to the Catholics. He would thus, beneath a cloak of enlightenment, advance his co-religionists to positions of influence and authority.

The king's infatuated confidence in the strength of his position was increased by the easy destruction of Argyle's and Monmouth's rebellions, in Scotland and south-western England in June-July 1685. Initially, therefore, James determined to try constitutional means, a decision which was all the more understandable in view of the almost servile nature of the Parliament (1685) which he had summoned after much hesitation. It was packed with Tories, who not only granted him an ample permanent revenue, but also overlooked the manner in which he had previously illegally proclaimed that the customs duties originally granted for his brother's lifetime should continue to be paid. Disturbed by Argyle and Monmouth's rebellions, they also granted James £700 000 for the maintenance of the standing army which he had inherited from his brother. When, however, James requested that they repeal the Test Act (originally passed against the Presbyterians in 1681), opposition and old suspicions raised their heads.

Parliament's uneasiness was increased by the arrival of 50 000 Huguenot refugees in England, following Louis XIV's revocation of the Edict of Nantes, and still more by their own Catholic king's request that he be allowed to appoint Catholics as army officers. They were willing to make some concessions, but only by act of Parliament (which would include the concessions in statute law), whereupon James, like his father and grandfather before him, lost patience and prorogued them. They were not to meet again during the remainder of his short reign.

James now (in 1686) took up the most powerful weapon left to the monarch by the Restoration Settlement, the right to appoint and dismiss the judges of the Court of King's Bench. He appointed a Catholic, Sir Edward Hales, governor of Dover, and when a test case was brought before the court, eleven of the twelve judges asserted that the king had every right to dispense with the laws, and the grounds on which they based their decision could be limitlessly extended! It appeared that nothing had been gained, since Charles I had evaded the consequences of the Petition of Right, and that Roman Catholics would soon control the army, navy, civil service and Privy Council.

His way having apparently been cleared by the outcome of the Hales Case, the king at once proceeded to make the utmost possible use of the dispensing power. During the period 1686-1687 the nation could do nothing other than watch and wait while this power was applied in four directions: an ever-increasing number of Catholic officers were appointed, while the rank and file took on a more Catholic tinge, as new recruits were brought in from Ireland; Anglican magistrates (Justices of the Peace) were dismissed and replaced by Catholics and nonconformists, for the king hoped to obtain the support of the latter in getting the Test Act revoked; Catholics were to lead the Privy Council; and finally, the Anglican Church itself was directly attacked when James allowed a convert to Rome to retain his London benefice. And that was not all. Magdalen College, Oxford, was forced to accept a

Catholic master, a papal nuncio was given a public reception (mid-1687), and James's Jesuit advisor, Father Petre, was admitted to the Privy Council. By actions such as these the infatuated king antagonized not only the Tory aristocracy who might have supported him, given reasonable behaviour on his part, but an ever-increasing proportion of the whole people. Many Catholics and nonconformists were themselves concerned, fearing that their ultimate position might be all the worse for his intemperate behaviour.

Whatever progress he appeared to be making, James knew that obtaining a favourable Parliament was essential for final victory, i.e. the formal repeal of the Test Acts by Parliament. The mere fact that he even considered the possibility is a startling revelation of just how hopelessly out of touch with popular feeling he was; some historians have even contended that the events of his mercifully brief reign show him to have been mentally disturbed! Be that as it may, the inquiry he ordered late in 1687, as to the feasibility of the project, did him nothing but harm by the way in which it revealed the extent and depth of his unpopularity. Men were no longer inhibited by fear of betrayal, for it was only too obvious that almost all were against the king. He had revealed his enemies' own strength to them. Meanwhile he had issued two Declarations of Indulgence: the first, issued on the 4th April 1687, had suspended all the penal laws which had been directed at Catholics and nonconformists alike, and amounted to a wholesale generalization of the dispensing power, which had been applicable to particular, individual cases; the second, on the 27th April 1688, was much the same but for the requirement that it should be read from the pulpits of all churches, without exception.

On the appointed day hardly any clergymen read the declaration, and in a few instances when an attempt to do so was made, congregations walked out. As a result of the Lambeth Conference of the 18th May 1688, Sancroft, archbishop of Canterbury, and six bishops, having remonstrated against the declaration on the grounds that the king was acting illegally, requested that the clergy might be excused from reading it. James chose to treat their petition as an act of rebellion, and the seven bishops were confined to the Tower, prior to being tried for seditious libel. The trial took place on the 29th and 30th June 1688 and was both a farce and a triumph for freedom in England. The judges were of course James's creatures, but their fear overwhelmed their prejudice; they lost control of the proceedings and allowed the jury to decide questions of law as well as of fact, relating not only to the point at issue, but to the whole of the suspending power. The result was the acquittal of the bishops – for the first time, since the great days of Coke, a case in which the rights of the prerogative were in question had been lost by the crown! The resulting outbreak of joy showed only too plainly how successfully James had managed to unite the nation against himself!

There were two reasons why he had got as far as he had: the English people looked back to the Puritan revolution, the civil war and Cromwell's military rule with dread; at the same time, they looked forward to James's death in the certainty that conditions would then improve, for he had no male heir and the heir-presumptive was his elder daughter, Mary, a Protestant, and married to a Protestant, William of Orange, stadtholder of Holland. That hope had been dashed on the 10th

June 1688, when James's queen had most imprudently produced a son. There was not the slightest doubt that the child was hers and James's, despite cynical assertions to the contrary.

England was now confronted with the possibility of a dynasty of Catholic kings, a prospect so daunting that on the day of the bishops' triumph an invitation, signed by seven leading Whigs and Tories, was sent to William of Orange, asking him to come with an armed force and ensure that England's grievances were redressed and the country's liberties defended against his father-in-law.

There was a good chance that William would accept, if the Dutch States-General was agreeable, for though it was by no means certain that he would become king of England and Scotland, an accomplished international statesman such as himself would be able to turn whatever new situation arose to his own country's advantage. Best of all, if he should gain a position of power, he would be able to end the island kingdoms' uncertain neutrality and enlist their full strength on the side of the Netherlands against France. The States-General understood that, and once it had become clear that Louis XIV was directing his attention and his army to the upper Rhine, partly because he had been offended by James II's haughty and foolish spurning of proffered assistance, and mainly because his threats to treat a move against England as one against France had only been bluff, they gave their approval to the English expedition. William's formal acceptance, on the 30th September 1688, as well as vigorous preparations in the ports of Holland finally made even James aware of the danger, and he strove to retrace his steps. But it was too late; his concessions were insufficient and too obviously inspired by fear. On the 5th November 1688 William landed a Dutch force, with many English and Scottish exiles, at Torbay. On the 11th December James fled, after a strange period of negotiation, during which it had become apparent that the entire nation wanted only to be rid of the foolish man.

WILLIAM, MARY AND ANNE, 1689-1714: A CROWNED REPUBLIC

The settlement which followed the "Glorious Revolution" falls into two parts: the formal and purely constitutional, contained in three great acts of Parliament, and the unplanned, almost unconscious, developments in custom and practice, which led to the shaping of institutions and precedents which, although essential to the government of the United Kingdom as it is today, have found no place in law. These developments continued through the reigns of William and Mary (1689-1694), that of William III alone (1694-1702), and of Queen Anne (1702-1714). They continued into Hanoverian and later times, and are going on now.

James II's welcome but precipitate flight had left his realm in a constitutional void. In the absence of the king there could be no Parliament; James had even hurled the great seal into the Thames. This legal dead-end was simply ignored; all members of the House of Lords, and of the Commons under Charles II, who were present in London, together with the Lord Mayor, the aldermen and fifty of the common council of the city assembled and requested the prince of Orange to assume the provisional government of the country, and to order all the constituent bodies of the kingdom to send representatives to a Convention Parliament, which would settle the nation's affairs.

The Tory majority in the Lower House of the Convention Parliament (which sat from the 22nd January 1689 to the 27th January 1690) was hopelessly divided, leaving the Whigs, the largest single body not encumbered with any exalted theories on kingship, in control. Split hairs as they might, the Tories could not escape the conclusion that their cherished doctrines of hereditary right and non-resistance bound them to, the conclusion that James was still king, and his son the heir apparent! The Whigs, on the other hand, were able to come out with the bold assertion that the nation had the right to expel a bad king, and to replace him with another, upon defined conditions. James, they argued, had by abuse of his power broken the (supposed) mutual contract between the king and his people, expressed on the one side by the coronation oath, and on the other by the oath of allegiance. By his flight James had abdicated the government, and left the throne vacant. The nation had the right to choose a new king and impose upon him conditions which would prevent a similar catastrophe in the future.

After prolonged debate, two resolutions embodying this Whig position, and utterly destroying any last traces of divine right and the hereditary principle were passed, on the 18th-19th January 1689, only to be rejected by the Tory majority in the House of Lords, most of whom favoured a regency, while rejecting the very idea that the throne could be vacant. Arbitrarily ignoring the existence of James's baby son, they insisted that Mary was already queen.

Deadlock between the Upper House and the Lower House threatened until the Prince of Orange intervened. He made it clear that he would return to the Netherlands, where Mary was and would remain, unless he was made king of England. Since Mary was essential if something of the hereditary principle was to be salvaged, the Tory Lords gave way and it was agreed that the prince and princess of Orange should be declared joint king and queen.

On the 13th February 1689 William accepted the crown, on behalf of Mary and himself, in accordance with the conditions set out in the Declaration of Right, which summarized James II's arbitrary acts, declared them illegal, and asserted, *inter alia*, that in fleeing, James had abdicated, leaving the throne vacant. There had therefore been no king for two months; the theory of divine hereditary right had been finally and irreparably destroyed. The one-time republicans understood that very well, and were satisfied that a precedent, that English monarchs were appointed by Parliament and could be deposed for misrule, had been established. Apart from die-hard supporters of the Stuarts and of the hereditary principle, henceforth known as Jacobites, the great majority of the nation accepted what had been done with joy and relief. The "Glorious Revolution" is one of the few in history, if not the only one, in which there was scarcely any violence, and which never got out of control, coming to a halt when it had reached its leaders' objectives.

The Convention Parliament having transformed itself into a regular Parliament, the formal and legal settlement was embodied in three major acts. The first of these was the Bill of Rights, of the 25th October 1689, which put the Declaration of Right into law, while extending and amending it. Together with the *Magna Carta* and the Petition of Right, it constitutes the foundation upon which the liberty of the British people rests.

The bill opens with a reference to how the Lords and Commons, fully and freely representing all the people of the realm, had presented the Declaration of Right to the then prince and princess of Orange, and then went on to recite the declaration in full, listing all the acts whereby James II had attempted to subvert the Protestant religion and the liberties of his people. Those acts were then declared to be contrary to the laws and freedom of the realm. All James's "pretended powers" were then listed and declared illegal, and the subjects' right to petition the crown affirmed. Important though all that certainly was, it did not amount to much of a parliamentary advance; it was rather a consolidation of an existing position. The only real innovation was the destruction of the crown's right to maintain a standing army in peace times, other than with consent of Parliament. Although that had not previously been illegal, Parliament, remembering Cromwell's Commonwealth, had been objecting to the practice since Charles II's time.

The Toleration Act of 1689, to give it its usual though unofficial name, may be regarded as a grudging reward granted to the Dissenters for refusing to co-operate with James II. Though still excluded from public affairs, they were granted a certain degree of religious freedom. As for the Catholics, it is possible that their affairs were even improved as a result of the revolution, for James II's provocative behaviour was brought to an end, and, as the result of an understanding between William III and Pope Innocent IX, they were left to conduct their religion in peace. The civil disabilities were maintained, but the penal laws were rarely enforced.

The Mutiny Act of 1689 regulated the size and disciplining of the armed forces which had to be kept in being owing to the Irish rising which had followed James's landing in that country on the 14th March 1689, and the outbreak of war with France on the 7th May 1689. It also made martial law inapplicable in times of peace and forbade the punishment of any man other than according to law.

The support James received in Ireland and the need to defeat him and his French allies convinced the English Parliament that the suppression of Catholicism in that country was necessary for the safety of England. A repressive policy was therefore carried out and attempts were even made to suppress the Ulster Presbyterians, despite the way in which they had co-operated against James. The Irish Parliament was utterly subservient to the English, which legislated for Ireland, too.

The only link between England and Scotland was the fact that both crowns had descended to the same monarch; the authority of the parliament at Westminster did not cross the border. The Scottish "Claim of Right" made it clear that James VII (as James II was known in Scotland) had forfeited his right to the Scottish throne by failing to take the coronation oath. The Convention of Estates went further and asserted their right to depose kings. Once he was convinced that maintaining Scottish religious institutions did not mean persecuting non-Presbyterians, William took the required oath, thereby becoming king of Scotland as well. In 1707, five years after his death, the Act of Union united the two kingdoms.

Although the wars with France guaranteed that Parliaments would be called annually, the Triennial Bill was eventually passed on the 22nd December 1694, which not only ensured that a Parliament be summoned at least once every three years, but also limited the Parliaments' duration to three years. This made it impossible for a monarch to retain an unusually tractable Parliament indefinitely. The periodic elections provoked a certain amount of interest in politics, although the system continued to be unrepresentative, riddled with patronage and wide open to manipulation through corruption or intimidation.

Within a week of the passing of the Triennial Bill, Queen Mary died, on the 28th December 1694, leaving William childless. When her sister, Princess Anne's, last surviving child, William, duke of Gloucester, died in 1700, it became urgent that further provision be made for the succession. The result was the Act of Settlement, of the 12th June 1701, which settled the crown on Sophia, the electress of Hanover (and granddaughter of James I) and her issue. In future monarchs of England could only be Protestant, and the country could not be involved in war in defence of their foreign possessions. Judges were to hold office for life, subject to good behaviour. The act, as the Whigs were quick to stress, amounted to a new compact laying down conditions under which the house of Hanover could rule.

Certain of its provisions were of the very greatest interest. One such provision prohibited any person holding an office of profit or a pension from sitting in the Lower House. This reflected suspicion of "place-men" in the House of Commons, men who provided a valuable link between the crown and that body. They were mainly ex-military officers, loyal to the crown, and in the midst of violent party feuds they not infrequently held the balance of power, and enabled the executive to influence the legislature. However, the clause affecting them was never rigidly applied, which was as well, for if it had been, the executive and the legislature would have been kept separate, and the further development of the nascent cabinet system would have been rendered impossible. In other words, the union of the powers later characteristic of the British constitution and those modelled upon it would never have come into existence.

Another clause which might have stifled the cabinet at the beginning was that which attempted to confine the formulation of policy to the decaying Privy Council. Parliament disliked the growing custom of informal meetings between the king and his ministers, which made it difficult to trace who was responsible for advice given to the sovereign. However, during the course of Anne's reign (1702-1714), the new informal practice developed so rapidly that the two provisions of the Act of Settlement which could have inhibited it were repealed by the Regency Act of 1705, without ever having been properly applied.

So much for the formal, legal settlement which followed the fall of James II. Quite as important is the growth of those institutions, customs and precedents which, though not formally recognized by law, have modified the practical working of the legal code enshrined in the *Magna Carta*, the Petition of Right and the Bill of Rights. The "Glorious Revolution" of 1688 finally destroyed royal absolutism and established the rule of Parliament, but custom and precedent influenced and shaped the mode of exercising that rule, i.e. parliamentary government through a responsible cabinet. So the greatest problem remaining from civil war times, from the mid-17th century, was ultimately resolved.

Much of this growth of custom and precedent was bound up with and profoundly influenced by the wars with France, which raged all through William III's and Anne's reigns. William's view of the crown was similar to Charles II's. Apart from what he had agreed to in order to mount the throne, he wished to preserve what he could of the royal prerogative. He also wished to thwart Louis XIV. The Whigs, on the other hand, wished to limit the prerogative, but were well aware that a victory for Louis XIV would result in the restoration of James II. William and the Whigs were therefore forced to co-operate in doing all they could to win the war, and both sides refrained from pushing disputes about the prerogative to extremes. In any event, and quite apart from such acts as it might pass, William's continuous and pressing need for funds made it certain that Parliament would be called every year and would get its own way in any serious dispute.

A great instrument of parliamentary control, which was established in William's time was "appropriation of supply"; the need, imposed by the war, to raise and spend money on a greater scale than ever before led to the evolution of a permanent system of estimate, appropriation and audit. There was an urgent need for a steady, rapid and ample supply of money, and since the income from taxation was irregular, systematic borrowing was resorted to in order to obtain and ensure the continuation of such a supply. Lending money to the government was the main function of the Bank of England, founded in 1695. All of this consolidated Parliament's hold on finances, for only Parliament could provide the secure control and stable conditions needed for large-scale borrowing. Parliament's assumption of financial control did not apply to extraordinary revenue only. The ordinary revenue of the crown (parliamentary grants) was incapable of bearing the new burdens which were placed on it, and the king consequently fell into debt and complete dependence on Parliament.

But if the war made Parliament's position impregnable, it also set limits to the growth of its power. William was his own first (prime) minister and he kept foreign affairs, of which he had a vast knowledge and in which field speed and secrecy were essential, under his own control. Parliament's claims to a share in matters which its members did not really comprehend, were simply ignored.

The most important informal development during the late 17th century and the early 18th century was beyond doubt the rise of the cabinet system. The financial dominance of Parliament, and especially of the House of Commons, brought the treasury and the legislature closer together. The former was supposed to control the king's finances in his interests alone, but his utter dependence on Parliament for money led to the treasury becoming a link between the king and Parliament, informing the latter of the former's needs, suggesting how to meet them and accounting for how money granted had been spent. So the king found it politic to appoint men who were both accomplished politicians and competent administrators, the sort of men who were most likely to gain a sympathetic hearing and who would know how to make the best use of it.

Since the division between the Whig and Tory parties was deep, a natural way for William to find support would have been to confine his choice of ministers to the party in power, but initially the thought that the sovereign should take the whims of the electorate into account was regarded as absurd. So at first William chose the ministers he wanted, regardless of their political affiliations. However, the strength of party feeling and the weakness of party discipline prevented mixed ministries from being really successful. After the death of Mary in 1694 the Tories became unreliable, for they were not as loyal to William as they had been to his Stuart queen, and the ministry therefore tended to become more and more Whig in character.

Under Anne (1702-1714) the "Lords of the Cabinet Council" went on from strength to strength, while the influence and importance of the Privy Council continued to dwindle. One significant indication of that was that Anne stopped dismissing councillors who were out of favour. Although she found it difficult, Anne remained effective head of her own government, and despite the increasing pressure of circumstances managed to avoid limiting her choice of ministers to the majority party. The members of the nascent cabinet were still the monarch's servants. Anne presided over their meetings, and her reign was not a period of cabinet government in the modern sense, although it had come to be understood, or circumstances had made it clear, that ministers had a dual function, combining the conduct of executive business with gaining parliamentary support for their actions.

The continued existence and growth of the cabinet had been assured by the amendment of those parts of the Act of Settlement which threatened it. The Place Act of 1707 altered the provision which barred holders of offices under the crown from sitting in the House of Commons. It did that by declaring that the ban only applied to persons who held offices or "places" which had been created after the 25th October 1705. The net effect of the change as it related to ministers was to cancel the ban imposed by the Act of Settlement.

In 1713 the cabinet was firmly established, for standing order no 66 of that year laid it down that no money could be voted for any purpose except on the motion of a minister of the crown. This in turn reflected the ever-growing complexity of the financial aspect of government and the consequent tendency for Parliament to depend on guidance as well as information from the treasury. As the cabinet had grown out of the treasury, and because the role of the treasury was changing and growing in importance, the leading cabinet position became associated with the treasury. So Godolphin, Lord Treasurer until 1710, was sometimes given the significant appellation of "prime minister".

The death of Queen Anne on the 1st August 1714 is a suitable point at which to sum up the results of the "Glorious Revolution", itself the climax of a century of constitutional struggle. A union had been established between the executive, the crown, and the legislature Parliament. Sovereignty had been grasped by the nation when, regardless of the fact that neither a Parliament nor any valid means for convoking one existed, arrangements had none the less been made to summon one. A struggle between despotism and liberty had been resolved in an ordered liberty. Since the throne had been regarded as left vacant after James II's flight, before a new king (William III) was invited to mount it, it had been finally and definitely established that in Great Britain the king ruled not by divine right, but by grace of

Parliament.

England or Great Britain, long preoccupied with her internal struggles, could and did at last take a major part in European affairs. The country entered upon what was to be its foreign policy for more than a century: alliances with various combinations of Continental powers against France. It was, of course, consideration of the part England could play in Europe that had been in William III's mind from the beginning, though not in the minds of those who had invited him!

The Bill of Rights is a final summing up and establishment of the legal bases of the constitution. Together with the *Magna Carta* and the Petition of Right, it forms the British code of government to which no formal additions of equal importance have ever been made.

Subsequent reforms, even the very greatest, such as the Great Reform Act of 1834, cannot be regarded as anything more than amendments, though fundamentally important, made to the existing constitutional machinery. Their intention was to enable that machinery to function more effectively and equitably, not to make innovations in basic principles that had been settled once and for all, in the 17th and the early 18th century.

CHAPTER 5

THE NORTHERN ALLIANCES, 1648-1721

THE EMERGENCE OF THE SWEDISH EMPIRE, BRANDENBURG-PRUSSIA AND RUSSIA

The period between 1648 and 1679 has aptly been described as "the age of puberty of European power politics".[1] Before this, for about one and a half centuries, there had been only two real powers in Europe, the Bourbons and the Habsburgs. But after the Thirty Years War there was a volatile situation when Europe became somewhat like a "political stock-exchange",[2] with numerous changes taking place in the balance of power in consequence of the fact that almost always a war was being waged somewhere in Europe, resulting in shifts in alliances and gains or losses of territories. Mainly owing to the achievements of its great soldier king, Gustavus Adolphus, Sweden emerged from the Thirty Years War as the strongest power in northern Europe. This was confirmed by the Treaty of Westphalia, according to which Sweden was awarded over 5 000 000 rixdollars for its expenses, western Pomerania, Wismar, the secularized bishoprics of Bremen and Verden, a seat in the *Reichstag* of the Holy Roman empire, and status as a guarantor of the peace, together with France.

With the acquisition of Pomerania Sweden placed a foot firmly on European soil, and became part of the European scene. To the Swedes this territory was a type of symbol – an indication that Sweden had become a great power. As a result, Swedish statesmen clung to it with great tenacity. Sweden had desired that territory mainly to prevent the Holy Roman empire from using it as a launching pad against Sweden's Baltic possessions. But after 1660 the emperor of the Holy Roman empire was too preoccupied with the question of the Spanish succession, the Turkish danger and the problem of Hungary to pose a threat to the Swedish empire. To its cost Sweden would, however, discover that its control of Pomerania entailed the enmity of Brandenburg-Prussia and Hanover.

The Swedish empire comprised three categories of territories, namely: former Danish territories, conquered and integrated into metropolitan Sweden; the Baltic provinces of Livonia, Estonia, Ingria and Kexholm; and the German acquisitions: western Pomerania, Wismar and Bremen-Verden.

However, Sweden's position of power was more apparent than real. Its empire was difficult to maintain, since the various parts were not bound together by racial or emotional ties and were scattered around the Baltic shores, making them vulnerable to attack on all sides. This strategic vulnerability and indefensibility was compounded by the fact that the empire was surrounded by vengeful and greedy neighbours. Moreover, until the 19th century, Sweden remained essentially a poor country, sparsely populated, underdeveloped, and the victim of a harsh climate. There were, in addition, years of demographic disaster during the period under discussion, for example, in 1648-1650; in 1696-1697 and in 1709-1711.

According to the well-known authority on Swedish history, Michael Roberts, the main motive behind Sweden's foreign policy was therefore "a feeling in her statesmen of insecurity and weakness: political weakness in one case and in the other an economic inadequacy which must be remedied if the state were ever to be safe".[3]

To understand the rivalry of the main protagonists in northern Europe, a few brief flashbacks into preceding periods are necessary.

In the first place, Denmark and Sweden were traditional enemies and centuries-old rivals for the domination of Scandinavia. Denmark had held the dominant position from pre-historic times until the 13th century. By the Union of Kalmar of 1397 the three Scandinavian kingdoms of Sweden, Denmark and Norway (whose inhabitants were all descended from the same ethnic stock) had been united under a single monarch, King Erik of Norway, though the real ruler was his aunt, the much respected regent, Queen Margaret. After Margaret's death the kings of the Union had placed Danish interests first and antagonized the Swedes. In 1521 Gustav Vasa had led the Swedes in a successful war of liberation. He was a man of stature who, after being elected Gustavus I of Sweden, had succeeded in uniting the refractory Swedes and securing their submission to his crown. Under his Vasa successors – Erik XIV (1560-1568), John III (1568-1592), Sigismund (1592-1599), and Charles IX (1599-1611) – Sweden was consolidated as a national state, but still had to find its place in the power structure of northern Europe.

Sweden embarked on the establishment of a Baltic empire as a result of the decline of the Teutonic Order of Knights which had long dominated the eastern shores of the Baltic. This order, established during the crusades, had secured from the Holy Roman emperor and the pope the right to all the land it won for Christianity and German civilization in northern Europe. After a century-long struggle the order had conquered a pagan Slavonic tribe known as the Prussians and had converted Prussia into a unique military-ecclesiastical state. By allying itself to the Hanseatic League, the order, headed by an elected grand master, became a commercial and maritime power on the shores of the Baltic. However, the renascence of the Polish kingdom under the Jagiellon dynasty during the 14th and the 15th century led to Poland's challenging the right of the Teutonic Order to be masters in a territory that cut Poland off from the Baltic.

A Polish state under a hereditary monarch had taken its place on the stage of history during the second half of the 10th century. But this first monarchy had not lasted long, and during the 12th and 13th centuries Poland had lapsed into unrest and disunity caused by scores of contending duchies, the harassment of Mongol-Tartar raiders and the expansionist policies of German rulers. During the 14th century the last of the Piast rulers had succeeded in reuniting Poland and establishing a personal union with the grand duchy of Lithuania in 1385. This had greatly extended the domain of the Jagiellonian monarchy and had made Poland one of the major powers of Europe.

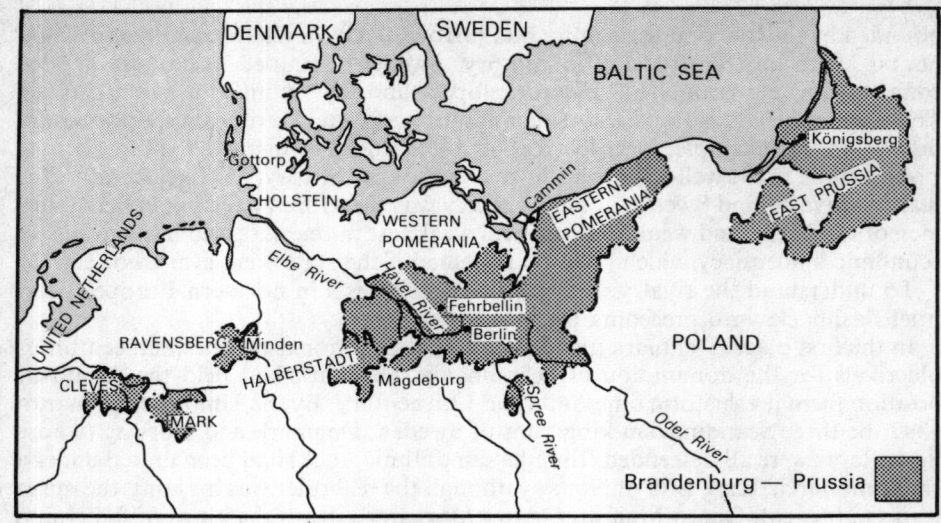

The territories of Brandenburg-Prussia, 1660

In the battle of Tannenberg (1410) the Poles defeated the Teutonic Order, and by the Perpetual Peace of Thorn (1466) western Prussia became a part of Poland, while eastern Prussia was left to the order as a Polish fief. This transformation of eastern Prussia into a Polish vassal state meant that it was no longer a part of the Holy Roman empire.

In 1511 Albert Hohenzollern, margrave of Ansbach, was elected grand master of the Teutonic Order and transformed eastern Prussia into a secularized, Lutheran duchy. In 1618, after much bargaining with Poland and shrewd arrangements of marriages, eastern Prussia was united with the electorate of Brandenburg under the elector, John Sigismund of Hohenzollern.

The history of the electorate of Brandenburg began with Charlemagne's subjugation of the Saxons when several marches were established as a protection against the heathen. In 1351 Emperor Charles VI elevated the march of Brandenburg to the dignity of an electorate of the Holy Roman empire, and in 1411 Frederick of Hohenzollern, burgrave of Nüremberg, was assigned the electorate of Brandenburg by Emperor Sigismund, in return for assistance in the latter's acquisition of the imperial crown.

The origins of the house of Hohenzollern can be verifiably traced back to counts who established the stronghold of Zollern in Swabia to which the epithet "high" or "hohen" came to be attached.

During the Thirty Years War Brandenburg was one of the main theatres of war and suffered great devastation, but with the accession of Frederick William as elector in 1640, the transformation of Brandenburg into a powerful, modern state began. Frederick William realized that the wide dispersal of Hohenzollern territories and their position in the centre of Europe made them vulnerable to attacks by powers such as Sweden, Austria, Poland and Russia. This made it imperative for the elector to strengthen Brandenburg-Prussia by establishing his unquestioned authority in his two states and building up a strong army. Consequently, Frederick William crushed the power of the local estates and substituted a single, centralized administration under his control. In addition, he built up an army, thus ensuring respect at home and abroad; he developed machinery for the extraction of ample military revenues and took measures to increase the population, productivity and prosperity of his lands. By marrying the daughter of the stadtholder of the Netherlands he also enhanced his diplomatic status.

At the peace negotiations after the Thirty Years War, Elector Frederick William made demands that he could back up with a considerable army. He wanted the whole of Pomerania which would have given Brandenburg-Prussia an extensive sea coast on the Baltic. However, the Swedes were in military occupation of Pomerania and claimed it as part of the spoils of war. The elector was awarded only the poorer, eastern part of Pomerania, but, as compensation for his dashed hopes, he demanded and obtained four secularized bishoprics: Camin, Cas, Halberstadt and Minden, as well as a claim to the archbishopric of Magdeburg. These territories greatly strengthened the central nucleus of his dominions. By insisting that Calvinists should be given the same political and religious privileges that the Lutherans had obtained through the Peace of Augsburg in 1555, the elector of Brandenburg-Prussia also won for himself the leadership of Protestant Germany. Brandenburg-Prussia therefore emerged from the Thirty Years War as the strongest Protestant state in the Holy Roman empire and as a potential threat to Austria and Sweden.

The weakening of the Teutonic Order as a result of the rise of Polish power and the spread of Protestantism meant that by the mid-16th century the Baltic littoral was ripe for plucking, and this brought Russia onto the scene as another contender for territories on the Baltic.

The origin of the Slavonic ancestors of the Russians is obscure. They apparently came from Asia and settled along the northern slopes of the Carpathian mountains in approximately AD 4. The Slavonic tribes probably divided into three groups during the 7th century: the southern or Balkan Slavs, the western Slavs (including the Poles), and the eastern Slavs who settled in the forested lands of northern Russia after having driven out or absorbed the Letts, Lithuanians and Finns who had earlier settled there. By the 8th century, trading cities had been established along the network of Russian rivers, and a confederation of city states existed. In the 9th century, wandering bands of Scandinavian warrior-traders subjugated many of these communities. In this way Rurik, a Danish chieftain from Jutland, became ruler of Novgorod in 862. Rurik subsequently returned to Denmark where he died, but Oleg, the leader of a band of Norwegians, was accepted as Rurik's successor. The sway of the Rurik dynasty eventually became so extensive that all the Slav tribes under its control came to be called Russians from "Rhos" or "Rus" which may have been a simplified form of "Rurik".

Oleg conquered the city of Kiev, making it the centre of the powerful Kievan state over which he ruled as grand prince. The golden age of Kievan Russia began in 980 when Vladimir became grand prince. He was an excellent soldier who enlarged and consolidated the Kievan state. He also adopted the Greek Orthodox religion and imposed it on all his subjects. The fact that the Russian church then fell under the authority of the patriarch of Constantinople led to the incorporation of many Byzantine elements into Russian culture, and this acted as a barrier to western influences.

After Vladimir's death the Kievan state was torn by fratricidal strife. The resulting unrest, as well as increasing pressure from Asiatic nomads who had settled in the southern steppes, caused the Russians to split into three groups. Large groups migrated to the west and south-west, settling in Poland, Galicia and adjoining territories. The one group was known as the Little Russians or Ukrainians, and the other as the White Russians. A larger group, the Great Russians, moved into the forests of north-eastern Russia where the state of Muscovy eventually arose.

During the 13th century the Russian city-states were subjugated by the Mongols (whom the Russians called Tartars), whose original home was in the region of Lake Baikal and the Gobi Desert. For nearly two and a half centuries the princes of Russia were tributaries of the Mongol khan of the Golden Horde.

The city-state of Moscow had a series of energetic rulers during the 14th, 15th and 16th centuries, who were determined to end Tartar control and unite the whole of Russia under their rule. The Muscovite ruler, Ivan III (1462-1505), also known as Ivan the Great, seized upon dissension in the Tartar empire to liberate Russia from Tartar domination. He married the niece of the last Byzantine emperor and assumed a style equal to that of the Holy Roman emperor, styling himself "by the Grace of God Czar (meaning Caesar), Autocrat of all Russia". The theory was developed that Moscow was the successor of Constantinople and therefore the "third Rome", with the divine mission to preserve and protect the Orthodox faith.

Ivan IV (1533-1584), also known as "the Dread" or "the Terrible" on account of his notorious cruelty and excesses, was the second outstanding Muscovite ruler. Through his conquest of Novgorod, the last eastern Slav state capable of checking the unification of Russia was eliminated. Division amongst the eastern Slavs disappeared.

As a child-tsar Ivan had suffered a great deal at the hands of boyars, or nobles, who had bullied and insulted him and plundered his patrimony. During his effective reign of some thirty five years he devoted his main energies to a ruthless terror campaign during which he destroyed the power of the boyars, appropriated the estates of disloyal ones and created a new aristocracy who accepted his autocratic rule. Russia was expanded by the conquests of the khanates of Kazan and Astrakhan and the exploration and settlement of Siberia. Ivan's reign was also distinguished by the opening up of trade links between Russia and western Europe via the White Sea as a result of a voyage to the shores of Russia by the Englishman, Richard Chancellor, who was attempting to find a northern trade route to the east.

Ivan realized the need to raise Russia to the technical level of western Europe and was anxious to obtain a warm-water port on the Baltic as a "window to the west". He invaded Livonia in 1558 and captured a number of cities including Narva which he attempted to make an entrepôt of Russian trade.

The grand master of the weakened Teutonic Order and the city of Reval appealed widely for aid. King Erik XIV of Sweden answered Reval's appeal by offering to incorporate the city. Reval had to accept and so the foundations of Sweden's Baltic power were laid, and Sweden, having staked out a position across the Gulf of Finland, was launched on a century of empire-building.

The Russian successes aroused the fear and hostility of other nations with interests in the Baltic, and Poland-Lithuania, Sweden, Denmark and the Teutonic knights all joined forces against the Russians. Ivan IV had to relinquish his hold on Livonia, which Poland annexed, while Sweden by the Treaty of Teusina (1595) acquired Estonia. Russia was completely cut off from the Baltic, but its desire to obtain an ice-free coastline along the Baltic remained and would revive strongly during the reign of Tsar Peter I.

A Swedish mercenary army captured Narva, and with this port as well as Reval and Viborg in its possession, Sweden controlled the trade through the Gulf of Finland. Sweden's subsequent restrictive trade edicts aroused the antagonism of its Baltic neighbours, and Denmark, Poland and Lübeck entered into an alliance against Sweden. The Seven Years War of the North (1563-1570) resulted, which was not noted for any great actions, and the peace mainly restored the status quo.

The death of Tsar Ivan IV and the succession of his sickly and weak-minded son, Theodor, resulted in a power struggle between various factions in Russia. There were years of anarchy, with several pretenders contending for the throne. Sweden seized the opportunity presented by Russia's weakness during its "time of troubles" to obtain more territories as a defensive buttress in the east. Sweden took Novgorod and obtained control of a large part of north-western Russia. King Sigismund of Poland also invaded Russia and seized Smolensk and Moscow.

Eventually a Russian national movement, under the banner of Prince Pozharski, succeeded in driving the Poles out of Moscow. A Russian general assembly or *Zemski Sobor* met in 1613 and decided to make the sixteen year old Michael Romanov tsar. He was found generally acceptable since he was too young to have taken part in the civil wars and because he was linked by marriage to the old Rurik dynasty.

Tsar Michael's government bought peace with Sweden and Poland. By the Peace of Stolbova of 1617 King Gustavus Adolphus of Sweden recognized Michael as tsar and relinquished Novgorod, but gained Ingria on the southern shore and Kexholm on the northern shore of the Gulf of Finland, which placed the whole shoreline of the gulf under Swedish control. Poland agreed to the Truce of Duelino (1619) in exchange for the White Russian provinces of Smolensk and Chernigov.

These agreements merely brought a temporary lull in the struggle for dominance in the eastern Baltic.

Besides the three-cornered rivalry of Sweden, Russia and Poland, Danish jealousy and resentment of Sweden's increasing power was another constant factor which complicated relationships. The Danes regarded themselves as the rightful heirs to the Hanseatic dominance of the Baltic and viewed Sweden as their chief rival. In 1611, seizing on Swedish preoccupation with Russia, Christian IV of Denmark declared war on Sweden and took Kalmar. This was a bid by Denmark to end Swedish rivalry, to eliminate the Vasas and restore the old Scandinavian union under the domination of Denmark. However, Christian IV was not able to achieve his goal before the winter set in. He withdrew his forces and negotiated the Peace of Knäred in January 1613, whereby Denmark restored some conquered territory but retained Älvsborg, the main entrepôt of Sweden's western trade, until Sweden had paid a ransom of 1 000 000 rixdollars. This was paid off by imposing crushing taxation and by raising a loan from the Dutch who, like the English and Germans, did not want to see Denmark dominate the entire north.

Once his conflicts with Russia and Denmark had been resolved, Gustavus Adolphus of Sweden could pay attention to Poland whose king claimed the Swedish throne. This claim arose because John III of Sweden had allowed his son, Sigismund, who had been raised as a Catholic, to be elected as king of Poland. On John's death Sigismund had returned to Sweden and was duly crowned king, but his attempts to introduce Catholicism had antagonized the clergy and the people. His uncle, Charles IX, a member of the younger line of the Vasa house, became king of Sweden, but the Polish Vasas refused to relinquish their claim to the Swedish crown, and for two generations the rulers of Sweden feared the restoration by force of the elder line.

A Turkish victory over the Poles in 1620 encouraged Gustavus Adolphus to take up the challenge to his throne by his Catholic cousin, Sigismund III of Poland, and Gustavus achieved considerable military successes in Poland between 1625 and 1627, conquering Livonia. After diplomats from France, England and Brandenburg-Prussia had achieved the Polish-Swedish Truce of Altmark, Gustavus turned away from his profitable conquests in the eastern Baltic area to involve himself in the Thirty Years War, partly to secure Sweden against the danger of a Catholic-imperialist conquest of northern Europe.

During the Thirty Years War Gustavus Adolphus seized an opportunity to try and end the ever-present Danish threat. Denmark was in a position to cut Sweden off from western markets by closing the Sound and endangering Sweden's only harbour to the open sea, Älvsborg. Moreover, from its provinces north of the Sound and the associated kingdom of Norway, it could launch attacks that could threaten Sweden's very existence. It therefore became a constant "axiom of Swedish policy that Denmark was the unsleeping enemy".[4]

Since the Danes had been heavily defeated in the Thirty Years War, Sweden decided in 1643 to make a pre-emptive strike against Denmark before its military strength had been rebuilt. Danish Jutland was attacked and the two Danish provinces of Scania and Halland north of the Sound were occupied. Christian IV of Denmark sued for peace and had to sign the Treaty of Brömsebro on the 13th August 1645. This provided Sweden with more natural geographic limits, for Denmark gave Halland in pawn to Sweden for thirty years and ceded the islands of Öseland Gotland, while Norway parted with Jämtland and Härjedalen. Nevertheless fear of Denmark remained, further reinforced by the possibility of Danish *revanche*. This fear affected Sweden's choice of territories at the Peace of Westphalia in 1648. Bremen and Verden were valuable in terms of the Elbe-Weser trade, but also because they were within striking distance of Denmark. They provided Sweden with a power base in north-western Germany from which she could exert pressure.

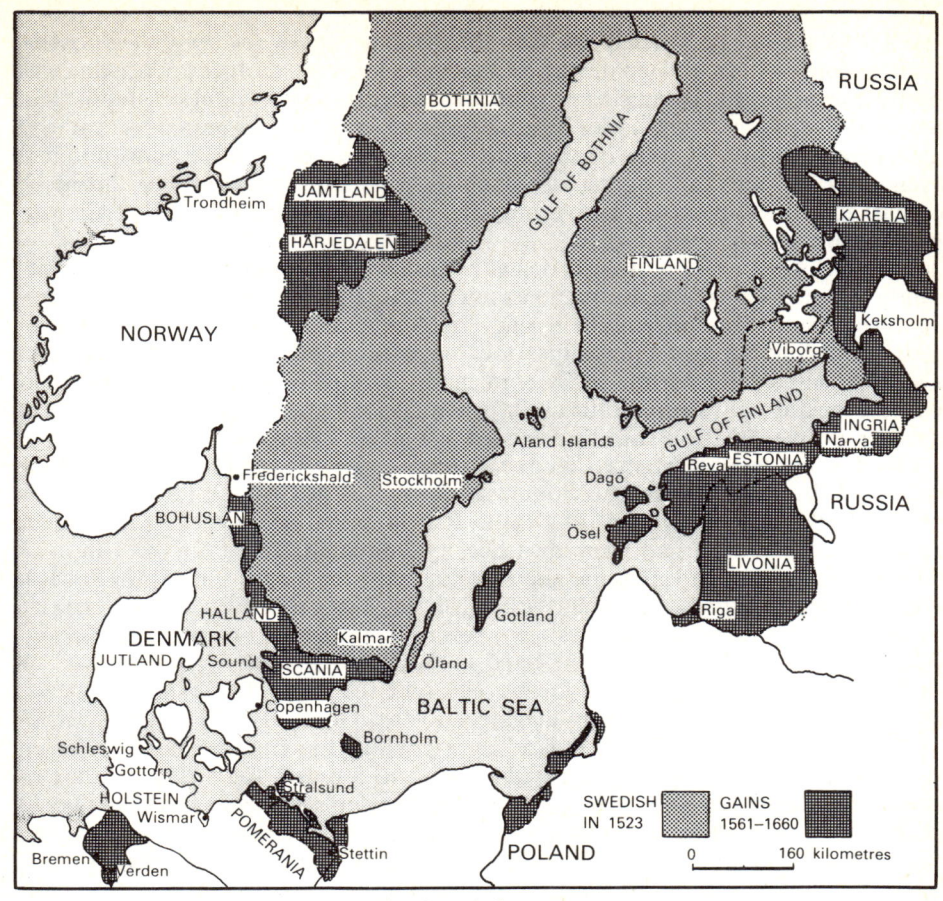

The Swedish empire

This would ensure the maintenance of the balance of power in northern Europe as established by the Westphalian peace settlement.

Since the only convenient means of access to Bremen-Verden was by land from Pomerania, it became essential for Sweden to remain on friendly terms with the intermediate duchy of Holstein-Gottorp in order to safeguard this access. This small dukedom formed the "keystone of Sweden's north-German arch",[5] and Sweden virtually became its political prisoner, since the Swedes were forced to support and maintain her against all threats.

When Gustavus Adolphus died in battle in 1632 his six year old daughter Christina succeeded him. In 1648, having come of age, she began her personal rule only to make known her conversion to Catholicism and abdicate in 1654 in favour of her soldier cousin, Charles Gustavus (son of the count palatine of Zweibrücken), who became Charles X of Sweden. He married the daughter of the duke of Holstein-Gottorp and so strengthened the ties between Sweden and this duchy. Christina was pacific by nature, and during her reign there had been a kind of political standstill in Sweden's foreign policy. Charles X, however, was an ambitious man of action who had spent most of his youth fighting with the Swedish troops in Germany and had eventually become their commander-in-chief. Soon after ascending the throne he embarked on a number of offensive and defensive wars to increase Sweden's power, prestige and safety.

Denmark was smarting over its defeat by Sweden and ready to seize any opportunity to redress the damage done to its interests by the Peace of Brömsebro; Brandenburg-Prussia was determined to end Polish suzerainty over Prussia, and Swedish control of western Pomerania; the son of Sigismund III of Poland, John Casimir, claimed the throne of Sweden; and the Romanov tsars of Russia had become increasingly aware of the need for Russian contact with the west. A potentially explosive situation therefore existed in northern Europe.

During the reign of Michael Romanov's successor, Alexis (1645-1676), a war broke out between Russia and Poland as a result of a Cossack rebellion in the Ukraine. The steppe country of "Little Russia", also known as "the frontier country" or Ukraine, had been absorbed by Lithuania, and after the Union of Lublin (1569) between Lithuania and Poland, had been incorporated into Poland. However, the Orthodox Ukrainians opposed the efforts of the Poles to catholicize them. Amongst these Ukrainians were several communities of adventurers and fugitives known as Cossacks who elected a new chief or *hetman* every year. In 1648 the *Zaporozhian* (translated, it means "beyond the rapids") Cossacks rebelled against Poland and offered their allegiance to the Russian tsar. The tsar's acceptance triggered off a war with Poland during which the Russian armies overran central Poland. These successes posed a threat to Sweden, for if the coastline of southern Livonia fell under Russian control, Sweden's strategic and commercial position on the eastern Baltic would be parlous in the extreme.

At the same time Poland's difficulties provided Sweden with an excellent opportunity to attempt to seize the Polish littoral and link up Swedish territories in Germany and Livonia. The war also provided Charles X with an opportunity to force the king of Poland to renounce all claims to the Swedish throne and recognize Charles's accession.

The outbreak in 1655 of the Northern War between Sweden and Poland posed a serious problem for elector Frederick William of Brandenburg-Prussia. As a vassal of King John Casimir of Poland he was obliged to support his liege lord. However, Poland was already showing signs of the weakness that was to lead to its dismemberment in the 18th century, while Swedish armies were advancing victoriously and casting a covetous eye on Prussia. Frederick William's offers of mediation were rejected by the Swedes, and he therefore decided to join them. The Swedes drove John Casimir out of Poland, and by the Treaty of Königsberg, signed on the 17th January 1656, Polish overlordship of eastern Prussia was replaced by Swedish suzerainty.

Shortly after this, however, the fortunes of war changed. In return for a Swedish promise of autonomy, the Cossack *hetman* deserted Russia for Sweden. Russia turned on Sweden and concluded the Truce of Androsovo with Poland, according to which Poland ceded Smolensk and the eastern bank of the Dnieper to Russia in return for the Polish territories that Russia had captured.

With the support of a popular movement and the church, John Casimir returned to Poland and fought to expel Charles X. This increased Brandenburg-Prussia's value as an ally to Sweden, and in the Treaty of Marienburg (signed on the 25th June 1656) Brandenburg-Prussia was promised a part of the Polish spoils after Sweden had defeated Poland.

In the battle of Warsaw the Brandenburg-Prussian army acquitted itself well, and the elector was in a position to raise his terms. Moreover, Austria and Russia began to rally to the support of Poland in order to keep Swedish ambitions in check. Sweden was on the defensive and Swedish resources proved inadequate to suppress national uprisings in the widely separated areas of Poland. Frederick William was in a position to demand that Sweden should revoke its bonds of vassalage and recognize the elector as sovereign duke in Prussia. This was agreed to in the Treaty of Labiau on the 20th November 1656.

Frederick III of Denmark decided that Swedish preoccupation in Poland provided an opportunity to avenge the Peace of Brömsebro, and Danish forces consequently attacked Bremen. Denmark, with a smaller population and economic resources, could hardly muster a third of the 90 000 men which were at the disposal of Charles X, and Swedish forces recovered Bremen and overran Jutland. Making use of the intense cold to cross the ice, Charles X, who had abandoned the long drawn-out campaign in Poland, also managed to capture some Danish islands. The demoralized Danes signed the Treaty of Roskilde, by which Sweden obtained the fertile provinces east of the Sound, Scania and Blekinge, which had long been Danish territory.

Meanwhile the Holy Roman emperor, Ferdinand III, had died on the 2nd April 1657, and the vote of the elector of Brandenburg-Prussia became important for the election of the next emperor. Under Habsburg pressure from Vienna the king of Poland agreed to recognize the independence of eastern Prussia and, since Charles X had withdrawn his troops from Poland, the opportunist elector was prepared to switch sides. By the Treaty of Wehlau, signed in September 1657, the elector allied himself with Poland and subsequently concluded an alliance with Austria in July 1658.

Charles X gathered his troops for an attack on Brandenburg-Prussia, but changed his plans when he could not persuade Denmark into an alliance. He suspected that the Dutch were egging on the Danes to take revenge, and, afraid of an attack in the rear, he decided to end the Danish threat for good. By subjecting Denmark, Sweden would also gain control of the Sound tolls which would provide the means to maintain a strong fleet and defy the trading nations of the west, especially the Dutch, and so bring about a Swedish monopoly of the Baltic.

Without a declaration of war Charles X launched a blitzkrieg against Denmark in August 1658, but Frederick III managed to hold out in Copenhagen with the aid of a Dutch fleet that broke through the Swedish blockade to bring relief.

Elsewhere the armies of Brandenburg-Prussia, Poland and the Holy Roman empire conquered most of Swedish Pomerania and expelled the Swedes from Schleswig-Holstein and from Poland.

At this critical stage for Sweden Charles X died suddenly in February 1660, leaving his four year old son, Charles XI, as successor.

The outcome for Sweden was better than expected. Fearing for their Baltic trade, England and the Netherlands urged Denmark to make peace. France objected to the occupation of western Pomerania by Brandenburg-Prussia, and, since the Peace of the Pyrenees had ended the French-Spanish War, Mazarin assembled an army of 40 000 to dissuade Poland and the Holy Roman empire from supporting Brandenburg-Prussian aggression. Both these states were prepared to make peace, since Polish territories had been liberated from the Swedes and the Holy Roman emperor was not interested in an involvement in war after France and Spain had come to terms. The result was a series of treaties that cost Sweden some of its more recent gains, but which left it generally stronger overall, since by the Peace of Oliva, concluded in April 1660, with France acting as mediator, John Casimir at last abandoned all his claims to the Swedish crown and to Livonia. Brandenburg-Prussia and Austria agreed to evacuate Swedish Pomerania and all the signatories acknowledged the elector of Brandenburg-Prussia's sovereignty as duke in eastern Prussia. Since eastern Prussia was not a part of the Holy Roman empire, this meant that with independent sovereign rights in one of his territories Frederick William had raised himself to a status above that of the other German princes who theoretically owed allegiance to the Holy Roman emperor in all their territories.

By the Treaty of Copenhagen, concluded in May 1660, Sweden had to return Trondheim and Bornholm to Denmark and the Danes withdrew their pledge made in the Peace of Roskilde to keep enemy fleets out of the Baltic. For the rest the provisions of the Peace of Roskilde were basically reaffirmed.

In the Peace of Kardis, signed in June 1661, Russia, pressurized by France, returned to Sweden all the Baltic areas it had conquered and acknowledged Sweden's rights to Karelia, Ingria, Estonia and Livonia.

The need for economy after Charles X's wars dictated an extremely cautious Swedish foreign policy aimed at protecting its extensive and vulnerable empire by alliances with powers outside the circle of those that would benefit from the collapse of Sweden's empire. The close ties between Denmark and the United Netherlands led to Sweden allying itself in 1665 with England, the chief rival of the Dutch. However, Louis XIV's aggressive policy in the Spanish Netherlands drove the English and Dutch together and in 1667 the regency for the young Charles XI of Sweden, against the wishes of the pro-French chancellor, Magnus de la Gardie, entered into the Triple Alliance with England and the Netherlands, aimed at countering French aggression. The situation changed when Charles II of England and Louis XIV of France concluded the Treaty of Dover in 1670, and, prompted by De le Gardie, Sweden concluded an alliance with France, thereby acquiring much needed French subsidies to strengthen its defences in its German territories. It was hoped that this move would dissuade the elector of Brandenburg-Prussia from joining France's enemies.

The French connection seemed a good bargain for Sweden because there appeared little likelihood of Brandenburg-Prussia entering a war against France. However, it almost proved to be Sweden's undoing.

Brandenburg-Prussia remained neutral during the War of Devolution, but when the Dutch War broke out, the elector rushed to the aid of the Netherlands by concluding an alliance with that country on the 6th May 1672. He was prompted by a sentimental attachment to his Dutch relatives and by fear that Catholic France might overwhelm this stronghold of Calvinism. This alliance led to an occupation by French troops of the elector's Rhenish provinces, thereby bringing home to him the vulnerability of his scattered territories. The quick collapse of the Netherlands enabled Frederick William to extricate himself from a war with France, and he concluded peace with France in 1673. He undertook to render no further aid to the Netherlands, while France returned most of the elector's territories it had occupied and promised him subsidies. Consequently, Brandenburg-Prussia did nothing when Louis XIV expanded his territory through the policy of so-called *"réunions"*.

However, when Spain and the Netherlands undertook to supply Brandenburg-Prussia with subsidies, the changeable Frederick William joined the Grand Alliance of Austria, Spain, Denmark and the Netherlands against France. Brandenburg-Prussia therefore participated in the campaigns against France on the Upper Rhine, but these campaigns brought the elector no laurels, and he hastily moved his troops northwards when Sweden, on France's instructions and in repayment for French subsidies, gave up its neutrality and invaded Brandenburg. To the surprise of Europe the forces of Brandenburg-Prussia won a decisive and unaided victory against the Swedes at Fehrbellin on the 28th June 1675. This victory shattered the Swedish record of invincibility and earned Frederick William the title of the "Great Elector".

The elector continued with a series of brilliant campaigns, as a result of which the Swedes were driven out of western Pomerania, and Stralsund and Stettin were captured. Only the lack of a fleet prevented the elector from continuing his success across the Baltic.

Meanwhile, however, the anti-French coalition had been defeated in the west. The Netherlands and Spain concluded peace with France in 1679, and the Holy Roman emperor also signed the Peace of Nijmegen. With only Denmark left as an ally, Brandenburg-Prussia could not maintain its position in northern Europe. It became imperative to bring hostilities with the triumphant Louis XIV to an end, and in the Peace of St Germain, concluded on the 29th June 1679, Frederick William was forced to restore to Sweden, as France's ally, all territory that Sweden had lost in fighting France's battles, namely western Pomerania, Stralsund and Stettin. This meant that after four years of victorious warfare Brandenburg-Prussia's only gains were the right bank of the Oder, tolls on the river and an indemnity of 300 000 thalers.

The elector felt very bitter that his allies, particularly the Holy Roman emperor, had left him in the lurch. As a shrewd and practical realist he decided to conclude a secret treaty with Louis XIV on the 25th October 1679. This brought him French subsidies, but entailed the subjection of his foreign policies to France's direction for as long as he remained its paid ally. He used the subsidies to strengthen his army and state so that he could change his policy when it suited him to do so.

Later the aggressiveness of Louis XIV's policies, especially the revocation of the Edict of Nantes, made Frederick William contemplate changing sides again. He was, in fact, preparing to join the Grand Alliance which was being formed against France by his nephew, William III of the Netherlands, when he died in 1688.

The Swedish defeat at Fehrbellin had encouraged the Danes and the Dutch to declare war on Sweden. A Dutch fleet secured control of the Baltic, enabling the Danes to cross into their former territory, Scania, where they could count on a considerable body of sympathisers, while the Norwegians invaded Böhuslan and Västergotland. However, the Swedish army redeemed its honour at the battle of Lund in 1676, where Charles XI (who had been declared of age in 1672) fought with great gallantry and personally led the army that drove the Danes out of Swedish territory. But the war dragged on during 1677 and 1678, and Sweden barely managed to hold out against Danish guerila depredations, while the Dutch were harrying Sweden's eastern shores. Mainly thanks to diplomatic pressure by Sweden's strong ally, France, Sweden only had to make minor concessions in Bremen-Verden and Pomerania, when peace was concluded with Denmark at Lund in 1679. Basically the status quo was restored.

Sweden, however, disliked its position as a French satellite, and the Danes were annoyed with the Dutch for making peace with France without consulting their Danish allies.

Charles XI's confidential adviser, Johan Gyllenstierna, therefore mooted the idea of a Swedish-Danish alliance to keep other powers such as the Netherlands out of the Baltic. Gyllenstierna conducted Sweden's peace negotiations after the Scanian War, and the Peace of Lund was accompanied by a Swedish-Danish defensive alliance, containing a number of secret articles involving mutual consultation before making an agreement with a third party, or entering a war of aggression. Gyllenstierna also promoted the marriage of Charles XI to a Danish princess, Ulrica Eleonora, the mother of the future Charles XII of Sweden.

Nevertheless Gyllenstierna's hopes of a close Swedish-Danish alliance never materialized because he died in 1680 and sources of disagreement outweighed the common interests of the Scandinavian powers.

The war had discredited the regents and the nobles in Sweden, but, since Charles XI had not been responsible for the policies that had imperilled Sweden, and since he had led Sweden very bravely at Lund, the prestige of the crown was enhanced. Sweden consequently followed what appeared to be the general trend in Europe towards absolute monarchy. The Swedish *Riksdag* lost its control over finances and administration, and the Declaration of Sovereignty in 1693 formally recognized the establishment of royal absolutism.

Charles XI used the enormous power which he acquired to restore the financial position of the crown and to build up Sweden's naval and military power. Through a policy of *reduktion*, 80 per cent of the lands alienated by the crown since 1500 were regained, and by the end of the 17th century about one-third of all the land in Sweden belonged to the crown. The result was that Sweden no longer had to hunt for foreign subsidies to maintain its empire, and a self-reliant Sweden could now follow a steadfast and more independent foreign policy.

Although Charles XI was cautious and peace-loving by nature, he realized that adequate means of defence were vital for Sweden to maintain its position as a great power. Consequently, he built up the largest fleet in Europe next to those of the leading maritime powers, England, the Netherlands and France. By the *indelningsverk* or allotment system of conscription he also raised a powerful army. At his unexpectedly early death from stomach cancer in 1679 he therefore bequeathed to his young son, Charles XII, an army, a navy and a financial system well equipped to wage war.

The sweeping reforms during Charles XI's reign had necessitated a period of peace. During the latter part of his reign Sweden's foreign policy was mainly directed by Bengt Oxenstierna (a distant relative of Gustavus Adolphus's great chancellor). Under him Sweden drifted away from France, which was threatening to disturb the balance of power in Europe, and in the 1680s Sweden concluded a series of alliances with the Netherlands and the Holy Roman empire, aimed at maintaining the existing settlement in Europe.

When the League of Augsburg, whose members were Spain, the Netherlands, the Holy Roman empire, Sweden and Bavaria, went to war with Louis XIV, Sweden did not wish to become actively involved, and tardily and reluctantly sent troops to the Rhine in terms of its obligations. This war dragged on until the Peace of Ryswick of 1697 where it was generally decided to preserve the status quo.

In 1689 Sweden had nearly gone to war with Denmark over the latter's expulsion of the duke of Holstein-Gottorp from his territory. Sweden had to protect this cornerstone of its foreign policy, and Denmark gave way to Swedish threats without fighting. The two Scandinavian powers even formed the Armed League of Neutrality in 1691 to counteract interference by Dutch, English and French privateers. However, this league petered out when both Scandinavian countries found it more profitable to deal separately with the maritime powers.

At the end of the 17th century the Swedish empire was still intact. "By proxy or on credit"[6] Sweden had been able to provide the men and money required to deal with its enemies, but the maintenance of its empire was also the result of a good administrative system, stability, military capability and leadership.

Sweden's administrative system was relatively sophisticated and modern in comparison with the systems that prevailed in the territories of its rivals. Throughout its age of greatness Sweden was a parliamentary state with a *Riksdag* which was remarkable for its inclusion of an Estate of Peasants. Although in times of crisis decisions were made by the sovereign, the *Riksdag's* consent was necessary for new taxes, and it had to be consulted on foreign policy. This created a sense of participation and "corporate responsibility" amongst nobles and non-nobles, making them more amenable to shouldering the burdens imposed upon them by Sweden's foreign policy.[7]

Swedish society was also remarkably stable and free from revolts owing to religious uniformity and the fact that in general the monarchy and nobles worked well together. Gothicism – the mystical-historical fantasy that the Swedes were descended from the ancient Goths, supposed to be the oldest nation (founded after the Flood by Magog, son of Japhet), and were retaining the original language spoken by God to Adam – had great propaganda value. It stimulated national pride and was an incentive to recover the lands the Goths were claimed to have ruled.

One of Sweden's main assets that made its age of greatness possible was the quality of leadership displayed by the kings who ruled between 1600 and 1718. They were strong rulers, with considerable administrative ability, and all were soldiers by temperament – in fact, Gustavus Adolphus, Charles X and Charles XII were amongst the greatest military leaders of the age.

During the closing years of the 17th century various changes took place in some of the states of north-eastern Europe that were to have fateful results for the Swedish empire during the 18th century. First of all, the enigmatic Tsar Peter I took control of Russia in 1694, and his reign until 1725 was to prove a turning point in Russia's history. He brought his ruthless energy to bear on trends started by his predecessors, and transformed the medieval Muscovite state into the modern autocracy of Russia which was to pose the greatest threat to Sweden. In 1697 Augustus ("the Strong"), elector of Saxony, was elected king of Poland, and with his rise in status his ambition increased. The elector of Brandenburg achieved a similar rise in status when the Holy Roman emperor, Leopold I, who was anxious to obtain the elector's aid in the impending war with France over the Spanish succession, agreed in 1700 to allow Frederick III of Brandenburg-Prussia to crown himself as Frederick I, king "in Prussia".

THE GREAT NORTHERN WAR: THE FIRST PHASE, 1700-1715

On the death of Charles XI of Sweden in 1697, the crown passed to his fifteen year old son. The youth and inexperience of Charles XII seemed to provide a golden opportunity for Sweden's ambitious neighbours to dismember the Swedish empire.

In Denmark, Sweden's traditional and "unsleeping enemy", Frederick IV, who succeeded Christian IV in 1699, wanted to recover from Sweden former Danish territories across the Sound. Denmark was also concerned about the close ties that had been established between the duchy of Holstein-Gottorp and Sweden through the marriage of the duke of Holstein-Gottorp to Charles XII's older sister, Hedvig Sophia, in 1698. Any offspring of this union could succeed to the Swedish throne and unite the two territories completely.

Augustus II of Saxony-Poland was bound by his *pacta noventa* with the Polish nobles to recover former Polish territories that had come under Swedish control. Moreover, Augustus was a dangerous schemer and opportunist. He is described by M. T. Florinsky as "one of the most unscrupulous scoundrels ever to ascend the ill-fated throne of Poland".[8]

History was to prove, however, that the greatest threat to the Swedish empire was Russia. As indicated, there had been attempts on the part of Russia to break through to the Baltic, but these attempts had been thwarted, and at the end of the Thirty Years War Russia had appeared to pose no threat to Sweden at all. In fact, in the Treaty of Osnabruck, which was one of the treaties that ended this war, Russia had merely been referred to in passing as one of the states "allied and adhering" to Sweden.[9]

Russia's potential was seriously underestimated by most western powers. Under Tsar Peter I Russia underwent a transformation that turned it into a major power. On taking effective control in 1694 Peter was determined to expand the Russian empire, establish easy contact with the west in order to westernize and modernize Russia, and acquire for that country a leading place in the European concert of nations.

The Polish-Russian Treaty of 1686 had given Russia final possession of Kiev and much of the Ukraine, and had marked the end of those Russo-Polish conflicts which had been a permanent feature of interstate relations in north-eastern Europe for about two centuries. It became obvious towards the end of the 17th century that Russian expansionist energies would in future be directed either southwards towards the Turkish (Ottoman) empire, in order to obtain access to the Black Sea, or westwards against the Swedish empire in a renewed effort to force an entry to the Baltic.

During the period 1695-1696 Tsar Peter I made two attempts to capture Azov, strategically guarding the entrance to the Black Sea. The first attack by land was unsuccessful, but the second, a combined assault by land and sea, succeeded.

After this Peter undertook a tour to western Europe, as a member of a delegation, to acquaint himself with developments in the west and to attempt to secure allies for further aggrandizement against the Turks. The Tsar's visits to towns, docks, schools, and other public institutions, particularly in France, Holland and England, confirmed him in his desire to modernize Russia.

The subsequent military, administrative, economic, social, educational and ecclesiastical reforms initiated in Russia by the tsar were intended mainly to improve Russia's offensive and defensive capabilities so that the tsar could achieve his expansionist aims and raise Russia to the status of a leading world power. Although few of these reforms made an enduring impact, they contributed significantly, in the short term, to Peter's successful foreign policy.

During his visit to western Europe Tsar Peter had met Augustus II of Saxony-Poland. The tsar found the tall, handsome and athletic Augustus congenial, and they became intimate friends.

Peter had no success in acquiring allies against Turkey, but Augustus persuaded the tsar to join a tripartite alliance against Sweden. The catalyst in bringing about this alliance was a Livonian nobleman, Johann Patkul, Baron Wallendorf. He nursed a personal grievance against the Swedish monarchy because his attempts to obtain redress for Livonian baronial estates attached to the Swedish crown had resulted in his exile. In his desire for vengeance he travelled from one northen European capital to the other, fomenting jealousy of Sweden's power and inciting greed for its possessions. Augustus of Saxony-Poland lent a ready ear to this incitement because he was an ambitious opportunist and believed that military action against the inexperienced Charles XII would involve no serious risks. Augustus wanted Livonia in order to present it to Poland in exchange for making his family hereditary rulers of Poland.

Augustus sent Patkul to Denmark, and the Danish king willingly agreed to an alliance according to which Denmark was to obtain what it could conquer from Sweden, while Poland obtained Livonia, and Russia was to have Ingria.

Tsar Peter deferred his open adherence to this anti-Swedish alliance until he had achieved a peace with Turkey. Meanwhile, by confirming the Russo-Swedish Treaty of Kardis in 1661, he lulled Sweden into a false sense of security regarding his intentions.

His visit to western Europe had convinced Peter that a warm-water port on the Baltic would be of greater value to Russia, as a window on the west and a naval base, than one on the Black Sea, since it was more accessible. The long journey across the steppes to the Black Sea was disagreeable.

Later the Russian tsar confessed that he agreed to involve Russia in the Great Northern War without realizing that his country was so unprepared and the enemy so strong. So in 1700 Sweden was confronted with the situation against which its diplomacy had tried to guard, namely an alliance of several neighbouring states bent on depriving Sweden of its empire and partitioning its territories amongst themselves.

Simultaneous attacks on the Swedish empire were to be launched from Denmark and Saxony. Consequently, in February 1700 Johann Patkul invaded Livonia with a Saxon force. At the same time Denmark invaded Holstein-Gottorp, thinking that the Danish navy held the Sound.

The members of the coalition expected little resistance from Sweden's young ruler, but they underestimated Charles XII who proved to be a military genius. He decided to move quickly and crush each member of the coalition separately.

The Danish invasion perturbed England and the Netherlands who dispatched a combined fleet to put an end to disturbances potentially harmful to their trading interests. While this fleet immobilized the Danish navy, led by a timid and irresolute commander, Charles XII managed to get his troops across the eastern end of the Sound which had been left unguarded by the Anglo-Dutch fleet because it was considered unnavigable.

In May 1700, having landed safely in Zealand with 11 000 men, Charles XII struck at the heart of Denmark and marched right up to the gates of Copenhagen. To avert an attack on his capital, and under diplomatic pressure from the maritime powers, Frederick IV capitulated and signed the Treaty of Travendal. Charles XII demanded only an assurance of Danish neutrality, and, having secured this and re-established the status quo, the young Swedish king immediately turned his attention to the eastern shores of the Baltic. Here, after the tsar had made a truce with the Turks, a vast Russian army had poured into the most northerly Baltic province, Ingria, and laid siege to Narva, the fortress on the Gulf of Finland.

Having transported his troops across the Baltic, Charles XII suddenly, under cover of a snow storm, attacked the besieging Russian forces at Narva on the 30th November 1700. Despite an enormous numerical superiority, the Russians proved no match for the well-disciplined and well-trained Swedish troops. The old-fashioned cavalry and the irregulars in the Russian army fled without fighting. Tsar Peter deserted his troops and took with him those officers who might be useful in raising a new army. It was one of the most ignominious defeats ever suffered by Russia, and Peter, who had surprised Europe by his victory over the Turks at Azov, became an object of derision.

Charles XII was advised to pursue Peter and compel him to accept a treaty that would render Russia harmless for a decade or more. But Charles's easy victory at Narva made him contemptuous of the Russians. He apparently stated: "There is nothing in winning victories over the Muscovites; they can be beaten at any time."[10]

Charles XII decided to deal with Augustus of Saxony-Poland first. This was perhaps the right decision militarily, since he could not invade Russia, leaving an army poised to attack his flank and disrupt his supply lines. Moreover, no superficial, quick action in the vastness of Russia was possible. Charles's great mistake was his underestimation of Russia's recuperative powers. For his campaign in Poland and Saxony he stripped his Baltic garrisons of the best men and left only about 15 000 troops to guard the over 900 km long Baltic frontier.

The Swedish king's spectacular successes had led to urgings that he should join the Grand Alliance against Louis XIV. But, as a staunch Protestant, Charles XII was opposed both to Emperor Joseph I of Austria who oppressed the Protestants in his territories and to Louis XIV who had persecuted the Huguenots. Also, elated by his military successes, he was determined to defeat and intimidate the aggressors in the Great Northern War and to ensure the preservation and security of the Swedish empire. Having found his undoubted *métier* as a soldier, he had the same assertiveness and thirst for military glory as Napoleon.

Convinced of his invincibility, Charles refused to listen to the advice of the Swedish chancellor, Bengt Oxenstierna, that Sweden had neither the men nor the money to indulge in foreign wars and should rather come to an agreement with Russia and Saxony-Poland and then assume the role of mediator between the rival claimants to the Spanish throne. This would enhance Sweden's prestige without undue sacrifice.

Since his childhood Charles XII had steeped himself in Nordic folklore and was strongly influenced by the Viking code of vengeance. He was determined to make Augustus II and Peter I pay for their duplicity.

Patkul's invasion of Livonia had not met with the expected success. He had overestimated the warmth of feeling for himself in his native country, and the Livonian gentry failed to join his invading Saxon force. Having no local rising to contend with, the Swedish garrisons in Livonia swiftly expelled the invaders.

Technically, the Poles were at peace with Sweden even though their king (as elector of Saxony) was at war with Charles XII. However, Charles invaded Poland, occupied Warsaw and Cracow and demanded the deposition of Augustus II and the election to the Polish throne of his own nominee, Stanislas Lesczinski. This tactlessness drove the reluctant Poles into supporting Augustus. Charles defeated a combined Polish-Saxon force at Klissow but, like others before him, found it difficult to impose his authority over the whole of Poland.

For several years the international situation prevented Charles XII from the one expedient that would have brought the war against Augustus to a speedy conclusion, namely an invasion of Saxony. He knew that England and the Netherlands would oppose such a move (which would complicate and weaken their position in the War of the Spanish Succession), and Charles XII relied on the two maritime powers to enforce observance of the Treaty of Travendal and make Denmark remain neutral.

The opportunist Augustus II was prepared to betray his allies and make peace provided he did not have to surrender the Polish crown which he had been at some pains and expense to acquire. He was not prepared to become a mere elector again, particularly after his "inferior" colleague of Brandenburg had become king in Prussia in 1701.

Charles XII's insistence on punishing Augustus by depriving him of his crown therefore resulted in a long, drawn-out struggle, and this lengthy involvement with Poland and Saxony was a mistake, since it gave Peter I of Russia a respite during which he could rebuild his army.

Peter's humiliating defeat at Narva made him determined to assemble a better-trained and better-equipped army. He strained his country's resources to the utmost to do so. The administration and finances were geared to war, European-style uniforms, equipment and discipline introduced and a conscription system was employed which required each Russian province to provide and maintain its quota and according to which nobles and peasants were drafted for life. This provided Peter with a standing army numbering 200 000 by the year 1725.

The tsar used his reconstructed military forces in two ways. First, he sent a Russian auxiliary force of between 15 000 and 20 000 men to help Augustus II. This support, and financial aid, enabled Augustus to maintain a long and stubborn resistance to Charles XII. Simultaneously, taking advantage of Charles's preoccupation with Poland and Saxony, Peter sent Russian forces into Livonia and Estonia which Charles had left with little protection. Russian forces captured the Swedish fortress at the mouth of the Neva, and Peter began constructing his new capital of St Petersburg there in May 1703. Other towns were captured as well, and Russia gained control over an important area along the Gulf of Finland.

Charles XII was not perturbed at these Russian conquests, since he felt confident of defeating the Russians and of recapturing their acquisitions.

In 1704, under Swedish pressure, the Polish Diet at last dethroned Augustus and elected Stanislas Lesczinski as his successor. Charles XII then treated Poland as a Swedish vassal state.

By 1706 Charles XII felt that his control of Poland was secure enough for him to invade Saxony. Going from defeat to defeat, Augustus finally signed the secret Treaty of Altranstädt on the 14th September 1706, terminating his alliance with Russia and recognizing Lesczinski as Poland's legitimate king. He also handed Johann Patkul over for execution and withdrew from the war.

However, Charles XII's onslaught on Russia was further delayed by a quarrel with the Holy Roman emperor over the latter's military aid to Augustus and over the persecution of Lutherans in Silesia. In September 1706 Charles XII entered Silesia and set up his standard as "Defender and Liberator of the Protestants" in the Holy Roman empire. The duke of Marlborough had to intervene to prevent war. In order to be able to concentrate on the struggle with France, Emperor Joseph I

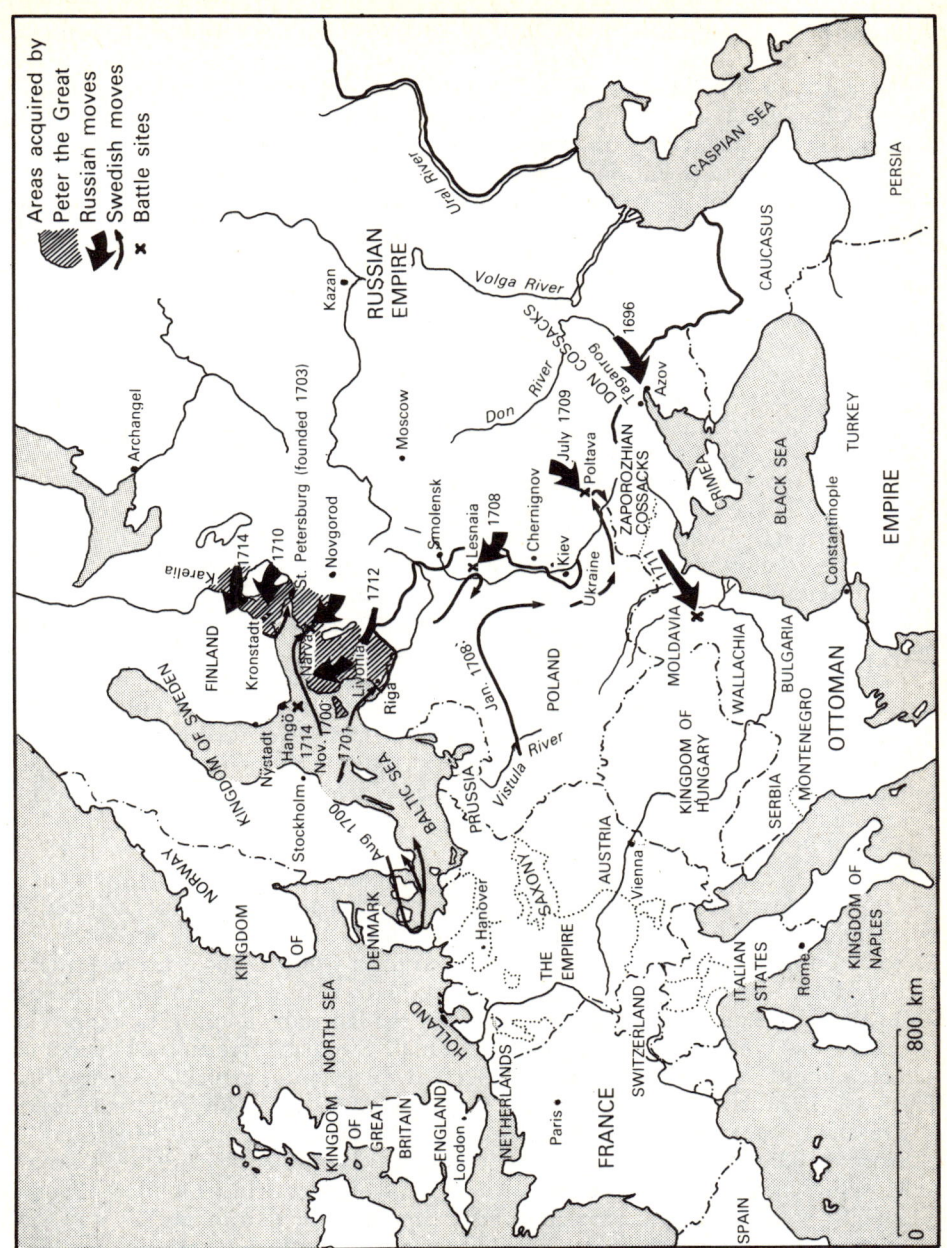

The Great Northern War, 1700-1721

agreed to humour the "mad Swede" and at Altranstädt in 1707 granted the required concessions to Silesian Lutherans.

There was a lull in the War of the Spanish Succession, and once again both sides sought Charles XII as an ally. But he had no interest in the politics of western Europe. He was intent only on wreaking vengeance on the tsar, and in September 1707 he left Silesia for Russia.

Peter I, finding himself without allies and faced by internal revolts in Russia, did his utmost to stave off the Swedish invasion. He offered the duke of Marlborough either Kiev or Smolensk and a pension of 50 000 thalers if he could mediate successfully. But Marlborough's efforts, as well as mediation offers by William III, came to naught because Peter was not prepared to surrender his outlet to the Baltic at St Petersburg and Charles XII regarded even a restricted Russian Baltic coastline as a danger to Sweden, since it would enable Russia to build up a powerful navy.

Leaving a Swedish division in Poland to protect King Stanislas, Charles XII crossed the Vistula with 44 000 men and invaded Russia in January 1708. A Swedish army of about 15 000 men under Count Löwenhaupt was sent to recover Livonia and collect supplies before joining the main army for an assault on Moscow.

Charles XII's army was well trained, well disciplined and very confident after their former easy victory over the Russians at Narva. In addition to this army, Charles had the promise of Cossack assistance. The Cossack *hetman,* Ivan Mazeppa, had negotiated with Charles XII and had offered him aid in return for securing the Ukraine's independence from Russia. The Swedish king also entertained the hope of acquiring Turkey as an ally against Russia.

Tsar Peter had an army of at least 70 000 men and enormous reserves, but he had learnt from his defeat at Narva not to trust in numbers alone. His policy was to avoid pitched battles and, by retreating, lure the enemy ever further eastwards, to separate Charles as much as possible from his communication and supply line. At the same time the Russians would prevent the Swedes from obtaining supplies by following a scorched-earth policy and using Tartar and Cossack horsemen to harass Swedish foraging parties.

The Swedes had an arduous campaign. Poor roads, made worse by a wet summer, slowed down progress. Field guns became bogged down in marshes and had to be abandoned. Charles XII defeated a Russian force at Golovchina and occupied Mogilev on the Dnieper river. Here he paused for a while to await Löwenhaupt's arrival. But Löwenhaupt had encountered an equally strong Russian force and had suffered a defeat on the 9th October 1708 near the Russian village of Lesnaia. The result was that when he eventually joined the main Swedish force on the Dnieper he had only about 8 000 of his 15 000 troops left and was minus artillery and supplies. This was a blow to the Swedes and a boost to Russian morale. Nevertheless Charles XII rejected peace offers, saying he would dictate his own terms at Moscow.

From the Dnieper Charles was advancing towards Smolensk on the direct road to Moscow when he was checked by a Russian force under Prince Golitsin. Charles XII might possibly have succeeded in his campaign if he had forced his way forwards and attacked Moscow, but instead he swerved southwards into the Ukraine where he hoped to find ample supplies for his hungry troops and the promised

Cossack reinforcements before launching a major offensive against Moscow.

Charles's calculations proved wrong. Peter had sent his trusted friend, General Menshikov, to the Ukraine to prevent the Swedes from receiving any aid there.

Disliking Peter's policies that were making inroads on cherished Cossack liberties, and banking on Russian ineptitude, and the military genius and good fortune of Sweden's soldier-king, *Hetman* Mazeppa had hoped to secure the independence of his Ukrainian homeland by siding with the "invincible" Swedes. However, Menshikov captured Mazeppa's capital, Bakurin, and the Ukrainian population was not prepared to rise up against the tsar until the Swedes had achieved a major victory. The result was that Mazeppa joined Charles with only 1 300 Cossacks instead of the promised 30 000.

Meanwhile Charles XII continued marching southwards, intending to rendezvous in Kiev with reinforcements ordered from Poland and possibly with Turkish troops as well, for he had sent an agent to Constantinople to solicit aid from that quarter.

However, Charles's campaign of 1709 opened for him under very poor circumstances. His army, already suffering from exhaustion and an acute shortage of food, had to endure an exceptionally cold winter. Exposure, starvation and disease took their toll and more than halved Charles's army. Charles endured the same privations and only his example and determination held the remnants of his army together. According to D. Maland,[11] the terrible ordeal served to make Charles mentally unbalanced, and the single-minded pursuit of vengeance which had characterized his campaigns against Augustus now became an obsession. He refused to retreat.

Still marching southwards, the weary Swedes reached Poltava on the Vorstka in June 1709. Charles hoped that a Swedish assault on this second-rate fortress would lure the tsar into a direct attack, so that the Swedes could defeat the Russians or keep them occupied until the expected reinforcements turned up from Poland and Turkey.

Since another Cossack group, the Zaporozhians under Hordienko, had revolted against him, Tsar Peter was prepared, even on the eve of the battle of Poltava, to discuss peace terms with Charles XII as long as this did not involve the surrender of St Petersburg. However, as Charles XII had undertaken not to make peace until the independence of the Ukraine was recognized and all Swedish territories had been recovered, while Peter would neither countenance the partial dismemberment of Russia nor the surrender of his "window to the west", peace was not possible.

The Swedes were still confident enough of their superiority to attack an army twice as large as theirs, in an entrenched position and infinitely superior in artillery.

Charles XII, with a bullet wound in his foot, was unable to take command when the battle of Poltava commenced on the 28th June 1709. However, he was carried around on a litter and kept on interfering with the disposition of the Swedish troops. The resulting conflicting orders caused confusion.

The Russian attack was accompanied by a devastating artillery barrage which took a tremendous toll of the Swedish infantry. The Swedes had only four guns with which to retaliate. The Russians closed in in a vast arc, leaving the Swedes little room to manoeuvre. A gallant Swedish charge threw the Russian right wing into disorder, but the left wing under Menshikov enveloped the small Swedish force, which suffered a complete defeat.

Charles XII was almost the last to leave the field. He and *Hetman* Mazeppa crossed the Dnieper by boat into Turkey where Mazeppa died three months later. The Swedish rearguard under Löwenhaupt, hotly pursued by the Russians, was unable to cross the river and surrendered.

Peter's unexpected victory at Poltava failed to bring about the result for which the financially overburdened Russian people longed, namely an end to the war. However, the defeat and flight of the reputedly invincible Swedish king made a great impression on Europe. Powers which before Poltava could not even be bribed into an alliance with Russia by the tsar's offers of generous subsidies were now eager to become allies of the conqueror of Charles XII. Peter was consequently able to resurrect the northern alliance destroyed by Charles XII.

Charles XII's defeat at Poltava also affected his protégé, Stanislas Lesczinski. The latter's hold on Poland had never been very secure, and in the summer of 1709 he fled to Pomerania. Augustus of Saxony was reinstated as king of Poland, and, after the pope had released him from the obligations placed on him by the Treaty of Altranstädt, he met Tsar Peter at Thorn on the 9th October 1709. The two rulers concluded the Treaty of Dresden, a new alliance against Sweden. A few days later a secret amendment declared Livonia to be the hereditary property of Augustus in his capacity as elector of Saxony. A military alliance between Russia and Denmark followed on the 11th October, and shortly afterwards Tsar Peter even negotiated a defensive alliance with King Frederick I of Prussia.

After the Holy Roman emperor had agreed to the elector of Brandenburg becoming king in Prussia the Prussian army had fought with the Grand Alliance against Louis XIV. Although Prussian troops participated in many of the historical battles of the Spanish War of Succession, the peace treaties of 1713-1714 ending the war did not bring Prussia compensation equal to the sacrifices she had made. Absorption in the western European struggle prevented Prussia from joining the northern coalition at the start of the Great Northern War. Prussia's real interests lay in the Baltic and with the valuable asset of his strong army Frederick I, by deserting the Grand Alliance and bartering his aid successively to Sweden, Poland and Russia could perhaps have acquired western Pomerania and western Prussia. But, having "neither the cynical courage, nor the unscrupulous egoism, nor the diplomatic versatility of his father's (the Great Electors') *Realpolitik*",[12] Frederick I kept out of the northern intrigues and struggles until after the War of the Spanish Succession had ended. He was probably wary of the soldiership of Charles XII until after the battle of Poltava and he was also influenced by the famous soldier and diplomat, Marlborough, to remain loyal to the Grand Alliance.

Since Charles XII was determined to avenge Poltava, he remained in Turkey, with the intention of persuading the Turks to take up arms against Russia.

Meanwhile Russian troops, encountering little opposition, conquered Estonia and Livonia, capturing fortresses and valuable harbours. These Russian victories during 1709 and 1710 gave the country a new international position and brought it into the broad arena of European politics.

During Charles XII's prolonged absence from Scandinavia a Danish force invaded Scania and in 1711 occupied Bremen and Verden.

Disturbed by Charles XII's anti-Russian intrigues in Turkey, Tsar Peter issued an ultimatum, threatening war if Charles was not deported. Much to Peter's dismay, however, Turkey refused to send Charles packing and on the 20th November 1710 declared that a state of war existed between Turkey and Russia. Turkey's actions were motivated by a desire for revenge over the loss of Azov and by Charles XII's promise of a Swedish assault on Poland simultaneously with a Turkish attack on Russia.

Tsar Peter tried to avoid war. He asked both France and the Grand Alliance to mediate, but when it became clear that war was unavoidable, he sent Russian agents to stir up revolts amongst the Turkish Sultan's Christian subjects in Moldavia, Wallachia, Serbia and Montenegro.

His victories had increased the tsar's confidence and ambitions. Counting on the support of Orthodox Slavs in the Turkish vassal states, he invaded Turkey with 40 000 men in July 1711. But support of a crusade for Balkan Slavs did not materialize. The Slav nobles in the Balkans were unwilling to take a stand until they were sure Peter would win. Near the Pruth river the tsar found himself, as a result of overconfidence and inadequate planning, with insufficient ammunition and supplies and surrounded by a Turkish and Tartar army vastly superior in strength. To escape certain defeat and possible captivity, Peter, whose entourage included several court ladies (amongst them the future Empress Catherine, who would become his second wife) asked for a truce on Turkey's terms.

The tsar was prepared to surrender all Russia's conquests except St Petersburg, but, as the Turks were not interested in continuing the war, particularly when no news was received of a supportive Swedish offensive in Poland, they proved surprisingly generous. By the treaty concluded on the 11th July 1711 Peter merely had to surrender all his strongholds on the Sea of Azov, promise to refrain from interfering in Poland or with the Cossacks and grant Charles XII a safe passage through Russia to Sweden.

As a result of this treaty, the settlement of the Black Sea question was left in abeyance for half a century. Tsar Peter decided to cut his losses on the Black Sea and concentrate on the Baltic area. Hereafter Russian military operations were twofold. On the one hand, Russian troops supported Peter's allies in their campaigns on the southern shores of the Baltic, and on the other hand, Russian forces also advanced into the eastern Baltic area and launched an attack on Finland in 1713.

During the Utrecht peace negotiations after the War of the Spanish Succession, attempts were made to induce Charles XII to accept the mediation of Britain and end the allied onslaught on Sweden's empire. But Charles was embittered against Britain for failing to uphold the Treaties of Travendal and Altranstädt as promised, and for endeavouring to counteract his attempts at inciting the Turks to renew the war with Russia. Instead, although as a staunch Protestant he personally disliked Louis XIV, Charles made overtures to him for French support, but to no avail.

With any political insight Charles XII should have forsworn Polish affairs and obtained at least the neutrality of Saxony-Poland by supporting Augustus's reoccupation of the Polish throne. Then he should have returned promptly to Sweden to try and recover Sweden's Baltic provinces. Instead, however, he remained in Turkey, refused to allow his ministers a free hand and ordered Swedish troops to be sent to theatres of war far from home. According to D. Ogg, he subordinated everything – including the best interests of his country – to his personal desire for vengeance.[13]

Sweden's reputation was upheld by capable generals and loyal troops. General Stenbock repulsed an attack by the Danes on the Swedish mainland and drove them out of Scania.

Encouraged by this news, Charles XII vetoed a suggestion by Britain and the Netherlands to form the Neutrality Compact with them, according to which Swedish possessions in Germany would be neutralized and guaranteed. This alienated the maritime powers who were anxious for peace in the Baltic to safeguard their trade interests. Charles XII ordered Stenbock to take a Swedish army into Pomerania to be held in readiness there for an attack on Poland or Denmark as required. Despite the fact that the Danes had destroyed his supply fleet, Stenbock managed to win a victory at Gadebusch in December 1712, but subsequently found himself in a very dangerous position between the Russians and Saxony-Poland in the east, and the Danes in the west. Lacking the strength to maintain himself in Germany, the Swedish commander attempted to invade Jutland, but was surrounded in the fortress of Tönnig in Schleswig-Holstein and forced to surrender his whole army in May 1713.

Stenbock's failure made Charles XII's position in Turkey untenable, and he was asked to leave. On refusing to do so, he was made a captive after a futilely heroic stand at Bender.

During 1713 Tsar Peter visited Berlin and tried to draw the new king of Prussia, Frederick William I (1713-1740), into an alliance with Russia. But Frederick William who had become king shortly after the Peace of Utrecht, did not immediately want to involve himself in the confused pattern of the Great Northern War. He gave priority to internal affairs and to consolidating what his predecessors had achieved. Nevertheless he not only commenced financial reforms, but immediately increased his army by seven regiments just in case he should decide to use it. He turned Brandenburg-Prussia into the best-run military state of his day. His main achievement was the establishment of a centralized monarchical nation with a strong army and an efficient administrative bureaucracy of career civil servants as its twin pillars. He also succeeded in attracting immigrants and increasing the prosperity of his state.

King Frederick William I is notorious for his harsh treatment of his son, the future Frederick the Great, but his aberrations were largely due to his suffering from porphyria and to the strong influence exerted on him by the Pietist movement, with its insistence on a disciplined and pious life of duty.

Inhibited by Pietist moral and religious scruples, and by temperament ill-equipped for diplomatic finesse, Frederick William I was rather timid in his foreign policy. In addition, he was reluctant to risk the army, of which he was so proud, in a major war. His attitude towards the Great Northern War during the early part of his reign was therefore rather hesitant and uncertain. He hoped to gain advantages for Prussia out of the war without having to fight. For this reason Prussia took no part in military operations against Sweden's German territories, and, for fear of becoming involved in hostilities with Sweden, he even refused to supply the allies with artillery when a combined Russian, Polish and Danish army besieged Stettin. Instead, he agreed to a scheme conceived by the Machiavellian George Heinrich, baron von Görtz, prince-bishop of Lübeck, who was administering the duchy of Holstein-Gottorp during the infancy of his nephew, Duke Charles Frederick. Görtz's plan was that a future marriage should be arranged between the young duke of Holstein-Gottorp and the tsar's daughter, Anne. The scheme also involved the sequestration of conquered Swedish German territories and their joint administration by Prussia and Holstein-Gottorp. In return for this bounty Prussia was to support the young duke of Holstein-Gottorp's claim to the throne of his bachelor uncle, Charles XII of Sweden.

The tsar approved of Görtz's plan and on the 6th October 1713 Frederick William I of Prussia concluded a treaty with the Russian general, Menshikov, whereby Prussia received in trust, until the cessation of hostilities, Stettin and western Pomerania up to the River Peene, while Russia was to have Baltic territories such as Estonia and Karelia.

Throughout the rest of the Great Northern War Prussia occupied this sequestered region which gave direct access to a major harbour on the Baltic, and from this time onwards Sweden ceased to be a German power.

The king of Denmark was very annoyed about this arrangement, since he had had designs on Sweden's German territories. He had to accept the settlement, but relations between Denmark on the one side, and Russia, Prussia and Holstein-Gottorp on the other became strained.

To give greater permanency to this temporary arrangement Frederick William I made a further supplementary secret treaty with Russia on the 12th June 1714, which guaranteed that at the conclusion of peace Prussia would obtain the territory it was occupying, while Russia could acquire Estonia and Karelia.

During the course of 1713 and 1714 Russian forces had advanced far into Finland and seized Viborg, Riga and Reval which gave Russia virtual control of the Gulf of Finland and secured St Petersburg.

On the 25th June 1714 the new and untried Russian fleet, with the tsar on board, also won an important naval victory over the Swedes at Hangö-Udd (Hanö) and captured the islands of Åland, only 24 km from Stockholm. The victory of Hanö was as great a triumph for Russia as was that of Poltava. It fulfilled Tsar Peter's dream of making Russia a naval power and showed the world that, in addition to having developed into a formidable military power, Russia had become a strong naval power as well.

The Peace of Adrianople between Russia and Turkey in June 1713 put paid to any further intrigues of Charles XII against Russia in Turkey, and he at last returned to an embattled Sweden in September 1714. Bearded and disguised he covered a distance of about 2 400 km in two weeks, mostly on horseback.

By this time several Swedish armies had been dissipated and, with annual deficits twice exceeding the national income, bankruptcy threatened. In addition, there had been a series of crop failures which could not be counterbalanced, as had been done in the past, by importing wheat from Livonia, the former granary of the Swedish empire. Moreover, an outbreak of plague had carried off about one-third of Stockholm's population. This, together with the tremendous drain on Sweden's manhood as a result of all the fighting, had caused a drop in production. So besides the worsening situation abroad, Sweden was faced with great internal problems. And yet the intransigent Charles XII stubbornly refused to consider peace.

Sweden still had enough talented statesmen and military leaders to have ended the Great Northern War on reasonably favourable terms at this stage. However, with an autocratic monarchical system, Sweden's leaders were powerless to use their initiative, and the country reaped the consequences of having an absolute monarch obsessed with war and revenge.

By 1715 every country at war with Sweden was willing to make peace, but Charles XII was determined to continue fighting until he had recovered all of Sweden's territories. This unyielding stance provoked a new alliance against Sweden and ushered in a second phase in the Great Northern War.

THE GREAT NORTHERN WAR: THE SECOND PHASE, 1715-1721

The death of Queen Anne brought about a dynastic change in Britain. In 1714 the elector of Hanover became King George I of Britain. He was anxious to acquire Bremen and Verden to link Hanover to the sea. He made a treaty with the tsar, in terms of which Russia was to have Ingria, Karelia and Estonia, while Bremen and Verden would be granted to Hanover. Denmark was prevailed upon to cede Bremen-Verden to George I, and in February 1715 George declared war on Sweden in his capacity as elector of Hanover.

In May 1715 the northern alliance was also joined, after much hesitation, by Frederick William I of Prussia. After Charles XII's return to Sweden, Frederick William had adopted an attitude of neutrality in the hope that Sweden would allow Prussia to keep on occupying Pomerania. But when negotiations with Sweden proved fruitless, Prussia declared war on Sweden on the 1st May 1715, mainly to prevent Charles XII from recovering Pomerania.

In July 1715 Charles XII attempted to save besieged Stralsund, but he failed, narrowly avoided capture, and returned to Sweden in December 1715. When in the next year Sweden lost Wismar as well to a combined Danish, Prussian and Hanoverian force, the Swedes no longer had a foothold on the south coast of the Baltic.

There was increasing division amongst Sweden's enemies, and if Charles XII had been willing to compromise and play up these differences, he might still have retrieved a part of the Swedish empire. But Charles was determined not to yield an inch of Swedish soil. It became clear that nothing less than the conquest of Sweden would bring an end to his implacability, and this placed Charles's enemies in a quandary, for Hanover and Saxony did not want Denmark to undertake this conquest and, by recovering control over the whole of Scandinavia, become too strong. However, neither Hanover, Saxony nor Prussia wished to invade Sweden themselves, and all the allies were becoming increasingly concerned about Russia's growing power.

The political balance in the north to which Europe had become accustomed since the Thirty Years War was disturbed. Clearly Sweden's eclipse as a great power was imminent and Russia was about to assume Sweden's former position as the dominant power in the north. This caused great uneasiness in most European capitals. However, none of the northern European powers was in a position to challenge Russia's domination of northern Europe. Poland, again ruled by Augustus II, was waning to such an extent that Frederick I of Prussia and Austria had already suggested a possible partition in 1710. Denmark was no match for Russia, and Prussia's new ruler, Frederick William I, wanted territories without risking anything to gain them.

Equally disturbing to the European powers was the fact that Tsar Peter was endeavouring to strengthen his position diplomatically as well by arranging marriage alliances designed to increase Russian influence in European affairs.

Before the 18th century, European royalty had been inclined to spurn marriage offers from the Russian royal house, but after Tsar Peter's military and naval victories he was able to arrange western European marriages for various relatives. His son, Alexis, married a sister of the empress of the Holy Roman empire in 1711. Two of the Tsar's nieces, Anne and Charlotte, married the duke of Courland and the duke of Mecklenburg respectively. In addition, Charles XII's nephew, Charles Frederick, duke of Holstein-Gottorp, and in direct line of succession to the Swedish throne, was being considered as a future husband for either of the tsar's two elder daughters, Anne and Elizabeth.

The tsar's dynastic ambitions even ran to achieving a *rapprochement* with France by arranging a marriage between his daughter, Elizabeth, and Louis XV. However, even a personal visit to Paris by Tsar Peter in 1717 failed to bring about the match.

The marriage alliances achieved by Peter entangled Russia in a web of dynastic intrigues and jealousies and served only to increase suspicions that Russia was trying to interfere in western European affairs, particularly those of Germany, to Russia's own advantage.

The Holy Roman emperor was very perturbed at the marriage links forged between Russia and various German principalities and was equally concerned about increasing Russian influence in Poland. The latter came about as a result of a revolt in Poland. The Polish nobles, exasperated at the depredations of Augustus's Saxon troops quartered in Poland, formed a confederation with the nobles in Livonia and rose up against Augustus II in 1715. Although Tsar Peter had reason to suspect Augustus of anti-Russian intrigues, he came to the rescue of his old ally and forced the confederates, who had appealed in vain to Sweden, the Holy Roman emperor and Turkey for aid, to make peace in October 1716. Having saved Augustus's Polish crown, Peter would not permit it to become hereditary, but insisted on the perpetuation of the system of elective kingship that would contribute so much to Poland's decline.

In April 1716 there was serious friction between Russia and its three allies, Denmark, Prussia and Hanover, over the city of Wismar. The tsar had promised the city to the duke of Mecklenburg as part of his dowry to his niece, Charlotte. However, Danish and Prussian troops had occupied the city, and they refused entry to Russian troops. To prevent an open breach with his allies Tsar Peter had to accept the situation.

The tsar became convinced that the best way to achieve a speedy end to the Great Northern War would be to land an expeditionary force on the southern shore of Sweden. A large fleet of Russian, Danish, British and Dutch ships assembled in Copenhagen in 1716, but the proposed expedition was postponed because Russia's allies showed little enthusiasm for the project.

The war dragged on amidst petty quarrels, mutual suspicions and abortive peace moves.

The Scandinavian historian Ingvar Andersson characterizes the period between 1716 and 1718 as a type of cold war, with the protagonists on either side equally determined to hold out longest.[14] Charles XII's reputation for inflexibility and stubbornness was well suited to a cold war situation. Sweden's domestic burdens and difficulties were increasing year by year, but so, too, were the problems of its adversaries, particularly Russia, and Swedish diplomacy could count on an ever-widening breach between the allied powers.

Britain was anxious to make peace with Sweden, since it needed Swedish exports, particularly iron, and was becoming increasingly concerned about Russia's inroads into northern Germany and Russian domination of the Baltic. Britain's Hanoverian king was also afraid that Swedish attacks on Norway could lead to support for the Jacobites in Scotland via the North Sea. These fears were not groundless, for the resourceful Baron Görtz had been introduced to Charles XII after the latter's return from Turkey and had won Charles's confidence to such an extent that he became the Swedish king's minister and trusted adviser. During a visit to the Netherlands, to raise a loan Görtz had intrigued with the Swedish envoy in Britain and some exiled Jacobites. Their machinations against the house of Hanover had been discovered, and, at the request of Britain, both Swedish diplomats had been imprisoned in the Netherlands in 1717. However, his Dutch captors had released Baron Görtz after six months and he had immediately set about trying to cause a breach between the allies by conducting separate negotiations with Russia and Hanoverian Britain and playing them off against each other.

Görtz was intelligent, ambitious and unscrupulous and he almost brought about a complete change in the situation of the participants in the Great Northern War. Since the unmarried soldier-king Charles XII was likely to die without an heir, Görtz expected the Swedish crown to go to his former employer and protégé, Charles XII's nephew, the young duke of Holstein-Gottorp. Görtz conceived a plot to restore much of Sweden's greatness with the aid of its powerful enemy, Russia. The proposed marriage of the tsar's daughter to the duke of Holstein-Gottorp, was part of the plan. For the rest Görtz proposed that, in exchange for ceding to Russia most of the territory Tsar Peter had conquered, Sweden should receive the full co-operation of the tsar to secure satisfactory territorial compensation at the expense of the other members of the anti-Swedish alliance.

After protracted preliminary negotiations Görtz and Russian representatives met at Lofö on the Åland islands in May 1718 to discuss the scheme. The negotiations proved difficult and the outcome was still uncertain when news was received of Charles XII's sudden death.

In the autumn of 1718 Charles XII had marched with a well-equipped army into south-western Norway and laid siege to the fortress of Frederickshald. Early on the evening of the 30th November he was inspecting the progress of operations from the trenches when he was fatally wounded in the temple by a bullet apparently fired at close range. Rumour has it that this was not a stray sniper's bullet, but an assassination. There were many people who desired Charles XII's death in order to bring about an end to the war. It has also been suggested that the assassin was an intimate of Charles XII's brother-in-law, Prince Frederick Adolf of Hesse, who hoped to succeed to the Swedish throne through his wife, Charles XII's younger sister, Ulrica Eleonora. Prince Frederick was, of course, aware of the fact that his rival for the Swedish crown, Duke Charles Frederick of Holstein-Gottorp, the son of Charles XII's deceased older sister, Hedvig Sophia, had the strong support of Charles's trusted adviser Baron Görtz. It was believed in Hessian circles that Görtz's negotiations with Russia on the Åland islands were succeeding and that Görtz would soon be presenting Charles XII with acceptable peace proposals that would finally have settled the succession in favour of the duke of Holstein-Gottorp.

With Charles XII dead, Frederick of Hesse immediately took further steps to outmanoeuvre his rival. Görtz was arrested, denounced as a hireling of the tsar and executed. To win support for herself in Sweden, Ulrica Eleonora announced her willingness to accept a constitution and renounce absolute monarchical powers. A *Riksdag* was convened and she was acclaimed *elected* queen of Sweden only to abdicate in March 1720 in favour of her husband, Prince Frederick of Hesse, who became Frederick I.

After the death of the intractable and vengeful Charles XII peace negotiations could proceed in earnest. These negotiations were facilitated by the fact that Russia's allies were becoming increasingly alarmed at the growing power and influence of Russia and that peace with Sweden could serve to check further Russian expansion.

Russia's close ties with Mecklenburg and the presence of Russian troops there alarmed the Hanoverians, since, from Mecklenburg as a base, the tsar could threaten much of northern Germany. If Russia controlled the entire Baltic coastline, Britain's source of tall pine masts, tar, hemp, and other supplies for the British navy and commercial fleet would be endangered. Britain was also concerned about Russia's growing navy, as well as the fact that the tsar was interested in the question of a Stuart restoration in Britain and had been in contact with Jacobites.

James Stanhope, the British secretary of state, hoped for a wide-ranging anti-Russian coalition of Hanover, (tacitly Britain), Sweden, Saxony, Poland, Prussia and the Holy Roman emperor.

British efforts to break up the northern alliance and isolate Russia were largely successful. A defensive alliance was made in Vienna in 1719 between Emperor Charles VI, George I as elector of Hanover, and Augustus II as elector of Saxony. The central objective was to drive the Russian forces out of Poland and prevent their return. However, this objective was not achieved mainly because Poland did not participate in the treaty, and, in fact, in February 1720 Tsar Peter I and Frederick William I of Prussia agreed to preserve Poland's existing political structure and neutrality. This was the first appearance of a policy that would unite Russian and Prussian interests for the next two centuries, namely the desire to keep Poland weak and disunited for their own expansionist ends.

In November 1719 the new Swedish government procured peace with Hanoverian Britain at the price of Bremen and Verden. Sweden also negotiated a preliminary peace agreement with Augustus of Saxony. Then, through the mediation of Britain and France, Sweden made peace with Prussia in January 1720. Sweden ceded Stettin and the neighbouring parts of Pomerania as well as the islands of Usedom and Wollin to Prussia, thus giving Prussia access to the coveted Oder estuary.

In June 1720 the mediation of Britain also brought about the treaty of Fredericksburg between Denmark and Sweden. Denmark returned all Swedish territories occupied by Danish troops, while Sweden renounced its exemption from Sound tolls and withdrew its traditional support of Holstein-Gottorp whose territories in Schleswig were given to Denmark. King Frederick I of Sweden was quite happy to renounce Holstein-Gottorp. He had no desire to aid the country of the rival claimant to the Swedish throne who had taken refuge in Russia and could count on Russian support since it was well known that the tsar intended the duke of Holstein-Gottorp to marry one of his daughters.

The various peace treaties had broken up the anti-Swedish northern alliance. Sweden had made peace with Russia's allies, but not with Russia, as the Swedes could not reconcile themselves to the loss of their Baltic provinces to Russia. A denuded Sweden now sought the backing of Britain to try and regain some of her former possessions from Russia. However, British support was to prove rather insubstantial.

King George I sent a British fleet to the Baltic, with orders to co-operate with the Swedish navy in order to force the tsar to accept British mediation in the Russo-Swedish conflict. The tsar retaliated by breaking off diplomatic relations with London.

The quick-moving, shallow-draught Russian galleys proved to be far better adapted to manoeuvring amongst the Scandinavian reefs and islands than the heavier British ships of the line. Consequently, in July 1719 a large Russian expeditionary force landed in Sweden and devastated the coast, while the advance Cossack detachment reached a point less than four kilometres from Stockholm. Faced with the South Sea Company financial crisis at home, Britain wanted to extricate itself with all possible speed from Baltic entanglements and urged Sweden to make peace.

Sweden was no longer in a position to continue the conflict with Russia. Russia used the threat of support for the duke of Holstein-Gottorp's candidacy for the Swedish throne against the insecure Frederick I and Ulrica Eleonora who, lacking heirs, were fearful of the intrigues of the Holstein party in Sweden and abroad. Russia, moreover, continued to pressurize Sweden by raids on the coasts of northern Sweden. Peace negotiations were commenced, which resulted in the Treaty of Nystädt on the 30th August 1721. This treaty assigned to Russia "for all time to come" the territories of Livonia, Estonia, Ingria, a part of Karelia with the city and district of Viborg, and the islands of Oesel and Dagoe. The expression "for all time" was an ingenious Swedish move to prevent any of the ceded territories from falling into the hands of the duke of Holstein-Gottorp.[15] Tsar Peter had endeavoured to promote and defend the interests of his future son-in-law, and his insistence that the duke should be declared heir to the Swedish throne had delayed the conclusion of the peace treaty. The tsar had later dropped this demand, but he never ceased intriguing to promote the duke's candidacy.

According to B. Pares, Tsar Peter had never intended to retain the whole of conquered Finland, but had conquered the territory in order to have something to bargain with.[16] Except for the south-eastern Finnish borderlands located strategically next to St Petersburg and the Gulf of Finland, and the portion of Karelia assigned to Russia, the whole of Finland was returned to Sweden. In addition, Russia agreed to pay Sweden 2 000 000 *Reichstaler* as compensation and to refrain from interfering with the internal affairs of Sweden, including the succession to the throne. As stated the tsar did not, however, observe the latter condition.

The Treaty of Nystädt was largely dictated by the tsar and constituted a magnificent victory for Russia. Russia was now firmly established on the shores of the Baltic and was to retain its Baltic provinces (to which Courland was later added) until the Treaty of Versailles of 1918 gave Latvia, Estonia and Lithuania a brief independence before they were swallowed up by Communist Russia during World War II.

The Treaty of Nystädt was the culmination of over twenty years of endeavour by Tsar Peter I. He dubbed the Great Northern War his "threefold school"[17] in which, fearing isolation, he had clung to allies that had repeatedly left Russia to do almost all the fighting.

As a result of the war, Russia had acquired a dominant position on the Baltic, a preponderant position *vis-à-vis* its ancient rival, Poland, became directly involved in German affairs, and emerged as a great European power.

The treaty confirmed a shift in the balance of power in northern Europe. In the Great Northern War Sweden had lost virtually all the territories it had acquired during the 17th century. Sweden's days as a great power were gone forever, and it sank to the position of a second-rate state no stronger than Denmark-Norway. Neither Scandinavian power could aspire any longer to dominion of the Baltic, but both had to live in the shadow of the Russian empire whose strength it could not match. In consequence, Swedish rulers became less involved in international disputes and confined themselves more to internal affairs. The war drastically affected the situation around the Baltic sea and the stimulation of trade, including the commerce of the Indies and China. Poland not only failed to regain the Baltic territories it had once controlled, but was further weakened by the war and found itself hemmed in by Russia, Prussia and Austria. Whereas Sweden had formerly dominated the Baltic area, Russia now controlled the eastern coast of this sea and Prussia a large part of the southern Baltic coast.

Both the War of the Spanish Succession and the Great Northern War can be seen as successful attempts to change the results of the Thirty Years War to respectively curb the powers of the two chief victors of the latter conflict, namely France and Sweden. However, because of the great discrepancy in the relative sizes, resources and populations of Russia and Sweden, the arrangements of the Treaty of Nystädt proved more durable than the settlement in western Europe after the War of the Spanish Succession. Russia's triumph over Sweden proved irreversible. Sweden had gone into the Great Northern War as the strongest power in northern Europe – an empire whose armies felt themselves invincible – while, in contrast, the powers of Europe had tended largely to disregard Russia and had held a poor opinion of its fighting capabilities. The war had reversed the position of these two states. Sweden had emerged from the war soundly defeated, with its empire irretrievably lost and contracted, to comprise only Sweden itself, thus reduced to a minor power. On the other hand, Russia, the old *terra incognito* Muscovite state, had emerged as an empire with a formidable military and naval reputation. Russia's isolation as a backward eastern state was ended for good, and the country became a leading member of the European constellation of states.

This dramatic change in Russia's status can be largely attributed to the efforts of Tsar Peter I, and that fact was recognized in Russia. The senate acclaimed him "Peter the Great" and conferred on him and his successors the title of "imperator" or emperor.

During the 18th century, Sweden would not accept the loss of its empire as final and made three attempts to change the situation. It was only towards the latter half of the 19th century that Sweden accepted the fact and, in the words of M. Roberts, adopted a new role, that of "professional neutral" and "self-appointed international *censor morum*".[18]

CHAPTER 6
THE ECONOMIC, SOCIAL AND INTELLECTUAL STRUCTURE OF EUROPE IN THE 17th CENTURY

INTRODUCTION

Frederick L. Nussbaum commented on the period 1660-1685: "In thought and in art, in science and in religion, in economy and in society, Europe in this period began a revolutionary process, the momentum of which is not even yet spent."[1] We can never underestimate the importance of the scientific revolution of the 17th century, together with its revolutionary implications for other spheres. Butterfield is of the opinion: "Since that revolution overturned the authority in science not only of the Middle Ages but of the ancient world – since it ended not only in the eclipse of scholastic philosophy but in the destruction of Aristotelian physics – it outshone everything since the rise of Christianity and reduces the Renaissance and the Reformation to the rank of mere episodes, mere internal displacements, within the system of medieval Christendom."[2] The scientific revolution therefore led to a complete revolution in the thought of western Europe. This intellectual revolution meant the secularization of thinking. D. Ogg declares: "... this period witnessed an emancipation so complete that while, at the beginning of the century, we are still in a half-medieval world, by its close, we are impressed by a comparative freedom of intellectual enquiry, and a vast range of achievements which includes the names of Bacon, Descartes, Galileo, Huygens, Newton, Boyle, Spinoza and Leibnitz. It may be doubted whether any other period of similar length can boast such giants as these."[3] What was the connection between the scientific revolution and the other aspects of life in the 17th century? The secularization of thinking went hand in hand with the work of the scientific revolution towards the end of the 17th century, but it would not seem as if secularization as such was altogether the result of scientific achievement. A certain decline in religion and morals apparently took place for other reasons. This period – the last forty years of the 17th century – was evidently one of the lowest points in the history of western Christendom.

There is another reason why it would be wrong to ascribe all the changes in thinking in this period only to the consequences of scientific discovery. Precisely at this stage, travel accounts began to have a remarkable influence on people's attitude – a retarded result of geographical discoveries and increasing acquaintance with far-flung countries. Western Europe now began to become aware of the widespread existence of peoples who had never heard of classical Greece or of Christendom. The view began to grow that the European perspective or culture, even its own religion, was not universal or central, but should be seen relatively. What was common to all cultures was the universal truth – the principles of natural religion or deism.

This critical view was nevertheless a consequence of the scientific movement. We should certainly not shut our eyes against the highly disruptive results wrought by the scientific revolution's upsetting of the authority of the Middle Ages as well as that of Antiquity.

On the other hand, we must take into account that, while the scientific movement was under way, other changes were taking place in society. Other factors were ready to combine with it to create what we call the modern world. Change was so rapid that it could be discerned with the naked eye, and the appearance of the world and of the activities of man would show greater change in one century than in the preceding 1 000 years. Sir George Clark declares: "Somewhere about the middle of the 17th century European life was so completely transformed in many of its aspects that we commonly think of this as one of the great watersheds of modern history, comparable with the Renaissance or the Reformation or the French Revolution."[4] There was a change of atmosphere between the earlier part of the century and the latter. The Puritan revolution and the Civil War brought about the sharpest break there had ever been in the continuity of English history. Virtually simultaneously a number of European countries underwent a revolutionary period, which was not altogether accidental. These revolutions differed as much in their consequences as in their circumstances and causes, but the change of the old world to the new was broadly the same everywhere. Almost simultaneously there were changes in every sphere of life. Within a few years after the beheading of Charles I and the Peace of Westphalia (1648) the lengthy economic process of the price revolution, which had increased the wealth of Europe, ended, to be followed by a new phase of restrictions and new trade conflicts between states, in particular Holland, France and England. The increase in overseas trade was the delayed result of the geographical discoveries of a much earlier period. A new world of finance was created. There is a tendency to look increasingly further back for the origins of the Industrial Revolution and the so-called agricultural revolution of the 18th century. In actual fact, these changes began to become clearly visible towards the end of the 17th century. The trend of extending the scientific method to every branch of thought was paralleled by the desire to let science serve the purposes of industry and agriculture, which was accompanied by great technological fervour. It is difficult to separate the search for pure scientific truth from inquisitiveness in connection with useful inventions. It has become a debatable issue to what extent the direction of scientific interest itself was influenced by technological requirements and interest in shipbuilding and other industries. The Royal Society in England certainly imitated Galileo's concern with the important topic of determining longitude at sea. The development of the steam engine is also a story which in fact begins in this period. These developments aside, it was probable that the possibilities of scientific experimentation themselves would be limited until certain forms of production and technique had developed in society in general.

Butterfield quite correctly says: "Indeed, the scientific, the industrial and the agrarian revolutions form such a system of complex and interrelated changes that in the lack of a microscopic examination we have to keep them all together as aspects of a general movement, which by the last quarter of the seventeenth century was palpably altering the face of the earth."5

The changes in civilization or culture which were brought about by this whole movement were localized and connected to the human activities which took place from about 1600 onwards, particularly in and between England, Holland and France. At this juncture cultural leadership was definitely moving away from the Mediterranean, where it had been for 1 000 years, to the territories further north. In France, and even more so in England and Holland, we find the power in intellectual matters at this time with the middle classes. Just as the Renaissance was associated in particular with the city-states in Italy, southern Germany and the Netherlands, where trade and economic development had created an exciting civic life, the intellectual changes of the last quarter of the 17th century were centred on the English Channel, where trade was reviving so remarkably and so much prosperity was being created. We find then an immense secularization of thought in every possible sphere in these countries in the same period, after the exceptionally strong religious character of much of the thinking of the 17th century.

We must note, however, that although the 17th century was a period of revolutionary progress in scientific and philosophical thought, it was also one of increasing absolutism in theory and practice in many countries. As such this epoch marked a division between speculative idealism and political materialism, a division which became that much more apparent as the 17th century blended into the 18th century and ultimately ended in collision in the century of revolution. The most important aspect of the Continental history of the 17th century is that, as politics grew more stereotyped, abstract thinking became more original. Stability was preserved only because the thinkers challenged everything except the authority of their rulers. The century of Descartes and Leibnitz regarded as sacrosanct those prejudices which would excite the scepticism of Voltaire and Rousseau. The gradual disillusionment of the 18th century was preceded by the trust and confidence of the 17th.

Before discussing the economic, social and intellectual life of the 17th century, it would be as well to look at that century's demography.

POPULATION

Although trustworthy figures are lacking, it has been calculated that the population of Europe in 1650 was about 100 000 000 or 18,3 per cent of the world population. There was apparently not a large increase in population in the 17th century. The real development of sanitation and medicine, trade and industry, which promoted population growth, still lay in the future. While there was a high birthrate, the mortality rate was also as high as a result of illness and famine. England, for example, was scourged by bubonic plague in the years 1603-1604, 1626 and 1664-1665, and France by famine in 1662, 1693 and 1709.

England was possibly the country with the most rapid population growth. At the beginning of the century the country was rather backward in trade and industry, but towards the end of the period it equalled or surpassed other countries in these spheres. Its population (together with that of Wales) was about 4 500 000 (one-tenth in Wales) in 1603, and 5 500 000 in 1696. Scotland possibly had 700 000 inhabitants in 1600 and 1 000 000 in 1700. Ireland's population was about 750 000 in 1700.

France had about 16 000 000 inhabitants in 1600 and by 1700 there were, according to the calculations of Vauban and others, about 19 000 000. This increase was probably the result of the annexation of new provinces, and not due to natural increase, as it was in England. Apart from these territorial gains, the population of France was most probably constant or may even have decreased, particularly as more than 200 000 Huguenots were driven from the country by the religious policy of Louis XIV.

Contemporaries agree that the population of Spain decreased during the 17th century. In 1586 the Venetian ambassador put it at 8 000 000. Spain's economic decline in the 17th century probably decreased its population to 6 000 000. The population of Portugal, too, possibly less than 2 000 000 in 1600, decreased in proportion.

As far as Germany is concerned, it can be accepted that the Thirty Years War decreased its population from roughly 21 000 000 in 1618 to less than 15 500 000 in 1648. The Great Northern War, it is surmised, similarly decimated Sweden's population by about 100 000 between 1697 and 1718.

With the exception of the Habsburg territories of Austria, where the population increased from about 5 500 000 to 7 500 000 – largely as a result of territories annexed – the other European countries showed no great population growth. Poland might have had a population of 6 000 000, while that of the Dutch republic remained at well under 3 000 000. The various territories of Brandenburg-Prussia possibly had 2 000 000 – in 1713 Prussia itself had less than 500 000. Sweden, Norway and Finland had about 1 400 000, Denmark about 600 000, and Switzerland about 340 000 inhabitants. Italy's population figure was about 13 000 000 (that of Naples about 3 000 000 in 1600, of Venice 4 850 000 in 1620, of Florence 649 000 in 1622, and of the papal states 1 880 000 in 1656). Calculating the Russian and Turkish populations is practically impossible, but it has been suggested that Russia had about 8 000 000 inhabitants in 1680.

A study of Europe's population in the 17th century is striking evidence of France's domination. Rich in natural resources, politically the most unified state on the Continent, it was numerically by far the strongest European power. By the end of the century France, with only slightly less territory, possessed about half of its present population. The Holy Roman empire was the only political unit which was numerically greater, but this was purely nominal. Such a loose association of heterogeneous states could never compete with France.

All countries, even where cities sprang up, were in essence agricultural and rural, and even in densely populated areas most people lived in small market towns, villages and hamlets, or were spread throughout the rural areas.

Throughout the century there were possibly never more than thirteen or fourteen towns with more than 100 000 inhabitants. Lisbon, Venice, Milan, Antwerp and other once large towns declined, but Paris, London, Amsterdam, Vienna and many other smaller towns flourished. It would appear that town life gradually became healthier, although sanitation remained primitive. The increased availability of hospitals and doctors by the middle of the century is possibly a partial explanation for this improvement in health. Another probable reason is that diets improved as trade increased the variety of foodstuffs in the towns. In any case, the mortality rate would seem to have decreased in English, French, German and Swiss towns between 1550 and 1720. Child mortality, however, was still high.

In the mid-16th century, Paris was easily the largest town in Europe, with a population of possibly 300 000, and while wars decreased the figure to 220 000 by 1590, it recovered rapidly and possibly stood at 500 000 by 1700. Of the provincial towns in France only Lyons had a population of more than 100 000.

London in 1631 had, according to the most trustworthy calculation, more than 130 000 people under the jurisdiction of the Lord Mayor, which possibly meant 230 000 for Greater London. By 1700 its population was considerably more than 250 000, which made it by far the largest town in England. By mid-century, Bristol was the second largest English town, with about 30 000 inhabitants. The largest Scottish town, Glasgow, had less than 12 000 inhabitants.

After Paris and London, Amsterdam was the next large city, with possibly more than 200 000 inhabitants by 1700. In the Spanish Netherlands Antwerp in 1550 had a population of about 110 000, but it declined when the Dutch closed the Schelde. The largest towns in Germany early in the century were probably Erfurt, Lübeck, Cologne, Nuremberg and Augsburg, each with possibly 40 000 inhabitants, while Hamburg had about 20 000 and Danzig and Munich possibly had a few more. The Thirty Years War probably cost Augsburg 20 000 and Munich 5 000 inhabitants, but Erfurt, Hamburg and some other towns showed a population increase. Berlin's population figure dropped to 6 000 by 1640, but rose to possibly 30 000 by 1688. In Geneva in Switzerland there were less than 20 000 inhabitants. Verona in Italy had 55 000. After the sack of Rome in 1527 its population decreased from 90 000 to 40 000, but in the 17th century it rose to above 100 000. Spanish and Portuguese towns declined, and Madrid, which possibly had 300 000 inhabitants in 1600, probably had a population of less than 200 000 by 1680.

The increase in population, if and where it occurred, was part of the larger fact that the 17th century was a period of economic progress. Europe became wealthier. The scale of economic life was growing. This change in dimension was not yet as rapid as it was to become in the 18th century, but it was gaining momentum. It was also more than a change in scale. As markets, business transactions and enterprises grew, their nature inevitably changed and therefore they underwent a change in system.

CAPITALISM

Coupled with the rising power of national states and the increasing importance of the middle classes was the development of capitalism in the Europe of the 17th century. As far as the meaning of this new system was concerned, there were naturally differences of emphasis, but its existence implied certain factors.

It meant the accumulation of wealth, the capital on which it was based; and because it had to be readily available, it also meant significant circulation of coins and a credit system for trade. Professor Earl Hamilton, the historian of the 16th century price revolution, has defined capitalism as the system which employs wealth other than property with the definite aim of procuring an income.[6]

Capitalism therefore means an economic system in which production takes place, whether of foodstuffs or consumer goods, not only to satisfy the needs of a community, but also to make a profit. Max Weber called capitalism simply "that approach which rationally and systematically pursues profit". It implies a class sufficiently wealthy, trained and competent to operate the capitalistic processes as well as a class sufficiently numerous to provide the labour for those processes. This, the manner in which the means of production are owned and the social relationships which derive from the production processes, is the meaning Karl Marx originally gave to capitalism. The profit motive entails that capitalism continually seeks larger markets and therefore needs traders who provide money to buy goods, also with the aim of making a profit by reselling them.

As such the 17th century is not a distinctive period in the development of capitalism. According to Henri Pirenne, medieval sources show the existence of capitalism as early as the 12th century. However, economic historians are agreed that 17th century capitalism is part of the period of "early capitalism", distinguishing it from the fully developed capitalism of the 19th century. Marxists sometimes call it the period of commercial capitalism, as capital was primarily employed for large-scale trade, rather than production, to produce a profit.

Increasing economic activity and wealth forced Europe to accept capitalism. The tempo of this movement was determined by the growth of the joint stock company – although increasing, it was a slow process in comparison with the subsequent period of capitalism, with its new forms of power and mass production.

The progress of 17th century capitalism was not equally rapid in every country. In fact, some countries which were pioneers of one or another aspect of capitalism had already declined and were to be replaced by others which would produce capitalistic institutions adapted to changing circumstances.

In the early 17th century, German prosperity was in a decline. Holland owned the mouth of the Rhine and traded in the Baltic sea territories, while the deterioration of the great harbour of Antwerp was an additional injury to the chief trading route of the German cities. At the other end of the route the decline of Venice and of the old connection with the east through the Mediterranean was also drastic. The new overseas routes were exploited by competing nations who had easier access to the Atlantic and a new spirit of enterprise which was not being equalled in Germany. The decline of Spain and the repudiation of the Spanish and French royal debts also hit the German banking houses. One after another they collapsed in the first part of the 17th century. Even the house of Fugger, which had a capital of 4 700 000 guilders in 1546, went bankrupt, with a debt of more than 8 000 000 guilders.

Italy and Germany therefore lost their previous leadership. Spain never developed capitalistic institutions, despite its empire, which was in any case increasingly being exploited by foreigners. Political circumstances and physical isolation prevented the spread of capitalism to the countries of the great plains of eastern Europe – Poland and Hungary. Capitalism did raise its head in Bohemia, Sweden and other countries, often with official encouragement, but its progress was nowhere more noteworthy than in the three great capitalistic countries of the century – Holland, England and France.

The 17th is possibly the most characteristically French century in Europe. As the most populous country and the one with the greatest diplomatic and military power, it took the lead in the economic changes which can be ascribed to state intervention. The growth of its army which set the standard for those of the rest of Europe was a major reason for the rise of capitalism. The revocation of the Edict of Nantes in 1685, however, did a great deal of harm to the economic prosperity of France. The flight of the Huguenots to Protestant countries was extremely important to the latter, and a milestone in their economic history. In Holland this meant that factories became general where they had previously been the exception. In England the results were less revolutionary, but still noticeable, particularly in the production of silk. Colbert's protectionist system was imitated in Europe as the standard attitude of the state towards trade and industry.

The Dutch influence was more purely economic. The Hollanders were the common freight shippers of the world, and in particular of the English, and had the best-managed merchant fleet in the world. Their ships were the cheapest to build and the best suited to their various purposes. Their trading policy was most suitable to stimulating trade and to make their country the "warehouse of the world". They did not have their equal in business management, either. The low interest rate in Holland, compared to that in England, was one of the most striking facts of the whole of the 17th century. The immigration of Hollanders to England after the Reformation played a large role; textile workers, in particular, gave this industry an impressive impetus. Then there were also fishermen, glass-makers, potters and dock labourers. It was not only in these many technical skills, however, but also in their social organization that the Hollanders in the 17th century surpassed the English by far. This also held good for life insurance and banking.

In the latter part of the 17th century, England also began to give a lead to other countries, but this was only after it had caught up with and overtaken the Dutch and French on the road to capitalistic development. This was the case in particular at the higher levels of financing and management.

The business world freed itself of some of the traditional ideas which hampered its actions. A large stumbling block in the path of free progress of capitalistic ideas and practices was the church's ban on usurious gain. In the Middle Ages there had been signs that this could be relaxed if required, but the pressure was never sufficiently strong to shake its foundations. In the 17th century a more liberal attitude in this regard steadily won ground. Bacon, in his *Essays* of 1625, regarded the ban on profiteering as utopian. The first unambiguous declaration of the modern principle on interest was made by Claude de Saumaise (subsequently known as Salmasius) in 1638-1640.

We should not, however, make too much of this. It did not mean that theoreticians had now surrendered economic matters to a reckless rationalism, or even that the spirit of the business community had grown predominantly individualistic. There were still restrictions to what was regarded as the businessman's true freedom. There was a definite and general view that certain types of profit were honourable and others morally inadmissible. Decency, the bourgeois virtue, began playing a larger role in the world. The most striking aspect – and the most easily forgotten – is that the spirit of industry was not yet competitive. The fact of competition existed, but was not regarded by writers on trade as the basis of the system.

MERCANTILISM

While capitalism as an economic system developed in the leading states of 17th century Europe, these states pursued a commercial policy known as mercantilism, a name it was later given by Adam Smith in his *The Wealth of Nations*, published in 1776.

In 1666 Colbert wrote to his nephew at the naval base at Rochefort: "Trade is the source of finance and finance is the fountain of life of war."[7] These words encompass one of the basic rules of the mercantilistic system (if it can be called that) or, in other words, of the economic presuppositions of the *ancien régime* at the international level.

The mercantilistic "system" of the 17th century has been represented by subsequent writers as much more systematic and much less intelligible than it was in fact. We must guard against accepting that it displayed anything of the consistency and uniformity which is ascribed to it in most of the short descriptions in modern works. There were many anomalies within the bounds of the "system". It was not the same thing to the French, the Dutch or the English. It was differently understood and applied by politicians and by traders. It meant one thing to the proponents of trade with East India and another to local manufacturers who were trying to compete with imported wares from the east. In the 17th century, therefore, mercantilism took on different forms in different countries and had changed somewhat in principle before the end of the century.

Even in any given period mercantilism was not the same everywhere. It developed in every state under different circumstances and with different aims. In England, under the Stuarts, as well as under the Commonwealth government, the trading classes persuaded the government to pursue a mercantilistic policy by protecting their foreign interests and passing laws against foreign competition at home. In Holland the republic's loose federal constitution hampered government action, and Dutch traders had to rely on their own initiative to achieve their mercantilistic aims. The more vigorous French policy under Colbert was launched according to a mercantilist programme which stood under strict government control and which was aimed at increasing the power of the state and its ruler. This was even more the case in Brandenburg-Prussia, when Frederick William accepted mercantilist ideas as part of his policy to turn his electorate into a powerful state. In Spain social circumstances were not favourable to mercantilistic ideas and prevented the rise of a merchant class which was strong enough to demand that the government implement such ideas.

What then, was mercantilism? Despite the differences, it is possible to define what the common features of mercantilistic policies were.

Adam Smith made a distinction between a trading and an agricultural economy and called the former "the commercial or mercantile system". He criticized the "system" of the time which preceded his own as one through which the state regulated economic matters, in the interests not of its subjects, but of the industrial and commercial minority. Although not generally accepted today, his views were long held by historians and others who damned mercantilism as a short-sighted, erroneous policy, detrimental to the state. It was, indeed, a "system" of political economy, that is, a "system" for the regulation of economic matters by the state. But mercantilists accepted that national wealth could be increased if the state encouraged its production methods and simultaneously protected them against foreign competition.

This idea held sway in the Middle Ages in every town or city, and municipal or guild regulations controlled production and protected it against competition from outside. When the individual importance of towns was diminished by the Renaissance rulers, mercantilism was aimed at a similar, national control of economic matters. The two elements of protection and regimentation – the individual was given a sheltered position in his trade, but had to submit to a system of regimentation – remained the fundamental principle of economic organization throughout the mercantilistic period. The big difference was that it was now the state, and not the town or its organ, the guild of medieval times, which accorded the privilege and protection against the non-privileged and the foreigner.

How did the rulers (such as Louis XIV who, it is alleged, had a great aversion to traders and their "disgusting" methods) find that mercantilism served their purpose? In the first place, they knew that all state activities demanded a sound economy as foundation. Their primary political need for order and security made it essential that the government should supervise every aspect of economic life. They needed money to be successful. And the state could be wealthy only if the population was wealthy and had money to yield to the state. Secondly, they needed troops for war, who had to be supplied with clothing, arms, ships, wood, pitch, tar, anchors, cables and the like, which in turn required able labourers who could manufacture the articles, as well as an efficient merchant fleet to transport the materials.

Thus it happened that the state became the vigilant and despotic guardian of the economic interests of its inhabitants. Briefly mercantilism can therefore be described as a system of control, exercised over home industries and the overseas or international trade of a state in such a manner as to produce the maximum of wealth as a power base. As the 17th century marched on, the states learned to apply their powers towards this end.

Initially there was a trend to limit wealth to the precious metals, and nations competed with one another for these valuable commodities over which Spain had had almost a monopoly in the 16th century. After the English revolution in 1688 and in the course of the war of William III against France this concept was, however, extended to include credit and paper money. Only in this way could England maintain itself against the wealthier and more populous France. In both countries the abuse of credit led to the financial scandals of the South Sea Bubble and the Mississippi Scheme. Despite these setbacks, wealth was still distinguished from money and was to be associated with the exploitation of the state's natural resources.

The inflow of precious metals to Europe from the New World – the silver mines of Mexico and Peru, and the gold mines of Brazil – and the consequent development of European currency systems certainly had an important influence on the economic policies of the leading states. Rulers needed money to pay for their households, administrators and wars; the nobility needed it to pay for their luxurious lifestyle or to extenuate their poverty; traders and industrialists needed it to provide capital for their business enterprises. Mercantilism attempted to provide it to the state in the form of bullion such as gold and silver.

Mercantilism has been criticized for its assumption that national prosperity was dependent on the accumulation of gold and silver and that it was based on the fallacy of equating gold with wealth. But, as has been said by a German writer, the mercantilists did not labour under the illusion that gold and silver were edible. The explanation for their attitude lies in the commercial circumstances of the time, when international trade was based on these precious metals. They were the major base for financial exchange. Bills of exchange had long been known, and trading in them – discounting by third parties – had begun, but bills were still employed only to represent goods, precious metals included. The capital which trade increasingly required therefore had to be obtained in solid form. It is a fact that there was a struggle between trading nations for possession of these metals and it is clear that the country which was, at any given moment, the wealthiest, was the one which had succeeded in owning the largest amount of them. There were doubtless additional reasons why the English, the French and the Dutch – who possessed no gold and silver mines of any consequence – made plans to acquire the gold and silver of America and Africa. The larger the amount of bullion a state possessed, the more its government benefited by taxes, and the greater its power grew internally and externally. The Dutch, and only they, also wanted bullion to resell at a profit. Their monetary policy was exceptional. They never prohibited the export of bullion, and from 1647 onwards export was actually permitted. In this respect, as in their tariff policy, the history of the Dutch stands as a warning against generalizations.

Mercantilism was therefore floated on the stream of precious metals from the New World. This process went through its crucial stages in the late 16th century. The price revolution which it caused was a major watershed in the fate of individuals and institutions and continued with gradually diminishing influence up to about the middle of the 17th century. Subsequently (though perhaps less so in England than elsewhere) the rise in prices was arrested, and the policies of governments and traders entered a restrictive phase during which they competed for what had already been acquired rather than opening up new sources. But the level at which the European economy stabilized was much higher than that at which it had begun in the time of Da Gama and Columbus.

Although the heroic period of Spanish-American silver exploitation was over by the middle of the 17th century, production was still significant. In addition, the activities of the Dutch and English on the west coast of Africa brought in further supplies of gold.

Despite the Spanish government's formal restrictions which limited trade with America to Spain, most of the American precious metals found their way from Spain to Holland, England and France through legal and illegal channels. The decline of Spanish industry required this country to import most of the goods needed for the American market. Before 1660 this profitable trade was virtually monopolized by the Dutch. In 1659 the Treaty of the Pyrenees gave the French preferential status in Spain. The treaty concluded in 1667 similarly opened the market of Cadiz to England. But the legal market also served as a screen for contraband trade, particularly in bullion. This was supplemented by the substantial increase in smuggling and piracy in the West Indies.

As a result of these activities, Holland, England and France were well supplied with money. Gold from Africa and silver from Spain flowed to Amsterdam in prodigious amounts. Every year between thirty and forty Dutch vessels carried silver from Spain to Holland which, according to estimates, represented up to half of the production of the American mines. According to an official survey in 1680, precious metals to the value of 20 000 000 *livres* entered France in 1679. Because of the primitive nature of the French financial institutions, much of this was handled by Amsterdam, rather than Paris or Lyons.

Holland and England also benefited by the immigration of refugees who had money. Those who came to England from Portugal and France were apparently particularly well supplied. It was, however, rather the development of a free market in money and bullion in Holland from 1647 onwards and in England from 1663 onwards which endowed these countries with the predominance they enjoyed in turn. It has been calculated that the inflow of precious metals into England rose from about £60 000 per year in the first few years after the Restoration to about £373 000 annually between 1667 and 1680.

Mercantilism created barriers against the kind of contact with other countries which was deemed to be undesirable. Nobody, however, went as far as to think that all contact with other countries was detrimental. Immigration and trade were welcomed. The "system" was one of regulation and even encouragement, not of abolition of trade. But it was based on a sharp differentiation between trade which was advantageous and that which was not.

According to one theory, only such foreign trade was profitable as led to an increase in the amount of precious metals in a country. The most desirable kind of foreign trade was export, in exchange for which the buying country shipped gold or silver; import which required payment in precious metals to foreign countries was the most undesirable. Between these two simple extremes there were a number of types of more complex and indirect transactions which were favoured or discouraged according to their ultimate effect on the national supply of money.

The chief prize for which mercantilist states competed was a favourable balance of trade. Mercantilism viewed trade in terms of competition or even war between states. The more precious metals a state obtained, the less there were for another. A favourable trade balance, it was believed, was the best way to ensure the desired inflow of treasure. A 17th century advocate of mercantilism, Thomas Mun, declared in his *England's Treasure by Foreign Trade*, published in 1664: "The ordinary means to increase our wealth and treasure is by foreign trade, wherein we must observe this rule: to sell more to strangers yearly than we consume of theirs in value." This meant, he continued, that the foreigner had to make good a trade deficit by paying in precious metals.[8]

The chief motivation of mercantilism was therefore the pursuit of power. If we take this into account, mercantilism was not such an extraordinary policy as is often assumed. The free trade episode of the 19th century was perhaps no more than a deviation from the normal trend. In the 20th century, with our foreign exchange control, regulation of imports and exports, our strong and weak currencies, we have returned to a more normal system with a view towards providing security as well as a high standard of living.

THE TRADING COMPANIES

Trade enviousness was initially expressed mainly in the passing of protectionist laws or the signing of advantageous treaties. Some of the laws, such as the English Shipping Acts and the protective tariffs of Colbert, went as far towards exclusivity as was then possible, but there was a further kind of commercial hostility apart from mere legislation – the large trading companies.

These companies of the 17th and 18th centuries expressed the requirements of a new era in trade. They were chartered joint stock trading companies which were operated by private enterprise, but – as a sign of the growing involvement of government in trade – were created by the state. The states created these companies by charter, as they could not themselves participate in trade. Trade could not exist without state support, but the companies were owned and managed by private enterprise because private individuals were still the only source of energy which such large undertakings required. Government aid was necessary particularly for the awarding of monopolies. It was the continuation of the medieval system of privilege; the state gave certain persons, and these persons exclusively, the right to operate within certain business sectors. In England and Holland the state sometimes took the initiative, but the major driving force for the establishment and extension of trading companies came from the commercial classes. The distinguishing feature of the French companies was their close dependence on the state.

When these three nations, which were the economic leaders of the 17th century, began developing a fairly far-flung trade, new kinds of trading organizations came into existence, broadly similar to, but also different from, their medieval forms. The joint capital enterprise established itself in the 17th century as the form for large-scale trade because of the change in the scale and extent of trading activities.

There were joint stock companies in Germany and Italy in the Late Middle Ages, but those of the 17th century were not their continuations. The joint capital principle appeared in England for the first time with the establishment of the Russia company and the first Africa company in 1553. From the legal point of view it was an amalgamation of the principle of the guild or association with the principle of partnership. Common measures were still taken, as was the case with the medieval guilds (defence against armed attack, for example), but to this was now added the new task of trading in concert. The members of the association were now also partners in an enterprise.

These companies, however, differed greatly in organization – many were rather like a modern joint stock company which divides profits amongst its shareholders in proportion to the capital which they contribute, while others were loose associations of traders who each traded for their own accounts.

The companies exported locally manufactured goods in exchange for raw materials which were not available in the exporting country, or which could be further processed. Amongst the raw materials sugar, tobacco, and later, cotton, were of particular importance, and for a long time spices were as sought-after as precious metals. The Dutch succeeded in almost totally monopolizing the spice trade and obtained their supplies from the East Indies. Later in the century the relative importance of spices declined, however, chiefly because, as new grasses and root plants enabled farmers to keep their cattle throughout the winter, the quality of meat improved and there was less need for spices.

In 1602 the Dutch established the Dutch East India Company. It operated on a far larger scale than its English counterpart which had been established two years earlier. By 1661 the DEIC was allegedly capable of equipping a fleet as large as that of France, and the company had an army of more than 10 000 men. From 1605 to 1648 the annual return on its capital was 22 per cent.

Of the many English companies the East India Company was the largest. These companies financed British shipping and colonization, developed and consolidated far-off foreign trade, arranged credit and practised the manufacture of new goods. They broke down the quasi-monopoly of trading capital as such, i.e. they enabled people other than merchants to invest their money in trade and thus enlarged the sources of available capital. They brought together various classes of people in their enterprises and were therefore in a position to combine the technical acumen of the merchant with the political influence of important personages.

The structure of the French companies differed greatly from that of other companies. They were artificial creations by the government, in which the kings and those around them took large blocks of shares. Colbert exerted administrative pressure to obtain capital for his companies. The king's financial advisers were heavily involved with their management. The monopoly was stricter than in Holland, which in turn was stricter than in England. The French companies were hampered by political interference, for instance those of Richelieu were not allowed to have Protestant members. Only in France were there cases of companies which handed over part of their functions to the crown. The Levant Company, established in 1676, had the most favourable area for French enterprise, but failed as a result of poor trading methods and in 1690 was given to an individual merchant. The relatively weak performance of the French companies in the 17th century was caused by their failure to use private enterprise, as did the English and the Dutch, and finally by the lack of a sufficiently viable trading community. France overwhelmingly demanded contributions to its war efforts from its inhabitants, with little left over for this less glorious work. The bourgeoisie, increasingly more interested in *rentes* (loans to the government) and *charges* (purchased posts) generally evaded the efforts of Colbert's agents to raise capital for the companies. Not one of the French companies was successful. The abortive East India Company was established in 1604. Between 1626 and 1642 Richelieu established a group of companies for Africa, Asia and America. They declined one by one, but all either revived or were imitated in the course of France's great mercantilistic period – that of Colbert – which was at its zenith from 1665 to 1673. The French East India Company and West India Company were both established in 1664 and the Company of the North in 1669. The wars of Louis XIV, however, did all these companies much harm. The Company of the North was ruined by the Dutch War of 1672; the East India Company suffered much in the wars from 1691 to 1713, which were chiefly wars of trade; and the Africa Company was practically destroyed by the struggle against the Algerians in 1682. Their heritage for the 18th century can therefore not be compared to that of the English and Dutch companies.

AGRICULTURE AND INDUSTRY

Mercantilism emphasized the importance of higher production, particularly in industry, but also in the agriculture of a country. Agriculture had to ensure that a country was self-sufficient and had no need for imported food, but manufactured goods were potentially the best sellers abroad. A flourishing industry had further advantages. It could support a larger population – and the state needed people and money – it enriched the important merchant class and it solved social problems such as poverty, unemployment and popular dissatisfaction, which were a threat to the peace and security of a state. Governments therefore encouraged exports with tariffs, export premiums, monopolies and other techniques. Colonies which were valuable for their supply of raw materials as well as being markets for manufactured products were forced to satisfy the needs of the mother country.

The efficiency of the various forms of mercantilism in 17th century Europe is evidenced by the commercial and industrial progress of the time. Expansion was slow in comparison with what was to follow, but it did prepare the way for subsequent development. It also took place without the stimulating circumstances of the previous century. As has been pointed out, the flow of bullion from the New World dried up in due course. There was no inflation to promote economic activity. International commercial competition, however, was on the increase.

By far the largest part of every country's population was still involved in agriculture, and 17th century farming was still essentially medieval. The changes which occurred influenced only a tiny part of rural Europe. In some countries the manor, as a feudal unit, was involved in the switching from payment by services to monetary payment, but as an agricultural unit it remained largely undisturbed.

France was one of the countries in which agricultural production remained at a low level. There were famines which cost the lives of thousands. Times of scarcity were exacerbated by transport problems and internal customs barriers. Food production was insufficient as a result of poor farming methods, and possibly as much as two-fifths of arable land were not being used. Feudal obligations and increasing taxes deprived the small farmer of the capital required to improve his activities. Even more important was that the nobility's indifference towards their estates deprived France of an enlightened land-owning class which was prepared to improve agricultural production. In addition, the urban bourgeoisie, which acquired a great deal of property, were no improvement on the nobility as landowners. Neither Sully nor Colbert could reform French agriculture. It is, in fact, possible that, instead of an increase in agricultural production, much of the land was left untilled.

Spanish agriculture was stagnant to an even greater degree. As has been discussed elsewhere, the *Mesta*, which monopolized sheep-farming, participated in the general decline of the Spanish economy until it was virtually bankrupt in 1685.

In comparison with agriculture, industry in the 17th century moved further away from medieval methods. The nation was replacing the town as economic unit, and supervision of industry passed from the guild to the state.

The usual form of industrial organization was the cottage industry where capitalistic middlemen provided raw materials and sometimes machinery to craftsmen who worked at home. In the course of the century many industries moved from the towns to rural areas to evade the limitations imposed by the guilds and to be closer to the two increasingly indispensable sources of power – wood and water. It was one of the century's most distinctive features that industries after the Middle Ages tended to be concentrated at the more favourable localities. New industries were initiated in rural areas to replace old ones. In the Spanish Netherlands this occurred before and at the beginning of the century. In France, Germany and England, too, rural areas gained at the cost of the towns. The metal industries with their developing techniques needed more water and fuel than was available in towns. Medieval industry and industry of the century of steam, the 18th, were predominantly urban. The 17th century was therefore an interim period in which the scattered factories and cottage industries existed along the rivers of Yorkshire or in the Silesian forests. This concentration had, however, not advanced much by the end of the century. It was not in accordance with the strongest tendency of the industrial geography of the 17th century, namely that of a national industry.

The "putter out" (Marchand, Verleger) who became of increasing importance in the 17th century, sought his labour in rural areas, far from the restricting regulations of the guilds in the towns. The hosiery or frame-knitting industries in England are a good example of the de-urbanizing effect of the practice of "putting out". By 1727 London had 2 500 frames, and the provinces 5 500; a few decades later the hosiery industry had virtually disappeared from the city.

In general 17th century industry did not adopt the factory system. At the end of the century, the cottage industry system held sway in the manufacture of most products. There were, however, certain industries in which the increasing costs of technical processes, raw materials or transport demanded large capital investments, which were most profitably operated by large enterprises. Spinning and weaving remained cottage industries, but by the end of the century some of the finishing processes in textile manufacture, such as dyeing, were being undertaken by large-scale organizations. In 1700 a wool firm in Glasgow had 1 400 workers and one in Saptes in France employed 800. Other industries which were increasingly organized by capitalism in this manner included printing works, saw-mills, shipyards, breweries and distilleries, manufacturers of soaps and candles, tanneries and various chemical and dyeing enterprises. New and necessarily large enterprises which were chiefly dependent on colonial raw materials, such as sugar, tobacco and cotton, also adopted the factory system and were inevitably based in the "colonial" ports – first Amsterdam, then London, Bordeaux, Marseilles and Le Havre.

Manufacture of textiles was 17th century Europe's chief industry. Up to 1700 East Anglia, and particularly Norfolk, was the largest English wool area, although Yorkshire grew steadily in importance. The Dutch wool industry was centred on Haarlem and Leyden, and the French centres were Amiens and Rouen, while Lyons, Nîmes and Tours were important for the silk industry. Early in the century Holland had the largest cotton industry in Europe, but by 1641 it was Manchester, and in the later years of the century England took the lead in cotton manufacture. It was, however, not yet a large industry: at the beginning of the 18th century, England was importing less than 2 000 000 pounds of cotton annually.

The iron industry increased in importance throughout the century. The Swedish iron industry grew rapidly and became the largest in Europe. Other metals mined in Europe included silver, tin and copper in Sweden, Saxony, Bohemia, Tyrol and Spain.

Increasing maritime activity created a steadily growing demand for wood which, in the course of the century, threatened to become problematic in the three great shipbuilding countries – Holland, France and England. Holland had no suitable indigenous wood and obtained it from Germany and the Baltic. Supplies of oak and pine in England were depleted by the 1680s, and wood was therefore imported from Courland, eastern Prussia and Scandinavia. Even the Navigation Acts were amended to enable foreign ships to bring wood to England.

The shortage of wood in these countries forced them to make increasing use of coal for fuel, and the production of coal increased throughout the century. Up to this stage coal had not been generally employed in Europe on a large scale for domestic or industrial use and it was therefore not mined to any great extent. The most important coal fields were in Northumberland, Yorkshire, Saxony, Silesia, and the Ruhr, which would all later increase in importance.

Industrial production of articles of silk, glass and other materials increased to satisfy the demands of the increasingly wealthier middle classes. Mounting production was achieved mainly by the gradual acceptance of previously developed techniques. Glass and tin manufacture, the refining of silver and gold with the aid of mercury, the saw-mill and the stocking frame serve as examples. Shipbuilding improved with experience, and the number of merchant ships increased radically. The telescope, developed by 1608, made a difference to navigation, and map-making gradually improved. At the beginning of the century Edward Wright discovered how maps could be drawn on Mercator's projection. In 1665 Kircher for the first time indicated ocean currents on a chart. The making of land maps was improved and a great variety were in use during the century. There were not, however, any great industrial inventions comparable to the printing press in the 15th century or firearms in the 16th.

The sum total of inventions and improvements (such as dyes, various kinds of glass, the megaphone, Turkish paper, fire hoses, fountain pens) looks scanty when seen against the general dynamism of the century, and needs explanation. Few of the inventions were derived from the scientific research for which the century is known. The one outstanding example of an invention by a great scientist is the improvement of watches by Huygens. Even in the metal industry, and still more in other industries, inventions were made chiefly by craftsmen and not by scientists. An example is William Lee, the famous inventor of the stocking frame. Savery, one of the two men who perfected the steam engine shortly after the end of the century, can be classed as a scientist, but he is an exception. Business and science were still worlds apart. Businessmen kept their knowledge to themselves, and there were many trade secrets. The most efficient contact between industry and the intellectual development of the time was not in technique, but in organization, such as in insurance and increased production.

There were also forces outside the industrial world which were antagonistic to technical development. In some cases states passed laws against technical development. Where machines threatened to create unemployment, the state sometimes took countermeasures, as in the case of the English proclamation against machinery for the manufacture of needles and bronze buckles. The same happened to the "devilish invention", the ribbon loom, which was prohibited. Protectionism was a reason for such prohibitions. For example, in the interests of the established textile industry – and of the importers of Indian goods – calico printing was for a time forbidden in France as well as England.

Although the growth of industrial production in Europe in the 17th century has at times been called the "first Industrial Revolution", it was, in terms of technical inventions and new forms of energy, not comparable to the great Industrial Revolution of the late 18th century. Still, the first was a precursor of the second. The 17th century "Industrial Revolution" made such increasing demands that new methods of development had to be found by the second Industrial Revolution.

EXPANSION OF TRADE AND COMMERCIAL COMPETITION

At the beginning of the 17th century the Dutch handled a large part of the total volume of European trade. The war against Spain destroyed Antwerp's prosperity, and the Dutch blockaded the Schelde. This opened the way for the rise of Amsterdam in commercial importance, to make it the entrepôt between the two old European trading routes of northern Europe and southern and western Europe.

To enable them to handle this trade, the Dutch had, by the middle of the 17th century, built up an enormous merchant fleet. Contemporaries differ on its size. Sir William Petty (1623-1687) thought it twice the size of England's and nine times that of France. In 1665 Colbert calculated that the Dutch had 15 000 or 16 000 ships out of a world total of 20 000, as against the 500 or 600 of France.

Early in the 17th century they developed the economic institution of capitalism to promote their overseas trade; their trading and shipping activities previously had been operated along primitive capitalistic lines. As early as about 1600 Amsterdam had already replaced Antwerp as Europe's largest financial centre. (London did not begin to take the lead before about 1700.) The Bank of Amsterdam was established in 1609, and the Amsterdam Exchange was founded in the same year to enable merchants to do business in goods as well as shares.

The Dutch republic was one state which remained solvent throughout the century. Although it had a large debt, it never lost the confidence of lenders. Between 1640 and 1655 the interest rate on loans dropped from six and one-sixth per cent to as low as four. Even in 1672, during the war which had such bad consequences for French and English credit, Holland could obtain money to pay for mercenaries, although French troops had overrun the country. Early in the 18th century, Holland was to experience serious financial problems, but in the 17th century there were no visible signs of this.

The republic was a merchant state, the lending class being the same as the regent class, the ruling oligarchy. They were not passive *rentiers*, but active businessmen whose business was loans to the state. As lenders and as businessmen they did business with people they knew. This was the most important point of all. Sound public finance does not easily come into being except on a basis of sound private finance. The general business world of Amsterdam was the best example in the whole of the 17th century of such a healthy business community. The Bank of Amsterdam played a leading role in the organization of European financing and credit from the start. It was never an issuing bank, like the Bank of England; its function was only to provide the mechanics for the best possible use of the bullion system. The exchange was essentially a personal meeting place for businessmen, and for all kinds of business purposes. One part of the exchange was trading in shares. It began with the shares of the large trading companies and speculation, not with the transfer of investments. By the end of the century the technique of speculation had to a large extent developed into its modern form ("bulls" and "bears", etc.).

With their large merchant fleet the Dutch supplemented their European trade by acquiring a share of the overseas trade over which Spain and Portugal claimed a monopoly. The Dutch took the lead in the attack on the commercial position of Spain and Portugal. Although England's seamen in the time of Elizabeth I had been the first to challenge the claims of the Spanish empire, the Dutch made the first successful attacks and, until about 1650, they were the more determined adversaries. Where the Spanish empire (which had taken over the Portuguese one) was still the only existing colonial empire at the beginning of the century, Spanish and Portuguese colonial growth had come to an end by mid-century. The big trading companies which had conquered the natives of the East Indies and the West Indies and on the coast of Africa, warred with one another. For many years an informal state of war existed between the Dutch, Portuguese and English on the seas where the Dutch and English had fought the Portuguese and Spanish in the previous century. The various governments were loath to involve themselves with the clashes between their merchants. For many years they gave them surreptitious aid by supplying arms and diplomatic support, but they had other matters to consider in the context of European alliances and hostilities. By about the middle of the century one of the great revolutions in European policy took place. First the conflict between the Dutch and the English, and then, a few years later, that of the Dutch and the Portuguese, came to a head in a European war. Throughout the last part of the 17th century, economic and colonial conflicts were the leading factors in the prelude to European wars. The wars of the 17th century, when they were not religious or dynastic, can be regarded as the logical result of an economic system which was nationalistic, exclusive, competitive or aggressive.

Colonial aggressiveness was a natural result of Dutch commercial enterprise and their struggle for independence. As they were at war with Spain, they also acted with less reserve than other countries. They insisted that the peace of 1609 had allowed them to continue their eastern trade. They began to fit out fleets for the East Indies and the West Indies. In the first half of the 17th century, Dutch colonization followed. With their small population, the Dutch obtained colonies to promote trade, and not to settle themselves overseas. Their greatest desire was to drive the Portuguese out of the Malay archipelago and to seize the spice islands. Early in the century Java, Sumatra, Borneo and the spice islands became Dutch. From 1616 onwards settlements were established in India, and in 1658 the conquest of Ceylon was completed. Jan Pieterszoon Coen, the great organizer of Dutch authority in the east, founded Batavia in 1619 as the seat of a governor-general and the Dutch capital of their empire there. The Dutch extended their trade to China and Japan and took possession of Formosa.

In the early days they were constantly opposed by the English who also wanted a share of the Portuguese trade, but the massacre at Amboina in 1623, which led to the destruction of the English trading post in the Moluccas, caused the English East India Company to withdraw from the Malay archipelago to India. The Dutch built up as much trade in Malaysia as they had in Europe. Not only were large dividends earned, but a reserve fund of about 20 000 000 guilders was built up.

In 1633 possession was taken of St Helena, and in 1652 the Cape of Good Hope became a victualling station for Dutch merchant ships.

In the Spanish and Portuguese empires in America the Dutch, in imitation of the English, raided settlements, impounded ships and smuggled slaves. In 1621 they launched their West India Company and settled in Guyana and along the Amazon. Pernambuco was possessed in 1628, threatening the Portuguese occupation of Brazil. In the same year Piet Hein captured the Mexican silver fleet and in 1639 Van Tromp defeated a Spanish armada near the English coast, destroying Spanish sea power as the Dutch had already done with that of the Portuguese. For some time the Dutch were almost as powerful in the West Indies as they were in the East Indies.

Meanwhile they had also established themselves in North America. They founded the colony of New Netherlands in 1623 and in 1655 they conquered the adjacent colony, New Sweden, on the Delaware.

By the middle of the 17th century the Dutch republic had an empire many times greater than the country itself, and trade which brought it a great deal of wealth.

The extent of the success of this small nation, however, made it difficult to retain these acquisitions. In the second half of the century Dutch expansion came to an end and they began to lose colonies. Portugal, having regained its independence from Spain, re-established its control of Brazil in 1654 after a long struggle. Formosa was yielded to Chinese refugees in 1661, and in 1664 the English conquered the colony of New Netherlands.

It was, in fact, the rise of England as a commercial and colonial power, coupled with the struggle against Louis XIV, which contributed the most to ending Holland's supremacy.

During the reign of the Stuarts in England (after 1603), financial matters went terribly awry after Elizabeth I had been the one solvent ruler of her time. James and his successors found themselves in the same problematic situations as did the French and Spanish kings and no more than temporary improvements were made up to the fall of the Stuart monarchy. During the reign of William III (1689-1702) trade developed rapidly and English finances were conspicuously well managed. Strengthened by the creation of the Bank of England, the constraints of the struggle against Louis XIV were successfully survived and England was firmly on its way towards creating an empire.

The first successful colony on the east coast of North America was founded in 1607, and in the course of the following 125 years the thirteen colonies were established there. In the West Indies the Spanish monopoly was successfully challenged under the early Stuarts. In 1623 St Christopher was the first island to be settled by the English. The uninhabited island of Barbados was occupied in 1627, and further settlements followed in the Bahamas, Nevas, Montserrat, Antigua and the British Honduras, while the Commonwealth government conquered Jamaica in 1655. These tropical colonies became permanent residences for English families; an early reason for British authority superseding that of the Dutch as colonizers.

The other area in which the English were active was India. The transfer of efforts of the English East India Company to India after the massacre of Amboina had the consequence that there were three chief settlements at the end of the 17th century – Bombay on the west coast, Madras or Fort St George on the east coast, and Calcutta or Fort William in Bengal. The English had neither the power nor the will to imitate the achievements of the Dutch there. They did not get involved in local matters and limited themselves to trade. This policy was not dropped until the next century, and then only after the English triumph in European waters, without which the whole East Indian effort would have failed.

Initially France fared no better than Spain in adapting itself to the problem of the new developments, namely the national control of money instead of supply by private finance houses. By 1575 the French king could no longer raise loans, and in 1580 existing obligations were repudiated. Italian creditors, however, carried the country until Sully, a really remarkable financier during the reign of Henry IV, could begin to put matters right. After him there was a period of confusion, during which the old system (loans from outsiders), which could not survive the state bankruptcy of 1648 and the civil war of the Fronde, was destroyed.

Colbert was the man of the new system. He strove for centralization, saving, increased income from taxation and payment of debts. His financing could not, however, counter the increasing costs of the wars. The Dutch War of 1672 forced him to raise new loans and to create new government posts for sale. None the less, he instituted financial reforms. In 1674 he began to obtain money directly from lenders amongst the French public, without the aid of middlemen, and thus it cost him less. By 1680, however, he expressed the opinion that the state's credit should not be exploited any further, and when he died in 1683 state credit was compromised far beyond its capacities. The remaining enterprises of Louis XIV were undertaken against a background of growing bankruptcy.

In the 17th century France had no true stock exchange. There was no trade in the shares of the French companies, partly because they largely employed the capital of the nobility, who were not merchants themselves, and who did not have the same contact with practical matters as the English investment class.

After the French, like the English, had started to make voyages of discovery in American waters in the 16th century and had begun undertaking commercial transport and fishing, they, with the support of the government and after the ending of the religious wars, began to pay attention to overseas expansion. French activity in the North Atlantic ocean dates from the early 17th century. In 1605 a group of French Huguenots founded Port Royal and Acadia – which remained French throughout the 17th century – and in 1608 Champlain established a settlement at Quebec. This was little more than a trading and mission station. The government made no effort to encourage colonization. There was no motive for large-scale emigration and the Huguenots were excluded from the colonies. In 1627 Richelieu gave charters to two new companies – the Company of New France and the Company of the Islands of America – which would have the monopoly of trade and colonization in the areas of the St Lawrence and the Lesser Antilles respectively. In the West Indies, Martinique and Guadeloupe (1635) and various smaller islands were occupied. Despite – or possibly as a result of – excessive state control, New France languished. When Colbert came to power, French colonial enterprises were given a new lease of life. The possibilities of New France were realized and the West Indian islands in French hands were important to Colbert's plan to deprive the Dutch of their sea trade. He drew up a grandiose plan to consolidate all the French colonies in the New World under one big company which would be controlled by the crown. The French West India Company (like the East India Company) was therefore established in 1664, with a monopoly over trade and shipping from Newfoundland to the Amazon, and with the intention to participate in the slave trade of West Africa. In 1678 the powers of the company were transferred to the crown, which excercised direct rule in the colony by means of military governors and civil intendants. In 1682 La Salle explored the Mississippi up to its mouth in the Gulf of Mexico, formally took possession of it in the name of the king and tried to establish a settlement in Louisiana (occupied in 1697). His activities gave the French the possibility of connecting Louisiana with Canada through a series of forts, which would mean that the English colonies on the coast would be cut off from the interior. By 1700 French possessions in North America stretched from Acadia and the Gulf of St Lawrence to the Gulf of Mexico, while in the north there were trading posts as far as Hudson Bay. But along these borders the French occupation, despite Colbert's encouragement of emigration, remained thin and the possessions were never consolidated as were the thirteen English colonies along the Atlantic coast.

The French were firmly established in the West Indies. Colbert would also have liked France to compete with Dutch trading in the East Indies, even destroy it, but little was achieved in the 17th century. After the founding of the East India Company in 1664, when the French began participating in eastern trade, two islands in the Indian Ocean, Bourbon (Réunion) and Ile de France (Mauritius), were occupied as naval bases. As the Dutch brooked no interference in the East Indian islands, the French entered the English "sphere of influence" by establishing trading posts at Pondichéry, south of Madras, and Chandernagar (1688) in Bengal. The Dutch took Pondichéry in 1698, but the Treaty of Rijswijk of 1697 forced them to return it. What was done was less than Colbert had hoped for, and the insufficient funds of the East India Company limited its activities. The French had made a start in India, but not much more.

The immediate causes of the overseas Anglo-French struggle can be traced back to the period when the Stuart restoration in England took place in the person of Charles II and the young King Louis XIV took over complete control of France.

After 1650 the Stuarts proclaimed their orders-in-council and the English Navigation Acts to eliminate the Netherlands from carrying the English empire's freight. The declining power of Holland and the increasing military and commercial power of France, however, led to the latter becoming England's most important competitor. Under the later Stuarts England was a French satellite, but in spite of their kings' subservience to France, English statesmen began having reservations about the French expansion of power which threatened the balance of power in Europe and even the safety of England. The lot of the Netherlands (the Dutch War 1672-1678/1679) had also always been of prime importance to England, and the early wars of Louis XIV caused concern about French aims in that territory. The French threat to England's lead in the colonial and commercial fields was to a large extent the result of Colbert's economic policy. When he began employing mercantilistic means to promote French trade and industry, for example by creating a tariff wall around the colonies, it led to a tariff war with the Dutch, which provoked a reaction in English trade circles and, in 1678, obliged the government to stop trade with France altogether for three years. It also caused intensified French-English colonial competition. Colbert's efforts to increase the number of overseas settlements, to expand the existing ones and to develop their resources, as well as to acquire for France a part of the trade of Africa and India, was a serious threat to English interests. In North America the bones of contention were particularly the fisheries along the coasts of Acadia and Newfoundland and the fur trade in the interior, which was also connected to problems of Indian politics. From the 1620s onwards there were frequent clashes. In the decade before 1688 a kind of balance of power seemed to prevail, but during the reign of James II relationships rapidly deteriorated and everything pointed to the probability of a French-English colonial clash.

The struggle began in 1689 with the War of King William, which involved England in the European struggle against Louis XIV. This meant that Continental wars were now also being fought at sea and in the colonies. This was a phase of the War of the Augsburg Alliance (1687-1697). The extent to which the English and Dutch fleets were weakened was evidenced by the French victory at Beachy Head (1690). Louis XIV did not, however, fully exploit his achievement. He spent more money on his armies and allowed his enemies to regain control of the sea (Cherbourg, La Hogue), although French privateers continued to do serious damage to English trade. The struggle in the colonies was as indecisive as that in Europe. The colonial clash was still purely a side-show, and neither country could spare forces for large-scale colonial enterprises. In America it was left largely to the colonists to settle their quarrels amongst themselves. In India there was a local agreement to keep the peace between trading posts, although the Dutch had captured Pondichéry. The Treaty of Rijswijk only restored the *status quo ante bellum*.

At the beginning of the 18th century the War of Queen Anne (the American aspect of the Spanish War of Succession) was to follow, which brought about England's indisputable superiority at sea.

THE SOCIAL STRUCTURE

The expression *ancien régime* is used for the social state system resulting from the reforms of the 16th century, consolidated and applied in the 17th century, and finally effaced by the revolutions of the years 1789-1848.

The 17th century inherited the moral and intellectual climate of the Renaissance and Reformation. These did not bring about a decisive change in society, but did strengthen the position of the rulers. As old ideas and the once powerful feudal and religious principles disappeared, people looked to their worldly rulers for security and maintained their prerogatives. The two classic 17th century authors who advocated the unlimited authority of the ruler on the basis of efficacy – and not of the Old Testament – were Thomas Hobbes (1588-1679) and Benedictus de Spinoza (1632-1677).

Monarchical government reigned supreme in the 17th century. It was a period of increasing absolutism in the theory and practice of government. Royal supremacy was characterized by a strongly developing bureaucracy of ministers, courtiers, officials and other important servants, as well as by an increase in royal expenditures on entertainment, buildings and patronage of the arts. Europe could bear these expenses as a result of its expanding economy. The acquisition of wealth, however, preserved society in its existing forms without causing great structural change. Some signs of resistance did, however, become visible in the 17th century, and there were protests by the Spanish *Cortes*, English Puritans and French *frondeurs* against expenditures in times of peace and war.

Although 17th century monarchy was frequently irresponsible and despotic, it saved Europe from a worse fate by keeping the aristocracy in check. The aristocracy or second estate as a ruling entity was the only possible alternative to the monarchy. The nobility imitated the spendthrift ways of the Renaissance princes, but this occurred at a time when their financial position was worsening. Unminted gold and silver from the New World caused rapid price increases. The nobility, as chief vassals of their feudal princes, still had to pay the customary dues which had in many cases been fixed centuries before, and their land consequently became less profitable. Many of them were therefore facing impoverishment.

Nowhere was this more true than in France where the nobility (calculated by Vauban at the end of the reign of Louis XIV at 200 000 or one per cent of the population) took advantage of the religious wars of the 16th century in attempting to take control of the crown and its revenues. Their failure to do so left them without work or a source of income in the 17th century. Many of them practically severed their connections with the land; estates were sold or mortgaged to the wealthy bourgeoisie. As the growth of royal absolutism deprived them of their feudal powers they made last-ditch efforts during the reigns of Richelieu and Mazarin to save themselves, but their poverty was largely responsible for their failure. Frequently forced to lead a hand to mouth existence, ruined by an extravagant way of life and debts, often obliged to pocket their pride and to marry into wealthy bourgeois families, not even the nobility could prevent the rising power of the monarchy. When they resisted, it was not so much to regain political power as to obtain gifts, privileges, pensions, offices and other sources of income from a weak government. When government was strong, as under Richelieu and even more so under Louis XIV, obedience to the crown was their only choice. Under Louis XIV, with his *intendants* who enforced royal authority in the provinces, the aristocracy found that only attendance at the court in Versailles and careful cultivation of the king's favour was financially beneficial. The once rebellious French aristocracy therefore became royal courtiers chiefly for economic reasons.

Generally speaking, the French nobility by the 17th century no longer held the predominant economic position which they once had as a result of their ownership of most of the land. Nominally they were still the lords of the land, which enabled them to raise feudal monies, but real ownership was limited to their demesnes, generally rented by tenants and seldom personally cultivated. In the western provinces there was a greater tendency for the nobility to retain their land, whereas the nobility of the eastern provinces mostly gave it up. In Burgundy it was about 35 per cent, in Picardy and Artois about 30 per cent and in Dauphiné about 12 per cent. Around the towns they, like the peasant farmers, yielded much of their land to the bourgeoisie.

In other countries – such as Spain and Denmark, and also most of the German states – the aristocracy also became politically ineffective courtiers. In Brandenburg-Prussia, however, circumstances enabled Frederick William to gain the obedience of his nobility by turning them not into courtiers, but into soldiers and administrators. By an agreement of 1653 he changed them from the most intransigent of his opponents into trustworthy supporters. In exchange for a monetary gift they received extensive privileges. Their feudal position was abolished. Their land would no longer be on loan; they would exercise full ownership rights. They were given posts in the army and in local and national government, to which they were appointed by the elector and not by feudal right. The same idea of an aristocracy which served the state was the motivation for many of Peter the Great's reforms in

Russia. The Russian nobility was, however, less compliant than the Prussian, and after Peter's death most of his most radical reforms were amended.

It must be kept in mind that during the *ancien régime* property preceded the person. What is termed personal status today was then calculated according to ownership, usually of freehold property. The society of the *ancien régime* therefore consisted of a hard core with privileges or monopolies based on ownership; around them there was an increasingly larger zone of people without property and therefore without rights. Political power was exercized chiefly on the basis of landownership. Not that land meant wealth. In truth the process was often the reverse, for the man who had made a fortune in trade or in a rewarding public office would often buy an estate which in turn would lead to a noble title, combined with a large degree of local influence or a government post.

Second in importance to the large landowners were the professions of which the clergy were the most important – according to the medieval feudal system, the first estate. It was characteristic that the most prominent amongst them, the archbishops and bishops, were large landowners themselves. The clergy in Roman Catholic countries enjoyed the same exemptions from taxation and other privileges as did the nobility. The higher clergy in these countries also kept their land grants, and French and Spanish bishops often lived like the aristocracy from which they had come. The lower clergy were, however, usually poorly paid and came from the lower social classes. The plundering of property in the course of the Reformation and the secularization of church property early in the 17th century frequently impoverished the Protestant clergy. None the less, the clergy in both Protestant and Roman Catholic countries still had great power and influence. Their religious duties aside, they exercized considerable control over education and welfare work.

Following the clergy was the military class of officers recruited from the nobility and the bourgeois classes. Then, after a large gap, followed the lawyers, and after them came the doctors, both representative of the learned professions.

This has brought us to the middle classes.

It has been said that every student of history knows that the particular and distinguishing feature of any century in modern history is the "rise of the middle classes". In any case, in the 17th century these classes acquired an increasingly important role in the politics of various states in western Europe. These classes included the professions, the merchants and industrialists. By the time they had grown strong enough to enter politics, they had considerable advantages – capability, education, wealth and, on occasion, the driving force and discipline of Calvinism – and they exercised a strong influence on the constitutional development of states. The "freedom" of a town could be obtained by the emancipation which followed the completion of one's apprenticeship or, in some cases, by marrying the daughter of a freeman. Merchants, particularly those involved in international trade, also rose on the social ladder. They could combine trading activities with ship ownership, banking or money-lending – vocations which had not yet been clearly differentiated.

Naturally the role of the middle classes was not the same everywhere. In Holland, as in England, they grew strong enough to gain effective authority in matters of state. The Dutch Revolt was partially a social revolution which transferred political power to a class which had, for a long time, possessed economic power without its political equivalent. Although the small provincial state bodies of the Dutch republic were all differently constituted, they generally consisted of wealthy urban citizens. The States-General, too, was elected from these citizens. This created a ruling class of rich merchants in the state, and the United Provinces became a bourgeois republic, a development which coincided with the zenith of Dutch capitalism in the 17th century.

The idea of a wide-ranging intermediate class, as well as the term which is usually applied to it, namely bourgeoisie, originated in France, but in the 17th century industry and trade in France were not as developed as that of England and Holland because the French merchant classes did not attain any important political or social positions. The aristocracy looked down their noses at merchants who were themselves embarrassed by their position and endeavoured to join the ranks of the aristocrats. For its requirements of administrators and money, the French monarchy exploited the bourgeois ambition to escape from trade and rise socially. The monarchy gained ministers and officials from the ranks of the bourgeoisie, as well as funds for the expenses of its court, government and wars. From the reign of Henry IV (1575-1589) onwards, many judicial, financial and municipal posts *(charges)* were created. In 1604 an annual tax, the *paulette*, was instituted; its payment ensuring that the officials' posts became hereditary. By the end of the century the appetite of the bourgeoisie for *charges* had apparently been satisfied and their sale decreased – but not before thousands of unnecessary posts had been created in France.

The French bourgeoisie, with its predilection for *charges* and *rentes* (loans to the government in return for acquiring nobility), differed from the English middle classes who invested their money in trading enterprises. Such government posts were in themselves a good investment, but even more important was the social distinction which they entailed – even the rank of nobility for the highest officials – and usually the remission of the *taille* and other taxes. Consequently, the old feudal nobility, the *noblesse d'épée*, which owned its property because of its military service to the king, was replaced by a new *noblesse de robe* – judges and administrators such as *intendants* and *financiers* in the department of finance and tax gatherers – who purchased from the king letters of nobility or high official posts, which elevated them to the noble class. In a single year, Louis XIV created 500 nobles at 6 000 *livres* apiece and his military expenses during the Spanish War of Succession forced him to almost equal this figure more than once.

This new aristocracy bought estates from members of the impoverished, old aristocracy and gave their sons a nobleman's education in their attempts to identify with feudal traditions. Amongst the *noblesse de robe* the members of the *parlements* (judicial courts) formed a wealthy and influential group which had bought or inherited their offices and were able to pay to bequeath these to their sons. The *parlementaires* increasingly became a closed order as their posts usually remained in the same family for generations, while tax levies and fees for lawsuits enriched them. They gradually bought estates, and by the 17th century much of the land near towns which had a *parlement* was in their hands. Many members of the new nobility made fortunes. It is alleged that Colbert and Louvois were both worth 10 000 000 *livres* (about R1 600 000) at their deaths. The old nobility loathed this new nobility and denied it equal status, but in the 17th and 18th centuries the two nobilities amalgamated, mainly as a result of intermarriage.

The bourgeois merchants in France had many opportunities to obtain wealth and power – by money-lending, providing war supplies and ships, finding capital for overseas trade, and acquiring government concessions for the development of colonies and the exploitation of resources. The financial requirements of the state made such people indispensable. They collected its indirect taxes and, because of insufficient credit facilities, supplied its precious metals.

This was in contrast to the position of the Hungarian and Polish middle classes. The towns in Hungary were not centres of trade and wealth, while the nobility filled virtually all professional positions. The traders in many towns were Germans, who were, however, not powerful enough to participate in the central government. In Poland the middle class was numerically weak, poor, and hampered by the privileges of the aristocracy which could not participate in trade, but was exempt from export tax and allowed to import goods for its own use free of tax. What trade there was, was chiefly in the hands of Jews.

Russia also had a small and unimportant middle class. Peter the Great, as part of his policy of developing Russian trade and industry, encouraged the rise of active and flourishing middle-class communities in the towns, and towards the end of his reign they constituted about three per cent of the population of his state.

The position of the labourers in cities and towns also merits attention. A change in human relationships took place in the industrial areas. The relationship between employer and employee and the circumstances of the working classes grew in importance during the 17th century. The rise of capitalism meant a change in the industrial function of the individual.

The time of the old guilds was passing, but when the nation became the economic unit, something of the old system was continued and extended into the new. As a result, particularly with the new paternalism of the state, attempts were initially made to stick to the principle of fairness between the individual workers in each industry, between one employer and another, but also between employers and employees. Industries and trade were largely organized in corporations and there was a multitude of rules which regulated mutual relationships in every industry. In the Middle Ages there were already exceptions to all these rules which, in the 17th century, were to begin to fall away. Their decay led to social unrest and certain obscure agitations and experiments which form part of the prehistory of the labour movement. This unrest, however, had little in common with the labour movements of subsequent times. Broadly speaking, it contained no socialism or theoretical philanthropism, no demands for a better social system and no doctrines about what social systems owed to individuals. The precursor of socialism in the 17th century was embryonic and was found mainly in periods of political and intellectual ferment. An example is the English interregnum, which even saw the advocacy of the vote for women and of communism. The social dissatisfaction of the 17th century was generally inarticulate, to the extent that one seldom knows where and to what degree the rise of capitalism improved or lowered the material standard of living of the working classes. There is not even any protest literature containing definite views on whether life for the poor went from bad to worse.

What is known for certain is that dissatisfaction amongst artisans was a clear cause of rebelliousness. In France the crown had to arbitrate in disputes between employers and workers. There are a number of records of workers' plots and rebellions although, it is said, not as many as in the 18th century. They resulted from immediate and practical grievances. In Thiers in 1688, between 300 and 400 paper workers demanded that their working hours, holidays and food rations should be determined. In Holland social dissatisfaction was indissoluble from politics and religion. It found expression in the communist ideas of certain groups and in political agitations in times of war, in particular the agitations in favour of the house of Orange and against the republican oligarchy. Direct and simple economic agitation was less general, but it did exist. In England the situation was similar: political parties and religious groups there also acquired power from a feeling which led to sporadic strikes and insurrections.

Sporadic protests, however, do not constitute a social movement and neither did any such movement exist. What we know of the workers of the 17th century makes it clear that they were not people who could easily unite in pursuit of positive goals. Most of them, it can be surmised, were ignorant people, satisfied with pure subsistence and crude pleasures. Those of more serious demeanours, which would subsequently be applied to social movements, devoted their energies to religion. The vitality of religious feeling, the absence of political democracy and the low level of education all contributed to the impossibility of a working-class movement. Much was to change in industry, religion and education before workers would unite as members of a class, with common aspirations and interests. They had not even reached a stage of effective combination in single trades or districts. The old corporations in which employers and employees both participated had decayed or were in the process of decaying; the new trade unions, for workers only, had yet to be born.

In England, in particular during the Puritan revolution, the artisans raised their voices, but after the restoration of Charles II their limited success was dissipated. In Holland workers' societies were forbidden, and they went underground. Stricter measures followed: in one case in 1692 such a rebellious group was even threatened with the death penalty. As was the case in England, repression met with success.

There is little evidence in other European countries that there was repression of such groups – there was simply nothing to repress. Neither were there, with the exception of England, any signs of the great change in social policy, which was one of the chief reasons for the alienation of the workers from their rulers. The paternalism of the Tudors and Stuarts simply came to an unheralded end. By the end of the century English industry had been left to the principle of *laissez-faire*. On the Continent, regimentation was still the aim of government. Under both systems there was neither the indignation nor the methods of protest which would make the life of the industrial worker the leading ethical problem of 19th century politics.

What of the peasants? In the 17th century the largest part of Europe's population still consisted of small farmers, each with a piece of land which in a normal year would be sufficient to support a family. Large numbers of the peasantry were, in turn, serfs who obtained their smallholdings from a landlord in exchange for labour and dues. These serfs were tied to the land and subject to other limitations on their personal freedom. Since the late Middle Ages growing trade, increasing circulation of money and other factors encroached upon the manorial subsistence economy and influenced the position of the peasant class. By this time there was no longer any serfdom in England, and similar developments took place in some Continental countries.

In 17th century France the peasantry represented about 80 per cent of the population. Serfdom continued only in one or two eastern provinces. About one twentieth of the peasants, possibly altogether 1 000 000, were serfs, tied to the land, with feudal obligations, but without any rights over their property. Less than one-twentieth owned their land, and less than a quarter were labourers with no land at all. The majority, possibly half, were now *métayers* who had to remit to the landowners part of the yield of the land. This varied from one-fifth to half and was payable partly in goods and partly in money. Most of the small farmers therefore made some form of payment to their landlords for their rented property which, however, was increasingly regarded as their own, of which they could dispose. Many of the nobility were forced by poverty to give part of their demesne (the personal part of the manor) to smallholders who, although they paid high rentals and even performed feudal duties, were in a completely different position as tenant farmers than the medieval serfs. The part of the land which in 17th century France was, for all practical purposes, owned by peasants (although they were still paying dues for it) varied from 50 per cent in Languedoc to about 20 per cent in Normandy and Brittany.

As they were the largest group of landowners in France, individual peasant holdings were generally small and frequently subdivided. By the end of the 17th century most small farmers enjoyed far better circumstances than before, but the remaining feudal obligations were onerous enough. A small farmer still had to use his lord's mill, wine press and bakery, which was often expensive and a nuisance. *Justice seigneuriale*, the landlord's right to try his tenants, continued in existence and made justice for peasant farmers always slow and often unobtainable.

The feudal monetary obligations, of which the amounts had been fixed centuries ago, were not very oppressive, but payment in goods deprived small farmers of part of their harvest which they could barely afford to lose. In the final instance they also had to pay tithes to the church, as well as national taxes.

The small farmer had to bear the brunt of virtually all direct taxation and the country's financial burden rested substantially on his shoulders. The most important of these taxes was the *taille*, which played the same part in the budgets of the 17th century as today's income tax. It was assessed, however, without regard to fairness or political economy. In the *pays d'état* (the last provinces added to the possessions of the French monarchy and which retained their state assemblies – Brittany, Burgundy, Dauphiné, Provence and Languedoc) which constituted about a third of the area and wealth of France, the *taille* was assessed on actual property, and it was not an excessive tax, since the landless escaped it. In the rest of the country, the *pays d'élection*, however, the *taille* was a most unfair tax. It was a poll-tax, paid almost exclusively by the peasants; and the nobility, clergy and incumbents of official posts jealously guarded their exemption from it. The *taille* ensured that peasant farmers would remain poor. Richelieu deprived Burgundy, Dauphiné and Provence of their privileges, and the remaining provincial assemblies only met to approve the *Don Gratuit*, the subsidies demanded by the king. By the time of Louis XIV these meetings were largely social gatherings.

It was the administration of the *gabelle*, the salt tax, however, that revealed the unfathomable depths of 17th century officialdom. Like the *taille* it was not levied uniformly, as some provinces (such as Artois, Navarre and Brittany) were completely exempt and others were either *pays de petite gabelle* (like Languedoc and Provence) or *pays de grande gabelle* (Ile de France, Orléanais, Maine, Anjou and Touraine), that is, they respectively paid little or much salt tax.

Salt could be sold only by licensed dealers or *regratteurs*, and a fixed minimum was mandatory. Whole villages were sometimes deserted because the peasants migrated from a province with a heavy *gabelle* to one where it was less onerous. The jails were filled with people who had violated the *gabelle* regulations. It needs to be kept in mind that salt was most important at a time when it was unusual to keep cattle through the winter and salted food was in much greater general use than it is today. In Roman Catholic countries salt fish was the staple food on Fridays and fast days. In addition, salt was in general use as a fertilizer and in various leather-tanning processes.

In the western parts of Germany the circumstances of the peasants were largely similar to those in the greatest part of France. They frequently met their obligations with money, were personally free, did not do much work on the demesne and owned their land on a hereditary basis, while the jurisdiction of their landlords was limited to smaller cases. In Prussia, however, as well as in other parts east of the Elbe and in Bavaria, where three-quarters of the population were small farmers, serfdom meant substantial labour service for the landlords, and they still exercised a considerable amount of jurisdiction. Serfdom continued to survive in Frederick William's agreement with his nobility in Brandenburg-Prussia in 1653.

In truth, the feudal obligations of peasants in central and eastern Europe were generally extensive, although there were differences between different countries. In Hungary they still paid levies in money and goods, performed weekly labour, gave part of their harvest to their landlord – who exercised exclusive jurisdiction over them – and paid the largest part of the national tax.

In Poland the years of war in the second half of the 17th century weakened the position of the 7 000 000 to 8 000 000 serfs. The population figure dropped and the increase in the serfs' weekly labour requirements did nothing to improve grain production. The nobility exploited the situation by curtailing the rights of serfs. Sometimes they demanded higher levies, and sometimes they took away part of their serfs' land.

In Russia about 60 per cent of the peasants were serfs on private estates. They did weekly labour or paid their landlords annual levies. The landlord could also sell serfs, with or without their property and even separately from their families. About 15 per cent of the peasants were serfs on church properties. Monks were frequently even more demanding landlords than laymen, and peasant uprisings on their estates were general. State serfs paid a small money levy and enjoyed better general conditions than other Russian serfs, although Peter the Great usually assigned them to mining, digging canals or building his new capital. By increased taxes, amongst other things, the general consequence of Peter's reign was to weaken the position of the Russian small farmer.

SCIENCE AND THOUGHT

Intellectual progress in the 17th century was most striking in those sciences which were based on mathematics. The men referred to earlier – Bacon, Descartes, Galileo, Huygens, Newton, Boyle, Spinoza and Leibnitz – were mostly mathematicians, physicists and astronomers. The 17th century was not only one of the periods of greatest progress in mathematics, but one in which mathematical knowledge had the greatest influence on knowledge in other spheres and consequently upon life in general.

It can be said that the scientific revolution as we know it would have been impossible without the achievements of the mathematicians. Where algebra and geometry were developed separately – the former by the Hindus and the latter by the Greeks – the amalgamation of the two, or the application of algebraic methods to the field of geometry, was the greatest single step in the progress of the exact sciences. The problem of gravity would never have been solved – indeed, the whole of the Newtonian synthesis never been reached – without, firstly, the analytical geometry of René Descartes and, secondly, the calculations of the infinitesimal by Newton and Leibnitz. The most important was that scientific research became experimental and thus the source of new discoveries. The experimental method, an essential of modern science, was gradually applied to several areas of research to produce one achievement after another.

In every country, however, a climax was achieved in philosophy before science made appreciable strides. This was because, before Europeans could investigate nature on any large scale, the philosophers first had to exceed the limits of medieval scholastic thought and develop the required method of free investigation. This entailed a reorientation in the ideas of western thinkers about man and the world which, for 2 000 years, had been based on a scheme developed in Greek antiquity, and by Aristotle in particular.

There was no medieval scientific movement, but rather a lack of interest in natural phenomena and, in its place, a mentality dedicated to the supernatural and other-worldly. Medieval thought was directed at the ordering of all knowledge and experience to produce an explanation of nature and the universe, which could transmit to man the purpose of his existence on earth. The most prominent medieval scholastic philosopher was Thomas Aquinas (1225-1274) whose greatest work was the *Summa Theologica*. Two sources of truth existed for him – reason and Christian revelation. The truths of reason were found by applying the logic of Aristotle and the truths of revelation in the Bible and the traditions of the church. The synthesis proposed by Aquinas endeavoured to show that, as God had made himself known in reason as well as by revelation, these two truths could never be contradictory. Reason alone, however, could not discover everything and was therefore inferior to revelation. Beyond reason, the act of faith was necessary to reach total truth through revelation.

The scholastic system therefore limited the sphere of reason to assumptions based on theological authority and all branches of human knowledge. In general, therefore, experimental science was impossible in the Middle Ages, because of the scholastic view of natural things as part of God's eternal plan. Attention was directed at the problems of man's relationship with God; relatively little consideration was given to nature.

The background to the evolution of the scholastic system was the all-encompassing feudal organization of medieval Christendom. Western Europe then lived in almost total isolation and had only poor and fragmentary knowledge of the great civilizations of Asia and North Africa. Its agriculture was largely committed to pure subsistence, its industry was insignificant, and its trade relatively unimportant. Its society was organized in a hierarchy which appeared to have divine sanction. This agreed with a philosopy which regarded the universe as permanent, designed to play its role in the divine will. This also explains the limitations to medieval science. Not only was the scholastic view unfavourable to scientific activity, but some of the inventions and discoveries which were made were forgotten and rediscovered more than once because there seemed to be no practical need for them. Medieval science therefore consisted largely of book-learning and disputation. Not before the disintegration of the old economy and community could a new, progressive, experimental science begin to replace the static, rational science of the Middle Ages.

Astronomy was to take the lead in challenging the medieval philosophical system. This was no coincidence. Royal regard for its associate, astrology, made astronomy the only truly practical science of the Middle Ages, one which performed sufficient observations, and scientifically tested its hypotheses. Furthermore, world voyages in the 16th and 17th century endowed astronomy with a practical purpose as a navigational aid and it gained renewed interest.

According to the Greek mathematician Ptolemy (AD 139-161), the earth was a stationary body in the centre of the universe, around which the sun, moon, planets and fixed stars revolved as satellites. The greater freedom of speculation which was encouraged by the Renaissance inspired astronomers to explore a more satisfactory explanation for planetary movements. The first progress was made by the Pole Nicolaus Copernicus (1473-1543) who postulated that the earth was only one of the planets orbiting the sun, and that it also revolved about its own axis. Although he did not exactly explain the laws governing planetary movement, and still thought that planets had circular orbits, he did manage to position them correctly. Although his *De Revolutionibus Orbium Coelestrum* was first published in 1543, it took nearly a century before the Copernican system would find wide acceptance in scientific thought. Initially it appeared as if his theory would be accorded religious sanction, but the Counter-Reformation caused the Roman Catholic church to stand by its traditional view. The work was suspended in the *Index* of 1612.

Subsequent development of the Copernican system by other astronomers aided its final acceptance. In 1577 Tycho Brahé (1546-1601), a Danish nobleman, became the first to suggest that a celestial body moves in a non-circular orbit. He was followed by his assistant in Prague, Johann Kepler (1571-1630), the first great Protestant scientist. In 1609 Kepler found that the only explanation for planetary orbits was that they were all ellipses. Ten years later he explained the speed of the planets in their orbits in his *Harmonices Mundi*. Through his discovery of the laws of planetary movement he developed the geometric model of the solar system and considerably increased the possibility of accurate astronomical prediction. Although the physical, dynamic explanation of his discoveries had to await the work of Newton, Kepler had struck the final blow against the conventional view of the universe.

Up to this point these new discoveries were properly evaluated by only a few who had no astronomical knowledge.

The world's attention was to be drawn to the most important scientific instrument of the 17th century – the telescope. Although lenses were generally known by the late Middle Ages, the possibility of using them for observation and in astronomical instruments was not realized until Dutch opticians discovered between 1590 and 1608 that a double convex lens and a double concave lens, placed at a specific distance from one another, would enlarge distant objects.

Galileo Galilei (1564-1642), a professor in physics and military engineering at the university of Padua in Italy, was a devoted follower of Copernicus. Interested in the movement of pendulums and the related problem of falling objects, he was inspired to build a powerful telescope for astronomical observation according to the Dutch model. He was the first to use the telescope as a scientific instrument, and within a few nights in 1609 his observation of the skies revealed enough for him to destroy the whole Ptolemaic system. He discovered the four moons or satellites of Jupiter, determined that Venus, Mercury and Mars showed phases, like the moon – as could be expected if these planets revolved around the sun – and he observed dark spots on the sun, which proved that this body also rotates.

The invention of the telescope and Galileo's use of the instrument was extremely important to the 17th century. The determination of longitude was an important technique in the century of great voyages of discovery, and until a reliable chronometer became available in 1760, the only method to determine longitude was to use celestial indicators, such as, for example, eclipses.

Galileo published his *Siderius Nuntius* in 1610 – a concise, simple exposition of his observations. He also endeavoured to justify the Copernican system and to reply to objections made against it. This entailed studies in mechanics, such as the movement of pendulums, the speed of falling stones and the like. These discoveries in mechanical physics had practical implications, such as the measurement of the pulse rate and the building of an astronomical clock.

In 1632 he published his *Dialogue concerning the two chief Systems of the World, the Ptolemaic and the Copernican*, written in Italian Latin, in which he criticized scholastic views with scathing ridicule. The Catholic church could not ignore his challenge. He was ordered to appear before the court of the Inquisition in Rome the following year and forced, under threat of torture, to recant "the false theory of the movement of the earth and the immobility of the sun because it is in conflict with the Holy Scripture". His sentence was rather lenient: he was nominally confined to the villa of a friend near Florence where he dedicated the remaining nine years of his life to the completion of his work on mechanics. Scholars in Catholic as well as Protestant countries deplored Galileo's condemnation. Although the *Dialogue* and other Copernican writings were not removed from the *Index* and the College of Cardinals did not approve of teaching the Copernican theory before 1882, the action taken against Galileo was the last of its kind. The Inquisition never again forced a scientist to recant his theories. All practical astronomers rejected the classic cosmology in favour of the new explanation of the solar system.

Although the astronomers had struck a blow at scholasticism by destroying its view of the universe, the system remained highly influential. Most European universities continued to teach ecclesiastic or Aristotelian dogma. The scientific method of investigation followed by the astronomers was far from being generally accepted. A new view of man and nature was essential if the scientific revolution was to continue making itself felt in practice. The implications of the new science had to be made clear not only to a few scholars, but to as many people as possible, and in particular to the rising classes – capitalists, manufacturers, merchants and politicians. Galileo attempted this, but he was writing in a country which was losing its economic and intellectual importance. After Kepler and Galileo, scientific activities in the 17th century shifted from Italy and Germany, the late medieval areas of commercial prosperity and Renaissance learning, to France, Holland and England, the countries favoured by the Atlantic trade routes. This is where the men were found who tried to give a general explanation of the scientific method in the first half of the century. Two of them were prominent members of the classes concerned in public affairs.

Francis Bacon (1561-1626), son of a Lord Keeper of the Great Seal of Queen Elizabeth I, was an able and ambitious jurist who rose to the office of Lord Chancellor. Throughout his varied career he enthusiastically attempted to formulate a philosophy of science. He wanted to replace the old, crumbling assumptions with a new view which would be generally acceptable and accord the scientific method its rightful place. The manner in which he set to work was to collect data, perform large-scale experiments and acquire results from a mass of evidence – essentially an inductive method. He believed that careful systematization of observations would create a new instrument – he called it the *novum organum* – with which to investigate nature. His work, *Novum Organum*, was published in 1620.

It has been said that Bacon's method was in essence that of the medieval philosophers, based on the classification of observable facts. He did not believe that a synthesis – a system of the universe – was yet within reach, but was trying to lay its basis.

Another objective of Bacon's from the beginning of his career was to explain the true purpose of science, i.e to enrich human life by new discoveries. He believed that scientists would be the benefactors of the human race if they were to increase its control over the forces of nature and brought it understanding of useful knowledge. His own few efforts in scientific experiment brought him no great discoveries; indeed, he did not regard himself as a scientist. He was, nevertheless, the first important writer to extol scientists as inventors and explorers whose work was essential to industrial progress.

His influence was considerable and not confined to his own country, for in the first half of the 17th century translations of his works were made available in French. In England the transition from medieval to modern thinking was frequently laid at Bacon's door, but it was not the work of a single person, and there can be differences of opinion about the exact timing of the transition. He was the herald of the scientific revolution, but not a representative of its mature phase, and neither did he ask the questions with which modern philosophy chiefly concerned itself. This was done by a much younger contemporary of his, the mathematician Descartes.

The Frenchman René Descartes (1596-1650) complemented Bacon's influence. He was educated in the Jesuit college at La Flèche and soon grew dissatisfied with scholasticism. He left for Paris to study mathematics. After serving as a volunteer in the Thirty Years War against the Protestants in Bohemia and Hungary, he entered the tolerant atmosphere of Holland where he wrote and meditated in great seclusion for twenty years. He died in Stockholm after having accepted an invitation from Queen Christina to visit Sweden.

Descartes was interested in physics, astronomy, biology, anatomy and, in fact, in every branch of science, but he was above all a mathematician. Typical of many contemporary thinkers, his view was that the natural world could be understood through mathematics, the science in which the universal certainty and exactitude could be found, which he regarded as the hallmark of the only true knowledge. It was crucial to subsequent thinking and did much to lend the science of his time its characteristic emphasis on mathematics and physics.

According to him, however, the secrets of nature could not be unlocked by Bacon's method of gathering facts and, by induction, postulating universal laws in the manner of the scholastics. In his *Discours de la Méthode* (1673) which had an enormous influence on European thinking, he did not emphasize the gathering and analysis of evidence, but the method by which it was viewed. His knowledge of scholasticism as part of French formal education convinced him that science was always hampered by an inability to distinguish between truth and lies because it had not yet achieved sufficient clarity of thought. For him the final test of a truth was the clarity with which it could be understood. He believed that clarity of thought would enable man to understand everything which was rationally discoverable and that experimentation was one of the methods to apply. His method was deductive rather than inductive. He began not with what was known, but with the fact of knowing the working of the individual mind. His point of departure was scepticism, and from there he continued his conclusions with a procedure as rigorous as that of mathematics. The one truth which could not be doubted was embodied in his famous thesis "Cogito, ergo sum" (I think, therefore I am), explained in his *Méditations* of 1641. He rejected every appeal to authority, whether it was Aristotelian or ecclesiastic, and in the *Discours* he postulated several rules which govern the free investigation of a problem: never to accept as true anything you do not certainly know to be true; to separate every problem under investigation into as many parts as possible; always to move in one's thinking from the simplest to the more complex; to make calculations so complete and synoptic that you can be assured that nothing has been left out. These principles, Descartes believed, were universally applicable.

From his certainty of human intelligence he derived the existence and nature of God as well as of the external world. For Descartes the existence of a thinking creature implied the existence of an eternal and perfect creature which is pure spirit or thought, in contrast to the finite, imperfect individual. Furthermore, there is the external world about which immutable knowledge is mathematical. Like Bacon, Descartes believed that a main objective of scientific knowledge was to ensure man's conquest of the material world.

Descartes made important progress in mathematical technique. In his *La Géométrie,* an addition to the *Discours*, he was the first to apply algebra to the methods of co-ordinative geometry. The essential innovation in Cartesian as opposed to Euclidian geometry was the introduction of the concept of "movement". Descartes therefore provided the basis for analytical geometry.

He also believed that he could apply mechanics to the formulation of a theory about the material world, in other words, the universe. The Cartesian theory about the "vortexes" of celestial bodies did not, however, explain well-known phenomena such as Kepler's laws of planetary movement, and Descartes's whole cosmology was superseded by Newton's simple, encompassing theory of gravity.

None the less, Cartesian philosophy was the first modern, total and logical system of thought. Descartes was the founder of modern philosophy, the precursor of thinkers who attempted to explain the universe purely with the power of their intellect. The new philosophy encouraged a more critical approach towards matters in which legend and tradition had prevailed up to that stage. Descartes announced a new "trinity": that of nature, reason and truth – phenomena which would soon be pursued in western Europe's "century of reason". He reflected the thinking of his time by combining rationalism (systematic thought) with empiricism (the search for truth by experience, in particular by observation and experiment). These two, together with the mathematical spirit, were the leading characteristics of the scientific movement. Those of his followers who accepted so many of his tenets as to become known as Cartesians insisted on the rationalistic aspect of his dogma. Among them were a number of people of considerable intellectual capability who attempted to find a satisfactory formula for the interaction of spirit and matter, and although no one today believes in this, it served the progress of thought.

The influence of his tenets was considerable amongst the leaders of philosophical thought, such as Spinoza. Cartesianism was regarded by contemporaries as a total and conscious break with the past, and in this sense it was the beginning of modern metaphysics. Although Descartes never broke with the church, there was considerable opposition to his theories from theologians and university authorities.

Benedictus de Spinoza and Leibnitz were to continue the rationalistic line of development of Descartes.

Spinoza, a Portuguese Jew who was born in Amsterdam in 1632, wrote remarkable books about political theory and about the interpretation of the Old Testament, but it was perhaps his purely philosophical works which gave greatest expression to his genius. The most important were the *Ethica* and the short dissertation *De Intellectus Emendatione*, both published after his early death in 1677. Their greatness was not appreciated until much later.

Spinoza followed Descartes in the lead he gave on method, but had a far greater desire to formulate an absolutely coherent system. To him the universe was a unity. His interpretation of the universe was pantheistic (i.e. God and the world are one – God is in creation), although he was unjustly regarded as an atheist in his own century and in the 18th century. He did not distinguish between two separate systems of laws in the universe – those of matter and those of the spirit – but provided an interpretation in which they were identical. Physical laws were what one knew of the functioning of the divine spirit. The human spirit, too, acted in accordance with the same divine law.

Like Hobbes, Spinoza regarded the good as that which one knows is good for one; man should love himself and pursue his own interests. He and Hobbes looked forward to a more enlightened, more tolerant society than that in which they lived. In his *Tractatus theologico-politicus* (1670) Spinoza declared that benevolence was the highest social virtue, as it enhanced the standard of the relationship with one's fellow man. He was moving in the direction of tolerance in thinking and religion in a strong and secular state. The *Tractatus* was condemned by the States-General and placed on the *Index* by the church.

If Descartes was the greatest intellectual power of 17th century France, Leibnitz was the greatest in 17th century Germany. He was born in 1616, the son of a professor of philosophy at Leipzig, and was a doctor of law by the time he was twenty eight. He spent some time (1672-1676) in Paris, where he devoted himself to mathematics with such distinction that he was elected a member of the French Academy and of the English Royal Society. Subsequently he lived in Hanover as librarian to the duke of Brunswick.

Throughout his life he made important contributions to science, mathematics, theology, history and law. As politician, pamphleteer, theologian, philosopher, historian and mathematician he was the most universal spirit of his time and the typical figure of the century. He was a well-read scholar, a believer and an audacious innovator. He displayed lack of enlightenment in only two respects: he was in favour of torture, and he retained a certain faith in astrology.

The key to his thinking was optimism. He advocated greater humanism than the cold, deistic rationalism of Descartes or the impassionate pantheism of Spinoza. Although he thought mostly in materialistic terms, he was more than a mere analyst; his speculation had practical and benevolent aims, and he looked toward the future as much as to the past. Throughout his life he was keen to find a great ruler who would share his enthusiasm and apply his proposals, for, like many of his philosophical successors, he believed that social amelioration had to be brought about by an enlightened ruler rather than by the initiative of a self-interested population.

In the construction of his system Leibnitz not only took note of the great mathematical discoveries, but also of the work of natural scientists. His view of the organism, for example, which is apparent in all his work, was partly derived from the work of microscopists. He set out with a far richer view of the universe as seen by science than any of his predecessors and did not, like them, make the erroneous simplification of distinguishing between matter and spirit. According to him, the universe consisted of "monads", substances which were a unity of spirit and matter.

After his death, his leading principles were reduced to a systematic form and became the ruling convention at German universities for the largest part of the 18th century. It was, however, limited to students of philosophy. Outside the universities, French thinking was to dominate in Germany.

The British philosophical school also originated with Descartes. John Locke (1632-1704), the founder of this school, agreed with Descartes where his faith in clear knowledge and in the fundamental difference between spirit and matter is concerned. Although he was as versatile as the other great philosophers of the century and had as great an influence on political and general thought as on philosophy, there was one significant difference between his views and those of Descartes, Spinoza or Leibnitz: he was the one great philosopher of the 17th century who was of no account as a mathematician. Consequently, he approached the problems of philosophy in his own fashion. The purpose of his *Essay concerning Human Understanding* of 1690 was practical or religious: he opposed the view of knowledge which was in conflict with reason and freedom. He wrote in the style of the common man and applied the methods of common sense. In comparison with the works of his predecessors, his were easy to read. They offered none of the problems created by a mathematical form, the Latin language or a technical vocabulary.

In spite of the ambiguity of his thought, he attained great influence over the educated classes of Europe in general and, paradoxical as this may sound, it was Locke, the empiricist, who began the trend which was to be labelled in the 18th century the "century of reason". The "reason" of Voltaire and Diderot was not the rationalism of the physicists, but purely common sense. Locke was the father of this utilitarianism. He admitted to no inborn ideas in knowledge which were above criticism. He wanted no arbitrary power in the state. He defended Christendom as being simple and reasonable, but claimed for religion the same freedom of the individual spirit which was the point of departure for his theory of knowledge.

Locke was closer to the 18th than to the 17th century. He stood at the turning point of what was a general transition, and displayed similarities to the thinkers of the 18th century, who were more concerned with political and human problems than with problems advanced by the scientific revival.

Meanwhile, however, we have neglected the scientific revolution, which reached its zenith with the synthesis of astronomy and mechanics in the system of Isaac Newton.

The general scientific movement in Europe apparently took its rightful place in the 1680s, when a handful of scientists in London and Paris topped everything with their remarkable achievements. In fact, these were the years which reached their high-water mark in 1687 with the publication of Newton's *Philosophia Naturalis Principia Mathematica*.

Sir Isaac Newton (1642-1727), the greatest scientific thinker of the 17th century, was born in the year in which Galileo died, five years after the publication of Descartes's *Discours* and exactly one hundred years after the publication of Copernicus's *De Revolutionibus*. Newton went to Cambridge in 1661 and became professor of mathematics when he was twenty seven. From 1703 until his death he was president of the Royal Society. His scientific work was done chiefly at Cambridge and his important discoveries were made early in life. Apparently he had little influence on the universities and never formed a school.

Almost all his work concerned astronomy, the predominating science of the century. His first achievement in physics meant practical advantages for astronomers: he improved the telescope by discovering the spectrum.

His principle of universal gravity was explained in his great work, *Principia*, published by the Royal Society and financed by Halley. This epochal work, destined to serve for more than two centuries as the frame of reference for physics and other sciences, was in itself a synthesis of the progress made during the two preceding centuries. His complete and coherent system of dynamics, as set out here, was his greatest single achievement. The publication of this, one of the greatest books in the world, characterized an epoch in the study of the effect of force on objects.

Newton's principle of gravity was the last and greatest of the triumphs of astronomy. The gradual development of mathematics which accompanied it enabled Newton to give an encompassing explanation of the mechanism of the universe in the light of this principle. His coherent system of the universe was based on the principle that the earth is moving; his own principle made it possible to explain how the earth remains in a state of movement. Furthermore his system, unlike the classic one which it replaced, described all movement on earth and in the heaven's expanse as manifestations of the same law. This and, in fact, the general trend of the scientific movement in the 17th century, encouraged a mechanistic concept of the universe which regarded nature as no more than a machine, subject to exact, discoverable and measurable rules even in disciplines such as biology, of which it is now known that purely mechanistic explanations do not suffice.

The great achievement of mathematics in the 17th century was the calculus, a system devised by Newton and Leibnitz. Pascal designed the first calculating machine. Apart from Newton, his great Dutch contemporary, Christiaan Huygens, improved the telescope, made pendulum clocks and also invented the balance spring for clocks.

What of the other branches of science?

Alchemy was left behind, and chemistry, although directly useful to medical science, to metallurgy and for other purposes, attracted little interest. By the middle of the century, gases were distinguished from air and water vapour. Robert Boyle (1627-1691) achieved most of his reputation for his work in chemistry, and his one work, *The sceptical Chymist*, published in 1662, is still read today. He brushed away a web of alchemistic theories and traditional, baseless theories and insisted on the importance of experimentation and sound conclusions. If it is said that he was the father of modern chemistry, this does not mean that this science had quite yet entered the modern period.

Amongst the biological sciences those that were concerned with the human body showed most progress. The discovery announced by William Harvey (1578-1657), an anatomist and physiologist of renown, in his book *De Motu Cordis et Sanguinis* of 1682, is often, although not altogether accurately, described as that of the circulation of blood. This was doubtless of substantial importance. Malpighi completed Harvey's work by discovering the capillary system.

Zoology and botany also made headway in the 17th century. The Dutchman Anthonie van Leeuwenhoek (1632-1723) was the greatest microscopist (although he was primarily a virtuoso in the production of lenses). Where Harvey merely deduced that blood circulated in the small capillaries, Van Leeuwenhoek and others actually observed it in circulation. Van Leeuwenhoek was the first to observe protozoa, bacteria and spermatozoa. This zoological work was, however, only the precursor to the great discoveries which had yet to be made to give biology its full status as a science. In botany as well, the investigators of this period have to be considered as precursors of the greater names of the 18th century. This holds true even more for other sciences. Only the merest beginning was made in palaeontology, while geology had hardly attained the rank of a science.

The European universities generally played but a minor part in the promotion of the scientific movement. Many of them remained committed to old ideas for a long time. Earlier on they had accepted Renaissance humanism only gradually, and they were even slower to show tolerance towards science. During the 17th century some universities, in particular those of Padua, Leyden, Oxford and Cambridge, had a number of thinkers and investigators who were followers of the "new philosophy", but scientists had to find a new type of organization to promote their work. This turned out to be the societies or academies which were formed to enable people of common interests and purpose to meet.

The earliest associations were literary and not scientific. This was because the various European vernaculars needed adaptation if they were to replace medieval Latin as the medium of scientific communication. Simple, unpoetic language was required to express exact scientific thought. The *Académie Française,* founded in 1634, disciplined the French language. In 1664 the Royal Society in England appointed a committee to adapt the English language.

The first scientific associations were, like the first literary ones, Italian. There was the *Accademia Secretorum Naturae,* formed in Naples in 1560, the *Accademia dei Lincei*, formed in Rome in 1603, and the *Accademia del Cimento* which the Medicis formed in Florence in 1651. Members of the latter were followers of Galileo. These societies were too late, however, to defy the hostility against science in Italy. They were all suspected by the papacy of practising the black art and were known as being hostile towards scholasticism. Not one survived for more than 30 years. Their work was continued by new associations in the countries where the leadership of science had established itself.

By 1645 a number of people in England, who were interested in the writings of Bacon were holding weekly meetings in London, calling themselves the Philosophical College, conducting experiments and discussing scientific problems. The civil war had recently ended, and of the ten members of the college who are known, six had Puritan and parliamentary sympathies. The next year most of them moved to Oxford. After the restoration, most of them left Oxford, or were expelled. London once again became the centre of England's scientific activities, and in 1662 The Royal Society of London for the Improvement of Natural Knowledge was formed under royal charter of Charles II. Apart from Newton, other prominent members were Sir Christopher Wren and John Wallis – immediate mathematical predecessors of Newton – Robert Hooke, a pioneer in mechanics, and Robert Boyle. In the early years this society relied on merchants and businessmen for its funds, and its early experiments dealt with practical matters such as the production of dyes through chemical combinations, the strength of metal wires and the manufacture of cloth materials. The Royal Observatory at Greenwich was founded in 1675.

The French *Académie des Sciences* also originated from an informal meeting of scientists, but it differed from the Royal Society. It was founded in 1666 when Colbert was in power and its members received salaries and grants from the king for their research. While members of the Royal Society – which received no support from the government – undertook individual research, Colbert planned collective projects for the *Académie des Sciences*. The most important, the design of a map of France, included data collection in France, voyages to the West Indies, South America and Africa, and required co-operation between astronomers, mathematicians and cartographers. It took decades to complete and was a great pioneering achievement. In 1672 a royal observatory was also founded in Paris. France was the first to publish a scientific magazine, an instrument which meant that information could be distributed more efficiently than by the correspondence which scientists had previously kept up amongst themselves. The *Journal des Savants* of the *Académie des Sciences* appeared in January 1665, while the *Philosophical Transactions* of the Royal Society first saw the light of day in March of the same year.

Various scientific societies were founded in other European countries in the course of the 17th century. The Berlin Academy of Sciences was approved in 1700 by Frederick I of Brandenburg-Prussia, mainly owing to the influence of Leibnitz. Only in 1725 was the St Petersburg Academy of Sciences founded by Peter the Great, after correspondence with Leibnitz and enquiries about the Royal Society and the *Académie des Sciences*.

The latter two, although imitated in other countries, did not live up to expectations in the 17th century. By 1690 both had reached their largest membership and greatest activity and were on the decline. They had originated because science seemed to the rising classes to be potentially important and profitable, but these hopes were set too high and could not be realized with any speed. The new science, still largely limited to mathematics and physics, certainly did make important practical contributions to astronomy and navigation. More had been expected, however, and the societies promised more than they could deliver. Many of their supporters were inevitably disillusioned. None the less, the societies, by organizing the application of scientific research, prepared the way for the great development of new manufacturing techniques which led to the Industrial Revolution of the 18th century. Even the outstanding feature of the Industrial Revolution, the steam engine, was the result of 17th century research. In France, Denis Papin (1647-1714) had discovered the expansive power of steam and designed a piston. In England, Thomas Savery (1650-1715) developed the first practical fire-actuated pump. The use of this new source of energy which was to transform industry and transport was brought about chiefly by the work of the scientific societies of the 17th century.

THE INFLUENCE OF THE SCIENTIFIC MOVEMENT

By the end of the 17th century scientists knew a great deal more than Aristotle: in anatomy, astronomy, mechanics and chemistry they found that he had sometimes erred or had not possessed the required knowledge. Simultaneously the new rationalism exposed laws of nature and systematic relationships between facts which had not been previously discovered. In these branches of science, it was no longer possible for the instruments of authority and censorship to ensure the survival of assumptions which had been abundantly disproved.

The overthrow of the scholastic systems not only decreased the regard for their exponents, but also struck the first blow at the Greek and Latin classics in general. Both were crowded out of the natural sciences.

Ecclesiastical authority in the intellectual sphere was weakened not only by the rejection of religious censorship in matters of science. The exposure of scientific laws changed the views about miracles, which had been so prevalent during the Middle Ages. The most striking change in astronomy concerned the comets. Until late in the 17th century it was believed that appearances of comets not only presaged vast disasters for mankind, but that they had no natural causes. Halley's calculation of the rotation of the comet of 1682 put an end to this. The critical spirit spread beyond the researchers and observers themselves, and authors such as Pierre Bayle (1647-1706), a Frenchman who settled in Holland, addressed the general public on the question of comets and used it as a lever for propaganda against the acceptance of assumptions which were backed merely by popular belief and irrelevant authority. The last execution of sorcerers occurred in 1712 in England, in France in 1718 and in Scotland in 1722.

In the churches themselves, particularly amongst the Protestants, there was a great deal of destructive criticism of the miracles of the church, and this led to the first examination of the subject in the Bible itself. Spinoza argued in his *Tractatus* that the apparent miracles in the Old Testament were manifestations of science. He, like other scholars, did not challenge the orthodox faith (Catholic or Protestant), but began the tradition of moderate scriptural criticism which was an extension of the scientific spirit. It was a forerunner of the conflict between this spirit and the churches.

Unlike Darwinian biology in the 19th century, the discoveries of the 17th century did not, however, cause serious conflict between the church and science. Virtually all philosophers and scientists viewed the world from the Christian standpoint and were therefore tolerated and favoured by the authorities. They could not imagine a contradiction between science and religion. Newton was unaware of any incompatibility between the two. Virtually all of the 17th century scientists regarded a belief in theism (divinity) as fundamental. They believed that any theory of the universe had to conform to such a belief and that their systems, in fact, did so. Newton, for example, although not orthodox in all his theological views, clearly had firm faith in God and never doubted that his scientific work confirmed that faith. Like Descartes he explained the existence of God. Even Hobbes, a philosophical materialist who regarded religion as "accepted superstition", thought it should be established and enforced by the state – and he was an exception!

In the 17th century it was believed that science could conclusively prove the existence of God by exposing the evidence of His wisdom and power in creation. He was, however, seen as an abstract "first cause" rather than the personal, omnipresent God of theologians and mystics. For Descartes, natural laws which controlled the universe and which were discovered by the researchers of the time were "the laws which God had placed in nature". Descartes assumed that God had decided on them at the beginning of time, and that once he had created and set the universe in motion, He did not – as believed by medieval philosophy – participate in its daily actuation, but left it to function according to those laws, without interference.

This new view of the relationship between God and His universe was generally accepted more readily by Protestants than by Roman Catholics, as was also the case with the new scientific inventions. The Roman Catholic theologians of the 17th century did not welcome the philosophy of Descartes, as this opposed the system of Aristotle – the basis of their scholastic theology. The Cartesian system claimed to be based on the discoveries of the time, while the Roman Catholic system of dogma was in apparent conflict with empirical science.

On the other hand, Protestantism rejected tradition – one of the two pillars of scholasticism – as a source of Christian revelation. It accepted only the authority of the other pillar, the Scriptures. Protestants could therefore reject classical cosmology as something which was not taught in the Bible, and until the biological discoveries of the 19th century showed that the organic species of the world had not been determined for all time in the variety in which they had originally been created, Protestants had few problems in reconciling the views of modern science with the Bible and their own views.

In fact, the Cartesian philosophy was highly acceptable to Calvinists. The Cartesian view of God as the "first cause" which had set the universe in motion according to immutable laws fitted well with the Calvinist doctrine of predestination. Consequently, the theories of Descartes were taught at the Dutch universities and at Cambridge, the more Puritan of the two English universities, in the 17th century. In France the theories found followers amongst the Jansenists in the Roman Catholic Church, who had much in common with the Calvinists.

None the less, the 17th century ultimately gave rise to a scheme of scientific thought, which had been designed by mathematicians for the use of mathematicians. Such a philosophical system was not satisfactory to some other thinkers. The Cartesian system was not as successful as the one it replaced in supplying a philosophy which could accommodate all the important views of modern thinking. The result was the separation of science, on the one hand, from philosophy and religion, on the other. The works of Newton and his contemporaries were still known as "philosophical investigations", but gradually, in the course of the next two centuries, such works became known as "scientific investigations", and the change in name indicated an important change in attitude.

What of philosophy, as we understand it today, in the 17th century? The scientific revolution of necessity had to lead to a change in philosophy. However much the philosophers of the 17th century retained of the language, methods and assumptions of their predecessors, they did not study their works as had been done previously. Even in the most conservative intellectual circles much of the best thinking of the Middle Ages was soon neglected and forgotten.

It is also important to point out that the scientific revolution concerned and interested only a small group of people, an intellectual aristocracy, and not the mass, with its prejudices and superstitions. Such an intellectual division was not new – educated people were always a conscious minority.

Although it is difficult to overemphasize the importance of the scientific and philosophical revolution in the history of human thought, it is easy to overestimate its consequences for the community of the 17th century. When all is said and done, these intellectual movements exerted their influence only on a small part of mankind; in civilization, as in nature, there is an inertia which resists sudden change. Even were we to argue, as does D. Ogg,[9] that the old order disappeared from the terrains of abstract and scientific thought long before it was even questioned in the political area, that the philosophical revolution preceded the political revolution of the 18th century, and that the lead was given not by statesmen, but by thinkers, it must be remembered that this influence was very limited and absolutist theory extremely strong.

The 17th century revolution was also incomplete because the biologists lagged so far behind the mathematicians – man was still clearly distinguished, in origin and in destiny, from all other living things.

Another factor limited the importance of the "revolution", even amongst intellectuals: this was the formulation, for the first time, of a theory of limited human progress.

The French author, Fontenelle (1657-1757), foresaw a great future for human knowledge, but not for the progress of society. His view was that knowledge entails power over the forces of nature, but never over the capabilities of the soul. Mankind's passions and instincts are unalterable, and governments would, in the final instance, always have to resort to force.

Fontenelle did believe, however, in the popularization of knowledge, particularly of scientific knowledge, to all those with enough sense to understand its importance. This stood in contrast to the theory of most of the religious teachers earlier in the century: that knowledge of scientific discoveries should be reserved for the few; should it become public, it would have a disruptive effect on faith. The latter view was quite justified as long as the Bible was taken literally and, together with Aristotle, was regarded as the total of the knowable. Fontenelle declared that knowledge ultimately had to trickle down to the masses and would thus destroy many cherished assumptions and prejudices.

Fontenelle was the most important person to attempt to impart the results of the scientific movement to the world at large. Together with the journalistic intellectual, Addison, he was a writer of "popular science". The appeal which had already been made by Galileo and which would reach its climax with Fontenelle and his successors, was an appeal against the learned world of the time, against both church and university, for a new arbiter in human thought: a larger general reading public. The bourgeoisie in France, by the end of the 17th century (after 1680), had begun to take the lead, and a number of prominent intellectuals – Corneille, Racine, Molière, Boileau, La Bruyère, Pascal amongst them – came from their ranks in the time of Louis XIV. One cannot say, however, that Fontenelle repaired the broken contact between the intellectuals and the general public. The crusaders for scientific education of the masses had yet to appear. It was only certain groups of people in the church (men as well as women) who spread knowledge amongst the poor. Although they were no longer the leading thinkers, it was the followers of the old theological ideas who kept alive the tradition of the medieval church to bring enlightenment to the masses. For many generations to come it was still one of the basic facts of European civilization that an educated person differed from others. Only powerful revolutions in thinking, in politics and in social organization would change this situation.

Another important fact is that the discoveries of 17th century science were hastily converted into a new view of life and the world (a "Weltanschauung"), not so much by scientists themselves as by the inheritors and successors of Fontenelle, who were literary people. Fontenelle was a writer who had turned to science and he achieved considerable success in poetry and drama as well as with works about physics and astronomy. He was not personally important as a scientist, although he was secretary of the *Académie des Sciences* from 1699 to 1741. He was a sceptic before he had contact with the scientific movement, and this he learned from Lucretius and the more modern writers such as Machiavelli and Montaigne. This scepticism imparted to the results of the 17th century scientific movement a tendency which was seldom seen amongst scientists themselves and which Descartes would have repudiated.

In this regard it is important to note that the great intellectual movement of the 18th century was to be a literary one. It was not the new discoveries of science which were to determine the next twist to the tale, and the direction of western civilization. Fontenelle was the most important single link between the scientific revolution and the *philosophe* movement of the 18th century and in a sense he was the first of the French *philosophes*. Together with Pierre Bayle, a strong opponent of religious hypocrisy and intolerance, he formed the intellectual bridge between the 17th and the 18th century.

CHAPTER 7

EUROPE: BALANCE OF POWER AND COLONIAL EXPANSION

THE IDEA OF A BALANCE OF POWER

One of the most important aspects of international politics in 18th century Europe was the application of the principle of a balance of power. A balance of power can be seen as a means to curb the pursuit of excessive power extension by states. It indicates the maintenance of a balance between states which will prevent one of them from becoming so strong as to become a threat to the safety or independence of others. Such a balance is often achieved by the establishment of alliances which create a balance of power between groups of states.

The English expression "balance of power" and the French equivalent, "équilibre européen" found general usage early in the 18th century. But neither the idea of a balance, nor its application, were innovations – even less a creation of the 18th century. Through the centuries states had been forming alliances against the lust for conquest of any strong state. Since the internecine struggle of the Italian states in the Middle Ages it had been a vital concept in European politics.[1]

In the 18th century, however, this idea was elevated to an acknowledged and clearly formulated principle in European statecraft. The principle was also applied after France, in her endeavour to obtain a position of power in Europe, had been defeated in the Spanish War of Succession and the balance restored by the Peace of Utrecht in 1713. This principle was subsequently used to thwart the covetousness of the major powers to some degree and to prevent the settlements at Utrecht from being endangered. As a result, no state in the 18th century succeeded in achieving a (politically) predominant position on the continent of Europe.

It should be emphasized, however, that although the principle was often quoted, its mere existence would not prevent acts of aggression by major powers. The system of the balance of power was violated on a large scale by the cynical policies of the rulers of Austria, Prussia and Russia. Frederick the Great maintained that the balance of power was only an expression and that great endeavours could only succeed if it was ignored.[2] Whereas the big powers quoted the principle and attempted to use it in their dealings with other major powers, they ignored it in their treatment of the lesser states. One has only to refer to their actions regarding Silesia, Poland, Turkey and Sweden. Where extension of authority was the major aim of the powers, any means were justified in achieving this goal. Diplomacy was corrupt and unscrupulous, and racial or national borders were of no account. "They cut and carve states and kingdoms," Alberoni wrote of the rulers of his time, "as if they are

Dutch cheeses." Large parts of Italy were taken away from Spain and given to Austria at the Peace of Utrecht, while the Spanish Netherlands were given to the distant house of Habsburg. War was regarded as a legitimate means of extending own power or territory. In a century of absolute (albeit enlightened) kingship, no war was a national one in the modern sense of the word; the aim was expansion of royal power.

European statesmen regarded the maintenance of the balance of power as the best policy for their own countries. In 1717 the British envoy in Paris, Lord Stair, told the French regent that the external policy of Lord Stanhope was based on the principle of a balance of power aimed at making Austria as strong as France and ensuring that neither of them became more powerful and influential than the other. For Britain the maintenance of the balance of power principle was the basis of its European policy. The principle was applied particularly by Britain – for her own reasons. The protection of Hanover and the Hanoverian succession was of the greatest importance to Britain after 1714. She was also highly sensitive to the welfare of Holland and Belgium and their ports for reasons of her own security. Britain was possibly the only power which would even have gone to war to restore the balance achieved at Utrecht. In Spain, however, Alberoni throughout his term of office desired nothing more than to have the agreements of Utrecht revoked as being in conflict with the balance of power and detrimental to Spain and Italy.

There were also those who rejected the idea of a balance of power in their political writings. The criticism stemmed from the proponents of peace projects, who argued that a method had to be found to curb the naturally aggressive tendencies of states. The balance of power, according to them, was a hopelessly inadequate instrument for this purpose. According to the best-known critic, the Abbé de Saint-Pierre, it was "that vain Idol to which the Nations have sacrificed so blindly, so fruitlessly, and for so long a Time, so much Blood and Treasure".[3] The solution lay, it was believed, in the creation of an effective international body. Not one of the proposals of this nature, however, had the slightest chance of being put into practice. The statesmen of the time and also popular opinion (partly protected against the realities of war by the use of professional armies) had no enthusiasm for peace and viewed the idea as highly unrealistic.

We have said that the forming of alliances was a method of maintaining the balance of power. A feature of 18th century alliances was, however, their fluidity. For the sake of self-interest or gain a state would recruit another which was not its traditional ally into an alliance, which would in turn lead to a regrouping to thwart its ambitions. In this regard the so-called "diplomatic revolution", about which more later, is one of the most striking examples.

At the beginning of the century the balance of power was still thought to be based on Bourbon-Habsburg rivalry, with France enjoying the support of Spain and some German rulers (Bavaria in particular), and Austria relying on Britain and Holland. This view of the balance of power was, however, superficial and misleading almost from the outset. A number of diplomatic episodes (particularly the Anglo-French alliance of 1717 and the Austro-Spanish combination of 1725) show that the assumptions of the previous century no longer held water. Furthermore, the fact that after 1713 there was no state in western Europe which was in a position to dominate the Continent, as France had done under Louis XIV, brought to the politics of the time a fluidity which had previously been absent. Above all, the traditional views of the balance of power were undermined by radical changes in the status of many European countries. This entailed the decline of some, such as Holland, Sweden and Turkey, and the rapid rise of large, new political powers in eastern and central Europe, namely Russia and Prussia. The full implication of the latter remained unnoticed, however, until the 1740s, and even till the diplomatic revolution of 1756 most observers still thought in terms of the traditional Bourbon-Habsburg struggle. It was only at the outbreak of the Seven Years War that the old balance of power irrevocably broke up. The short-term changes in European diplomacy after 1713 must be seen, however, in the light of the immediate aims of the rulers and on the whole had little influence on the fundamental changes which were taking place. Where Britain on occasion temporarily co-operated with France, or Austria and France engaged in war, this has to be taken into account.

INFLUENCE OF THE EXPANSION OF EUROPE

Apart from the Continental balance of power there was a second one of increasing importance: the power relationships of the European states overseas where the British-French competition for trade and colonies was of particular importance – a struggle which had already taken on considerable dimensions by the end of the 17th century. Holland had fallen out of this race at the beginning of the 18th century, and Spain in this century was never numbered amongst the leading sea powers.

This struggle particularly influenced Britain's participation in European politics. Britain traditionally interfered on the Continent to restore the balance of power against a dominant state. Because of the increasing competition for trade and colonies she saw even greater advantage in a number of more or less equally strong powers or power groupings, whose attention would be occupied to such an extent by mutual envy and fear that they would not compete with her in her expansion abroad. The predominance of one country on the Continent – in particular if it, like France, possessed a considerable naval power and was situated right across the Channel – was a threat to Britain's trade interests. As early as the end of the War of the Spanish Succession an English pamphlet described the Continental balance of power as a prerequisite for British world domination.

It can be said that the application of the balance of power principle thus underwent a shift in emphasis. Where the Bourbon-Habsburg struggle was the axis on which the European balance of power revolved in the 17th century, the Anglo-French competition for trade and colonies became increasingly important in the 18th century, and this also, to some extent, determined the power groupings on the continent of Europe.

Most contemporaries realized that these two aspects were intimately related. In particular they believed that a state which could control the sea and Europe's trade with the outside world would largely be able to make itself the master of the

European continent. From this assumption grew the idea – enunciated as early as 1720 – that the existing balance between the maritime powers of the European states should be maintained on the same basis as that between their European territories.

In the majority of Continental states this aspect of the balance of power evoked anti-British feelings. They (and particularly France, normally supported by Spain) endeavoured – in the main unsuccessfully – to limit the enormous growth of Britain's maritime power and overseas possessions and, if it were possible, to bring about decline. The zeal, sometimes brutality, with which Britain in times of war harnessed her sea power to interfere on a large scale with neutral shipping which was carrying contraband or was trading with her enemies did much to increase the hostility which she was now generally experiencing. French propaganda emphasized the danger of Britain's dominance at sea, as well as the necessity for Europe to unite against it. Propaganda of this kind was particularly vicious during the Seven Years War, and the idea of a *balance de commerce*, which had to be protected against the excessive power of Britain, was propagated. The British, the duc de Choiseul alleged, professed to be protecting the balance on land, which was being threatened by no-one, but was totally destroying the balance at sea, which no-one was defending.

After the Spanish War of Succession Britain was the most powerful force at sea as a result of her strong fleet and trade. In 1715 she had about a third of the world's fighting ships, France and Holland together another third, and Spain, Portugal, Denmark, Sweden and Russia the remaining third. In subsequent years there was, apart from the decline of the Netherlands, an appreciable increase in Russian maritime power, particularly as a result of the endeavours of Peter the Great. At the time of his death in 1725 Russia was one of the leading naval powers. France, like Holland, had to sacrifice her maritime needs to her military requirements on the Continent during the later wars of Louis XIV, and she could never, in spite of the efforts of her statesmen, achieve naval parity with Britain.

The struggle for trade and colonial supremacy between Britain and France in the Mediterranean and the Levant, India and the coast of Africa, North America and the West Indies, continued unabated after Utrecht. After a period of peaceful competition it broke out in a world-wide struggle in 1744. Only after half the century had passed was it determined that Britain and not France would reign supreme in India and America.

BALANCE OF POWER AFTER THE PEACE OF UTRECHT: A PEACEFUL ERA

The signing of an international peace treaty is never generally satisfactory and is followed by a period of tension between the powers who have an interest in its maintenance on the one hand, and those who strive for its revision on the other. The years after the Peace of Utrecht – which includes the Peace of Rastadt and Baden (1714) and the Barrière Treaty (1715) – was no exception. At least two of the participants in the Spanish War of Succession were not satisfied with the end result.

Emperor Charles VI of Austria did not regard his gains in Italy (Sardinia, Naples and the Spanish territories in northern Italy) and in the southern Netherlands, which were ceded to him at Utrecht, as sufficient recompense for the crown of Spain which he had hoped to unite with his possessions in Germany. He was hoping for a rearrangement of the Italian division (he wanted Sicily in particular) and he hoped to exchange the southern Netherlands for Bavaria. The alternative to the latter – to acquire for Austria a share of world trade through the Belgian Ostend Company – would result in opposition from Britain and Holland.

The Spanish Bourbons were not satisfied with the terms of Utrecht either. During the reign of the first Bourbon king, Philip V, Spain had an aggressive policy. Although Philip had formally renounced his claim to the Bourbon throne of France at Utrecht, he still felt that he, rather than Louis XV, was entitled to it. Neither could he reconcile himself to the loss of the Spanish possessions in Italy and the Netherlands. His dissatisfaction was nurtured by the ambitions of his second wife, Elizabeth Farnese, who lived in the hope that her sons, Don Carlos and Don Philip, would be provided for by the restoration of Spanish rule in Italy, from where she stemmed. (The children by Philip's first marriage were the heirs to the Spanish throne.)

Although Holland was not happy with the Barrière Treaty, with the position of Austria and with the conduct of Britain, she had reached the end of her golden century by 1715 and was of necessity compelled to support Britain and Utrecht.

France supported the balance of power achieved at Utrecht. Not that she was satisfied with the settlement: she was determined to dispute British supremacy in North America, where she had lost important colonies. Although France was apparently still the most important power in Europe, she was facing a variety of problems, amongst them the threat of national bankruptcy. She therefore needed time to recover from her exhausting wars. The Duc d'Orléans, who was acting as regent for the young Louis XV, feared that any disturbance of the balance of power would provide Philip V with the opportunity of removing him from office.

After the Peace of Utrecht Britain, under the able leadership of Stanhope, took the lead in the effort to maintain the peace and the balance of power. Although she had emerged as potentially the strongest power and many of the terms of peace were to her advantage, Britain also had her problems. The advantages were: controlling the Mediterranean sea through the acquisition of Gibraltar; obtaining Newfoundland, Nova Scotia and the Hudson Bay territory from France; getting the *Asiento* (monopoly in the provision of slaves to the Spanish colonies), as well as the right to send one ship annually to trade with the Spanish colonies. One of the problems was that in the years following the peace there was considerable dissension in the country. Queen Anne died childless in 1714 and was succeeded by the elector of Hanover who became George I. To many Britons he was a stranger. His inability to speak English contributed to the establishment of parliamentary government in Britain, which meant that national interests (and particularly trade interests) increasingly determined foreign policy. The king's attachment to Hanover, however, also increasingly drew Britain into Continental politics, and remained a constant and important consideration in this respect. The presence on the Continent of a claimant to the British throne (the so-called Pretender, James Edward, son of James II) who enjoyed the support of the French court and of many Britons, particularly those in Scotland, was a further bedevilling factor. His attempted insurrection in Scotland in 1715, it is true, was suppressed without too much trouble, but he could not be ignored, and the position of the house of Hanover remained weak.

The war-weariness of France and Britain, the peace policies of Walpole and Orléans (and later Fleury), and the maintenance of an uneasy balance of power contributed to keep the general peace in Europe and to curb the ambitions of the aggressive states such as Spain, Austria and (up to 1719) Sweden. The most important reason why there was no large-scale conflict was, however, the British-French alliance of 1716. Although commercial and colonial competition between them continued, the domestic situations in both countries made peace a necessity. *Rapprochement* came from the French side. Orléans feared that if Louis XV were to die, Philip V would attempt to claim the succession. A strong alliance was ranged against France and consequent isolation was also a danger. Stanhope had succeeded in 1715 in creating the Third Barrière Treaty which was acceptable to Holland, as well as Austria, and this was followed in 1716 by a British-Austrian treaty. Spain could also become involved in this alliance. As a result of the continued activities of the Pretender, the new regime in England was as unsafe and in need of an ally as was the regent of France. Secondly, Britain had to cope with the unfavourable course of the Northern War, where Russia was in the process of winning the struggle against the Swedes. Peter the Great was in garrison in Mecklenburg, on the border of Hanover, constituting a threat to this territory. George feared that France and Russia would come to an agreement – there were rumours of negotiations – and saw a French alliance as the only way to counteract this new danger. The alliance of Hanover between Britain and France became the Triple Alliance when Holland joined it in January 1717. France withdrew its support of the Pretender, and the three powers pledged themselves to honour the terms of Utrecht, in particular the agreement that the house of Orléans would succeed to the throne of France if Louis XV were to die without issue.

As long as the Triple Alliance existed, it strove for peace in Europe. For almost a generation – up to 1733, when another general war broke out – Europe was by and large peaceful. It was clear, however, that a revival of hostilities could be averted only by wise and firm action amongst the leading powers. The resolve of various states to rid themselves of the limitations imposed by Utrecht, together with the rise of Russia, pointed towards future sources of friction in the north and east, as well as in the south and west of Europe.

For a few years Britain dominated Continental politics. Apart from the Triple Alliance of 1717, Whig statesmen also endeavoured to retain the friendship of Austria. A return to the system of the Grand Alliance was, however, hampered if not made quite impossible by the dissatisfaction of the court of Vienna with the Peace of Utrecht, the Barrière Treaty and the Anglo-French alliance. The Jacobites, who had been driven out of France, were allowed by Charles VI to shelter in Belgium. In January 1718 George I paid the emperor a sum of money to solve this problem, which opened the way for the Quadruple Alliance which was effected in August 1718.

This alliance was made between France, Britain, Austria and Holland to bring about peace in southern Europe. Elizabeth Farnese (supported by Alberoni) was threatening the peace in this area with her desire to regain for her sons some of the lost possessions in Italy at the cost of Austria. As tension between Spain and Austria mounted, Stanhope tried to satisfy them by a revision of the peace treaty, but when Austria was once again at war with Turkey, Philip V struck, and Spanish troops occupied Sardinia and Sicily, from where southern Italy could be invaded. The countries of the Quadruple Alliance, however, caused the failure of Spain's plans. French troops invaded Spain, and Admiral Byng destroyed the Spanish fleet at Cape Passaro in the Mediterranean. The Spanish had to admit defeat and accept Stanhope's plan. Philip V and Charles VI recognized each other's titles and Philip recognized Orléans as heir to the French throne and George I as king of England. Charles gained Sicily and in return relinquished Sardinia to Savoy. Don Carlos was recognized as the heir to the Italian duchies of Parma and Piacenza.

Britain wanted peace in southern Europe to enable it to resist the dangers which had developed in the north. Events in the north were a constant source of concern to Britain and a steadily increasing threat to peace in Europe. The Great Northern War between Russia and Sweden, which ended in 1721 with the Peace of Nystadt, brought about a radical change in the northern balance of power. Russia was now in control of a large part of the eastern Baltic states. It was the beginning of the rapid growth of Russia, which would subsequently exploit the weakness of Sweden, Poland and Turkey to extend her borders and become involved in the politics of Europe. Henceforward Russia, together with Prussia under Frederick William, would dominate north-eastern Europe and in due course compete with Britain, France and Austria. The destruction of the balance of power in the Baltic area did not suit Britain and France – particularly not Britain, whose supremacy at sea depended on the naval supplies from these territories, and who was always concerned about Hanover.

Spain's joining of the Quadruple Alliance in 1720, followed in 1721 by the ending of the war in the north, served to create a pretence of peace, and in the years after 1720 two European congresses, which met first at Cambrai and then at Soissons, attempted to settle the remaining questions at issue.

The ten years from the death of Orléans and Dubois (1723) to the outbreak of the Polish War of Succession, form an uneasy and complicated period. The alliance between Britain and France was maintained by both Bourbon and Fleury (who governed on behalf of Louis XV from 1723 onwards), but the existence and increasing importance of a strong party at the French court, which was opposed to the link with Britain, foreshadowed future complications. The growing coolness between Britain and Austria and between Austria and Prussia tended to weaken the position of Charles VI. The emperor was endeavouring to obtain guarantees for such chimeras as his Pragmatic Sanction (which gave his own daughters precedence over his elder brother, Joseph I, the previous emperor) and the establishment of an East India company at Ostend. The conduct of Charles was the chief reason for tension amongst the members of the Quadruple Alliance.

The most serious problem in Europe, however, was that created by Elizabeth

Farnese. Hassall wrote: "During the ten years from 1723 to 1733 Elizabeth Farnese was the pivot upon which the diplomacy of Europe turned."[4] It is understandable that Spain was totally dissatisfied with the terms which the Quadruple Alliance compelled her to accept. Spain's three major grievances were: Sicily and Naples in the possession of Austria; Gibraltar and Mahon in the hands of Britain; and the immense contraband trade by British merchants and ships in Spanish America. Britain was the active supporter of all these irritations and therefore Spain's special enemy. From 1713, Spain therefore tended towards an improved relationship with France. Offended at Britain's refusal to negotiate about her possession of Gibraltar, Spain sought *rapprochement* with France in 1719. A tripartite marriage agreement was concluded. Amongst others, the three year old Spanish infanta, Maria Anna Victoria, was betrothed to Louis XV of France and sent there to be educated as the future French queen.

The duke of Bourbon, however, alienated Spain in 1724 by returning the infanta and betrothing Louis XV to the immediately marriageable Maria Lesczynski, the daughter of the exiled king of Poland. Elizabeth Farnese, already impatient with the delay at Cambrai in achieving anything tangible for her sons, decided to make representations directly to the emperor. He lent a ready ear, as he was in conflict with the British about his Ostend Company, and as Britain and Holland would not endorse his Pragmatic Sanction. In April 1725 Europe was surprised by the news of the signing of the first Treaty of Vienna between Austria and Spain. It was an offensive and defensive alliance between the two antagonists in the Spanish War of Succession. An attack on Gibraltar and its restitution to Spain were proposed. The two kings abandoned all claims to each other's territories, Don Carlos was to marry Maria Theresa (and was also to succeed in Parma and Piacenza), and Don Philip another daughter of the emperor. Spain guaranteed the Pragmatic Sanction and promised trade preferences to the Ostend Company.

It was a great triumph for Elizabeth Farnese. It led to a diplomatic revolution which, however, unlike those of 1717 and 1756, did not lead to a permanent change in the relationships between the various powers. In fact, the Viennese agreement was not a great danger. The aims of Charles and Elizabeth were too conflicting to ensure long-term co-operation. However, the western powers met again to counter the threat to the balance of power in Europe and to their own commercial interests. France, Britain and Holland joined with Sweden, Prussia and Denmark in the defensive Treaty of Hanover of 1725. Spain doggedly but fruitlessly besieged Gibraltar, but the war between Spain and Britain did not spread. Both Walpole, who came to power with the succession to the throne of George II, and Fleury desired peace to enable them to build up their national strengths, and they co-operated to this end. The emperor withdrew from the alliance with Spain and under British pressure (through the merchant classes) also relinquished the idea of an Ostend Company. Frederick William of Prussia, however, soon left the western alliance and joined the emperor in the Treaty of Wüsterhausen of 1726. In the same year the emperor found another ally in Russia. Catherine, disturbed by the penetration of the British fleet into the Baltic, undertook to guarantee the Pragmatic Sanction.

Elizabeth Farnese, disillusioned by the Austrian alliance, turned to her enemies, and in 1729 Spain, France and Britain concluded the Treaty of Seville. The birth of a son to the French king had removed the major bone of contention between Spain and France. Britain was favourably disposed, as the treaty between Prussia and Austria had made Hanover vulnerable to an attack by Austria. By this treaty Spanish troops were to be sent to the duchies, Spain was immediately to revoke her concessions to the Ostend Company, renew the *Asiento* and relinquish her claim to Gibraltar.

Spain's *rapprochement* with France and Britain incurred the wrath of Charles VI, and on the death of the duke of Parma he sent Austrian troops to occupy that duchy. Walpole averted war by bribing the emperor with an acceptance of the Pragmatic Sanction. In return, Charles finally dissolved the Ostend Company and allowed Don Carlos to take over Parma and Piacenza in the second Treaty of Vienna (1731).

Elizabeth Farnese was, however, not quite satisfied. The question of the Polish succession would provide her with a further opportunity.

THE WAR OF THE POLISH SUCCESSION

The chronic anarchy in Poland resulting from its constitution (which stipulated that the nobility should choose the king), and the egoism, lawlessness and recalcitrance of the nobility were ideal circumstances for surrounding states with aggressive tendencies. Every election turned into a struggle of foreign interests and intrigues.

This was the case in 1732 when Augustus of Saxony, who was also king of Poland, died. Poland now took the place of Italy in becoming the apple of discord between the European powers. The tsarina as well as the emperor supported the candidacy of Augustus III as his father's successor, while Louis XV was in favour of his father-in-law, Stanislaus Lesczynski. The latter was elected with the help of French bribes, but then Russian and Austrian troops invaded Poland and forced the Diet to elect Augustus as king.

War was inevitable. France had recovered from her financial crisis and was resuming her old, active role in Europe. Fleury was personally not in favour of war, but the war group under the leadership of Chauvelin, minister of foreign affairs from 1727 onwards, was traditionally anti-Austrian, and Fleury could not prevent them from embroiling France in a war. The French were also keen to sign a treaty with Spain which would unite the Bourbons against Britain. Spain, which also welcomed war, concluded the First Family Agreement with France in 1733. The two powers agreed to drive Austria out of Italy, where all conquests, with the exception of Milan (which was promised to their ally, Savoy), were to be given to Don Carlos. They would also attempt to curb British overseas trade and colonization.

Britain and Holland, however, remained neutral on account of a promise made by France, namely that she would not attack the Austrian Netherlands. One of the fears of the British government was that the outbreak of a European war would be followed by the occupation of the Austrian Netherlands by French troops and an attack on Hanover. Since Walpole had begun dominating Britain's foreign policy from about 1730, Britain was for some time to restrain herself from active interference in Europe. According to Walpole and other Whigs, Britain should preferably keep the peace and develop her trade unless there was a major crisis.

The war was fought in Poland, on the Rhine and in Italy. In Poland Russian troops drove Stanislaus from the country, and the struggle on the Rhine was indecisive. In Italy, Austria was no match for the combined forces of France, Spain and Savoy. Spain conquered Naples and Sicily on her own, and Don Carlos became Carlos III of this Bourbon kingdom.

The war ended in 1735 when Fleury agreed to peace with the emperor and Spain and Savoy had to follow his example. The third Treaty of Vienna was, however, only concluded in 1738. According to this, Parma and Piacenza again became Austrian possessions, but Don Carlos kept Naples and Sicily. Francis of Lorraine, who had married Maria Theresa in 1736, received Tuscany. Stanislaus renounced the Polish throne for ever and was given the duchy of Lorraine in compensation. France recognized the Pragmatic Sanction.

A period of complex and somewhat confusing conflict and diplomacy, resulting from the problems of Utrecht, was concluded by this peace.

Austria was worst off. Although she managed to place her candidate on the Polish throne, she lost Naples and Sicily, as well as a great deal of prestige. It is important to note that Vienna was highly dissatisfied with Britain's neutrality. Walpole did indeed leave an old ally in the lurch. The alliance between Russia and Austria was also of first-rate importance, as these two powers successfully implemented their policy in Poland. The appearance of Russian troops on the Rhine for the first time in European history proved to a surprised Europe how valuable a Russian alliance could be, and undoubtedly it speeded the peace.

The war also indicated the increasing coolness between Vienna and Berlin. Frederick William, in accordance with his obligations under the treaty, had sent 10 000 men to join the imperial army, but was extremely irritated at the course of events in Poland. He was completely ignored throughout the peace negotiations and declared that he had been let down by Russia and Austria. The Polish War of Succession was a definitive epoch in the history of the increasing conflict between Austria and Prussia in Germany.

The success of Elizabeth Farnese was the most remarkable feature of the time. She had promoted the interests of her sons with every peace since Utrecht and finally gained a royal crown for the eldest.

The effect of the war on British-French relations was also of great importance for the future. The alliance was seriously weakened by the war. Louis's determination to see Lesczynski on the Polish throne was a warning to Europe that France was ready to return to the policies of Louis XIV. The French would not be satisfied with subjecting themselves to British leadership and to play a secondary role in the affairs of the Continent. The able Cardinal Fleury quietly and successfully strove to restore French leadership on the Continent by cultivating the friendship of Spain and reviving the traditional enmity towards the Habsburgs. As long as Fleury desisted from reviving the territorial ambitions of Louis XIV, as long as – above all –

he did not disturb the status quo in the Netherlands, Walpole was prepared to let peace reign. None the less, France's position was strengthened with Lorraine (which it would get after the death of Stanislaus), as well as by the transfer of commanding positions in the central Mediterranean to an ally.

The efforts of Walpole and Fleury to promote the development of trade in their respective countries also impeded Anglo-French friendship. France recovered strongly and competed strenuously with Britain, which ruffled British merchants no end. The secret clause in the French-Spanish alliance which was aimed against Britain's trade supremacy was sufficient evidence of France's eagerness to unite the Bourbons against Britain. United, France and Spain could mount formidable opposition against the colonial expansion and commercial aggression of Britain and simultaneously act in concert against the emperor. The possibility that the French and Spanish Bourbons might dominate Europe haunted British statesmen up to the French Revolution. Spain was just then harming British trade in Spain and Spanish America with its *guarda costas*, and in the colonies British-French competition was continuing unabated. Although Bourbon arms during the war had been pointed chiefly at the emperor, Spain's open hostility towards Britain would surface in 1739 for all the world to see. The link between Britain and France, which had prevented a major war in 1713 and in 1740, had worn thin over the years. Walpole and Fleury were fighting a losing battle against the war-mongers.

THE WAR OF THE AUSTRIAN SUCCESSION AND THE STRUGGLE FOR TRADE AND COLONIES

The peace which was made in 1738 was not to last for long. It was a commercial difference between Britain and Spain which would once again inflame hostilities.

The countermeasures Spain took against British methods to break the Spanish monopoly in their colonies (the West Indies and Spanish America) reluctantly compelled the British government into a war with Spain. Walpole, aware of the increasingly friendly relations between the French and Spanish royal houses, and fearing that war with Spain could rapidly be followed by war with France, tried in vain to keep the peace. When Captain Jenkins, master of a British vessel, testified that a Spanish coast guard in the Caribbean had detained him and cut off one of his ears, a popular movement developed in Britain, and this, at the insistence of Walpole's opponents, led to a declaration of war against Spain in October 1739 – the so-called "War of Jenkins's Ear".

The war was characterized particularly by British attacks on the Spanish West Indian islands and on Spanish trade in the Pacific. Vernon's attack on Cartagena (1740) was, however, an expensive failure, and Anson's activities in the Pacific, although partially successful, had no lasting results. As Spain was an ally of France, the war was to escalate to one between France and Britain at sea. Britain allowed France to expand on land as long as she did not arouse the jealousy of the British people by competing at sea. This suited Fleury, who was in favour of consolidating France on land and who neglected the French colonies and navy.

Every colonial conflict found its counterpart in a European war, and the Spanish-English conflict soon became a wider European struggle. Two events in 1740 led to a European war which impinged on the one already being fought and which extended it into the War of the Austrian Succession. These events were the death of Charles VI in October 1740 and the conquest of Silesia by Frederick II, who had become king of Prussia in May 1740. These two events constituted a new threat to the balance of power and inaugurated a new era in European history.

The succession of Maria Theresa in the Habsburg territories, the goal to which Charles VI had dedicated himself for 20 years, had been guaranteed by all the major European powers, but the apparent weakness of Maria Theresa's position fired the ambitions of other rulers. A number of states, despite the Pragmatic Sanction, began staking claims. The elector of Bavaria, Charles Albert, claimed the imperial crown, and was supported by France. (His wife was the eldest daughter of Joseph I.) Augustus III of Saxony-Poland in turn claimed Moravia and Silesia; Charles Emmanuel of Sardinia wanted Milan; Elizabeth Farnese desired a further part of Italy for Don Philip; and Frederick II claimed Silesia.

Frederick set the ball rolling by invading and conquering Silesia. With the battle of Mollwitz (1741), when Frederick defeated Austria, he demonstrated the efficiency of the Prussian infantry, and this encouraged other claimants to Habsburg territories to strike as well.

In France Fleury was in favour of co-operation between the Bourbons and the Habsburgs, but the war party under the duke of Belleisle set the tune. In contrast to the peace policies of Fleury, Belleisle advocated a return to the policy of Henry IV, Mazarin and Richelieu: to humiliate the Habsburgs, to rule over Germany by keeping her divided and to extend the boundaries of France to the Rhine. He was also opposed to the alliance with Britain. In May 1741 France agreed to the Treaty of Nymphenburg with Charles Albert, supporting his claimancy. The next month the Treaty of Breslau with Frederick followed, recognizing his possession of Lower Silesia. Spain, Saxony, Sardinia and Sweden joined the alliance of France, Bavaria and Prussia.

Only Britain, Holland and Hanover ranged themselves on the side of Austria. Britain did this not merely as an ally of Austria, but as chief guardian of the balance of power. If Austria were to be divided by its enemies, there would not be a single large military power on the Continent to serve as a counterbalance to France. Of course, there was also the question of competition for trade and colonies with Spain and France. The prospect of a revival of French aggression moved Walpole to allow Maria Theresa a British subsidy, but not military assistance. The reason for the latter was that George II feared a French or Prussian attack on Hanover. He therefore, in September 1741, concluded a treaty of neutrality for his electorate with France. George saw the position in Germany from the point of view of a German prince and was, like many other German princes, opposed to the domination of Germany by the Habsburgs – he was not at all averse to seeing Charles VII of Bavaria crowned as emperor. On the other hand, although tied to Prussia by marriage (the mother of Frederick II was the sister of George II) and by religious sympathies, the relations of George I as well as George II with the Prussian kings had seldom been friendly up to the Seven Years War, and Hanover was continually attempting to deprive Prussia of her position of leadership in northern Germany.

Maria Theresa bribed Frederick to break up the coalition against her. Through the good offices of Britain, where Walpole was striving for peace between Prussia and Austria, the secret agreement of Klein Schnellendorf was reached between Maria Theresa and Frederick, by which the latter was given Lower Silesia and undertook to demand no further concessions from Austria.

When the French-Bavarian army invaded Prague, however, Frederick broke his agreement with Austria to fight once again with the French, fearing that he was on the losing side. He had cynical contempt for promises and treaties which were not to the advantage of his own interests. The position of Maria Theresa, with six major powers ranged against her, was therefore critical. Amongst her allies, Britain's attention was wholly taken up with her war at sea against Spain, aided by France (there was as yet no official war between Britain and France), while Holland was interested solely in her own safety. Maria Theresa could expect no help from Russia, which was incapacitated by a dynastic crisis and a Swedish attack on St Petersburg.

Shortly after February 1742, when Charles of Bavaria was crowned emperor in Frankfurt, Britain began playing an active part in the war. Walpole's reign came to an end when the failure of the Spanish-American expeditions roused popular opinion against him. Britain, now under Carteret's ministry, openly became an ally of Austria. Mercenaries were sent to the Austrian Netherlands. Carteret succeeded in luring Sardinia from the anti-Austrian camp, and the British fleet forced Don Carlos of Sicily to remain neutral. As a result of pressure from Britain, which preferred to aim her war effort against France, Maria Theresa concluded the Treaty of Berlin (1742) with Frederick, thereby ceding him the whole of Silesia.

The French army had to fight its way out of Bohemia with heavy casualties, and an allied army, consisting of British, Dutch and Hanoverian troops under George II, defeated the French at Dettingen. Bavaria was once again occupied.

Although the tide had turned in Maria Theresa's favour, she preferred revenge to peace. She united with Britain and Sardinia in the Treaty of Worms (1743), with the aim of driving the French and Spanish from Italy. Thereupon France and Spain concluded the Second Family Agreement.

Now a new phase of the war began. Britain was no longer merely an aid to Austria, but a major participant. In London and Versailles it was realized that the point at issue was no longer the maintenance of the Pragmatic Sanction, but supremacy at sea and in America and India. France was now pre-eminent as Austria's opponent on the Continent, and of Britian at sea and in the colonies. France formally declared war on Britain on the 15th March 1744, and on Austria on the 4th April. The struggle between Austria and Prussia over Silesia, the French-Austrian conflict and the mercantile struggle between Britain and the Bourbons of France and Spain were now being fought simultaneously.

The Second Silesian War began in May 1744 when the Alliance of Frankfurt (Prussia, Bavaria, etc.) against Austria was formed. At the beginning of 1745, however, Emperor Charles VII died, ending the alliance. Britain, saddled with a Jacobite revolt when Charles Edward landed in Scotland on the 4th August 1745, and George II, fearing that Hanover would be exposed to an attack by Frederick, (British troops were required to quell the rebellion), signed the Convention of Hanover on the 26th August. In this he guaranteed Frederick's possession of Silesia and confirmed the Treaty of Berlin, also on behalf of his allies. In September 1745 Francis of Lorraine was elected emperor. The Second Silesian War was ended by the Treaty of Dresden in December 1745. The Convention of Hanover was confirmed, and Frederick kept Silesia and recognized the new emperor, Francis I. Frederick thus gained a dominant position for his kingdom in Germany, and Prussia withdrew from the struggle.

For the rest of the war, hostilities were practically confined to a conflict in Italy and the Netherlands between Austria on the one hand, and France and Spain on the other, and between Britain and France in North America and India.

In North America the French Canadians recaptured Port Royal, but volunteers from New England, supported by a British naval force, struck back by occupying Louisburg (1745). The rest of the war here was little more than an intensification of French and Indian raids along the northern borders of the British colonies.

The French fleet was gradually weakening, and two naval battles in 1747, at Cape Finisterre and Belle Ile, sealed its fate.

In India, Dupleix, assisted by a naval force under La Bourdonnais, occupied Madras. A British naval force besieged Pondichéry, but did not succeed in capturing it.

In 1748 a war-weary Europe began peace negotiations, and in October the Peace of Aix-la-Chapelle was effected.

EUROPE AFTER AIX-LA-CHAPELLE

The settlement at Aix-la-Chapelle in 1748 ushered in a brief interlude of uneasy peace amongst the nations of Europe. The treaty solved little and in general represented a return to the pre-war position originally established by the Utrecht agreements of 1713-1715.

Territorial restitution and the resumption of former privileges and guarantees were to a large extent the guiding principles at Aix-la-Chapelle. France undertook to return Madras to Britain, to dismantle her seaward fortifications at Dunkirk, to expel the Stuart Pretender and to recognize the British Hanoverian succession. The military achievements of Maurice de Saxe and Löwendal in 1747-1748 were sacrificed in a French withdrawal from the Austrian Netherlands and the restoration to the United Provinces of the defensive barrier fortresses. In exchange for Madras, Britain handed back Louisburg on Cape Breton Island to France, but was confirmed by Spain in possession of the *Asiento* slave-trade contract for the period of its suspension during the war. Austria, however, not only had to accept permanent Prussian occupation of Silesia and Glatz, but was also forced to confirm the cession of the Ticino frontier to Sardinia, and of Parma, Piacenza and Guastalla to the Spanish prince, Don Philip. On the other hand, the Pragmatic Sanction was endorsed by all signatories to the peace treaty, and Maria Theresa's husband, Francis, was acknowledged as Holy Roman emperor.

Although so much of the old order had been re-established in 1748, a new Europe had, however, emerged from the War of the Austrian Succession. For the moment, traditional alliances held good, despite the stresses to which some of them had been subjected during the recent conflict. However, the balance of power after Aix-la-Chapelle underwent a significant change, and this circumstance, combined with the continuing Anglo-French rivalry for a colonial empire, brought about a new alignment of states in which national interests took precedence over dynastic issues. It is pertinent, therefore, to review at this stage the position in Europe on the eve of what came to be called the diplomatic revolution.

The Dutch republic, pursuing a course of qualified neutrality in defence of its commerce during the War of the Austrian Succession, and bound by treaty to Britain as an auxiliary, had visibly declined in stature. Financially weakened, its economy exposed to increasing foreign competition and invaded by French forces in the closing stages of the war, the Dutch state had turned, as it had done in 1672, to the house of Orange for salvation. But Prince William IV, first member of his family to be chosen as Stadtholder in all seven provinces, proved incapable of achieving real unity. The power of the urban oligarchs remained unbroken, and the scheme of economic reform which he espoused in 1751, shortly before his death, encountered insuperable opposition from vested interests. Nor was he able to do more to support his ally, Britain, than to provide limited assistance to Boscawen in the British admiral's ineffectual campaign of 1748 against the French in the Indies. Britain, indeed, no longer regarded the United Provinces as a reliable Continental bulwark in her foreign and colonial policy, and the Dutch came increasingly to resent Britain's failure to defend their own interests. Despite pro-British Orangist sentiment, many in the republic looked to France for future help. It was the beginning of the end of an old alliance and certainly the end of Dutch significance in European politics, if not in the fields of commerce and banking. The French threat of 1747 had, however, raised fears in mercantile circles for the Dutch position in East Indian waters, diverting capital and expertise in 1751 to Prussia's short-lived Asiatic Company of Emden, which joined Denmark and Sweden, also enjoying Dutch financial support, as a new competitor east of the Cape of Good Hope in the potentially lucrative China trade.

Spain had failed to wrest Gibraltar and Minorca from Britain, but had emerged from the War of the Austrian Succession as a respectable naval power, well able to hold her own against British attacks on its American colonies. Spain's military intervention in Italy had been less successful, but Aix-la-Chapelle had at least satisfied the ambitions of Philip V's widow, Elizabeth Farnese, in providing a modest dukedom for her son, Don Philip. By 1748, however, Elizabeth's star was waning. Ferdinand VI (1746-1759) was married to Barbara of Braganza, a union which linked the royal families of Spain and Portugal, and for the immediate future Spanish policy was to follow the example set by her neighbour in avoiding international involvement. Better relations with Portugal's ally, Britain, were one of the results of this new approach by the Spanish government.

Another, foreshadowing a coming change of direction in European politics, was Carvajal's *rapprochement* with the Italian Habsburgs in 1752 to preserve the status quo in that politically fragmented region and to allow it a respite from the clashes of foreign armies. Two other consequences of the war for Italy deserve passing comment: Sardinia, whose recent policy had been a classic illustration of "geography making conscience impossible",[5] had found opportunism profitable, and the island's devious involvement in the struggle between Bourbon and Habsburg left it in a much stronger position on the northern mainland. The republic of Genoa, however, forced into alliance with France and Spain at Aranjuez in 1745, suffered invasion, unrest and a temporary loss of independence. A further stage towards total eclipse was reached in 1768, when continuing insurrection in Corsica led Genoa to sell the island to France. Italian unity was still far distant, the Spanish Bourbons were firmly established in the Two Sicilies under Elizabeth Farnese's other son, Don Carlos, and the Habsburgs in the Milanese and Tuscany, but the germ was there and Sardinia's house of Savoy was destined to provide the Italian kingdom of 1861 with its first monarch.

Opportunism on the Sardinian model had also been the keynote in divided Germany. Saxony and Bavaria had both found themselves in the Austrian camp after first seeking that country's dismemberment. The former, whose elector-prince, Augustus III, had dual interests as king of Poland, came to see Prussia as a dangerous ally, while Bavaria only retained her independence by accepting Austrian dictates and renouncing imperial claims advanced by the Wittelsbach ruling line. Maria Theresa's turncoat allies of "slender resources and equally slender fidelity"[6] emerged from the war with no enhanced status or reputation, although Bavaria remained neutral after making peace with Austria at Füssen in 1745.

It was the Prussia of Frederick the Great which gained most from the war, although not represented at the peace. By 1748 Prussia was set on the road to future greatness and the ultimate leadership of a united Germany. Her high standing amongst the powers had been won by the achievements of a disciplined army, and the acquisition of Silesia, with its valuable industrial resources, had immeasurably increased her potential. The Hohenzollern territories, extending over northern Germany in isolated segments from Cleves to east Prussia, with Brandenburg at their heart, were not yet a nation-state, but their ruler had made them a force to be reckoned with.

Austria had good cause to fear her upstart German rival, and it is not surprising that the alliance she had concluded with Russia in 1746 contained the secret clause that any attack by Frederick on Austria would mean the retrocession of Silesia. For the loss of this province had deprived Maria Theresa of the dominant position she had hitherto enjoyed in the German empire. Austria nevertheless remained a great power and the unresolved question of German hegemony gave her breathing space to overhaul the administration and reorganize the army for the next round of the struggle. There were, however, internal weaknesses. Austria was a patchwork confederation, largely land-locked and lacking a strong sense of national unity. Bohemia was subject to an oppressive despotism, although Hungary, whose separatist tradition might have been a serious obstacle to Austrian regeneration, had been effectively won over by Maria Theresa in 1741 at the price of accepting partial Magyar autonomy. It was a concession which prefigured the dual monarchy of the following century. In the peripheral dependencies in Italy, together with the southern Netherlands, there was little interference with existing institutions, and government by viceroy in Milan and Brussels was generally benevolent. The Austrian Netherlands were reasonably prosperous, despite the restrictions on sea-borne commerce imposed by the maritime powers. The Austrians, however, did not regard this part of their dominions as defensible in time of war and declined to pay for the continued upkeep of the barrier fortresses after 1749. This refusal ran counter to British ideas on the importance of the Low Countries and further inclined the Dutch to seek friendship with France, or at least to preserve a strict neutrality in any future conflict. It was, moreover, a further indication of a growing rift between the Austrians and a British government which had carried a heavy financial burden in war subsidies to support its Continental ally.

Britain after 1748 was a war-weary nation, shaken by the Stuart threat in 1745 and defeat by the French in the same year at Fontenoy, and resentful, like her New England colonists across the Atlantic, of the restoration of Louisburg to France. There were some, like William Pitt, the future earl of Chatham and as yet on the threshold of his parliamentary career, who subordinated European interests to the drive for Britain's supremacy as a colonial power. Elder statesmen, however, of whom the duke of Newcastle was one, still clung to the old system of European alliances, with Britain playing a leading part in maintaining the Continental balance of power. Britain, too, had her special interests: the protection of the Low Countries, and especially the defence of Hanover, a preoccupation which in the late war had immobilized thousands of troops – to the exasperation of her allies. But whether Europe or the wider world came to dominate in British political thinking, France remained the rival and the threat; this at least remained an island of firm ground in the shifting sands of mid-century diplomacy.

France was still the greatest power in Europe, with important colonial interests in the West Indies, Canada and India. Despite the crippling effect of British blockade and naval strength in the War of the Austrian Succession on her overseas trade, France's astonishing vitality can yet be seen in the triumph of her armies in Flanders as the war drew to a close. The fact that these late French successes in a part of Continental Europe of special concern in British policy did much to bring the war to an end and to spare France possible further humiliation in the colonial and commercial spheres is an indication that Britain had not yet made the colonial struggle a priority. "France had literally reconquered Cape Breton and the West Indies in Europe."[7]

COLONIAL RIVALRY

Aix-la-Chapelle did not result in a colonial cease-fire. In India which was not yet an integral part of the imperial system and less important than the West Indies in international commerce, Anglo-French rivalry was a contest between the trading monopolies of the two nations, although both sent out naval forces in 1754. Territorial dominion, however, formed part of the Dutch East India Company's policy in its commercial empire based on Batavia (Jakarta), and the French began to follow suit in southern and central India, a change in policy whose possible advantages were not lost upon the British. Dupleix, French governor-general at Pondichéry, soon gained political ascendancy in the Carnatic, and his success was duplicated by Bussy, his able and scholarly lieutenant, in the Deccan. British commerce at Madras and Fort St David was threatened and the London company sought allies hostile to Dupleix's Indian supporters. In Stringer Lawrence and Robert Clive the British had officers of outstanding ability, and the latter's triumphs at Arcot in 1751 and at Srirangam in the following year led to the recall of the French governor-general in 1754. An uneasy truce ensued, but the French company remained paramount in the Deccan, in a large part of the Carnatic and along the Orissa coast and the Circars facing the Bay of Bengal, as well as in its west-coast factories and at Chandernagore above Calcutta. The principal British centres outside the Carnatic were at Bombay and Calcutta. It has been well said, however, that Dupleix "was obliged by circumstances to apply his energy and his resources in the wrong part of India".[8] The area which offered the greatest commercial and political advantage was not the relatively barren hinterland of the southern coastal strip, but the fertile and teeming Ganges valley in Bihar and Bengal. Clive was to appreciate the possibilities.

In the West Indies the French began to infiltrate certain islands declared neutral at Aix-la-Chapelle. In 1749 they fortified Tobago, but were compelled to withdraw. Some years later they took St Lucia in retaliation for British aggression on the high seas. Britain, however, continued to dominate the West African slave trade, so important to the West Indian sugar-planters, although the French share was considerable and growing.

It was in North America that the cold war of 1748-1756 reached its greatest intensity, although initially neither side wished to provoke an open conflict which might well precipitate another European war. The diplomatic scene was too fluid for certainty of success on the Continent, and British public opinion was opposed to a further defence of Hanoverian interests in Germany. Barrin de la Galissonière, appointed French governor-general in Canada in 1748, spelled out his country's immediate objective: to gain control of the Ohio and Mississippi valleys, linking Canada with French Louisiana and its port of New Orleans on the Gulf of Mexico, thus confining the British colonies from Massachusetts to Georgia to the coastal regions east of the Appalachian mountains. It was a bold design, but already out of date. Canada, with a population of at most 70 000, could not hope to settle so vast a region, whose only economic significance to France lay in the activities of the scattered fur-traders. The British colonies, with perhaps 1 500 000 inhabitants, were already poised for further westward expansion. French arms, colonial disunity and British lack of resolve could possibly delay this movement, but could hardly check it permanently. In colonial terms, "the military fur trade frontier was about to clash, head on, with the Anglo-American land settlement frontier".[9]

For the duration of the cold-war period at least, fortune favoured the French in this part of North America. After the appointment of Duquesne as governor-general in 1752, France gained control of the Ohio valley and completed the construction of defensive positions south and west of the Great Lakes, including Fort Duquesne, the modern Pittsburgh. In 1754 Robert Dinwiddie, lieutenant-governor of Virginia, sent young George Washington to challenge the French at Fort Duquesne, but after a small initial success his undisciplined militiamen were forced to capitulate at Great Meadows.

The defeat caused alarm in the colonies and strengthened the hand of the war party in Britain, led by the duke of Cumberland, Henry Fox and Pitt. Reinforcements were disembarked at Philadelphia in January 1755 under Edward Braddock, who was placed in supreme command in North America. A planned offensive met with only limited success, however. Braddock, of whom it has been unkindly said that "his experience as an officer extended no farther than a review, and the parade in St James's park",[10] lost his life in a defeat before Fort Duquesne in July 1755, when his army was routed by a far smaller Franco-Indian force under Daniel de Beaujeu. Attacks on Fort Niagara and at Lake Champlain under the general direction of William Shirley, governor of Massachusetts, resulted in stalemate at best, while Boscawen's attempt in June 1755 to intercept French reinforcements for Quebec and Louisburg led only to the capture off Cape Race of two stragglers from Du Bois de la Motte's considerable fleet. Only in Nova Scotia, the former French Acadia, could victory be claimed. There the British had established a valuable base at Halifax in 1749, but France retained Forts Beauséjour and Gaspereau, protecting the gateway to Canada across the narrow neck of land between the Bay of Fundy and the Northumberland Strait. These were captured by a colonial force with regular assistance in June 1755, while at the same time French fortifications on the St John's river were demolished. The deportation of Acadian peasant farmers and fishermen from Nova Scotia, considered a potential fifth column, caused widespread indignation in France and Canada.

Boscawen's naval action off Newfoundland, moreover, was blatant aggression in time of peace and was followed by the illegal seizure of some 300 French merchant vessels in the last months of 1755. France, thoroughly alarmed, began to restore the Dunkirk fortifications, to strengthen her fleet at home and abroad, and to assemble troops for a possible invasion of England. This threat to British security, coupled with acts designed to disperse her enemy's formidable navy, seemed to offer the best chance of maintaining French supremacy in North America in the conflict which was obviously looming. Accordingly, in April 1756, the former governor-general of New France, La Galissonière, and Armand de Richelieu began an attack on the British island of Minorca in the Mediterranean. Britain now had ample pretext for her declaration of war on the 17th May.

THE DIPLOMATIC REVOLUTION AND THE SEVEN YEARS WAR

The colonial struggle had begun, but Europe was still at peace. Neither France nor Britain, Hanover apart, had strong motives for involvement in a European conflict, unless dragged in by the system of alliances. France, in the first years after 1748, had continued to tread a well-worn path. Austria remained the enemy, with Prussia as Louis XV's chief ally. Friendship with the Turks helped to hold a dagger at Hungary's back, while alliances with Poland and Sweden served to keep Russia out of central Europe where she might act in concert with Austria. Crumbling powers these secondary allies might be, but the Swedish alliance at least had served its purpose in 1741-1743, when Sweden attacked Russia at French insistence and was badly mauled in the process. If a European conflict should break out, it would clearly be to Britain's advantage to see France as deeply involved as possible; the traditional policy of British subsidies to allies to defend that country's Continental interests would take care of Hanover, while Britain prosecuted the colonial war with vigour. Austria, however, had shown herself reluctant to exert herself on Britain's behalf once again, and in September 1755 the British government came to an agreement with Austria's old ally, Russia. In return for a subsidy, Russia was to maintain an army on the eastern Prussian border to intimidate Frederick and, should the need arise, to protect Hanover.

This subsidy treaty, designed to keep the peace in Europe while Britain concentrated her energies on defeating France abroad in an imminent war, did more than anything else to set in motion the diplomatic revolution. Not that the reversal of alliances was in any sense of British conception – credit for that must go to the astute diplomat, Count Kaunitz, former Austrian envoy to Versailles and chancellor in Vienna from 1753. Nor was Hanover a major issue in European politics; the main question after 1748 was Austria's reaction to the loss of Silesia and the challenge of a powerful Prussia. Kaunitz had expounded his views on the inadequacy of existing alliances in restoring Austrian dominance in central Europe as early as 1749. Friendship with Britain and the United Provinces meant more to those countries than it did to Austria. What the Habsburg monarchy needed was French support for its policies in Germany and Italy, support which would also remove the fear of a Turkish attack on Hungary. Alliance with Russia could be rewarded, in case of war, by the gift of east Prussia, which lay outside the imperial borders, and such smaller powers as Saxony, Sweden or Denmark might also obtain territorial compensation for acceptance of the Austrian plan.

If the influence of Prussia were to be countered effectively, the Franco-Prussian alliance must be broken and France be convinced that a continuing Bourbon-Habsburg dynastic hostility had no place in the present circumstances of central Europe. What could Austria offer France in exchange for her support? Acceptance of French influence in Poland and Italy came into the picture, but more important would be Austrian neutrality in any Franco-British colonial struggle and, in the event of French assistance in a European conflict, territorial gains in the southern Netherlands, Austria's poor relation. When Kaunitz first broached the idea of a reversal of alliances at Versailles in 1750, he met with a cool reception; even at the end of August 1755 the French were unwilling to break with Prussia, although impressed by Austria's determination to give no further aid to Britain on the Continent.

The Anglo-Russian agreement, however, introduced a new dimension into the balance-of-power problem. A subsidized Russian army at the gates of East Prussia seriously compromised Prussian security, and a combined Austrian and Russian onslaught on Prussia seemed more than a vague possibility. Frederick the Great in his dilemma turned to Britain for support and on the 16th January 1756 signed the Convention of Westminster, pledging with George II the neutrality of Germany and joint opposition to the entry of foreign troops – French or Russian – into the empire.

Prussia and Britain saw their agreement as complementary to existing alliances, but at Versailles and in St Petersburg treachery was the cry. France was driven into the arms of Kaunitz and on the 1st May 1756 signed the first Treaty of Versailles, a defensive agreement guaranteeing the signatories' territorial integrity and promising the support of 24 000 men if either were attacked. Elizabeth of Russia was impatient to open hostilities against Prussia and proposed an offensive alliance with Austria, Sweden and Saxony for an immediate war. Kaunitz counselled patience, but on the 29th August 1756 Frederick anticipated the inevitable and invaded Saxony. The Seven Years War in Europe had begun.

The odds against Frederick were overwhelming, for the Treaty of Westminster did not require Britain to come to his aid. Not until 1758, after Pitt's rise to power, did the Great Commoner overcome his distrust of German entanglements and provide Prussia with troops and a subsidy. Frederick stood alone in 1756, and in the following year the second Treaty of Versailles completed the diplomatic revolution by committing France to active participation in the war against Prussia and the payment to Austria of a substantial subsidy, although the French foreign minister, Choiseul, limited French aid at the third Treaty of Versailles in 1759. All France was to receive in return was territorial aggrandizement in the Austrian Netherlands. It seems a small return for restoring Habsburg power, but it must be remembered that France was backing the favourite in the Seven Years War and entered the conflict in a dominant position in India and the Americas. The Franco-Austrian alliance endured until the French Revolution and was further cemented in 1770 by the marriage of Marie Antoinette, Maria Theresa's daughter, to the future Louis XVI. Her unpopularity in France was a measure of the general dislike for the Habsburgs.

The Seven Years War was really two separate contests, and the colonial struggle between France and Britain may appropriately be divorced from the Continental conflict, despite their obvious interaction. Frederick's campaigns began well with the capture of Dresden, although he met with unexpected Saxon resistance. In 1757 he invaded Bohemia, but was beaten by the Austrians at Kolin, and driven out. The Russians invaded East Prussia, Austria overran Silesia, and a large Swedish army took the offensive in Pomerania. The French advance from the west was greatly facilitated when in September 1757 the duke of Cumberland and Richelieu signed the Convention of Klosterzeven, a virtual capitulation by the defender of Hanover, which was repudiated by George II later in the year. The gloomy picture for Prussia was relieved by two brilliant victories: over a Franco-German army threatening Leipzig at Rossbach in November, and over the Austrians at Leuthen in December 1757, allowing Frederick to regain Silesia. He was unable to loosen the Russian grip on East Prussia, but effectively prevented a joint invasion of Brandenburg by the Russians and Swedes by defeating the former at Zorndorf in August 1758. Despite an Austrian victory at Hochkirch in October of that year, Frederick was able to

Central Europe in the Seven Years War

drive his major opponent out of Saxony and Silesia, the main Austrian objectives. Britain's greater measure of assistance to Prussia paid dividends in Ferdinand of Brunswick's victories over the French, with Anglo-Hanoverian help, at Krefeld in the Rhineland in 1758, and at Minden and Warburg in Westphalia in 1759 and 1760. From the British point of view, these campaigns against the French in western Germany not only saved Hanover, but also had diversionary value in the colonial struggle.

Frederick the Great's skill and courage in the conduct of the war inspired a new sense of Prussian patriotism, but his armies were not invincible, and his success owed much to the chronic inability of the coalition facing him to work together, despite all Choiseul's efforts in that direction. The dreaded union of Austrian and Russian forces occurred in 1759, and in August of that year Frederick was heavily defeated by the combined troops of Laudon and Saltikov at Künersdorf. However, despite an Austrian occupation of Dresden, the success was not followed up. Prussian victories over the Austrians at Liegnitz in Silesia on the 15th August 1760 and at Torgau in the following November, leading to the reoccupation of much of Saxony, showed that Frederick was still a force to be reckoned with, although he was hard pressed elsewhere. The Russians occupied Berlin for a few days in October 1760 and in 1761 advanced with their Austrian allies into Silesia. Further attacks by the French on Hanover were foiled, but the fall of Pitt in October 1761 led to the withdrawal of the British subsidy and the unpalatable advice from Pitt's successor, the earl of Bute, to end the war and cede Silesia.

Frederick was saved by the death in January 1762 of the Empress Elizabeth of Russia. She was succeeded by the pro-Prussian Peter III who placed the Russian armies at Frederick's disposal. Prussian resources were revitalized and Frederick went over to the offensive, defeating the Austrians at Burkersdorf and regaining Silesia. Frederick had withstood every onslaught, and his enemies – and his allies – were exhausted. Peter III's deposition and assassination brought his wife, Catherine, to the Russian throne in July 1762, and one of her first acts was to withdraw from the war. France had lost all interest in the European struggle, and the financial burden proved too much for Sweden, now under attack in Pomerania. Adolphus Frederick signed a separate peace with Frederick the Great on the basis of the status quo. Austria was unwilling to continue the fight alone, and on the 15th February 1763 the Treaty of Hubertusburg was signed by Prussia, Austria and Saxony. Frederick retained Silesia and Glatz and promised the Brandenburg vote to Maria Theresa's son, Joseph, as a candidate for the imperial crown. Saxony, restored to Augustus III, received no compensation for the considerable financial help she had been compelled to give Prussia. The long war had achieved nothing, and Kaunitz saw his plans for Austrian supremacy in ruins. Frederick the Great's reconstruction policy soon allowed Prussia to recover from the ravages of war, and with the decline of French influence in European affairs the balance shifted to the east, where Russia was to play an increasingly important part.

While the great powers had been fighting to a stalemate in Europe, Britain and France had continued their colonial and maritime struggle for world domination. The war began badly for Britain. Minorca fell in June 1756, a disaster unfairly attributed to the negligence of the British admiral, John Byng, whose execution at Portsmouth in March of the following year elicited from Voltaire the famous remark that it was British policy so to eliminate unsuccessful naval commanders in order to encourage the others.[11] In North America during 1756 and 1757 Montcalm took Fort Oswego on Lake Ontario and Fort William Henry on Lake George. The French and their American Indian allies, moreover, ravaged the British colonial frontiers from the Carolinas to New York, causing great distress and widespread destruction of property. In India the war against the French was preceded by troubles in Bengal, where the nawab, Siraj-ud-Daula took Calcutta in 1756, incarcerating some of the defenders in the infamous Black Hole from which only a handful emerged alive. And always in the background was the very real fear of a French invasion attempt on the English coasts, a scheme which attracted the French for a number of years until growing British naval superiority rendered it impracticable.

It was, indeed, British strength at sea which helped to turn the tide, together with Pitt's implacable resolve to destroy France as a colonial and commercial power. In Bengal, Clive retook Calcutta and, after defeating Siraj-ud-Daula at Plassey in 1757, placed his own nominee, Mir-Ja'far, on the throne. In the same year Clive captured the French factory at Chandernagore and in 1759 used force to counter Dutch resistance to his control of the province. The war in southern India began in earnest when Anne-Antoine d'Aché arrived in 1758 with a French fleet and rein-

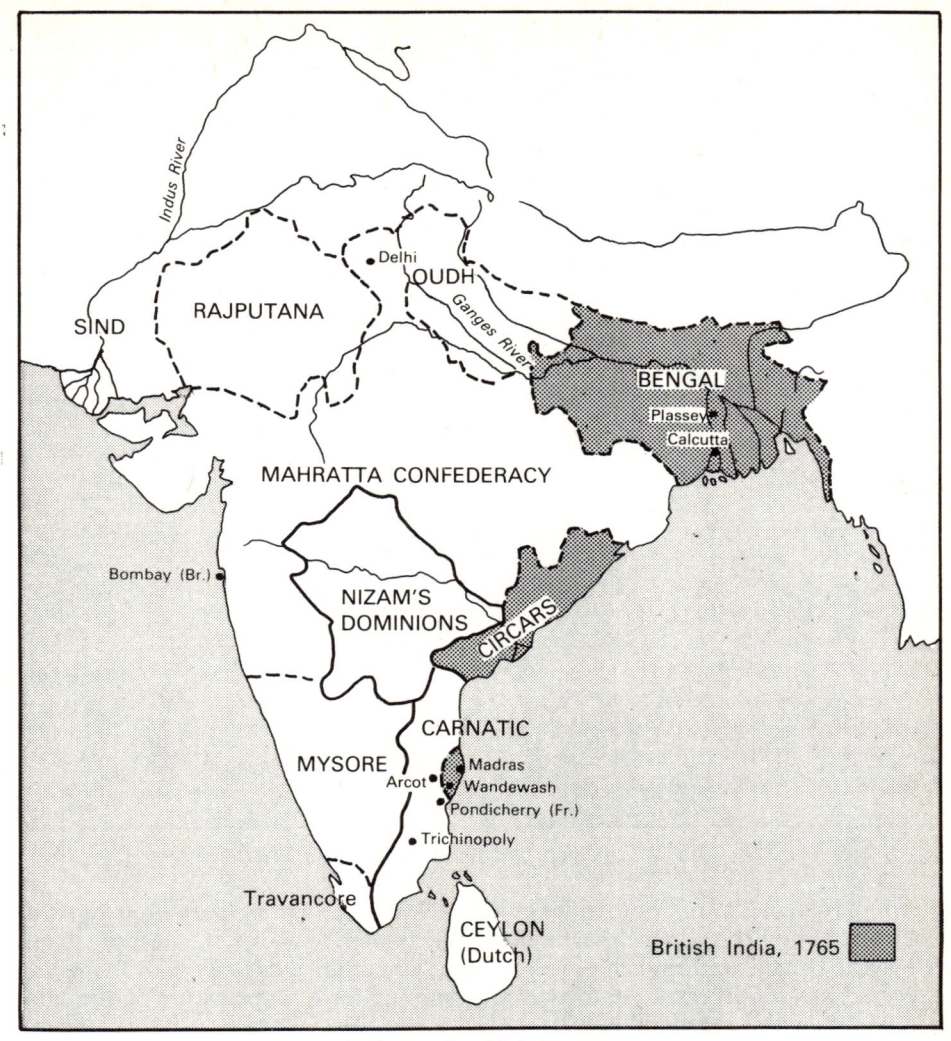

India in the 18th century

forcements for Lally de Tollendal, recently appointed to the command in French India. Lally abandoned the Deccan and concentrated on driving the British from the Carnatic, achieving initial success by capturing Cuddalore, Fort St David and Arcot. Even with the aid of Bussy's troops from the Deccan, however, he was unable to take Madras, and Admiral Pocock successfully deprived him of naval support. Meanwhile the British had occupied Karikal and had driven the French

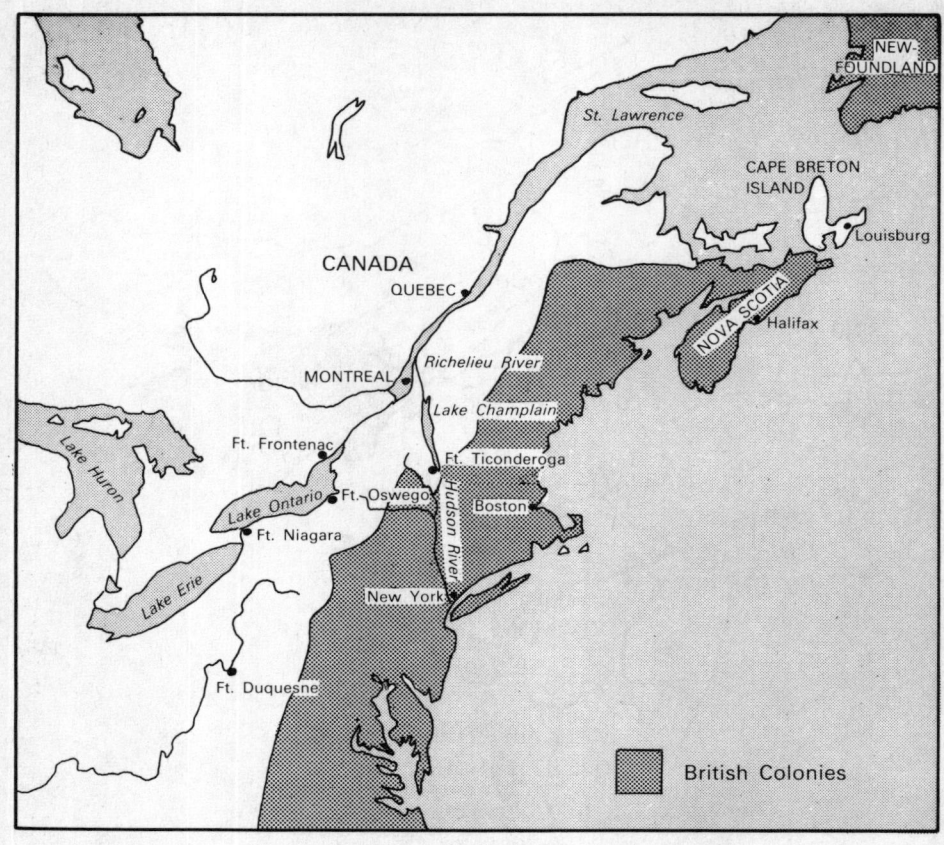

North America and the Seven Years War

out of the Circars. Eyre Coote routed Lally at Wandiwash in January 1760, opening the way to Pondichéry, which surrendered a year later. Mahé on the west coast also fell to the British, and French power in India was at an end. Lally, like Byng, was executed in 1766 in response to popular clamour for a scapegoat. Voltaire later played a part in his rehabilitation.

To bring the war in North America to a successful conclusion, Pitt decided to attack New France with overwhelming force from all sides. Louisburg surrendered in July 1758 after a combined operations assault led by Amherst and Boscawen, and in the following month Bradstreet's colonials, with a stiffening of regulars, took Fort Frontenac on Lake Ontario. In November the French destroyed Fort Duquesne before the advancing troops of General Forbes, but the British initiative on the Lake Champlain frontier had earlier been lost when James Abercromby, commander-in-chief in North America, was defeated by Montcalm near Ticonderoga on the 1st July, despite the British troops' enormous superiority in numbers. But the French were beginning to fall back on Canada. In 1759 they abandoned Ticonderoga and Crown Point, and surrendered Forts Oswego and Niagara, thus losing control of the territories south of the Great Lakes. On the 13th September Wolfe took Quebec in a spectacular battle in which both he and its defender Montcalm were killed. All was not yet lost and in April 1760 Lévis defeated Murray at Saint-Foy outside Quebec and laid siege to the city. Reinforcements, however, failed to arrive, the siege was abandoned and the British advanced on Montreal, where the capitulation of the governor-general, Vaudreuil-Cavagnal, on the 8th September marked the end of French resistance.

It was the same story in the West Indies, where between 1759 and 1762 the British captured Guadeloupe, Dominica, Martinique, St Lucia, St Vincent and Grenada. In addition, Keppel's capture of Gorée off the West African coast in 1758 dealt a crippling blow to the French slave trade and to the city of Nantes whose prosperity depended so much upon it. The favourable terms granted to the French planters in the West Indies led to a glut of sugar on the London market and a fall in prices little to the liking of the British West Indian interest. It was, however, widely held that the West Indian conquests alone enabled Britain to weather the financial strain of the war.

Not surprisingly, France began to think of peace in 1760, but Pitt's refusal to guarantee French rights to the St Lawrence and Newfoundland fisheries suggested to Choiseul another road to salvation, the revival of the Franco-Spanish Family Compact. Charles III of Spain, the Don Carlos of the Two Sicilies, agreed to this Bourbon alliance in August 1761, but to avoid giving that country time to mobilize its resources, Britain declared war on Spain in January 1762. Spain's object in joining France was in part to diminish British influence in the West Indies; the Spaniards could also expect the restoration of Minorca. Spain's participation, however, merely emphasized her weaknesses. Pocock and the earl of Albemarle took Havana in August 1762, and Manila in the Philippines fell to Cornish and Draper in the following October. The refusal of the Portuguese minister, Pombal, to close his country's trade to the British brought Portugal into the war and its armies, with British assistance, foiled a Spanish invasion attempt. A last echo of the war in northern latitudes was Ternay d'Arsac's cruise of 1762 against the British Newfoundland fisheries, which for three months left the port of St Johns in French hands. The achievement was "a glimmer of success amid the misfortunes attending the end of the war".[12]

With Pitt in office and Anson at the admiralty, the British navy made a remarkable contribution to the defeat of France in the colonies and to the frustration of that country's schemes to invade the British Isles. The French coast was blockaded from Dunkirk to Toulon, while amongst the many engagements on the high seas the destruction of La Clue's fleet by Boscawen at Lagos Bay off southern Portugal in August 1759, and Hawke's victory over Conflans at Quiberon Bay in the following November, were of crucial importance in maintaining naval supremacy. The British navy also supported a number of moderately successful raids on the French coast from Cherbourg to Rochefort, although the British suffered a reverse at Saint-Cast in September 1758. The most significant venture of this nature was the capture in June 1761 of Belle Ile off the southern coast of Brittany, a strategically important island commanding the approaches to Nantes and Lorient. In contrast, all that France could show for her plans to invade Britain was François Thurot's brief occupation of Carrickfergus on Belfast Lough in February 1760. This scheme to rouse the disaffected in Ireland failed completely, and the surviving ships of the squadron never regained France.

Peace preliminaries were signed at Fontainebleau in November 1762 and the definitive Peace of Paris between France, Spain, Britain and Portugal took effect on the 10th February 1763. Britain's gains were considerable, but Choiseul snatched something for a badly defeated France, despite the virtual exclusion of that country from North America. French fishing rights were respected, and that country retained the island group of St Pierre and Miquelon off Newfoundland, but Cape Breton Island and Canada to the left bank of the Mississippi went to Britain, and Louisiana with New Orleans to Spain as some compensation for losses in an unfortunate alliance. French navigation rights down the Mississippi were also ceded. In the West Indies, Guadeloupe and Martinique were restored to France, but Britain kept all the neutral islands, except St Lucia, which became a French possession. In Africa, France ceded Senegal to Britain, but Gorée was returned to that country. The French factories in India on the Malabar and Coromandel coasts and in Bengal, shorn of their fortifications, were restored. In Europe the Dunkirk defences were again dismantled, Minorca returned to Britain and Belle Ile to France. Spain kept Cuba and the Philippines, but ceded Florida to Britain. Spain also lost her Newfoundland fishing rights and acknowledged British logging privileges in the Gulf of Honduras. Portugal received compensation in South America with the retrocession by Spain of the Sacramento colony on the river Plate, ceded in a boundary adjustment of 1750.

COLONIAL PROBLEMS AND AMERICAN INDEPENDENCE

Britain had emerged from the war a major power indeed, feared by competitors who had not given up all hope of challenging her supremacy. The French continued to nurse hopes of revenge and of a possible invasion of Britain, counting on Spanish support. However, in the only threat to peace in the immediate post-war era Spain took the initiative without French backing. The Falkland Islands group in the South Atlantic was shared between that country and Britain, but in 1770 a powerful expedition from Buenos Aires forced the British to surrender West Falkland. Louis XV, however, dismissing Choiseul, refused to co-operate, and in 1771 Spain bowed to British demands for restitution without renouncing her claim to the entire group.

These were years of administrative and commercial reform in Spanish America and in the French West Indies, and free trade concessions – sugar excepted – in the French colonies of St Domingue, Guadeloupe and Martinique benefited British colonials in North America, despite the mother country's mercantile restrictions. Britain also had to face administrative problems concerned with the integration of her newly acquired North American territories into the empire and with the inefficiency of company rule in India, where Lord North's Regulating Act of 1773 and the younger Pitt's India Act of 1784 progressively limited company activity to the commercial sphere.

It was, however, in her relations with her thirteen seaboard colonies in North America from Georgia to Massachusetts that Britain encountered her greatest challenge after the Peace of Paris. Her problems were compounded by political changes at home after the accession of George III to the throne in 1760, which saw the increasing involvement of a court party, inimical to colonial interests, in parliamentary life. On the American frontier, a reluctance to open up new lands to settlement irritated the colonists, who now numbered well over 2 000 000. On the other hand, colonial collaboration in the serious Pontiac Indian revolt of 1763 was lacking, and it seemed that Britain would still have to provide the military forces needed to keep the peace on the frontier. The British, impoverished by the Seven Years War, expected the colonies to share the burden of defence expenditure, and a series of taxes and import duties were levied on them by the Westminster parliament. These caused widespread dissatisfaction and the flame of protest was fanned by radical politicians in America. Parliamentary action of this kind was entirely constitutional, but in view of the home rule enjoyed in the colonies it was, as British statesmen such as the elder Pitt and Edmund Burke appreciated, impolitic in the extreme. The cry of "no taxation without representation" was raised, and colonial attitudes, despite strong loyalist undercurrents, hardened from an early anticipation of dominion status to the open defiance of all British authority in the Declaration of Independence of the 4th July 1776. "The coercive steps of the British government served perfectly the purpose of those who sought to overturn the outmoded system of imperial relationships" and "generated a degree of emotional fervor in favor of unity of action that men previously had thought to be quite impossible".[13]

The War of Independence which began with the skirmish at Lexington on the 19th April 1775 produced an able general in George Washington, the future first president of the United States, and some disastrous tactical blunders on the British side before the virtual end of hostilities on the 20th October 1781, when Cornwallis surrendered to Washington and his French ally, Rochambeau, at Yorktown, with a French fleet under François de Grasse at his back in Chesapeake Bay. For by 1781 the Americans were not fighting alone. Their defeat of Burgoyne at Saratoga in October 1777 convinced the French minister of foreign affairs, Vergennes, that independence was within their grasp, and in February 1778 he concluded a treaty of alliance. This inevitably led to a British declaration of war, and in June 1779 Spain entered the contest as the ally of France. Dutch sympathies lay with the Americans and their refusal to sacrifice the advantages of non-belligerency caused Britain to declare war on them in December 1780. Russia, Denmark and Sweden established the League of Armed Neutrals to defend the principle of free navigation for neutral vessels and although Britain refused to abandon her right of search, she took pains to avoid confrontation.

For Britain's position in this latest colonial and maritime struggle was a difficult one, made more serious by temporary loss of the command of the sea in home waters, off the American coast and in the Caribbean and Mediterranean seas. In Europe, a threatened Franco-Spanish invasion of Britain in 1779 was a fiasco, although the Scottish-born American raider, John Paul Jones, was active around the British coasts and in April 1778 had carried out a daring attack on land at Whitehaven. Gibraltar withstood a Franco-Spanish siege, but Minorca fell in 1782. A French fleet under Suffren de Saint-Tropez operated with great success in Indian waters, reversing British gains at Dutch expense in Ceylon after first guaranteeing the security of the Cape of Good Hope in June 1781. However, Pondichéry, Chandernagore and Mahé fell to the British in 1779, although the governor-general, Warren Hastings, found himself with a full-scale war on his hands in the Carnatic against the pro-French Hyder 'Ali. In Africa, French forces took Senegal in 1779.

In the Americas, Spain's dynamic governor of Louisiana, Bernardo de Gálvez, took every British garrison town in West Florida between 1779 and 1781. A Spanish force moved north to capture Fort St Joseph towards Lake Michigan in January 1781 and another expedition temporarily secured the Bahamas in 1782. Britain's only permanent wartime gain in the West Indies was St Lucia, captured in December 1778, but the French took a string of islands from St Kitts to Tobago between 1778 and 1782. The sombre picture of British naval decline was relieved by Rodney's victory over the Spanish off Cape St Vincent in January 1781, thus saving Gibraltar, and by his capture of Grasse in the battle of the Saints off Dominica in April 1782.

The Treaty of Versailles of the 3rd September 1783 brought the war to a close. The independence of the United States of America was recognized, and the excellent terms that country obtained owed much to the tenacity of the American negotiators, and in particular Benjamin Franklin. The United States retained the old colonial Newfoundland and St Lawrence fishing rights; the boundary with Nova Scotia and Canada was so determined that the new nation had access to the west; Anglo-American freedom of navigation on the Mississippi was guaranteed; and the United States were not compelled to compensate loyalists for property losses, a burden which fell upon the British government's shoulders. Spain recovered Minorca and the Floridas, east and west, but French gains were of a minor nature, including only Tobago and Senegal. Most territorial accessions made during the conflict by force of arms, whether in the West Indies or in India, were restored to their original owners.

The loss of Britain's transatlantic colonies did not, as her competitors hoped, ruin the British economy. America remained a large and expanding market and the world at large was far from being closed to further colonial expansion. Already Byron, Carteret and the Frenchman Bougainville had begun to open up the Pacific, and James Cook's explorations in the Antipodes were to lead to the settlement of New South Wales in 1788. On the American west coast a British fur trading base on Vancouver Island was forcibly closed in 1789 by the Spanish, who claimed jurisdiction in the region. Britain's early start in the Industrial Revolution also stimulated the demand for Indian cotton and imports increased almost twentyfold in the last half of the 18th century. Side by side with this continuing expansion ran new currents of thought on the economics of colonialism, reflected in the views of the

French physiocrats and in those of the British economist, Adam Smith, who questioned the value of trade restriction and company monopoly. From the 1770s, international finance was at the disposal of new trading ventures to the east, masquerading under such national flags as the Austrian, Danish and Portuguese, while the East India monopolies were further challenged in the next decade by the Americans. The old colonial system, too, was under fire from the humanitarians in their campaign against the evils of slavery and of the slave trade. A new imperialism was to emerge in the 19th century, but in 1789 Europe stood on the brink of international tensions born of fundamental political change, and colonial issues would play no more than a secondary role for over two decades.

EUROPE AFTER 1763

While Britain's thirteen American colonies moved towards independence after the Peace of Paris in 1763, the expansionist drive of Catherine the Great's Russia dominated the European scene. The death in that year of Augustus III, Saxon elector and Polish king, provided Catherine with the opportunity of extending Russian influence in Poland by placing her nominee and former paramour, the Polish nobleman, Stanislas Poniatowski, on the throne of that country. This was achieved after agreement had been reached in April 1764 with Frederick the Great of Prussia. Frederick saw in a Russian alliance a bulwark against Austrian pretensions in Silesia, the chance of territorial gain at Poland's expense and a guarantee of the status quo in Sweden, where political turbulence under the weak king, Adolphus Frederick, would effectively prevent any resurgence of Swedish power inimical to his own and Catherine's interests.

Division in Polish politics was also much to the advantage of expansionist Russia and Prussia. Poland was already a battleground between reforming Czartoryski supporters and the reactionary opponents of that noble house, the Potocki and Radziwill families; religion, too, was involved, in that there were grievances of the Orthodox and Protestant minorities in the predominantly Catholic state. Catherine and Frederick exploited these differences with a cynical disregard for the welfare of Poland. Catherine sent troops to support the conservative Confederation of Radom of 1767, but at the same time encouraged the demands of the dissident religious minorities for the full political rights denied them by the strongly Catholic Polish Diet in 1766. However, she compelled the Diet to abrogate the reform measures it had passed and in 1768 had herself made protector of what was by then no more than a puppet state. Frederick acquiesced and Poland's continuing instability was ensured by the refusal of that country's powerful neighbours, east and west, to sanction two measures which might have done much to end internal strife: the substitution of a hereditary for an elective monarchy, and the abolition of the *liberum veto* by which a single dissenting vote in the Diet was sufficient to prevent the passage of any legislation proposed.

In 1768 Polish Catholic noblemen, hostile to the new dispensation, formed a resistance movement, the Confederation of Bar in the province of Podolia, and appealed to France for assistance. The French, who had recently gained Lorraine and the adjoining Barrois on the death in 1766 of an earlier claimant to the Polish throne, Stanislas Lesczynski, persuaded the Turks to go to the aid of the confederates. The Russo-Turkish War of 1768-1774 revealed the weakness of the Ottoman empire. By 1770 the Russians had occupied most of Bessarabia, Moldavia and Wallachia north of the Danube and had gained a window to the Black Sea. In 1770 a Russian fleet from the Baltic entered the Mediterranean, took control in the Aegean archipelago and destroyed the Turkish navy off Chesmé. In the following year the Russians advanced into the Crimea and in 1774 crossed the Danube to threaten Constantinople. In Poland they took the former capital, Cracow, in 1768.

In Austrian eyes, Russia's easy victories tilted the balance of power, although the Austrians themselves were not averse to the prospect of gains at Polish and Turkish expense, annexing the Polish province of Zips on a dubious claim in February 1769 and, as the Russo-Turkish War ended, taking over Bukovina on the northern frontier of Moldavia. Kaunitz, however, flirted with the idea of an alliance with Turkey and Prussia to curb Russia's expansionist drive. Frederick the Great was unwilling to become involved in a general conflict and proposed the cynical solution "of a tripartite Prussian, Austrian and Russian action simultaneously to end the war against Turkey and make Poland pay the price of peace".[14] Catherine, faced with a peasant revolt at home and a stronger monarchy in Sweden on Russia's northern borders under Gustavus III, was prepared to sacrifice some of her Turkish gains for compensation in Poland, and as a result the first partition treaties were signed at St Petersburg on the 25th July 1772. Poland lost about one-third of her territory and almost half her population and was left a weak buffer state at the mercy of her neighbours. Austria acquired Galicia and retained Zips, Russia advanced to the Dvina and the Dnieper in White Russia, taking over the eastern regions of the old Lithuanian state, and Prussia was permitted to consolidate her territories by incorporating Polish West Prussia, with the exception of Danzig and Thorn. The Turks sued for peace in 1774, and by the Treaty of Kutchuk-Kainardij of the 21st July Russia limited her territorial aspirations, but gained access to the Black Sea and control of the Sea of Azov, with freedom of navigation in that region. The khanate of the Crimea became an independent state which Russia promptly annexed in 1783, at the same time extending her influence in the Caucasus, the back door to the Ottoman empire.

Continuing Russian expansion precipitated the Russo-Turkish War of 1787-1792, with Austria joining the attack on the Ottoman empire in 1788. Again the Turks, despite an invasion of Hungary, were soon forced onto the defensive. The Russians captured Ochakov on the Black Sea and overran Moldavia and Bessarabia, while the Austrians took Belgrade and Bucharest. Gustavus III of Sweden used the opportunity of Russian involvement in Turkey to declare war on Catherine the Great in 1788, but an army mutiny and a Danish invasion of southern Sweden restricted his offensive. The Swedes won a naval victory at Svenksund in July 1790, but the status quo in the north was restored at the Treaty of Verela in the following month. Austria, fearing Prussian intervention, made peace with the Turks at Sistova in August 1791, at which Maria Theresa's son, the emperor Leopold II, gained territory in the Banat, north of the Danube. Tension with Prussia and Britain, who feared Russian power and growing trade advantages in the Black Sea region, led to the Russo-Turkish Treaty of Jassy in January 1792, by which the Russians retained Ochakov. The Turkish wars not only reflect the almost total eclipse of France in the eastern balance of power struggle, but also the beginnings of British interest in what was to become known as the Eastern Question of the following century as the Ottoman empire began to crumble under nationalist pressures.

Poland's cup of misery had not yet been drained. Between 1788 and 1791 members of Poland's reforming nobility took advantage of Russia's preoccupation with Turkey to design a new constitution with a hereditary monarchy and a parliamentary system in which decisions were taken by simple majority vote. Urban representation in the Diet was granted, peasant reforms initiated and the cultural life of the nation revived. Reform owed a little to Jacobin influences from a France in revolution since 1789, although there was nothing revolutionary in the new dispensation by 18th century standards. The Poles concluded the Reichenbach agreement with Prussia in March 1790 in order to gain outside support, but Catherine the Great encouraged Polish malcontents to form the Confederation of Targowica in 1792, which pledged to overthrow the new government. Frederick the Great's successor, Frederick William II, unwilling to risk war with Russia when his quarrel lay with revolutionary France, repudiated the Polish agreement and marched troops into Thorn and Poznan. The Russians occupied Warsaw, and on the 23rd September 1793 the Diet agreed to cede Poznan, Thorn and Danzig to Prussia and a large area in the east to Russia.

This second partition of Poland excluded Austria, but with the Polish kingdom on the verge of extinction, Russia saw the Austrians as more valuable allies in her quarrels with the Turks. Their reward was not long in coming. The old order, including the *liberum veto*, was restored in the truncated Poland, but a patriotic movement under Tadeusz Kościuszko briefly seized Cracow and Warsaw. Prussian, Russian and Austrian armies invaded the country and a third partition of 1795 put an end to Polish independence. Prussia took an area on the Silesian border and a large tract of territory adjoining East Prussia, including Warsaw; Russia incorporated eastern Poland from Courland to the borders of Galicia; and Austria annexed West Galicia, thus gaining the cities of Lublin and Cracow. In the long term, the significance of the Polish partitions of 1793 and 1795 lay in the creation of an eastern conservative and absolutist bloc to counter the new currents of political thought flowing through Europe as a result of the French Revolution; in the short term, however, it was France which benefited most from the rape of Poland, since Austrian and Prussian forces were unable to make an adequate contribution to the formidable coalition ranged against the French.

The revolutionary wars, do not, however, fall within the scope of this chapter; we may none the less appropriately conclude our survey with some account of events which, although of minor importance to the balance of power, serve as a link between the international issues of an older age, in which relations between church and state, and dynastic questions played so important a part, and the modern world of secular power politics.

Although religious fanaticism was still in evidence in the 18th century and can be seen in action in London's violent anti-Catholic Gordon riots of 1780, more tolerant attitudes were gaining ground in government circles. Maria Theresa's son and successor, Joseph II, virtually abolished religious discrimination in the Austrian dominions in 1781; the dissenting Old Believers of Russia obtained relief in 1785; and two years later, Louis XVI extended a wide measure of tolerance to French Protestants who had been deprived of all rights for more than a century.

In Catholic Europe relief for Jews, Protestants and Orthodox Christians was a by-product of campaigns to diminish papal influence, thus binding the Catholic church more closely to the secular state. This policy was particularly marked in Austria and Spain between the years 1763 and 1789. The campaigns in Portugal and the Bourbon lands were closely associated with attacks on the Society of Jesus, wealthy, influential, conservative and a bastion of papal authority. The Jesuits were expelled from Portugal in 1759, from France in 1764 and from Spain in 1767, the Bourbons of Naples and Parma followed suit, and their example was followed by the ruling powers of Modena, Venice and Bavaria. Pressure was applied to Pope Clement XIII to abolish the Jesuit order, French troops seized the papal enclave of Avignon, and Benevento in the Two Sicilies was also occupied. Clement XIII's successor, Clement XIV, finally agreed to dismantle the order in 1773, whereupon Avignon and Benevento were restored to papal control. The bull, *Dominus ac Redemptor*, which dissolved the Society of Jesus was rescinded in 1814, but that legacy of the Middle Ages, the direct political involvement of the papacy in European statecraft, was virtually at an end. The papal adversary of old, the Holy Roman empire, had equally little significance in the later 18th century with the development of rival nation-states. It was to disappear in 1806, when Francis II of Austria relinquished the imperial title.

One last flicker of imperial ambition, although equally a question of Austrian political power, came with the death in December 1777 of Maximilian Joseph, the elector of Bavaria. His heir was Charles Theodore of the Palatinate, who was persuaded by Kaunitz and the emperor, Joseph II, to partition his newly acquired territories with the Habsburgs. This alarmed Prussia, and Frederick the Great invaded Bohemia. France refused to involve herself on behalf of the Austrians, despite the offer of the Austrian Netherlands as a reward, and the almost bloodless war dragged on, the *Kartoffelnkrieg*, in which two hungry armies were reduced to digging up frozen potatoes in order to stay alive. Finally, in May 1779, the Peace of Teschen was signed. Charles Theodore kept the title of elector of Bavaria, thus creating a union with the Palatinate, much to Prussia's advantage as a check to the Habsburgs. Austria retained a slice of territory along the river Inn and agreed to the future incorporation by Prussia of Bayreuth and Anspach.

Joseph did not lightly give up his scheme to exchange the Austrian Netherlands for Bavaria and entered into negotiations to that end with the French and Charles Theodore in 1784. France, however, held aloof, and Frederick the Great emerged as the protector of the smaller German states against Austrian encroachments by forming the *Fürstenbund*, or League of Princes, in January 1785. At the same time Joseph sought to make his dominions in the Netherlands more profitable. Using the excuse of a minor border infringement by the Dutch, he proposed to open the Scheldt to imperial navigation. Again, the anticipated support of France was not forthcoming, and in 1785 Austria had to accept French mediation in settling the Dutch dispute. By the Treaty of Fontainebleau the United Provinces indemnified Austria for the violation of neutrality and agreed to demolish the barrier fortresses at the mouth of the Scheldt. Austria, for her part, gave up all plans for freedom of navigation on the river and also dropped her claim to the strategically important city of Maastricht on the Meuse.

Joseph II was an enlightened reformer whose aims struck at the foundations of ancient privilege. His policies led to revolt in Hungary and in the southern Netherlands. His visit to the latter region in 1781, the first by a reigning monarch since the days of Philip II of Spain, was followed by reforms which took no note of local traditions and alienated many sections of the population. But the Austrian Netherlands had been influenced by French ideals of a just society and by trends across the Atlantic which had culminated in the formation of the United States of America. The result was the Brabançon revolution of 1789, the occupation of Brussels and the declaration of independence of the United Belgian States on the 11th January 1790. Success was short-lived. Dissension in the insurgent ranks destroyed the confederation, and Austrian rule was speedily restored. The movement, however, was to inspire a later surge of national feeling.

Events in the United Provinces also reflected a changing political climate. At the same time they brought Britain back into the European system of alliances from which that country had been excluded since 1763. Her international and colonial policies had reached their nadir in 1780, when the Commons, sitting in committee, passed the motion proposed by John Dunning, the later Lord Ashburton, "that the power of the Crown has increased, is increasing, and ought to be diminished". After 1783 Britain took action to end her isolation. A commercial treaty with France in 1786 was a first step, but this implied no political *rapprochement* in that direction, and its value depended entirely on the maintenance of peace in Europe through French inaction. But Vergennes had concluded an alliance with the United Provinces in the previous year, and in the confusion of Dutch politics at that period, the French were giving their support to opponents of the Stadtholder, William V, and the pro-British Orangists around him.

In the van of the attack on the Orangists were the radical republicans calling themselves Patriots, influenced by the political idealism of the French *philosophes* and critical of the lack of effective leadership in the Dutch state. William V's passivity allowed the Patriots to gain control in the United Provinces, but William's wife, Wilhelmina, sister of Frederick William II of Prussia, was made of sterner stuff and attempted to reassert the authority of the house of Orange. She was, however, humiliated and briefly detained by the Patriots of Utrecht in July 1787, an incident which aroused the ire of her brother. Prussian troops under the duke of Brunswick swept into the United Provinces, Amsterdam fell in October 1787, William V was restored to power, and many of the Patriots fled to France. Prussia was assured of British goodwill in this short campaign. The Royal Navy stood off the Dutch coast, and Pitt compelled the French to repudiate any intention of assisting their Dutch allies. France, in any case, faced an internal financial crisis and could do nothing to aid the Patriots.

For Britain the days of isolation were over. Both Britain and Prussia signed separate alliances with the United Provinces and on the 13th August 1788 a defensive treaty between Britain and Prussia established a triple alliance. Within five years all three nations would find themselves at war with revolutionary France; within seven, French arms would bring the Patriots in exile back to their native land and compel William V to seek refuge in Britain. The French Revolution of 1789 brought an era to an end, even though the coalition which came into being to oppose France was to fight for the defence of the existing order. To preserve the balance of power remained, as always, a chief priority, but the French Revolution was not merely a national phenomenon – it was of universal significance. Its influence was to affect the entire social and political world structure when the guns fell silent on the fields of Waterloo more than a quarter of a century after the storming of the Bastille on the 14th July 1789.

CHAPTER 8

THE FIRST INDUSTRIAL REVOLUTION: IRON AND COAL

THE STEAM ENGINE

A commonly held assumption, even today, amongst all too many students of the British Industrial Revolution appears to be that the revolution can be dealt with primarily in terms of scale and rate of economic growth, with little if any emphasis on the technological nature of that growth. According to Phyllis Deane, for example: "It was the sheer scale and persistence of economic change that was new."[1] As this chapter will attempt to emphasize, what was new in the Industrial Revolution was not simply economic change, but, more fundamentally, technological change. It was in particular the adoption of the steam engine which gave industrial growth after 1775, and particularly after 1830, the character of revolution instead of simply accelerated evolution.

What exactly was the Industrial Revolution? It involved engines (initially only the steam engine) which converted heat into mechanical energy or "work". It combined two principles: it substituted inanimate engines, such as the steam engine, for human and animal muscle power; and it replaced the more traditional inanimate sources of energy, wind and water power, by steam. Human or animal labour was not as efficient as the steam engine. Men and animals tire easily, while the steam engine did not. More important, the steam engine relied on mineral fuel (coal) which at that time was far more abundant and cheaper than the organic fuel (food) necessary to sustain men and animals. Moreover, it has been calculated that in 1870 Britain's steam engines had a working capacity equivalent to that generated by 6 000 000 horses or 40 000 000 men. Had a work force of so many men actually existed, it would have consumed some 8,7 billion kilograms of wheat a year, or more than three times the annual output of Britain at that time. This figure does not even include the large number of people who, while not themselves contributing to the work force, would have depended on it, notably the families of these workers; nor those people upon whom the workers themselves would have depended – the service sector of the economy, including the merchants and professionals (doctors, lawyers, clergymen).[2]

At the same time, the steam engine was also more effective than the more traditional sources of inanimate energy, wind and water. While it was, other things being equal, obviously cheaper to use wind and water, these sources of power were not reliable. Wind might not blow, or a water source might dry up or freeze. The steam engine, on the other hand, could be used at all times. Also, it depended upon mechanical power which, because it was converted from heat, could be created (synthesized) in quantities large enough to fulfil any demand. Water mills and windmills, in contrast, depended upon limited, locally available, mechanical power. The water wheel could not count on easily increased supplies of energy – its size would have to be enormously increased in order to expand such supplies even moderately. The largest water wheel was probably that built at the French court of Versailles, in the late 17th century. It served to supply water for Louis XIV's fountains. Fourteen large water wheels, each about fourteen metres in diameter and driven by the river Seine, worked 221 pumps which raised water by stages (steps), with the water at each stage collecting in a reservoir. And yet the output in energy in terms of water actually raised amounted to only sixty kilowatt-hours – the output of the engine of a 3 500 kg truck. Steam engines, on the other hand, eventually came to provide up to 15 000 kilowatt-hours; and they were far cheaper to produce than the Versailles water wheels had been.

While the steam engine would eventually largely replace wind and water, these two energy sources, during the six centuries prior to the Industrial Revolution, were beginning to replace human and animal sources of energy. Thus, for example, the water wheel was already used during Roman times, but only to grind corn into flour. With the Middle Ages, particularly from the 12th century onwards, water wheels were used for a whole range of industrial processes, most notably in textile manufacturing and in metallurgy, the two branches of industry which, subsequently, in the late 18th century, would most distinguish Britain's economic growth at the beginning of that country's Industrial Revolution. Already during the High and Late Middle Ages, water wheels were used for fulling (the process by which woollen cloth is beaten in water, and thus shrunk, so as to improve its durability). A process which hitherto had been performed by human muscle power (hands, feet and/or wooden clubs) was therefore mechanized. Similarly, water wheels began also to operate forge hammers and forge bellows for metallurgy.

Sailing boats (thus named because they use wind power for navigation) had existed since ancient Egyptian times. None the less, down to the end of the Middle Ages, they were to some degree a misnomer: they relied largely on human oarsmen, and only secondarily on sail (wind) power. It was only from the 15th century, with the voyages of discovery and navigation on the open seas (in particular in the Atlantic) that ships, dispensing with oarsmen, and powered only by sail, became common.

Even after the Middle Ages, however, the use of inanimate sources of energy (wind and water) remained relatively limited, even if they were much more important than ever before. As Carlo Cipolla suggests: "Eighty to eighty five per cent of the total energy income at any time before the industrial revolution must have been derived from plants, animals and men."[3]

The more direct background to the invention of the steam engine can be traced to the growing preoccupation, from the time of the late Middle Ages, with drainage and land reclamation. Unlike the water wheel, the windmill continued to be used only for corn grinding during the Middle Ages. From 1400, however, windmills came to be used, via their applicability to drawing water, for draining land, particularly in the Netherlands. During the 16th century, drainage found further use in the mining industry. As mines became deeper, they tended to flood. In Germany, drainage techniques became particularly advanced with new kinds of pumps being used. Drainage techniques had, of course, existed in classical times. Since about 600 BC, the water-raising wheel had been used, but it was driven by human or animal power. In contrast, the Germans in the 16th century used suction pumps, driven, after 1545, by water power (water wheels rotating under the impact of a fast-moving stream). Pumps suck up water by creating vacuums into which the water then rushes. In 1643, Evangelista Torricelli, a pupil of Galileo, gave a more precise explanation to this phenomenon, in terms of air pressure: when a pump creates a vacuum, the surrounding water is forced into this vacuum by the pressure from the surrounding atmosphere which pushes it into the vacuum. Torricelli also showed that atmospheric pressure itself is limited, so that it could only force water up to a height of some nine metres. In the 1650s, Otto von Guericke invented the air pump which not only created a vacuum, but could maintain it at will.

As early as 1600, vacuums had also been created by condensing steam. In 1606, Battista della Porta had used steam pressure to raise water. By the end of the century, these principles were finally applied to the first steam engine. As in 16th-century Germany, it was the mining industry which provided the chief incentive for improved drainage technology. The mining of coal in particular brought deeper and deeper mines in its wake: between 1700 and 1750 the maximum depth of coal mines increased by 50 per cent, correspondingly increasing the pumping problems. The first steam engine, the Savery engine, patented in 1698, turned out to be inadequate for mines, although it was used to pump water for country houses. By 1712, however, Thomas Newcomen, an associate of Savery, had perfected a workable, reasonably efficient steam engine for mines, which, by 1730, was being used all over Europe. The basic principle was that the expansion of steam could drive a piston up a cylinder while the subsequent condensation of that same steam would create a vacuum, drawing the piston down again. Although the Newcomen engine was used largely to pump water, in 1776 it was supplanted by a more efficient model, patented by James Watt – one which, soon after, was adapted to driving rotary machinery. Thus, whereas there had been more than seventy Newcomen engines in operation as late as 1778, by the year 1790 all but one had been replaced by Watt steam engines. Yet even Newcomen and Watt steam engines were still primarily atmospheric engines, working at little more than atmospheric pressure. Such engines therefore derived most of their power, not from the force of the steam, but from the vacuum created. By 1800, however, Richard Trevithick and others had created the high-pressure engine working on at least two atmospheric pressures. A crucial advantage of the high-pressure engine was that with more steam pressure it could be built relatively lightly and cheaply because it did not need as large a piston to do the same amount of work, and it used far less water. This saving of space and materials was extremely important for the subsequent construction of movable engines such as the locomotive and the steam boat.

It can, however, be argued that the Industrial Revolution, at least in a narrow sense, did not begin with the steam engine, but with the advent, some four centuries earlier, of the cannon, itself based on military fire power (the explosive force of burning gunpowder, propelling a cannon ball). As early as the 14th century, it had been discovered that the same technology used for casting church bells could be applied to casting cannons. It was realized that the new fire power was more effective for smashing down fortifications than the older siege engines. Originally, siege engines had been developed by the Greeks and Romans. The medieval version was the catapult, powered by torsion – by the elasticity of two thick cords twisted to a high level of tension, like a giant spring coil or slingshot which could suddenly release a large stone aimed at walled fortifications. The cannon, unlike the catapult, was powered by heat energy derived from an explosive, so-called gunpowder, itself a compound of potassium nitrate, sulphur and charcoal.

The cannon, like the subsequent steam engine, was a "heat engine" powered by a chemical reaction whose heat was converted into mechanical energy. In the case of the cannon, the heat was given off by the burning of gunpowder and was then converted into mechanical energy in the form of fire power. In the case of the steam engine, coal replaced gunpowder, while steam power replaced fire power. Just as the cannon, because of its relatively high heat energy emission, was more destructive than the catapult, so the steam engine, for the same reason, was more effective than the windmill or water mill. Only the use of heat would permit the release of mechanical energy above those levels readily available (through torsion, wind or water) in the everyday environment. One could therefore, in a strictly technological sense, identify the beginning of the Industrial Revolution with the 14th century invention of fire power. The reason this is not usually done is perhaps that the direct economic (as opposed to technological) impact of the cannon, in contrast to that of the steam engine, was nil. Even in a technological sense, moreover, one should keep in mind that the cannon was a far more primitive "heat engine" than the steam engine. In the cannon, fire power was harnessed to propel a simple missile of destruction, the cannon ball. In the steam engine, on the other hand, steam power was harnessed to operate relatively sophisticated machines: pumps, spinning machines and weaving machines, foundries and forges.

The subsequent history of fire power and the origin of the steam engine were, during the century prior to the Industrial Revolution, intimately intertwined. Around 1660, Robert Boyle studied vacuums and the atmosphere (air) from two perspectives: firstly, in the tradition of Otto von Guericke, he constructed an air pump which permitted him either to create vacuums or to increase air pressure. His study into the nature of both vacuums and atmospheric pressure would become a fundamental contribution to the subsequent science of the steam engine. Secondly, Boyle studied the impact of the atmosphere and vacuums on combustion. He found that whereas charcoal and sulphur could not burn in a vacuum, saltpetre (potassium nitrate), when mixed with either sulphur or charcoal, thus forming gunpowder, did burn, even when heated in a vacuum. In this way Boyle implicitly illustrated a key chemical difference between an ordinary fuel such as carbon (or coal) and an explosive such as gunpowder. An explosive, unlike ordinary fuels, contains its own oxygen and can therefore burn even in a vacuum. Such an oxygen-containing fuel is also known as a propellant, and many propellants today are used in space rocketry.

In 1680, Christian Huygens attempted to operate a piston-and-cylinder engine by means of gunpowder explosion. While this approach failed, it directly influenced the advent of the steam engine during the following two decades. Already in 1690, Huygens's assistant, Denis Papin, substituting steam for gunpowder, constructed the first steam engine. Built in miniature, it had no practical use. Yet it did serve as a model for Savery's own steam engine eight years later. Huygens's gunpowder engine for its part anticipated the eventual development, in the late 19th century, of the internal combustion engine, the basis of the automobile. The internal combustion engine would derive its name from the fact that, unlike in the steam engine, the combustion of fuel, generating the heat, would take place directly inside the cylinder of the engine, rather than outside via a furnace and boiler. Here again, we can see the link between the invention of fire power and the subsequent Industrial Revolution: the 14th century cannon was in effect the first internal combustion engine.

The casting of iron cannon, common in England from the time of Henry VIII, was itself a major, if indirect, stimulus to the eventual development of the steam engine. The timber required as fuel for the casting of iron cannon, together with the timber required for shipbuilding, depleted England's forests, causing an acute timber shortage by the 1630s. This was reflected in a steady long-term rise in the price of charcoal, which became particularly sharp after 1630:

INDEX OF PRICES IN ENGLAND, 1560-1670[4]

	General	Charcoal
1560	46	60
1610	90	95
1620	87	100
1630	100	100
1640	106	135
1650	133	225
1660	121	220
1670	102	250

The growing timber shortage in turn stimulated the exploitation of coal as the obvious alternative source of energy, although, as we shall see later, the use of coal, prior to the 18th century, would not extend to the smelting or refining of iron itself. In turn, the digging of deep mines, with their tendency to flood, opened up a demand for better pumping mechanisms: the Newcomen steam engine was the eventual answer to this demand. In the third quarter of the 18th century, war-time demand for better cannon stimulated the iron master, John Wilkinson, to devise, in 1774, an improved method for boring cannon. A year later, this technique was adapted to more accurate cylinder boring which in turn was to be used in the Watt steam engine. Watt used the improved cannon-boring method to produce higher-quality cylinders which now could prevent leakage of steam, until then a major defect of the Newcomen engine; for the next twenty years, most Watt steam engines had a Wilkinson cylinder.

IRON AND COAL

Until iron machinery could be easily and cheaply produced, there could be no Industrial Revolution. Originally, machines were constructed largely from wood. The essential metal (brass or iron) parts were made, and were joined to the wood by the local blacksmith. The steam engine, however, created the need for iron machinery. Iron, unlike wood, would provide a machine with the necessary tensile strength to resist the increased mechanical pressures exerted by the higher speed which steam power, as opposed to water, wind or muscle power, afforded. Moreover, machines constructed from iron could be more accurately and more tightly fitted for running at these higher speeds. While early steam-driven machines (e.g. the first models of Thomas Newcomen's steam-driven water pumps) were built partly out of wood, they were perforce severely limited in size. In particular they could not be efficiently constructed beyond a certain diameter, without the risk of being shaken to pieces by the force of the steam. Furthermore, iron machines could be turned out by semi-skilled workmen and were therefore cheaper than wooden machines which had to be handmade by skilled wheelwrights and carpenters. Finally, iron machines, because of their greater resilience to temperature, humidity and mechanical pressure, could be more precisely made and therefore, where parts wore out, these could be more easily replaced than was possible with wooden parts.

Brass, a compound of copper and zinc, was, outside the armaments industry, the most popular construction material apart from wood, prior to the Industrial Revolution. In particular, brass was used for precision instruments: watches, clocks, mechanical toys, navigation instruments, microscopes, and models of the solar system. The art of precision-instrument manufacture went back as far as the 14th century, but had only become fully developed by the 16th. In effect, a whole applied science of precision engineering had developed during this period. Many of the machines of the mid-19th century machine tool industry were already understood in principle, and had been described and illustrated, as early as the 16th century, in Leonardo da Vinci's notebooks. At the time, however, none of this pre-industrial precision engineering was translated into steam-powered machine building, but only into toys and scientific instruments, run by torsion-powered steel springs. The reason, at least in part, was one of cost. Miniature precision goods were handmade luxury items, but the costs, although relatively high, were still kept within acceptable bounds since the products were small. Moreover, brass, as opposed to iron, could for the purposes of small objects be worked cold, without the need for expensive fuel. For large machines such as the steam engine, on the other hand, expensive smelting processes were required.

Prior to the 18th century the main stimulus to the adoption of cast iron as a construction material was war. The cannon, in contrast to the steam engine, did not have to pay for itself economically and was therefore used long before the steam engine. Nor, before probably the 19th century, did cannons have a sufficiently rapid rate of fire to subject their cylinders to pressures as intense as those in the steam engine (particularly once it had been adapted to manufacturing, as opposed to just pumping). And, as opposed to the steam engine, the cannon did not have to endure the continuous pounding of the three-shift day. Although brass and bronze (a compound of copper and tin, greatly resembling brass) provided the original metals for cannon, they were, being each a compound of two separate metals, relatively expensive to use. Consequently, by the mid-16th century the cheaper iron cannon came to be preferred, despite the fact that initially it was more brittle (as iron has less tensile strength) than its bronze and brass counterparts.

While iron-making had existed since the time of the ancient Hittites (1400 BC), the products involved were, prior to the 16th century, almost all from so-called "wrought" iron, whose impurities were hammered out at the forge, and which was subsequently beaten by blacksmiths into nails, horseshoes, locks, picks and spades. In contrast, it was only in the 16th century, under the stimulus of the English armaments industry, that so-called "cast" iron began to be produced to a significant degree, even though its actual origins dated back as far as the 15th or 14th century. Cast iron, because of its relatively high carbon content, was hard and brittle, in contrast to wrought iron, and therefore not susceptible to being shaped into assorted hardware. However, it could, at the blast furnace (or "foundry"), be poured molten into moulds (castings) to form large objects such as cannon cylinders and cannon balls. Originally, the art of gun-casting had been most highly developed on the Continent, and England's first iron cannons themselves were made during Henry VIII's reign, by French founders living in England.

From 1560 English cannons were eagerly sought on the Continent, notably by the Dutch, now cut off from the cannon-producing centres of Flanders because of their war with Spain. The growing need in England for armaments, as a result of the subsequent English civil war during the 1640s, and the constant wars with France during the late 17th century and the entire 18th century, created a rapidly expanding market for cast iron. The greatest consumer, of course, was the government itself. Whereas at the time of the destruction of the Spanish armada (1588), total expenditure by the Crown was probably not more than £600 000 per year, by the battle of Blenheim (1704), government spending per year had reached ten times that amount, two-thirds of which was military expenditure.

Until the 18th century, wood was not only a key construction material but, in the form of charcoal, also continued to provide the main source of fuel. It is true that already during the late 16th and 17th centuries, coal, as charred coke, had replaced charcoal in a broad range of industrial activities, e.g. in brewing, in salt and sugar refining, brick and pottery making, in the manufacture of soap, nails and glass, as well as the smelting of non-ferrous metals such as copper and tin. The application of coke to iron, however, remained impractical for a long time, because coke, unlike charcoal, contaminated the iron with added chemical impurities, silicon in particular. While this did not affect the quality of cast iron, it did affect that of wrought iron (itself now most profitably obtained from the same raw material as cast iron), in turn necessitating still more heating and hammering at the forge in order to get rid of these added impurities: the result was a rise in the cost of the final manufactured product. Therefore, just because the cast iron manufacturers themselves were now not only using their crude ("pig") iron for castings, but were also sending it to the forges as a source of raw material for wrought iron products, charcoal, instead of coke, continued to be used for the making of cast iron, too.

The first breakthrough in coke iron technology occured in 1707 when Abraham Darby devised a new technique for manufacturing cast iron pots. He discovered that the very same silicon with which coke contaminated iron, could, ironically now also be used to make cast iron products at half the cost and with a far higher quality than under the charcoal process, so that they could also be sold at a higher price: Darby's iron pots and his other castings not only consumed less iron, but were less likely to have defects such as cracks or holes. While coke, until the mid-18th century, would continue to be a more expensive fuel than charcoal for the production of wrought iron, Darby's substantial profits from cast iron were compensation enough. His invention was of fundamental significance, since for the first time it provided a construction material, coke iron, which was strong enough, and, in the long run, also cheap enough, to permit the mass application of heat engines to industry. Not only was coke iron cheaper than bronze or brass, but it also greatly surpassed them (not to mention charcoal iron or wood) in tensile strength. Originally, Newcomen steam engines had had their cylinders made of brass, and other parts, such as the main beam, made of wood but within a decade of Darby's invention, Newcomen was ordering Darby's cast iron cylinders and beams. No longer were Newcomen's pumps limited in size as a result of weak and/or expensive materials. This dependence on coke iron for Newcomen's steam engine would be greater still for the subsequent Watt variety, since its greater efficiency in steam consumption would naturally also expose it to greater stress. In the Newcomen engine much steam was wasted because the cylinder could not be kept hot permanently: half the time it had to be cooled in order to permit the steam to recondense, which would create the necessary vacuum, whereby the piston would be allowed to drop back to its original position. Furthermore, steam was further wasted through leakage resulting from low-quality cylinder construction. Consequently, Newcomen engines could pump only gently and slowly. Because Watt engines resolved these engineering weaknesses, and were consequently functioning much more rapidly and diversely, they were subjected to far greater steam and atmospheric pressure.

It was, however, not before 1750 that other ironmasters began to emulate Darby. As long as the price of charcoal remained lower than, or even the same as, that of coke, ironmasters, traditionally established in wooded as opposed to coal-bearing areas, were discouraged by the initial high costs of having to transfer their manufacturing enterprises to completely new sites. By 1750, however, the steady, long-term depletion of Britain's timber reserves was pushing charcoal prices high enough to encourage the widespread shift to coke. Whereas in 1750 coke was used in only 5 per cent of total raw ("pig") iron output, by 1760 its share had risen to 28 per cent, and by 1775, to 55 per cent. By the end of 1791 coke would account for 90 per cent of the total pig iron output. Thus, as Charles K. Hyde has so effectively shown,[5] even before the advent of the first Watt steam engine in 1776, coke was eclipsing charcoal in iron metallurgy. Indeed, the Watt steam engine itself was an outcome of this new coke iron technology. In turn, according to Hyde,[6] the Watt steam engine permitted the ironmaster to increase furnace size, and thus the pig iron output per individual furnace. Coke itself could, in any case, support a much heavier load of iron ore in the furnace stack than could charcoal, so that the size of the furnace was now in practice limited only by the strength of the blast required for combustion. For its part, the application of the more powerful Watt steam engine to metallurgy could provide the very powerful blasts required to operate substantially larger furnaces. The incentive for building larger furnaces appears to have been mainly one of economies of scale, including, for example, fixed costs (in initial site construction and in the maintenance of a core of competent management personnel). Not surprisingly, within less than fifteen years of the advent of Watt engines, steam had largely replaced water power in the running of coke blast furnaces. By 1815 the average coke furnace produced five times as much iron per year as its charcoal predecessor of a century earlier had done.

The cost of producing wrought iron with coke was itself dramatically reduced when in 1784 Henry Cort's "puddling" (or stirring) process altogether eliminated the need of costly hammering at the forge to remove impurities from the metal. If as a result of the Watt steam engine, economies of scale had cut costs in the cast iron sector; conversely, Cort's puddling process, by dramatically cutting costs in wrought iron production, permitted output there to rise to a scale far larger than before. In addition, larger forges must have encouraged the extension of the use of the steam engine to this sector as well.

Wood, both as a fuel and as a construction material, could now be fully replaced by coal and iron. The first iron (cast iron) bridge was built in 1779, appropriately enough by Abraham Darby III, and the first iron-framed (cast iron) building was erected in 1793. By the end of the century all rails and tramways for transporting coal out of the mines had been iron-plated (wrought iron). After 1825, similar iron rails would be used for steam engine trains. Whereas between the 1740s and the 1780s pig iron output had increased at 2 per cent per year, during the following fifty years the rate tripled to 6 per cent. Between 1788 and 1805 the output of British pig iron almost quadrupled, thus freeing Britain from her dependence on overseas iron: until then, Swedish and Russian iron had been imported in large quantities because the ample forest reserves of these two countries had made the charcoal fuel for their manufacture of iron and iron products relatively cheap. In 1812 Britain for the first time became a net exporter of iron, and that country's share of world pig iron production grew from 19 per cent in 1800 to 40 per cent in 1820 and 50 per cent in 1840.

THE HERITAGE OF THE COUNTRYSIDE: CONVERTIBLE HUSBANDRY AND ENCLOSURE

While the transformation of British agriculture was not an intrinsic part of the Industrial Revolution, it contributed to a climate of general economic growth favourable for this revolution. In particular, rising agricultural productivity would mean a higher standard of living, and thus purchasing power for both the town and the countryside, which in turn provided a rapidly expanding domestic market for industry.

As late as the 18th century, in most of Europe, the traditional three-field, "open-field" agrarian system was still prevalent. Even in England, where agriculture was modernizing more rapidly, about half the arable land was still cultivated under the open-field system as late as 1700. In northern and central Europe village agriculture followed a traditional three year cycle of crop rotation. A given field, for example, might be sown one year with wheat, the following year with oats, while the third year it would lie fallow, permitting the soil to be restored. This meant that one-third of all arable land was always left uncultivated at any one time. Besides the two fields and the fallow, each village had its common land where every villager had the right to pasture his animals and collect wood for fuel. The villagers' animals were also allowed to graze on arable land that had just been harvested, thereby manuring the land.

How did the system work in practice? All the land occupied by the village community was divided into three large fields. Each field followed the three year pattern of crop rotation, but synchronized with the other two fields in such a way that at any given time, there was no duplication of a particular phase of the cycle. When one field would be growing wheat, the second would therefore be growing oats, and the third would lie fallow. Each villager would have strips of his land in each of the three fields. His strips, moreover, were not fenced off, but were openly interspersed with those of his neighbours – hence the term "open field". This system, of course, prevented more efficient, compact (consolidated) holdings. Much time was wasted by the villagers having constantly to walk back and forth from one field to the next. The advantage of the system was that, within each field, it permitted (in fact, encouraged) the collective use of all available farm equipment and draught animals. This made sense at a time when animals and equipment were scarce and no one villager was wealthy enough to possess a full plough team of eight oxen. At the same time, by discouraging individual initiative and innovation, the system protected the masses of undynamic peasants against competition from the potentially more dynamic.

The prevalence, throughout Europe, of fallow land complemented the open-field system. Both symptomized a subsistence agriculture in which animals were scarce. Because animals were scarce, the soil was starved of manure fertilizer; regular fallowing was the means of preventing the exhaustion of the land. Not only had this agrarian system adapted to the scarcity of draught animals, but it had also developed a built-in resistance to improving the herds: spring-sown crops such as oats and barley were discouraged in France as late as the 17th century, since they were only a second-rate food for humans and were really fit for horses only. Although the horse was faster and more powerful than the ox, the latter continued to be used side by side with the horse, even in northern Europe, and, in fact, was often preferred, presumably because oxen were cheaper than horses to maintain, and particularly because they did not need to be fed on special, spring-sown crops. In some areas, such as the middle Rhineland, the three-field system was actually shunned in favour of the even more primitive two-field system. The two-field system required a fallow of half, rather than only one-third, of the land, thus cutting down agricultural production. However, it had, in the eyes of many peasants, the advantage that it dispensed with spring sowing, permitting full concentration on the autumn-sown wheat and rye, more desirable for human consumption. Finally, it should be pointed out that while draught animals were in great demand (for transporting crops and especially for drawing the plough), few animals were kept for their meat. Only aged animals which could no longer work were eaten.

Agricultural technology remained primitive, reflecting the state of agriculture as a whole. The plough had not changed since the Middle Ages. In northern Europe it was heavy, made of oak wood, and only its cutting blade was made of iron. Not before the end of the 18th century would the wooden plough begin to yield to the iron plough. The plough was usually drawn by a team of oxen. In contrast, in Mediterranean Europe, with its lighter soils, the plough was lighter and drawn by only one or two oxen. In southern (Mediterranean) Europe, because of the less favourable climate (relatively little summer rainfall), agriculture was even more primitive than in the north. A two-field, rather than a three-field system, prevailed, which meant the absence of a spring-sown crop, and therefore the absence of oats for horses. Because it was always being cultivated with the same single crop, the soil was even more prone to exhaustion than in northern Europe, and fallow assumed a correspondingly greater importance: half, rather than one-third, of the arable land was at any one time devoted to lie fallow. Already in the Middle Ages, one could see how southern Europe's economic development was beginning to fall behind that of northern Europe. Still, as already mentioned, this distinction was one of degree only. Even in the north, resistance to widespread use of the horse, and at times to the three-field system itself, persisted.

Traditional historiography has seen European agriculture change in dramatic terms: the so-called agricultural "revolution" was supposed to have occurred quite suddenly in Britain at the time of its alleged counterpart, the Industrial Revolution of the late 18th century. Since the 1950s, a newer interpretation[7] has maintained that agricultural change was much less revolutionary and much slower and gradual than industrial change. For agriculture there was, in fact, no counterpart to the steam engine. Agricultural change was an evolutionary process dating back, in England, to the mid-17th century at least. Moreover, it is now accepted that even the agricultural innovations in 17th-century England were themselves only adaptations of even earlier innovations from Flanders and southern Holland, which date back to the 14th century. At the same time, even this newer view emphasizes that outside of England and Flanders, agricultural innovation in Europe remained largely alien prior to the 19th century.

In the traditional, medieval open-field system of cultivation, crop land (the arable land) and pasture land (for raising livestock) were treated as two separate and rival ways of exploiting the land. If the arable land expanded, then pasture land must contract. In such a system, as has been discussed, arable land was usually favoured at the expense of pasture. Animals, aside from a minimum of draught animals, were seen as an expensive luxury. As already mentioned, extensive fallow land was a means of rejuvenating the soil without having to depend on animal manure as fertilizer. What small supply of animal manure did exist was often used by the poor for fuel, thus avoiding dependence on relatively expensive timber. Gradually, however, arable and pastoral cultivation became mutually reinforcing instead of mutually exclusive. Under the traditional open-field system, the fallow was simply land left barren in order to rest and restore its productivity. Fallow land would be ploughed, but not sown. As such, it was useless for animal grazing. With agricultural innovation, on the other hand, the fallow began to be planted with specialized forage crops – lucerne (alfalfa), vetch, sainfoin. These forage crops were crucial because they restored the arable land and at the same time fed the cattle, thus in effect supplementing the pasture. This new type of agriculture, because it served both the arable land and the pasture, came to be known as "convertible husbandry". It now became possible to produce enough forage to increase the herds and eventually to produce livestock not only for draught purposes, but specifically for high-quality meat as well. In contrast, under the open-field system, "the ox was eaten when it could no longer draw".

Since the Middle Ages, Flemish and Dutch farmers had used fertilisers to improve the yield of their crops. Because animal manure was scarce, night soil (human excrement) and garbage were purchased from nearby towns. From the 14th century these fertilizing techniques began to be supplemented with a more sophisticated approach. The earliest innovation, during the 14th century, was a system of crop rotation in which pasture played a prominent role for the first time: autumn-sown crops (wheat and rye) one year, spring-sown crops (oats and barley) one year, fallow one year, and pasture three or six years. As can be seen, this meant a reduction in emphasis on both fallow and cereal crops, although not in cereal output because the land, rejuvenated by long rests from cereals, and well manured during the time it served as pasture for cattle grazing, was actually able to produce a higher cereal output per square hectare, not to mention its ability to sustain more livestock. From the 15th century the new cycle of cultivation was made more efficient: the practice of laying land fallow was dropped altogether and, along with pasture, fallow was replaced by specialized fodder crops (leguminous grasses): turnips and vetches were probably the first used, to be eventually supplemented, in the 17th century or earlier, by sainfoin, lucerne, clover and rye-grass. Thus, in the space of some three centuries, there was a breakthrough in productivity in all sectors: cereal, vegetable and livestock. Whereas, for example, in the Middle Ages, a harvest yield of four to one for seed originally planted was standard, by the 18th century the ratio had risen to ten to one.

All these innovations originated in the Low Countries and subsequently spread to England in the 17th century, in particular to the east coast county of Norfolk, situated on the North Sea, across from Holland. It was in late 17th century Norfolk that there developed the famous Norfolk system of crop rotation (wheat-turnips-barley-clover), itself a variant of Flemish rotation systems developed earlier. With convertible husbandry, the horse increasingly began to supplant the ox. The horse, while more expensive to feed, was stronger and faster. It was powerful enough to draw the heavier, more expensive, but more efficient, iron plough. The Norfolk plough drawn by two horses became particularly well known. It must once more be emphasized, however, that these changes, however radical, were largely confined to the Low Countries and certain parts of England prior to the 19th century. Elsewhere, the horse was still less popular in agriculture than the ox. The chief significance of the horse remained in military operations and for rapid transport. In many respects, agriculture in the rest of Europe was still influenced by the persistence of traits such as the two-field system (of which the three-field system was only a more productive variant), the ox and the wooden plough, which harked back not only to medieval but actually to classical times. Changes began to come about from the mid-18th century onward, but at first only slowly and hesitantly.

With the steady penetration into the English countryside of convertible husbandry, there occurred the waning of the open-field system, itself effected through the so-called "enclosure" of the land. Under the English open-field system the cultivation of the land was done collectively, from ploughing to harvesting. There was therefore little if any spirit of individual enterprise. Enclosure, on the other hand, meant the rearrangement of the open-field system into individually exploited, self-sufficient private land units. The strip system of intermingled landholdings was replaced by a pattern of compact, consolidated holdings, facilitating individual initiative in agriculture. By the early 18th century about half the arable land in England was already enclosed. Most of the remainder became enclosed during the next hundred years, a process virtually complete by 1830.

Enclosure, like convertible husbandry, was a long-term, evolutionary process, dating back to the 16th century. Since the High and Late Middle Ages with the growth of trade, English peasants had commuted their traditional labour dues owed to their landlord into money rents. This meant that they no longer worked directly for the landlord several days a week on his part of the manor (the so-called "demesne"), but, instead, paid him cash rents from the proceeds of the sale of their own produce on the market. At the same time their legal status changed: from being hereditary serfs, attached to the land, many became hereditary free tenants, so-called "copyholders". Others became "leaseholder" tenants. Whereas copyholders leased land which they had occupied since the days of serfdom, leaseholders leased land not on a hereditary but on a short-term basis, and their lease was renewable only with the landlord's consent. With the increasingly marked inflationary price rise, particularly from the 16th century, copyholding became discredited, since it did not permit rents to be raised in tandem with the rise in prices. By the late 17th century, copyholds had either been replaced by leaseholds or else must have merged into small (peasant) property holds with full ownership rights for the holder.

By the 18th century one could divide English rural society into four classes: (i) landlords who lived off the land but had others working it for them; (ii) large and small tenants (leaseholders) who were able individually to lease property ranging from small parcels of land to entire estates from the landlord. The larger tenants saw their leases as a purely commercial investment: they themselves did not directly work the land any more than did the landlords, but lived from the rents. The small tenants, however, lived like peasants but lacked the latter's security of tenure; (iii) small peasant landowners. A peasant holding was for the most part cultivated only by the peasant and his family, although hired labour might temporarily be used at harvest time. Often such small landowners supplemented their land by leasing extra land from the local landlord; and (iv) a landless agricultural proletariat, itself divided into cottagers and ordinary labourers.

The replacement of copyholding by leaseholding established the legal framework permitting the landlords' subsequent enclosure of the land. A landlord could now force his small tenants off their strip holdings simply by refusing to renew their leases. However, it would be misleading to think of enclosure simply in terms of landlord pressure against tenants. Often the initiative might originate with some of the tenants themselves. In particular, the more enterprising might take this initiative by making the landlord especially attractive rent bids in exchange for his permitting them to enclose their holdings. The rest of the tenants would then be obliged to adapt to the system of enclosure. Those unable or unwilling to adapt would lose their holdings; their former strips of land would be merged with the newly consolidated holdings of more enterprising or richer tenant neighbours, while they themselves would be forced to abandon renting land altogether and seek work as paid (wage) labourers on one of the newly consolidated tenancies. In the long run, enclosure was therefore tending to encourage concentration of land tenure.

A factor which slowed down the enclosure movement was that the open-field land within a given village was usually divided amongst a number of landowners, ranging from landlords to small peasant landowners. As a result, before an owner could pressure his tenants to consolidate their holdings, he first had to obtain the co-operation of the other local landowners. This co-operation was not always easy to obtain. Landowners, like tenants, tended to be divided between the dynamic and the undynamic, the innovative and the tradition-bound, the rich and poor, the large and the small. Therefore, enclosure by private arrangement proceeded slowly and piecemeal. From the middle of the 18th century, enclosure came to be enacted through formal acts of Parliament. The new system had the advantage that it could afford the wealthier landowners (the ones most likely to want enclosure and the ones also the most likely to have influence in Parliament) the legislative means to override any local opposition emanating from other, smaller, and therefore less influential landowners.

One reason enclosure has attracted so much attention in historiography is because its study originally formed an essential part of Karl Marx's politico-economic analysis. In *Das Kapital* (Capital), volume 2[8] Marx devoted a whole chapter to "primary (capitalist) accumulation": "The so-called primary accumulation . . . is nothing other than the historical process whereby the producer is divorced from the means of production" (p. 792); ". . . The expropriation of . . . the peasants, their severance from the soil, was the basis of the whole process" (p. 793). Thanks to this process of expropriation, "urban industries were supplied . . . with masses of proletarians . . ." (p. 826). While this analysis is not entirely incorrect, it is necessarily an over-simplification, a telescoping of a complex process which must be analysed in greater detail. While enclosure did in the long run facilitate the massive uprooting of the rural population, including its displacement to the towns, this same rural population, prior to the mechanization of agriculture from the third quarter of the 19th century, did not diminish in absolute numbers. Enclosure itself provided new need for farm labour. Fencing, hedging and ditching had to be done. The increase in the herds of cattle and sheep required more stockmen and shepherds, as well as labour to build new sheds and buildings for the enlarged and consolidated farms. Furthermore, the cultivation of turnip and green fodder crops necessitated more intensive labour than used for the old cereal crops. Also, the breaking up of the common pasture into individual holdings and often its conversion into arable land required in itself a massive labour force.

There was, of course, a constant and growing flow of people from the countryside to the towns, but this was not due so much to enclosures as to the general growth in rural population, outstripping rural employment possibilities. Between 1800 and 1820 the population of the rural areas was growing almost as fast as the total population. Rural employment, while growing, simply could not keep up with population. To be sure, there was a long-term decline in the relative number of people employed in rural occupations: from 33 per cent in 1811 to 25 per cent in 1831, and 22 per cent in 1851; however, in absolute terms, rural employment grew: from 1 700 000 in 1801 to 2 100 000 in 1851. Moreover, for many years even the new migrants into industry would temporarily return to the countryside every year, to work in the harvest. In the late 18th century, the Midland iron trades and the Yorkshire textile firms were therefore obliged to stop production for several weeks each summer at harvest time. The statistics of poor relief bear out the fact that the distribution of poverty bore no relationship to the extent of recent enclosure, but rather to the availability of work outside farming for the growing population. Certain counties which were not particularly affected by 18th century enclosure spent as much or more on relief as the most heavily enclosed counties. Within the heavily enclosed counties, moreover, those which remained agricultural spent much more on poor relief than those which had become already partly industrialized. Presumably this reflected the fact that few people migrated to the towns simply because they were unemployed, but because of the actual employment opportunities awaiting them there. Nor does there appear to have been any connection between rural unrest and enclosure. It was not the recently enclosed Midlands, but the impoverished counties of southern England, where enclosure had occurred before the 18th century, that witnessed the last agricultural labourers' revolt of 1830. However, although enclosure did not reduce rural employment (in fact, enclosure increased it) the question remains as to what degree the landholding population lost their leasehold farms, and became a proletariat. In fact, the ratio of the agricultural proletariat to landholders rose very slowly and gradually from 1,7:1 in 1688 to 2,5:1 in 1831. And some of this increase, like the growth in urban proletariat, came not from enclosure, but from population growth. The custom of primogeniture, prevalent in Britain, meant that only the eldest son inherited the land, forcing the younger, particularly in poorer families, to seek wage employment.

While enclosure only moderately encouraged the growth of an agricultural proletariat, it had a marked effect by changing the nature and composition of that proletariat. As already mentioned, this class was itself divided into cottagers and labourers. Cottagers were a hybrid between ordinary landless agricultural labourers and small tenants. They were, in fact, live-in labourers, living permanently on the premises. They occupied no fields, but as part of their labour contract were given the use of a cottage and perhaps a small vegetable garden. Of particular importance was their custom of using the common pasture and woodland for grazing their flocks and for collecting fuel. With enclosure, the pasture and woodland and vegetable gardens were apt to be taken away from them, as both the commons and the open fields were first divided up and then consolidated into compact farms. In the new regime of intensive farming, land was too valuable to be allowed under such easy terms as had been hitherto available to these cottage labourers. As a result of enclosure, they therefore became fully proletarianized: their source of income was now uniquely derived from the wages they earned.

Small landowners and small tenants, for their part, were, at least prior to 1850, not being proletarianized, so much as being (willingly or unwillingly) pressured to adopt new, more efficient and more effective patterns of cultivating the land. Small tenants and small peasant landowners who were dynamic enough to adapt to the systems of convertible husbandry and enclosure, thus becoming independent of open fields and village commons, and who, in the case of tenants, could thereby afford to pay higher rents, were able to survive. Landlords did not want fewer tenants so much as more productive ones. Of course, enclosure was expensive, and this in turn challenged the small agriculturists who lacked capital. The costs included the expenses of surveying and valuing, of fencing in the land, and often of the building of new farmhouses and roads. But since enclosure was apt to increase the value of land by making it more compact and thus more efficient, it was usually possible, at least for someone owning his own land, to obtain the money through a mortgage. In 1832 there were, in fact, as many small owners as there had been in 1780, and this after a period during which the enclosure movement as a result of parliamentary support had reached unprecedented proportions. It is, on the other hand, likely that small tenants did not fare as well as small owners. Not only could they not count on being able to mortgage their land to tide them over the costs of enclosure, but, unlike owners, and like cottage labourers, they could not claim any land compensation as a result of the enclosure of the commons. At the same time, as Chambers and Mingay have pointed out, "to a considerable extent the pace of enclosure was determined by the availability of farmers able and willing to change their methods and pay the higher rents . . ."[9] Suitable tenants were after all not so easily obtainable. This last point is particularly important in suggesting why enclosures contributed only modestly towards the growth of an agricultural proletariat. While a landlord might be able if necessary to evict some of his tenants if these showed themselves unable to adapt to enclosures, he could hardly have evicted the majority without suffering financial ruin, if not also risking armed insurrection. The growth of enclosures therefore did not simply cause agrarian modernization, but was itself a symptom of the English small landholders' increasing dynamism and receptiveness to such modernization. As we shall see, this pattern was in sharp contrast to what was happening in France: there the peasantry's large-scale and continued opposition to modernization remained manifest.

It should finally be emphasized that, before the third quarter of the 19th century, the Industrial Revolution had little technological impact on agriculture. The rise in agricultural productivity, however substantial, was not due to a technological breakthrough, but to improvements in agriculture itself. While from the 1780s the iron plough began in England to replace the wooden one, its effect was isolated and therefore hardly decisive. There was still no decisive mechanization of the stages of agricultural production. The harvest in particular continued to be a long, drawn-out process, requiring much labour. Ploughing and sowing were not speeded up prior to the middle of the 19th century, either. As a result, agricultural employment continued to rise. Only as a result of the penetration of the Industrial Revolution, after 1850, into agriculture did the type of population shift out of agriculture into the cities, alluded to by Marx, occur. Yet even this shift was to be small in comparison with the population already in the towns.

WOOL AND COTTON

Britain's production of textiles changed radically during this period, too. While, as in the case of agriculture, the textile sector was not an intrinsic part of the Industrial Revolution, it, too, helped provide a climate of general economic growth favourable for the revolution in iron and coal.

Prior to the Industrial Revolution, England's chief export was textiles, in particular wool. The production of wool for weaving into cloth had originally been encouraged in 1138 by the arrival in England of the Cistercian monastic order. English wool soon came to be of the highest quality in Europe. Yet the English did not originally manufacture wool into cloth. They sold the raw material to foreign (initially Flemish and Italian) merchants rather. This revealed England's industrial backwardness *vis-à-vis* the Continent, prior to the mid-16th century. England was originally simply a supplier of raw materials for the Continent – in particular of wool, tin, lead, animal skins and hides. Already by the 1330s, however, a native cloth industry had evolved, especially in East Anglia. The monarchy encouraged this industry by inviting Flemish weavers to come and settle in England. Even so, for the next two centuries the new cloth industry concentrated on only semi-finished cloth which was sent to the Continent for the final manufacturing processes. Woollen, semi-finished cloths and raw wool continued to characterize English trade, amounting to 86 per cent of exports (80 per cent for cloth and 6 per cent for raw wool) as late as the mid-16th century. The English merchant marine, during this entire period, remained insignificant. The trade routes were dominated by the Hanseatic League, the Dutch and the Spanish. Much of the country's foreign trade, even when handled by English merchants, was carried in foreign vessels. As late as Henry VIII's reign, the Hansa and other foreign merchants controlled some 50 per cent of English cloth exports even at their London source. Only from the 1550s did the native merchants' control of London's cloth exports rise substantially above this figure, reaching 70 per cent. Long-distance overseas trade routes continued to be dominated by foreigners, in particular by the Italian city-states of Genoa, Florence and Venice, as well as the Hansa ports of northern Europe. Even when Genoa and Florence lost their commercial pre-eminence in the late 15th century, it was the more efficient Spanish and the Dutch, and not the English, who filled the gap. More generally, 15th century England was considered a backward rural area, in contrast to, for example, highly urbanized Renaissance Italy. England's only important commercial city, London, was overshadowed in wealth, size and culture by the great cities of the Continent, in particular Paris, Venice and Florence. It was, in effect, of the same rank as a second-class town such as Verona or Zurich. Before 1650 there were no English banks or bankers. The great banking enterprises were on the Continent. In the 15th century, London banks were just branches of the Florence-based Medici banking empire. English mining and metallurgy could not match their German counterparts, nor could English shipbuilding compete with the Spanish or Dutch. In paper, linen, silk, leatherwork, hosiery, iron founding and glass-making, the market was controlled by the Continent. If England, none the less, had been an important power since the 11th century, this was due to the country's relatively advanced level of political centralization in comparison with its continental rivals, which compensated for its economic backwardness. By the late 15th century, however, even this compensatory advantage was rapidly diminishing, as continental powers such as France and Spain consolidated their own national unity. During the 15th century and the 16th century, therefore, England's military insecurity grew.

For the English woollen industry the turning point seems to have been reached with the devastation of Flanders in the 1560s. The revolt ended the region's economic importance. Flanders, which until then had been Europe's economic heartland, was crushed by the Spanish, which crippled her economy until the 19th century. Holland managed to survive, but even that country remained, because of her war with Spain, commercially inactive for twenty years. A commercial vacuum was now created, which England was able to fill. With the extinction of the famous Flemish cloth industry, England now began to produce finished instead of semi-finished fabrics. She was assisted in this endeavour by the emigration to England of Flemish skilled weavers fleeing Spanish persecution. By the 17th century the English had become world leaders in the dyeing and finishing of cloth. Parallel with England's new economic assertiveness, her merchant fleet began to grow from only 50 000 tons in 1570 to 115 000 in 1629, and 150 000 in 1640. England now actively began to penetrate overseas markets. England also began to innovate in the woollen industry: to produce so called "new draperies", or lighter woollens. These were of lighter texture and cheaper, albeit of lower quality and less durable.

The English consequently found a broader market, particularly in southern Europe. As with the more traditional woollens, here again, the Flemish played an important role. The Flemish had originally pioneered the new draperies in the early 16th century in order to exploit the markets of southern Europe opened up by the decline of the Italian textile industry.

Whereas these "new draperies" were still woollen, albeit of a lighter quality, by 1600 cotton had begun to be used for the first time. Again, the new techniques appear to have been introduced by Flemish refugees. The cotton was imported from the eastern Mediterranean and was combined with linen, itself made from Irish flax, to produce a linen-cloth combination known as "fustian". Markets for these new lighter textiles were found in England's American tobacco colonies and in her

Caribbean sugar colonies. In contrast to a century earlier, England was, by the seventeenth century, no longer an economic colony of Europe, but had herself become a colonizer. For some time, however, only the lighter woollens (the result of England's long experience in the woollen industry) were, amongst English textile exports, able to compete in European markets. For their part, English fustians were competitive only in England's own home markets, not being able to compete with the better-established linen and cotton centres of continental Europe.

While pure cotton began to be manufactured much later – only in the 18th century – the market for cottons was potentially much broader than for woollens or even new draperies and fustians. Pure cotton provided a cheap, washable textile, so that it was no longer the wealthy few alone who could afford hygienic underwear (until then probably only available in the form of relatively expensive linens). The poor who until now had worn only coarse, dirty outer garments could now also buy cotton drawers and chemises which were comfortable to the skin and which were easy to clean and maintain, and could therefore be frequently changed. During the 18th century, England's production of cotton began to rise noticeably, paralleling that of iron. From the first decade of the century to the 1740s, the rate of growth was about 1,4 per cent per year. Then it suddenly doubled to 2,8 per cent until the early 1770s, following which, it tripled to 8,5 per cent, remaining at that level until the early 19th century. At the same time, the position of wool *vis-à-vis* cotton was dropping sharply. In 1750 wool still accounted for one-third of the total industrial production. By 1780 it accounted for only 25 per cent, and by 1812 for only 11 per cent, already just below cotton's share of 12 per cent. The share of wool in total exports also declined markedly *vis-à-vis* that of cotton. In the early 16th century, semi-finished woollen cloth, as we have seen, comprised, along with raw wool, 86 per cent of England's exports. That figure had not substantially changed as late as 1650, although by then, of course, the cloth was manufactured and sold in a fully finished state. By 1700, however, that figure had dropped to 70 per cent. The following figures[10] illustrate the long-term change in the relative export positions of wool and cotton during the subsequent century:

	Cotton (%)	*Wool* (%)
1700-1709	–	70
1750-1759	1	48
1770-1779	3	43
1780-1789	7	35
1790-1799	15	30
1800-1809	39	24
1810-1819	53	16
1820-1829	62	12

As with iron, the expansion of cotton production was linked with a series of technological breakthroughs, each corresponding with a particular key phase in the production process. For iron, there had been a breakthrough in 1707 in cast iron production and, after the perfection of the process through the Watt steam engine, a second breakthrough in wrought iron production in 1784. For cotton, the two phases of production were spinning the raw cotton into yarn, and then weaving the yarn into cloth. As opposed to the breakthroughs in iron production, which had ultimately improved the quality of the finished product while reducing its cost and increasing the scale of production, those in cotton production involved cost and scale but not quality. The first breakthrough in cotton production occurred in 1733 when John Kay invented the "flying shuttle", thus greatly speeding up the weaving process. However, the spinning process remained relatively slow. As a result, within a few years, the weavers' increasing demand for yarn led to a shortage in supply, so that in 1760 it took eight spinners to keep one weaver supplied. In 1769 this production bottleneck was removed with Richard Arkwright's "water frame" which greatly accelerated the spinning process. The water frame was essentially an enlarged version of the late medieval spinning wheel, adapted to power drive. At first, this power came from large iron-clad water wheels, but soon the water frames also began to use Watt steam engines as an alternative.

The adaption of steam power to the cotton industry was slow and considerably less essential than in the iron industry, if only because the advantages were less. As mentioned, coke-heated iron, produced with the help of steam-powered (as opposed to water-powered) furnaces and forges, was produced on a larger scale and more cheaply. The Arkwright water frame, however, as the name implies, could quite effectively be driven by water. While cotton textile production rose dramatically after 1775, for the first half century, this growth, while coinciding with the steam engine, owed relatively little to the latter. As late as the 1830s only 30 per cent of the weaving looms were driven by non-manual power, let alone by steam power. In 1800 less than one-third of Arkwright spinning mills were steam-powered; for other kinds of spinning mills, such as the by then more prevalent Crompton "mule", the percentage was even lower. Nor did these machines themselves provide a market for iron since, prior to their adaptation to the steam engine, they were largely made of wood. The revolution in cotton production, in short, might well have occurred without an Industrial Revolution, as had, by the 17th century, if not earlier, happened in India.

POPULATION AND STANDARD OF LIVING

Another form of growth coinciding with (but not intrinsic to) the English Industrial Revolution was a sudden long-term population rise. This population rise was, however, probably not due to rising agricultural productivity. While the population rise was ultimately helped by improvements in agriculture, its immediate cause lay elsewhere. It is, of course, true that agricultural output was steadily increasing so that by the early 18th century perhaps twice the number of people could be fed as had been the case 200 years before; presumably, the difference in agricultural output between the early 18th century and the Middle Ages was at least as great, if not greater. Yet this growth had not been reflected in terms of long-term population trends. Between 1300 and 1700, England's population rose from just over 4 000 000 to just over 5 000 000, an increase of less than 25 per cent. Moreover, the population growth during the 17th century, the very period when agricultural improvements were becoming particularly marked, had actually been slower than during either the 16th century or during the two centuries prior to the traumatic demographic disruptions of the Late Middle Ages.

The most important reason for the relatively modest size of population growth was the high death rate resulting from persistent and widespread disease. Even wars created relatively few casualties. If armies were wiped out, it was usually through disease. Disease, moreover, seemed to occur independently of the level of food supply. During the second half of the 17th century, harvests were good, yet epidemics of typhus and smallpox were common, not to mention the great bubonic plague of London in 1665-1666. But while there were still widespread violent attacks of typhus and smallpox as late as the 1730s, such epidemics declined sharply thereafter. This was reflected in a steady drop in the death rate. Between 1740 and 1800, the population rose by more than 50 per cent. Moreover, the drop in the death rate affected all segments of the population, even the well-fed aristocracy:[11]

Life expectancies at birth of aristocratic women

1700-1724	1723-1749	1750-1774	1775-1799	1800-1824
36,3	36,7	45,7	49,0	51,7

As has been suggested, most notably by J. D. Chambers,[12] diseases probably owed their disappearance to the spread, during this period, of cotton fabrics. Typhus, like bubonic plague, originated amongst rats and, once established in humans, was spread elsewhere by fleas and lice which thrived in the warm, moist layers of woollen clothing. With the advent of cheap cotton underclothing and bedding, the situation changed. Cotton fabrics, unlike heavier woollens, could easily be washed and boiled, thus killing the typhus-carrying louse. In contrast, prior to this time, women wore undergarments which "were never washed although worn day by day for years. The wives and grown daughters of tradesmen, and gentlemen even, wore petticoats of camlet, lined with dyed linen, stuffed with wool and horsehair and quilted; these were also worn until they were rotten".[13]

Once it was realized that typhus could be brought under control, it might further be argued, there must have been more incentive to deal with smallpox as well. After 1765 the inoculation against smallpox came into widespread use. General improvements in hygiene followed: the spread of cheap soap, regulations against the dumping of night soil and refuse, and attempts to cover open sewers. While many of these measures, including even the inoculation against smallpox, were not difficult to achieve, there was no obvious cure for typhus or the bubonic plague, prior to the spread of cotton fabrics. And as long as certain epidemic diseases were inevitable anyhow, there must have been little incentive to eliminate the others. What was the use of a cure for smallpox if the gap would be filled by typhus in any case?

The new population growth, much sharper than before, in turn must have affected agriculture. Whereas prior to the mid-18th century, agricultural modernization, including convertible husbandry and enclosures, must have been influenced by growing trade rather than by growing population, from now on trade and population growth would both exert an influence on increasing agricultural output. As will be recalled, enclosures had the effect of not only facilitating the spread of convertible husbandry and of arable farming, at the expense of pasture and woodland, but also of requiring more agricultural labour than before: for the restructuring of the farm buildings and land, for the new labour-intensive crops, and for the husbandry of the larger animal herds. The population growth therefore satisfied the increasing manpower needs of the rural sector. Also, sharply growing population, particularly in the towns, must have initially driven up the price of food, creating a strong incentive, after 1750, for the accelerated spread of enclosures and of convertible husbandry. Until 1663, England's export of cereals had been restricted by law so as to avoid famine. Then perhaps under the cumulative influence of agricultural improvements, greatly reducing chances of famine, this legislation was repealed, permitting exports to rise rapidly. With the new upsurge in population growth from around 1740, however, cereal surpluses vanished and Britain became a net cereal importer. As a result of a series of protectionist "corn laws", these imports were kept under sufficient control to keep cereal prices high enough to encourage the continued growth of domestic agriculture.

To what degree did the greater longevity and population increase reflect the workers' standard of living during the Industrial Revolution? The discussion of this issue has existed at least since Friedrich Engels's *The Condition of the Working Class in England* (1845). The issue, of course, is related to the controversy, already discussed, about the effects of enclosure upon the working class's source of living (employment). Whatever the case for the short term, there is no doubt that in the long run, the living standards for the mass of the population definitely rose. As we have seen, the advent of mass cotton apparel in the mid-18th century was itself responsible for the sharp drop in deaths from epidemic disease. Hygiene and sanitation in the new industrial towns were substantially worse than in rural areas, but infinitely better than in either the town or the country of a century earlier. British mass standards of living were also, from at least the late 17th century, higher than French standards of living by some 25 per cent. During the 18th century the French were less well dressed and less well fed than the British. During the 19th century this difference persisted, although it probably narrowed because of Britain's relatively increasing commitments to military and capital goods investment. Within Britain itself, while initially the influx of a rural population to the towns must have caused rents to go up, the increasing mining and improved transportation of coal must have compensated by providing cheaper fuel. Manufactures in particular became ever more accessible: cotton goods, pots and pans, soap and candles.

Generally it is accepted that the period 1795-1815 showed a temporary drop in the mass standard of living owing to the Napoleonic wars. In the coal mines, the influx of cheap Irish labour after 1815 may have lowered miners' living standards for a generation. In other branches of industry, the long-term rise in the standard of living was temporarily checked by the rise in the cost of food imports, itself perhaps reflecting the population rise abroad and at home, as well as the effects of the import duties imposed by the corn laws. For the first third of the 19th century the price of bread was at its peak. A more fundamental reason for the levelling off, if not the actual drop, in standards of living between 1795 and 1840 was that this was the very period when Britain was for the first time investing relatively heavily in capital goods, necessarily at the expense of the short-term consumer standard of living: in new textile mills and iron works, and in canals and railways. After 1840, although such investment actually grew even more, it could now be financed more from the returns of the first generation of industrial investment. Thus the strain on consumption was lessened, and the standard of living rose once more.

In terms of the less tangible "quality of life", it is likely that much harm was done at an individual, psychological level. Child labour not only increased, but became harsher. Child labour had always existed, notably in domestic spinning and weaving as well as in agriculture. But at least in the old days children had tended to work for their parents. Now, in the early 19th century, they were employed outside the home, in textile mills and in coal mines, where their work conditions were apt to be more harsh. Coal mining came to employ children to a far greater extent during the 1840s than during the previous century: industrial modernization appeared to encourage child labour. In the early 18th century the transport of coal from underground was too heavy for anyone but adult men. With the introduction of horses into the mines, however, boys began to be employed as drivers. With the introduction of tram rails and wheeled corves or trolleys, the task of the transport was made light enough to employ children even to push the corves along rails. In fact, it was in the more backward coal fields where, as late as 1842, tramways had not been introduced, that child labour was unknown. Urbanization also meant often the break-up of family life. Infants and small children in particular were more likely to be a burden to their parents in an urban environment where the parents were obliged to work far from home every day. As a result, many small children were given away to orphanages where they grew up emotionally deprived.

For adults, working conditions were more insecure, not to mention more monotonous, than in farm work. The traditional farm servant was hired at the great hiring fairs. He earned little, but had relative security of employment. The urban industrial worker, on the other hand, was hired only by the week or even by the day. As late as the 18th century, English workers expected to get a fair day's wage in return for a fair day's work. In case of dispute, the local justice of peace was supposed to provide arbitration. The industrial setting of the 19th century, on the other hand, did not provide such safeguards: wages were set by the free market, which meant, at least in theory if not in practice, no minimum limit to wages. The labour force was largely unskilled, many of them women, adolescents and children, and therefore in a relatively weak bargaining position. Their position was further undermined by the rapid growth of the labour population, augmented, in the 1840s, by the influx of the destitute Irish, fleeing the potato famine. Paradoxically, while the early 19th century worker must have enjoyed a substantially higher material standard of living than his forefathers had done, he was also more insecure, constantly facing the prospect, if not the reality, of permanent unemployment: he had more, but could take it less for granted.

ON THE EVE OF THE RAILWAY AGE: BRITAIN IN 1830

If coal and iron were the heart of the Industrial Revolution, the Industrial Revolution ultimately found its most eloquent expression in the steam engine railways. Coal production, like iron, rose steadily and with greater rapidity during the 18th century, from 2 500 000 tons in 1700 to 6 000 000 tons in 1770, and 11 000 000 tons in 1800. Canal development, which preceded and led to the railroads, was, like the railroads, closely bound up with coal mining. Coal was by far the most important canal-carried commodity: of the 165 canal acts passed between 1758 and 1801, ninety had coal transport as their prime objective. Canals were much cheaper modes of transport than the more traditional road-bound pack horse-and-wagon. Rivers, for their part, were not dependable, being subject to floods, droughts, tidal action, or silting of the river bed. The first great upturn in canal construction came in the 1760s, and by 1800 most viable canals had been completed. Originally, the need to link mines with rivers led to the development of railways. Actually such railways had been built as far back as the 17th century. By 1750 most important collieries had railways operated by horse-drawn wagons. By the second half of the 18th century, canal companies were beginning to take the initiative in building horse-drawn railways where ground was hilly and unsuitable for canals. Such railways had the advantage over roads that they did not tear up under the weight and friction of heavy coal wagons. Yet, since one horse could not draw more than one loaded wagon at a time, it was an expensive method of carriage. Not only would a locomotive steam engine draw, if necessary, many dozens of wagons, but each wagon could be twice as long as one driven by horse.

As mentioned, the Industrial Revolution can be considered to date from the steam engine's adaptation to industrial purposes (in particular the manufacture, on a large scale, of cheap, high-quality coke-smelted iron) from 1776. For the following fifty years, however, the Industrial Revolution existed in many respects more in theory than in practice. Although the economy was changing rapidly, much of that change was happening, it could be argued, independently of the Industrial Revolution. In transport, canals, while relatively recent, owed nothing to new industrial technology. Canal locks, for example, had been invented in the 14th century. By 1815, steamship navigation had become well established only on the rivers of the USA; it had not spread to Europe. Ocean voyages continued to be by sailing ship at least as late as the middle of the 19th century or later because of low engine efficiency.

Cotton production grew spectacularly during this period, but, as already suggested, the cotton industry, prior to the second quarter of the 19th century, was still largely independent of the steam engine. In fact, its relative initial growth only served to emphasize this independence:

Cotton (raw cotton) (retained imports in 000 pounds)[14]		Iron (pig iron in 000 tons)[15]	
1750-1759	2 820	1750	28
1760-1769	3 531	1760	35
1770-1779	4 797	1775	44
1780-1789	14 824	1790	90
1790-1799	28 645	1805	258
1800-1809	59 554	1820-1824	428
1810-1819	96 339	1825-1829	658
1820-1829	173 000	1830-1834	689
1830-1839	302 000	1835-1839	1 150
1840-1849	550 000	1840-1844	1 278
1850-1859	795 000	1845-1849	2 000
1860-1869	803 000	1850-1854	2 757
1870-1879	1 244 000	1855-1859	3 526
		1860-1864	4 152
		1865-1869	4 904
		1870-1874	6 378

These two sets of figures suggest a significant difference between the pattern of growth of cotton and that of iron, particularly for the first quarter of the 19th century. From 1800-1809 to 1830-1839, cotton production rose some 400 per cent, at about 13 per cent a year. During the subsequent forty years (from 1830-1839 to 1870-1879) its growth rate, while still impressive, was much lower: only 300 per cent, or about only 7,5 per cent per year. The rate of growth of cotton production was therefore actually higher prior to its full mechanization with steam power than subsequently. The rate of growth of iron production itself, while impressive at the end of the 18th century (when iron works were just completing their transition from charcoal to coke and from water to steam), grew much more slowly between 1805 and the early 1830s: some 180 per cent in just under thirty years, or about 6,5 per cent per year. In contrast, during the ensuing forty years (from 1830-1834 to 1870-1874), its growth rate was about 800 per cent or 20 per cent a year. The relatively slow rate of growth of iron production during the quarter century prior to the steam engine railway therefore indicates, in contrast to cotton, its much closer dependence upon steam engine technology: if the advent of the Watt steam engine had been indispensable for the initial surge in pig iron *supply*, the coming of age of the railway, a half century later, permitted an even more spectacular surge by suddenly providing a greatly increased source of *demand* for iron products.

A comparison between the percentage shares of iron and cotton of Britain's total exports during this period provides a similar picture:[16]

	Cotton	*Iron*
1750-1759	1	5
1760-1769	2	6
1770-1779	3	7
1780-1789	7	6
1790-1799	15	7
1800-1809	39	5
1810-1819	53	4
1820-1829	62	4
1830-1839	48	11
1840-1849	45	15
1850-1859	36	18
1860-1869	36	15
1870-1879	33	16

Here, even more graphically, we can see the change after 1830: from then on, the proportion of exports in cotton began to drop, while that of iron rose substantially. In short, the significance of the steam engine's widespread application to long-distance passenger and freight rail transport, from around 1830, is that it was only from then on that the Industrial Revolution and general economic growth became synonymous.

THE STEAM ENGINE RAILWAY

Although the first railroad (the Stockton-Darlington line) was built in 1825, it was not until around 1850 that the railways were to play a decisive role throughout the different branches of the economy. The first generation of railway transport was geared predominantly to passenger service: freight was relatively neglected. The first to suffer from railway competition were the stage coaches, oriented towards passenger transport, and not the canals, since these specialized in freight. As late as 1843, passengers still provided two-thirds of railway income. Not until 1852 did freight income finally surpass income from passengers. While early passenger carriages were similar in design to stage coaches and therefore presented few new problems in construction, there was no similar precedent for the transport of, for example, livestock which had hitherto travelled "on the hoof". Apart from coal wagons, already familiar in mining areas since the 17th century, there was no precedent for the new rolling stock which was now to deal with other categories of freight. Moreover, in contrast to goods and livestock, passengers obligingly loaded and unloaded themselves. Most railway companies of the 1830s still operated on a small scale, with under 80 km of line each. It was generally the responsibility of the professional carriers, who paid a toll for the use of the railway companies' wagons, to make all necessary arrangements for the transfer of goods from the wagons of one company's train to those of another. The system was cumbersome and led to innumerable disputes and delays. A through goods traffic system did not come into operation before 1847. Then too, prior to the early 1840s, locomotive technology remained rudimentary so that locomotives were still not powerful enough to haul heavy goods trains.

During the second quarter of the 19th century the advantages of the railway over land transport, even for freight, became ever more apparent. The most obvious advantage of the railway was speed. Not only would passengers and freight reach their destination more rapidly, but this in turn would permit a more intensive and therefore a more effective utilization of rolling stock, thus reducing costs. Speed notably also stimulated agricultural improvement, since relatively perishable crops and fresh meat could now be marketed even at long distances. The railway was a cheaper form of transport compared with road travel, not only because of its greater speed, but also because it reduced the cost of raw materials required to transport a given ton of commodities. There was a marked saving in manpower, animals, animal foodstuffs and timber in particular. In other words, the railway, like so much of the Industrial Revolution, was able to reduce costs by replacing animal and vegetable products, increasingly scarce, by more abundant and therefore cheaper mineral inputs, in this case coal and iron. A particularly striking example of the effects of cost reduction is the transport of livestock. Costs to farmers of sending cattle, sheep and pigs by rail were about half the costs of the traditional mode of marketing, namely droving (sending cattle "on the hoof"). Cattle lost a substantial amount of weight when travelling in this manner to their destination of slaughter. With the railway, they could be transported by freight, thus avoiding weight loss. Alternatively, they could be slaughtered locally and their carcasses sent by freight, since, as mentioned, the new high speed of transport reduced the chance of spoilage. The savings in weight loss more than offset the added expense of rail freight charges for the transport of the animals. It must be emphasized, moreover, that by the 19th century the costs of droving were actually increasing. For example, the improvement of roads worked against the drovers, since it necessitated toll charges to pay for initial costs and upkeep. Hard-surface roads in turn necessitated costly shodding of cattle. Enclosure, largely complete by 1820, had eliminated much of the open grazing land, forcing cattle to walk along fenced roads which lacked grass and water. By facilitating cheaper and more effective fattening of cattle, the railway stimulated more intensive agriculture. Railways, by reducing costs, also permitted large-scale purchase of imported fertilizers. In 1841, only 1 700 tons of guano were imported into Britain. By 1847, the quantity imported had increased more than one hundredfold, to 200 000 tons.

A rival to the railways, considerably more effective than road travel, was the waterway, in particular the canal, perhaps because, as we have seen, the origins of the canal and the horse-drawn railway were so closely intertwined, notably in response to the stimulus of the expanding coal trade. The sudden and dramatic construction boom in canals, during the last third of the 18th century, was itself largely a response to the rapidly growing coal trade. Even with the advent of the steam locomotive, railways continued until the mid-1830s primarily as extensions of or tributaries to existing rivers and canals. To the degree that these early steam engine railways did carry freight, this was, like canal freight, largely coal. As late as 1842,

80 per cent of railway freight tonnage was coal. By 1847, this share had dropped, but was still 60 per cent, at which level it would permanently remain. Just as in 1852 railway income from freight had first surpassed income from passengers, it was also in the early 1850s that the tonnage of freight carried by railways first exceeded tonnage carried by waterways. By 1856 the traffic controlled by railways was twice that controlled by canals. To be sure, throughout the 19th century, freight tonnage carried by canals continued to rise in absolute terms, but at a rate far slower than that of the railways. By 1898, most canals had become mere local feeders of traffic to the main railways. Thus the relationship between railways and canals existing prior to about 1835 had been reversed exactly.

As with road transport (before the 20th century internal combustion engine), the most obvious advantage the railway had over canals was speed. Travel by canal was extremely slow, no faster, in fact, than walking, probably because of the relatively little space for manoeuvrability afforded the long barges by the narrow width between canal banks. In comparison with railways, canal construction tended to raise more complex engineering problems. Depth and breadth of each individual canal varied according to the possibilities allowed by the surrounding topography, as well as to the local commercial requirements. Then, too, canals, like rivers, were often separated from each other by differences of altitude, necessitating complex lock systems. Such problems could only further delay traffic, particularly over long distances. It was, in fact, claimed that it sometimes took longer to ship goods by canal from Manchester to Liverpool than it did by ocean from New York. Problems of speed were compounded by problems of distance. Rail links were often less circuitous than links by canal. Moreover, the very engineering difficulties which might force a canal to zigzag (thereby adding distance), might also in this way force it to avoid many small centres of production which the more flexible railway lines could reach. Eventually the rail network was to be at least five times as extensive as the entire system of rivers and canals. Because of its low speed, canal transport, like road transport, was unsuited to conveying perishable goods (meat, fish, fresh milk, vegetables). Nor was it suited to transporting livestock, since beasts were apt to suffer from the long confinement required by such slow journeys. Because canals were much less able than railways to benefit from the advent of steam engine locomotion, they were not able to diversify their services and were forced to continue, as during the late 18th century, to concentrate solely on mineral transport.

Largely because of their greater speed, railways operated at lower costs than either roads or canals. For example, even for coal, English railways decreased freight costs by 70 per cent, compared with canals. Even so, canal costs, in the long run, were much cheaper than costs of road transport. Road transport, as already indicated, was extremely wasteful of resources. It could not provide the large-scale bulk transport of canals either, not to mention railways. Whereas the advent of the railway almost immediately rendered road transport insignificant, canals were therefore less easy to put out of business, in spite of their substantial handicaps. In certain respects, canal costs were lower than railways, particularly with respect to maintenance. The upkeep of a waterway was cheaper than that of a railroad, and canal barges cost less than railway wagons. Also, a unit of tractive power could haul a greater weight of cargo on a canal than the same unit could haul on rails. But all these advantages were more often than not outweighed by the engineering difficulties of building the canal in the first place, as well as by the cost savings of the railroad's greater speed, and thus the more intensive utilization of existing stock.

Just as the railroad gradually supplanted the canal as the main conveyor of coal, the key fuel of the first Industrial Revolution, so, too, the railway acted as an important market for the main construction material of that revolution – iron. The expansion of the iron industry was closely tied to the British railway boom of the 1840s. Between 1844 and 1851, some 29 per cent of pig iron used domestically was consumed by the railway for track ("permanent way") alone. In the peak year of 1848, this share rose as high as 40 per cent. The increase in British (domestic) pig iron consumption during the period 1845-1847 was therefore probably largely due to the growth in the demand for "permanent way". Moreover, locomotives and other rolling stock, as well as accompanying equipment, must have increased total demand by another 20-25 per cent. A further substantial impact on the iron industry must have been exerted through the railway's stimulus upon the coal and engineering industries. True, this close and direct correlation between the growth of the iron industry and the expansion of the railway was especially short-term. After 1851, the impact of railway iron consumption became less impressive. Its share of total domestic iron consumption during the next two decades dropped to about 16 per cent or only just above one half of the level reached during the 1840s. For the total British iron output (including not only the domestic, but also the foreign market) the foreign railway demand, particularly the continental European railway boom, exerted the more decisive impact. During the period 1844-1851 the export market's share of British pig iron production amounted to one-sixth more than that claimed by domestic demand. Again, between 1852 and 1869, the export market's lead became particularly noticeable: its share of pig iron output exceeded the domestic demand by two to one. In sum, the domestic and foreign railway demands together claimed as much as 39 per cent of British pig iron output for the period 1844-1851, and 24 per cent for the 1850s and the 1860s. Britain's railway iron production in turn reflected the world leadership of mid 19th century Britain in the iron industry. The total British iron exports (of which railway iron amounted to about one-third) increased more than twenty times between 1830 and 1870, while the share of these exports of pig iron output jumped from 25 per cent to roughly 60 per cent. As late as 1873, Britain must have produced as much pig iron as the rest of the industrialized world (Europe and the USA) combined. British iron exports alone during this period were almost as high as the entire iron output of continental Europe.

In the USA, railroads at first reflected a more rural, less industrialized society than in Britain. From the very beginning, British railways operated on coal, whereas before the Civil War (1861-1865) most American locomotives, as well as steamboats, used wood as fuel. Nor, at least until the Civil War, were most of the rails in America produced domestically; 40 per cent were imported from Britain and another 9 per cent were made from imported pig iron. Still another 21 per cent were simply rolled from old rails, many of which in turn must have themselves been imported originally. Whereas the peak railway construction years in Britain were in the 1840s, the peak years in the USA came some thirty years later. In America, railways were, in contrast to Britain, initially linked to agriculture rather than to industry. The American Industrial Revolution was still only in its infancy, so that the railroad's impact there was substantially less than in Britain.

Another reason why there was less emphasis on the railways in America was the more extensive river network existing there. As a result, transport costs by water were at first substantially less than by rail, so much so that, in contrast to Britain, water transport, even as late as 1850, was used not only for freight, but for passengers as well. In 1851-1852 American inland waterways carried six times as much freight as the railways. Only by 1861 did water and rail freight traffic become approximately equal, whereas a comparable situation had occurred in Britain already a decade earlier. It was in particular the factor of "economies of the long haul" which gave American water transport such an advantage over rail transport in comparison with the situation in Britain. Because distances were greater, canals that were built could be far longer than those in Britain. The best-known example of such a canal was the Erie canal, opened in 1825 and connecting the Hudson river with the Great Lakes. As late as the 1850s it was still the principal transport artery between the eastern seaboard and the Midwest. Canal rates fell sharply after 1830 and, twenty years later, canal rates were only 25 per cent of railway rates. During the period 1820-1850, as a result of the Erie canal in particular, the population of Ohio, Indiana, Illinois and Michigan rose from 8 per cent to 18 per cent of the national total. In other, less important, respects, however, American water arteries suffered handicaps as great as or even greater than those in Britain. For example, the Mississippi-Missouri river system, in spite of its length, breadth and depth, was very difficult to navigate, being full of reefs and sandbanks, severely reducing navigation speeds. Furthermore, the impact of adverse weather on canal transport was far stronger in America than in Britain: canals and rivers in America were plagued during some five months a year with either summer water shortages or winter frost.

It was only after the Civil War, when the American Industrial Revolution, as well as agricultural exports, greatly accelerated in tempo, and when, simultaneously, the USA expanded into the western half of the continent, that the role of the railways finally eclipsed that of the rivers and canals. West of the Mississippi, the climate was much drier and the country more mountainous; there were fewer rivers, and canal-building was much more difficult. While in 1852 the railways carried only one-sixth the freight of waterways, by 1890 the railways were carrying five times as much freight as did the waterways.

BRITAIN AND FRANCE

Two hundred years before the cast iron Watt steam engine, Britain, as we have seen, had begun to outdistance her neighbours in military technology, becoming for a time the leading power manufacturing cast iron cannon: since 1560, the country had replaced Flanders as a key cannon exporter. Still earlier, under the Tudors, the English had become enthusiastic developers of a new, more modern type of war ship, the "galleon", itself developed in the mid-15th century with the onset of ocean sailing. The more traditional war ship, the "galley", was a relic from Greek and Roman times and suitable only for closed-sea (Mediterranean) navigation. Its use of sails was only partial, being supplemented by oarsmen. For the more extreme Atlantic winds, it proved necessary to develop galleons: these were operated purely by sail power and, for defence, were mounted with cannon. Although the cannon had been used sporadically since the early 14th century, particularly for siege-warfare, it was only with the advent of the galleon that its impact became decisive. The first two English galleons had been built in 1487 by Henry VII, and, under Henry VIII and Elizabeth, the galleons became the basis of the English war fleet.

In contrast to the English, their rivals, in particular the Mediterranean powers, were, if also adopting firepower, much less innovative. The Turks did not generally use artillery on land except for siege operations, at least not before the 17th century; in contrast, since the early 16th century, field artillery had come into widespread use in western Europe. In naval warfare the Turks likewise clung to the traditional galley, throughout the 16th century.

Like the Turks, the Spanish, too, lagged behind in armaments. For example, Spain suffered from a shortage of skilled labour; yet, unlike England, Spain did not encourage foreign technicians to settle and pass on their skill to domestic industry. Rather, Spain found it cheaper to obtain cannon from her European possessions in Flanders and Germany. With the Flemish insurrection of the 1560s, however, Spain underwent an acute armaments shortage. On sea, in contrast to the English, Spain clung to the tradtional galley ship with its ramming and boarding tactics and its sparse use of cannon because the room was needed for oarsmen. The comparative English naval headstart was reflected, in 1588, in the humiliating defeat of the Spanish armada.

The French armaments industry had flourished during the first century of widespread cannon power (1450-1550), but then it, too, had declined. The decline seems to have been associated with the ensuing period of religious civil wars, involving the consolidation of the national Catholic church, with its rural, anti-industrial outlook; the result involved the flight abroad of many skilled technicians, themselves supporting Protestantism in reaction to the Catholic establishment. In France, as in Spain, traditional landed interests proved victorious. In England, the reverse trend was evident.

England's dynamic armaments industry and the growth of that country's navy (and merchant marine) were interrelated. By the middle of the 18th century the British mercantile marine was several times the size of its main rival, that of the French. British armed naval superiority permitted Britain to dominate the seas increasingly to acquire new colonies at France's expense, and to protect her own trade. The population of British North America increased tenfold between 1700 and 1774, by which time it comprised well over 90 per cent of total British and French White colonial populations. In contrast, the colonial market for French manufacturers was, by 1774, simply the French West Indies. The British colonial system was vital for developing Britian's still immature iron industry. Through the navigation acts of 1651 and 1660, half the nails produced in England were said, during the mid-18th century, to have gone to the colonies. For the country's raw cotton supplies, Britain came, as of the early 18th century, to rely on her West Indies colonies. In the 1790s, with the invention of the cotton gin, and by 1803, with the Louisiana purchase, the southern USA became Britain's key source of cotton. Economic links with America, in fact, grew even more rapidly after the American revolution than before. British exports to America rose from £2 100 000 in 1765-1770 to £7 000 000 by 1796-1800. Significantly, by 1800, these exports included a growing and significant share (31 per cent) devoted to cotton fabrics and iron manufactures, the two most characteristic products of Britain's early 19th-century industry. During the 18th century, Europe's share of Britain's exports fell from 82 per cent to 21 per cent, while North America's rose from 6 per cent to 32 per cent. The shares of North America and the West Indies together rose from 10 per cent to 57 per cent. The French, too, developed a market for their own manufactures, but this market was in European countries rather than in the colonies, and in the more traditional textile products of woollens and linens (as opposed to cottons). Having decisively defeated Spain in the mid-17th century, France had since become Spain's protector and had thereby penetrated the Spanish market, including Spanish America. To be sure, this could hardly rival the British North American market in importance. English trade with European countries, on the other hand, was less impressive than France's. Between 1715 and 1783, it rose by 140 per cent, while the French trade rose by 200 per cent. Only with Britain's breakthrough in cotton production in the 1770s did Britain's competitive position begin to improve, even in Europe. The significance of the Eden treaty of 1786 is that it permitted British cottons to enter the French market tariff-free for the first time. To the extent that, during the subsequent generation, France was almost continuously at war with Britain, the revolutionary and Napoleonic period can be seen as a reaction, on the part of the French bourgeoisie, against the *ancien régime's* policy of ultimately having accepted free trade with Britain. Conversely, Waterloo was a victory for both Pax Britannica and free trade.

If, prior to the French Revolution, England's military and naval superiority was not yet paralleled by a corresponding superiority in manufacturing, this was only because France's population was so much larger. In 1781, France's population was about 26 000 000; in contrast, Britain (England, Wales, Scotland) had a population of only 8 900 000. Even if we add to this figure the population of Ireland (4 100 000) and White North America (2 200 000 in 1774), the total would still have been a potential internal market of only some 60 per cent the population of France. However, in *per capita* terms (amount of manufactures consumed per person), Britain was already ahead of France. And by 1800 the share of Britain's industry in the gross national product was one quarter, as opposed to one-fifth for French industry. The most important difference, by the late 18th century, between the manufacturing (and even trade) sectors of Britain and those of France was not so much one of quantity as one of quality. As already mentioned, French exports tended to be in the more traditional woollens and linens. France also began to manufacture cottons in the early 18th century, and until the last quarter of the century, France's cotton industry held its own against Britain's. (In France, as in Britain, the spread of cotton fabrics, more hygienic than traditional fabrics, may well have contributed to the drop in the mortality rate and the resultant population rise at this time.) By 1786, however, Britain was clearly in the lead: her net imports of raw cotton were two-thirds higher than France's. In the production of cast iron, France, on the eve of the revolution, was actually producing twice as much as Britain. But French iron was being smelted with charcoal, not coke; in contrast to Britain, France was poorly endowed with coal, but much better endowed with large forests. France's iron industry was therefore technologically more primitive than Britain's. As already mentioned, the coking of iron was crucial, not simply because of cost-saving (in England if not in France), but because coke, in conjunction with the Watt steam engine, permitted iron manufacturing on a large scale; moreover, coke produced a cast superior to that produced by charcoal, a cast indispensable in particular to heat engines, such as the steam engine, subject to high pressures. The French economy, as Francois Crouzet pointed out, was, by 1789, "not basically different from what it had been under Louis XIV: it simply produced much more".[17] In England, on the other hand, growth was not only in the economy, but in technology as well, symbolized by such key innovations as the Arkwright water frame, and, much more significantly, by Darby's coke process for the smelting of iron, and by the steam engine.

As has been suggested, even the British economy, prior to 1830, was in most respects not revolutionary at all. It was showing rapid accelerated economic growth in its textile industry, in its transport system and in its agriculture, but its technology was still based on traditional principles. Only in the armaments and metallurgical sectors was there a technological revolution. The French economy was, however, technologically even more archaic. While showing dynamism, particularly during the 18th century, it did not show, even in its metallurgical sector, any revolutionary technology. And while the French textile industry was showing rapid economic growth, its technology was not affected by the Industrial Revolution, and even lacked the innovativeness shown by the Arkwright water frame.

Like French industry, French agriculture before 1800 did not fall behind its British counterpart so much in quantity as in terms of modernization. French agricultural output, during the ninety years prior to the revolution, grew rapidly – at least as rapidly as British agriculture, if not considerably more so. In terms of structure, however, the differences between the two agrarian systems were marked and would remain so until the 20th century. France, in contrast to Britain, remained a country of small cultivators, producing relatively little (less, in any case, than the British agriculturist) for the market, and working according to more traditional patterns of cultivation. Even in the late 17th century, small peasants in England and Wales controlled not more than 25 per cent of arable land. As late as 200 years later, by contrast, the French peasantry still controlled 40 per cent of French arable land. If anything, the trend in France towards small peasant proprietorship actually grew from the 18th century to the 19th century. In Britain, the trend was in the reverse direction: the New Domesday Survey of 1873 showed that 80 per cent of the land was owned by 7000 individuals. Similarly, in terms of average size of land cultivated per agricultural worker (including presumably peasants, tenants, and labourers) during the 19th century, the land per worker in France kept shrinking, while that in Britain kept growing:[18]

	France (ha)	*Britain* (ha)
1815-1824	6,7	8,2
1845-1854	5,9	7,9
1905-1914	5,4	9,8

A key factor in assuring the triumph of the French smallholding was, of course the revolution of 1789. The revolution led to a redistribution of land expropriated from the king, from nobles who had fled the country, and from the church. While many recipients were not peasants but middle-sized landholders and urban bourgeoisie seeking to buy land, these purchasers were themselves smaller landowners than those whose lands had been expropriated. Most importantly, the revolution abolished seigneurial dues; this in turn favoured the broad masses of the peasantry, forcing many large landowners to either sell part of their lands or face bankruptcy.

As opposed to the steady advance of enclosure in Britain, during the 17th and 18th centuries, French agriculture continued to be dominated by the open-field system, based on strip cultivation and the three-field rotation. When, in the 1760s, some landlords began to advocate enclosure, the movement allegedly caused serious peasant discontent. In this respect the French Revolution might be seen as a peasant "counter-revolution" against attempts, however belated and hesitant, at agricultural modernization. In turn, the revolution left largely unchanged the traditional communal techniques of cultivation and the layouts of fields and simply reinforced the pattern of small peasant landownership. Whereas enclosure appears to have foundered against the resistance of the French peasantry, enclosure was passively accepted by the British smallholder. One reason for this passivity must have been that enclosure in England did not necessarily mean proletarianization. As mentioned, prior to the second quarter of the 19th century the growth of such a proletariat relative to landholders rose only slowly, so that much of this same increase could be accounted for simply by an increase in population. Even more significantly, because the practice of convertible husbandry had long been penetrating the English countryside, many small cultivators may well have been acquainted with the new agricultural techniques even before enclosure reached their own particular village, and may therefore have been able to adapt relatively easily. The French peasant, on the other hand, was unlikely, even in 1789, to have heard much of convertible husbandry. For him, therefore, enclosure and proletarianization were synonymous.

The persistence of open-field three-field cultivation and small peasant landholdings was reflected in French animal husbandry, which was much less extensive than that in Britain. In France, a smaller share of farmland was allocated to stockrearing, and this in turn made for lower yields of cereals and vegetables than in Britain. Between 1815 and 1914 about 54 per cent of cultivable land in Britain was used as pasture, as opposed to only 23 per cent in France. In reality, even this striking difference tells only part of the story, since these figures do not include acreage in convertible husbandry devoted to specialized fodder crops. Since in Britain such acreage was far more important than it was in France, its inclusion in our comparison would make the difference between the two countries in acreage devoted to stock-rearing more striking still. Britain's far more advanced animal husbandry also showed itself in the quality of that country's draught animals in contrast with those of France. In Britain, the more efficient horse was prevalent, in contrast with the more traditional and less efficient ox common in France. This distinction was furthermore compounded by the fact that, in terms of sheer numbers of draught animals, the ratio of draught animal power both to arable land and to the worker employed in agriculture was substantially higher in Britain than in France. The following figures are for 1892, but they would obviously have been just as relevant at the beginning of the 19th century:[1][9]

	Draught horses 000s	*Draught cattle 000s*	*Ratio animal power: ha of arable land*	*Ratio animal power: worker employed in agriculture*
Britain	1 027	–	1: 6,4	1:1,6
France	1 322	1 387	1:11,4	1:2,6

The relative differences between animals (both in quality, and in animal power) in the two countries was further evident in the quantity of organic fertilizer available per hectare. In the 1830s, for example, 188 kg of fertilizer was available per hectare of British arable land, as opposed to only seventy kg per ha of French arable land.

The archaic traits of both French industry and French agriculture were paralleled by the quality of France's internal trade, which was both more primitive and less dynamic than Britain's. Britain was favoured by geography more than was France: France's size was two and a half times that of Britain, making internal communications, particularly prior to the advent of the railway, correspondingly more difficult. Britain also had much more coastline relative to her surface area, making her harbours that much more accessible to her hinterland; Britain was also relatively better endowed in harbours and rivers. While northern France enjoyed the same advantageous maritime climate as Britain, large parts of southern France suffered from inadequate summer rainfall. This drier, Mediterranean climate in turn resulted in less productive arable land, as well as in low yields of hay from pasture. The less productive (and therefore less dynamic) agrarian sector served to reduce internal trade. In countries such as Spain and Turkey, whose climates were even drier than southern France's, shortcomings in agriculture, and therefore in internal trade as well, were even greater. As early as 1688, *per capita* income in France was estimated at 20 per cent less than in Britain.

While both Britain and the Continent, by the 18th century, had large cities, the quality of urbanization was significantly different. The cities of Europe tended to be administrative, judicial and ecclesiastic rather than commercial centres. Notable examples were Madrid, Rome and Paris, as well as the provincial towns. In Germany, too, the many small principalities and duchies each had their bureaucratic-military capitals. In Britain, by contrast, the newer provincial centres, such as Birmingham, Liverpool, Leeds and Manchester, were strictly trade-oriented, as was, to a large degree, London itself. Another distinction was the transport system. Since the later 17th century, under Louis XIV, France had begun to develop trunk roads. From the 1730s, a national plan for such trunk roads was being gradually implemented. After 1750, French roads were actually of a higher quality than were the British roads. Like its towns, however, France's roads were built for military and administrative, not commercial, reasons. The roads emphasized speed of travel, but did not lessen the costs of transporting heavy bulk goods. Nor did they penetrate geographically remote (and therefore economically unproductive) regions. In contrast, as we have seen, Britain emphasized canals which, while not providing as rapid a transport as roads, provided transport which was cheaper, not requiring as much horsepower or such expensive maintenance. The relative absence of canals in France reflected the fact that the countryside was so much more hilly and mountainous than that in England. More significantly, however, France's canals were few also because there was little coal produced, and therefore little need of heavy bulk transport so suitable for waterways. As mentioned, canal-building in England had served primarily to transport coal. France's lack of canals was therefore in part an index of France's more modest potential for heavy industry.

France's more underdeveloped internal market was a product not only of the country's climate and geography, but of her history as well. England's tradition of political (and therefore economic) unification was much stronger than France's. England had been firmly centralized both politically and economically by the Norman conquest of 1066. France's national unity, on the other hand, while existing in principle since the early Middle Ages, if not since late Roman times, existed much more in theory, less in practice, than England's did. Prior to the early 13th century the rulers of France had often lacked effective control of most of the country. After that date, the government's extension of effective control to the southern half of the country (much of it controlled by England) still took another 250 years. Even after 1450, the shadow of incomplete national unity lingered until the French Revolution: in the form of bitter and protracted religious division, as well as in persistent economic division in the form of internal tariffs and tolls. The river Loire alone had seventy five tolls, and this was France's main commercial artery. France, moreover, was also, until the revolution, divided into different tariff areas, even though northern France, at least, had had its internal tariffs abolished since Louix XIV. England's far more developed economic unity was paralleled by a correspondingly more unified social structure. In particular, there was lacking the antagonism between the landowning nobility and the urban middle classes, which existed in France and which would ultimately precipitate the revolution of 1789. The English aristocracy was heavily involved in both agriculture *and* commerce and industry. The British Parliament of the 18th century was dominated by the great landowning aristocracy; and it was this same Parliament which passed the protectionist navigation acts, passed legislation initiating turnpike roads, and passed tariff legislation protecting domestic industry. In France, such legislation was passed by the central government, itself often viewed with suspicion if not animosity by many members of the nobility. The English nobility furthermore encouraged agricultural modernization, itself permitting greater trade with the towns. The average French nobleman, on the other hand, like the French peasant, was more tradition-bound, and therefore reluctant to risk enclosures and convertible husbandry. While the practice of simply raising rents antagonized the peasantry, enclosure risked antagonizing them even more. The legacy, for the 19th century and the 20th century, of France's comparatively archaic economic growth was that, while the country's economy could provide an adequate standard of food consumption for its inhabitants, the manufactures, particularly those involving heavy industry, remained inadequate. France could provide herself with butter, but not with guns. Britain could provide herself with both.

CONCLUSION

As has been discussed in this chapter, the Industrial Revolution, particularly in its initial phase, was not synonymous simply with accelerated economic growth. It was the particular quality of the growth involved, namely growth involving heat engines such as the steam engine, which gave this "revolution" its character. Only the use of heat would permit the release of mechanical energy above those levels readily available (through torsion, wind or water) in the everyday environment. Most of Britain's economic growth prior to the second quarter of the 19th century (in agriculture, textiles, population and transportation), while facilitating the development of the Industrial Revolution, was not, strictly speaking, an intrinsic part of it. The Industrial Revolution, prior to the steam engine's massive spread to transportation and textiles around 1830, was, it has been argued, circumscribed largely to the heavy-industry sector of manufacturing, in particular to iron metallurgy: coke-smelted iron was indispensable to the manufacture of the steam engine, and in turn the steam engine provided the technology for the large-scale manufacture of cheap, high-quality cast iron and wrought iron products. Moreover, this early Industrial Revolution owed is origins not to economic growth *per se*, but specifically to the military sector of that economy. The cast iron cylinder of the steam engine was the descendant of the cast iron cylinder of the 16th century cannon and the bronze cylinder of the late medieval siege cannon. It is also hardly a coincidence that England, the country which pioneered the development of the 16th century iron cannon, was the country which, 200 years later pioneered the steam engine. It is therefore not possible to understand Britain's 18th century Industrial Revolution without studying its 16th century antecedents.

CHAPTER 9

ENLIGHTENMENT AND ENLIGHTENED DESPOTS IN THE 18th CENTURY

THE ORIGINS OF THE ENLIGHTENMENT

The 18th century is often called the Century of Enlightenment. The French *philosophes* of the century themselves called their time *le siècle des lumières*. The term "Enlightenment" was used in England for the first time only in about 1865, analogous to the original German word *Aufklärung,* as a description of the spirit and aims of the French *philosophes* of the 18th century.

The most numerous and prominent protagonists of the 18th century Enlightenment, those in France, appropriated the name *les philosophes* for themselves. As the French forms of the Enlightenment dominated in Europe, one can describe the followers of this intellectual movement as *philosophes* whether they were French or not. And certainly there were *philosophes* in other countries such as Scotland, England, Italy and Germany! One must keep in mind that there were national differences between these thinkers. Even more important is the fact that they were philosophers in a particular sense. They were not dedicated to the meditation, abstraction and logical consistency which is associated with philosophers today, but were concerned with the application of ideas about social and political change. Yet they were philosophers, both in the loose, 18th century sense of the term as well as in the fundamental sense in general, as they asked the basic questions about God, man and nature and were in search of the causes and understandable realities underlying these phenomena. They combined the vocations of philosopher and intellectual, as they felt that the most fundamental ideas were of necessity applicable, communicable, effective and socially relevant.

L. Krieger writes: "The Enlightenment was a movement which actually first assumed an identifiable form between 1715 and 1748, and then only as a loose collection of like-minded individuals, engaged in the most various kinds of intellectual enterprises but associated through mutual recognition in the common task of turning the philosophies of secular reason and natural science into a real cultural force competitive with contemporary orthodoxies and the emotive arts. Not until the intellectual generation of 1748-1776 did these protagonists of Enlightenment develop the organized communication and doctrine which endowed them with a comparative unity among themselves and a clear pre-eminence over their cultural competitors. And even this halcyon phase was short-lived, yielding to the unraveling of the Enlightenment itself and to the cultural pluralism which featured in the last quarter of the eighteenth century."[1]

A number of important aspects regarding the origins, nature, development and conclusion of the Enlightenment are contained in the above.

First, it should be noted that the *philosophes* did not form a coherent movement for many decades. They did not adhere to a fixed, uniform doctrine. Amongst the "members" of the Enlightenment were: atheists, deists, Protestants and Roman Catholics, aristocrats, democrats and admirers of enlightened despotism, idealists and materialists, withdrawn scholars and propagandists, wise as well as foolish men. Very few of its great figures were typical of the movement. By as late as 1748 the Enlightenment was not yet a coherent intellectual movement supporting a common programme, but only a concept taking shape in the minds of a scattered handful of writers and social critics. But after about 1750 the situation would change to a great extent, as will be seen later. It should also be mentioned that the *philosophes* did, however, form a closely knit social group and were in constant communication with one another. Their voluminous correspondence aside, they often met and had incessant conversations. The leaders of the Scottish Enlightenment – David Hume, Adam Ferguson, William Robertson and Adam Smith – frequently visited each other and their French counterparts on the Continent. The men of the Enlightenment often travelled – it was the century of the "grand tour". One must remember that the Enlightenment was essentially cosmopolitan. The *philosophe* viewed himself as a world citizen and believed in the universality of his own values. French became the language of a civilized way of life.

Secondly, there is the place held by reason and science in the thinking of the Enlightenment. Many of the *philosophes* put their faith in human reason, a philosophy known as rationalism, which was almost a religion. During the 17th century intellectual "revolution" the view that human reason provides the means of determining truth (as the classic Greek philosophers also believed) was already revived amongst thinkers such as Descartes, Hobbes and Spinoza. To the rationalists it was clear that man was meant by nature to be happy, but that only through reason could he attain true knowledge and thus achieve happiness. This confidence in human reason was, to them, justified by the discoveries of the scientists in the 17th century. In the course of that century, philosophers attempted to combine the results of these intellectual developments in a new philosophy, distinct from the Christian view of the world of medieval theology.

The German philosopher, Immanuel Kant, in an article written in 1784, explained to the general public that the Enlightenment was man's "appearance from his immaturity". This immaturity, according to him, was not caused by a lack of intellect, but by a lack of determination and courage to use this intelligence without somebody's guidance. *"Saupere aude!"* he declared – in other words: be courageous enough to use your intelligence. Kant and his fellow-thinkers wanted man to reject the authority of tradition in every sphere of knowledge and to think for himself. The common aim of the leaders of the Enlightenment was therefore to enlighten others, to bring their fellow man the light of their own knowledge. Education of man was therefore extremely important to them.

Let us take note of the intellectual basis of the Enlightenment. In a certain sense, the Enlightenment began as far back as the Renaissance. Like the rationalists, the humanists of the 16th century also predicted the dawn of a new era, a millenium in which reason would disarm prejudice and make man master of his fate. Like the rationalists, the early scholars emphasized the necessity for social reform and thought that this task should be undertaken by enlightened rulers. They also shared a critical approach to medieval Christian philosophy and a general curiosity about the here and now, as opposed to the world hereafter. Even the Protestant Reformation helped to pave the way for the Enlightenment by shattering the unity of western Christianity and weakening the authority of the church.

In 17th century Europe authority inevitably meant the authority of the church, which held sway over every aspect of intellectual investigation. Although Descartes did his best to avoid a conflict, this was inevitable in the long term, and it would be one of the chief features of the struggle of the Enlightenment. It took several forms, as some of the Protestant churches (and many individuals in the Roman Catholic Church) were prepared to go a long way on the path towards rational deism or "reasonable" Christianity, and thus to reach a compromise with the spirit of the Enlightenment. This happened, for example, in Scotland, where many of the leading figures of the Enlightenment were also prominent theologians. In those Roman Catholic countries, however, where the church was intolerant and authoritarian, and where, in addition, its wealth roused the dissatisfaction and jealousy of its opponents, the struggle was to be bitter. This was the case in France.

The rejection of authority would not, however, have led to this clash if it had not gone hand in hand with a positive belief in an alternative method of discovering truth, namely the method of scientific research. The principles of this method can be related to Bacon and Galileo and can be taken even further back, but they were formulated with remarkable clarity by Descartes in his *Discours de la Méthode*, one of the most influential and radical rejections of the accepted approach to science and philosophy. These principles were to be revised in the course of the 17th century, and the revisions were to culminate in the works of Locke and Newton who were to become the acknowledged fathers of Enlightenment thinking.

Newton, the greatest scientific genius of his time, was in many respects not part of the movement he had begun. In the first place, he was a mathematician and physicist. In this sense he clearly belonged to the 17th century rather than to the 18th century. His works – in particular the *Principia Mathematica* of 1687 – meant above all that only patient and sceptical investigation could provide reliable results. The philosophical systems of the 17th century metaphysicians and the tales of saints were therefore under suspicion. Secondly, Newton's thinking meant that the scientific method could, with care, be applied to non-scientific disciplines: theology, history, politics and ethics. Thirdly, Newtonian thinking meant that man could concentrate on practical problems, on the improvement of his lot in this world.

Locke, in contrast to Newton, displays all the hallmarks of the transition from one century to another. Although no mathematician, he was a man with scientific interests (he had had medical training), and an admirer of Newton. He did not, however, concentrate on the physical sciences, but rather on studying man and society.

In his *Two Treatises of Civil Government* (1690) the central ideas – criticism of absolutistic theories, laying claim to a social contract and the right of a people to depose a monarch who violated this contract – were not new in the late 17th century. He was not revolutionary; his purpose was not to begin a period of political instability, but comprised a rationalization of the revolution of 1688. What he did achieve, however, was to create a new test for good government, namely the happiness of its subjects and the prosperity of the state. Coupled with his theories about the natural "sociability" of man and more emphasis than before on the rights of private property, his points of view boiled down to a justification of constitutional government, which had a strong attraction for Europe's middle classes.

In his *Letters Concerning Toleration* (1689-1690) and *The Reasonableness of Christianity* (1695) Locke treated two other themes which were central to the Enlightenment. His insistence that superstition, intolerance and dogma should be rejected in religious thinking characterised most of the Enlightenment thinkers. In the *Letters Concerning Toleration* he said that a person's religious views were no business of the ruler, as long as that person was a good citizen. Written a few years after the revocation of the Edict of Nantes by Louis XIV, this undermined the intellectual foundations of intolerance.

Locke's third influence was more rigorously philosophical. With the *Essay Concerning Human Understanding* (1690), his most influential work, he became the father of modern psychology by making the following statement: man can make his own way with the help of his reason and in the light of his experiences. The ultimate test of good and evil is the happiness of man. Although Locke was no materialist, but a sincere Christian, his arguments had a powerful influence on deism and the whole thinking of the *philosophes*.

Together with Leibnitz and Bayle, Newton and Locke were the most important figures in the general "crisis" in European thought at the turn of the century. The final stages of 17th century thinking would provide the transition and challenge which was to result in the Enlightenment. A late development of 17th century culture was the extension of the critical spirit from theoretical to practical matters. This entailed that the criticism shifted from the foundations of institutions to their functions. Thus the specific policies of church and state became subjects of intellectual discussion in the decades around the turn of the century.

A new level of discourse also emerged in the late 17th century, aimed at popular consumption. The greatest popularizer who set the tone for the Enlightenment and can perhaps be regarded as the first *philosophe* was Bernard de Fontenelle. In writings such as the *History of Oracles* and *Dialogues about the Plurality of the Worlds* (both written in 1686), he moulded the insights of the new science and its philosophical implications concerning the regularity and autonomy of nature into a gracious and entertaining form.

Two cultural tendencies, quite different from the Enlightenment, also made a successful transition from the 17th century to the new era, namely religious orthodoxy and the cult of feeling. They would provide the competitive background against which the young Enlightenment would develop in the first half of the 18th century. Although the Enlightenment did not have an intellectual monopoly in the 18th century – it was also a century of pietism and religious revival in the form of

Jansenism in France and Methodism in England – this movement can none the less be regarded as the central cultural theme of the century.

One must keep in mind that the content of the culture of the Enlightenment was determined not only by the intellectual ingredients provided by the generation of the turn of the century, and which the *philosophes* were to attempt to combine into a relevant philosophy of life, but also by the circumstances in which the *philosophes* lived.

THE EARLY ENLIGHTENMENT

The early Enlightenment became identifiable for the first time in the midst of the changing circumstances of cultural production which followed the disappearance of the Stuarts and Louis XIV and the war-torn atmosphere with which these monarchs are associated. The stimulus and focus of creative activity shifted from the royal courts to the educated classes in society as a whole. In France as well as Britain the development of wealth, leisure time and self-confidence in the middle classes by 1715 coincided with an appreciable decrease in the cultural influence of the royal courts as a result of the death of Louis XIV and the enthronement of the Hanoverians.

Particularly France and Britain saw the social organization of intellectual life at its most advanced, and this is where the early Enlightenment was chiefly concentrated. The characteristic channels of communication were the academies (in the capitals as well as the provinces), salons, magazines, books, pamphlets, unpublished manuscripts and correspondences. All these, at this point, served a writing community within a limited circle of intelligentsia by providing forums for exchanging and debating ideas. The literary forms in which this community of writers communicated were highly divergent and included formal theses, informal essays, poetry, dramas, novels and literary criticism.

What did the society look like from which the Enlightenment originated and which it tried to change, that is to say, the social environment which explains the ideas of the thinkers?

It was a relatively stable and prosperous time. Although there were wars, these were not as destructive as those of the previous century had been. Although there was famine (as in France in 1709) and there was always the possibility of the plague (as in Provence a decade later), not one of these two visitations had the fateful consequences they had had in previous centuries. Civil wars continued, but great religious civil wars were a thing of the past. Agricultural production which had been static in the 17th century and had even decreased, revived again in the 18th century and the population was to increase. Above all, western Europe was experiencing an unparalleled increase in commercial prosperity. All of these developments provided grounds for the optimistic view that social prosperity was more possible than ever before.

Those who contributed the most to the progress and who reaped the greatest benefits were the middle classes. In England, as a consequence of the Great Rebellion and the Revolution of 1688, they acquired a share of the political power. Similar developments took place in Holland. In France, under the authoritarian regime of Louis XIV, they at least replaced the aristocracy as the chief agents of royal authority.

The rise of the middle classes was therefore important in the intellectual revolution subsequent to 1660. To describe the Enlightenment as essentially bourgeois, however, would be dangerous. The 19th century concept of class struggle was alien to 18th century thought. In some countries limited political and social reforms would be undertaken primarily by "enlightened" despots. In France the aristocracy would make an important contribution to the ferment of ideas which were to characterize the regency and the immediately preceding period. But it was in those countries where the middle classes were the strongest and the most numerous – England, Holland, France and parts of Germany – that the Enlightenment first took root. Where France is concerned, this can be disputed, as will be seen later. In central and eastern Europe there was no middle class worth mentioning.

The ideals propounded by the Enlightenment were certainly chiefly those of the middle classes. Technological progress was close to the heart of the movement. Although the *Encyclopédie ou Dictionnaire Raisonnée des Sciences, des Arts et des Métiers* of Diderot and d'Alembert is today chiefly consulted for its "undermining" views on politics and religion, it was intended primarily – as its subtitle clearly indicates – to be a dictionary of the sciences, arts and crafts. The English Royal Society, in its promotion of the study of astronomy and geographic discovery, never lost sight of the interests of sea-trading merchants. The more abstract virtues expounded by the "Enlighteners" also tended to be those of the middle classes. Tolerance, benevolence, cosmopolitanism, hate of war, and the defence of economic and political freedom, all found particular empathy in the rising middle classes.

To associate the ideals of the Enlightenment with those of the middle classes does not mean, however, that those who propounded them had only their own interests in mind. Their repugnance of cruelty, intolerance, and barbaric torture originated in a deeply felt resentment, and by proclaiming these ideals, they frequently exposed themselves to – and sometimes had to endure – persecution.

It also has to be pointed out that the tool created by the 17th century – the method of investigation which became known as the "geometric spirit" – was seized upon by the Enlightenment and used in a radically different manner, namely to solve social problems. The *philosophes* not only intended to understand the world, like the scholars of the 17th century, but also to change it. Traditional religious views were to be investigated in the light of reason and morality, and social institutions would be subjected to similar investigation and, should they fail the test, be rejected as spurious and harmful. The function of reason therefore changed as far as the men of the new Enlightenment were concerned. From the uninvolved explication of natural reality, and of mankind as part of it, reason now became the weapon of an aggressive creed aimed at mastering nature for the benefit of a wiser and better mankind. The function of reason had become more concrete, practical, flexible and dynamic and was directed at utility and the free will. This happened because bourgeois materialism had saved man from supernatural determinism, and he was not prepared to subject himself to the determinism of nature. This is why Hampson says that the century could more correctly be described as one of reasonableness rather than of reason or rationalism: "It valued good-natured sociability rather than the vigorous pursuit of logic to extreme conclusions."[2]

The favourite fields of investigation of the early *philosophes* were natural religion and moral values.

In the field of natural religion the most characteristic innovation of the early Enlightenment was deism, the anti-theological movement which had been announced as early as 1642 by Herbert of Cherbury, and which flourished in England after 1660. The deists did not deny the existence of God. According to them, He was the creator, but was like a great watchmaker who had made the world, had given it laws according to which it had to function and had then withdrawn from it to function on its own. This view of God excluded the possibility of miracles. Secondly, it implied that there were universal moral laws which all reasonable people could discover, that the ethical teachings of all the great philosophers – eastern or western, Christian or not – ultimately converge to the same issues: goodness, benignity, honesty and sincerity, and that these were all that man required to shape his course through life. This led to the third aspect of deism: rationalism. Mankind finds religious truth only by means of his rational abilities. Deism also meant anti-clericalism and a frontal attack on all ecclesiastical dogma, ritual and practice.

It is easy to see why deism was so popular during the Enlightenment, and equally easy to understand why it led to more radical beliefs which excluded God altogether. In France deism had its fullest, widest and most prolonged effect, for here it was not only the central theology in the intellectual community of the *philosophes*, but included a powerful attack on every institutional aspect of Christianity, particularly because of the strength of the Roman Catholic church. The first generation of *philosophes*, which included Montesquieu and Voltaire, were deists. So were some of their younger contemporaries such as Rousseau. In fact, deism remained popular throughout the 18th century. About the middle of the century, however, two other philosophies which were to become of greater importance won a following. One of these was David Hume's scepticism, and the other the atheism of a group of philosophers of whom the central figure was the rich German nobleman-in-exile, Baron d'Holbach.

There are various reasons why the *philosophes* concentrated on religion. Tactically, they could reach greater consensus amongst themselves in their argument against established religion than on any other subject. In spite of their differences in temperament, style, social status and political loyalty, Montesquieu and Voltaire found agreement in their common deism. In the course of the early Enlightenment, furthermore, there were highly important assumptions internal to their thinking behind the focus of the *philosophes* on religion. The early *philosophes* were unanimous in that their shared antipathies – uninvestigated faith, blind obedience, unearned privileges, ignorance, superstition, intolerance, fanaticism – had their common denominator in organized religion. The struggle for natural religion as against organized religion was symbolic of the struggle for greater individual freedom from traditional institutions. Even more important, the *philosophes* concentrated on religion because their own ideas at this stage had less to do with changing things than with changing the manner in which things were viewed. Conditioned by the apparent impenetrability of social realities and their own stubborn conviction that should man turn to things in this world, his reason would do the rest, the main message of the *philosophes* was that mankind had to reject the dogmatic and ecclesiastic restrictions on free thought as the indispensable first step towards any freedom whatever.

FRANCE

In the course of the 18th century the Enlightenment, although originally English, became increasingly French in character. The English ideas spread to France in the first half of the century, amongst others through the Huguenots after they had settled in England, and in the 1740s through the works of Bacon, Shaftesbury and Berkeley.

The shift from the early British environment to the headquarters in France, and specifically in Paris, which dominated the mature Enlightenment, had special consequences for the extension and intellectual character of the movement. In France the spreading of ideas from the French intellectual creators to the educated public went further than elsewhere in Europe, and the practice of writing for a fairly extensive reading public gave the French Enlightenment its special qualities of universality and social consciousness, explaining its pre-eminence in 18th century European culture.

The advantage the French had in the communication of ideas was partly a question of intellectual institutions. The ideas of the *philosophes* became a subject of general discussion for the first time in the salons of Paris, for example those of Mlle. De Lespinasse, a deist, and Mme. Necker, a Christian. These salons and the academies of the French provinces surpassed their British, Dutch and Italian counterparts in the intensity and continuity of the intellectual exchange they provided. At one stage during the reign of Louis XIV there seems to have been only a single cultural centre in France: Versailles. But in the 18th century the aristocracy and the rich returned to Paris and immediately established centres of pleasure and refinement. The French also had a greater predilection for the art of correspondence, and in France, more than elsewhere on the Continent, authorship was a profession. After 1750, when De Lamaignon-Malesherbes became chief censor and proved to be a friend rather than a judge of the *philosophes*, publication replaced the circulation of manuscripts as the chief method of distribution for the French Enlightenment.

But not one of these institutions – a reasonably free press, a free choice of *avant garde* salons and coffee houses, lively urban cultural centres in the provinces, the publication of intellectual correspondence, the freelance writer – were exclusively French. There were more important factors. The French intellectuals occupied a special place in their community which encouraged them to produce and publish ideas with the widest possible impact – a place which involved them in the urgent interests of their society.

The leaders of the Enlightenment in France, as elsewhere, were orientated towards the middle classes. Most of them were from the upper middle class and from the mobile sector of the aristocracy, that is the upwardly-moving, property-owning classes (e.g. Montesquieu, Condillac, Mably, d'Alembert and d'Holbach). The French middle classes had a distinctive position which made their relationships with the higher and lower classes more enduring and at the same time more problematical than elsewhere in Europe. They were linked to the court because of the widespread bureaucracy and the flourishing practice of selling offices. They were linked to the aristocracy because the 16th century and the 17th century bourgeois lawyers were the fathers of the 18th century nobility of the cloth. By the recruitment of wholesale merchants as members of the free professions from the ranks of the abler master craftsmen, retailers and small farmers the middle classes were also increasingly – as a result of France's prosperity in the 18th century – tied to the working masses. As part of this encompassing middle class, the French *philosophes* were encouraged to act as representatives of a large part of society. The fact that the middle classes had no traditional status or particular function in that society established them in the generalized nature of their outlook. By the middle of the century the desires of the middle classes for social mobility were frustrated by the reaction of the aristocrats. In this situation the majority were left in a state of embittered but impotent demoralization. The intellectuals accepted their position of leadership in the middle classes by producing a bourgeois type of criticism within the established order. But they also proved their loyalty to this order! The concentration of *philosophes* in the property-owning classes is a definite indication of their standpoint in favour of reform rather than revolution, in favour of an ordered society which would accord their talents due recognition.

We referred above to the reaction of the aristocrats and must add that France's role in the development of Enlightenment thinking was decisive precisely because by the middle of the century it possessed an entrenched aristocracy on the one hand, and a vital middle class on the other. The role of the aristocracy in France should therefore not be minimized. In the first half of the century there were, it is true, few signs of any popular or middle class opposition to equal the particularly outspoken aristocratic opposition. The middle-class lawyers who had left *mémoires* gave their support to the *parlements*, but tended to concern themselves more with religious than with political matters. The aristocracy had developed an aversion to the restrictions to which they were already subjected in the time of Louis XIV and were waiting for an opportunity to regain their lost feudal privileges as soon as possible. It was only when the traditional enmity between the *noblesse d'épée* and the *noblesse de robe* had largely disappeared and the *parlements* provided a new focal point for dissatisfaction, that the aristocrats formed an organized opposition. The so-called *thèse nobilaire* – the belief that life, freedom and the pursuit of happiness could best be ensured by the existence of strong *parlements* and a powerful aristocracy as a bulwark against royal despotism – grew in force and was to find its greatest exponent in Montesquieu. The opposing belief was the *thèse royale*, which held that the aristocracy was essentially concerned with the preservation of its own privileges, and that necessary social change could be brought about only by a centralizing, reforming royal government. This belief also had its followers, amongst them important ministers such as Machault and Turgot. It was not before the Austrian War of Succession had caused the financial problems to become acute, however, that the opposition between these two contentions clearly manifested itself in terms of actual politics.

Just as the revolution of 1789 could not have taken place without the aristocratic revolution which preceded it, the political and social doctrines of the French Enlightenment were as much the product of aristocratic dissatisfaction as of the aspirations of the rising middle classes. It would be naive to accept that the dissident aristocracy held the tenets they did merely in their own interests. Their attempts to regain their privileges were not divorced from a general concern about the welfare of the state, and, by defending their own liberty, they supported the cause of freedom in general.

It can be averred that no 18th century French thinker produced a philosophic system which was original and sufficiently profound to be compared to those of Descartes, Spinoza and Kant. One work of the early Enlightenment was, however, a milestone of 18th century thought. This was Voltaire's *Lettres Philosophiques*, published in England in 1733 and in France in 1734.

As background to this it can be mentioned that in 1726 Voltaire (François Arouet) had a quarrel with De Rohan-Chabot, member of a prominent aristocratic family. After he had been given a hiding by the nobleman's servants, Voltaire objected and threatened revenge. This led to his being sent to the Bastille (for the second time) by the government, and eventually he was exiled. He went to England and returned in 1729 with his mind full of English religious, philosophical and scientific ideas and a feeling of mortification – against Rohan, against the government for his imprisonment and exile, and against the whole structure of a society which could allow such things to happen. All this led to the *Lettres Philosophiques*. In England he had enjoyed the company of Pope, Swift and Gay, and had discovered the works of Bacon, Locke and Newton. There he had been drenched in English empiricism and free thinking, and in France he devoted himself to enlightening the French and ultimately the whole of mankind. To this end he wielded his pen and produced dramas, poems, pamphlets, histories, novels, dissertations and translations, altogether more than seventy volumes.

He became the best-known and most respected author of his time and was the acknowledged leader of the *philosophes*. More than any other *philosophe* he synthesized their views about the use of reason to discover the just and ideal order of society, as prescribed by nature, in an ideology.

Although Voltaire was of middle-class birth he was a royalist. He was convinced that the kind of reforms France required would never occur by means of the *parlements*, whose aristocratic members confused their own interests with those of the state. These reforms – such as free speech, a free press and civic freedom – could only be instituted by the king. Properly advised by informed ministers, the king could rise above the level of personal interests to order what was good for the state. He was a prominent supporter of the efforts of Machault and later of Turgot, also a *philosophe*, to institute sorely needed financial reforms, and when the latter had to resign in 1776, the "Patriarch of Ferney" was dealt a blow from which he never recovered (at least in the political sense) until his death in 1778.

One could argue, however, that Voltaire did not so much champion "enlightened despotism" (that is, an autocratic but benevolent monarchy), but was a proponent of political pragmatism. He argued that the traditions, culture and historic circumstances of every country differed and had to be taken into account. Thus he approved of Britain's strong House of Commons, the Netherlands' commercial aristocracy, the liberal republicanism of Geneva, and Frederick the Great's autocracy in a poor and poorly educated Prussia.

What was of primary concern to Voltaire was not who governed, but how they governed. In various articles he defined the ideals for which a government should strive: the abolition of the remnants of feudalism, limitation of the authority of the church (his famous slogan was *Ecrasez l'infâme* – smash the awful thing), provision of education to all who could benefit from it (not the lower classes), the abolition of legalized maltreatment and barbaric punishment, the extension of the rights of property-ownership, and freedom before the law. This list could be expanded, for in his writings one finds a whole programme of bourgeois-liberal reforms.

He did not indicate in his *Lettres Philosophiques* how the desired reforms were to be brought about in his own country, but he illustrated quite clearly what he wanted done. There is probably no briefer formulation of the essential grievances of the French middle classes up to the Revolution itself. According to Lanson, this was the first "bomb" thrown at the old *régime,* particularly because Voltaire made the point that the purpose of the English civil wars had been freedom.[3] The "bomb" went off, however, in a period of peace and relative calm and therefore caused less immediate destruction than might otherwise have been the case.

Voltaire was, however, like all the other *philosophes*, unsure of how the masses should be treated. He referred to them as "a cruel and blind monster" and maintained that he had never professed to enlighten shoemakers and servants. To a friend he wrote that he doubted whether the masses would ever have the time or the ability for education and that he regarded it as essential that there should be unenlightened poor. They only needed guidance. Yet his attitude did not prevent him from anger at the injustice of hanging a servant girl for the theft of handkerchiefs. He was, in truth, a champion for the victims of intolerance and injustice and thus for the cause of humaneness.

Voltaire's historic importance lies in his undermining of the foundations of the *ancien régime*, his popularization of philosophical scepticism and his proclamation of a new philosophy of humanism. His works also contradict the view that most of the *philosophes* were impractical dreamers who were infatuated with a dogmatic vision of a perfect society. Recent research emphasizes his political realism and his distrust of such dogmatic abstractions as natural law and natural rights.

As a result of the specifically bourgeois standpoint in the *Lettres Philosophiques* one is inclined to agree that this work was the first bomb aimed at the old *régime*. Yet it was in some respects less outspoken than an equally successful work which had appeared more than a decade earlier. This was the *Lettres Persanes* (Persian Letters) by Charles Louis de Secondat, Baron de Montesquieu, of 1721. It contains, in the guise of a dialogue between two naive Persians, a satiric description of France in the last years of Louis XIV and during the regency, and pokes fun at contemporary religious views and political institutions.

In terms of practical politics, however, this work did not offer a programme. This would be offered only in Montesquieu's *De l'Esprit des Lois* (The spirit of the laws) which appeared more than a quarter of a century later, in 1748. The latter was a work of remarkable importance in which Montesquieu endeavoured to describe the laws governing society. He also attempted to some extent to describe what society should be like, and in particular he sketched certain guidelines along which a society such as his own should develop. It was therefore a work of social science as well as of liberal propaganda.

Montesquieu was not, however, a democrat. Although he admired the republican ideal, he did so from a safe distance. He regarded republican democracy as impossible in most European states. Those democracies of which he approved most were the classic republics which divided their citizens into "classes" and gave greater political power to those with the greatest wealth and status. His ideal was therefore far removed from one with equal rights for all. Compromise, moderateness and tolerance were closer to his heart and although he felt the necessity for reform, he was also, as aristocrat and *parlementaire*, deeply attached to the political traditions of his country. Consequently, his real sympathies lay with the monarchy rather than with democracy. To him, monarchy and despotism were, however, worlds apart. Despotism is the arbitrary rule of a single individual who exercises absolute power over the lives and property of his subjects. Monarchy is also the rule of an individual, but of one who rules through intermediate powers and according to fundamental law. The basic psychological "principle" behind despotism is fear; monarchy, on the other hand, is permeated with the spirit of *gloire* (glory). Montesquieu also wanted to see the reactivation of the nobility as the politically responsible class in France, but it was to be an aristocracy of merit, independent of the crown.

His "admiration" for the constitutional monarchy of England can also be seen in the light of the above (although his political ideas are open to more than one interpretation). In his attempt to explain the English constitution, he did, however, also have a great deal of criticism for English political practice. Traditionally the essence of his thinking was seen as the doctrine of the separation of powers: freedom can best be assured by a constitutional structure in which the legislative, executive and judiciary powers do not dominate one another. Yet he never himself used the phrase "separation of powers" and, although he certainly emphasized his contention that they were to possess a degree of independence, he also – with apparent approval – pointed out examples in English practice where this was not the case, where the king had a legislative as well as an executive role, and Parliament could act as a judicial body. What he was most probably propagating was not so much a constitutional separation of powers (although this was to an extent preferable) as the general distribution of political power throughout the various classes of society. In England all the social strata (excepting the very lowest, and Montesquieu never dreamed that they should be enfranchised) had a role to play.

As a conservative monarchist, Montesquieu believed in the role of the aristocracy, and he emphasized the social necessity for religious institutions. He even defended the Spanish church. But, like Voltaire, he hated despotism, cruelty and intolerance, condemned religious persecution (in particular that of the Inquisition), and slavery.

Although Montesquieu and Voltaire were great admirers of British institutions, they did not advocate the implementation of the British system in France. They merely wanted an efficient, fair government. This was within the grasp of the monarch if he reformed every aspect of life within the *régime* – from religion to the legal system, and from education to politics.

Montesquieu's theories, particularly that of the rule of law as a prerequisite for good government, were to pave the way for modern democratic thought. In the later 18th century, political science would progress beyond the point at which Montesquieu had left it, but it would take place largely on the pattern he had drawn. Political thinking in a wider sense would, however, be reshaped, as people such as Rousseau would lay the foundations of a modern democratic philosophy by asking fundamental questions about the rights of all people, something which Montesquieu had not mentioned.

THE MATURE ENLIGHTENMENT

It is roughly correct to say that the first half of the 18th century was intellectually predominantly destructive, and the second half constructive. At the outset, as evidenced in the work of Bayle, the young Montesquieu and the English deists, the emphasis lay on negation: the myths which clouded man's view of society, religion and history had to be exposed. Subsequently, the Enlightenment endeavoured to contribute more positively to what Lessing called "the education of the human race".

After 1750 the *philosophes* became, in spite of the many issues which still divided them, what Peter Gay called "the Party of Humanity". They began to participate in joint ventures of which the greatest was the *Encyclopédie*, but which also included the stream of books flowing from the "propaganda factory" controlled by d'Holbach. They began forming organized pressure groups in the academies and elsewhere and supported one another's efforts to gain admittance to societies or achieve promotion. Voltaire, for example, made serious but unsuccessful efforts to have Diderot elevated to the *Académie française*. The *philosophes* joined ranks against people like Fréron, the editor of *L'année Littéraire*, and Pallisot, the author of the satiric drama *Les Philosophes*, who attacked and ridiculed them. They also occasionally defended one another in times of persecution. Their noblest achievement was to combine, usually under the leadership of Voltaire, in sustained campaigns for the defence of victims of injustice and intolerance such as Jean Calas.

Their acceptance of a more active role was apparently the natural consequence of their growing strength and increasing self-confidence. There were also, however, other reasons. They were not only drawn closer to one another through their common ideals, but also driven closer to one another by the increasing hostility of the political and religious authorities. From about 1750 the Sorbonne and the government, which had previously been far more concerned about getting rid of Jansenism than about the dangers of "philosophy", began regarding the latter with more suspicion and in this they had the support of the *parlements*. The arrest of Diderot in 1749 was an indication of the direction in which things were moving. In the same year Montesquieu as well as Buffon got into trouble with the Sorbonne. Voltaire, after the death of Mme. Du Châtelet, felt that the time had come to accept the invitation of Frederick the Great and to escape to the safety of Berlin. In the same year d'Argenson spoke of the French Inquisition, although he was certainly exaggerating. The religious devotees, in particular the Jesuits, gained increasing power at the royal court, and although their power was subsequently to be curbed by the influence of Mme. De Pompadour and her allies, they remained a dangerous threat to the *philosophes*.

The Austrian War of Succession, which ended in 1748, left the government with a financial crisis. Machault, the minister of finance, tried to solve it by instituting the *vingtième,* an income tax on all classes. This was immediately opposed by the nobility, the *parlements* and the clergy, under leadership of the latter. Confronted with this opposition, undermined by enemies in the government, and without any positive support from the king, Machault perforce had to withdraw his proposals and he resigned. The same pattern would be repeated more than once before 1789.

Machault had his champions amongst the *philosophes*, particularly Voltaire. Yet the majority of them were not unduly concerned, as they were not "politicians". With the publication of Montesquieu's *De l'Esprit des Lois* in 1748, however, their active interest in politics was aroused, marking the beginning of the mature Enlightenment. From then onwards, freedom would replace order as the dominating virtue on which their thinking was focused – this was to be a fundamental break with the early Enlightenment, and a new point of departure in western thinking. In 1748 La Mettrie's *L'Homme machine* (Man a machine) also appeared. Diderot's *Lettre sur l'homme aveugle* (Letter about the blind man) followed in 1749. In 1750 there was Rousseau's first *Discours* (the second appeared in 1755), and also that of Turgot (which laid the basis for the theory of progress). In 1751 the first volume of the *Encyclopédie* was published, and in 1755 Morelly's *Code of Nature*, the first modern conception of a communist society.

Brumfitt writes: "The list could be extended but it is already long enough to show that, by 1755, the main positions of the French Enlightenment were clearly established. It is true that Helvétius, d'Holbach and Condorcet were still to come; that Voltaire and Rousseau had still to produce the works by which they are best remembered; that the economic theories of the physiocrats ... had yet to be elaborated ... Yet by 1755, the great period of discovery was over. The tasks which remained were those of co-ordinating the newly found truths into more systematic bodies of doctrine, of disseminating them amongst all educated men, and of setting them to work in order to achieve the practical amelioration of society."[4]

The *Encyclopédie* was the greatest literary effort of the *philosophes* and the most enterprising intellectual venture of the century. It provided them with a public forum and was largely instrumental in uniting them in a movement. During the thirty years of its production virtually every leading thinker in France was involved in it at one time or another. The editor, Denis Diderot, had the co-operation of nearly two hundred experts and writers, including Montesquieu, Voltaire, Rousseau, Helvétius, d'Holbach and d'Alembert. The first volume was published in 1751 and the twenty eighth and final one in 1772 – seventeen volumes of text and eleven of illustrations.

The *Encyclopédie* had a triple purpose: to serve as a reference work with information about the crafts and sciences, to serve as a means of education and instruction in every sphere of knowledge and practical activity, and to be a clearing house for new ideas about religion, politics and society. The work not only intended to express public opinion, but also to shape it – "to change the general form of thought", as Diderot put it.

The most important themes were the autonomy of man, the secularization of knowledge and thought, faith in reason and experience, science and progress; briefly: the credo of the Enlightenment.

As far as its influence is concerned, the following must be said: although 4 000 copies found wide distribution in France, it was, with its original subscription price of 280 *livres* (about R14), clearly a work only the wealthy could afford and its circulation was therefore limited, even amongst the well-off.

It was meant as a vehicle of reform, but Diderot's comments and actions indicate that this was not the case. From the beginning he emphasized the scientific and technological importance of the work. Although it is true that daring "philosophical" ideas were sometimes "hidden" in lesser articles, and that there was a note of reform in some of the major articles (the *Collège* and *Genève* by d'Alembert, for instance), the majority of articles about politics and religion were very moderate. There was no direct attack on religion or politics, although articles were clearly formulated from the new point of view. (Fanaticism and superstition were severely attacked.) As far as politics are concerned, Montesquieu's ideas were largely repeated, or the beneficial properties of the philosopher-king stressed. Even a supporter such as Voltaire felt that the *Encyclopédie* was rather watered down.

Jean Jacques Rousseau merits more than passing attention. Rousseau has acquired the reputation of a utopian dreamer who wanted to get rid of organized society, and advocated a "return to nature" and the state of the "noble savage". In fact, Rousseau never used either phrase. He did not argue that primitive man was superior to the civilized variety – the former, to him, was rather a whole man as opposed to modern man, who is alienated from himself by the immorality of his culture. He repeatedly declared – at his most eloquent in *Le Contrat Social* (The Social Contract) – that once man has entered society, he can never leave it. What he had in mind was therefore a moral rather than an anthropological situation, a return to a society in which the simple virtues, those of family life and altruism, would be the highest values.

As far as Rousseau's emphasis on the emotional life is concerned, it must be remembered that it was important to him because it exercised a restraining influence on reason. He was not championing emotion against reason and his view of the emotional life was also not new in the Enlightenment. Voltaire, Diderot and Hume all believed that the emotions were basic to the functioning of reason, but Rousseau's emphasis on emotions had a new and socially radical implication:

love for virtue which could restore the unity of mankind, a culture of citizenship.

The well-known "general will" of *The Social Contract* is not merely the will of the majority or the sum of all the individual wills, but that which takes into account only the general interest. It is general because the goal is general: the general welfare. It finds expression only in a system of laws to which all people voluntarily subject themselves. The general welfare was defined by Rousseau as "freedom and equality". He advocated the total sovereignty of the state, but the state was to take its lead from the general will. If not so led, the state would lose its legality. The good society, for Rousseau, was a democratic republic in which everyone would be equal. Freedom, the primary political right, rested on equality, the primary social right.

Although Rousseau came closest to liberal democratic principles by combining absolute equality, legislative sovereignty and positive morality in the idea of consent, he was not a revolutionary. His *Discours sur l'Économie Politique* (Discourse on Political Economy) (1755) and *The Social Contract* were proposals for a political dispensation which would enable an individual to develop his personality in accordance with the principle of social equality. He believed that man, without turning to revolution, could realize his potential of self-perfection.

He did not, in fact, differ that much from other *philosophes*, but took their thinking to its logical conclusion by insisting that not only the *bourgeoisie,* but all people, had to be free, and that a benevolent society had to be benevolent to everybody. As Rousseau was the son of a watchmaker and someone who led the life of a poor wanderer, one can understand his point of view.

It is true that he influenced other republicans such as Diderot and d'Alembert, but up to the French Revolution the idea of democracy remained a concept rather than a force, a political form without effective political content. *The Social Contract* had no discernible influence until the revolution actually began. (Brissot, Danton and Robespierre were amongst Rousseau's devoted disciples.) Krieger[5] maintains that this was the least influential of his works in the 18th century. Harris[6] alleges that Rousseau's influence before 1789 was moral and not political, and according to Anchor[7] Rousseau exercised little influence before the last quarter of the century when the lower orders began stirring.

Account must also be given of the physiocrats. They were a school of intellectuals fathered by François Quesnay who published his *Tableau Économique* (Economic Model) about *laissez-faire* (free trade) in 1758. He and his followers called themselves *économistes*, but their doctrine was later dubbed "physiocracy", meaning the rule of nature. The physiocrats developed into the dominating school of political economy in Europe and laid the groundwork for the policy of economic freedom. They were opposed to the royal policy of mercantilism and any interference in trade from the government.

The physiocrats (like the proponents of socialism, Morelly and Mably) saw society as being governed by its own laws. The methods and laws of the natural sciences were applied directly to society by these economic doctrinaires. They did not derive from an industrial society and did not direct themselves at one, but were in favour of agriculture, the most conservative economic activity. They also did not speak for a particular class, as the traditional groups whom they favoured were not prepared to involve themselves in the competitive economic process which they had in mind. The policy they proposed, according to which the prices of goods, property and labour were to be determined "naturally", that is without interference, was obviously in the best interests of the middle classes. It was not, however, the conscious aim of the physiocrats to serve these interests. In fact, they regarded the bourgeoisie as economically sterile, although useful in other respects, and recommended that capitalism should be applied to agriculture rather than to trade and industry. Because of their economic worthlessness, so they argued, the bourgeoisie should be allowed to go their own way, free of economic limitations. The aristocracy, however, was to be reactivated as an economically useful and politically responsible property-owning class.

The agrarian capitalism which the physiocrats propounded received so little attention that the school was deteriorating by the 1770s. Voltaire ridiculed their doctrine, which contained a fair amount of mysticism parading as science. Their doctrine of *laissez-faire* was, however, taken up by others.

What is of importance here is that with the exception of one or two – Mirabeau (not the one of the revolution) and Morellet – they were unanimously in favour of enlightened despotism and were, in fact, its most influential supporters. According to them, despotic power was necessary to restore the natural order. The exercise of authority should not be arbitrary, but legal. The law which should lead the ruler was that of logic.

Enlightened despotism as a form of government was, in fact, up to Rousseau, supported by most of the "Enlighteners". This idea originated with Thomas Hobbes and his utilitarian and rationalistic justification of despotism, namely that absolutism only had to promote the welfare of the people.

This preference for enlightened despotism must, however, be understood correctly. From the correspondence of a Voltaire or a Diderot with such "enlightened" despots as Frederick II, Joseph II or Catherine II it is clear that they appealed to the autocrats to create the circumstances for a *régime* in which there would be democracy, *laissez-faire* and socialism. It was therefore a liberal ideal which they upheld in the midst of political practice. In France the gap between the two was much larger than in Britain. In Germany, Austria and Russia the doctrines of a fair constitution and a free society were unattainable ideals. As the power in most countries was in the hands of monarchs, the *philosophes* endeavoured to influence them to institute reforms from above.

For the *philosophes* there were two methods of renewing a society. One was slow, relying on the gradual spread of enlightenment until it had reached all (or rather, most) classes and individuals. The second (which found the greatest following) promised quicker results, and could be instituted if a wise ruler in one fell swoop were to create the required laws of social harmony. Such a ruler could reorganize the life of a nation and revitalize it by a few well-calculated edicts and thus earn the thanks of his people, thereby clothing the title of despot in glory. As his laws on their own merit would gain the acceptance of all right-thinking people, they would hardly need the support of his absolute authority. The standpoint of many thinkers was that the art of government could, for the first time in history, be elevated to an exact science and that human affairs could be regulated with perfect order and efficiency. The monarchy of the 18th century was offered a unique and enviable opportunity: the privilege of organizing society according to the new discoveries.

Between 1770 and 1789 three kinds of intellectual movements brought the Enlightenment to an end. First, there was the so-called "radicalization" of the Enlightenment, which was really the one-sided development of its rational principles in the inflexible systems of atheism, determinism and inescapable progress, represented by such figures as d'Holbach and Concordet. Second, there was the one-sided development of its individualizing, liberalizing and dynamic principles in the utilitarian, sentimental, idealistic, naturalistic and evolutionary doctrines, represented by such figures as Bentham, Rousseau and Kant. Thirdly, there was the authentic resistance against the Enlightenment which was a rejection of the *philosophes* and all their works, on behalf of individual, anarchic and demonic forces outside the Enlightenment syndrome. Represented by the German school of *Sturm und Drang*, anarchists such as Burke and mystics such as Blake, this revolt was a pre-Romantic movement with an aesthetic character, but it absorbed ideas from the sentimental, classic and dynamic tributaries of the Enlightenment.

D'Holbach, under various pseudonyms, published a series of works about natural and moral philosophy from 1770 to 1776, which extended the characteristic views of the Enlightenment about reason, nature, utility and humanism to a simple atheism, materialism and fatalism. He was increasingly supported by Diderot – who was also an atheist – and Joseph Priestley. Materialism, determinism and even atheism as such were nothing new – see, for example, La Mettrie and Helvétius (who was the first true utilitarian). Yet these views showed a marked difference from the reasonable aura of the Enlightenment. Nonetheless, these *philosophes* were not radicals either. Although d'Holbach liked to appeal to mankind to throw off the combined yoke of priests and kings, he made it clear that he was not insisting on the people to stage a revolt. The revolution he wanted was basically technocratic rather than democratic. Similar views were expressed by utopian socialists such as Morelly and Mably. D'Holbach shared the general tendency of 18th century Europeans, relying on established rulers to take the initiative in social and political reform, although he subordinated politics to his notions about natural law. Diderot and Priestley also shared the 18th century suspicion of the masses and tended to trust only the property-owning middle classes with political rights. The subordination of all individuals to natural law, however, endowed their moderate political proposals with a radical egalitarian undertone which announced the beginning of the post-Enlightenment.

The "radicals", Concordet and Raynal, were tuned to the heated social and political scene of the 1770s and 1780s, and in their writings sympathized with the agitators – the Americans, the British parliamentary reformists and the French anti-aristocratic pressure group around Turgot. This sympathy took the form of a sharper tone, a more encompassing critique, a more categorical condemnation of the established church and state than ever before, as the intellectuals became impatient with the compromising of rational principles. The notorious "radicalism" of Raynal and his supporters, such as the older Voltaire, therefore confirmed the hardening of anti-clericalism in a rationalistic dogma. Yet even they were all in favour of limiting political rights to property-owners.

In their deepest nature the *philosophes* were not radicals. Even as more and more of them began to devote their attention to the form which essential and far-reaching social change would have to take (that is to say after the Seven Years War had brought with it new military and economic disasters, and after the gap between the aristocratic *parlements* and the reforming ministers of the crown had increased), the "philosophic" group never became a party in the modern sense of the word. The policies they advocated were as dissimilar as they were numerous. A majority of reformers, in fact, held relatively authoritarian points of view. Change was essential, but it had to come from above, not from the fickle population. There was, however, deep division about how much change would be required and what was meant with "from above". The general idea (popular early in the 19th century), that they were a group of democratic revolutionaries, can be summarily dismissed. Democracy was propagated by a small minority of which Rousseau was the most important figure. Revolution, although increasingly regarded as a possibility, was not propagated as a practical policy. In general, the political rationalists were prepared to welcome revolutions when they occurred (Raynal was not even prepared to accept this), but they did not create the kind of doctrine which was to cause revolutions. Not one formulated a programme in which popular political action was demanded, although all of them laid new emphasis on the right of people to political representation as an inviolable universal right which kings – one day – would have to grant. The rapid tempo of events after 1776 – which they had not caused – in general increasingly alienated the "radical" rationalists further and further from the real world which they could not master. Only the future leader of the Girondist party during the French Revolution, Jacques Pierre Brissot de Warville, was a true revolutionary before the revolution.

The other chief inheritance of the Enlightenment in the latter third of the 18th century, namely the intense focus on individual freedom, was a trend between radical rationalism and the pre-Romantic aversion to the Enlightenment, and combined the characteristics of both. We have already referred to Rousseau, who represented this direction. Another was Kant, who serves as a good example of the German Enlightenment. German thinkers, for lack of the cultural and intellectual ferment of Paris and London, tended towards seeing a major contrast between the world of thought and that of social reality, and between the ideal past (Greek or medieval) and the real present. They tended to let inner freedom take the place of political freedom. Romanticism, as a form of escape from the present, would find its home in Germany. Although Kant fully subscribed to the ideals of the French Enlightenment, he saw them as more real than the empirical world.

To the pre-Romantics such as Herder, Goethe and Schiller, passion and emotion were highly important in their idea of individuality. Their new humanistic view of nature, which was also partly inspired by Rousseau, found its highest expression in Goethe. His first novel, *Die Leiden des jungen Werthers* (The Suffering of young Werther), written in 1774, meant the transfer of artistic and intellectual supremacy from France to Germany. The theme was the conflict of the individual in himself and with society as a whole. Goethe believed in individual freedom – his own – thus personal rather than social freedom. In the period before the revolution, the pre-Romantics felt themselves alienated from the *philosophes*.

An aspect which deserves attention is the 18th century theory of progress. The *philosophes* attempted to create their "heavenly city" in the second half of the 18th century. The idea of progress can be traced back to the Renaissance, and in the 18th century a consciousness of the necessity of progress was the basis to a great deal of Enlightenment thought.

Rousseau was enthusiastic about this, and his *Le Contrat Social* would be regarded by later generations as a blueprint for the future progress of society. Yet he presented his ideas in an intellectual framework which was totally hostile towards the idea of progress. The two *Discours* also proved that, to him, progress meant decay and degeneration. None of the so-called political radicals – Rousseau, Helvétius and d'Holbach – in fact adhered to any theory of progress. Educated people did not have any doubt that they were living in what they described as a *siècle de lumière*, an *Aufklärung,* or an enlightened period. When the French writers looked at the future, however, they were pessimistic. Cyclical theories of history were the norm (such as those of Condorcet, the last *philosophe*), and as the current period was regarded as a kind of zenith, many were inclined to think that the future would be downhill. Not before the last quarter of the century was there much confidence in progress in any sphere. The advocates of material determinism such as d'Holbach and, at times, Diderot, apparently saw life as a continuing condition of instability rather than as an evolution in a particular direction. The static, short-term view of society taken by the majority of thinkers made it difficult for them to envisage future changes, except as an educational process through which a large part of the population could be elevated to the level of the fortunate minority. In this respect the Enlightenment gives no indication of any consciousness of the social and economic forces struggling to break through traditional limitations to begin a period of revolutionary transformation. The utopia the *philosophes* had in mind had to be a replica of 18th-century society in which, however, man would be freed from all vexatious interference and would attain a more honourable status. It is this acceptance, that the future at best would be an improved version of current times, which at its clearest distinguishes the 18th century from modern times, despite the apparent similarity in many respects. The French Revolution was to prove the virtually universal conviction that the social order was static. There was increasing talk of the possibility of a revolution in France, but what the prophets seemed to have had in mind was a political revolution, and the example of 1688 in England fostered the suggestion that it need not have far-reaching social consequences. Property-owners were always uncomfortably aware of the danger of a hungry population which was not controlled by an effective police force. But apparently nobody believed that there was, or could be, any connection between such traditional outbursts of violence and the writings of the *philosophes*, which were certainly not read by the revolutionaries.

The writers themselves accepted the existence of an ineducable majority as self-evident. Voltaire, in particular, liked to enlarge on this, as has been discussed. The more radical d'Holbach also emphasized that he wrote only for the élite. In the *Système de la Nature* he argued that atheism, like philosophy and every other profound and abstract science, was totally unsuited to the common man.

Brumfitt says: "In varying degrees, most of the *philosophes* had subscribed to the so-called double doctrine. 'Not in front of the servants' had been their motto. Truth was for the élite, the geniuses, the *philosophes*; so too was power. The majority might be allowed to cling to their superstitions, or they might be provided with new ones; but in any case they were to be conditioned, led and ruled (however benevolently) by the enlightened minority."[8] This attitude of the *philosophes* did not necessarily imply aversion of or hostility towards the lowest classes, but they hoped that the slow process of education would gradually elevate the more intelligent amongst the common people to participate in a political community, the stability of which they accepted as an accomplished fact.

This has brought us to the influence of the *philosophes*, especially on the coming of the Revolution.

INFLUENCE OF THE *PHILOSOPHES*

We have indicated that the *philosophes* were not as radical as is sometimes alleged. It could also be advanced that the "radicalism" of the *philosophes* cannot be ascribed to a growing protest of the middle classes against a "feudal" social order. Many of the writers were themselves members of the privileged orders of the church and nobility. They did have an enthusiastic public amongst the professional classes, but less readers amongst the merchants and traders. They themselves, in fact, claimed that they could not be accused of responsibility for social unrest, as they wrote for a very limited audience. Hampson writes: "Whatever the actual consequences of their work, and whatever, after the death of almost all of them, they may have contributed to influence a revolutionary movement that had started for other reasons, the overthrow of the traditional social hierarchy was no part of their plan. On the contrary, the conviction of their own inability to do more than to spread enlightenment, tolerance and humanity amongst the educated seemed to them to guarantee that their beneficial teaching could do no harm to anyone."[9] These circumstances must be taken into account when pointing out the criticism of the old *régime* by the *philosophes* – in the form of values which would subsequently be incorporated in the revolutionary slogan: liberty, equality and fraternity.

As far as the dissemination of their ideas is concerned, certain factors must be kept in mind. First, there is the limited influence of their writings. According to available evidence, literacy was fairly widespread by the end of the century, even in rural areas. In France facilities for a good secondary education were surprisingly plentiful. A recent investigation into literacy in Toulouse, as indicated by the number of legibly written signatures on marriage contracts in 1749 and 1785, shows that between 90 per cent and 100 per cent of the men of the lower middle class, and from 67 per cent to 75 per cent of their wives, could read and write. For the upper working class the figures were 51-54 per cent for men and 18-19 per cent for women. On the lowest level it was 19-26 per cent for men and 0-4 per cent for women. But literacy was no proof of "enlightenment". In a recent survey the existence of a flourishing trade in cheap popular literature, which remained quite inaccessible to the changed attitudes of the 18th century, was demonstrated.[10] The question also remains: how many people, in rural areas in particular, did any reading even if they were able to do so? Voltaire wrote in 1770: "Go to a small town in the provinces and you will seldom find one or two books there ... judges, priests, the bishop ... no one has books, no one has a cultivated spirit; they are no more developed than in the 12th century." This situation has to be taken into account when it is pointed out how many books appeared in the second half of the 18th century. There were twenty two editions of Montesquieu's *De l'Esprit de Lois*, which meant sales of about 35 000 copies. There were eight editions of Voltaire's *Candide* in 1759 alone, and 4 000 subscribers to the *Encyclopédie*. Other works of equal importance to the modern reader were, however, known to relatively few people, for example all the writings of La Mettrie. Diderot was famous as editor of the *Encyclopédie* and well known as dramatist, but his most adventurous works were not published before his death in 1784. Hampson advances: "Any attempt to assess the diffusion of the ideas of the Enlightenment must therefore start by recognizing that even the best-informed readers, who had invested heavily in expensive banned books, had a somewhat limited acquaintance with what had been published, and *a fortiori* with works circulating in manuscript within a limited circle. On the whole, despite exceptions such as Helvétius's *De l'Esprit*, which achieved considerable notoriety, it was the most radical works which took longest to reach an extensive public."[11]

Even if one limits one's survey to books which enjoyed a wide circulation, the problem of the extent to which the ideas of the writers were, in fact, disseminated throughout Europe is not a simple one. The social dissemination of the ideas of the Enlightenment was determined in the first place by the high cost of books, which to a large degree limited potential readership, even if one rejects as pessimistic Grimm's calculation in 1757 that in Paris itself only a few hundred people concerned themselves with literature, the arts and philosophy. Important works such as Rousseau's *Émile* and d'Holbach's *Le Système de la Nature* cost about 15 to 18 *livres* (roughly R1,50) if they could be bought on the open market. Once such books had been banned, their price could rise fourfold or fivefold.

As far as newspapers and magazines were concerned, it must be noted that France lagged behind England and Holland. (The first Dutch monthly magazine was established in 1686 and the earliest English newspaper in 1702. By 1750 there were ninety newspapers and magazines in England, and by 1780, 158.) Between 1740 and 1770 there was an increase in newspapers and magazines in France, but some of them were short-lived. In 1770 there were nineteen of them, such as the *Journal Encyclopédique, Journal Économique* and *Journal de Physique*. The *Mercure*, in particular, propagated the ideas of the *philosophes*. In 1748 it was available in twenty six towns, and by 1774 in fifty five. The magazines were also, however, expensive, and did not reach more than a few thousand people. The provincial press only began after 1770. France got its first daily newspaper, the *Journal de Paris*, only in 1777, but two years later there were thirty five newspapers and magazines, and in 1789, 169.

Other channels of communication were the academies, universities, literary societies, salons and Freemasons' lodges. In France, as in England, the universities were generally at a low ebb. It cannot be said that a single one of France's twenty two universities – least of all the Sorbonne in Paris – was a centre of Enlightenment. The other methods of dissemination were certainly lively. The most fruitful of these were perhaps the Parisian salons with leanings towards literature and philosophy. After the early 1770s the Freemasons' lodges, under patronage of the nobility, were popular discussion forums. There were also the provincial academies such as those in Toulon, Bordeaux and Marseilles, where educated clergy, nobles and merchants imitated the practice of the Paris salons, and which increased from fifty in 1750 to twice as many by 1770. Then there were the Parisian *cafés,* the clubs and the much more numerous literary and "philosophical" societies which increased rapidly after 1770 and, by the late 1780s, were to be found in every town of average size in France.

Finally it must be said that it is doubtful whether before 1770 the new ideas of the Enlightenment went any further than the intelligentsia and a select group of the aristocracy. Apart from the inevitable exceptions, it is possibly not far from the truth to say that those who lived in the towns of Continental Europe were touched by the Enlightenment only in as much as it influenced the manner in which they were treated by their social superiors.

The application of 18th century ideas to political and social realities was made not by intellectuals, but by practical people who were consumers of these ideas. It was the "enlightened" rulers who first attempted to apply the intellectual matrixes of the Enlightenment by trying to find a role for rational order and civic virtue in the sphere of the true interests which were their primary concern. This political version of the Enlightenment dominated European life up to about 1780, when another kind of political practitioner transformed the dynamic, radical and freedom-seeking trends, which arose in the last phase of 18th century culture, into a movement of social revolution. The rise of fundamental opposition to the monarchy coincided with the shift from philosophy to ideology, and with the end of the "Enlighteners".

The Enlightenment finally died, after a lingering illness, in 1789, when the French Revolution destroyed the movement's intellectual, social and political philosophy. It has been said that the Enlightenment contributed to its own destruction and to the rise of the revolution because the *philosophes*, with their attacks on traditions and institutions, undermined confidence in the existing order. But was the Enlightenment a cause of the revolution? Brumfitt's opinion is: "The question whether, and if so, how far, the Enlightenment may be considered a 'cause' of the Revolution, has been debated endlessly and largely fruitlessly. However, at the extremes of the debate, two points at least can be fairly firmly established. Firstly . . . the Revolution was in no sense a 'philosophic', 'Encyclopedic' or 'Masonic' plot. Secondly, the creation of the National Assembly, and the legislation enacted by it and its successors, were deeply indebted to 'philosophic' thought. To attempt to go beyond such general conclusions is to involve oneself in another of Diderot's 'chicken and egg' debates, or to indulge in a futile search for a balance in which to weigh, say, the *Encyclopédie* against the price of bread."[12]

ENLIGHTENED DESPOTISM

It is often alleged that a number of European rulers in the second half of the 18th century were influenced by the writings of the *philosophes*, and applied their ideas in their government practices. It is said that the young rulers prepared themselves for their royal duties by enthusiastically reading the works of the *philosophes*. They were also said to have corresponded to compare their programmes of reform. Diderot is quoted: "There is no prince in Europe who is not also a philosopher." He spent some time, in fact, at the court of Catherine II of Russia, where he discussed matters of state and philosophy with the tsarina. It is pointed out that Frederick II of Prussia preferred to write and speak French and, like Catherine, eagerly corresponded with Voltaire. It is also pointed out that the most important tutor of Joseph II, namely Martini, was a leader of the Enlightenment in Austria. Joseph himself, in 1780, allegedly declared on becoming the sole ruler: "I have made philosophy the legislator of my empire; its logical principles will reshape Austria."

The point is then made that rulers throughout Europe undertook their task of reform with zeal and devotion *because*, under the influence of the Enlightenment, they had come to realize that their power entailed duties as well as responsibilities, and that it was their duty in particular to improve the management of the state and to promote the material well-being of their subjects – to be the first servant of the state.

This view deserves attention, namely that there was a kind of absolutism in Europe during the second half of the 18th century, motivated by the Enlightenment and characterized by autocratic government, which was essentially aimed at governing on the basis of the best of contemporary knowledge, in accordance with rational planning and towards the achievement of benevolent social goals. This was the historiographic meaning retrospectively given to the 18th century by monarchistic and systematically minded German historians of the 19th century. This view predominated during the first third of the 20th century, and still has its followers today. We can maintain, however, that it is not possible today to hold literally to this historic meaning of enlightened despotism – certainly not in terms of the achievement of benevolent social goals. Since the revisionist historiography of the 1930s, this view has been subjected to many attacks. In particular the differences between the ideas of the *philosophes* and the practices of absolute rulers have been pointed out. (As has already been discussed, most *philosophes* relied on a philosopher-king – and not on mass uprising – to bring about the reforms they desired.) It has been pointed out, for instance, that Diderot himself rejected enlightened despotism, although he had at an earlier stage praised the powers of the philosopher-king (Plato's ideal). In 1774 he told Catherine the Great that two or three successive reigns of just and enlightened despots would be one of the greatest disasters that could visit a nation, as any despot, however excellent a person he may be, is a good shepherd who lowers his subjects to the level of animals. Rousseau's reference to the contradiction in the term "enlightened despotism", which held no meaning for him, has also been quoted.

The paradoxical term is precisely another issue which has been examined. In his

In search of humanity, A. Cobban rejects the concept as a useless text-book category. German historians, such as Fritz Hartung, prefer using the term "enlightened absolutism", as they regard absolutism as a form of government which, although it had no place for any institution to represent the people, did recognize the force of law and the rights of subjects, while despotism indicated an unfettered arbitrariness. Absolutism could therefore according to Hartung, be enlightened, but despotism not. However, Stuart Andrews writes about the term "enlightened despotism": "The phrase is, of course, a calculated paradox. Even if we speak of 'Enlightened Absolutism'... the term remains an implied contradiction of Lord Acton's famous dictum that absolute power corrupts absolutely."[13] In contrast to the abstract concepts created by historians, the term "enlightened despotism" was, in fact, used in the 18th century. Not one of the rulers regarded as examples of enlightened despots apparently ever used the term themselves, but the expressions *despotisme éclairé* and *despotisme légal* appear in the writings of the physiocrats from about 1760 onwards. Diderot, too, used the phrase *despotisme éclairé* in his letters in 1760, while Raynal, in 1770, wrote about *un despote juste et éclairé* (a just and enlightened despot). Although arguments of political logic, linguistic analysis and historical fact can be raised against the term "enlightened despotism", we can keep to the term used in the 18th century. It is not the term, in any case, which is of importance, but rather the nature of government practice in the period under discussion.

It has been mentioned that rulers enthusiastically read the writings of the *philosophes*. There can be no doubt about this. It is particularly true of the great "enlightened" despots of central and eastern Europe, who had much to catch up with in the westernization of their more "backward" nations. Catherine II, Joseph II and Frederick II all enjoyed periods of enforced leisure before they became rulers of their countries. Catherine spent eight years as archduchess of Holstein-Gottorp and wife of the unattractive successor to the throne of Russia before the palace revolution of 1762 brought her to power. In this time she turned to the works of the Enlightenment, in particular those of Locke, Diderot, Voltaire and Montesquieu, and became one of the best-read women of her time. Joseph, who lived in Vienna in extreme impatience while Maria Theresa reigned, was crown prince for twenty four years and co-regent for another fifteen before he became the sole ruler in 1780. He therefore had enough time to acquaint himself with the leading ideas of his time. As crown prince, Frederick was excluded by his father from government, and he spent seven happy years in Rheinsberg before he succeeded to the throne in 1740. In this time he corresponded with Fontenelle and, in particular, with Voltaire, and developed the reading habits which were to be associated with the philosopher-king of Sans Souci.

To have read the writings of the *philosophes* did not, however, necessarily mean that the ideas they contained were applied in the government practices of the rulers. The *philosophes* who were collected at court were favoured by the rulers not as tutors, but as entertainment artists, sycophants and publicity agents. Good relationships between them were frequently short-lived and always fragile. The rulers chose those enlightened ideas which happened to suit their particular circumstances. R.J. White writes: "If enlightenment paid off in terms of strength, unity and material success, they (the rulers) were enlightened. Otherwise they kept enlightenment as a private hobby, a pose, a courtly fad. They were fond enough of posing as enlightened, sometimes genuinely rejoicing (as who would not?) in the writings of the Philosophes, but always going about their hard-headed and ambitious projects with as much, or as little, unconcern for intellectual theories as suited them."[14] They therefore paid only lip service to the thinking of the Enlightenment.

According to White, it is therefore misleading and absurd to think of this period in terms of a group of despotic monarchs suddenly touched by a passion for reason, suffering attacks of enlightened benevolence, having "a change of heart" which metamorphosed them from wilful autocrats into virtuous confessors of enlightened principles, fathers – or mothers – of their people, magnanimous abolishers of the traditional deficiencies in tyrannous reigns, practitioners of humane and self-sacrificing virtues. He goes on to say that what really occurred was that certain European rulers, crowned or otherwise, like most educated people of their time, took to the fashion of the Enlightenment and, inasmuch as it served their ends as rulers, accepted some of the self-evident and elementary reforms which were propagated by its philosophic exponents. After all, the practical advantages of certain forms of Enlightenment were easy to see and would have come to the notice of an intelligent ruler, even if he or she had never opened a "philosophic" book. The application of reason held the promise of efficient organization. The more rationally a state is organized, the easier it becomes to govern, and the more profitably its resources can be employed in terms of wealth and power. For example: religious tolerance attracted skilled workers as refugees from "unenlightened" states.[15] There was therefore a great deal about the well-ordered state recommended by the *philosophes* which had its attractions also for despots. Principles such as rationalism, religious freedom, secularism and utilitarianism would therefore be employed in the interests of the state, or rather of the ruler, but not so the principles of enforceable limits to the ruler's power, or representative participation in the legislative process.

Why did the so-called "enlightened" monarchs reject these constitutional principles? Firstly, they were subjected, exactly like their predecessors, to the general rule of western politics that power is not spontaneously relinquished. Secondly, because the socially static areas in which enlightened despotism flourished – that is, in central and eastern Europe – by comparison did not produce any pressure worth mentioning for ceding such powers. Thirdly, because the pressure which did exist emanated from the nobility, which demanded influence over or exclusion from the power of the state, rather than sharing it. Fourthly, because international competition made the concentration of political power a continual responsibility of the ruler. Fifthly, the distinguishing principle of the enlightened despots was: in the predominantly agricultural and conservative context of central and eastern Europe, liberal principles could not be implemented without becoming self-denying. The "enlightened" ruler was the sole ruler, who could not institute reforms which would jeopardise this sole rulership. A despot could be enlightened only up to the point where his own power was assailed. Therefore the implementation of the more radical ideas of the Enlightenment, which would ultimately mean participation of the people in the governing of their country, was impossible. That is why a halt had to be called when even moderate reforms endangered the position of the ruler. The interests of the state also had to be taken into account. This still weighed heavier than the "utopian" ideas of the *philosophes*. Not "freedom", but "order" was the watchword. That is also why a radical reshaping of existing social relationships was undesirable, as foreign action demanded the greatest possible degree of peace on the home front. This is also why mercantilism existed for so long in the form of external tariff arrangements (although most of the so-called enlightened despots had a policy of internal free trade) – proof that the physiocrats had little influence on economic or political practices.

It has been said that the need for order, peace and security was greater than ever before to enable preparations to be made for participation in international competition, or to head off social revolutions at home. The "enlightened despots" therefore adapted government measures to the needs of the times (apart from the Enlightenment). According to this argument, there were, enlightened thinking apart, other factors which contributed to the urge for reform. Europe was in a phase of transition. New intellectual, political and economic forces were threatening to upset the existing order and adaptations had become imperative. Acton referred to the monarchy at this stage as the "repentant monarchy", endeavouring to justify itself on the eve of its overthrow by more efficient use of its power – a ruler trying to prove himself the first servant of the state by energetic and predominant concern with the interests of the nation as a whole. This is, however, as White points out, a dangerous academic idea. To mention only one point: the monarchs and their subjects had no reason to suppose that royal authority was on the point of being replaced or even of being seriously challenged. White thinks that absolute monarchy became more determined in its absolutism, more intolerant of competitors for its authority, as the Revolution approached. He says: "If there is one feature of monarchy in the last years of the *ancien régime* that strikes the historian more forcibly than another, it is its sublime self-confidence. Absolutism was never more arrogant than on the eve of its fall in the person of Louis XVI..." [16] We can argue, however, that although there was no idea that open opposition was in the offing, European rulers still thought that they could improve on the circumstances which caused insurrections, by applying the new ideas. There is therefore a fair amount of truth in the argument that the monarchy instituted reforms to retain its power in a century of change. Enlightened despotism was therefore reactionary, and not revolutionary, in its reforms.

Another point of importance is that the generation of rulers preceding the "enlightened" despots was also guided by practical considerations. Both generations were motivated by the same needs for greater internal strength and stability of their states. Absolute monarchy, in fact, had its origins in the monarch's need for internal as well as foreign action. This need for security necessitated a permanent army under control of the crown, which in turn required increased taxes for its maintenance. This again led to the need for intensified economic growth and the creation of a central and efficient bureaucracy to rule the state. These requirements were not limited only to the "enlightened" despots, but applied to most monarchs of the 18th century (and to rulers of other times).

The reforms of the "enlightened" despots were, in fact, virtually all further developments of what had been planned or begun by their predecessors. There was little which was truly new in the policies of these monarchs, and what innovations there were can seldom be ascribed to the influence of the Enlightenment. It must also be kept in mind that reforms cannot automatically be seen as "Enlightenment". This must be remembered when reference is made to the new bureaucratic administrative techniques, the codification of laws in a rational manner, the reform of legal organization and procedures, the regulation of all economic activities in the interests of the state, the subjection of the church to the state, the dissolution of religious orders, the encouragement of the latest techniques in agriculture and industry, the provision of incentives for immigrants, the building of roads and canals, the removal of internal tolls, the standardization of weights and measures, the patronage of the arts, and even the establishment of schools.

Frederick II, Catherine II and Joseph II all had predecessors whose policies were similar to theirs. Frederick William I of Prussia, Peter the Great of Russia and Maria Theresa of Austria all brought about fundamental reforms which led to centralized states. Similarly, the "enlightened" despots followed in the footsteps of their forebears in the respect that they were determined to enforce their authority on every aspect of life in their states. Most European monarchs could not afford the luxury of clinging to an ideology, not even one as loosely defined as that of the Enlightenment. They were all inevitably prisoners of history, as their actions were largely determined by economic, political and military forces which were the products of past events. Totally "enlightened" government was a goal which, even had they wanted to achieve it, would have been beyond reach because of the internal complexities of their own countries and the external pressures applied by others. Only small states, free of the burden of playing a role in international affairs and frequently economically and socially more homogeneous than their more powerful neighbours, could afford to apply the remedies of the Enlightenment with any measure of thoroughness. Consequently, the Margrave Charles Frederick of Baden was the only European ruler to institute the *impôt unique* (a single land tax for all – the most practical innovation suggested by the physiocrats), albeit on a limited scale. This experiment was, however, a failure. With the exception of Joseph II, the rulers of the largest states in the late 18th century were not prepared to face the problems involved in truly radical changes of this nature. Both Louis XV and Louis XVI had neither the desire nor the ability to be "enlightened" despots. In Britain such a government had always been out of the question. In practice, neither Frederick II nor Catherine II displayed any evidence of having been profoundly influenced by the ideas of the Enlightenment.

The viewpoint can be held that the Enlightenment had little or no influence on the government practices of the so-called enlightened despots except perhaps for Joseph II and other smaller rulers. And Joseph was to pay dearly for his fundamental reforms. The other despots easily rationalized their way out of the restrictions to which they did not want to subject themselves. As long as rulers had no general opposition to their policies, as long as they had a measure of public order and could squeeze enough money from their subjects to maintain their courts and armies, they really had little interest in the reform of their states in a utilitarian manner. More often than not, enlightened reforms were instituted only to enforce absolutism. The typical 18th century state was a *Herrenstaat*, a state governed by and in the interests of the feudal aristocracy. Its guiding principle was not the welfare of its people, but rather the conservation and increase of the power of the state. This principle required a constant strengthening of the state's position within a system of other competing *Herrenstaaten*. The interests of the state were indeed approached rationally (as always) in its relationships with other states. The replacement of the old Bourbon-Habsburg struggle by an Austro-French alliance (the so-called Diplomatic Revolution) is evidence of the replacement of dynastic interests by state interests. But the "enlightened" despots certainly did not apply enlightenment in their foreign policies. These were absolutistic, and took no account of principles such as reason, peace, humaneness, international law, universal morality and cosmopolitan unity.

Were the "enlightened" despots really absolute? It has been argued that only a totally absolute ruler could be altogether enlightened. It is true that the despots of the 18th century were less absolute than they pretended to be. Even the most enlightened of the 18th century monarchs were powerless to implement the whole programme of the *philosophes* in a semi-feudal society. It was as unrealistic in Prussia as in France to expect that the property-owning classes would voluntarily relinquish their powers and privileges. Vested interests and historically-rooted conventions therefore set limits to enlightenment.

Krieger sums up the argument against enlightened despotism as follows: "What has been called enlightened despotism, it has been argued, was neither enlightened nor despotic. It was still simply absolutism as such, now adjusted to the particular tone of the later eighteenth century, *but essentially continuous in its forms and its goals with the absolutism that preceded it*. The statements of principle, policy or purpose that are usually taken as proof of a different, enlightened form of absolutism, these critics conclude, were in respect of policies, either rhetorical or irrelevant: monarchs used the fashionable terms of the Enlightenment to rationalize irrational policy or to express cultural interests other than policy, but in either case such terms had, and were intended to have, little bearing on the realities of government."[17] The contention that the governments of many European states in the generation or two before the French Revolution can be distinguished from the practice of the first half of the century by the existence of something called "enlightened despotism" therefore, in our view, does not hold water.

As a stage in the development of western politics, "enlightened" despotism is conceivable only in connection with a group of late 18th-century reforming monarchs in central and eastern Europe whose differences in policy were at least as obvious as the similarities. In reality they had less in common with one another than each had with his or her own immediate predecessor and successor. We are dealing here with the monarchs of the half-century 1740-1790, who operated in differing geographic, social and economic milieux. Just as the case was with all absolute rulers, their characters determined their actions. It is therefore necessary to consider who the "enlightened" despots were, what kind of people they were, and which measures they applied.

Apart from Frederick II, Joseph II (and possibly also his mother, Maria Theresa) and Catherine II there were also, for instance, Charles III of Naples and Spain,

Gustavus III of Sweden, Leopold of Tuscany (subsequently Holy Roman emperor) and various German sovereigns who are classed as enlightened despots. Ministers such as Pombal of Portugal and Struensee of Denmark are also included here.

We shall pay attention only to Frederick the Great, Joseph II and Catherine the Great, the best known representatives of this "form of government". It is noticeable that their countries (Prussia, Austria and Russia) were land-locked in comparison to the countries of north-western Europe, England and Holland. In the latter, where maritime trade reached such importance, the middle classes were predominantly capitalistic and increased in power so rapidly that they overwhelmed the monarchy, while in the former states, where the middle classes were professional and bureaucratic, they remained much weaker in comparison to the nobility and the monarchy. France covered the geographic middle ground. Here the middle classes and the nobility had roughly equal power, and the monarchy was unsuccessful in solving the problem of a revitalized aristocracy and a rising bourgeoisie.

About the lip service these three rulers paid the Enlightenment, White justifiably remarks: "The most equivocal of them was undoubtedly Catherine II . . . The most academic, and at the same time, one of the best-intentioned, was the Emperor Joseph II . . . The most reactionary of them was Frederick II of Prussia, who delighted to be thought the Philosopher-King *par excellence*."[18]

FREDERICK II

Much is made of the correspondence and friendship of Frederick II with, for instance, Voltaire and d'Alembert. Between 1740 and 1743 Voltaire visited him on four occasions at Sans Souci at Potsdam, but by his fifth visit in 1750, this friendship had begun to show signs of strain. Frederick subsequently complained: "Voltaire is the most good-natured mad man I have yet met; he is good only to read." It is said that he declared to his nephew and successor, "I have done everything possible to acquire a reputation in literary matters. I was luckier than Cardinal Richelieu, because, thank God, I pass muster as an author, but, between us, the *beaux esprits* are an abominable lot. They are unbearably haughty people." Of d'Alembert's songs of praise about him, Frederick said that he liked to be praised.

After 1740, when he succeeded to the throne, he did not allow himself much leisure to attend to his literary and philosophical interests. Possibly there was a watershed in 1756 (the outbreak of the Seven Years War) after which he subordinated cultural interests to power politics, and also changed his attitude towards French culture in the radical form which it had been given by d'Holbach. Where the reforms advocated by the *philosophes* might be helpful in governing his military and mercantilistic state, Frederick was prepared to accept them, but where they were inimical to his absolutism, they were rejected.

In his *Political Testament* of 1752 Frederick noted: "A well-planned government must possess an underlying concept which is so well integrated that it can be compared to a philosophical system. All actions must be well considered; finance, politics and the army must be managed to the same ends: the reinforcement of the state and the promotion of its power. Such a system can flow only from a single brain. This must be that of the king. But such a ruler cannot be self-willed or lazy; the prince is the first servant of the state." This definition of the king as the *premier domestique du peuple*, which is often quoted, originates in classic times. Frederick was, however, the first monarch to use the words. But they have to be correctly understood! In his famous description Frederick revealed as much about the ruler's supremacy – which he did not emphasize – as about the obligation to serve, where he did let the emphasis fall. He took his view of himself as first servant of the state very seriously, for his power was legitimized by the duties he accepted and his superior responsibilities. Just as with other "enlightened" rulers, his absolute political power was justified as being the only common bond between the competing rights in society and the only power that could guarantee what was fundamental in these rights against any social force.

Frederick was not particularly original. For the greater part of his reign he followed in the footsteps of his predecessors as far as internal policies were concerned. Despite superficial differences from his father, and despite their personal clashes, he was, throughout his life, in many respects the political executor of Frederick William I. He was certainly more aware than his father of the state as an entity separate from the person of the ruler, but his only important addition to the system of government he inherited was a series of legal reforms which were principally the work of one of his ministers, Samuel von Cocceji. "His flute playing, the reams of bad French poetry he wrote, his friendship with Voltaire, which have so impressed many historians, are no index to his attitude to matters of real importance. This is seen rather in his snobbish preference for aristocratic ministers and officials, in his unyieldingly mercantilistic ideas on economic affairs, and in his lack of any real interest in education. It is no accident that so many contemporary German writers and scholars – Wieland, Winckelmann, Lessing, Gottsched – disliked both him and Prussia; and it is hard to point to any aspect of his activities which would have been very different if the idea of the Enlightenment had never existed." Such is the view of M.S. Anderson. [19]

There was, in fact, little opportunity for the realization of Enlightenment thought in Prussia. It was rather a caricature of "enlightened" government under the cynical reign of Frederick. Lessing even called the Prussia of Frederick "the most enslaved country in Europe". Free speech meant little more, according to him, than permission to crack anti-religious jokes. Kant advised his readers: "Argue as much as you like, but be obedient." Frederick himself declared in his *Histoire de mon Temps*: "I trust posterity will do me justice, and know how to distinguish the king in me from the philosopher, the good person from the political one."

Frederick's all-encompassing activities and reforms in many spheres left no place for the least independence in any of the branches of government. Prussia did not even possess a pretence of popular representation, and although a number of provincial assemblies still met, it was only to receive the instructions of the royal officials in the districts concerned. It must be admitted that Frederick took his task as absolute ruler very seriously, and devoted his energies to revitalizing the country after the Seven Years War. He was really "the first servant of the state" (but not of the people) and his government in Prussia was an example of absolutism (and not enlightenment) at its best. He issued numerous decrees which regulated every aspect of the nation's life and undertook personal tours of inspection to ensure that they were implemented. He devoted himself to the mastery of every department of his government. It is said that he rose at four in the morning in summer, and at five in winter, and spent ten hours a day on matters of state, four on study and writing, and two on relaxation. He certainly did not lack zeal and devotion, but precisely because everything had to receive his personal attention, the durability of his reforms was suspect. The weakness of his highly centralized system was that it was centralized in his own brain. Mirabeau foresaw this danger when he wrote: "If a foolish king should ever mount this throne, we will see the formidable giant collapse, and Prussia will come to a fall like Sweden." His words did not altogether come true, but Frederick's successor, his nephew, was a spendthrift and incompetent, and many of Frederick's measures died with him. This is, of course, the problem with hereditary absolute rulership – it cannot provide a continuous series of able rulers.

Frederick intended to give content to the idea that it was the duty of the ruler to strengthen the state. His first concern was consequently to supply himself with major financial resources and to gain control of all the forces which he might find useful. He was literally the absolute ruler of his country and his subjects, as he was the largest landowner in the kingdom – a third of it belonged to him personally. Many of the reforms he made must be seen against this background. The French doctrines favouring individual property rights, and of which Voltaire was the great champion, could have been nothing but unacceptable to Frederick, as they would weaken the state and the monarchy. He meant to remain a landowner and to derive personal benefit from agricultural progress, which he diligently promoted. The technical developments which improved the productivity of the land and the work of agriculturalists were of great interest to him as they contributed to increasing his wealth. This is why he busied himself with an Academy of Sciences – it was, in fact, an academy of technology which enriched him. His establishing of small towns and his support of settlers with loans and temporary exemptions of taxes and military service can all be seen in this light. He acted like a landlord when he erected grain stores which he filled in good years and emptied in times of scarcity, thus creating controlled reserves. It was monopolistic, and the *philosophes* criticized him for it, and also because he did not sub-divide the land, which would have been to the benefit of small and medium-sized farmers.

The backward nature of the Prussian economy was most useful to Frederick, as its development ensured his power, and prevented the emergence of a new society. His personal views had a decidedly limiting influence in the sphere of economic policy. There is no reason to believe that he ever systematically studied economy or took note of the newer ideas of the physiocrats. In practice he never deviated from the mercantilistic system he had inherited from his father. The question whether changing times demanded a different economic policy never seems to have occurred to him, even though the general application of mercantilist principles gradually injured trade to such an extent that everyone suffered. When his ministers cautiously raised the subject, he summarily dismissed their suggestions without considering their arguments. The great increase in agricultural production did not profit the peasants. Industry and trade certainly revitalized the capitalistic zeal of the urban entrepreneurs, but Frederick's strict control measures dashed the hopes of the producers. Fiscal measures weighed heavily on producers and consumers alike. Military requirements had precedence in public finance, as war was, in fact, Prussia's national industry. Of the 22 000 000 or 23 000 000 Reichstaler in government income in 1786, between 12 000 000 and 13 000 000 were spent directly on the maintenance of the gigantic army of 195 000 soldiers. Therefore, because he was the kingdom's landlord, Frederick had at his disposal an economy which was totally at the service of the overriding goal of his reign: successful wars.

His attitude towards the peasantry was particularly peculiar. He was clearly aware of the contradiction between his theory of the original equality of all men and the true situation of the peasants, but did nothing to change matters substantially. Even in the royal domain his reforms remained limited to one important innovation: the transformation of the uncertain property rights of small farmers into a hereditary right in 1777. Nothing was done, however, for those who lived on the estates of the aristocracy. The strict legal relationship between *Junker* and peasant was not alleviated. Of course, Frederick's dependence on the nobility in matters of statecraft and military leadership had a great deal to do with this. The protection the crown offered the peasantry was effective only in that it prevented the nobility from acquiring peasant land – protection for the class as a whole, and not for the individual farmer. This was done in the interests of protecting his source of peasant recruits, who made up half of his armed forces. The inherited practice of total or partial exemption from taxes for the old, privileged social classes placed the tax burden on those who were least equipped to bear it. Government saving, expenditure on agriculture and industry, and the maintenance of a large army, were all paid for by taxes wrung principally from the poor.

The mass was excluded from the handling of local matters. The townsmen hated the royal officials who served a state which was so far removed from them, foreign to their expectations, as well as indifferent to their needs.

Frederick's interest in the Prussian system of education was lukewarm, even after 1763. He hardly bothered about the education of the broad masses. It is true that there were parts of his writings in which he declared himself to be in favour of the dissemination of enlightenment, or at least denied that it is easier to govern an uneducated people. But deep down he was quite unmoved by the optimism of the Enlightenment that the spread of knowledge and the struggle against prejudice would lead to the moral progress of mankind. On the contrary, he became ever more convinced of the irremediable evil of mankind, the majority of whom were stupid at best and cruel at worst. He did believe, however, in the education of the aristocracy, as they could furnish the state with moral and social services.

His policy of religious tolerance is often referred to, and it gained him, in fact, greater prestige amongst his enlightened contemporaries than his military achievements ever did. This is easy to explain. One reason for this tolerance was his scepticism about the doctrines of all Christian churches as revealed in his own definition of tolerance: "Everyone in this kingdom will go to heaven in his own way." But it was also the result of the Prussian tradition of religious freedom which Frederick William, the Great Elector, had had to accept a century earlier through force of circumstance. The old Hohenzollern motives were to attract suitable immigrants, and to maintain peace between local minorities while fomenting unrest amongst majorities abroad. Frederick's attitude to religion was thoroughly opportunistic. He claimed to be the pope of the Lutherans and was convinced that "a Protestant prince is a greater master in his state than a Catholic one". His main aim in the control of the Lutheran church was to prevent any surfeit of dogma and fanaticism from endangering the civic peace. Churches were, to him, political institutions, but religious freedom an individual right. He sheltered French Jesuits to counter the pro-Austrian Jesuits in Silesia. His refusal to suppress the Jesuits could also have been motivated by his need for teachers. He was tolerant of Jews because of their economic activities. His general view is summarized in his *Testament* of 1768: "It does not matter to the state which metaphysics dominate the thinking of man; it is sufficient that everyone acts as a good citizen and patriot." To grasp Frederick's opportunism, one need only note his actions before he invaded Silesia, when he abolished censorship, decreed religious freedom and forbade torture in prisons.

His aversion to the broad masses went hand in hand with a pronounced preference for the aristocracy. He turned Prussian absolutism away from the direction which had been followed by the Great Elector, namely to suppress the demands of the nobility. Such a struggle with the aristocracy had, it is true, become unnecessary, as they had subjected themselves to absolutism and voluntarily accepted the duties of military service as officers.

Although Frederick could show great achievements, and he was a successful and dynamic ruler, he was not an "enlightened" despot in practice, but a reforming reactionary. The obvious contrast between his enlightened theory and absolutistic practice was, according to Hartung, largely the result of the urgent demands of power politics. Prussia's position as the youngest and weakest of the great powers was too insecure to risk endangering it by the unrest which a radical break with the traditional order of society would have entailed.

JOSEPH II

Joseph is usually regarded as the most enlightened of the 18th century despots, but also as the least successful ruler. Was he, however, all that interested in the Enlightenment? Was it the Enlightenment which induced him to institute his many reforms?

Although it is said that he acted out of intellectual conviction in his dedication to emancipation, he was particularly suspicious of the *philosophes*. He remained a good Roman Catholic – his education was strictly supervised by his pious mother – and he had no desire to meet Voltaire when he visited France. Although it is doubtful whether he read Voltaire, he certainly had knowledge of the works of the *philosophes*. None the less we can say that his claim of having made philosophy the legislator of his empire was empty boasting. It has to be admitted that he endeavoured to do much more than Frederick, but the thinking of the Enlightenment was just as little of a guide to him as to Frederick. It was certainly not an excess of enlightenment which caused his failure.

We can accept, like Ernst Wangermann has done,[20] that Joseph instituted reforms as a consequence of circumstances within and outside his empire, and not as a result of the Enlightenment. Wangermann argues that Maria Theresa and Joseph made reforms because Austria lagged behind in the power struggle with Russia and Prussia, whose powers were increasing through state centralization. The loss of Silesia was one symptom of this. Maria Theresa was determined to win Silesia back by a fresh display of force, and this determination was the starting point for a series of great reforms which she and Joseph instituted regarding central administration, local government, finance, the peasantry, education and religion. It began with the reform of the armed forces. This implied reforms in other spheres: maintenance of the new armed forces required a substantial increase in taxes, which in turn could only be effected by far-reaching reforms of a constitutional, political, economic and administrative nature. To implement these reforms, a new public service was needed, and to train public servants, a new educational system, devoid of ecclesiastical control and censorship, had to be built up. Wangermann says: "A policy of enlightened despotism thus appeared in Austria no less than elsewhere in response to certain practical and urgent necessities, and not as the fruit of philosophical persuasion ... the 'revolutionary' Emperor undertook little that was entirely new in principle. But his obstinate consistency and enthusiasm have always provided historians with an additional temptation to impute philosophical motives to him, which has resulted in a longstanding and sterile controversy as to the theoretical origin of his reforms."[20]

Centralization in Austria, as in Russia, was motivated by the needs of warfare. And in Austria, as in France, a sound financial system depended on the limitation of aristocratic privilege and the encouragement of the progressive middle class. Joseph was the only one amongst the so-called "enlightened" despots who was prepared to hazard a frontal attack on the privileged classes, but his well-meant attempt to raise the status of the peasantry to that enjoyed by their counterparts in France before the Revolution, was foiled by the reaction of the peasants themselves. (His mother had already begun the emancipation of the peasants.) His introduction of a single land tax and the commutation of feudal obligations, such as the *robot* or labour services, to cash payments, unleashed opposition amongst the peasants because they found that their new taxes were a heavier burden to them than their old obligations. Consequently, Joseph had to suspend the implementation of this idea. His successor, Leopold, revoked the land tax and reinstituted the *robot*, which also, however, led to a peasant revolt.

Joseph's far-reaching measures favouring the peasants earned him the hatred of the estate-owners. It must be mentioned, however, that the measures were not applicable to all of the small farmers, for example not to those who had terminable tenure on the landlord's own domain. Secondly, the landlord's authority of fatherly jurisdiction, which gave him local judicial and police powers over the peasantry, was left untouched, and the public basis of his privileges thus continued.

Joseph did, it is true, agree with the physiocrat Turgot, that nothing was more important than freedom in trade and industry. He therefore relaxed government measures concerning industry, but before his death they were reintroduced in the case of the textile and metal goods industries. Agriculture in the German-speaking provinces also continued to be protected by tariffs imposed on Hungarian grain and wine. Mercantilism regarding foreign countries was discarded, but Austria's traditional self-sufficiency did not really demand such trade. Many of the efforts in these spheres were never realized, and many of the expectations came to nought. Joseph's goals were frustrated by what he regarded as the excessive demands of the middle classes.

He granted religious freedom, and his policy of tolerance seems to have been based on principle rather than on opportunism, as was the case with Frederick. His Edict of Tolerance of 1781 granted private practice of religion and full civil rights to Lutherans, Calvinists and Greek Orthodox, as well as improving the circumstances of the Jews. (Deists were, however, not tolerated and were given corporal punishment.) On the other hand he placed the Roman Catholic church under the control of the state. Consequently, all communications between the pope and Austrian Roman Catholics were subject to royal consent, the powers of the bishops were increased, and they were obliged to swear an oath of loyalty to Joseph, new bishoprics were established, lay monastic orders were abolished and subordinated to local bishops. Yet the Roman Catholic religion expressly retained its supremacy in the interests of the unity of the state, and therefore the oath of loyalty was, in practice, of lesser importance. The measures concerning tolerance and greater control over the Roman Catholic church formed a coherent policy in two political functions, namely the fiscal function of increasing the taxable population and production, and the government function which accorded the king the determination of the respective rights of church and state. The establishment of the state's authority over the Roman Catholic church in Austria had, in any case, been sustained Habsburg policy since the Thirty Years War, and under Maria Theresa – orthodox in religious thinking and intolerant in religious principles as she was – this policy was extended in practice to encroach upon Roman Catholic privileges and to make concessions to industrious religious minorities. To Joseph, religion was more of a central concern than to Frederick and Catherine, but, like they, he combined greater state control over the established church with tolerance regarding other churches. Yet, he earned nothing but the hatred of the papal supporters and the ridicule of the free thinkers for his religious policy. Amongst the people it was the most unpopular of his reforms, and he was dumbfounded at the "ludicrous enthusiasm, particularly amongst women" which met Pope Pius VI when the latter visited him in Vienna in 1782 in a fruitless effort to reverse Joseph's religious measures.

As far as education is concerned, it was typical of his policy that all educational institutions were subject to strict state control, and typical of his character that he issued numerous decrees which regulated their discipline and teaching. His narrow-minded consciousness of state interests frequently led to extremely limited views. In the secularization of high schools and universities, short-sighted goals were set. The education of public servants was limited largely to the study of administration and economics.

In 1781 Joseph promulgated a law which went a long way towards creating a free press, but after 1785 he applied censorship to counter free-thinking tendencies. Like Catherine, he later began to react against radical opinions. Therefore state censorship replaced censorship of the church. The broadly-based magnanimity which is so essential to a thorough flowering of intellect and literature was missing. Usually the demands of the state in this respect, as in many other spheres, were the decisive factor, although the measures were dressed up in modern clothes. In his political fanaticism, Joseph neglected the appreciation of intellectual and artistic values.

As far as the administration of justice was concerned, a general code was issued in 1787, and a criminal code in 1788, applicable to all Habsburg territories. Class differences in law were abolished and legal costs were reduced. Torture was forbidden, and the death penalty reserved for a smaller number of crimes. Many religious courts were abolished, and marriages became civil contracts. But the number of crimes against the state grew drastically, and there was little amelioration of the brutal treatment of prisoners.

Joseph's policies, in particular his religious, political and agrarian reforms, provoked increasing opposition from his subjects. This opposition from all sides, unrest in the Netherlands and Hungary, and his unfortunate Turkish campaign, forced him to revoke many of his reforms shortly before his death, and others were set aside by his successor, Leopold II.

There were various reasons for his failure.

As for Frederick, sovereignty to Joseph meant unlimited authority which he could exercise at will. The power conferred on him by his subjects, to be exercised on their behalf, was absolute. A biographer has called him the Ignatius Loyola of the idea of the absolute state. No subordinate authority in his territories could have any validity unless it derived from him, or had been confirmed by him. To him, the institutions between himself and the people, which, in reality, were still quite strong, were altogether unimportant. His zeal for reform can be deduced from the more than 6 000 decrees and 11 000 laws which appeared in the ten years of his sole reign. He wanted to change everything in one fell swoop. It was his conviction that reform was for the good of the nation, and he brooked no delay or opposition, or allowed it to deflect him. He took no account of people's prejudices or their opinions. He told the Bohemian State Assembly in 1784: "This is my system, it is not for you to discuss whether it is desirable or not – only to design the best means to implement it."

His personality was therefore one reason for his failure. He lacked tact, patience and understanding of human nature; he was too hasty and self-willed, and undertook many reforms without previously preparing public opinion for them or training an officialdom which was able to implement them. "Joseph always wants to take the second step before he has taken the first," was Frederick the Great's perspicacious comment. Possibly he was too much of an idealist to take into account tradition, time and circumstances. The fact remains, however, that in his reformatory zeal he lost sight of the force of individual, group and national interests, and of the traditions of centuries. A person with his character was bound to provoke opposition.

His failure, however, also suggests that the limitations imposed by vested interests or historically-rooted traditions could not be exceeded by "enlightened" despotism (or rather, reforming despotism). This could only occur with the compliance of those involved, but absolutism made no provision for this. The opposition he experienced must then partially be ascribed to the fact that virtually every one of his reforms was detrimental to some historic right or privileged class or vested interest. All the established interest groups in his territories – church, nobility, states, privileged cities – were finally opposed to him. His endeavour to simplify and centralize the government of the empire and to introduce German as the official language throughout the Habsburg possessions, foundered on the provincial racial pride of the Magyars, Flemings and Italians, and generated a sense of national feeling among them. The composition of his empire, which in essence was a mere group of provinces, was therefore also a large problem. The nobility was enraged because their rights and privileges were encroached upon. The religious reforms provoked the opposition of pope and priests. Even the oppressed classes, who had most to gain from his reforms, were suspicious of him. They were disappointed in the limits to the usefulness of his reforms, and to their centralizing oppressiveness. The farmers regarded him as a tyrant who overthrew good old customs and forced them to serve in the army. Jews feared that compulsory education and military service would undermine the orthodoxy of their children. In the face of all this opposition, he increasingly employed force, and in his last years instituted a system of secret police, abolished the limited degree of press freedom which he had previously granted, and made use of armed force to keep large territories under control.

Possibly all this illustrates that the case of Joseph shows the vital weakness of "enlightened" despotism: the monarch was never sufficiently absolute to succeed in being "enlightened" – there were, after all, too many limits to his power. He attempted in vain to enforce reforms from above, while simultaneously new and, to him, incomprehensible middle-class ideas about freedom began to emerge from below. He tried to reform Austria into a rational western state, but finally left a weaker and much less united empire, and had even undermined the foundations of his own throne.

CATHERINE II

The interest Catherine had in the Enlightenment thinking has been referred to, as well as the fact that she was one of the best-read women of her time in Europe. She later informed Voltaire that she owed him a great deal since 1746. Their correspondence did not begin, however, before 1763, when he was sixty nine and she was thirty four. They never met, but their exchange of ideas continued up to Voltaire's death in 1778. Diderot visited her once, in 1773, when she was overwhelmed by his verbosity. She also bought his library for the Hermitage Palace.

These connections had, however, practically no influence on Catherine's reign in Russia. Although she continually vaunted her enlightened ideas, and extolled her own authorship (which was versatile, but not original), she implemented few of these ideas, and then only those which were unimportant and which she could control. In practice she was an absolute monarch, and the reforms which she did introduce in Russia, hid a "despotic" goal behind a front of "enlightenment".

In reality she was, at least as much as any of her contemporaries, the prisoner of the historic situation in which she found herself, a situation which prevented her from instituting any radical change in the internal organization of Russia. Her dependence on the land-owning nobility was an important limiting factor in the legislative innovations of her reign. Under the dubious circumstances in which she ascended to the throne she had, in any case, no choice but to seek the goodwill of the emancipated aristocracy. She was, therefore, pro-aristocratic from the beginning, and not just later (after the Pugachev Rebellion) as has often been alleged, and her measures strengthened the position of the aristocracy against that of the peasantry – for example through the charter to the nobility in 1785.

The dichotomy between theory and practice must also be sought in Catherine's personality. She was much less adventurous and far-seeing than Peter I and lacked the sincerity, intellectual honesty and even humility which did so much to balance his cruelty and recklessness. She was notorious for her whims and opportunism, and even confessed that she could begin things, but not complete them.

The central fact in her economic policy, as in those of her "enlightened" contemporaries, was the necessity of obtaining men and money for her army. If the interests of the nobility were a stumbling block on the path to a liberal policy, her own interest in territorial expansion was another. Annual expenditure during her reign rose from 17 000 000 to 70 000 000 or 80 000 000 roubles. Much of this was spent on conquests which, it has been calculated, added almost 570 000 km^2 to her empire.

The government system she built up was totally Russian and owed little to French or other foreign influences. Like Frederick, she largely implemented policies which had been suggested or begun before. Her reforms of 1775 concerning local government had been in prospect during the reign of Elizabeth. The same holds good for the great survey of landownership which she began in 1765, and even for the legislative commission which she appointed two years later. The idea of limiting the obligations of the Russian serfs to their owners by legislation, which engaged her attention during the early years of her reign, was already suggested in the thirties. Her secularization of land owned by the church in 1764 was the completion of a process which Peter I had begun.

An interesting example of her methods is her "attempt" to have Russian law investigated and modernized. She appointed a legislative commission (*Zemstvo*) for this purpose, which met in Moscow in 1767. It consisted of 564 members: 208 representatives of the cities, 161 of the nobility, seventy four of the peasants (but not one of the serfs) and twenty eight government officials. The remaining eighty eight were from the border territories, in particular the Cossack communities. To guide the commission, she drew up instructions (*Nakaz*) in which the main ideas were borrowed from the Enlightenment and in particular from Montesquieu's *De l'Es-*

prit des Lois. Reforms were proposed, which included an insistence on the equality of all before the law, an emphasis on the prevention of crime rather than the infliction of punishment, a total ban on torture, as well as religious freedom and the right to own land. There was, however, no indication that these high principles would be applied by a representative assembly. The *Nakaz* also declared: "The ruler is the source of all civic and political power." It is therefore hardly surprising that not a single law emerged from the more than 200 sessions of the commission from August 1767 to April 1768, when it was suspended – with the Turkish War as the excuse. Although Catherine maintained that the commission had only to blame itself, current historians agree with contemporaries that the appointment of this body was a propagandistic trick to counter the unfortunate impression which had been created abroad by the *coup d'état* which had set her on the throne. Catherine refused to act on any of the matters which were mooted in the discussions.

Although she professed her sympathies for the peasants, she did nothing to ameliorate their plight (although they made up 95 per cent of the population, or 34 000 000 of an estimated population of 36 000 000, of which almost 20 000 000 were serfs). She needed the support of the nobility, and thought that any attempt to ease the burdens of the small farmers would upset the established social order and thereby endanger her own sovereign authority. Where peasant uprisings occurred, they were cruelly suppressed. Rather than attempt to remove the grievances which caused the uprisings, she delivered these people to the cruel whims of the nobility to a much greater extent. Her reign is therefore generally regarded as a period in which the fate of the peasants reached its lowest ebb, as the control of the estate-owners over their serfs was set out in greater detail than ever before, and the rights which they had previously enjoyed were legally abrogated. Millions of such peasants were consequently degraded to serfdom.

As far as her religious policy is concerned, Catherine seemed to have shared the faith of the *philosophes* in tolerance, but undoubtedly also regarded it as good politics. Like Frederick, she practised tolerance *de facto*, and justified it by referring to the civic peace in a population with differing convictions. She extended freedom of religion to the Jesuits, but repealed it for the Jews. By depriving the clergy of the Orthodox church of their financial independence, and making them paid servants of the state, she completed, as has been pointed out, a process begun by Peter I. For the rest, she encouraged the formal observance of Orthodox ceremonies, which suited the political motives of her nominal conversion to the Russian church.

She paid lip service to universal education. Although far-reaching decrees were issued in 1764 and 1786, few of them were seriously implemented as a result of the limitations which were imposed by administrative necessity and social privilege. By 1790 there were no schools of any kind in the smaller towns, which meant that at least half of the country's population had no access to education. Children of the nobility were, however, provided for.

Finally, it must be kept in mind that Catherine was the only exponent of "enlightened" despotism who lived long enough to experience the more serious excesses of the French Revolution. Under these impacts, her reign began to be truly repressive. Her restrictions on intellectual freedom were worst of all. She had earlier on already acted against disciples of the radical phase of the Enlightenment such as Alexander Radishchev who wrote about conditions in Russia and was sent to Siberia for his pains. While her early tolerance can be attributed to her own pretensions as an author, she even forbade her own *Nakaz* in the end.

It can be argued that "enlightened" despotism represented the zenith of absolutism. Possibly it can be regarded as an effort to adapt absolutism to the needs of a changing world. If so, the effort failed in any case. Absolutism was obsolete, and "enlightened" despotism represented its last agonies – the twilight of the gods who had borne the fate of Europe and its people in their hands for so many centuries. The inability (or mostly unwillingness) of the "enlightened" despots to bring about any meaningful change in the social order can be partially blamed on the reaction of the aristocrats, who also became prominent in this period. While the nobility were frustrating efforts towards reform, the bourgeoisie were insisting on even greater reform of government as well as society. By 1790 progressive political thinking in Europe had discarded the idea of absolute monarchy and moved in the direction of constitutional government – even of sovereignty of the people. When reform from above proved to be insufficient, reform from below became inevitable.

CHAPTER 10

THE FRENCH REVOLUTION

THE *ANCIEN RÉGIME* IN FRANCE

The French Revolution was in the vanguard of the European movement in the last quarter of the 18th century and the beginning of the 19th century, which aimed at radical reform in the political and social spheres. The aims of the movement, which in due course became a revolution, were embodied by its motto: liberty, equality and fraternity. Liberty was meant to be, in the first place, the freedom of the individual to do whatever he pleased as long as it was not injurious to other individuals, in the second place, protection against arbitrary state control, and in the third, that people should have a voice in legislation – in other words, a democratization of state authority. Equality meant in the first place the overthrow of the class system with its class privileges which had been inherited from the Middle Ages, and in the second place, equality of opportunity for everyone, irrespective of the class into which he was born or to which he belonged. Fraternity, a relatively vague concept, more or less stood for a greater measure of humaneness and fairness towards less privileged people and the abolition of class and racial differentiation. The French Revolution was therefore an important event which adapted political, social and religious institutions to new demands. In action and reaction the ideas of the French Revolution, together with the effects of the Industrial Revolution, dominated the history of the 19th century. It is a powerful factor even today.[1]

With the exception of England and the Netherlands, the rise of national states in most of the European countries in the early modern age went hand in hand with the consolidation of royal absolutism. It was generally accepted that the king ruled not by permission of the people, but by divine right, and that all powers of government vested in the king himself.

This development of royal absolutism reached its zenith in the last half of the 17th century under Louis XIV, and France's standing in Europe at that time seemed to justify this. Under the successors of Louis XIV, absolutism, however, degenerated – internally into a form of tyranny, and externally into weakness and loss of prestige. No effective leadership could be exercised. In addition, the strict class system which characterized society meant favouritism of the first and second estates – the clergy and the nobility – over the less privileged or totally unprivileged third estate.

Although the king theoretically exercised absolute authority, in practice he had to rely on officials acting in his name. Even Louis XIV, the best example of an absolute king, could therefore not supervise the whole of his state administration, and the government of France under his slack successor, Louis XV (1715-1774), was, in fact, in the hands of the *conseil du roi*. This royal council consisted of about forty members and was subdivided into smaller councils, such as the council of state, the council of finance and trade, the war council and the council of despatches.

The central government had thirty *intendants* as provincial agents. As local representatives of the king, their authority was practically absolute, particularly in the provinces closest to Paris, called the *pays d'élections,* which had no local representative assemblies. In the remote provinces, called the *pays d'états,* local representative assemblies controlled by the nobility had a measure of authority.

The administration of government already displays the seeds of revolution, namely arbitrariness and confusion. In arrogant fashion the pleasure of the king or his privileged officials was the decisive factor, rather than the spirit or even the letter of the law. Government machinery was so unwieldy and complicated that confusion and delay were the order of the day.

This confusion was perhaps most noticeable in the administration of justice. Royal, feudal, municipal and ecclesiastical courts dispensed justice alongside of each other, a confusion exacerbated by the absence of a uniform code of laws. There were, in fact, on the eve of the Revolution, more than 300 codes in force. Many justice officials were extremely inept and corrupt. It is therefore not surprising that administration of justice was a confusing, expensive and time-consuming process and, moreover, that it paralysed control of the country's administration and caused general embitterment amongst those who were wronged.

The highest courts were the thirteen *parlements*. Of these, the *parlement* of Paris, which had existed since 1302 and frequently took the lead amongst the other twelve provincial *parlements*, was the oldest. Their judicial function aside, these courts also had the right to register all royal laws and decrees. This included the right of remonstrance and even the refusal to register any royal law. Although the king could enforce registration of legislation by means of a *lit de justice*, this right of the *parlements* was still a measure of limitation on royal absolutism. As the nobility manned and controlled the *parlements*, they were particularly careful in registering any new legislation aimed at curtailing their privileges.

The king had the right to withdraw any case from the customary courts and to have it heard by the royal council. In addition he could, in terms of a *lettre de cachet* (a warrant under the royal seal) have anyone locked up without giving reasons, and without a hearing or an opportunity for defence. The administration of justice, therefore, also showed a striking element of arbitrariness.

In the highly important sphere of finance, administration was equally characterized by confusion, arbitrariness and privilege. Direct and indirect taxes were raised. The *taille* was the basic direct tax of the French crown before the Revolution. This was the most oppressive tax for the third estate, the peasants in particular, but the clergy and the nobility (the first estate and the second estate) were exempt from it. To pay the *taille* was not only a financial burden but also a social affront. The *capitation* was a poll tax imposed according to income, and the *vingtième* or "twentieth" was originally a tax of 5 per cent on income. The privileged and influential groups such as the church, the nobility and certain associations of the bourgeoisie watered down these two taxes so effectively that they were practically exempted. They took the point of view, in fact, that, as they were not represented in central government, they were under no obligation to pay taxes, an attitude of "no representation, no tax". The *corvée* was a direct road tax in terms of which only the peasants had to provide labour and transport.

Occasionally the convocation of the church voted the government a *don gratuit*, but this was substantially lower than their fair share according to their wealth and property. What it really amounted to was that whatever the clergy and the nobility did not pay, also rested on the shoulders of the third estate.

Under such circumstances the monarchy depended heavily on indirect taxes. In principle all classes paid them, but as general consumer articles were taxed, the less wealthy sectors bore the burden. Indirect taxes included import tax and the *gabelle* or salt tax. The collection of these taxes was farmed out, that is to say, the government gave the right of tax collection to the highest bidder. The resulting collection therefore brought about anomalies and an arbitrary distribution of tax. Once again, the weak and the unprivileged bore the brunt. The nobility, the clergy and the rich bourgeoisie escaped lightly, while the pressure on the lower classes, the peasants and labourers, was unbearable and, in fact, exceeded their capabilities.

The division of society into three classes, namely the clergy, the nobility and the third estate was a heritage of the Middle Ages. This was a period in which the division corresponded to the division of labour or social obligations, but by the 18th century the first two (privileged) estates no longer fulfilled any particular obligations. Yet they still enjoyed all the privileges to which they had previously been entitled on the basis of their services to the community. This feudal division of society had, in fact, become unfair and illogical.

Out of a total population of about 23 000 000 there were probably no more than 130 000 priests, monks and nuns (the so-called first estate) and 400 000 nobles (the second estate). The remainder, at least 97 per cent of the population, made up the third estate.

The clergy enjoyed tremendous privileges and their influence extended far beyond what their small numbers would seem to indicate. The Roman Catholic church was responsible for the registration of births, deaths and marriages, and controlled poor-relief and education. It was, in fact, a self-governing institution, almost a state within a state, with its own administrative officials, own courts of law and an own representative assembly which, amongst other matters, determined the attitude of the church towards the monarchy.

The church was extremely wealthy. Its income was derived from its properties, numerous donations and levies, and the tithe which was levied on all harvest yields. It was not subject to the ordinary direct taxation, but in its stead, on its own authority, determined the "free donation" to the king mentioned previously.

The king had the right to appoint bishops and archbishops. These high offices in the church were consequently filled exclusively by the nobility, and ability or religious devotion hardly played a part. This circumstance contributed to the waning power of the church and engendered bitter criticism.

In reality members of the church were not a class, but members of a profession. Socially speaking they could be distinguished as the higher clergy, such as the bishops and abbots, and the lower clergy such as the priests and parish priests. These lower clergy were from the common people, amongst whom they worked. In general their exemplary life contrasted sharply with that of their superiors. They were poorly paid, and during the Revolution they were to make common cause with the third estate.

The nobility can be divided into two groups: the old medieval nobility, or the nobility of the sword *(noblesse d'épée)*, and the new nobility of the robe (*noblesse de robe*) which had obtained its titles by marriage or the purchase of administrative or judicial posts. Unlike the clergy, they were therefore not corporately united. As far as their financial status was concerned, the nobility ranged from the greatest wealth at the royal court at Versailles (at most 4 000 in number) to the greatest poverty on rural estates. Legally, however, they were united, and socially, in particular, they existed as a separate, privileged class. Their rights and privileges included, amongst other things, exemption from the most burdensome direct taxation, the *taille*, preferential tariffs for other taxes, the right to be tried by their own special courts, a monopoly of the highest offices in the administration of the state and offices in the church and military and diplomatic services, and the exclusive right to the traditional sports of hunting and fishing. Those living in royal favour were, moreover, in a position to wheedle numerous gifts and favours from the monarch for themselves and their friends.

The nobility was not satisfied with its privileged social and financial position, and strove for further privileges for itself. Politically it wanted to take over local government as well as participate in central government, as can be seen by the actions of the *parlements* detailed below. Furthermore, they wanted to extend certain of their manorial rights and privileges, increase the taxability of their properties and revive earlier privileges.

The ambitions and position of the nobility and the clergy must be viewed against the background of a centuries-old power struggle between the aristocracy – meaning the nobility as well as the clergy – and the French monarchy. Since the Middle Ages the aristocracy had been a stumbling block in the extension of the monarchy's powers, and it was really only in the 17th century, under Henry IV and particularly under Richelieu and Louis XIV, that the aristocracy was relatively effectively placed under the king's authority. Under Louis XIV it seemed as if the battle had been won: the aristocracy was subjected to direct taxation, and saw local government taken from its hands. The successors of Louis XIV did not, however, continue his work in this respect, and the aristocracy, by the end of the 18th century, had won back some of its earlier social privileges and had in mind a further strengthening of its social and political position. This would, naturally, cause a confrontation with the monarchy. Although the 18th century can be described as the period of the rise of the bourgeoisie and the triumph of "reason", it also saw, in the words of Lefebvre, the last offensive of the aristocracy.[2] And yet they held a privileged position in the social hierarchy.

The largest part of the population, the third estate, can basically be divided into three groups: the bourgeoisie or middle classes, the urban craftsmen and labourers, and the peasants.

The bourgeoisie represented about 10 per cent of the total population of France, or about half of the population in cities and towns. They owned about one-fifth of the land in the country, somewhat more than that belonging to the nobility.

The rise of the bourgeoisie must be ascribed to the rise and progress of capitalism, trade and industry in Europe since the 14th century. The bourgeoisie gained in strength through the voyages of exploration of the 15th and the 16th century and the resulting exploitation of the newly discovered lands, and also by supplying the monarchy with money and able officials. By the 18th century trade and industry were playing an important part in the national economy, and it was the bourgeoisie which kept the treasury going in times of crisis. They therefore took the side of the king in the last offensive mounted by the nobility to regain, or at least maintain, its privileges. Where the nobility and clergy were the social and legal superiors, the bourgeoisie possessed economic authority, its personal talents, and confidence in the future.

The bourgeoisie can be divided into a broad spectrum of classes. There was a higher bourgeoisie, consisting chiefly of the wealthy new business élite and government officials, a middle bourgeoisie of independent craftsmen, wealthy merchants, booksellers and printers, and members of the rapidly increasing "liberal" professions such as authors, scholars and lawyers, and the petite bourgeoisie – small shopkeepers and local merchants. It is often difficult to distinguish the latter group from the working class or lowest part of the populace, such as day-labourers, apprentices, clerks and domestic servants. This influenced the direction the revolution was to take, as the bourgeoisie was not averse to accepting the support of the lower classes rather than coming to an agreement with the aristocracy.

The bourgeoisie stood, however, in life-style and expectations, at a considerable remove from the working class. Their influential positions enabled them to avoid, at least partially, some of the heaviest taxes. Although they accepted the class division and the subdivisions in the third estate, they strove – somewhat paradoxically – for upward social mobility, for instance through marriage, the purchase of offices entailing the privileges of nobility, or the purchase of noble estates. The wealthy and educated bourgeoisie was therefore strongly opposed to the endeavours of the monarchy and the nobility to thwart its opportunities of social advancement. They demanded, in fact, that the social, legal and political privileges of the aristocracy be abolished. They read the *philosophes* and the economists, and prepared themselves for an onslaught on a system of government which discriminated against them unfairly and which, in addition, was wasteful and inefficient.

The craftsmen, retailers and urban labourers did not share in the wealth of the higher bourgeoisie. Their existence in general was poverty-stricken. The craftsmen were fast losing their independence and descending to the level of mere wage-earners. Industrial production was increasing and both the master craftsmen working for the guild masters and the labourers in the new capitalist industries worked long hours at low wages, with little prospect of improvement. When a crisis occurred, thousands were beggared. Their daily struggle consisted of warding off unemployment and hunger, and during the Revolution they were to play an active role in the popular insurrections.

Although trade and industry progressed well, France was still in the main an agricultural country, and four-fifths of the population were employed in soil and animal husbandry. Most of these were peasants.

Like the other groups, these peasants are difficult to see as an entity. Possibly about 25 per cent of them were tenant farmers, 50 per cent were share-croppers, 20 per cent were landless agricultural labourers and only five per cent were landowners. Serfdom had practically disappeared from France by the end of the 18th century, and a minimal percentage of the rural population consisted of serfs.[3]

It is not so easy, however, to determine the overall landownership of the peasants. The feudalism of the *ancien régime* still exerted too strong an influence. If the number of landowning peasants with the right to leave their land to their children is included who simultaneously had to pay all kinds of feudal taxes and levies to the church, to the nobility or the wealthy bourgeoisie, then the percentage of "landowners" amongst the peasants can be increased from 5 to more than 30 per cent.[4]

Even the small group of direct landowners found that they did not have enough land to guarantee subsistence. They then tilled additional property which they, like the share-croppers and tenants, had to lease, or on which they had to pay feudal taxes. Therefore their obligations to the state, the church and the manorial lord were an oppressive burden. Under these circumstances most peasants in times of prosperity barely managed to keep their heads above water. Times of crisis created a ready breeding-ground for revolt.

The conditions under which France's peasants lived were highly disadvantageous, but there is little doubt that they were better off than similar classes in certain parts of Germany, Italy, Spain, Ireland and England. The best proof is possibly that the number of famines and their intensity in the French rural areas decreased during the 18th century, that there was a slow increase in the population figures and that, during the last two governments before the Revolution, there were no serious insurrections amongst the peasants.

Yet dissatisfaction amongst them was growing, and would become an important factor in the Revolution. Primitive agricultural methods, famines and epidemics were partially responsible, but there were two reasons in particular for their dissatisfaction. These were the heavy taxation, which was levied so unfairly and took most of their income, and secondly, the oppressive and irritating obligations they had towards the landowners. This entailed obligations such as unpaid labour, tolls, and the exclusive hunting and fishing rights of the nobility, and the *banalités,* i.e., all grain had to be ground in the manorial mill, all wine pressed in the manorial winepress, and all bread baked in the manorial bakery at prices fixed by the lord.

The aspirations of the peasants were therefore simply ownership of more land, freedom from manorial obligations and limitations, a lower tax rate and continued market stability for their produce.

THE REFORM MOVEMENT UNDER THE *ANCIEN RÉGIME*

One can hardly explain the origin and course of the French Revolution without tracing the part played by the Enlightenment and the writings of the *philosophes* in it. These must be seen as long-term causes of the Revolution.

One of the most noticeable features of the Enlightenment was its harsh criticism of all existing institutions and its subjection to "reason" by a new kind of intellectual, the *philosophe*. (See also Chapter 9.) In many persuasive works, with heart-felt eloquence, the *philosophes* pilloried and condemned the abuses of the *ancien régime*. No institution or established view was spared. Confidence in the ability of man to change things for the best was the most important part of the belief. The result was that the social structure, the church and the government were exposed to continued and harsh criticism.

As the largest part of the French population was illiterate, the *philosophes* directed their propagandistic writings at the developed bourgeoisie. It was not difficult to persuade them to the cause. The bourgeoisie was receptive to the political and fiscal reforms which the *philosophes* championed, and to their defence of free enterprise. As a group, the bourgeoisie was sufficiently wealthy to strive for a continually improving dispensation and for greater privileges. The *philosophes* desired a society in which undeserved privilege would be abolished. This doctrine naturally appealed to the talented members of the middle and lower bourgeoisie, whose social mobility was thwarted at the outset because of their descent. As the revolutionary leaders were from the bourgeoisie, the influence of the *philosophes* cannot be underestimated.

Obviously the *philosophes* did not share the same opinions. The greatest exception was perhaps Jean Jacques Rousseau who exchanged rational thinking for human emotions or intuition as a guide towards exploring the truth. Voltaire, although on the one hand a champion of enlightened despotism through reason, was on the other devoted to the concept of the sovereignty of the people, and therefore of pure democracy. Yet the *philosophes* had one thing in common: their criticism of the abuses of the *ancien régime*.

The ideas spread by the *philosophes* undoubtedly gave direction to the Revolution and exercised an important influence on it. When their contemporary writings are analysed, it is clear that a number of theses and principles were accepted as virtually axiomatic. These theses are frequently repeated in the speeches of the revolutionary leaders and in the Declaration of the Rights of Man.

It is not true that, as is often believed, the *philosophes* in general strove for a political revolution. Most of them either pleaded for enlightened despotism, in which a strong central ruler governed the people to their greatest benefit, or a constitutional monarchy, in which the king governed according to a constitution drawn up by representatives of the people. They did demand that the monarchy should be "enlightened" and institute extensive reforms. These included civic freedom, equality or the abolition of aristocratic privileges, equal taxation, religious tolerance, a uniform and fair judicial system and the abolition of state monopolies. Social distinctions were only to be founded on public utility.

As they thought that "reason" should be purged of prejudice and superstition before it could be accepted as a guideline, most of the *philosophes*, with Voltaire in the vanguard, sharply attacked Christianity, and in particular Roman Catholicism, as if these were the greatest source of human confusion and befuddlement. In this manner the *philosophes* succeeded in undermining and destroying the bases of faith, religion and Christian morality. The result was frequently quite different from what the *philosophes* had in mind, because through their attacks on authority and tradition, the respect for absolute monarchy and the aristocracy was similarly undermined, and the way was prepared for the destruction of all traditional institutions in the course of the Revolution.

To what extent the *philosophes* were responsible for the Revolution remains an open question. One can state with certainty, however, that the defects and abuses of the *ancien régime,* and not the *philosophes*, were the chief cause of the radical change. As Ergang rightly puts it, these defects and abuses were so clear that no *philosophes* were required to point them out. [5] While we cannot blandly contend that there would have been a revolution without them, it can be asserted that, with them, it was to take a somewhat different course.

From the foregoing it is clear that in the years preceding the Revolution there was a certain collective mentality active in France; one might almost call it a pre-revolutionary mentality. On the one hand, the *philosophes* were responsible for it, and on the other, the successful American Revolution should be duly acknowledged. The struggle for independence of the British colonies in America from their motherland gripped the imagination of the French public from the outset. The *philosophes* and their followers were enthusiastic about the American Declaration of Independence and in particular about its claim to the "natural rights of man". This mentality was not confined to the bourgeoisie. Members of the French aristocracy, who were to become the leaders of the liberal elements during the first phase of the French Revolution, served as officers in the American army. Possibly more important than the relatively small officers' corps was the rest of the 18 000 French veterans who assisted the colonies. They returned to their fatherland as followers of liberty and critics of the existing government of France after they had seen how the common man in America was a free tenant on his land and enjoyed his prosperity and freedom. Various historians contend, in fact, that in those areas in France where there was a geographical concentration of these French veterans from the American Revolution, the beginning of the French Revolution was more radical than elsewhere. [6]

Whatever influence the American Revolution may have had on the mentality of its French participants, the most important point is surely the fact that France's participation dramatically doubled the French royal debt. This brings the state of the French economy into focus, an aspect which is open to various interpretations.

It must be an accepted point of departure that the economy of France experienced a period of steady growth in the half-century before the Revolution. This is proved by the increasing industrial output of the period, the expansion of foreign trade and the increasing prosperity of the merchant class or the higher and middle bourgeoisie. This favourable circumstance must not, however, be over-emphasized.

There were three extremely important deficiencies which totally overshadowed the positive influence of this prosperity and which would finally determine the course of events. [7]

The first deficiency was that the prosperity was not equally shared. The prosperity of the merchant class was, to some extent, shared by the aristocracy who, as landowners, benefited by the rise in food prices in the years before the Revolution. This rise was largely an effect of the population growth from the middle of the 18th century onwards. The problem was therefore that prosperity did not extend to all layers of society. As wages did not nearly keep abreast of price rises, artisans and wage-earners lost purchasing power. The peasants were as badly off, if not worse. Although more than 30 per cent of the land in France belonged to them, they did not benefit from the rise in food prices because individual plots of land were too small to produce enough to send anything to market after the family had been fed, the church paid and the feudal obligations and taxes imposed by the monarchy and the manorial lord had been absolved. As the purchasing power of the masses was so drastically reduced, it was out of the question that taxes, and indirect taxes in particular, would yield sufficient income for the monarchy.

The second deficiency was that the general expansion of the French economy since the 1730s was interrupted by periodic economic crises which hit the unprivileged the hardest. In particular, it was the crop failures and consequent crises of the years 1787 to 1789 which led to food shortages, corresponding sharp rises in prices, a decrease in textile production and widespread unemployment in cities. The misery which resulted in the cities as well as in rural areas from these short-term economic crises and crop failures created an explosive situation which could be ignited by unpopular political decisions. [8]

The third deficiency in the French economy was the financial crisis in which the monarchy had found itself since Louis XIV (1643-1715). A clear differentiation has to be made between the finances of the monarchy on the one hand, and those of the French population – and more specifically of the privileged groups – on the other. The annual revenues of the crown were not nearly sufficient to its needs. The deficit and the current debt increased every year. Waste and extravagance at the royal court, increased costs of living and new administrative responsibilities contributed only a small amount to this deficit. It was France's aggressive foreign policy in particular which set the country on its road to bankruptcy. The wars were continued after Louis XIV. Between 1733 and 1783 France waged four wars which cost, in total, about 4 000 000 *livres*. All the major wars were financed by enormous loans, until the interest on the debt amounted to more than half of the royal expenses by 1788. [9] It was, as shown above, particularly France's participation in the American Revolution which was the last straw by doubling the crown debt. This was probably the most important factor to lead to the final fiscal and economic crisis of the French monarchy in the 18th century.

In March 1788 Calonne, the French comptroller-general, submitted the first and, as it happened, the last budget of the *ancien régime:* expenditure was estimated at 629 000 000 *livres* and income at 503 000 000 – a deficit of 126 000 000. The actual expenditure and income for the ensuing year are not known, but the deficit must have been even larger than anticipated, for the economic crisis of 1788 must have decreased income and increased expenditure. Grain even had to be imported from abroad. Whatever the facts were, the deficit could not, as in the past, simply be written off, as the *parlements*, and in particular, the financial classes (the higher and middle bourgeoisie) would refuse any further support of the treasury. This is, by the way, an indication of the large influence which the bourgeoisie already wielded. It was out of the question to finance the deficit by increasing the existing taxes. The purchasing power of the tax-payers, particularly that of the masses, had already shrunk by too much.

As the cost of leasing land had risen by 98 per cent, and in comparison, prices by only 65 per cent,[10] peasants were at a further disadvantage, while the aristocracy, landowners on a large scale and exempted from most of the taxes, gained most of the advantage. It amounted to the fact that, the richer people were under the *ancien régime,* the less they paid.

From the foregoing it is clear that financial chaos in France was due not only to the lack of a proper financial system, but also to the combination of a medieval social structure based on differentiation between classes and the absence of effective judicial and administrative systems. Effective financial reform in France would therefore of necessity entail changes which amounted to a social and political revolution. Privilege was so interwoven with the social contract (or the medieval agreement of mutual obligations between the nobility and the peasant), and the higher social classes were so closely identified with special favours that the king, with the best will in the world and even with the most absolute authority at his disposal, could hardly have solved the problem. How did Louis XVI fare?

If France had ever had need of a great king, it was in 1774 on the death of Louis XV, who wore the crown for sixty years in a profligate, irresponsible and extravagant manner. His successor, Louis XVI, was a man of moral behaviour (which cannot be said of his queen, Marie Antoinette), a man who took his duties seriously and who was honest, benevolent and religious without being intolerant. He really wanted to improve the lot of his subjects, and tempered the expenses of his court. But these virtues were quite overshadowed by the inability of Louis, as absolute monarch, to govern a country as large as France, with is enormous social, political and economic problems – problems which, moreover, threatened to come to a head simultaneously. His serious character defects included, amongst others, a slowness of grasp, indecision and a lack of self-confidence, and consequently an inability to pursue a determined course.

In his fervour to institute reforms Louis appointed able ministers. But as he was easily influenced by his wife, his family and the court circle which saw its privileges threatened, he withdrew his support from his ministers at critical moments. Thus he only impressed the people more clearly with the need for reform and his inability to bring it about.

His queen, Marie Antoinette of Austria, was highly unpopular. She was the symbol of the hated Austrian alliance which had, with the Seven Years War, cost France its colonial empire in India and America. Marie Antoinette did not understand the French and, possibly more important, she did not understand the needs of

Execution of Louis XVI in 1793.

Napoleon as Emperor. Portrait by Ingres.

the time, and therefore frequently exercised a wrong or harmful influence on her husband. Louis's closest kinsmen, his two brothers, the count of Provence and the count of Artois, and his nephew Philip – the later duke of Orléans who was also known as Philip Egalité – were frivolous and irresponsible. Together with the queen, they frequently had a detrimental effect on Louis's decisions.

The Revolution cannot simply be ascribed to the king and his court. Yet the personalities of the royal pair can be described as one of the immediate causes of the Revolution. A strong and able ruler, such as Henry IV or even Louis XIV, could possibly have controlled the course of events and channelled the forces of reform correctly and safely.

At the beginning of his reign Louis XVI had raised great hopes. He had begun by re-instituting the *parlements* which his father had abolished. It was a very popular measure, but unwise, for these *parlements*, controlled by the nobility, soon proved to be one of the greatest stumbling blocks on the road to essential reforms.

The most pressing issue was undoubtedly the chaos in financial administration. Louis immediately appointed the able and popular intendant, Turgot, as comptroller-general of finance. Turgot began by introducing thrift at the royal court and abolishing thousands of useless posts. Next he removed abuses in the collection of taxes, abolished the *corvée*, and replaced it by increasing the *vingtième*. Although the nobility and clergy were practically exempt from these taxes, it was still an attempt to impair their privileged position. Turgot encouraged agriculture, and endeavoured to bring about a decrease in food prices by instituting free trade in grain and wine.

Turgot succeeded in decreasing the deficits and restoring France's credit-worthiness within two years. But everybody whose privileges or vested interests had been detrimentally affected by his measures was mobilizing their powers against him. The *parlements* were in the forefront, as they had the right to register governmental measures. If they refused, they could be forced to do so only by a royal *lit de justice*. Once they had won the support of Marie Antoinette, Louis gave way to pressure and dismissed Turgot in 1776, at the same time revoking his reform measures. Had Turgot been allowed enough time and been given sufficient support, he could possibly have solved the problems of the royal exchequer. But he realized himself that the chances of continued political support for his extensive reform measures were rather slim.

Towards the middle of 1777 Louis appointed Necker, a Genevan banker and a Protestant, as director-general of finance. Necker made a determined effort to strengthen the royal treasury's control of finances. When he took office, the annual deficit was 24 000 000 *livres*, and, like Turgot, Necker attempted to cancel this by purely financial reform measures. This included economizing at court, decreasing royal gifts and abolishing useless posts. A further step was the introduction of provincial assemblies with advisory powers in four provinces. As the third estate made up half of the members, however, the nobility and the clergy opposed these institutions.

Necker's measures decreased the usual state expenditures substantially, but France's participation in the American Revolution entailed enormous new expenses. To finance the war effort, Necker took up large loans. In his five years in office, in fact, he borrowed 530 000 000 *livres*, thereby undoubtedly setting France on the road to bankruptcy.

Although he was widely popular, some members of the higher clergy and the nobility began to plot against Necker. The king's prime minister, Maurepas, was also keen to get rid of him. In an attempt to regain some of his lost prestige, Necker obtained the king's permission in 1781 to publish a financial report, the well-known *compte rendu*. This report, for the first time, lifted the veil of secrecy under which financial administration had always been hidden. The relieved French public was highly satisfied, but the report unfortunately sketched an incorrect picture of the financial position. It is true that deficiencies were pointed out, but Necker, in a hitherto unheard-of phenomenon in 18th century France, showed a financial surplus of 10 000 000 *livres* instead of admitting to a deficit of 46 000 000. The immediate result was the procurement of a new loan. In this manner he only created problems for his successors, for if he could show a surplus in time of war, it would be difficult to understand a growing deficit in peacetime. Necker's enemies exerted more pressure, and he tendered his resignation in the same year. He left the country's finances in a worse state than when he took office.

In 1783 Louis appointed Calonne, an intendant of Lille, as comptroller-general. In his three years of office Calonne was to contribute, more than anyone else, to the hastening of the advent of the Revolution. The basis of his administration was the peculiar notion that the government should create a pretence of prosperity by spending money freely and thus re-establishing its creditworthiness. In this he was temporarily successful. His enthusiasm was catching, and he was able to borrow large amounts of money which were lavishly spent. At court it was a period of prosperity, and even the masses benefited by the construction of public works.

By 1786, however, he had run out of gunpowder: the annual deficit amounted to 112 000 000 *livres*, and no banker was prepared to grant any further loans. The only solution was new taxes. Calonne realized that successful tax reform would have to go hand in with political and administrative change. When he therefore proposed a new, general land tax, from which no one would be exempt, to replace the *vingtième*, he meant it to be administered by provincial assemblies. It is important to note that their members were to be elected by landowners, without differentiation between the three estates, and that the chairman could be from the third estate. Furthermore, he counted on extending stamp duties with the effect that these, like the envisaged land tax, would be borne chiefly by the privileged and wealthier classes. Simultaneously, he intended easing the burden of the lower classes by commuting the *corvée,* abolishing the *gabelle* and decreasing the *taille.*

Although the nobility would continue to be exempt from the *taille*, and the clergy from the *capitation*, and both from the *corvée,* Calonne's envisaged reforms were decidedly revolutionary. They entailed an abolition of privilege and a large-scale dismantling of the structure of the *ancien régime.*

Calonne held no illusions about the reception his proposals would receive from the *parlements* controlled by the nobility. Had he been able to depend on Louis XVI, he could possibly have challenged them openly to register his proposals as legislation. Instead, he persuaded the king to revive an old custom and to call an assembly of 144 "notables" to approve his tax and reform measures. This Assembly of Notables would consist of the aristocracy – members of the nobility and the clergy. Meanwhile, demands were made that the old Estates-General, which had last met in 1614, should be assembled to solve the problems.

The Assembly of Notables met on the 22nd February 1787. In effect it was the first capitulation of the *ancien régime*. The king was consulting the aristocracy, rather than informing them of his wishes. The manner in which the aristocracy reacted, was the beginning of the pre-revolution or revolution of the aristocracy.

Calonne had hoped that his personal nomination of the members of the Assembly would influence the course of events, and that patriotism would take precedence over class interests. It was a dire miscalculation. He had been over-confident of the king's support, and also failed to load the Assembly with his supporters. It was soon obvious that his enemies, led by De Brienne, the archbishop of Toulouse, dominated the Assembly. De Brienne was in no mood at all to approve Calonne's proposals. The problem of the measures was their disregard of privileged status and social precedence in the envisaged new, elected provincial assemblies. This would rob the aristocracy of the opportunity of exerting the same dominating influence in the local government of the *pays d'élection* (the provinces near Paris), as they were already exercising in the *pays d'état* (the remoter provinces). When Louis realized that Calonne was making no headway with the Assembly of Notables, he dismissed him on the 8th April 1787.

The fall of Calonne was a triumph for the aristocracy. It was an indication that reform was possible only if efficient financial control were given to the aristocracy, and if their political ideals enjoyed attention. De Brienne, Calonne's successor, soon found that the success of the notables incited them to such an extent that they increased their political demands and that their willingness to compromise was destroyed. They refused all co-operation, and De Brienne was forced to dissolve the Assembly on the 25th May 1787. The monarchy therefore suffered a substantial reverse at the hands of the aristocracy. The financial problems were still no nearer any solution, and it now depended on whether De Brienne could persuade the *parlement* of Paris – or intimidate it – to accept his views.

De Brienne experienced no problems from the *parlement* with reform measures such as the commutation of the *corvée* and the institution of provincial assemblies, for the magistrates, although basically conservative, had begun to woo the common people at the cost of the monarchy. The *parlement* refused, however, to register the land tax and stamp duties. This left De Brienne no choice. He had to enforce these tax measures on the 6th August by employing a *lit de justice*. The *parlement* declared it null and void, whereupon the king banned its members to Troyes.

Without money, and with public opinion squarely behind the *parlement* and against the crown, Louis was soon obliged to reinstate the *parlement* in its functions and to withdraw the tax edicts. The opposition of the *parlement*, however, continued, and the magistrates directly attacked the concept of royal absolutism in a petition of protest. Circumstances became so untenable that Louis decided on the 8th May 1788 to deprive the *parlement* of its right of registration, offering instead much-needed judicial reforms. The most important aspect of the reform programme was the creation of a new judiciary, the *Cour Plénière,* which was nominated and paid by the crown and would have the sole right of registration. Provincial *parlements* would in future have to limit themselves only to the administration of justice.

The establishment of the *Cour Plénière* met with considerable opposition. The magistrates of the *parlements* held it up as an attack on "provincial freedoms" and as a royal pretext to avoid or delay the assembly of the Estates-General. The people, who at this stage still regarded the conservative, aristocratic *parlements* as the champions of the national interest, resisted the edicts which abolished the right of registration in various provinces. This was the so-called May riots. In the hurly-burly the cry for "liberty" was often heard. It was uttered in defence of the local rights and privileges of the *parlements* and other local representative assemblies. What they strove for was freedom in the sense of release from "ministerial despotism".

Although there had been little bloodshed in the May riots, the situation in the provinces had clearly got out of hand. The monarchy could not rely on military discipline, and its executive power appeared to be impotent. The king treated the revolt with remarkable leniency and revoked the May edicts. Encouraged by this success, the three estates of Grenoble took it upon themselves to revive the old provincial assembly. It was decided that the third estate would have as many representatives as the first and second put together, and that they would all deliberate and vote together. This was nothing less than revolt, and the king sent troops under General De Vaux to bring it to an end.

De Vaux found public opinion so unanimous and determined, however, that he gave the assembly permission to meet. It then demanded the abolition of the *lettres de cachet*, as well as the convocation of the Estates-General to solve the financial and other deadlocked issues.

Louis XVI gave way to the pressure. He recalled Necker as director-general of finance, and ruled that the Estates-General should meet at Versailles in May 1789. This opened the way to something which very few members of the *parlements* could have foreseen: a revolutionary change in French society. In fact – but this was not clearly realized – the French people were now to be consulted on their desires.

The *parlement* of Paris now showed its true colours as mouthpiece of the aristocracy. At the registration of the edict summoning the Estates-General, it set the condition that the assembly was to take place like the previous one in 1614, namely that the estates were to deliberate separately and vote according to estate. This would ensure the continued majority of the two privileged estates, rendering any drastic reforms impossible.

In this, the *parlement* failed to appreciate the social and economic development which the bourgeoisie and even the masses had undergone in the previous 150 years. The popularity of the *parlement* evaporated overnight, and the bourgeoisie, which had been its partner in the struggle against royal absolutism, broke away from it. A radical regrouping of forces followed. The bourgeoisie, also called "patriots" or "nationals", was reinforced by a small group of supporters from the liberal wing of the *parlement*, and they formed the Committee of Thirty to launch political actions. This included influential leaders such as Lafayette, Mirabeau, Talleyrand, Condorcet and the abbot, Siéyès.

On the eve of the first meeting of the Estates-General the Revolution had therefore started to undergo a change in character. The aristocracy had overshot its mark. They had begun the struggle against royal absolutism in the name of the people, but in the determination of ruling the people from above and not to be ruled themselves. The consequence was that they had simultaneously undermined the monarchy, on which they depended for their privileges, and had woken the bourgeoisie, by whom they were detested. The future was in the hands of the bourgeoisie.

The decision to summon the Estates-General precipitated heated discussions about the manner in which the three estates should be represented. The higher clergy and the majority of the nobility, which desired only to break the deadlock of 1788, maintaining the social privileges of the *ancien régime,* welcomed the proposal that the representatives of the different estates should meet and vote separately, as in 1614. The patriots, who demanded total political and social reform were, however, dismayed, and began to agitate for a more liberal adjustment of the Estates-General to the exigencies of the times. They demanded double representation for the third estate, in other words, as many representatives as the other two estates put together, joint sessions and voting by head count instead of by estate. Should voting be by estate, chances were that the two privileged estates would close ranks against the third, and defeat it by two votes to one. In a vote by head count, however, the third estate, with doubled representation, would have an excellent chance of gaining victory for its ideas.

The government agreed to the doubling of the third estate, but did not solve the question of procedure. Louis, and in particular Necker who had been entrusted with the organization, failed in remarkably short-sighted manner to direct the course of events. With no political experience to fall back on, a large assembly would have had to feel its way. This gave the more radical reformers the opportunity to realize their aims.

A direct result was the avalanche of pamphlets which made their appearance in the winter of 1788-1789. They contained three basic tenets: a declaration of human rights, the concept of national sovereignty and the necessity of providing France with a constitution. In his famous pamphlet *What is the third estate?* Siéyès came to the conclusion that the French people should be identified exclusively with the third estate, and that only this estate could provide the country with a constitution. These basic thoughts, which were to influence the course and character of the events unambiguously, were, in effect, the answer of the third estate to the political ambitions and social privileges of the first two estates.

Early in 1789 millions of Frenchmen went to the polls to elect their representatives to the Estates-General. The privileged estates elected their representatives directly on the basis of general male franchise. Elections for the third estate were more complicated. Virtually all male citizens of twenty five years and older who were on the tax roll had the vote. The elections were, however, indirect, in other words, there were three or four rounds, and with every one a certain percentage of the voters fell away until only a nucleus had the final vote.

Altogether 1 201 members were elected to the Estates-General: 300 clergy, 291 members of the nobility and 610 of the third estate. The greatest majority of the clergy were parish priests whose sympathies lay with the third estate. Ninety of the nobles were liberals who had participated in the American Revolution, while the rest of the representatives of the nobility were traditional and conservative landowners who would not easily make concessions to the third estate. The representatives of the third estate were the liberal bourgeois lawyers whose background enabled them to act as spokesmen for the masses. Some individuals from the privileged classes were elected as representatives of the third estate, such as Siéyès and Mirabeau.

The king had no intention of relinquishing his legislative authority. According to him, the Estates-General should meet merely to act as an advisory and money granting assembly, as before 1614. The three estates were therefore requested to put their grievances and desires in writing for submission to him.

These memorials or *cahiers* are a good indication of the grievances and proposals of the various estates in 1789. On the one hand, there was a surprising amount of unanimity between the three estates. All were in favour of retaining a hereditary monarchy, disapproved of royal and ministerial despotism, and desired a constitution which would guarantee the rights of the individual. It would mean a constitutional monarchy, in which the king would act as executive officer. The *cahiers* requested that the constitution should place matters such as taxation and new legislation in the hands of the Estates-General, which should meet periodically. Furthermore, there should be decentralization by giving the provincial assemblies administrative tasks.

On the other hand, the *cahiers* of the clergy and the nobility show that the privileged classes were only prepared to relinquish their tax privileges under certain conditions and that they had not yet agreed to accept social and political equality with the third estate. The third estate, however, insisted on equality. Consequently, the first two estates wanted to maintain the class differentiation in the Estates-General, with separate sessions and voting by estate, while the third estate wanted joint sessions and vote by head count. Although they all demanded legal reform, it was the third estate which went the furthest: they wanted ready access to the courts for everyone, simplification of court procedure, abolition of the sale of judicial posts, appointment of judges for life, the replacement of fees by salaries and the abolition of manorial courts. As far as the church was concerned, the clergy, although they were willing to pay taxes, wanted to preserve the corporate structure of the first estate. They also wanted to retain church control of education, poor relief and registration of births, deaths and marriages. The nobility was somewhat more tolerant in religious matters, but the *cahiers* of the third estate indicated to what extent the church had lost the respect and goodwill of the people. They demanded religious freedom, a decrease of the tithe, and even state control of the church. There were also large differences in the approach to the agrarian system. Where the nobility and church wanted to see all feudal privileges retained, the third estate demanded the abolition of all these irritating measures.

In summary it can be said that the Revolution was, above all, a striving for equal rights.

These were the circumstances under which the formal opening of the Estates-General took place on the 5th May 1789. Without any firm guidance from the government, the assembly was immediately embroiled in the issue of procedure. Amongst others, Necker delivered himself of a long speech in which he proposed that the custom of voting according to estate should provisionally be retained. This left the impression that change in the future was a possibility. This was confusing enough, but Necker had made no mention of any constitutional change.

The third estate followed by insisting on joint sessions and joint voting. The nobility and the clergy, however, went away to meet on their own, and therefore initiated a policy of no compromise. The delay this caused sowed the seed for future confusion and discord.

On the 10th June the third estate, under the leadership of Siéyès, issued a formal "invitation" to the other two estates to hand in their letters of accreditation jointly as representatives of the people. The invitation was not heeded.

When all efforts to persuade the privileged estates to accept their point of view had failed, the representatives of the third estate (that is, the bourgeoisie) decided to assume full powers. After some parish priests had joined them, they decided on the 17th June 1789, by 489 votes against 89, to call themselves the National Assembly. This was a decisive moment in the struggle between the three estates, for it was clear that the initiative which the nobility had previously held had now fallen into the hands of the bourgeoisie. It was now no longer the aristocracy involved in a struggle with the king, but the bourgeoisie in confrontation with the privileged classes. The revolution of the bourgeoisie took place without the use of violence. Thus the convention of the Estates-General had provided them with a platform for further action. They now appropriated overall national authority for themselves. Previously, the assembly had arrived at "decisions", but now, for the first time, it issued "decrees", and also appropriated the right to revise the constitution without the king's permission. [11]

The National Assembly declared all existing taxes illegal, but ordered tax-payers to continue paying until the National Assembly was to be dissolved. In this way they wanted to prevent the king from collecting taxes, should he dissolve the National Assembly before its work was completed.

Disconcerted by events, Louis XVI approved Necker's proposal that a royal session be held on the 23rd June to reach a compromise. The assembly hall of the National Assembly had to be spruced up for the occasion. With the characteristic lack of consideration shown on numerous occasions to the third estate, no formal notice was given of the closing of the hall. When the members of the Assembly arrived on the 20th June, they found the hall locked. Their immediate fear was that Louis was planning to dissolve the National Assembly. Acting on the proposal of Dr Guillotin, they adjourned to a nearby building which was used as a tennis court, and there took a solemn oath not to part until they had provided France with a constitution.

It now depended on Louis whether the issue could be resolved, but he was not up to the task. At the royal session he declared that the differentiation between estates was to be maintained. Joint sessions could take place, subject to mutual agreement and royal approval, but discussions of the feudal rights of the nobility and the clergy, or the constitution of the Estates-General, were expressly excluded from joint sessions. In addition, the king declared the events of the 17th and the 20th June illegal. In reply to their decisions, he then had his programme of reform read out: abolition of all exemption from taxation, no new taxes or loans without permission of the Estates-General, annual reports of income and expenditure, provincial assemblies of the estates, the abolition of *lettres de cachet*, and conditional freedom of the press.

Although the king had solved the political problem in principle by his willingness to accept a constitutional monarchy, he attempted to protect the socially privileged classes by ordering the three estates to meet separately. This was the ultimatum of the *ancien régime*. By choosing to side with the privileged, the king missed the opportunity of leading the Revolution himself.

When the king left the hall, most of the nobility and some of the clergy followed him. The others defiantly remained seated, and when they were reminded of the king's order, Mirabeau answered that they were there on the instructions of the people and would not leave except by force of the bayonet. This was the ultimatum of the new *régime*.

The king took no steps to enforce his will. Gradually the other members of the nobility and the clergy joined the delegates in the hall. By the 2nd July 1789 the National Assembly was fully attended. The Estates-General was something of the past. A new era had begun.

THE NATIONAL ASSEMBLY, 1789-1791

With the crop failures of 1788-1789 and the resultant rise in prices, the misery and restlessness of the populace in cities and rural areas increased. There was a growing fear of a conspiracy by the aristocracy. In the midst of these threatening circumstances, and under the influence of the court circle, Louis had already on the 26th June begun to concentrate troops, in particular mercenaries from Germany and Switzerland, at Versailles and around Paris. The next day he was informed from the capital that a mob of 30 000 would storm the palace if he did not order the amalgamation of the estates by royal decree. He immediately gave way to this demand. The peaceful revolution of the bourgeoisie was therefore promoted by the threat of the masses.

In reality Louis was paying only temporary heed to the storm. The rumour quickly spread that his troop concentrations were meant to thwart the victory of the National Assembly and to enforce the announcements made at the royal session. By the beginning of July it was clear that violence was to determine the future of the Revolution. The deputies of the third estate became apprehensive and unleashed country-wide agitation. The most intense reaction came from Paris, where the situation was already dangerous. Fearing that the soldiers would dissolve the National Assembly by force, the members made representations to the king. The Parisian working class and the lower bourgeoisie were, in turn, apprehensive that the soldiers would suppress their demonstrations and make them pay for their part in the agitation against unemployment and the rapidly rising price of bread. Unemployed and starving people from all parts of the country were beginning to throng together in the capital. Criminal elements were strong and active, and created a condition of unrest.

All this constituted fertile soil for revolutionary propaganda. Scores of extremist pamphlets appeared daily, and people such as Desmoulins and the duke of Orléans – who himself aspired to the throne – incited the people to resistance. As the newspapers remained silent, there would have been few sources of information in the provinces if no information agencies had been formed. Members of the National Assembly kept officials throughout France abreast of developments. Their letters were read to the populace in public, which gathered from all over at the stations of the mailcoaches.

The power behind the rebellious movements throughout the Revolution was the lower bourgeoisie – the artisans and supervisors of workshops, and small merchants. Day-labourers and other workers ranged themselves behind them, not as a separate class, but as allies in oppression.

The mob could not, however, have been driven to revolution if it had not been for the economic crisis which made life unbearable. The poor crops of 1788 not only caused incessant rises in prices between August 1788 and July 1789, but also drastically reduced the purchasing power of the people and hampered international trade. Unemployment was therefore rife at the precise moment when the cost of living was rocketing. Lefebvre quite justifiably asks: "How can anyone fail to suspect a connection between this ordeal and the fever of insurrection that gripped the population at the time?" [12]

When the dismissal of the popular Necker on the 11th July became known in Paris the following day, riots broke out. The police force was quite inadequate, and the sympathies of the French Guard lay with the people. The mob plundered shops, broke open gaols, and finally stormed the Bastille on the 14th July to obtain arms. The French Guard played along, and after a half-hearted defence by the garrison on duty, the Bastille was won. The first blood had flowed.

There was an attempt to combat the riots. The municipal government of Paris, controlled by the nobility, collapsed, whereupon the bourgeoisie established its own city council, the Commune of Paris, and the National Guard, under Lafayette. Other cities followed the example of Paris. This so-called communal revolution in France replaced the old administration everywhere with administration by the bourgeoisie.

Even before the fall of the Bastille, large-scale riots also occurred in rural areas. News of the fall gave the movement added momentum. Particularly when it was rumoured that the frightened aristocracy was inciting "brigands" to attack the peasants, a panic, known as the Great Fear, befell France. The Great Fear finally subsided, but not before the peasants, armed against non-existent brigands, had wreaked their vengeance on the hated aristocracy. Castles and manors were attacked and there was large-scale looting.

Meanwhile the king had been forced to send away the troops, and to recall

Necker. On the 17th July Louis visited Paris, where he recognized the new city council and the National Guard, and placed the new tricolour *cocarde*, the emblem of the revolutionary government, on his head.

When reports of the riots reached the National Assembly at Versailles, mixed feelings of enthusiasm and fear seized the members. In the dramatic session of the 4th August 1789, one member after another of the nobility and of the higher clergy rose to voluntarily renounce his feudal rights. It was, quite obviously, a decisive moment in the Revolution. These decisions were embodied in the August Edicts, which abolished the old feudal rights, partly with and partly without compensation. In this manner a great social revolution was brought about almost overnight.

A number of members of the nobility and the court circle, who feared for their lives, went into exile. They were the first of the émigrés, to be followed by many more in the course of the Revolution.

The preceding events freed the National Assembly of any fear of reactionary or violent steps by the court circle. As the communes and the detachments of the local National Guard were, in any case, restoring order in rural areas, the National Assembly could continue its reform programme for France. On the 26th August 1789 the foundation for a new government was laid by the approval of the Declaration of the Rights of Man. The first clause begins with the words: "Men are born free and remain free and equal in their rights." In essence, this summarized the achievements of the Revolution to date. The rest of the declaration is merely an extension of this statement. It laid down fundamental principles such as social equality, sovereignty of the people, civic freedom, sovereignty of law, religious freedom and the freedom of the press, equality of taxation and the division of powers.

Order returned to France. Louis's vacillating attitude, however, cast suspicion on him, and the fear arose that he would leave for the provinces and try to annul the work of the Revolution. He was led by the nose by his advisors, and delayed approval of the Declaration of the Rights of Man and the clauses which revoked feudal rights. As the National Assembly had cornered him on these issues, he ordered a detachment of his Flemish regiment to march to Versailles.

The Parisian mob, already suffering from the scarcity of bread and increasing unemployment, were further incited by reports that the Flemish regiment had trod the Tricolour underfoot in the palace. On the 5th October hundreds of Parisian women walked to the palace in a procession, and forced the royal family to return to Paris with them. In his palace in Paris, the Tuileries, the king would henceforth be a virtual prisoner. Ten days later the National Assembly followed him to the capital.

With their immediate future safeguarded, the members of the Assembly continued their work of creating a constitution for France according to the principles in the Declaration of the Rights of Man. In the two years it took to complete the constitution, the *ancien régime* in France was overthrown and revolutionary changes occurred in the constitutional, economic, social and religious spheres. Never before had old institutions been so totally destroyed to make way for new ones.

Political parties in the modern sense were non-existent in the National Assembly, but the deputies soon showed a tendency towards separating into groups. They sat in a semi-circle around the chairman, and so the concepts of "left", "centre" and "right" originated to indicate political groupings. The advocates of the *ancien régime* took their places at the extreme right. These were the court nobility, the *noblesse de robe* and the higher clergy. They had extensive contact with counter-revolutionaries inside and outside France. In the centre to the right sat those members of the nobility who sympathized with the reform movement, but who thought that the Revolution had gone far enough. They wanted a constitution modelled on that in England. At left centre were such outspoken reformers as Mirabeau, who desired reform of the obsolete social order, but simultaneously wanted to retain strong royal authority. They called themselves the patriots, and formed the majority in the National Assembly. Directly to their left the outspoken revolutionaries took their places, those who wanted to construct a constitution on democratic principles. At the far left wing there was a group of radicals, people such as Robespierre, who strove for a total social and political revolution on the principles of Rousseau's theories.

Outside the Assembly, the groupings inside were supported with action programmes by newspapers and clubs. The Jacobin Club in particular, with a network of branches throughout France, had the most influence. The cream of the bourgeoisie was represented in this leftist pressure group. The labourers outside the Assembly initially accepted the lead of their bourgeois representatives, but they, too, soon had their own leaders, societies and daily newspapers, and an action programme which was more democratic than that of the patriots inside the Assembly, or of the Jacobins outside.

The changes wrought by the National Assembly covered a wide field. Most important was the abolition of the feudal system, embodied in the so-called August Edicts of 1789. Serfdom, tithes, the *corvée*, the exclusive hunting and fishing rights of the nobility, and the manorial rights were all abolished, with or without compensation. The principle of equal taxation was announced, the sale of judicial and municipal offices prohibited, and all citizens without discrimination had access to all offices.

As far as legal and administrative reforms were concerned, the royal courts, including the *parlements*, were abolished. A new system of regional authority began to take shape. In an attempt to break down deeply rooted provincialism and to obtain uniformity, the Assembly did away with the old provinces and divided the whole country into eighty three "departments" of more or less equal size. Each department was subdivided into districts and cantons, which in turn included communes or municipalities. A new system of local government was also introduced and adapted to this regional division. Elected councils in the communes, districts and departments replaced the intendants and provincial assemblies of the estates.

The ecclesiastic measures of the National Assembly were indicative of the dismantling of traditional authority which characterized the revolutionary period. The August Edicts abolished the tithes payable to the church, without compensation. To ward off bankruptcy, the Assembly shortly afterwards seized church property and issued paper money (*assignats*) to serve as security. The next step was to dissolve most of the monasteries. Ultimately the whole ecclesiastic system was reorganized by the so-called Civil Constitution of the Clergy, which was proclaimed on the 24th August 1790. It did not change any religious dogma, but purely coordinated the administration of the church with the new civil administration. First, the old number of 135 bishoprics was decreased to eighty three, corresponding to the number of new departments. Second, priests and bishops would henceforth be elected, which meant that non-Roman Catholics and apostates would be able to vote. Further, the clergy became paid state officials. Fourth, the ties between the French bishops and the pope of before 1789 were broken by forbidding the clergy (and all French people) to recognize the authority of the pope. All clergy had to take an oath of loyalty to the new constitution.

This new measure had far-reaching consequences. Not only was it rejected by Pope Pius VI, but more than half of the clergy (most of the bishops and the majority of parish priests) refused to take the oath. Many church members subsequently received the sacraments from the so-called constitutional clergy, but many sided with the nonjuring or refractory clergy. No other measure did the cause of the Revolution as much harm as this. France was torn apart, and the counter-revolution gained popular support. Gershoy quite rightly says, "The fires of religious fanaticism were lighted, as from each side came increasing violence and persecution". [13]

Paris, Louis saw the foundations of the old and well-known political and social order crumble without offering any resistance. The measures against the church, however, roused him to action. He had signed the Civil Constitution of the Clergy with a heavy heart – the break with Rome was highly inconsistent with his religious convictions. He began to think about placing the fate of the French monarchy in the balance by leaving Paris. From some city on the border he would be able to appeal to the loyal section of the population, and call on aid from foreign rulers (absolute monarchs) to stem the revolutionary tide. Mirabeau dissuaded him, for although he was a great proponent of radical social reform, Mirabeau was convinced of the necessity for strong executive authority, and he warned the king against the possible consequences of the step he was contemplating. Mirabeau died in 1791, however, and Louis fell under the influence of Marie Antoinette once again. In June a dramatic escape attempt to reach Metz near the eastern border failed when the royal family was recognized and arrested at Varennes.

The flight of the royal family can be seen as a turning point in the Revolution. In the first place, it revealed Louis's attitude towards the Revolution. It was clear that he was an unwilling collaborator in the matter of reforms. The failed escape also for the first time really drew the attention of the French people to the issue of republicanism by widening the breach between the moderate and the democratic leaders of the Jacobin Club even further. In the National Assembly a number of republicans demanded that the king be dethroned, but the majority was still in favour of monarchical government. They feared that the deposition of the king might unleash a new revolution. When the mob gathered to demand the king's deposition, the National Assembly had them dispersed, and merely suspended the king until he should have ratified the new constitution, which was fast nearing completion. A final indication of the turning point created by the flight to Varennes was the fact that European monarchies – Austria and Prussia in particular – realized afresh that they would have to show solidarity in opposing the new revolutionary order.

Meanwhile the National Assembly continued its work of providing France with a constitution. Most of the reforms which are referred to above were implemented immediately. Ultimately they were combined in a single document, known as the Constitution of 1791. On the 3rd September 1791 it was approved by the Assembly, and Louis accepted it in public eleven days later. It was the first written constitution in Europe. In its terms, France became a constitutional monarchy, in other words, the king was bound by a constitution which had been compiled by representatives of the people.

An important principle was the separation of the legislative, executive and judicial powers, as advocated by Montesquieu. This differed totally from the position in the *ancien régime,* which had united all three powers in the absolute monarch.

Legislative power was in the hands of the Legislative Assembly, which was to consist of 745 deputies. Only "active" citizens had the vote, that is to say, male land-owners of twenty five years and older, whose annual direct taxes were equal to three days' wages. (Interestingly enough, Rousseau was, in these terms, a "passive" citizen!) More than 4 000 000 people qualified for enfranchisement, and about 3 000 000 were excluded.

The Legislative Assembly would be elected for two years, and the king would have no powers to adjourn or dissolve it. Neither could the king nominate a deputy as minister. The king's participation in legislation was limited to the "suspensive veto", in other words, he could delay legislation, but not prevent it. This veto was not in force for fiscal and constitutional measures. The Legislative Assembly controlled both the determination of taxes and the expenditure of national income.

The king was to be head of the executive authority, but his powers were strictly limited. The reason was the fear that he might reinstitute the *ancien régime* should he have sufficient power. Now he was unable to introduce legislation, and could also not conclude treaties or declare war without the consent of the Legislative Assembly. He had no judicial powers, and could not appoint judges. He had no control over local authorities, and there were no longer agents in the provinces, such as the old intendants, who represented the monarch's authority. This lack of a strong executive authority was a grave defect. It was to become the most important factor in the success of the Paris Commune and the Jacobins in their abolition of the monarchy and the institution of a republic. In its fear of the king's reaction from the right, the National Assembly's constitution ensured a new revolution of the Jacobins from the left.

Administration of justice was to be independent of both the executive and the legislative authorities. The hodge-podge of royal, administrative, ecclesiastic, feudal and manorial courts which bedevilled justice to such an extent, was abolished. Procedure was simplified and made uniform for the whole country. Judicial officers who had previously bought their offices were replaced by elected officers. Judges were elected for only six years and received relatively low salaries, which (alas!) made it difficult for them to ignore the pressures of public opinion. Administration of justice would be free, and all citizens, irrespective of their religious or social status, would be equal before the law. The Constitution of 1791 was not in operation long enough for the legislature to include all the legislation concerning persons and property in a single legal code.

As indicated above, local authority was adapted to the new division into eighty three departments. Local assemblies were given extensive powers, and central government exercised relatively little control over them. It was one of the most serious flaws in the constitution in terms of policy-making and implementation of authority.

In a drastic review of the tax system, the salt and other indirect taxes were abolished. In accordance with the principle of equal, proportional tax, three direct taxes were levied: a land tax, a tax on income from industry, and a tax on trading enterprise.

The Civil Constitution of the Clergy which has been discussed above, was technically part of the Constitution of 1791.

In a spirit of self-denial, the National Assembly determined that not one of its members would be eligible for the Legislative Assembly. The new assembly, to which members were moreover elected on a limited basis, therefore displayed a lamentable lack of experience, and had no access to the broad base of political authority on which its predecessor had leaned so heavily. Furthermore, the continued exclusion of members of the legislative authority from any ministerial office meant that there was no minister of any quality. The ministers were mere puppets. If they had been appointed by the king, they were distrusted by the Legislative Assembly, and if they had been forced on the king by the Assembly, he simply ignored them.

Seen as a whole, the chief feature of the Constitution of 1791 is its bourgeois character. The dominant group in the National Assembly had represented the wealthy and enlightened bourgeoisie. Because the Assembly had removed power from the previously ruling and privileged groups, and had placed the vote and incumbencies of office in the hands of the wealthier groups, the rule of the bourgeoisie was thoroughly established. It was the *feuillants* above all who indicated the course, a group which broke away to the right of the Jacobins. The bourgeoisie had certainly entrenched itself against the threat from above (that is to say, from the king, or in the form of any offensive the aristocracy may still have mounted) as well as against the threat from below (from the masses or the lowest class of the third estate). Proofs of this are the extreme limitations to the king's authority, which made his position as head of the executive power almost untenable, and in the limitation of the franchise to "active" citizens. The express delineation of the principle of the people's sovereignty in the Declaration of the Rights of Man therefore, in certain respects, remained an unrealized ideal.

As a result of its servitude to the political ideas of the *feuillants* and the wealthy bourgeoisie, the National Assembly concluded its activities in September 1791 in great disfavour. The deputies thought the Revolution was over, but the next few months were to show whether the National Assembly had really halted it. There were disturbing signs that this was not the case. The people as a whole were not satisfied. The lowest classes were becoming mistrustful of the attitude and policies of the bourgeoisie, and the radical Jacobins were determined to take the Revolution further. At the other side of the spectrum, the counter-revolutionaries, the clergy, the nobility and the émigrés abroad, were waiting for their opportunity to restore the *ancien régime* with the help of foreign rulers. In addition, Louis would find it difficult to co-operate even with the moderates in the new Legislative Assembly, because of his dissatisfaction with his role as constitutional monarch and the Civil Constitution of the Clergy, which weighed heavily on his conscience.

THE FAILURE OF THE CONSTITUTIONAL MONARCHY, 1791-1792

Of the 745 members of the new Legislative Assembly, 264 were *feuillants* or rightists who were in favour of a constitutional monarchy, although not necessarily of the existing constitution. They had no strong leaders. The left wing in the Assembly consisted of only 136 members, the Jacobins and the Girondins. (Most of the members of the latter group were from the department of Gironde. They were also known as Brissotins, after their leader, Brissot.) They wanted the continuation of the Revolution and the deposition of the king. The large majority of members, 345, sat in the centre, and had no definite political convictions. Further forming of factions shrunk the Jacobin numbers, but the radical Jacobins, led from outside by Robespierre, were extremely active inside as well as outside the Assembly. They persuaded the Legislative Assembly to open its galleries to the public, and to cause every member to vote verbally and audibly. After that it was easy to pack the gallery with the rabble of Paris or the radical bourgeoisie, and to "persuade" the moderate leaders to their point of view at critical moments. Outside the Assembly, the Jacobin Club, with its network of affiliated clubs throughout France, formed active centres for the distribution of revolutionary ideas. Robespierre also had able assistants in Danton and Marat.

Within a few weeks of the first session, the Assembly paid attention to the elements fostering a counter-revolution: the nonjuring clergy in La Vendée and the hostile émigrés in the Netherlands and the Rhine territories. As the Assembly regarded them as the most dangerous enemies of the constitution, two decrees were proclaimed in 1791 – one ordering the émigrés back to France by the 1st January 1792 on pain of death, and the other depriving all priests who refused to take the oath of allegiance of their offices and emoluments. When the king vetoed both decrees, the tension between the legislative and the executive authority almost reached breaking point. Louis's veto, in fact, benefited the radicals, as the supporters of the constitution suspected him of collusion with the enemies of the Revolution.

While the revolutionary changes in France rumbled along, international politics also took its course. A divided France represented no threat to the European balance of power, but it did not prevent the powers from mutual trials of strength. By 1791, however, there was reason for anxiety. France was subtly threatening the monarchs of other powers by its abolition of feudalism and the institution of a constitutional monarchy. The king's flight to the eastern border of France, and his suspension and subsequent imprisonment, gave rise to thoughts of intervention amongst the threatened monarchs. In addition, Leopold II of Austria was under pressure because of the safety of his sister, Marie Antoinette. Gradually the rulers began to see the wisdom of burying their hatchets. *Rapprochement* between Austria and Prussia resulted in the Declaration of Pillnitz on the 27th August 1791, which declared that the restoration of the monarchy in France was a matter of common interest to all the monarchs of Europe.

The Declaration of Pillnitz was a gesture rather than a serious threat, and the restoration of Louis XVI to his throne, once he had approved the constitution in September 1791, provisionally ruled out any reason for intervention. The language of Pillnitz was, however, provocative, and the émigrés continued to foment war.

In France, too, a strong mood of war was beginning to develop. As a result of the deteriorating economic conditions, there was a spirit of restlessness in the country which could easily be turned into a desire for war. The *feuillants*, led by Lafayette, were in favour of war because they hoped that a short and glorious campaign would restore the prestige of the king in the eyes of the people, and reinforce the Constitution of 1791. The leftists were divided. The Girondins were in favour of war, not only because it would win all classes for the revolution and bring their true attitudes to light, but also because their large shipping and trade interests would benefit. The faction of the Jacobins led by Robespierre feared that a long, exhausting and wasteful war would, in case of defeat, destroy the fruits of the revolution, while a victory would strengthen royal authority. Louis himself was in favour of war, as he expected France to be defeated, and thought that the people would then rally behind the throne again.

Under the influence of the Girondins, the Legislative Assembly took the first step towards war in December 1791. It ordered the king to concentrate an army on the eastern border, and to demand from the electors of Trier and Mainz that they disband the organizations of émigrés within their territories before the middle of January 1792. Although Leopold had promised both principalities support, both submitted to the demand. The Legislative Assembly was still not satisfied, and requested a statement from the emperor, Leopold II, about his attitude towards the Revolution. His reply included a sharp attack on the Jacobins. The Assembly protested strongly against this provocative reaction. Those of Louis's ministers who were opposed to the war policy were forced to resign, and the king appointed his new ministers from the ranks of the Girondins. Government had now gone over into the hands of the most radical war party, under the leadership of Dumouriez.

In March 1792 Leopold II died. His successor, the youthful Francis I, was rather inclined towards a military adventure, a policy in which he was supported by the veteran imperial chancellor, Von Kaunitz. Francis rejected the demand of the French government that he revoke his alliance with Prussia. On the 20th April 1792 the French government declared war on him. Prussia entered the war on Austria's side, although Frederick William's problems with the second partition of Poland, which was current, prevented the immediate active participation of Prussia.

The French army of only 130 000 men entered the war totally unprepared. Many officers had emigrated, and the gaps in their ranks had not yet been filled. Discipline was extremely slack, military equipment was poor and the economy not prepared for war conditions.

Early military reverses immediately exerted an influence on the political state of France. Suspicion of the royal family and Marie Antoinette in particular rose to new heights, and in Paris it was rumoured that an Austrian committee was working from the Tuileries. Mindful of counter-revolutionary actions, the Legislative Assembly had determined, amongst other matters, that the nonjuring clergy should be banned, and that an army of 20 000 *fédérés* (voluntary contingents from the departments) should be concentrated in Paris. Ostensibly the *fédérés* were to participate in the Bastille Day festivities, but in reality they were there to intimidate the king and the moderates. Louis vetoed these decrees on the 13th June, and dismissed the majority of his Girondin ministers.

The dismissal of the ministers had, to some extent, the same effect as that of Necker in July 1789. It stimulated the radical element in Paris, but, unlike three years previously, the dissatisfaction could be channelled into the assemblies of the forty eight *sections* into which Paris had been divided for administrative purposes in the middle of 1790. (These assemblies, as an aside, had received representations to allow "active" as well as "passive" citizens membership – an indication of how radical the Revolution was becoming.) The assemblies consequently supported a people's movement, which ostensibly wanted to commemorate the Oath of the Tennis Court on the 20th June.

On the day concerned the mass procession, consisting mainly of "passive" citizens, forced their way into the Legislative Assembly, submited petitions against the dismissal of the ministers and the use of the royal veto, and set off for the Tuileries. They stormed into the palace, but Louis placated them by wearing the revolutionary cap and drinking to the health of the people. He bore the humiliation with dignity, but refused to withdraw his veto. For a moment there was a reaction in his favour, but the revolutionaries now redoubled their organizational efforts in Paris.

On their arrival in Paris, the *fédérés* went along with the political demands of the members of the *sections*. A secret committee of five members began planning a revolt against the monarchy. It was the *fédérés* who, on the 17th July, were the first to demand that the powers of the king should be suspended, and shortly afterwards that they should be revoked altogether.

The last event preceding the fall of the monarchy was the manifesto of the duke of Brunswick, commander-in-chief of the Austro-Prussian forces. The contents became known in Paris on the 28th July 1792. The manifesto declared that the allies were invading France to suppress anarchy and restore the king to his rightful position of authority, that any members of the National Guard who resisted would be shot and their homes demolished, that if the Tuileries were to be stormed again or the slightest harm befall the royal family, revenge would be taken on Paris. It seemed to confirm the suspicion that the émigrés and foreign rulers were secretly hand in glove with counter-revolutionary groups within France.

Nothing could ever have been better calculated to unite all patriotic Frenchmen and to make the position of the king untenable than precisely the Brunswick manifesto. The *fédérés* batallion from Marseilles marched into Paris, and for the first time the capital heard their marching song. It was to become the famous French national anthem, the Marseillaise. A popular revolt was imminent.

On the 9th August the representatives of the *sections* took over the municipal administration with an unofficial and revolutionary city council (commune). As the

Legislative Assembly itself did not demand the deposition of the king, the council the following day ordered an attack on the Tuileries by the *sections* and the *fédérés*. The royal family sought shelter at the Legislative Assembly, while the National Guard, infiltrated by the *sansculottes*, joined the attackers and cut the Swiss Guard to pieces. These *sansculottes* were action groups from the lowest classes of the petite bourgeoisie and the higher stratum of the populace: craftsmen, shopkeepers and industrial labourers. The republic had not been officially proclaimed, but *de facto*, it already existed.

The Legislative Assembly had therefore lost control of the situation. Leadership now rested in the hands of the revolutionary city council of Paris, which in reality became the government of France. Its control of the police and the National Guard, amongst others, ensured this. Its members were chiefly from the lower bourgeoisie of small shopkeepers and craftsmen. A provisional government was chosen, in which Danton played the leading role. His aims were to save the principles of the Revolution which seemed in danger. The council provisionally maintained the Legislative Assembly, but forced it to keep the king suspended and confined until such time as the National Convention, elected on the basis of universal male franchise, could draw up a new constitution.

The shift in political authority went hand in hand with profound social and economic change. By the end of August the feudal land tax was abolished – something the National Assembly had omitted to do. Property laws were changed by abolishing the principle of inalienable inheritances. The registration of births, deaths and marriages became the responsibility of the city council instead of the clergy.

The council felt that although the king was confined, his collaborators were still at liberty. This forced the Legislative Assembly to enact drastic measures against "enemies" and to institute a revolutionary court. Paris was diligently searched for suspects, and these, together with the nonjuring clergy, filled the prisons.

On the 1st September 1792 the alarming news reached Paris that Verdun was surrounded and that enemy cavalry was on its way to the capital. Panic seized the city, and new volunteers were hurriedly recruited. To prevent the detainees from escaping and organizing a counter-revolution, the gaols were stormed on the 2nd September and the suspects and priests indiscriminately murdered. Various provincial cities followed the example of Paris. In the course of four days, some 1 200 victims died, most of them criminal lawbreakers.

The September massacres had far-reaching results. The events strongly influenced the election of delegates to the National Convention. Monarchists hardly dared to vote, and many moderates also stayed away from the polls, in fact, only 10 per cent of the qualified voters registered their votes. This ensured a thoroughly republican Convention, and the election of extreme revolutionaries, such as Marat, Danton and Robespierre. With one exception, all twenty four members for Paris were Jacobins, while the Girondins found most of their support in the rural areas. A second important result was a further worsening of the relationship between the state and the church. The state now once more encroached on the traditional rights of the church. Clerical dress was forbidden, except at church services, and no religious processions and other church ceremonies would in future be allowed in public. Thus the foundation was laid for the de-christianizing movement of 1793.

Meanwhile, Verdun had fallen, and the Prussians were marching on Paris. To the surprise of friend and foe alike, Dumouriez checked them at Valmy on the 20th September 1792, and they began to retreat. On the same day the National Convention assembled for its first session in Paris to draw up a new constitution for France.

THE CONVENTION, 1792-1795

The 782 deputies can be divided into three groups according to their political views. On the right were the Girondins who, in the Legislative Assembly, had been on the left. It was not that they had changed their point of view – only, the other groups in the Convention were more revolutionary than they. On the left, on the "Mountain", were the radical Jacobins or *Montagnards*. The centre once again, also known as the "Plain" or the "Marsh", had no specified policy. All three groups were avowed republicans, who differed only over the issue of how far the Revolution was to go. The Jacobins of 1793 were more definitely the representatives of the proletariat, and were strong supporters of a powerful unitary state under the leadership of Paris. Therefore they were – not unjustifiably – accused of propagating a dictatorship of Paris. Their strength lay in their forcefulness, their good organization and their unity. The power of the Girondins lay in the provinces, where they represented the landowning bourgeoisie. As they were axiomatically advocates of greater influence by the provinces in state matters, they were accused of federalism, precisely at the point when the Republic was proclaimed as "united and indivisible". In contrast to the *Montagnards* (Jacobins), they had no efficient and widespread organization to fall back on. They were men of words rather than of deeds, and frequently they acted in disunity in times of crisis. It is no wonder then that the Plain, under the influence of the powerful action of the Jacobins, and in fear of the Parisian mob which filled the galleries, usually supported the extreme left at critical moments.

During the initial stages of the Convention, circumstances favoured the Girondins' endeavour to develop the Republic on a moderate basis. They had a majority in the Convention and almost a monopoly in ministerial posts, as well as control over most of the Parisian newspapers. The excesses of the previous September had shocked general opinion, and had brought the Jacobins into disfavour. Even in Paris there was a reaction in favour of moderation. But through their lack of organization, coupled with their inability to cope with the problems at home and abroad, the Girondins were defeated by the Jacobins in the struggle for control of the state. Although it certainly was a struggle, the political history of the Convention has traditionally, and possibly erroneously, been seen purely as a struggle between the Girondins and the Jacobins. This, however, ignores the constructive reforms of the Convention, particularly in the areas of legal codification and the progress of education. Whatever the case may be, personal envy also played an important part in the mutual differences between the Girondins and the Jacobins. Girondins such as Brissot and Condorcet hated people such as Robespierre, but it was particularly Roland's personal attacks on Danton, virtually the leader of the "Plain", which prevented the deputies on the "Plain" from supporting the Girondins.

The first action of the Convention was to abolish the monarchy on the 21st September 1792, and to declare that the first year of the French Republic began on the 22nd September 1792. The question was what to do with the king. The Girondins wanted to spare his life, but the Jacobins demanded his death as a matter of political necessity and not so much of justice. After a trial of more than six weeks, Louis was unanimously found guilty of high treason. With a majority of seventy votes, he was sent to the guillotine, where he died on the 21st January 1793. It was the first victory for the Jacobins, for the idea began to take root that the Girondins were no longer faithful to the Revolution.

After their success at Valmy, the French took the offensive along the entire border, from the Mediterranean to the Baltic. Nice and Savoy were occupied, as well as Speyer, Worms, Mainz and Frankfurt. The Austrian Netherlands (Belgium) were invaded and the Austrian troops driven out. The French armies were welcomed everywhere as liberators by a large part of the inhabitants. In the first flush of victory, the Convention decreed in November 1792 that all nations who wished to rebel against their rulers would be offered assistance. Here was a challenge indeed to all the monarchs of Europe.

Shortly before, the Convention had declared that the river Scheldt was open to the shipping of all nations. It was a challenge and a severe blow to the Dutch, who, since the Peace of Westphalia in 1648, had held the sole navigation rights over the river, as well as to their British protectors. Savoy, Nice, Belgium and the Rhineland were incorporated into France. In December it was announced that wherever territories had been invaded by the French armies, the tithe and feudal taxes would be abolished, political rights would be limited to the non-privileged classes, and provisional governments would be established under French control. The execution of the king further brought matters to a head.

The Convention took the initiative on the 1st February 1793 by declaring war on Britain and the Netherlands. Austria, Prussia, Spain, Portugal and Naples joined Britain and the Netherlands in the so-called First Coalition against France.

Matters took a serious turn for France almost immediately. The defeat and treason of Dumouriez were followed by the loss of the Netherlands. Spanish troops crossed the Pyrenees. In La Vendée in the west of France the peasants, incited by the local nonjuring priests, rebelled against the recruitment of troops. In Paris and elsewhere the price of bread, which had been stabilized the previous year, rose sharply. Necessities such as soap, sugar and coffee were unobtainable.

The threat to the Republic posed by foreign armies and internal revolt had an immediate effect on internal politics. The Convention entrusted all executive authority to a secret committee of nine members, known as the Committee of Public Safety. The most important member was Danton. The committee controlled the ministers as well as the various committees of the Convention, and was virtually a despotic authority with the Convention as its willing instrument. By means of political commissioners it kept a close watch on local governments in the provinces and incited them to action. A Committee of General Security controlled the police, investigated the reports of secret informants and arrested conspirators and suspect persons. These were tried by the Revolutionary Tribunal, a special court not bound by the ordinary rules of court and legal procedures.

Meanwhile the struggle between the Girondins and Jacobins intensified daily. Dumouriez's treason caused the distrust of the Girondins. Their resistance to attempts to peg food prices further antagonized the starving mob of Paris. On the 2nd June 1793 the National Guard, on the order of a new so-called Insurrectionary Commune which had taken over the authority in the mean time, forced the Convention to have a score of Girondin leaders arrested. Some escaped, and the rest were put under guard in Paris. Thus the Girondins' blocking of parliamentary development came to an end without bloodshed. The Jacobins were now in power. In terms of liberty the revolution of the 2nd June paid a high price: parliamentary immunity had been flagrantly violated, and force had the upper hand.[14]

The first action of the Jacobins was an attempt to reconcile public opinion in the provinces by drawing up a new constitution. A draft was ready within a few weeks, and on the 24th June the Convention approved the Constitution of 1793. More than the constitutions of 1791 and 1795, it embodied the idea of direct representation by the people. There would be no property qualification for voters or candidates, and every male citizen of twenty one years and older would have the vote to elect deputies to the Legislative Assembly. Executive authority would be in the hands of a committee of twenty five members, chosen by the Legislative Assembly from a list of candidates which, in turn, had been elected indirectly. A Declaration of Rights promised freedom of worship and of labour, while public support would be given to the disabled. It also viewed public education as a necessity. The local assemblies received the Constitution with enthusiasm throughout the country, but no attempt was made to implement it. It would not have worked, as the executive authority was ineffectively set out, and local government remained undetermined.

Even as a political manoeuvre aimed at the Girondins, the Constitution was a failure, as the violence of the Jacobins in Paris in June shocked the country. Revolts broke out in about sixty departments south and west of Paris, where royalists, Roman Catholics and Girondins made common cause to overthrow the Jacobin reign. The Jacobins, who regarded the Republic as "united and indivisible", described the Girondist revolt as a "federalistic" and counter-revolutionary attempt to institute a loose federal government of wealthy Girondin followers in the provincial cities in the place of the central authority of the Convention, with its democratic followers in Paris. Initially the revolt was certainly not counter-revolutionary, but as it widened, it obviously began to include elements of this nature.

This crisis was aggravated by a simultaneous invasion by Prussian, Sardinian and Spanish forces, while the British fleet began a blockade of French harbours. There was an unparalleled shortage of food, and the *assignats* dropped to only about 30 per cent of their nominal value. It was clear that only drastic measures would save the Republic.

The Jacobins proved equal to the crisis. On the 10th July 1793 the Committee of Public Safety assumed even greater dictatorial powers for itself and Danton, who had advocated conciliation with the Girondists, was left out. During the next month the Convention, on the comittee's recommendation, proclaimed a general mobilization for military service and labour. It was an important step in the direction of a full-scale war. An army of 750 000 men was soon raised, and in September, stringent measures were taken to ward off the financial crisis, amongst them a compulsory levy of 1 000 000 francs on the rich.

The actions of the Committee of Public Safety were to lead to the so-called Reign of Terror. By this is meant the period in the Revolution when the government of France as embodied in the Convention, would deliberately adopt a policy of terror in order to instil fear of the Republic in the hearts of the royalists, traitors, counter-revolutionaries and war profiteers. Up to that stage, the policy of terrorism had been sporadic, but from then onwards is was to become official and permanent, until the fall of Robespierre in 1794. The Comittee of Public Safety achieved such success with its vigour and energy that the Convention accepted its leadership. In the provinces, the local revolutionary committees also exercised effective control, supported by the Committee of Public Safety. This cooperation was to enable France to overcome the threatening dangers at home, and the onslaught from abroad, with a great measure of success.

The Reign of Terror was to make itself felt in the economic, religious and political spheres. The purpose of the economic terror was really to organize the people with a view to the state of war. In this manner military supplies could be obtained at reasonable cost, and the clashing interests of consumer and producer could be co-ordinated. A central Food Committee contributed to the success of the policy. Bread was rationed, and food and war supplies were commandeered for the war effort at fixed prices. As a result, the value of the *assignats* remained fairly firm. This contributed to the military victory over the First Coalition.

In religious matters, the payment of salaries to priests was left in abeyance, and the Christian religion was increasingly viewed with suspicion and scorn. The Hébertists, a small group of fanatics under Hébert and Fouché, who controlled the Paris commune, wanted to take matters even further. Nonjuring as well as loyal priests were now engulfed by the wave of revolutionary patriotism. All the churches in Paris were closed, and steps were taken to institute atheism as the official religion. In the cathedral of Notre Dame, an actress was crowned as the Goddess of Reason. The provinces followed the example of Paris, and thousands of churches were closed, or converted into "temples of reason".

A republican calendar replaced the Christian-Gregorian. The twelve months of the year were re-named after seasons, and the names of saints in the calendar replaced by names of plants, trees and fruits. Every month was divided into three periods of ten days, so that the Christian Sunday fell away. These measures were, however, not as popular as the anti-clericalists had hoped. Many of the loyal priests refused to celebrate High Mass on the new sabbath day, while the workers found, to their dismay, that their day of rest only occurred every tenth instead of every seventh day.

Robespierre, who personally held deistic convictions, regarded the excesses of the Hébertists as a blot on the name of the Republic, and feared that there would be serious repercussions abroad. The Committee of Public Safety also realized that the majority of the French were still loyal to the Roman Catholic church. In addition, there was the possibility that the religious terror could become a source of social confusion and political disunity. With the support of Danton, the Hébertists were consequently accused, condemned by the Revolutionary Tribunal, and sent to the guillotine.

The political terrorism of the Reign of Terror was extensive. The Law of Suspects determined that all suspects should be charged immediately. Suspects were described as all persons who showed that they sympathized with "tyranny" or "federalism". As a result, few royalists, Girondins or people who were in the slightest dissatisfied with the Revolution, escaped. In Paris, the Committee of General Security had the task of arresting suspects, while in the provinces, vigilance committees were responsible. It has been calculated that about 500 000 people were arrested. Between January 1973 and June 1795 the Revolutionary Tribunal sent about 2 800 people, amongst them Marie Antoinette and the duke of Orléans, to the guillotine. Many others were the victims of a senseless butchery, while their property was confiscated. The worst atrocities occurred in the provinces, but in some parts of the country the Reign of Terror merely took the form of a systematic suppression of all personal liberty.

While these measures frequently were senselessly cruel, they had an important effect. The Reign of Terror was viewed by normal and civilized citizens as an imperative to overcome a national state of emergency. Not only treason, but even indifference or laxness towards the Republic became dangerous. In addition, the greatest internal dangers, as well as the threats from abroad, could be countered during October 1793 with a good measure of success.

Through the energetic efforts of Carnot, the ill-disciplined and ill-equipped French troops were transformed into efficient armies.

France ended the year 1793 with excellent victories. The enemy was repulsed across every border, and the counter-revolutionary revolt in La Vendée was finally suppressed. In the spring of 1794 French armies made renewed attacks on neighbouring countries. As previously, they took the principles of the Revolution with them, and instituted social and judicial reforms which would, in most cases, become permanent.

As the tide of war turned, there seemed to be no justification for continuing the Reign of Terror in its atrocious form. That it was continued none the less, was due to the fact that the war against the First Coalition had not yet ended, to the leaders' fear of revenge, and to Robespierre's desire to realize the "ideal" republic in the spirit of Rousseau.

After the removal of the Hébertists, Danton and his followers became the next victims. Danton was in favour of reconciliation with the Girondins and was sharply critical of the unnecessary excesses of the Reign of Terror. Where the Hébertists had been regarded as dangerous because of their radicalism, the Dantonists "sinned" by their moderation and tolerance. In April 1794, Danton and fifteen of his followers died under the guillotine. The Revolutionary Tribunal had become a political weapon, and the Revolution was beginning to devour its own children.

Robespierre and his like were now supreme, and the Reign of Terror continued unabated. Robespierre's greatest desire was still the ideal republic in which all citizens accepted moral purity, high ideals and disinterested patriotism as the highest spiritual values. The view of the *philosophes* – that man was perfectible – is clearly discernible. Robespierre believed in the binding force of religion, but he did not want to reintroduce Roman Catholicism. He championed a religion which would be free of "corruption" and "superstition". Consequently, he began to introduce a new deistic religion, in which the two positive articles of faith were faith in a Supreme Being, and in the immortality of the soul. At the first ceremony of the new religion, Robespierre himself acted as a kind of high priest.

In the month Thermidor of the revolutionary calendar, however, the Reign of Terror reached a turning point, which is known as the reaction of Thermidor. The fear that Robespierre was heading for total dictatorship had rapidly been growing.

Robespierre's introduction of the so-called Law of Prairial in June 1794, by which he wanted to silence all criticism, finally alienated him from the other members of the Committee of Public Safety. This law stipulated the death penalty for "enemies of the people"; gave the Revolutionary Tribunal the right to pronounce a verdict without trial or investigation of evidence; accused were denied the right to legal representation; and the immunity which members of the Convention had enjoyed up to this point, was abolished.

The Law of Prairial was in force for seven weeks, and on average thirty people a day were guillotined in Paris during this period. Everyone who did not belong to Robespierre's inner circle felt themselves threatened. Collusion to get rid of him began to take shape. His downfall can be ascribed to his losing control of the Convention. Many members of the Convention never forgave the Jacobins for the fate which had befallen the Girondins and the Dantonists, but the majority were particularly dismayed over the mass executions which followed in the wake of the Law of Prairial.

Meanwhile a military victory over Austria and the resultant occupation of Belgium left the moderate members of the Convention convinced that the the Reign of Terror was redundant. The tyranny of Robespierre and the Committee of Public Safety had become unbearable. On 9 Thermidor (that is, the 27th July 1794) he was arrested. Although the populace of Paris tried to intercede for him, the insurrection was suppressed, and he died on the guillotine the next day, with twenty one of his followers. The Committee of Public Safety and the Commmittee of General Security lost their despotic powers, the Revolutionary Tribunal was abolished, the Jacobin Club closed and the revolutionary committees reorganized. The Convention regained its grip on the Revolution, and the remaining Girondins regained access to the Convention. The economic tyranny was relaxed, and forced loans were abolished. Most of the laws against nonjuring priests and against émigrés were revoked, and religious freedom reinstituted. The National Guard, purged of the *sansculottes*, safeguarded the Convention against the threat of the populace.

This reaction against Jacobin terrorism and radicalism and the desire for a strong and permanent government were, in fact, so strong that the royalists began to have hopes of restoring the Bourbon monarchy. The son of Louis XVI, who would have been Louis XVII, had died in June 1794, and the émigré brother of Louis, the count of Provence, laid claim to the title of Louis XVIII. The efforts of the émigrés to land in Brittany with the assistance of the British fleet failed, and the revolt was easily suppressed.

To a large extent the so-called reaction of Thermidor (that is, the period July 1794 to the end of October 1795) featured the bourgeoisie regaining the political control which it had temporarily lost to the rash efforts to establish a republican democracy. To forestall any further attempts to restore the monarchy, this group in the Convention drew up the Constitution of the Year III (1795).

Meanwhile the French armies had continued to be victorious. Belgium was annexed and General Pichegru invaded the Netherlands and occupied Amsterdam. The Stadtholder fled to England, and the Batavian Republic, which would henceforth act in alliance with France, was proclaimed. In April 1795 the Prussians concluded peace at Basle, and in June Spain followed suit. The First Coalition against France now consisted solely of Britain, Austria and Sardinia, and they were on the defensive.

In October 1795 the Convention was dissolved, having been in session since September 1792. Although it left memories of bloodshed and terror, the achievements of the Convention were hardly insignificant. It had saved France from invasion and had made it the dominant power in Europe. It had also completed the destruction of the feudal *régime*, and had introduced important social, cultural and legal reforms.

THE DIRECTORY, 1795-1799

In the Constitution of the Year III (1795), indirect elections on the basis of a limited franchise replaced Robespierre's idea of universal male suffrage. Provision was made for a legislative authority which consisted of two chambers: the Council of Five Hundred and the Council of Elders (250 members). The latter would function as a kind of senate. Only those of twenty one years and older who paid direct taxes or who fought for the Republic, had the vote. About 5 000 000 males qualified, as against 7 000 000 under Robespiere, and 4 000 000 in terms of the Constitution of 1791. The indirect election meant that these voters could vote only for so-called "electors" who, in turn, would elect the deputies of the two legislative assemblies. Property qualifications for these electors were higher than in 1791, and only about 20 000 people qualified as electors. [15] The executive authority was vested in the Directory consisting of five members, elected by the Council of Elders from a list of names submitted by the Council of Five Hundred. Local government was organized more or less on the basis of the Constitution of 1791, except that the district as an administrative entity fell away.

Because a third of the members of the legislative assemblies had to resign annually, but only one of the members of the Directory, this body ran the danger of being thwarted by a hostile legislative authority. To eliminate a deficiency in the Constitution of 1791, and to prevent revenge, it was determined that two-thirds of the members of the Convention would have seats in the new legislative assemblies.

The Constitution of the Year III was approved by plebiscite, but Paris refused to accept the two-thirds decree because it violated the principle of representation by the people. The royalists, backed by the economic motive that only a third of the bread ration was being distributed, organized an insurrection for the 5th October 1795 in the midst of the general dissatisfaction. The army, however, immediately suppressed it. One of the officers was a youthful Corsican, Napoleon Bonaparte, who had distinguished himself at the siege of Toulon and now opened fire on the masses with his artillery. It was a political fact that the revolutionary government no longer depended on the support of the people, but on military force.

The Directory inherited most of its problems from the Convention. As it could not altogether solve these problems, it is sometimes judged somewhat harshly. Yet the Directory had a fair amount of success. Many of the reforms Napoleon was to make later were made possible by the preliminary work of the Directory. A three-fold task awaited the government: to place the finances on a sound footing, restore order in France, and to create general peace in Europe.

France had tremendous financial problems. The treasury was bare, and the troops needed clothes and food. The whole economic system was, in fact, falling apart because of the devaluation of the *assignats*. By November they had dropped to 1 per cent of their face value! A new form of paper money, *mandats*, replaced the *assignats*. In 1797 the government made an effort to balance the budget by reducing government expenditure by a third, chiefly by abolishing interest on two-thirds of the national debt. In addition, the revised taxation system functioned better than ever before.

The restoration of order in France and the creation of universal peace in Europe were important aims of the Directory. The Revolution had taken its toll, and most of France desired peace and quiet. The peasants wanted it in order to pick the social fruits of the revolution, the working class in the cities needed regular work and income, and the business interests desired stability to be able to exploit the free trade which had been established in France.[16]

Armed bands of robbers terrorized rural areas, and insurrection in La Vendée broke out anew. The Directory created "tolerant order and obedience", but was not as successful in this respect as in other matters. Highway robbery was curtailed to some extent, and the insurrection in La Vendée was suppressed.

Politically speaking, the legislative authority was divided into revolutionaries (that is to say, republicans) and constitutional monarchists. The latter were the moderates who wanted to bring the revolution to an end, and, as their name indicates, restore a constitutional monarchy. Furthermore, they wanted to restore peace at home and abroad, and give France the opportunity to recover. Further to the right, there was even a large group of pure royalists. At the other extreme, the revolutionaries wanted to continue the revolution as a means to retain power, thus preventing a reaction which may have been dangerous to them. At the outset of the new government, they were in the majority, as the Assembly consisted largely of members of the former Convention. In the Directory they also had a majority – three representatives – of whom the corrupt and ambitious Barras was one.

The chief threat to political stability originated from both extremes. Babeuf's assault from the left on free enterprise was warded off in 1796. The threat from the right came from within the government itself. The election of the Year V (April 1797) gave the constitutional monarchists and royalists a large majority in the two legislative chambers. It was obviously a protest against the inability of the government to restore credit or to alleviate the widespread social misery. They had the support of two members of the Directory, and were determined to revoke the revolutionary laws and restore normal conditions.

The three Directors supporting the revolutionaries had their own safety in mind. However, they had no authority to dissolve the hostile legislative chambers. The only solution was a *coup d'état*. They declared that there was a royalist conspiracy against the Republic, and appealed to Napoleon Bonaparte for military support.

Napoleon had, in the mean time, achieved great success against the Austrians and Sardinians in Italy. He was aware that the royalists would probably end the war. Consequently, he sent his lieutenant, Augereau, to Paris, who purged the legislative chamber of royalists. A commission revised the election results in favour of the revolutionaries, while the freedom of the press was abolished and the laws against the émigrés and nonjuring priests were reproclaimed. There was even a small revival of the Reign of Terror. This so-called *coup d'état* of Fructidor (the 4th September 1797) once again saved the Republic at the expense of liberty.

Prospects for general peace in Europe had meanwhile grown quite favourable. The republican generals had achieved victories on all fronts, and had thus gained for France its "natural borders" – the Rhine, the Alps and the Pyrenees. With the elimination of the Netherlands, Prussia and Spain, the campaign was now directed at Austria and Sardinia. A threefold assault would be launched on Vienna. French armies under the leadership of Jourdan and Moreau would advance along the Danube and Main rivers respectively, while the third assault would be made through northern Italy by Napoleon Bonaparte.

Napoleone Buonaparte (as he wrote it up to 1796) was born on the 15th August 1769 in Ajaccio on the island of Corsica, barely a year after Louis XV of France had bought the island from the Republic of Genoa. The Buonapartes were of noble Florentine descent, and most of them were lawyers, officials or clergy in established Italian society.

From his mother, Letizia Ramolini, Napoleon learned discipline and perseverance, thrift, and a love for his family. From his father, Carlo Buonaparte, he inherited personal charm, to be exploited when he deemed it necessary, and an opportunism which was to stand him in good stead. After his education at Brienne and the École Militaire in Paris, he was promoted to lieutenant in 1785, qualified as an artillerist. The young lieutenant subsequently educated himself extremely well by reading widely in the works of Plato, Aristotle, Thucydides and the *philosophes*. He also extensively studied the campaigns of Alexander the Great, Caesar, Charlemagne, Condé and others.

The authoritarian aspects of the works of *philosophes* such as Montesquieu, Voltaire and Rousseau probably had the greatest influence on him. Rousseau advocated government by "general will", but he defined this as being that which was best for mankind, whether mankind approved of it or not. Napoleon was later to share a similar point of view by declaring that sovereignty was embodied in the French people in so far as everything, without exception, should be done in their interest, for their prosperity and their glory.

In 1793 Paoli, governor of Corsica, declared the island independent. The Buonapartes and other French sympathizers were exiled, whereupon the former fled to France in June 1793. At last Napoleon Bonaparte, who had been see-sawing between the French army and the Corsican National Guard, became a devoted Frenchman.

In the same month the city of Toulon revolted against the Reign of Terror because the moderate Girondins were expelled from the Convention. The rebels were supported by a British naval task force in the harbour. Napoleon, as acting commanding officer of the artillery, spotted the key British position, took it, and from there beat off the British fleet.

Although Napoleon was promoted to brigadier-general at the age of twenty four, this was not really exceptional. Worth mentioning, however, is the fact that Carnot, the military member of the Committee of Public Safety, was busy replacing all older and incompetent officers, or presumed royalists, with younger men who had proved themselves on the battlefield.

With the beheading of Robespierre in 1794, some of his followers were arrested, but Napoleon was released within two weeks on the grounds that as military officer he had merely been executing the orders of the Committee of Public Safety.

Subsequently the revolt of the 5th October 1795 (in the month Vendémiaire) took place, during which Napoleon dispersed the crowd with gunfire. With the establishment of the Directory, Napoleon was to give France a taste of the glory of victory, for almost simultaneously with his marriage to Josephine Beauharnais in March 1796, he was made military commander of the French army in Italy.

In Italy a formidable task awaited Napoleon. Certain circumstances counted against him. He had little experience against foreign enemies, and because of his descent and slight Italian accent, he was regarded by many as a foreigner. Then, at 1,53 m he was 5 cm taller than the average French soldier, but most French officers were much taller than he, and literally looked down on him. His officers and men, however, soon experienced what Connelly calls the "Napoleonic presence". He describes it as: "The eagle-sharp stare of the blue-grey eyes, the coiled-spring air of suppressed violence that demanded attention." [17] The officers soon discovered that Napoleon knew more than they did of the French army in Italy. In fact, a secret of his success was his thorough preparation and hard work.

With the aid of his elder brother, Joseph, who was consul in Genoa, and Salicetti, chief of the commissariat, he obtained better food, clothes and arms – and prompt pay – for his soldiers, and promised them the riches of Italy. What he achieved can be described as a miracle of leadership. Within a month he had changed a sulky rabble into a battle-hungry army, inspired with the will to win.

At this early stage Napoleon was demonstrating his ability to influence people, which he would subsequently display in civil as well as military matters. His mere presence and energy, his charm, intelligence and his incredible mind for detail, stood him in excellent stead.

In Italy Napoleon achieved great success and more than made good the fact that the other two French armies were checked by Archduke Charles. After heavy battles he managed to separate the Austrian and Sardinian forces, and then eliminated the Sardinians by concluding the Armistice of Cherasco with them. He could then continue with his main task, which was to drive the superior Austrian force from Italy. After months of hard campaigning, he succeeded. He pursued the Austrians up to 130 km from Vienna and, in April 1797, there concluded the provisional Peace of Leoben with them. Meanwhile he had also forced the pope to cede Bologna, Ferrara and Romagna to France, and to pay a large indemnity.

The *coup d'état* of Fructidor ensured that peace negotiations with Britain would break down, but in October 1797 the Treaty of Campo Formio with Austria brought about peace on the European continent. It ratified the annexation of Belgium (the Austrian Netherlands) by France, determined the Rhine as France's eastern border, and gave Austria the largest part of Venice in exchange for Lombardy, which was annexed to territory taken from Venice and the pope to form the Cisalpine republic.

The Treaty of Campo Formio eliminated Austria from the First Coalition. Only Britain remained. This had far-reaching consequences for Italy and would eventually lead to the unification of this disrupted country. With the partition of Venice between Austria and France, Venice ceased to exist as an independent state. In addition to the forming of the Cisalpine republic, the Ligurian republic was born, because Genoa was encouraged to overthrow its oligarchic government. Both republics were under the influence of France. The following year the Roman republic was born. The Revolution paved the way for republicanism in territories which had previously been ruled by princes, dukes and other sovereigns.

Now France could devote its attentions to Britain. Because of Britain's naval domination, an invasion of the British Isles was out of the question. Instead, it was planned to weaken it by an assault on its route to India. The conquest of Egypt would cut off the artery of its prosperity and power, and form the basis of a great French empire in the east. The Directory was also fortunate, of course, to be able to rid itself of Napoleon in this manner, as his abilities and popularity in France could elevate him to a dangerous opponent.

The French army embarked in February 1798. Militarily speaking, however, the expedition was a failure. Even though Malta was conquered *en route*, the Egyptian cavalry was beaten in the Battle of the Pyramids, and Cairo was occupied, Admiral Nelson annihilated the French fleet in Aboukir Bay in August 1798. Napoleon and his army were completely cut off from France. He could do no more than establish the authority of the French republic in Egypt as firmly as possible. Meanwhile, French scientists investigated the art and antiquities of Egypt. Amongst others, the Rosetta Stone was discovered, which was to make possible the deciphering of Egyptian hieroglyphs.

While Napoleon was in Egypt, the Directory attempted to change the map of Europe, making use of France's increasing power and prestige. In addition to the existing republics, the Swiss cantons were recreated as the republic of Helvetia, and Naples became the Parthenopean republic.

France's enemies were not prepared to put up with this. Austria felt itself threatened by French control of Italy, and by the subjugation of Switzerland. Tsar Paul of Russia was enraged by the occupation of Malta, of which he was the protector. Thus the Second Coalition, consisting of Britain, Austria, Russia, the Ottoman empire and the exiled princes of Naples came into being to counter France's new diplomatic and military aggression.

In the war which broke out in March 1799, the French were defeated practically everywhere in Europe. In Italy, in particular, the joint Austrian and Russian forces were successful in driving out the French. In the Ottoman empire, matters developed more favourably for France. When Napoleon, then in Egypt, heard that the sultan was arming, he invaded Syria, conquered one city after another, and defeated the Turks at Jaffa.

The loss of his artillery and an epidemic of bubonic plague among his men forced Napoleon to break off the siege of Acre and retreat to Egypt. In Cairo he re-established his authority and defeated a Turkish army which had been shipped by the British fleet. The news of the French setbacks in Europe, which had reached a zenith with the loss of Italy in the summer of 1799, decided Napoleon to return to France immediately. He left his army in Egypt, and arrived in France in October 1799, where he was received with great enthusiasm as the conqueror of Egypt.

Meanwhile, the prestige of the French armies was restored by Masséna, who saved the Helvetian republic against an Austro-Russian onslaught, and by Brune, who defeated a British army in the Batavian republic. But the French were weary of war. They wanted a leader who could transform the eternal war into an honourable peace. To them, Napoleon, whose reputation had increased through his Egyptian campaign, was that man.

There was also growing dissatisfaction with the Directory, which was under suspicion of exploiting the war in its own interests. The setbacks in Italy and the repressive measures which followed the *coup d'état* of 1797, further fanned feelings against the Directory. The election of 1799 showed a strong swing to the left in the legislative chambers. They immediately nominated a new Directory, which was in a weaker position than ever before in its dealings with the legislative authority. This situation anew offered Jacobins as well as royalists the opportunity of overthrowing the constitution. There was a general desire for a strong government which could restore internal peace, consolidate the social gains of the Revolution and restore French prestige abroad. Moderate republicans as well, under a new member of the Directory, the Abbé Siéyès, sought somebody to help them to review the constitution.

Napoleon's arrival in Paris could not have been better timed. He was soon plotting with Siéyès for the overthrow of the government. Both were of the opinion that confidence had to come from below, from the people, and authority from above, but Siéyès had not taken into account Napoleon's lust for power.

The *coup d'état* took place on 18 and 19 Brumaire (that is, the 9th and the 10th November 1799). The Council of Elders, where most of the deputies supported Siéyès, determined on his secret recommendation that the assemblies should meet in St Cloud to prevent the intervention of the Paris mobs. Three members of the Directory resigned, and the other two were arrested. This necessitated the institution of a new executive authority. Napoleon was put in command of the troops in Paris. The plan almost miscarried when the Council of Five Hundred resisted and threw Napoleon out of the hall after his speech. Napoleon's brother, Lucien, the chairman of the Five Hundred, however, saved the *coup d'état*. He called on the soldiers to save their general, and the recalcitrant members of the Five Hundred were simply driven out of the hall at bayonet point.

The remaining members subsequently entrusted the authority to a provisional executive committee of three consuls, consisting of Siéyès, Ducos and Napoleon. A commission was also appointed to assist the consuls with the administration and revision of the constitution.

The Directory had come to an inglorious end, and the first step towards the dictatorship of Napoleon had been taken. The failure of the Directory was an indication of the weak parliamentary tradition in France. But it proved in particular that a strong executive power was necessary in a post-revolutionary France, which remained sharply divided along social, political and religious lines.

CHAPTER 11

NAPOLEON BONAPARTE

THE CONSTITUTION OF 1799 AND THE WAR AGAINST THE SECOND COALITION

Napoleon was aware that the French, after ten years of revolution and war, were more interested in stability and security than in equality or even liberty. In his whole approach he took account of this, but he also identified himself with the will of the French people as reflected in the *cahiers* of 1789. In those terms, they did not demand the abolition of the monarchy, but a more efficient government, equal taxation, justice and the elimination of privilege. He was to curtail liberty in France, but exert himself for greater equality before the law, and for equal opportunities.

His conduct is clearly delineated by the manner in which he had the Constitution of the Year VIII (1799) ratified. In February 1800 the people were asked, after a propaganda campaign of two months, to vote for the Constitution in a plebiscite – two months after it had been put into operation, and the legislative bodies had already been appointed. Although 3 000 000 votes were for the Constitution, and only 1 500 against, about 4 000 000 Frenchmen did not vote at all. None the less, Napoleon took the result as a vote of confidence in himself.

Although it was republican in form, the Constitution did not guarantee the sovereignty of the people, and gave the executive authority wide powers. Nominally, executive authority was vested in the Consulate – the committee of three consuls – but the actual authority rested with the first consul, Napoleon himself. Although he could consult the second consul and the third consul if he pleased, his decision was final. With the exception of judges, who would be elected, the first consul personally appointed or dismissed the ministers and all other high government officials, including military personnel. He also gained the right to conclude peace and declare war, subject to ratification by the legislative authority. The consuls were assisted by a Council of State, which drafted and introduced laws and ordinances, and whose members were nominated by the first consul, as well as by a senate of sixty (later eighty) life members, which had no legislative powers, unless it was a matter of constitutionality.

The senate's task was to nominate the members of the legislative authority, namely the Tribunate of 100 members and the Legislative Body of 300 members, from a list of "notables". These notables were indeed elected by universal male suffrage, and not only by "active" citizens, but the franchise was now actually more

The Congress of Vienna. Painting by Jean-Baptiste Isabey. Metternich stands left of the table, pointing towards Castlereagh, who is seated at the table with his legs crossed. Talleyrand is the third figure from the right at the rear of the table, while the Duke of Wellington is standing at the extreme left.

The invasion of the Tuileries palace by the Paris mob in 1848.

limited than in the Constitutions of 1791, 1793 and 1795. All the voters in a commune could elect one-tenth of their number to a communal list. These elect could then again vote one-tenth of themselves onto the departmental list, which in turn elected a tenth to the national list. These were then the so-called notables of France, from whom the senate nominated the members of the Tribunate and Legislative Body. Out of something more than 6 000 000 enfranchised voters, there were therefore only 6 000 on the national list.

The Tribunate had the authority to discuss legislation which had been introduced by the first consul or the Council of State, but it had no vote in the matter, and could not initiate legislation. The Legislative Body, in turn, could vote on proposed legislation during its four-month sessions, but no debate was permitted.

The whole arrangement was a denial of popular government, although this was not generally perceived at once. It was, in fact, calculated to place the supreme authority in the hands of the first consul, Napoleon. As the first consul made appointments to the Council of State, and as this council could also carry through urgent legislation (and all legislation was, to Napoleon, a matter of urgency), and as he appointed the members of the senate, which in turn nominated the members of the Tribunate and the Legislative Body, Napoleon in fact also controlled the legislative authority. The separation of powers as embodied in the Constitution of 1791 therefore continued only in theory. Although universal male suffrage had been introduced, it was virtually meaningless, as the members of the assemblies were nominated and not elected. In addition, the legislative bodies were, in subsequent years, increasingly stripped of their already limited power. Napoleon defended himself on the grounds that the people gave him a mandate from time to time through the plebiscites, but this method was employed merely to confirm decisions which had already been taken.

The powers which had been exercised in the time of the Reign of Terror by the Committee of Public Safety were therefore now concentrated in the hands of one man, and this was more than Louis XVI ever had in the *ancien régime*. "Napoleonic parliamentary institutions were from the beginning little more than window dressing for what was essentially a dictatorship," is Breunig's laconic comment.[1] Indeed, the Council of State, for example, was nothing other than a revival of the *conseil du roi* (royal council) of the *ancien régime*.

His choice of subordinate consuls, Cambacérès and Lebrun, reveals Napoleon's true attitude. Lebrun was a royalist who had kept himself aloof during the Revolution, while Cambacérès had been a member of the "Plain" (the centre) during the Convention and now proved to be loyal to Napoleon. Subsequently, Napoleon gradually increased the number of ex-royalists in the government, thereby moving step by step in the direction of a monarchy.

One should, however, guard against judging Napoleon according to modern views of democracy. Justifiably Thompson puts the case that the French would not necessarily have condemned the franchise issue the way a modern voting public would do: "Indeed, few people still thought in terms of 'rights'... It was thought more important that there should be elected assemblies than that they should be elected in any special way; and indirect election had long come to be accepted as the normal method."[2]

Although the introduction of a new constitution and peace at home were Napoleon's priorities, action against the Second Coalition – Britain, Austria, Russia, the Ottoman empire and the exiled sovereigns of Naples – was no less important. Napoleon also needed victories in battle to entrench his internal position, against the Jacobins on the one hand, and the conspiring nobility on the other. Consequently, he launched his campaign against the Second Coalition.

With characteristic speed and self-confidence he crossed the Great St Bernard Pass in the Alps in May 1800 and invaded Italy. On the 14th June he scattered the Austrians at Marengo. This time he consolidated his forces and drove his enemies into a corner. Five days later a French force under Field Marshal Moreau defeated the Austrians at Ulm, following this with the important victory at Hohenlinden on the 2nd December 1800.

To save Vienna, Emperor Francis II was forced to sign the Peace of Lunéville in February 1801 on Napoleon's conditions. Basically it was a confirmation of the Treaty of Campo Formio (October 1797), while the independence of the Batavian, Helvetian, Cisalpine and Ligurian republics was guaranteed. The pope and the king of Naples were left in possession of their states. Austria was compelled to recognize French annexation of the left bank of the Rhine, but retained Venice. France had restored its lost foreign prestige. With the absorbing of Piedmont into France in 1801, the pattern became quite clear: a league of Continental vassal states under French hegemony was replacing the traditional balance of power. In January 1802 the Cisalpine republic became the Italian republic, with Napoleon as its president. It was clear that Napoleon was no longer confining himself to the natural frontiers of France.

With the elimination of Austria, the Second Coalition collapsed. Napoleon's conciliatory policy towards Russia and the accession of a new tsar, Alexander I, offered Russia the opportunity of withdrawing from the struggle. Once again, Britain was the only remaining member of the coalition. Notwithstanding British successes at sea, such as the reconquest of Malta in 1800, the driving of the French army out of Egypt, and the occupation of the Dutch and Spanish colonies, the British government desired peace. British merchants wanted to gain access to Continental markets. Napoleon himself strove for an honourable peace, which would enable him to consolidate his position in France and Europe.

In March 1802 the two powers signed the Treaty of Amiens. Britain gave France or its allies (Spain and the Batavian republic) back all the territories which it had conquered since the beginning of the war, with the exception of Trinidad and Ceylon. France agreed to vacate the kingdom of Naples and the papal states, return Egypt to Turkey and, in concert with Britain, recognize the restitution of Malta to the Order of the Knights of the island. France was left in control of the Batavian republic, Belgium, the left bank of the Rhine, Switzerland, and the largest part of the Italian peninsula. The independence of the Italian mini-republics which had been established under French authority, was not recognized. It is important to note that France was left a free hand in reshaping Germany.

British merchants who had been looking forward to the restoration of trade with Continental ports were the greatest opponents of the treaty, as it made no provision for this, and as, moreover, most of these harbours were now in French hands.

Although the treaty with Britain lasted only just over a year, France enjoyed a breather from war on the Continent for almost five years (1800-1804). During this period, Napoleon's *régime* was highly beneficial to France. With half his aims – peace on the Continent – achieved, Napoleon now had the opportunity to create internal peace and stability.

THE RECONSTRUCTION OF FRANCE AND THE EXTENSION OF NAPOLEON'S POWER, 1799-1815

If the French nation had sacrificed its political liberty with the Constitution of 1799, at least it had gained an energetic and efficient government in exchange. Napoleon's watchwords were order and authority. Two important tasks were to combat brigandage and to pacify the western area around La Vendée after unrest had broken out again for the umpteenth time towards the middle of 1799. However, military detachments acted with great determination, and as a result, the numerous bands of brigands which had plagued France were eradicated by the spring of 1800. Policy regarding the insurrectionists in La Vendée was more conciliatory. Most political detainees, as well as rebels willing to submit within a given deadline, were granted amnesty. The émigrés, with the exception of the most notorious, were allowed to return, and permission was given for public religious services.

After ten years of political unrest France enjoyed a competent, honest and energetic government. The Revolution of 1789 had been a social, administrative and political revolution; by 1800 the French were ready to bury the political side of the Revolution in order to consolidate its other two aspects.

The first few years of the 19th century, when Napoleon was able to devote his attention to the internal reorganization of France, were of the most important periods in the country's history. The financial, judicial, administrative and religious innovations which would form the basis of France in the 19th century, fell into this era.

On the 19th February 1800 Napoleon moved into the Tuileries and immediately went to work. Although he had not been trained for his task, he succeeded in teaching himself very rapidly. His strong point was to recognize capable men and organize them to his own advantage.

Just like the Directory, the Consulate set out with an almost bare treasury. With his first law of 3 Frimaire (the 24th November 1799), Napoleon countered the financial problems, which the Directory had been unable to solve, or which it had created, by means of centralization: a director of taxation was put in control in Paris, to whom deputies in each department and agents in each *arrondissement* and commmune were responsible. In this manner the whole tax machinery was put on a firm footing, which enabled the government to make a better estimate of its revenue. Direct taxation was kept at a steady level, while indirect taxation was increased as the need arose. As his power increased, Napoleon instituted more and more indirect taxes, such as the tax on alcohol in 1804, and on salt, two years later.

Yet the French hardly complained, although their taxes were the highest in Europe. The franc was the most stable currency in Europe – and this included Britain in this period.[3]

In order to relieve the high interest rates on government loans and stabilize the currency, Napoleon established the Bank of France in February 1800 with a capital of 300 000 000 franc in 1 000-franc shares. In 1803 it gained the exclusive right to issue bank notes in Paris. In due course its influence spread across the whole of France. The shareholders included the first consul, members of his family and leading government officials. The Bank of France is still today the country's central financial institution, although it was nationalized in 1945.

The results of this economic policy were favourable, and there was a noticeable improvement in public finances. After the resumption of hostilities in 1803, the military victories helped to relieve the pressure on the treasury, because the French armies under Napoleon provided for themselves outside France. Regular tax collection and economizing on government expenditure even balanced the budget for the Year X (1801-1802). French industries grew by 25 per cent, and various new industries – in metals, wool, sugar-refining, tobacco-processing and cotton – were established. Unemployment was low or unheard-of, thanks to the industrial growth, larger European markets, protective tariffs and military service. Trade was promoted by improving roads, canals and harbours. The purchasing power of the bourgeoisie in particular, benefited from these measures.

Agriculture also expanded. The growing population, a series of crop failures and military requirements forced price increases, thereby increasing the purchasing power of the landowning peasants. The general public was impressed with the payment of debts, which was, to them, the most important. Thus Napoleon bound all classes closer to him. He had become, indeed, "the bulwark of society".[4]

These financial reforms of the Consulate did not, however, bring about a large measure of financial stability. Napoleon was unable to create full confidence in government policy, as his measures were arbitrarily taken, and not openly. As a result, the market value of government stock was, on average, rarely more than half of its face value.

As far as central administration was concerned, Napoleon demanded regular ministerial reports from his ten ministries. A department of internal affairs served as a central bureau to the various ministries, and also transmitted Napoleon's instructions to them, thus relegating the ministers to the status of ordinary clerks. In addition, general managing boards which were directly responsible to Napoleon were created within certain ministries to facilitate administration and to further decrease the authority of the ministers.

An important aspect was local administration. Although the Revolution's geographic division into departments was retained, (there were now 98, which were soon to increase to 102), Napoleon reversed a characteristic principle of the Revolution by returning to the centralization of the Bourbon monarchy. A law of the 17th February 1800 replaced the local self-government and elected officials of the years 1789-1792, with officials appointed by the first consul, to whom they were also responsible: prefects for the departments, subprefects for the 400 *arrondissements* (previously called districts), and mayors for the 40 000 communes. Although local assemblies continued to assist these officials, chiefly in an advisory capacity, they were also nominated in Paris, and no longer elected. The prefects were nothing other than a revival of the intendants of the *ancien régime*. As with the central government, the chief aim of reform here was to eliminate election by the people. Thus Napoleon paved the way for his centralized despotism. Centralization, the creation of the Bourbon monarchy, had been partially destroyed by the Revolution, but was being restored in 1800. The fairly simple and centralized system exists to this day, more or less in the shape it was given by Napoleon, although currently mayors are elected.

Reform of the judicial authority began in March 1800 when the election of judges was ended. Napoleon now appointed them for life. A chancellor and the Council of State supervised judicial authority. Initially, the council interpreted the legislation, but later, during the empire period, this authority was shared with the emperor's Privy Council.

An early achievement was Napoleon's religious settlement. Religious issues had seriously divided France since the Civil Constitution of the Clergy had been promulgated in 1791. Two important causes of the unrest and friction were the breach with Rome, and the tension between loyal priests, who had accepted the Civil Constitution, and the nonjuring priests who had refused to do so and who had also cooperated with the royalists in La Vendée.

Although Napoleon had no strong religious convictions, he appreciated the value of religion for the people. He was aware of the religious revival amongst the bourgeoisie, and realized that the masses were basically still Roman Catholic. His declared support of Roman Catholicism would therefore be useful in gaining the people's obedience to law and order. An agreement with the pope would drive a wedge between royalism and Roman Catholicism, finally subjugate La Vendée, and reassure buyers of church lands about their property.

Following lengthy negotiations with Pope Pius VII, the Concordat was signed in 1801. Although it was a compromise, the French government benefited most. All French Roman Catholics were granted religious freedom, on condition that they obeyed police regulations. Roman Catholicism was recognized as the religion of the three consuls, in other words, of the government of the Republic, and of the "large majority of the French citizens". It was not recognized as the state religion, as such a measure would be a denial of a principle of the Revolution, namely liberty of conscience. In exchange for this semi-privileged status of the Roman Catholic church, the pope in the name of the church relinquished all claims to church property which had been declared forfeit. All bishops had to resign, and new ones would henceforth be nominated by the first consul and canonically installed by the pope. The lower clergy would be appointed by the bishops, subject to ratification by the state. As the loss of church property and the abolition of the tithe had drastically reduced the income of the church, the state agreed, as with the Civil Constitution of the Clergy, to pay the salaries of bishops and priests who, in turn, had to take an oath of allegiance to the government. The French also recognized the papal states.

The phrase dealing with "police regulations" gave Napoleon further opportunity to curtail the activities of the church. Once the pope had proclaimed his bulls about the Concordat, Napoleon issued a set of regulations, known as the Organic Articles, in April 1802, as if they were part of the Concordat. The authority of the state over the church was thus unequivocally confirmed, and the connection between the pope and the French bishops further weakened. It was a return to the Gallicanism of the 17th century, according to which all clergy had to swear allegiance to the French government which was to pay their salaries. The government also forbade the publication of papal bulls or the decrees of ecclesiastical councils, without its approval.

Although ardent republicans were opposed to the compromise represented by the Concordat, and saw it as a retrogressive step, the largest part of the population welcomed reunion with the Roman Catholic church. Napoleon, too, was satisfied, as his most important aims had been achieved. The differences in the church between the loyal and nonjuring priests were, to a large extent, settled, (although there were still thirty eight of the nonjuring ninety three who refused to recognize the Concordat). Purchasers of church lands, who now had property rights, became loyal to Napoleon in gratitude. The success of the Concordat formed a firm foundation for Napoleon's rule.

The Civil Code (the *Code Napoléon*) is undoubtedly Napoleon's most important and lasting achievement. Such a code was essential. When Napoleon came to power, there were 366 local codes in force throughout the country, containing Frankish, Roman, royal, provincial and feudal elements. In addition, the Revolution had radically changed the system of ownership by the abolition of feudal privilege and the sale of church properties. The new situation had to be defined and stabilized.

The idea of creating order in the chaotic administration of justice did not originate with the First Consul. At the beginning of the Revolution, the National Assembly had passed a resolution to codify the legal system, but nothing had come of it. Napoleon, with characteristic drive and single-mindedness, completed the task.

In August 1800 Napoleon nominated a committee of four jurists to draft a civil code of laws. As he had a great interest in family law, Napoleon personally attended about half the sessions of the Council of State, during which the draft was discussed in detail. Although it was completed as early as January 1801, the proclamation of the Code was delayed until the 21st March 1804 because the Tribunate and the Legislative Body opposed certain provisions. This was one of the few occasions on which these assemblies delayed proposed legislation.

The final draft, consisting of 2 281 articles, is characterized by precision and clarity. It was a compromise between the most important ideals of the Revolution and the authoritarian views of Napoleon himself. On the one hand, it made provision for a uniform legal system for the whole country, the freedom of the individual, equality before the law, the right to private property, secularization of the state, liberty of conscience and the freedom of everyone to choose his own profession or work. It confirmed the abolition of all aspects of feudalism, and, amongst others, ratified the land settlement of the Revolution.

On the other hand, the Code incorporated Napoleon's authoritarian views by promoting the interests of the state or a figure of authority at the cost of the individual. The family was of great value to the state, as it was one of those units which disciplined the behaviour of the individual. In this spirit, the patriarchal authority of Roman Law, which had been weakened by the Revolution, was re-established. A father could make his children serve up to six months in gaol purely on his own evidence, and had total control of their property. Furthermore, he could administer his wife's property and, as common ownership was law, he could do with it as he pleased. To prevent families from becoming too powerful, the family was put under the guardianship of the state. The Code determined, for example, how property inheritances were to be arranged. Civil marriages, which meant that marriages had to be registered with the state, were compulsory, even if the couple had been married in church. Divorce by mutual consent was possible, or in the case of adultery, after a criminal offence, or by reason of insanity. But as the legislation strove to preserve the family as a unit, divorce was difficult to obtain. In other respects, too, women were regarded as "less equal" than men and discriminated against. For example: should a woman detect her husband in adultery and kill him or his partner, she was guilty of murder, but in a reverse situation the man could not be charged.

Like all other legislation this (concerning control over wife and children) should be viewed in the spirit of the time. Although it was a return to the social discipline of pre-revolutionary France, the French laws were only adapted in the 1960s to provide a reasonable measure of equality for women. The divorce law was changed as recently as 1965, and only in the following year were women permitted to own businesses.

The Civil Code was silent about those who owned nothing, except that their personal freedom was protected by forbidding the permanent leasing of services. Freedom to work and equality before the law in fact exposed the wage-earner to the risks of competition.

The Code in reality therefore rejected the Jacobin ideal of the individual's right to existence. As only the employer's word was taken in wage disputes, the Code even departed from the principle of equality by discriminating against the wage-earner. In addition, the state employed its police powers to enforce labour discipline. The reason for this was that the Code could not offer employers sufficient protection, as the workers, because of their poverty, were immune to court cases. The law of the 22nd Germinal of the Year XI (the 12th April 1803) renewed the ban on trade unions, and on the 1st December 1803 a decree obliged workers to carry a labour pass issued by a local authority, without which they could not be employed. Thompson compares the Code to the Concordat, and comes to the conclusion: "Both recognised and exploited the need that most Frenchmen feel for a power which will control and an authority which will decide."[5]

An important feature of the Code was its concern with land as property. The right to private property, as has been pointed out, was recognized. It was still regarded as the most important form of wealth, while industrial prosperity, business undertakings or credit were disregarded.

From the foregoing it is clear that the code was bourgeois-oriented. It was, as Lefebvre puts it, "the product of the evolution of the French society insofar as it created the bourgeoisie and carried it to power".[6]

The Civil Code was followed by the Code of Civil Procedure (1806), the Commercial Code (1807), Criminal Procedure (1808) and the Penal Code (1810). These codes were increasingly reactionary and illustrated the growing extension of Napoleon's powers. There was a return to the laws of the *ancien régime*. Heavy penalties were imposed for political offences against persons and property. The branding iron and severing of a hand were accepted as the penalty for patricide. The pre-revolutionary principle, according to which the onus was on the defender to prove his innocence, was reinstituted. The intention was to protect the state, and not the individual. The argument went that it was better to punish the innocent than that society should suffer. Although arbitrary arrest and detention were forbidden, people could, on the strength of a warrant, be detained for virtually unlimited periods. Plaintiffs had more rights than defendants, while judges could order retrials if juries had acted "illegally". Torture by the police was allowed under judicial restraint, which meant that the police acted rather brutally.

Once again the interests of the employer were carefully guarded, and the organizing of trade unions and the calling of strikes – the workers' only defence against exploitation – was forbidden. The Commercial Code was not well adapted to the demands of 19th century capitalism, and was therefore not a success. The Rural Code, on which a commission began in 1804, and which was promulgated only in 1814, after the abdication of Napoleon, remained a dead letter, in company with the Industrial Code.

The Revolution had its most far-reaching consequences in the sphere of law. The Napoleonic Codes, with extensions or amendments, still underlie the laws of France. The Civil Code also influenced the legal systems of Belgium, the Netherlands, Luxemburg, Bavaria, Baden, Westphalia, Switzerland, Italy, Rumania, Egypt, Canada, Louisiana, Haiti, Bolivia and even Japan. Napoleon himself regarded it as his greatest achievement. On St Helena he remarked: "My true fame does not lie with the forty battles I have won. Waterloo will erase the memory of those victories. But what can never be erased, what will continue in existence, is my Civil Code."

Napoleon believed that education had to agree with the established social order and the authoritarian nature of his régime. It should "embrace the nation" and be the "first concern" of the state, a "source of power" by which he could control the political and moral opinion of the youth and raise the able officers and obedient officials which he needed so badly. He did not believe in education for its own sake, but in education as a service to the state.[7] The result was a national, government-controlled educational system at all levels, although this was not applied in practice in every respect.

The principle of free elementary education for all children had already been embodied in the Constitution of 1791 and had been confirmed by the Convention, but little progress in its establishment was made in the course of the Revolution. The Napoleonic government was not much more successful in extending the principle. Elementary education was left to the municipalities, as in the days of the *ancien régime*. In more than one department, half the communes had no teachers, and there were no funds for teacher training. In rural areas illiteracy persisted. It has been calculated that only one out of every eight children of school-going age was accommodated in the existing primary schools in 1813. Like Voltaire before him, Napoleon took the view that education for the poor was politically and socially "inconvenient".

As far as secondary education was concerned, the state-supported central schools of the Convention were initially allowed to coexist with the *prytanées,* which were also controlled by the central government, and whose syllabuses included classical grammar, mathematics and French literature. The standard was high, and education flourished in the initial years of the Consulate. Seemingly because they promoted independent thinking,[8] Napoleon allowed the central schools to die out. With the education ordinance of Fourcroy on the 11th Floréal of the year X (the 1st May 1802), the central schools and the *prytanées* were replaced by forty five *lycées* (of which only thirty nine were ultimately established) as well as 700 *écoles secondaires* (secondary schools), which were privately administered, but government-controlled. The *lycées* were nothing other than colleges of patriotism for the training of future leaders. The government prescribed the syllabuses, appointed teachers and enforced regulations by means of inspectors. The schools were controlled with military discipline, and retired officers even lectured on military matters. There were 6 400 bursaries available, of which 2 400 were reserved for the sons of officers and government officials, and the rest for the ablest scholars. Most of the poor were therefore excluded, but this system opened the way for talented members of the petite bourgeoisie to carve out a career for themselves. It was an attempt to bring this social class closer to the notables or upper bourgeoisie,[9] the class which benefited most from Napoleon's measures. Church schools were also permitted, but when they subsequently began to compete with the *lycées* because of the difference in cost, Napoleon returned to total government control of education.

In order to ensure control of education, Napoleon centralized this control by establishing the Imperial University in 1808. It was not a university in the usual sense of the word, but a kind of government department, a corporation of all the education personnel in France, aimed at promoting loyalty to the government. It drew up syllabuses, determined the nature of examinations, and controlled grading. In this manner the tradition of a strong central bureaucracy in the French national education system came about, a tradition which remained almost untouched up to the student riots of 1968.

Napoleon paid little attention to education for girls. According to him, their mothers were their best educators. Their role was at home, not in public life. He did, however, approve a finishing school for girls, where they were given some education. Most of their time was to be devoted to religious instruction, good manners and practical subjects such as needlework.

Napoleon's rule was also marked by drastic limitations on the freedom of expression and speech. This was clearly in violation of the Declaration of the Rights of Man. Napoleon accused "irresponsible intellectuals" of confusing the people. "Troublemakers", such as Madame de Stael, were banned from France. Napoleon advocated public harmony in political matters, but achieved it at the cost of freedom of expression.

In January 1800 Napoleon closed down sixty of the seventy three newspapers in

Paris. By the end of the year, only nine remained, and ultimately, only four were permitted. Only one newspaper could appear in each department. Newspapers became little more than mouthpieces for the government, carrying official news. A watch was also kept for any works of literature which may put the government in a bad light. Theatre was subjected to the strict censorship of agents who minutely examined all performances. Fixed censorship was instituted in February 1810 by the appointment of a director-general and imperial censors. The next year Napoleon instructed his censors to act more leniently and less arbitrarily.

It is customary to condemn the system of censorship under Napoleon, but in reality censorship was nothing new in France, and not stricter there than elsewhere in Europe. Besides, it was subsequently continued under the parliamentary government of the Restoration.

In order to enforce all the censorship regulations, a large and efficient police force was required. The notorious Fouché who, during the Reign of Terror had been relieved of his post because of excessive cruelty, was appointed as its chief. In 1810 he was succeeded by the less subtle Savary. Fouché established an effective espionage system to watch over the personal lives of thousands of individuals in all walks of society, who might be suspected of undermining sympathies. Daily police bulletins, spies and informers kept Napoleon abreast of public sentiment, while his "black cabinet" kept a strict watch on private correspondence. Because he was suspicious of Fouché, Napoleon preferred to have more than one parallel police organization. As a result, these organizations, striving to outdo one another, operated at the cost of the man in the street. Denying the principles of the Revolution, the system of *lettres de cachet* of the *ancien régime* was once again openly employed, following a decree of 1810. Its terms permitted the Privy Council to authorize detention without trial, and state gaols were established in which, in 1814, there were about 2 500 political prisoners. Other political opponents were kept in asylums for the insane. Consequently, the atmosphere in Paris by the end of Napoleon's reign was similar to that during the Reign of Terror and, according to Breunig, "certainly at odds with the principles of individual liberty and freedom of speech proclaimed in 1789".[10]

It is clear that Napoleon's reign became increasingly despotic. Yet there were profound reasons why the French did not oppose his laws. The National Assembly's policy of decentralization during the Revolution had exposed France to grave danger in times of war. The Committee of Public Safety, in its reaction to this, had then taken a firm hold of the reins of government. Under the Convention there had been a relaxation, until Napoleon took firm control once again. That he was able to satisfy his personal desire for domination in this manner was only possible because he had won the French to his cause by his victories on the battle front, because they enjoyed prosperity at home, and because he respected the social arrangements of the Revolution. The people were satisfied with and proud of their leader, but they had not yet realized that he was abusing his power, and that his aims were a threat to their interests. If his regime was acceptable to the people, says Jones, "it nevertheless showed an approach to government and administration that was at once in the tradition of Enlightened Despotism and yet also prefigured the pattern of the twentieth-century fascist state".[11] To his contemporaries, however, he was the soldier of the Revolution who had created order from chaos.

The more firmly the Consulate established itself, the more desperate grew the royalist and Jacobin plots against Napoleon. Every failed plot, however, gave him the opportunity of eliminating his opponents and extending his authority. The delaying tactics of the legislative bodies, concerning the Concordat and the Civil Code, also convinced him that these bodies had to be purged.

Between April and August 1802, a series of laws openly turned the Consulate into a dictatorship. The opportunity to do this was offered to Napoleon by the enthusiasm engendered by the Concordat and the Peace of Amiens. He requested the senate to elevate him to consul for life. When the senate, in a rare display of courage, refused, the Council of State proclaimed a plebiscite. On the 2nd August 1802 the voters, with a poll of more than 3 500 000 in favour and less than 9 000 votes against, approved Napoleon's consulship for life. Two days later the senate passed an amendment to the Constitution of the Year VIII. It was the so-called Constitution of the Year X.

This Constitution extended the legislative authority of the senate. It was empowered to nominate the second and the third consul, dissolve the Tribunate and the Legislative Body, and to review the Constitution by means of a *senatus consultum*. The Tribunate was reduced by half to fifty members, and would henceforth meet *in camera* in three groups, each discussing quite different legislation. In this manner the efficiency and political power of the only nearly representative body of the people was undermined. In 1807 the Tribunate was finally dissolved. Although the authority of the senate was increased, its subservience to the first consul was ensured. He nominated the candidates for the senate and acted as its chairman. Members of the senate were favoured with senior administrative posts and estates to tie them to the Napoleonic regime. The principle of the *senatus consultum* was therefore nothing less than a method by which Napoleon could legislate personally and by means of decrees.

The Constitution retained universal male suffrage, but elections were reduced to a minimum. A new system of electoral colleges, consisting of the 600 wealthiest citizens, replaced the national lists which, in fact, had never been put into operation. Thereby the election system was brought more directly under the control of Napoleon.

Meanwhile, more and more important appointments of chairmen, magistrates and various public officials came under Napoleon's control. A nominally democratic government was thus reshaped into an oligarchy of officials and experts who were appointed or dismissed at the will and whim of a single person.

The Constitution of the Year X and his life-long consulship practically gave Napoleon the powers of an absolute monarch. All that remained was to formally institute an imperial crown. In 1804 Napoleon's prestige stood very high as a result of his domestic and foreign successes. When a conspiracy to assassinate Napoleon, hatched by a group of émigrés in London under the duke of Artois, with the Breton leader, Cadoudal, and the royalist general, Pichegru, came to light, there was a strong reaction in France. All who favoured the continuance of the existing order –

the peasants who had received confiscated church lands during the Revolution, the merchants and businessmen who benefited by the order of the Consulate, and the bureaucrats and militarists whose fate was bound up with Napoleon's – were only too prepared to go along with a *senatus consultum* of the 18th May 1804, that Napoleon should become the "Emperor of the French", and that his office should be made hereditary. Only the heredity was tested in a plebiscite, of which the result (3 500 000 for, and 2 500 against) was once again an overwhelming confirmation of what was already a *fait accompli*.

The Republic had become an Empire. Napoleon did not regard the Revolution as irreconcilable with a monarchy. He now formally obtained the powers which he already exercised in practice. The second consul and the third consul now became, respectively, an arch-chancellor and an archtreasurer. Napoleon's brother, Joseph, was designated his successor in the absence of a direct heir. The old form of address, citizen (*citoyen*), was now abandoned as being anomalous in an empire.

On the 2nd December 1804 the coronation of Emperor Napoleon I took place in the cathedral of Notre-Dame. Pope Pius VII had a place of honour during the ceremony, but because he had been forewarned, he did not crown the emperor. In dramatic fashion, Napoleon crowned himself, an act immortalized by the skilled painter, Jean-Louis David. At Napoleon's side was the sword of Charlemagne, an indication that Napoleon was not a successor to the Bourbons, but to Charlemagne himself. An imperial court was established to lend more dignity to the office. However, this cut Napoleon off from his people: the constitution was now embodied in one man, and that man was no longer national or part of the people.

Napoleon employed architects, painters and sculptors to contribute to the illustriousness of his regime and to depict him as a hero. Particularly in Paris, numerous striking and geometric constructions were erected within a short time, amongst them the Arc de Triomphe. New bridges spanned the Seine, a number of streets were widened, and Paris sewerage and fresh-water provision were improved. Apart from the building and furnishing of such museums as the Louvre, numerous art treasures from conquered territories were brought to France. Artists such as David and Goya enjoyed Napoleon's patronage, while a number of scientists came to the fore, such as Gaspard Monge, the father of descriptive geometry, and the zoologist, Jean Baptiste Lamarck.

As was the case with his other measures, Napoleon's social policy thrust in two directions: on the one hand, he continued a principle of the Revolution by opening careers to talent, but on the other, this led to the creation of a new social class, the "aristocracy of merit". The idea of a "career open to talent" was not at odds with revolutionary principles. The first article of the Declaration of the Rights of Man stated that all people were from birth free citizens with equal rights, and social distinction arose purely on the grounds of usefulness, meaning talent.

Following the *coup d'état* of Brumaire in 1799, a select group of notables constituted the national list of voters. This list provided the appointments to the various legislative bodies and officialdom. There was therefore a dictatorship of the notables from the start. They were a group which were, so to speak, "more equal" than the rest of the population. Napoleon also made it clear to them that they had been saved from the "dangers of democracy", and that they held all the most important positions. It was from their ranks that Napoleon built up his aristocracy of merit. He held the view that a whole social hierarchy should be created with wealth and talent. Careers were opened to talent, but such people should preferably be wealthy, as Napoleon shared the suspicion of the rich of needy people with talent.[12] The notables were therefore from the bourgeoisie, where one could find talent coupled with wealth.

The most talented members of the petite bourgeoisie were equally incorporated into these notables, as their appointment as government officials or economic leaders would stifle any dissatisfaction.

Although Napoleon made the rise of the bourgeoisie possible, he did not trust them. Against his own growing ambition to institute a monarchy, the bourgeoisie brought forth individuals who were, firstly, proud that financially they owed nothing to anyone but themselves, and secondly, all the more determined not to lose their independence. Consequently, Napoleon moved further and further away from the Constitution of the Year VIII (1799), which provided the bourgeoisie with an important voice in government.

With the Constitution of the Year X (1802), Napoleon extended the power of the notables by instituting the electoral colleges. This simultaneously meant that he won the loyalty of the senators and higher officials and made them dependent on his person. The Penal Code even went as far as subjecting all organizations of more than twenty persons to Napoleon's authority. He was therefore aiming at extending his government control over important organizations, consisting of the aristocracy of merit. As they had an influence on the wage-earning classes, these organizations had to ensure the loyalty of the population in exchange for their privileges and honours. The electoral colleges and the legislative bodies aside, the Legion of Honour was such an organization.

On the 19th May 1802 Napoleon founded the Legion of Honour. He had come to the conclusion that mankind desires distinction, and consequently, he had already awarded swords of honour for meritorious service during the Directory. When he became first consul, he began to plan an organization which would reward merit in the civil and military spheres. In defence of his scheme, he declared to the Council of State, "I do not believe that the French love liberty and equality. They have not been changed by ten years of revolution ... They have only one feeling, and that is honour. We must nourish that feeling." [13]

The members of the Legion of Honour were to be chosen by a so-called Great Council. The fact that Napoleon was its chairman, agrees with his train of thought that the award of any honour or privilege should be under his control.

The Legion of Honour indeed consisted of a host of meritorious citizens who made up part of Napoleon's new aristocracy of merit. On the other hand, the principle of equality was maintained, as anyone who had given exceptional service to the state or society could be rewarded with membership.

An increasing bureaucracy of notables was added to the social organizations such as the electoral colleges and the Legion of Honour. Initially they were drawn from the wealthy bourgeoisie. In April 1803 Napoleon created the so-called *audi-*

teurs as a new set of officials. They were connected to the ministers and the Council of State, and formed the core of the high administration which had no ties with the Revolution. In fact, Napoleon now thrust aside national interest and brought about a reconciliation with the counter-revolution, as seen with the creation of the empire.

Between 1804 and 1808 the new aristocracy of merit was turned into an imperial aristocracy at court and in the salons, with medieval titles which went back to the Holy Roman empire. A number of returned émigrés received important posts in the imperial regime, and the Tuileries soon breathed the atmosphere of the old monarchy.

A *senatus consultum* of August 1806 permitted Napoleon to award hereditary fiefs (feudal estates) in Italy and Germany to generals and senior officials. This was a deliberate attempt to bind them more closely to the government. In July 1807 the title "great" was officially conferred on Napoleon. It was a title Louis XIV had last held.

In March 1808 the new aristocracy was formally established: at the top was the "royal" family (that is, the Bonapartes) who were swamped with princely titles, money and the opportunity of gaining new kingdoms. They were followed by dukes, counts and barons, each with a sum of money and inalienable hereditary estates. Below them were the knights who received a sum of money, but no estates. It was still an aristocracy open to talent, and several of Napoleon's military commanders, in particular, benefited.

Unfortunately for Napoleon, the new aristocracy looked no further than its self-interest. It simply endured the empire's gaudiness and was determined not to give up its privileges. The returned émigrés even awaited the fall of Napoleon. Napoleon had strengthened the pre-revolutionary aristocracy without tying it to his regime. In fact, he robbed his supporters of Brumaire of the authority which the new aristocracy wanted to exercise. His empire was busy reducing the base of its support. In addition, there were to be many foreign problems.

THE REORGANIZATION OF EUROPE, 1803-1807

The Peace of Amiens (March 1802) could be little more than a truce, for its terms failed to recognize the most important point. This was that British and French imperialism could not co-exist. The British prime minister, Addington, certainly viewed Amiens as more than a truce, but the same cannot be said of Napoleon.

The resumption of the struggle between Britain and France in May 1803 must be almost exclusively blamed on Napoleon. In the first place, he soon made it obvious that he no longer desired to maintain the status quo on the European continent. The absorption of Piedmont into France, and Napoleon's conversion of the Cisalpine republic into the Italian republic, with himself as president, virtually made him the ruler of northern Italy, clearly a violation of the Peace of Lunéville of 1801. His intervention in the discord in the Helvetian republic and the resulting creation of the Swiss confederation, caused further alarm amongst the states of the former Second Coalition. Napoleon's drastic reorganization of Germany in 1803 – in which 112 states of the Holy Roman empire disappeared from the map and their territories were incorporated in larger states such as Prussia and Bavaria – had the greatest negative effect on Austria. The ecclesiastical states, which traditionally supported Austria, were eliminated. In the next decade Bavaria, Württemberg and Baden would look to France for guidance. Napoleon's actions on the Continent therefore contributed to the dissolution of the peace.

A second reason must be sought in Napoleon's refusal to accept British commercial and colonial dominance. As long as Britain predominated in these areas, Napoleon could not exercise economic control of the Continent. For the rest of his regime Napoleon aimed at the destruction of this mastery of the British. It can be seen as an important reason for his fall. When his attempt to establish a colonial empire in the west failed, he attempted to undermine the British commercial dominance by mercantilism. His refusal to conclude a trade agreement with Britain, and his high import tariffs on British goods, virtually amounted to their exclusion from French markets. He also endeavoured to extend this policy to France's allies, thereby foreshadowing his subsequent Continental System. Probably no other action of Napoleon's did more to unite British opinion in favour of a resumption of the war with France.

In the third place, the British were justly disconcerted at Napoleon's renewed interest in the eastern reaches of the Mediterranean. It seemed that Egypt could easily be reconquered by France because of its weakened military position. With control over Italy and Egypt, it would not be difficult for Napoleon to turn the Mediterranean into a French sea. The profitable trade with the Levant would fall into French hands, and Britain's position in India would be threatened. In addition, Napoleon's authority in the Batavian republic, which gave him control over the strategically important Cape of Good Hope, made Britain unwilling to abandon another key to the east, namely Malta.

Under these circumstances Britain not only refused to vacate Malta, as determined at the Peace of Amiens, but furthermore demanded that Malta should remain occupied by British troops for ten years, and that France recall its troops from the Batavian republic and Switzerland.

War began officially in May 1803, when a French army invaded Hanover, which had as its ruler George III of Britain. Simultaneously, Napoleon sent another force to the mouth of the river Elbe to cut off British trade with the interior of Germany.

The idealistic but vacillating tsar, Alexander I of Russia, took the lead in the creation of the Third Coalition against France. Napoleon's reorganization disconcerted not only Russia because of its trade with and influence in the Balkans, but also the Austrian emperor of the Holy Roman empire, Francis II. Napoleon's crowning himself as emperor in 1804 was a further blow to Francis. In addition, Napoleon transformed the Italian republic into the kingdom of Italy early in 1805, with himself as hereditary king. This was an unlawful appropriation of a Habsburg title. In Britain the beginning of William Pitt's term of office in 1804 was decisive to the formation of the coalition. In April 1805 the Anglo-Russian Convention was signed in St Petersburg, and Austria joined the Third Coalition in August. It was determined that the Batavian republic would be given Belgium, while Savoy and Genoa would go to Piedmont.

The weak link in the entire political and military framework of the Third Coalition was the stubborn refusal of Frederick William III of Prussia to relinquish his neutrality. He took this attitude because he hoped that Napoleon would give him Hanover, because he was suspicious of Russia's aims in Poland, and because Prussia was dissatisfied with Britain's treatment of neutral shipping.

Napoleon did little to prevent the formation of the Third Coalition. Undoubtedly he regarded himself as strong enough to act against the old governments of Europe and to finalize his reorganizational plans for the territory. He stood strongly indeed. In May 1805 he crowned himself in Milan as "King of all Italy", and the next month incorporated the Genoan republic into his empire. He provisionally left Rome and southern Italy in peace, but these were nevertheless at his mercy. He controlled the Batavian republic and Switzerland, and could rely on the support of Spain which had been driven onto his side by the British treatment of their shipping. Furthermore, he forged an alliance with Württemberg and Baden, and with Bavaria which was threatened by Austria's plans in southern Germany.

Shortly after the resumption of hostilities between Britain and France in 1803 Napoleon concentrated an army at Boulogne, apparently to invade Britain. By 1805 it was certainly no longer his intention. Any possible invasion plans across the English Channel were, in any case, thwarted by Britain's mastery of the sea, and by Admiral Nelson's destruction of the combined French and Spanish fleets off Cape Trafalgar on the 21st October 1805. The battle of Trafalgar confirmed Britain's domination at sea and enabled her to make war on Napoleon for a further ten years. In 1805, however, the significance of the battle was not quite as clear, and news of it was almost swamped by reports of Napoleon's successes on the Continent. In fact, his concentration of the army opposite the English Channel enabled him to launch surprise attacks on Austria in Germany. On the 15th October 1805 he imposed a crushing defeat on the Austrians at Ulm, from where he proceeded to occupy Vienna.

Tsar Alexander did not fare much better than the Austrians. In an attempt to cut Napoleon off from Vienna, the Russian army was led into an ambush at Austerlitz on the 2nd December 1805. At the end of the bloody battle, the French had lost about 9 000 out of an army of 73 000, as against 27 000 Russians and Austrians in an army of 87 000. It was probably Napoleon's most famous victory, and an excellent first commemoration of his crowning as emperor.

The rest of the Russian and Austrian forces were totally demoralized, and the Third Coalition collapsed. Emperor Francis had no choice but to sue for peace. At the Peace of Pressburg in December 1805 Austria ceded Venetia, Istria and Dalmatia to the kingdom of Italy, and her Tyrolese and Swabian possessions to the dukes of Bavaria and Württemberg, in exchange for Salzburg. By her recognition of Bavaria, Württemburg and Baden as independent kingdoms, Austria lost her last foothold in Germany.

The campaign of 1805 is important, particularly because of its lasting influence on the political and social systems of southern and central Europe. It meant, in fact, the end of the 1 000 years of the Holy Roman empire for the German people, and of the loose federation of German states under the Habsburg archduke as elected emperor.

Francis II took the hereditary title of Francis I of Austria, hoping thereby at least to unite southern Germany and Austria. After Ulm and Austerlitz, however, it was clear that the task of organization and consolidation would not emanate from Vienna, but from Paris. Moreover, it was to take the form of a social and political revolution which was to unite the Germans in a large federation under the leadership of Napoleon. In fact, he declared shortly afterwards that he was the successor not of Louis XVI, but of Charlemagne, of which his coronation in December 1804, with Charlemagne's sword and imperial insignia from Aix-la-Chapelle, had already given notice. Napoleon dreamt of restoring the old medieval empire under French leadership. This was a means of excluding Britain from the Continent, and also to control and reform European society. The reconstruction of Europe had to follow the reconstruction of France.

A new era had begun, and this was symbolized by the reintroduction of the Gregorian (Christian) calendar as from the 1st January 1806. Also in January 1806, shortly after Pressburg, Napoleon declared Ferdinand of Naples deposed and instated his own brother, Joseph, as king of Naples. The occupation of the papal states by French troops brought the whole of Italy under the authority of Napoleon. In June 1806 he turned the Batavian republic into the kingdom of Holland, with his brother, Louis, as king. The next month the Confederation of the Rhine was established under the protection of Napoleon. Sixteen west German and south German sovereigns somewhat reluctantly renounced the Holy Roman empire and entered the Confederation. They would leave foreign policy to Napoleon and support him with troops. Each state retained independence in domestic affairs, and matters of common interest were dealt with by the Federal Diet at Frankfurt.

Prussia was beginning to realize that the neutrality had allowed Napoleon a free hand in Germany. Consequently, Frederick William III began to take a more provocative stance. His suspicions were fed by Napoleon's refusal to sanction a north German confederation under Prussian leadership. Furthermore, Frederick William learned that Napoleon had secretly offered Hanover to Britain in exchange for peace – after Prussia had received Hanover in 1805. Moreover, Napoleon forced Prussia to suspend its trade with Britain. Totally overestimating his power, Frederick William concluded an alliance with Russia in July 1806, mobilized in August and, without waiting for his ally, marched on the Confederation of the Rhine. The aged duke of Brunswick and Prince Hohenlohe, however, did not co-operate, and on the 14th October 1806 the Prussians were crushed at Jena and Auerstädt. Two weeks later Napoleon was in Berlin.

Frederick William, who had fled to the Russians, found the peace terms unacceptable, and decided to continue the war with Russian aid. In order to prevent the Russian army from joining the Prussians, Napoleon marched in an easterly direction. During the winter of 1806-1807 the French pursued the retreating Russians across the vast expanse of Poland and east Prussia. In February 1807 a fierce but indecisive battle was fought at Eylau. Having called up reinforcements from every part of his empire, Napoleon resumed his march and, on the 14th June 1807, won a resounding victory over the Russians at Friedland.

Without consulting his ally, Tsar Alexander opened peace negotiations with Napoleon, and Frederick William perforce had to submit. Two treaties, known as the Treaty of Tilsit, were signed on the 7th July 1807, one between France and Prussia, and another between France and Russia. Prussia was forced to pay a large indemnity and to maintain a French army of occupation until the indemnity had been paid. Prussia also lost all the territories it had gained in the three partitions of Poland in the previous century. These territories were transformed into the grand duchy of Warsaw and placed under the rule of the king of Saxony. The latter had previously been the duke of Saxony and, as such, an ally of Prussia until, after Jena, he switched sides and was made a king by Napoleon. Poland subsequently continued to provide Napoleon with troops, and was the eastern bulwark of the empire until 1813. Prussian territories west of the river Elbe were united to form the kingdom of Westphalia, with the youngest Bonaparte, Jerome, as king. Danzig became a so-called free city, under the command of a French general.

Russia was much more leniently treated, because of the plans Napoleon had with Alexander. Napoleon claimed virtually only the Ionian Islands, and relinquished part of Prussian Poland to Russia.

At the signing of the Treaty of Tilsit, Napoleon and Alexander also concluded a secret agreement for future joint action. Napoleon thus gave the tsar the impression that, in exchange for recognition of French hegemony in German and Italy, he was recognizing the Russian claim to an eastern European empire. The open Treaty of Tilsit therefore also made provision for Napoleon to act as mediator between Russia and Turkey in the war which had broken out in 1806. Secretly it was now agreed, however, that should the mediation fail, Napoleon would assist the tsar in a war, and that the Turkish European provinces, Moldavia and Wallachia, would be given to Russia. On the other hand, the secret agreement provided that the tsar would act as mediator between Britain and France. Should Britain refuse to hand back all the conquests she had made since 1805 and to recognize the freedom of the seas, Russia would declare war on Britain, close the Baltic ports to British products, and persuade Denmark, Sweden, Austria and Portugal to do the same. This undertaking of Alexander's was in accordance with Napoleon's Continental System, about which more will be mentioned later. In the knowledge that it was unlikely that Britain would accept these conditions, Napoleon knew that he could rely on Russian support in his efforts to eliminate British trade with the Continent. [14]

Both rulers parted highly satisfied. Alexander had cancelled the defeat at Friedland, but soon realized that Napoleon would not allow him to make substantial gains in the Balkans, nor hand him Constantinople. The Russian nobility, moreover, saw the Treaty of Tilsit as treason. For Napoleon, however, the treaty was a triumph. He had added an important ally and had made progress in isolating Britain and closing the Continent to British trade. Furthermore, he had gained the peace he so badly needed to control Austria, consolidate his position in central Europe and rest his battered army. In any case, neither Alexander nor Napoleon were to keep their promises. The newly found friendship evaporated within a few years.

The Third Coalition had collapsed, and Prussia was also defeated. Only Britain remained to offer resistance. In their attempts to dominate Europe, a way of eliminating Britain had been a problem to French rulers for centuries. Britain's domination of the seas and her entrenchment behind the English Channel and the North Sea exacerbated the problem. The French defeat at the battle of Trafalgar in 1805 had shattered the last hopes of a direct invasion. Some other means had therefore to be found for bringing Britain to her knees.

Napoleon's sense of realism failed him in economics, just as it had in naval strategy, and he acted according to doctrinaire principles and prejudice. He was convinced that Britain's large national debt was a symptom of vulnerability and weakness. He therefore thought that France could bring Britain to her knees by discrediting her balance of trade and consequently undermining confidence in her paper currency. This would not only eliminate Britain, but also stop the subsidies to her allies. The method Napoleon thought most suitable was the closing of the Continent to British manufactured goods. The state of the depleted and battered French fleet prevented Napoleon from following the reverse course, namely of blockading British harbours.

The idea of mercantilism (protectionism in trade) was not new by any means. France had a strong tradition of mercantilism since its application by Colbert in the 17th century. In 1793 French ports had been closed to British goods, but France had controlled too few ports at that stage to affect British trade to any degree. The extension of Napoleon's authority over the Netherlands and Italy, however, enabled him to deal British trade a sensitive blow. Furthermore, the establishment of the Confederation of the Rhine and the victory over Prussia meant that France controlled virtually the whole of the North Sea and Baltic coast. As a result, Napoleon could apply the Continental blockade much more effectively and, in fact, transform it into an all-embracing system, the so-called Continental System.

The Berlin Decree of November 1806 formally launched the Continental System. Britain was declared to be in a state of blockade, and all states were forbidden to trade with the country. British subjects on the Continent were henceforth liable to arrest, and their property to confiscation, as well as all goods belonging to Britain or which originated from her factories or colonies. Likewise, any ship, of whatever nationality, which arrived directly from British ports or colonies, would be refused entry to Continental ports. As the decree applied to all France's allies and dependent states, Napoleon was, in fact, aiming at erecting a barrier against British goods, running from the north German ports to the Italian peninsula. After the Treaty of Tilsit, the blockade included even the extended frontiers of Russia. By this measure Napoleon was also attempting to ensure exploitation of the markets which had previously been controlled by Britain, by the manufacturers and merchants of the Continent, and particularly by France.

In January 1807 Britain reacted with an Order-in-Council. It forbade all neutral ships, on pain of confiscation, to call at ports which were closed to British vessels. A further Order-in-Council of November 1807 determined that neutral ships would be permitted to call at Continental ports provided they had previously been to a British port to pay a tax on their cargo and obtain a licence from the British government. Napoleon's reaction was his Milan Decree of December 1807, in which he threatened to confiscate all neutral ships which complied with the British instructions.

The struggle between Britain and France now developed into a commercial war between a sea power and a land power. It lasted from 1806 to 1812, but was mostly not fully enforced. On the occasions when it was, that is from July 1807 to July 1808, and from April 1810 to November 1812, Britain suffered heavily under the restriction of her Continental trade. Nevertheless, Napoleon never achieved his main objective with the Continental System, which was to destroy British trade. His plan was certainly formidable. Had he succeeded in excluding British trade from the Continent, British credit would have collapsed. There were, however, a number of factors which doomed Napoleon's efforts to failure, and simultaneously contributed substantially to his fall.

In the first place, British goods were never totally excluded from the Continent. They managed to enter Europe in various ways. The problem was that the European coastline, from the eastern Mediterranean to the furthest reaches of the Baltic, was too long. Honest and competent customs officials and military officers were not always available to apply the system effectively. As a result, there were constant instances of large-scale smuggling. Contraband came to mean big business in Europe. The island of Heligoland in the North Sea served as a British depot. British merchants quickly imitated French packaging to prevent the identification of contraband. Small islands on the French coast, and Malta, Sicily, and the Ionian Islands, served as springboards for smugglers, while Louis in Holland and Murat in Naples openly contravened the Continental System.

A second reason for the failure of the system was the fact that it disrupted the French economy at least as much as it did the British. It is true that some major undertakings such as agriculture flourished, but others experienced a serious recession. Enterprises which depended on foreign trade collapsed completely. Serious shortages of certain raw materials and manufactured goods arose. Napoleon's first opposition came from the French ship-owners, merchants and bankers. Instead of French trade increasing at the cost of the British, it declined sharply. The problem was that the British blockade was succeeding. It was not aimed at preventing imports to the Continent, but at beating the French by destroying their shipping and, consequently, their trade. Numerous French ship-owners and merchants faced financial ruin because their ships were trapped in Continental ports by the British fleet. The large harbour cities such as Marseilles in France, and also Venice and Genoa, as well as the Dutch and Hanseatic ports, suffered extensively. In 1807, for example, Marseilles had 330 seagoing vessels, but four years later there were only nine. The population of Bordeaux decreased from 120 000 to 70 000 in the same period. [15]

A third reason, connected with the foregoing, was the fact that Napoleon himself undermined the Continental System. By 1809 the system was functioning so badly that Napoleon decided to issue licences for trading with the enemy. His objective was to complement shortages in France, to get rid of the surplus of wheat and brandy, and particularly to drain Britain of bullion. A licensing system with high tariffs for colonial goods was instituted in 1810 by the decrees of St Cloud and Trianon. That French businessmen were permitted to trade within a system which was directed against such trade, was telling proof of the failure of the Continental

System. By 1813, it had been abandoned, as Napoleon urgently needed the licence revenue for his war efforts.

An important cause, but also a result of the failure of the Continental System, was that Napoleon lost the support of the bourgeoisie. This was the social group who had brought him to power, and derived the greatest benefit from his government. They blamed the Continental System for the economic depression of 1810-1811, and their indifference to the fate of the government and the Napoleonic dynasty dates from this period. The emperor was to experience this in the last years of his reign.

The reason for the failure of the system must also be sought in the fact that neutral shipping suffered greatly. If ships failed to obey British regulations, they were liable to seizure on the high seas by British warships. If they complied, they were liable to seizure on arrival in European ports. This led to much dissatisfaction and to various retaliatory measures by neutral countries. The USA, in particular, were alienated from Napoleon for this reason. Had he obtained the support of the USA in 1808, or again in 1811, he could have seriously embarrassed Britain. The USA's war against Britain in 1812 was too late to sway the effect of the Continental System in favour of France.

Because of her sea power, Britain found it easier to implement her Orders-in-Council than Napoleon his imperial decrees. The lengthy colonial and commercial trade wars of the 17th century and the 18th century had made Britain the world's foremost trading country. She possessed more ship-owners, sailors and merchants than any other. In addition, Britain became the undisputed leader in the Industrial Revolution of the 18th century. (See Chapter 8.) The country experienced unheard-of progress in large-scale mechanized manufacturing, which enabled her industrialists to manufacture products of higher quality and in larger quantities at lower cost, and to sell them more readily on the Continent at lower prices. It was this "nation of shopkeepers", as he called them with contempt, that Napoleon was up against. Against the cheaper British products of higher quality and in larger quantities, the decrees of the Continental System were of no effect.

Equally serious was the dissatisfaction amongst the nations controlled by France or regarded as her allies. This was particularly the case in the countries where there was less industrialization, but a surplus of agricultural products – which had to be exported – such as those in eastern and south-eastern Europe. The Decree of Trianon in 1810, and the Decree of Fontainebleau in the same year, created tension, with its clause instituting a special customs court to trace smuggling and to destroy all contraband. The Confederation of the Rhine and Prussia were heavily guarded, and after a thorough investigation, irregularities in Frankfurt were heavily penalized as a cautionary example. Bankruptcies in Dutch and Hanseatic ports caused panic and led to loss of production and increased unemployment. Wheat prices soared as a result of failed crops. Where the French could still be encouraged by patriotic appeals to respect the Continental System, the subservient states and allies could see no reason to take note of such measures. European merchants were simply no longer prepared to do so in the hopes of an eventual Napoleonic victory. His appeal that Europe should stand fast and suffer temporarily in order to finally free itself of British trade domination, sounded less and less convincing as it became clear that there was no difference between British and French economic imperialism.

No imperial decree could suppress the demand for familiar and inexpensive British or colonial goods, and there was increasing opposition to Napoleon's economic tyranny throughout Europe. The merchants of Europe were only too keen to take to smuggling. In this they had the support of consumers and of military chiefs. One state after another was to challenge Napoleon over the continued application of the system. Spain was to set the example. On the 31st December 1810 Tsar Alexander opened Russian ports to neutral shipping in protest, and by doing so sealed the fate of the Continental System.

It is clear that the system had sprung leaks which had to be plugged. This was precisely the problem, for Napoleon's personality did not allow him to tolerate opposition or undermining.

That Napoleon possessed remarkable qualities which set him far above many excellent leaders down the centuries cannot be doubted. There was his magical charm, which could win over opponents within moments. Then, he had the ability to understand the psychology of his soldiers and to win their confidence. The duke of Wellington himself said that the moral effect of Napoleon's presence on his army was worth as much as 40 000 men. No setback or defeat could break the bond between Napoleon and his soldiers. But then it is true that while certain personal qualities helped him to achieve great heights, they were equally responsible not only for the failure of the Continental System, but for his fall.

One such quality was Napoleon's romantic and unbridled ambition to surpass the careers of all the heroes of history. On St Helena he declared that it was during the Italian campaign of 1796, after the success at Lodi, that he had realized that he was an exalted being. That was when he first formulated for himself a clear picture of his ambitions to attain great heights which, previously, might have seemed to him to be merely fantastic dreams. Now his ambition was to force his archenemy, Britain, to her knees, and to shift the axis of trade to France. This made him launch the Continental System. Because of the smuggling and the leaks which developed, Napoleon sought retribution. He would not tolerate any opposition and therefore demanded absolute obedience. It was his conviction that power could only be exercised through fear and constant supervision. [16] This attitude ultimately gave rise to the Spanish reaction, the disastrous Russian campaign of 1812, and the wars of liberation of 1813. The failure of the Continental System preceded the fall of Napoleon.

REACTION AND THE FALL OF NAPOLEON, 1807-1815

Ostensibly the Treaty of Tilsit, which was a result of the Continental System, left Europe at the mercy of France. But the far-flung empire was by no means easy to control. For the first time Napoleon began to realize that he could not effectively counter every foreign threat.

A new situation arose in Europe which, for the first time, presented Napoleon's enemies with a united front. This was the growing opposition to the increasingly oppressive French imperialism. These repressions consisted of the growing demands for recruits to extend or complement existing armies, various tax burdens, the garrisoning of troops, and the pressures of the Continental System. All levels of society in Europe were affected by this: the masses and the bourgeoisie, which had previously welcomed the French armies, as well as the established aristocracy. A revival of Romanticism was nurturing a new cultural nationalism amongst intellectuals. It fed on political and economic discontent, and gave moral force to resistance. [17]

After the Treaty of Tilsit, Napoleon could devote his attention to Spain. With the Continental System in force it was, moreover, essential to control the coastline of the Iberian peninsula. Spain had been an ally of France since 1795, but did not mean much to Napoleon. There was discord between King Charles IV and Godoy, the queen's lover and real ruler, and also the successor to the throne, Prince Ferdinand. The Iberian peninsula was not profitable, and it was dangerous. Portugal ignored the Continental System, and although the latter was applied by Spain, smuggling was the order of the day. Furthermore, there was the danger that the extensive coastline would offer a springboard for British troops against Napoleon. It is clear that Napoleon did not trust the Spanish dynasty, and wanted to drive it out in favour of a ruler who would be subservient.

In October 1807 Napoleon sent Marshal Junot to subjugate Portugal. The Portuguese royal family fled to Brazil. A month later Junot occupied Lisbon. Meanwhile Napoleon had become convinced that Spain could be revived by efficient French administration, and, with the excuse that he wanted to safeguard Junot's position, he sent Marshal Murat to occupy Spain in March 1808. At the same time, Ferdinand rebelled against his father and proclaimed himself Ferdinand VII. Napoleon brought the royal family together for negotiations. The final outcome was that both Charles and Ferdinand renounced their claims to the throne, and that Napoleon installed his brother, Joseph, as king. Murat took the place of Joseph in Naples.

In the long run, this step proved to be a fatal blunder. The proud Spanish nation found it an intolerable insult to its honour, and for the first time Europe experienced that a nation, rather than a government, rose against the conqueror.

Fearing the loss of their traditional leadership, the Spanish aristocracy took the lead. The religious peasants and the labourers, particularly in the harbours which had been ruined by the Continental System, joined the movement without hesitation. In the Spanish middle class there was a core which remained loyal to Joseph, but the rest, fearing that they would be branded as traitors, rebelled against French authority. The Spanish were provincially orientated. They regarded themselves as Catalonians, Aragonese or Castilians. They fought not for Spain, but for the crown and the church. It was a medieval kind of nationalism, but nevertheless powerful.[18]

Juntas (people's committees) were formed everywhere, with a central *junta* in Madrid to lead the rebellion. The aid of Britain was also sought. Although Britain was still in a state of war with Spain, George Canning, the British secretary of state, declared that any nation resisting Napoleon was a British ally. Thereupon a British force under Sir Arthur Wellesley (known after 1809 as the duke of Wellington) was sent to help the rebels liberate the peninsula.

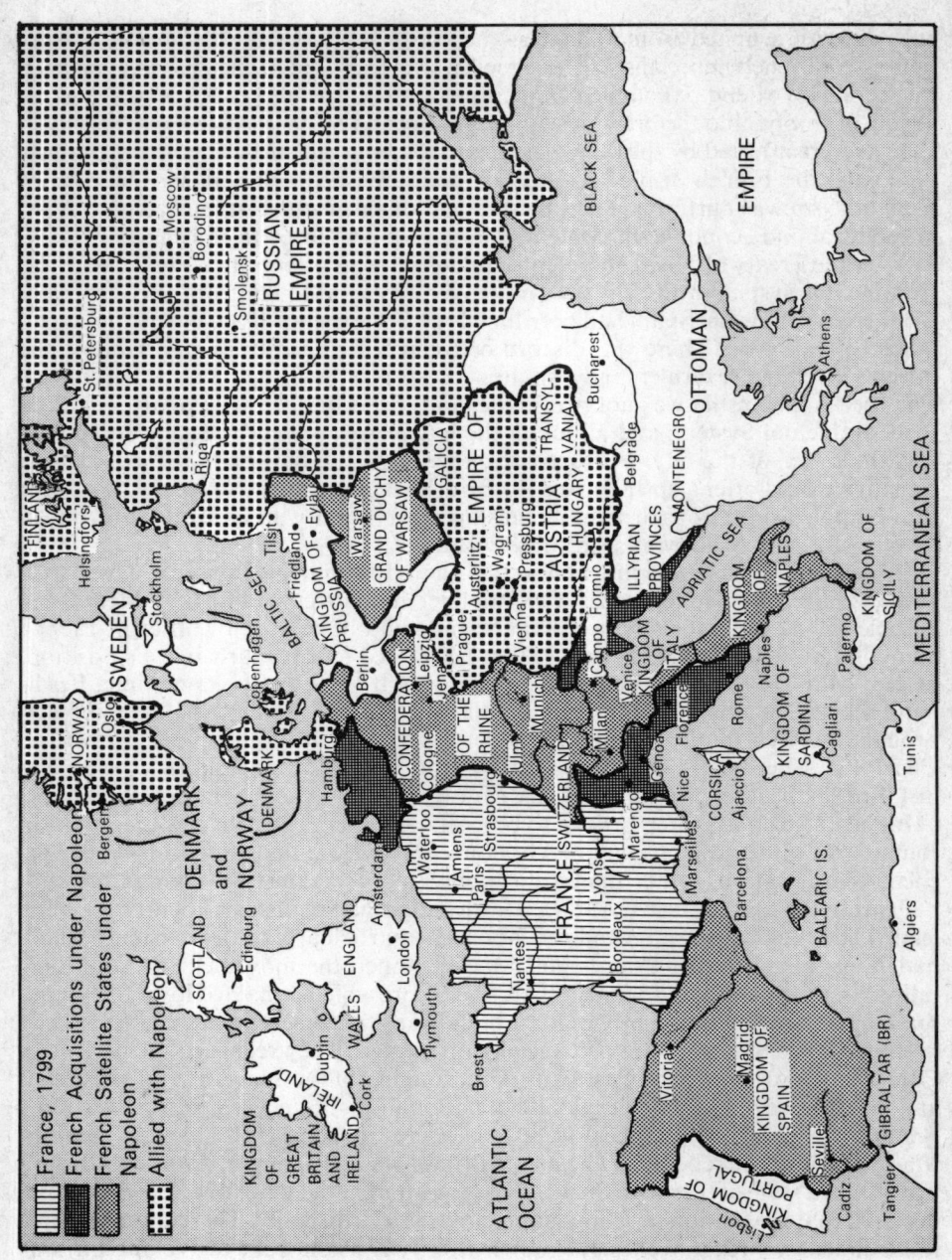

Europe in 1810 at the height of the Napoleonic empire

In July 1808 the Spaniards forced 30 000 of Dupont's troops to surrender at Bailen. Joseph had to flee Madrid and seek shelter behind the Ebro Line. Napoleon finally realized that he had a full-scale war on his hands, and ordered the largest part of his Grand Army to leave Germany for Spain. Shortly afterwards Wellesley drove Junot out of Portugal, freeing himself to co-operate with the Spaniards. The war in the peninsula had begun.

Meanwhile Napoleon had his hands full elsewhere. Tsar Alexander was becoming impatient because the secret agreement at Tilsit had not been fully implemented. Napoleon arranged a meeting at Erfurt to satisfy Alexander. A secret treaty was signed here, of which the most important clauses were recognition of Alexander's conquest of Finland, Wallachia and Moldavia, and permission for Russia to incorporate the Danube provinces. Further, it was agreed that if Turkey were to resume her war with Russia, France would remain neutral. Alexander undertook from his side to keep Austria in check while Napoleon ended the struggle in Spain.

Napoleon could now devote all his attention to Spain. He was not prepared simply to end the war, because he continually hoped that he could corner and annihilate the British army in Spain. He therefore restored Joseph to the throne and, to make his government more popular, instituted several radical reforms. Feudalism and class distinctions disappeared, and feudal courts, provincial customs barriers and the influential Inquisition were abolished. The number of monasteries was reduced and church property was confiscated. All this meant nothing, for the Spaniards were not prepared to accept any reforms at the hand of the hated conqueror.

Napoleon aimed at subjugating the south of Spain, but a British force under Sir John Moore advanced from Portugal and threatened his lines of communication. He was forced to return to face Moore. However, after reports reached him that Austria was busy arming, he returned to Paris as soon as possible.

The Spanish rebellion was extremely important for various reasons. In the first place, it offered Britain a convenient base against Napoleon on the European continent. The British dug in at Lisbon, which was highly important from a strategic point of view. Secondly, the Spaniards' guerrilla warfare occupied large numbers of French troops in the critical ensuing years. Spain became a permanent problem area, as it drew off equipment and men required elsewhere. "The Spanish ulcer destroyed me", Napoleon said later, as a second army was needed at a time when Napoleon was not in a position to levy further French troops. He consequently relied on his satellite states for troops, and thereby not only weakened the quality of his army, but also earned himself the animosity of the satellites. A third consequence for Napoleon was that the Spanish example had an inspiring influence on the European nations, particularly the Germans. It has been interpreted as the first example of national resistance against Napoleon's domination, but this view is not quite correct. As has been pointed out, the Spanish rebellion was more of a religious nature, and it had little in common with the awakening of the national consciousness of Europe in the 19th century. The latter was the work of the liberal middle class, stimulated by the principles of the French Revolution. While the Spanish rebellion was not a typical example of national resistance to Napoleon, it did indicate his attitude towards nationalism and popular movements. He always feared the masses, and the Napoleonic empire was, in the last years in particular, a clear denial of nationalism. In other words, the Spanish rebellion demonstrated that France was no longer the champion of liberty and democracy, but had rather become the suppressor of liberty, trampling national honour underfoot. Moreover, it showed that Napoleon was not invincible, and the good news resounded throughout the German territories.

In an over-confident moment, Austria once again resumed hostilities against Napoleon. After the Peace of Pressburg in 1805 Austria was in an unenviable position. Together with the loss of her traditional influence in Germany and Italy, Austria now also saw her trade languishing because of the Continental System. Austria regarded the Spanish rebellion as an opportunity to rid herself of her heavy burdens, and to regain her influence in Germany, as well as her prestige in Europe. In April 1809, therefore, Austria resumed hostilities against Napoleon, appealing to all Germans to reject the French tyranny.

The other German states did not, however, react. Prussia remained neutral, while the rest supported Napoleon. Within a few weeks he was in Vienna, and although he experienced a setback with the battle of Essling-Aspern, he won the bloody battle of Wagram, between the 5th and the 7th July 1809, which caused 20 000 casualties on each side. Although the Austrians had by no means been crushed, Emperor Francis sued for peace. The Treaty of Schönbrunn in October 1809 robbed Austria of 3 500 000 subjects. These included the Illyrian provinces in the Balkans (directly opposite Venice and the kingdom of Italy), which became an integral part of France; Salzburg, which was given to Bavaria; western Galicia and Cracow, which went to the grand duchy of Warsaw; and a strip of eastern Galicia, which was given to Russia. In addition, Austria had to pay a huge war indemnity, and give a renewed undertaking to comply with the Continental System.

Notwithstanding the Spanish rebellion and the signs of national resistance elsewhere, the Napoleonic empire had reached its zenith, and France held the undisputed hegemony of Europe during the years 1809 to 1812. The Empire was enlarged by new additions: Piedmont, the Ligurian republic, Tuscany, the papal states, Holland, and the harbours of Hamburg, Bremen and Lübeck were all incorporated into France. Napoleon's direct control also extended to other territories, such as the Illyrian provinces and the north of Spain. He was not only ruler of a France which stretched from the North Sea (Holland) to the river Ebro in northern Spain, and from the English Channel to the Bay of Naples in Italy – he was also king of Italy and patron of the Confederation of the Rhine which, by 1810, included all the German states except Prussia and Austria, both of which were, however, allies and tributary to him. His brothers, Joseph and Jerome, were, respectively, kings of Spain and Westphalia, and his brother-in-law, Murat, king of Naples. The grand duchy of Warsaw was governed by his ally, Saxony. In addition, Denmark and Norway were also allies. In brief, virtually the whole European continent lay at his feet.

After divorcing Josephine, as she was unable to provide him with an heir, Napoleon married Marie-Louise, the daughter of Francis I of Austria, in March 1810. By so doing Napoleon entered one of the oldest dynasties in Europe. The birth, exactly a year later, of a son who received the proud title of "king of Rome", seemed to ensure the survival of the dynasty Napoleon had created.

In spite of its outward appearance of strength, the Napoleonic empire had inherent flaws which appeared one after another. The empire was kept together by military force, and there was almost no firm national support. Continuous wars substantially thinned the ranks of the veterans who had received their baptism of fire in the revolutionary wars. Less than a third of Napoleon's army in the campaign against Austria in 1809 consisted of veterans. Napoleon was increasingly obliged to make use of foreign troops and young, inexperienced French conscripts. In addition, the lead Britain enjoyed over France in the Industrial Revolution manifested itself in the quality and manufacturing of arms, and of artillery in particular. Napoleon's early victories had given him inordinate self-confidence, and he no longer planned his campaigns with his earlier care. His happy marriage to Marie-Louise influenced him into rather sending his generals to Spain, where his own presence could possibly have been decisive. His almost boundless ambition also led him into tackling extremely reckless ventures.

As Napoleon's judgement and the quality of his armies deteriorated, opposition to him gained in strength. Britain was still supreme at sea, and was carving out a firm foothold for herself on the Continent through Portugal and Spain. Dissatisfaction with the Continental System, the commandeering of victuals and supplies, and the increasing recruitment of troops, gained in momentum throughout Europe. Napoleon failed to recognize the strength of national sentiments which he had excited. The growing spirit of nationalism could no longer tolerate foreign domination. As has been pointed out, the French armies were now regarded as the tools of a much more effective despotism. Nobody put it more succinctly than Ergang: "On all sides the forces were gathering for that great popular insurrection of Europe which was to result in the collapse of Napoleon's colossal Empire and in his dethronement."[19]

The reaction against the Napoleonic yoke found its most fertile soil in Prussia. The two-fold reaction, namely reform measures by the government and an intellectual revival amongst the people, complemented and promoted each other. A regeneration of Prussia was the result.

After the humiliating conditions of the Treaty of Tilsit in 1807, Frederick William III realized that only a drastic programme of reform could still save Prussia. Consequently, he appointed Baron Von Stein, an advocate of a unified Germany, filled with ideals of reform, and also a follower of Turgot and Adam Smith, to undertake the enormous task of Prussian political and social reform. Stein's drastic reform measures not only saved Prussia from the social disruption which characterized the downfall of feudalism in France, but in the popular imagination also linked the royal house of Hohenzollern with the cause of social equality. Of all the European countries, therefore, Prussia was the only one in this period which implemented the necessary reforms without breaking with the past. The social reforms included the abolition of serfdom and the division of land into property-ownership by the nobility, the bourgeoisie and the peasantry. Free trade was now also possible.

In the constitutional sphere a beginning was made by reforming local government. Cities were freed of the irksome control of the central government or the manorial lord. The fact that the cities would henceforth elect their own executive officers and representative councils to control local affairs, contributed substantially to the revival of civic pride and national enthusiasm. Stein's term of office was too brief to carry these measures through to their logical conclusion, namely the reform of central government. At Napoleon's insistence, he was dismissed in 1808. He did, however, succeed in paving the way for the institution of provincial councils by his successor, Hardenberg, who was appointed in 1811.

The reform of social and political life in Prussia went hand in hand with innovation in the military system. The army was to be a national institution, founded on the principle that it was the duty of every citizen to defend his country. All citizens had to undergo military training, and thereafter be enrolled in the national reserves, the *Landwehr* and the *Landsturm*. To keep abreast of the times, improvements were also made to military training, uniforms and weaponry. Scharnhorst and Gneisenau, and the well-known military strategist, Clausewitz, undertook the military reforms which were completed by 1813.

Stein therefore achieved in Prussia within a short while what the National Assembly had done in France, namely to turn a medieval state into a modern one, but this was accompanied by a revival of national sentiment amongst the people themselves. By the beginning of the 19th century the rationalism of the Enlightenment in Germany made way – as in France – for the Romantic movement. A conservative reaction and religious revival emphasized the priority of an own, uniquely German culture. Before 1806 this cultural nationalism was limited to only a group of intellectuals, but Prussia's humiliation in 1806 turned cultural nationalism into political nationalism. Although it left the greatest German writer, Goethe, unmoved, works such as Schiller's *Wilhelm Tell* (1804) and Fichte's *Reden an die deutsche Nation* (Appeals to the German Nation) inspired the people to a new patriotism. Fichte's influence led to the establishment of the *Tugendbund* in 1808, which strove for the revival of religion, morality, serious taste and eagerness for public service. Under the leadership of the great classical scholar, Wilhelm von Humboldt, the gymnasia (excellent secondary schools) were established in 1809, and the universities of Berlin and Breslau founded. The new German patriotism was fully echoed in the schools and universities.

One has to guard against overestimating the value of the Prussian-led German nationalist revival as one of the factors in the fall of Napoleon. Justifiably, Markham is of the opinion "that the spirit of nationality, receiving its first stimulus from the Napoleonic domination, was still too feeble and obscure to exert a powerful influence on Napoleon's policy or on his downfall". Napoleon, says Markham, was to be defeated by his own over-reaching ambition and by dynastic rulers who, after repeated and painful lessons, learned to combine and modernize their military effort.[20]

Meanwhile, Napoleon's "ulcer", Spain, would not heal. After the conclusion of peace with Austria in 1809, Napoleon did not return to Spain. Large French forces under Soult and Masséna tried in vain to crush the Spanish rebellion and to drive the British from the peninsula. Wellington had built an impregnable line of defence at Torres Vedras, from where he could launch attacks on the French armies. Spanish guerrillas ravaged the French lines of communication, overwhelmed isolated detachments and seized convoys with arms and supplies. By the end of 1811 the French armies were becoming demoralized, and Wellington advanced deep into Spain to seize their strongholds. In 1812, when Napoleon began to recall his veterans for the invasion of Russia, the British were on the point of driving the French from Madrid.

Relations between Napoleon and Tsar Alexander of Russia had meanwhile rapidly deteriorated. Various factors contributed to this estrangement. The Russian nobility thought the Treaty of Tilsit a humiliation of Russia. Alexander was, like all the tsars before and after him, conscious of the power of the Russian nobility. To differ from them would undermine his own position. Moreover, there was sufficient reason for Alexander to reconsider his connection with Napoleon. There were the failed negotiations about an intended marriage between Napoleon and Alexander's sister, Catherine. Napoleon's marriage shortly afterwards to Marie-Louise of Austria probably meant that Alexander would not be able to expand at the cost of Austria. Furthermore, Alexander was dissatisfied with Napoleon's refusal to let him take Constantinople. The grand duchy of Warsaw was a continuous problem area and, when Austria ceded western Galicia to her in 1809, Alexander demanded a guarantee from Napoleon that there would not be another independent Poland. This, Napoleon refused to furnish. Alexander was suspicious of Napoleon's intentions in eastern Europe, where he was apparently trying to establish a federation of Balkan states under his patronage, as he had done with the Confederation of the Rhine. The resistance movement in Spain and Germany was contagious. It was clear that the Franco-Russian accord was on unstable ground. By the end of 1810 the injurious influence of the Continental System on Russia's agricultural economy was so obvious that, on the 31st December, Alexander opened his ports to neutral shipping and imposed customs duties on French products.

As Napoleon brooked no opposition from anyone, and demanded absolute obedience, Alexander's violation of the Continental System was a challenge which simply could not be ignored. The tsar had to be humiliated. Napoleon therefore resolved to reduce Russia to a state of complete submission. This would also offer France the opportunity of taking Constantinople and of controlling the Levant.

Napoleon fully understood the risks of a Russian campaign. He had studied Russian maps, as well as Charles XII of Sweden's invasion of Russia under similar circumstances in 1707. He had equipped his army well, and had made extensive logistic preparations. It would be a brief campaign.

In June 1812 the Grand Army, with a troop strength of 611 000 men, was concentrated at the river Niemen in East Prussia and further south in Poland. It included only 200 000 Frenchmen, plus 100 000 men from new French departments. Every satellite state and ally was also represented.

By the end of June the Grand Army, which was obviously difficult to victual, crossed the Niemen. Napoleon's objective was to encircle the two Russian divisions waiting for him, and to defeat them separately. Then he would force Alexander to make peace at Smolensk. If the tsar should refuse, he would winter at Smolensk, and continue the advance on Moscow in the spring of 1813.

The Russians, however, avoided contact and began to fall back across the endless plains without offering resistance. Napoleon was eager to get to grips with the enemy, with the result that he entered ever more deeply into an area which the Russians had denuded of all food supplies. Thousands of soldiers fell by the wayside owing to heat, exhaustion and hunger, and were killed by the local population or the Cossacks. By the middle of August, Napoleon was in Smolensk. His subordinates entreated him to call a halt, but he was determined to do battle with the Russians. He therefore took the fatal decision to march on Moscow.

In an attempt to check Napoleon's advance on Moscow, Field Marshal Kutuzov lay in wait for him at Borodino on the 7th September. One of the bloodiest battles of the Napoleonic wars followed. The expensive victory cost Napoleon 30 000 men, while Kutuzov lost nearly 50 000.

To Napoleon's surprise the road to Moscow was now open, and a week later the Grand Army (or what remained of it) marched into the city. It was a hollow triumph. The city was deserted, and soon a fire reduced three-quarters of it to ruins.

The shortage of food made it impossible for Napoleon to winter in Moscow. Alexander rejected the offer of a truce, and Napoleon waited in vain for the tsar to sue for peace. Forgotten was the plan of a lightning campaign, and because of the desperate circumstances, the morale of his troops deteriorated rapidly.

By the middle of October, Napoleon had no choice but to begin the retreat, with only 100 000 men left. The Russians forced him to retreat along the same bare route by which he had come. Heavy snowfalls, temperatures of thirty degrees below freezing, typhus and pneumonia, and the merciless attacks of the Russians, devastated the French army. By the end of November Napoleon got his army across the Berezina River under murderous Russian gunfire in one of the most brilliant manoeuvres of his military career. In the confusion of the ensuing flight, all organization went by the board. Probably not more than 20 000 or 30 000 men out of an army of over 600 000 finally straggled across the Niemen. The rest had paid with their lives for Napoleon's grand ambitions.

Napoleon himself left the remains of his army early in December and hurried back to Paris. Full details of the disaster were not known there yet, but rumours had already reached the city, and he wanted to be present personally to forestall "unnecessary fears" and any attempts at a *coup d'état*. His main reason was, however, to build up a new army. He was not personally crushed by the enormous defeat he had just sustained, and in his insensitivity and sickly egotism, he was determined to continue the war against his two enemies, Russia and Britain.

By the beginning of May 1813 Napoleon had already raised another army of 300 000 men. It consisted chiefly of inexperienced recruits who did not have the courage and tenacity of their predecessors. Yet the prospects for the campaign of 1813 were not unfavourable. Although the British were liberating Spain, Britain was simultaneously involved in a war with the USA. Napoleon would restore the kingdom of Poland again to keep the Russians at bay for the time being. His troops still occupied the Prussian fortresses, and the emperor of Austria was his father-in-law. But there was one factor of which he took no account: the possibility of a national uprising in Germany.

Tsar Alexander again set himself up as the liberator who was to free Europe from the Napoleonic yoke. The Russians invaded East Prussia and occupied Königsberg. Stein, who was now in the tsar's entourage, began recruiting a number of Prussians despite the king's subservience to Napoleon. This forced Frederick William to act, and in February 1813 he concluded the Treaty of Kalisch with the tsar, in which they bound themselves to fight until "the independence of Europe" had been achieved. This was, in fact, the cornerstone of the Fourth Coalition, which was to defeat Napoleon. They appealed to the other German princes to join them, and uprisings occurred in some of the smaller German states. Chancellor Metternich of Austria decided, however, to adopt a waiting attitude.

As a consequence of the blunders of his field marshals, the victories Napoleon achieved at Lützen and Bautzen over the Prussians and Russians in May were expensive. He then agreed to a truce, which in the long run was more advantageous to the allies than to himself, for by the time hostilities were resumed in August, Metternich had decided to join the coalition against him. Britain also undertook to subsidize the coalition heavily. For the first time in his career, Napoleon was confronted with the joint forces of four large powers. Apart from his French troops, he had only detachments of the Confederation of the Rhine in support. Three large armies, under Bernadotte and Moreau (previously Napoleon's marshals), Blücher and Schwarzenberg, descended on Napoleon. Bernadotte and Moreau persuaded the allies to utilize Napoleon's proven tactics of dividing the enemy, and to fight the separate commanders, and not Napoleon himself. In this they were successful. Moreover, Bavaria had broken away from the Confederation of the Rhine early in October and had joined the coalition. Ultimately the allies cornered Napoleon at Leipzig. They had 320 000 men, and Napoleon half that number. In what the German nationalists later in the 19th century somewhat optimistically were to call the "Battle of the Nations" (the 16th-19th October 1813), Napoleon suffered a crushing defeat. He retreated across the Rhine with barely 60 000 men. Behind him the Confederation of the Rhine crumbled away, as his former allies joined the enemy.

In the next few months Napoleon's once mighty empire collapsed. All of Germany threw off the French yoke. A revolt in Holland, followed by an invasion of the allies, replaced the prince of Holland on the throne. Napoleon's former stepson, Eugène de Beauharnais, was defeated by the Austrians in northern Italy. Most of Italy was thus freed from French rule. One setback after the other battered the French in Spain, as the duke of Wellington advanced on a French army weakened by the transfer of important divisions to the German front. In June 1813 Wellington decisively defeated Joseph Bonaparte, and after driving the French army across the Pyrenees, he opened a new front against Napoleon in the south of France.

Suspicious of one another, and hesitant to invade France, the allies made Napoleon another peace offer in which France was guaranteed the retention of her natural borders (the Rhine, the Alps and the Pyrenees). Napoleon rejected it, but the French people were weary of war, and their discontent began to manifest itself in plots and uprisings against the emperor.

Early in 1814 the allies, with a force of 200 000 men, invaded France across the

Rhine. With only 90 000 men, many of them striplings, Napoleon conducted a brilliant defensive campaign. He won one skirmish after the other, but he was faced by overwhelmingly superior numbers. He could not prevent Alexander and Frederick William from entering Paris on the 31st March.

The tsar invited the senate to form a provisional government under Talleyrand. Early in April the senate deposed Napoleon and restored the Bourbon monarchy to the throne, with the count of Provence, brother of Louis XVI, as Louis XVIII. Napoleon wanted to continue the struggle, but his field marshals convinced him that the position was hopeless. On the 11th April he relinquished the throne with the Treaty of Fontainebleau. The allies gave him the island of Elba in full sovereignty, an annuity, and the right to retain the title of emperor.

Before Louis XVIII arrived in France, the senate had drafted a constitution which incorporated most of the reforms of the Revolution, but which strengthened the authority of the Lower House of the legislature. The Bourbons were restored, but in a constitutional monarchy.

Louis XVIII, surrounded by a group of embittered émigrés, at first refused to accept the constitution, but under pressure from the tsar he promised his people a liberal *chartre*. When this was promulgated, it was found that it hardly differed from the senatorial draft, except that the wording had been revised to adapt it to the principle of the divine right of kings. Louis was, however, not particularly interested in politics, while the people were indifferent to his government, and took exception to the replacement of the Tricolour by the white cockade of Bourbon.

The king's next step was to accept the terms of peace offered by the allies with the first Treaty of Paris. In the interests of the balance of power, Britain resisted every effort aimed at unduly weakening France and thus making her vulnerable. Although France was restricted to the borders of the 1st January 1792, she was not expected to pay any war indemnity or to maintain an army of occupation, and she regained most of the colonies that had been captured by the British fleet. The terms were generous indeed, and France remained one of the great powers.

While the allies were negotiating at Vienna to arrive at a settlement in Europe (see Chapter 12), the Bourbon monarchy in France was falling into further disfavour. There were the usual post-war problems, but their solution was bedevilled by the increasing tension and distrust. Louis XVIII was anxious to please his subjects, but he increasingly fell under the influence of the returned nobility and clergy, who viewed the restoration as a victory for their faction. A number of reactionary measures alienated the general goodwill, and aroused the fear that feudalism and absolute monarchy were to be restored.

Napoleon, who was well informed about the growing dissatisfaction in France and the disunity of the allies in Vienna, decided that the time had come for him to reassert himself. On the 1st March 1815 he landed in France to be greeted with general jubilation. The ensuing period, before he was finally defeated at Waterloo, is known as the Hundred Days. In Paris he proclaimed the *Acte Additionnel*, which provided for a liberal constitution similar to the *chartre* of Louis. He promised to forgo conquests, honour the Treaty of Paris, and to govern as a constitutional monarch, and at the same time to secure the fruits of the revolution in France.

The allies settled their disputes to plan an invasion of France with an army of altogether 700 000 men. Napoleon quickly raised an army of 200 000. There was a lack of horses, arms, ammunition and money, and the war-weary population displayed an alarming indifference.

Napoleon's campaign plans against Wellington were masterly, and the speed with which they were implemented emphasized his competence. He aimed at keeping apart the forces of Britain under Wellington and Prussia under Blücher, and to destroy them separately, and then, playing on Metternich's fears of Russian domination, possibly to obtain the aid of Austria against the tsar. His initial lead was eliminated, however, by weak staff work and officers who did not execute their tasks properly. It is also clear that Napoleon underestimated Wellington and the British infantry. In addition, there is evidence that Napoleon, who was only forty five years old, could no longer stand the physical and mental strain after twenty five years of warfare. He himself said later that he no longer harboured that feeling of certain success within himself. On the 18th June 1815 the end came with the battle of Waterloo, just south of Brussels.

Napoleon returned to Paris, still hopeful of winning the struggle, but the French Chamber had lost its confidence in him and requested him to renounce his throne. He tried in vain to escape to the USA. On the 15th July 1815 he was forced to surrender himself to the captain of the British warship, the *Bellerophon*. The British government exiled him to the island of St Helena, where he died on the 5th May 1821.

The exile and death of Napoleon were the beginning of the Napoleonic legend which depicted him as the ideal emperor who extended himself unselfishly in aid of mankind. Napoleon was personally responsible for this glorification. In a purposeful effort to influence posterity, he gave an illustrious account of his battles in his conversations and in his dictated memoirs. In addition, he presented himself as the disinterested advocate of liberty, equality and national rights against the suppressive forces of the *ancien régime*. This image, however, does not quite agree with the facts.

There lies tragedy in the fall of Napoleon. It coincided with the fall of France, a country which since the 13th century had held a strong position in Europe, but which, with the fall of Napoleon, lost its predominating position. This must be ascribed chiefly to the rise of the leader in the Industrial Revolution, Britain, who thereby filled the vacuum left by France. There is almost something inevitable in this, for it would appear as if the rise of Britain was unpreventable in any event, and that Napoleon's aggressive foreign policy therefore merely hastened the fall. Although Napoleon III made a brief effort at a restoration of France after 1850, that country could never really return to its glorious past.

CHAPTER 12

REVOLUTION AND COUNTER-REVOLUTION, 1815-1848

INTRODUCTION

Following the French Revolution and the subsequent Napoleonic wars, the forces of liberalism, nationalism and industrialism rose to prominence, threatening to overthrow the existing order. The years from 1815 to 1848 are therefore characterized by endeavours of the major powers to keep these forces in check and, where possible, to eliminate them.

A clear distinction has to be made between the current and the 19th century meaning of the concepts liberalism and nationalism. The liberal of the previous century also agitated for constitutional and social change. For that era, the insistence on representation in government seemed highly radical. Liberalism was therefore merely a reflection of the political aspirations of the middle classes, who questioned the arbitrary powers of the privileged classes. The average 19th century liberal was not sufficiently democratic, however, to approve of universal suffrage.[1]

Nationalism was of a more penetrating nature than liberalism, as it appealed to all classes of society. The French Revolution caused a drastic shift in emphasis in the people's idea of a state. Loyalty was now accorded a particular country, rather than a specific monarch. The term "citizen" replaced "subject". Nationalism as a binding force therefore stood in direct contrast to the view of the statesmen of the *ancien régime* that the monarch's interests were paramount. For this reason, Italy and Germany had remained disintegrated to provide for all the various rulers.[2]

The third force threatening the old order was industrialism, probably the most dynamic and penetrating of the three. The increasing utilization of machinery, and the revolution in sea and rail transport radically changed the structure of society. The growth of industrial cities resulted in new class distinctions, represented by the smug industrial aristocracy standing in direct contrast to the dissatisfied industrial proletariat. Where labourers had previously lived in dispersion on farms, the concentration of a strong working class in the cities promised to be troublesome to the equilibrium of any government.[3]

The first half of the 19th century was a period of relative peace and stability – the result of careful statesmanship. Within the borders of important geographic areas such as France, the German states, Austro-Hungary, the Italian states and Great Britain, the new forces again and again threatened to overthrow the existing structures.

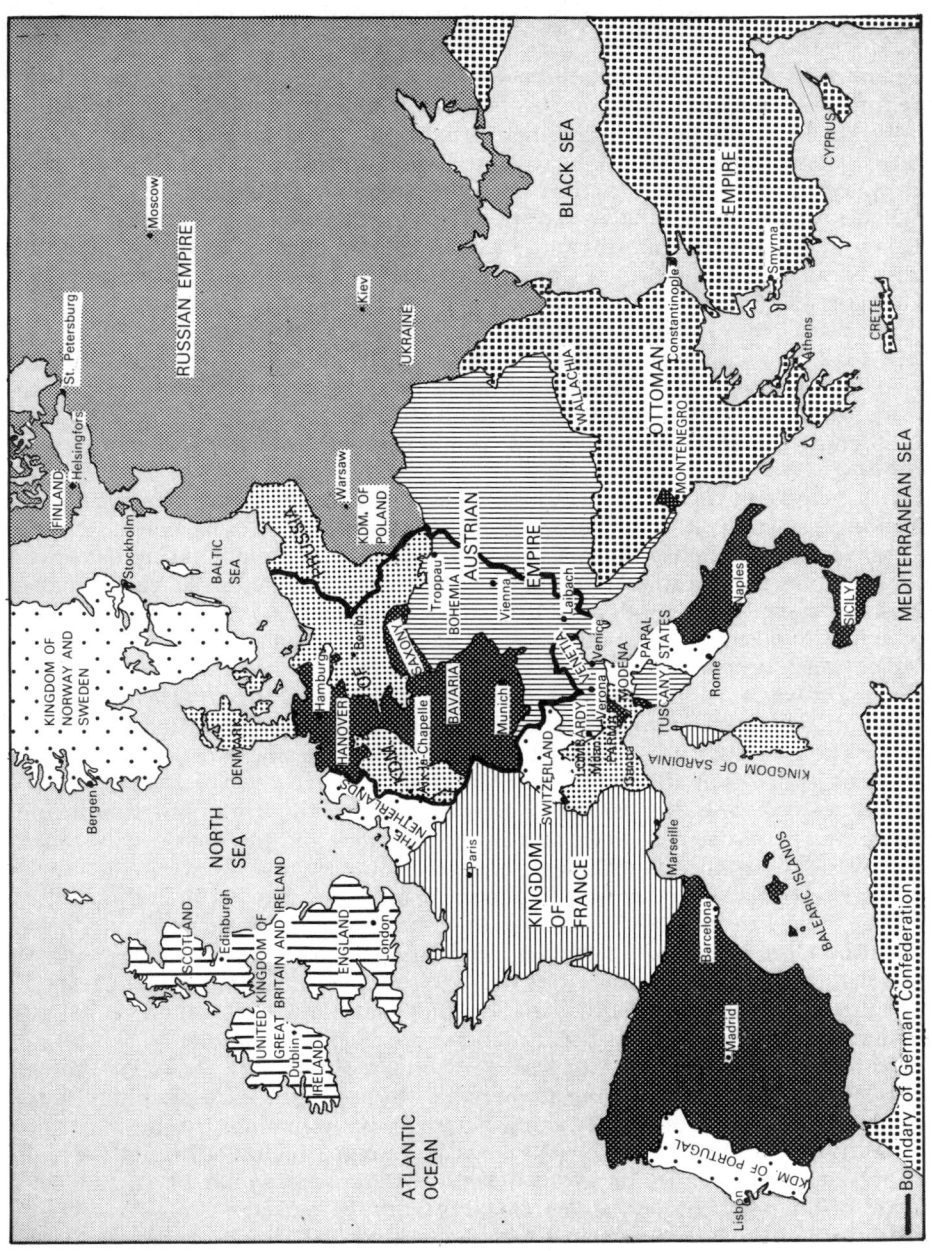

Europe in 1815

THE TREATY OF PARIS AND THE CONGRESS OF VIENNA

The era of Napoleon also introduced a new, unheard-of interdependence and cooperativeness between the major European powers. With the Treaty of Chaumont on the 9th March 1814, Austria, Great Britain, Prussia and Russia formally concluded an agreement, undertaking to unite in a quadruple alliance for twenty years and, amongst other matters, to overthrow the Napoleonic dynasty. The underlying objective was to create a balance of power in Europe, which was to prevent any single state from ever again reaching such a dominant position as France had held under Napoleon. The Treaty of Chaumont also paved the way for the later system of congresses.

Paris was already in the hands of the allies when Napoleon formally abdicated in April 1814. According to the Treaty of Fontainebleau (signed on the 13th April 1814), he was obliged to relinquish all claims he and his family had to the French throne. Napoleon furthermore undertook to settle on the island of Elba, where he would enjoy full sovereignty. He and members of his family would also receive pensions.

With Napoleon out of the way, the allies could devote their attention to the creation of a lasting peace for European society. The Bourbon dynasty was restored in France, and the clumsy Louis XVIII was placed on the French throne as constitutional monarch. The allies' terms of peace were set out in the First Treaty of Paris, which was signed on the 30th May 1814. It was a very lenient agreement which did not aim at imposing revenge on France. The treaty determined that the country's borders were to revert to those of 1792. France was further exempted from the payment of war damages, and was even permitted to keep the art treasures which Napoleon had seized, as well as certain territorial gains along the Rhine. As far as France's possessions outside Europe were concerned, the allies were somewhat less indulgent. Britain was allowed to keep Mauritius, Tobago and St Lucia, which she had occupied during the war, while part of San Domingo was given to Spain. France was permitted, however, to keep her colonies and trading posts in India. Moreover, she regained Guadeloupe, and her fishing rights in Newfoundland waters were recognized. France also had to undertake to vacate her military bases in the East Indian territories. France was therefore militarily weakened in her colonies, although her trading wealth remained largely untouched. The allies realized full well that their task was still a long way from completion with the First Treaty of Paris, and therefore Article XXXII stipulated that a congress would be held in Vienna in September 1814 to order matters in Europe as a whole.

The formal opening of the Congress of Vienna took place on the 1st November 1814. It was a glittering gathering accompanied by appropriate elegance and festivities. It was a meeting of royalty and diplomats who were aiming to negotiate the greatest possible advantages from the envisaged reconstruction of Europe for their various countries. It was therefore inevitable that there would be friction and clashes of interest between the peacemakers from the outset.

Although all the European states, with the exception of Turkey, were present, the real decisions were made by a committee of five, representing the major powers,

Austria, Russia, Britain, Prussia and France. France gained access to the inner circle only as a result of the argument of her representative, the shrewd Talleyrand, that the major powers could not hold his country responsible for the actions of Napoleon.

Clemens von Metternich, the Austrian chancellor, acted as chairman, chief planner and host of the congress. He liked to see himself as the "coachman of Europe", who wanted to expunge all signs of the French Revolution by restoring the peace and security of Europe under the domination of Austria.

The Russian delegation was led by Tsar Alexander I. He was an enigmatic figure who frequently vacillated between liberal and authoritarian convictions. Despite his sporadic liberal views, he never lost sight of the interests of Russia. Lord Castlereagh, Britain's Secretary of Foreign Affairs, led the British delegation. His objective was to restore the balance of power in Europe so that no single power would ever attain a position which threatened the peace in Europe. As Britain had no territorial ambitions in Europe, and concerned herself solely with protecting her trading interests, Castlereagh played a decisive role in settling disputes between the Continental statesmen.

Prussia was represented by her king, Frederick William III, who entrusted the actual negotiations to his prime minister, Hardenberg.

The Polish-Saxon question was one of the most vexatious issues with which the congress had to contend. Russia and Prussia had already reached an agreement at Kalisch in 1813, regarding their respective aims in Poland and Saxony. The broad outlines were that Prussia would claim Saxony, while Russia would extend her authority to Poland. Great Britain and Austria, however, soon opposed this arrangement. Castlereagh feared that Russian authority extended in Europe would hamper the creation of a balance of power, while Metternich was also not in favour of a reinforcement of Russia and Prussia. Talleyrand fully exploited the dissension between the allies to the advantage of France, and ranged himself on the side of Britain and Austria. At the beginning of 1815 the issue came to a head when Austria, Britain and France concluded a defensive pact, aimed at opposing the demands of Prussia and Russia. At this point, war looked very likely. A timeous compromise was reached, however, by allowing Russia to extend her authority over a large part of Poland, which included Warsaw. Prussia watered down her initial demands and accepted about half of Saxony.

The statesmen at Vienna made no effort to restore the old Holy Roman empire or the numerous German principalities. During the Napoleonic wars the number of German states had been reduced from about 350 to thirty nine. The congress united these states into a loose German confederation under the chairmanship of Austria. In this way Metternich ensured that he had a voice in matters concerning Germany.

Meanwhile the disconcerting news reached the peacemakers that Napoleon had returned to France. The four big powers immediately put their disputes about the territorial arrangements aside, and once again combined their forces to check the recalcitrant Corsican. Nine days before Napoleon's final defeat at Waterloo, on the 18th June 1815, the peacemakers concluded the final agreement. Napoleon's

Hundred Days therefore had little influence on the deliberations of the allies. It is clear that the primary objectives of the Vienna statesmen were to neutralize future aggression and to ensure the security of Europe. In their striving for lasting peace, the peacemakers took as guidelines the principles of legitimacy and compensation. According to the principle of legitimacy, the legal rulers who had been forced from their thrones by Napoleon's conquests, were to be restored to their positions. But the principle was not always consistently applied. Although it applied in the restoration of the Bourbons in France, it was disregarded in states such as west Germany, the Austrian Netherlands (Belgium), Norway, Poland and Saxony.

The countries which lost territories as a result of the arrangements were compensated elsewhere. Thus Austria, in return for relinquishing the Austrian Netherlands to Holland, was generously rewarded in Italy, where Lombardy and Venice were put under Habsburg authority. In addition, Austria also kept Galicia. Members of the royal house of Habsburg were appointed as rulers in the Italian duchies of Tuscany, Parma, Modena and Lucca. Genoa was incorporated into the kingdom of Sardinia or Piedmont. The kingdom of the Two Sicilies in the south of Italy was restored, and the papal states were given back to the pope. As in the case of the German states, the congress made no effort to unify Italy.

The congress appointed a committee to pay attention to the Swiss question, and it was decided that a federation of twenty seven cantons was to be established in Switzerland.

Great Britain's claims to Helgoland, Mauritius, Tobago, St Lucia, part of Trinidad, Malta, Ceylon and the Cape of Good Hope (for which the Netherlands were paid £6 000 000) were recognized.

Coupled with the principles of legitimacy and compensation, there was the desire to reward those states which had opposed Napoleon, and to punish those which had supported him. Although the Vienna statesmen used the principles of security, legitimacy and compensation as guidelines, they never forgot to think of the interests of their own countries.

The most important criticism usually levelled at the Congress of Vienna is that the dynamic forces of nationalism and liberalism were underestimated, and that the peacemakers were too reactionary in their deliberations. It should be kept in mind, however, that the Vienna statesmen were representatives of the old order. The new forces, unleashed by the Napoleonic wars, largely passed them by. It was their task to restore order in Europe, and it was only natural that they should be guided by the stability of the old *régime* with which they were familiar. In their striving to create a balance of power, the diplomats paid little attention to the interests of smaller states whose national aspirations they did not hesitate to ignore. The dawning nationalism was to overthrow many of their territorial arrangements. The unification of Norway and Sweden lasted ninety years, but that of Belgium and the Netherlands only managed fifteen.

In defence of the Vienna statesmen it can be argued that few people realized and understood the real extent of the forces of nationalism and liberalism in 1815. The period of peace which Europe enjoyed up to 1854, until the beginning of the Crimean War, can be ascribed chiefly to the fact that the peace arrangements, unlike the later Treaty of Versailles, did not bear in them the seeds of a further war.

With Napoleon finally out of the way, the victorious powers met in Paris again, amongst other matters to conclude a new peace treaty with France. Although the Second Treaty of Paris was very similar to the first, the allies were less lenient with France. The country's borders were now narrowed to those of 1790, and the art treasures which Napoleon had seized were to be returned. France was obliged, moreover, to maintain an army of occupation until damages of 700 000 000 franc had been paid.

The statesmen of Vienna realized that certain means had to be created to ensure the permanency of the territorial arrangements and to forestall the threat of future wars. The Holy Alliance and the Quadruple Pact were attempts to meet this requirement. The Russian tsar, strongly under the influence of the religious revival of the 19th century, surprised the hard-bitten diplomats with a proposal that all monarchs of Europe should undertake to rule their countries in accordance with Christian principles. Consequently, the Holy Alliance was formally signed on the 26th September 1815 by the Prussian king, the Austrian emperor and the Russian tsar. The ultimate objective of the alliance was to persuade all European rulers to subscribe to its aims. With the exception of the sultan of Turkey, who was not a Christian, and Pope Pius VII, who regarded Alexander as an heretic, the European rulers in due course signed the alliance. Few of the signatories took it seriously, but signed merely out of respect for the tsar. Metternich called it a "resounding nothing", but regarded it as valuable none the less, as it placed the tsar under an obligation towards those powers which had signed. Talleyrand found the alliance laughable, and Castlereagh regarded it as mystical nonsense.

THE CONGRESS SYSTEM

The Quadruple Pact, signed simultaneously with the Second Peace of Paris, by Austria, Great Britain, Prussia and Russia on the 20th November 1815, was of more practical value. Based on the Treaty of Chaumont, the pact reconfirmed the co-operation of the major powers. The statesmen agreed to combine their forces for the next twenty years to maintain the territorial agreements which had been reached in Paris, Chaumont and Vienna. France was not drawn into the pact, as one of its objectives was the safeguarding of Europe against future French aggression. An important objective was to prevent a Bonaparte from ascending the French throne. The four powers also agreed to meet at fixed times, and to deliberate jointly about peace and order in Europe. The result was the origin of the congress system, which represents the first attempt at international government. Just as Alexander I was the creator of the harmless Holy Alliance, Castlereagh was the initial exponent of this new diplomacy. Peace in Europe was of paramount importance to Britain's trade interests, and therefore Castlereagh regarded the congress system as a valuable means of maintaining the Quadruple Pact. For almost a decade the congress system made a valuable contribution towards the solution of European problems.

The years after 1815 are characterized by violent reaction in most European states. At the head of the conservative reaction stood Metternich who had a deeply rooted aversion to all revolutionary movements. He was a great proponent of the congress system, as it created the possibility for negotiation around a conference table, and because it was a means for maintaining the status quo. Metternich took the view that the members of the Quadripartite Pact were entitled – with the necessary mutual deliberations – to employ armed force to suppress revolution in any country. By contrast, Castlereagh regarded the congress system as an opportunity to maintain the balance of power on the Continent, to thrash out differences amongst the major powers, and to facilitate diplomatic intercourse. Metternich therefore differed from Castlereagh in that he wanted to use the congress system to exercise a wider supervisory function over European matters, thereby protecting conservative interests. Britain's trade interests were a more important consideration to the British government than the solution of domestic problems of the European states. British aversion towards interfering on the Continent can therefore not be ascribed simply to sympathies for the revolutionary movements of Europe.

The members of the Quadripartite Pact held their first congress in Aix-la-Chapelle in 1818. The Russian tsar and the Austrian emperor were present in person, while Castlereagh represented Great Britain. Metternich and Hardenberg spoke for Austria and Prussia respectively. The immediate aim of the meeting was to review the position of France. The news that the situation in France was satisfactory and that the major part of the damages had been paid, made the congress decide to lift the occupation of north-eastern France. Although France was further invited to join future discussions of the allies, the Quadripartite Pact was secretly renewed and strictly maintained as a safeguard against any possible French aggression.

With the French issue settled for the moment, the allies could continue with a discussion of general European problems. A difference between Sweden and Denmark was settled, and border disputes in the German states were also resolved. Tsar Alexander made the proposal to establish an alliance of solidarity to enable existing governments to deal even more forcefully with revolutionaries, and to send an allied force to the Latin American colonies to aid Spain to suppress the revolutions there. Alexander's proposals found little favour with Castlereagh, as Britain could not be bound by any system of international control. The tsar had to drop his *Alliance solidaire*, and provisionally, Castlereagh's policy of non-intervention was victorious. Up to this point, the experiment in international government seemed to be working out well.

Two years went by before the powers met again. During this time, Alexander's attitude towards liberalism underwent a radical change. A series of assassinations in Germany, the rise of secret organizations in the Russian army and the murder of the duke of Berri in France gradually convinced Alexander that the tenets of liberalism were inherently dangerous to the existing order. The Spanish rebellion of 1820 meant a turning point in the attitude of the unpredictable tsar. He believed that the revolution was a potential threat to every throne in Europe, and that it could also destroy his treasured Holy Alliance. Metternich was very slow to react to the tsar's request to call a congress to discuss the Spanish question, as it did not represent a direct threat to Austria. When the revolution was followed, however, by rebellions in Portugal, Naples and Piedmont, the situation changed rapidly. Austria's interests were now directly involved, as Habsburg authority in central Europe was being threatened. Metternich therefore took Alexander's side and also called for the convening of a congress. Consequently, the major powers met at Troppau on the 29th October 1820.

Castlereagh was still of the opinion that the pact did not have the right to combat revolution wherever it was found. He set out Britain's point of view in the famous State Paper of 5 May, 1820, which became the basis of British foreign policy in the 19th century. The memorandum makes it explicit that the purpose of the pact was to keep France in check, and not to intervene in the domestic affairs of other states. He emphasized that, as Britain had also shaped its statehood through internal revolution, other states could not be denied the same right.

The emperor of Austria, the king of Prussia and the Russian tsar were present at Troppau. Metternich and Hardenberg once again acted as spokesmen for their countries. The aloofness of Britain and France was emphasized by the fact that they merely sent observers to the congress. In Tsar Alexander, who had now totally abjured his liberal sympathies, Metternich found an important ally against revolutionary sentiments. The absence of the moderate Castlereagh also enabled him to dominate the meeting. The co-operation between the three monarchies reached its zenith when they agreed, in the Troppau Protocol of 19 November, 1820, to suppress revolutions anywhere if they threatened the peace of other states. France was careful not to reject the protocol in its entirety, while Castlereagh uncompromisingly stuck to the position taken in his State Paper.

The Congress of Troppau adjourned, to meet again in January 1821 at Laibach, where the Italian question was the most important point on the agenda. At the behest of the congress, Austrian troops invaded Italy in March 1821, destroyed the revolutionary constitutional government of Naples, and restored the legal ruler to his throne. Britain protested bitterly against this action, and increasingly dissociated itself from the congress system.[4]

Revolutions in Spain and Greece were the reasons for the next congress, which met in Verona in 1822. Castlereagh had planned to be present, but in a moment of insanity he committed suicide in August 1822 by cutting his throat. He was succeeded by George Canning as minister of foreign affairs, who made no bones about his aversion to the congress system. The old warhorse, the duke of Wellington, represented Britain at the congress. When it became clear that the allies were going to persist in their policy of intervention, and were planning to send French troops to suppress the Spanish rebellion, Wellington protested and dissociated himself from the congress. This was a severe blow to the system. Great Britain's aloofness did not, however, destroy the experiment in international government. After the successful suppression of the Spanish rebellion, the Spanish king appealed to the allies in December to devote some attention to the rebellious Spanish colonies in South America. Canning wanted no part of any congress which would offer the European powers the opportunity of restoring the old order in South America. Such a step would pose a serious threat to Britain's growing trade interests in the area. His attitude is reflected in a letter of the 3rd January 1823 to the British ambassador in St Petersburg, in which he summarizes the European situation as "Every nation for itself, and God for us all".[5] Helpless before the power of the British navy, the European powers had to shelve their intervention plans. Meanwhile the United States of America had also recognized the independence of the Spanish colonies, and in December 1823, President Monroe formulated his famous doctrine, according to which any European interference on the American continents would only be regarded as "a manifestation of an unfriendly disposition towards the United States".[6] The attitudes of Britain and the USA struck the death blow at the Spanish empire in South America.

In 1824 the congress system was revived by Tsar Alexander, who called on the allies to discuss the Greek rebellion. Canning refused to send a delegate. The congress, which met in St Petersburg in January 1825, clearly demonstrated that co-operation between the major powers was something of the past. The delegates parted in May 1825 amidst general ill-feeling, and without having taken any decisions.

THE RESTORATION OF THE BOURBON MONARCHY IN FRANCE 1815-1830

In the years following Waterloo and up to the end of the 19th century, France underwent five clearly demarcated constitutional changes. Between the years 1815 and 1830 there was the first restored Bourbon monarchy under Louis XVIII and Charles X. In 1830 the *Bourgeois* or July monarchy of Louis Philippe followed, which met an inglorious end with the revolution of 1848. The short-lived Second Republic (1848-1852) was followed by the Second Empire of Napoleon III (1852-1870), and the Third Republic was established in 1870. Some of the changes went hand in hand with rebellions which echoed widely around Europe.

The restoration of the Bourbon monarchy was in accordance with the principle of legitimacy. Louis XVIII, elder brother of the unfortunate Louis XVI, was living in exile in England when he heard the good news of the restoration of his dynasty. The obese, sickly Bourbon king was already fifty nine years old then, and apparently bore no grudge against the French people. The situation was different though, with the hundreds of *émigrés* which followed the king into France. They were out for revenge, striving for the restoration of their previous privileges and the total extinction of the heritage of the revolution. The king, however, realized from the beginning that it would be impossible to restore the old *régime,* and therefore complied with the wishes of the allies by accepting a constitutional form of government.

The charter (*Chartre constitutionelle*) reconfirmed the divine right of kings, but simultaneously recognized the revolutionary principle of people's sovereignty. Basically the charter was conservative, although the Bourbons knew full well that the social revolution could never be undone. The charter contained three important clauses. Firstly, the executive power lay with the king. Secondly, the government would be composed of an upper house whose members would be nominated for life by the king, and a chamber of deputies, which would be elected by those who were enfranchised. The vote was given only to those who paid more than 300 franc per year in direct taxes, and who were older than thirty years. To be eligible for election, a male had to be older than forty years and be paying over 1 000 franc per year in direct taxes. This stipulation limited voters to about 100 000, while only about 12 000 were eligible for election out of a population of 30 000 000. The largest part of the population was therefore as unrepresented as it had been before the revolution. Where the aristocracy had been privileged by birth under the old system, the new *bourgeois* class now had the advantage of wealth. It is understandable that the prosperous middle class would do everything in its power to strengthen and maintain the constitutional monarchy. Thirdly, the charter provided that the king reserved the right to introduce legislation. Although the charter confirmed the freedom of the press, the king also had the reserved right to correct anomalies of the press, and papers could only appear by royal sanction. Religious freedom was permitted, and the Roman Catholic church would be recognized as the state church. Civic freedom was basically left untouched, and the Napoleonic Code was recognized. The Bourbons were therefore sufficiently careful and wise to accept the judicial, social and administrative heritage of the revolution.

Political groupings under the Bourbons were to a large extent a reflection of the currents left from the revolution. On the right were the Ultra-royalists, an embittered and influential group consisting of returned *émigrés* and clergy. They had a deep aversion to the constitutional government, and their objective was to undo the heritage of the revolution. The king's brother and successor, the count of Artois, acted as leader of this group. On the outer left wing there was a group of diverse elements, the Independents, who were unanimous in their aversion to the Bourbon monarchy, but could not agree on an alternative form of government. In the middle was the large group of Constitutional or Moderate Royalists, who supported the principles embodied in the charter. They were mostly from the ranks of the prosperous *bourgeoisie*.

The unpopularity of the anti-democratic Bourbon *régime* was clearly demonstrated by the wide support Napoleon enjoyed after his return from Elba. The Bourbon monarchy was restored a second time after the Battle of Waterloo. This restoration was followed by an intense reaction of the Royalists, which manifested itself in the political persecution of Bonapartists and Republicans. The murders and intimidations which accompanied this White Terror ensured a substantial victory for the Royalists in the first election of 1815. As successor to Talleyrand, who could not see his way clear to promote the vengeful cause of the Ultras, Louis appointed the moderate Richelieu. The extremely right-wing ministry immediately began to undo the work of the revolution. A number of laws were passed which provided for the persecution of Bonapartists, Republicans and all who were disloyal towards the Bourbons. These highly reactionary measures, which legitimised the White Terror, not only alarmed the king, but also the large powers. A second large-scale revolution had become a real danger.

Encouraged by the allies, Louis curtailed the power of the Ultra-royalists by dissolving the Chamber of Deputies in September 1816. He further employed his authority to manipulate the composition of the chamber and the election procedure to ensure the election of a Constitutional majority. By these actions the king hoped to create a government which would support the charter and bring about greater unity in France.

The Constitutional Royalists, who ruled from 1816 to 1820, supported the Richelieu ministry to the hilt, which enabled constructive legislation. A new electoral law was passed (1817), which favoured the liberal urban *bourgeoisie;* important financial and military reforms were tackled (1818), which returned France to its place of honour among the major powers; and in 1819 a liberal press law, similar to that of England, was promulgated.

The new electoral law, which provided for the annual election of one-fifth of the chamber, resulted in a gradual shift of power towards the Independents. This growing power of the Bonapartists and liberals alarmed Richelieu to such an extent that he pleaded for a review of the electoral laws and reconciliation with the Ultra-royalists. His pleas fell on deaf ears, however, and he consequently withdrew from public life, to be succeeded by Decazes. The murder of the duke of Berri, son of the successor to the throne, the count of Artois, caused such a storm, however, that the king was forced to appoint Richelieu again, heading a strongly Ultra-royalist cabinet.

This rightwing ministry immediately made every effort to undo the liberal measures of its predecessors. Press censorship was re-instituted, and the electoral laws revised to benefit the governing party. The reactionary actions of the Ultra-royalists, which intensified with their take-over of power, substantially widened the gap between them and the supporters of the revolution. In 1821 the government found the moderate Richelieu's liberal foreign policy unacceptable, forcing him to resign to make way for Villéle, who danced more to the tune of the Ultras. The government's drastic measures led to all kinds of demonstrations by the people, plots in the army, student riots, and the establishment of secret revolutionary societies like the *Charbonnerie*, based on the Italian *Carbonari*. The government successfully overcame these undermining activities, however, and when Louis XVIII died in September 1824, it was still firmly in the saddle.

When the duke of Artois succeeded to the throne as Charles X, the government became even more reactionary than before. Unlike his predecessor, Charles was an implacable opponent of the Revolution, and had no desire to govern as constitutional monarch. The reactionary element won a great victory when the government decided to make the Roman Catholic church responsible for education once again, and to compensate the *émigrés* for their losses by reducing the interest rates on state debts from 5 to 3 per cent. This step was taken at the cost of the wealthy bourgeoisie, who were the largest holders of government stock. The benefiting of clergy also caused some of the Ultras to join the opposition parties. The election of 1827 indicated a clear weakening of the position of the Ultra-royalists, forcing the king to become even more reactionary in his efforts to resist the opposition. He dissolved the National Guard, increased the membership of the upper chamber, and dissolved the First Chamber (lower chamber). At the election of 1828, the opposition succeeded in further increasing its majority in the new chamber, and to force Villéle to resign. His successor, Martignac, could satisfy neither the right nor the left, and consequently the king decided to appoint the extremist Polignac as prime minister.

Polignac was of the same ilk as the king, and made no secret of his desire to restore the pre-revolutionary *régime* in its entirety. His appointment motivated the opposition groups to join forces in an attempt to bring him to a fall. The opportunity soon arose, when Charles, at the opening of Parliament in March 1830, expressed his full support for his ministers and gave evidence of his aversion to parliamentary government. The Chamber of Deputies replied by passing a motion of no confidence in the government by a majority of 221 out of 402 votes. The king reacted by dissolving the chamber on 16 May, 1830. At the new election, the opposition groups were further strengthened, increasing their seats from 143 to 274.

Despite the unmistakable rejection of his government, Charles X apparently did not realize the gravity of the situation, and continued to refuse to heed the will of the people. In his judgment all the problems were caused by a small group of politicians – the majority of the population was indifferent towards the form of government as long as its material prosperity was not assailed. Soothed by the supposition that the mass of the people would not rise to save a few journalists and the bourgeois voters, the king promulgated a series of arbitrary ordinances on 26 July, 1830 to safeguard his throne. The four well-known July Ordinances abolished the freedom of the press, dissolved the recently elected chamber, reduced the electorate by 75 per cent, and provided for a new election in September 1830. This measure, with which the king really envisaged a *coup d'état,* sealed the fate of the Bourbon monarchy.

Contrary to the king's expectations, the working class of Paris did not receive the ordinances in silent resignation. Restlessness among unemployed printers soon spread to other working classes, and grew to such an extent that civil war broke out within a few days of the July Ordinances. The July revolution forced Charles X to recognize the seriousness of the situation, and he attempted to save his position by revoking the offending ordinances and dismissing the unpopular Polignac. He also relinquished his throne in favour of his grandson, the young count of Bordeaux (Henry V). But these concessions came too late, as the Chamber of Deputies was already in control of the revolution. The insurrection was virtually bloodless, and hardly spread beyond the city limits of Paris. On 30 July Thiers published a manifesto in which Louis Philippe, the duke of Orléans, was proclaimed king. Charles X left the country as an exile. With this, the failure of all efforts to fully restore the old *régime* became accomplished fact.

THE JULY MONARCHY IN FRANCE, 1830-1848

The new dynasty was also known as the July monarchy, the Bourgeois or Citizen's monarchy, and the Orléans monarchy. Louis Philippe's assumption of the reins of government occasioned little enthusiasm among the majority of Frenchmen. The nobility of wealth had replaced the nobility of descent, still excluding the largest part of the people from political power. It soon became clear after the July revolution that a bourgeois plutocracy could be just as oppressive as the most corrupt hereditary kingship.

Louis Philippe's reign was weak from the beginning, as his kingship was not based on either divine right or election. The bourgeois reign was, moreover, not acceptable to all the political parties. The Legitimists, consisting chiefly of Ultra-royalists of the previous reign, refused to recognize the new king's claim to the French throne, supporting the duke of Bordeaux as the legal successor. The republicans, who played a big role in the success of the July revolution, equally rejected the Orléans monarchy – they felt that the opportunistic bourgeois politicians had robbed them of victory. Progressive and conservative groups had co-operated to place Louis Philippe on the throne, but could not reach agreement whether the charter should be maintained unchanged. At this time, socialism was also rapidly gaining ground in France, and it became a real threat to the stability of the monarchy. It is therefore hardly surprising that the first ten years of the citizen-king's reign were characterized by a proliferation of secret societies, riots and assassination attempts.

Louis Philippe's extremely cautious foreign policy further contributed to his unpopularity. His ingloriousness stood in shrill contrast to the glory of the Napoleonic era, and thus Bonapartism rapidly gained ground. The government itself promoted the revival of the Napoleonic legend by completing the Arc de Triomphe, which Napoleon had been unable to do. Streets and bridges were named after Napoleon's battles, and in 1840 his mortal remains were brought from St Helena to Paris and laid to rest in a mausoleum. The Tricolour and the National Guard were also revived.

Under the extremely conservative Guizot, who succeeded Thiers as prime minister in 1840, the corruption of the government began to attain large proportions. Guizot was indifferent to the needs of the lower classes, and did not hesitate to manipulate elections by means of bribery. The repeated appeals of the liberal opposition for parliamentary and electoral reforms fell on deaf ears. The weakening of the country's economy in 1847 and 1848, together with the increasing social and political problems, hastened the demise of the bourgeois monarchy.

As the government maintained its opposition to reform, the Monarchists in 1847 conceived the idea of organizing a "reform" banquet to publicise their political aims. A stiff entrance fee would ensure the exclusion of the proletariat from the proceedings. The success of the first dinner, which was held on the 9th July 1847, soon encouraged the Socialists and Bonapartists to organize similar political banquets to mobilise public feeling against the government.

The banquet campaign initially made little impression on the government, and it appeared as if the dissatisfied elements would have to change their strategy. A turning point was reached, however, when a group of reformers decided to present a banquet in honour of a group of radical officers of the National Guard on the 22nd February 1848. The banquet, due to take place in one of the poorer areas of Paris, caused the government to fear that it would give rise to restlessness. Guizot's consequent ban on the meeting made the reformers persist with their plans, and a confrontation became inevitable. The reformers finally yielded to the government's threats and called off the meeting. On the appointed day, however, students and labourers, incited by a hostile press, gathered in the streets of Paris and rowdily demanded the dismissal of Guizot. Matters took a serious turn when the king's troops attempted to disperse the crowds. Red flags and barricades appeared on the streets, fanning the flames of revolution.

The next day, the 23rd February 1848, the government hoped to suppress the demonstrations with the additional help of the citizen's force. The National Guard, however, was sympathetic to the insurrectionists, and therefore prevented the royal troops from acting with any force. It seemed as if the crisis was over when the king dismissed Guizot. A skirmish between celebrating demonstrators and some of the king's soldiers, however, developed into a bloodbath, and sealed the fate of the Citizen's Monarchy. Now the dissidents no longer insisted on reform, but demanded a new government. Louis Philippe, who did not see his way clear to unleash a civil war for the sake of retaining his throne, tried to save his dynasty by abdicating in favour of his grandson on the 24th February, and fleeing to England. He could have saved himself the trouble – France no longer wanted a king. A provisional government, led by the poet Lamartine, was formed.

With men such as Louis Blanc at the head, the social factor gained in importance. The Socialists had also formed a provisional government, but, after negotiations with the government of Lamartine, the two merged to establish a republic. The objectives of the groups were, however, irreconcilable, as the Socialists saw the republic as a means of bringing about a profound social revolution. Supported by the populace, the Socialists initially had the whip hand. The provisional government immediately began launching a programme of social and political reforms. Working hours were reduced, and to fulfil its promise of the "right to work" for every labourer, Louis Blanc established national workshops. Press censorship was abolished, as was control of civic freedom. With the institution of universal suffrage, the electorate was increased from about 200 000 to 9 000 000.

At the first general election on the 23rd April 1848, the Socialists suffered a severe reverse which showed that their support was limited to Paris. With the temporary loss of their power, experiments such as the national workshops also went by the board. The republican revolution was the overture to the dictatorship of Napoleon III.

THE GERMAN STATES, 1815-1848

Before the French Revolution, Germany consisted of more than 300 small principalities which were jointly part of the Holy Roman empire. Napoleon is often described as the founder of German unity, as it was he who did away with the Holy Roman empire and reduced the German principalities to thirty nine, thereby rousing a German national sentiment. The Congress of Vienna did not leave behind it a unified German empire, but a loose confederation or alliance, with a permanent assembly in Frankfurt under the chairmanship of Austria. The only mouthpiece of the confederation was the Diet, whose members were nominated delegates of the various states. There was therefore nothing resembling representation by the people at this point. The particularism of the various states was the most important stumbling block on the road to national unity.

The period 1815-1848 is known as the *Vormärz* period, that is to say, the period preceding the outbreak of revolutions in Vienna and Berlin in March 1848. It was a period of political stagnation during which reaction ruled, and all national and liberal movements were nipped in the bud. In the economic and social spheres, however, the picture was somewhat different. Extensive industrial development had resulted in a prosperity which aided political change. In 1818 a *Zollverein* (customs union) was established, which destroyed the hampering tariff walls between the various provinces. By 1834 the whole of Germany, with the exception of a few smaller states and Austria, were unified in the *Zollverein*. This greater co-operation between the states inevitably reinforced the sentiment of German unity, and thereby increasingly impeded Austria's task of maintaining its political grip on Germany. The *Zollverein* ultimately prepared the way for the political conquest of Germany by Prussia.

The German desire for unity found strong expression at the University of Jena, where the students united in a national movement known as the *Burschenschaft*. The objective of the *Burschenschaften*, which rapidly spread to other universities, was to nurture amongst members a sense of religion, of patriotism and of moral principles. In 1817 the Jena students invited all the *Burschen* of Germany to attend a patriotic festival at the castle of Wartburg – where Luther had translated the Bible – to commemorate the Reformation and the battle of Leipzig. In the course of the festivities, the students displayed their aversion to the reactionary powers by burning military codes, the writings of Kotzebue (the most hated of reactionary authors), a corporal's baton and similar symbols of autocratic government. The students' actions dismayed Metternich to such an extent that he feared widespread revolution.

When Kotzebue was murdered in 1819 by a member of the *Burschenschaft*, the Austrian chancellor was convinced that his fears had come true. He therefore had little trouble in persuading Frederick William III of Prussia to promulgate extremely repressive measures against all liberal elements. A conference of princes – held at Karlsbad in 1819 – drafted a number of reactionary decrees which were immediately approved by the diet. The Karlsbad decrees initiated a period of political suppression and threw a heavy yoke of despotism on the whole of Germany. The *Burschenschaft* and other societies which were regarded as undermining were banned, the universities placed under more direct control of the government, general press censorship was instituted, and a central committee was appointed to investigate secret organizations and to expose revolutionary movements.

When Frederick William IV of Prussia ascended to the throne in 1840, hopes rose amongst the liberals for a new dispensation in political life. These hopes were further raised when the new king freed political detainees, relaxed press censorship, and once again summoned provincial assemblies. It soon became clear, however, that the new king shared his predecessor's opposition to any form of constitutional government, and would nip all developments in this direction in the bud. The reaction against the suppressive policy was to reach its zenith in the revolution of 1848.

The February Revolution in France soon spread to the other European states, encouraging liberal elements to agitate for greater constitutional freedom. The success of the revolutions in the lesser German statelets was largely determined by the course of events in the two larger ones, Prussia and Austria. The vacillating attitude of the Prussian government in paying attention to the demands of the liberals resulted in riots in the Prussian capital, Berlin. The initial success of the insurrections in Austria and the news of the fall of Metternich further incited the revolutionary spirit in Prussia. These events made the king realize to the full how shaky his throne was, and on the 17th March 1848 he announced in a manifesto that he was accepting the liberals' demands for constitutional reform. This period, known as the March Days, therefore seemed to represent a resounding victory of the people over the army, the crown and reactionary forces in general.

An election, based on universal male suffrage, created a Prussian National Assembly which met in Berlin on the 22nd May 1848. It soon became clear, however, that the king had no intention of relinquishing his sovereign power to the assembly, and regarded this body purely as advisory. As the revolutionary movements in central Europe weakened, the king began to act more forcefully, until the Prussian National Assembly was formally dissolved on the 5th December 1848. The next day Frederick William submitted a constitution to his subjects, which was promulgated in its final form on the 31st January 1850, and endured up to 1918 as Prussia's constitution.

The liberal stirrings and the apparent impotence of the German princes had meanwhile also encouraged renewed hopes of a unified Germany amongst nationalists outside Prussia. In March 1848 they took the opportunity to call a provisional assembly, the *Vorparlament*, in Frankfurt. The idea was to create a national assembly in which all German states would be represented. The most important task of the assembly was to draft a constitution for the whole of Germany.

The new Parliament, consisting of almost 600 elected deputies, met in Frankfurt in May 1848. The assembly lacked any executive authority from the outset, and was therefore doomed to failure. The Parliament decided to organize the new German empire on a federal basis, without Austria. The federal constitution provided for an elected National Assembly, with an emperor as head of state, and the parliament decided to offer the crown to Frederick William IV of Prussia. The Prussian king declined the honour, however, and thereby ensured the shipwreck of the federal experiment. The more moderate groups also withdrew from the National Assembly, handing it over to extremist elements which saw armed force as the solution for the achievement of German unification. Discord amongst the leaders of the assembly caused its rapid decomposition, until it was completely suppressed by conservative forces, and peace was re-established by August 1849.

AUSTRO-HUNGARY, 1815-1848

The multiracial composition of Austro-Hungary and its consequently varying national aspirations complicate the history of this state in the 19th century beyond that of every other European country in the same period.

Following the Congress of Vienna, the structure of the empire was still largely feudal. Apparently the influence of the French Revolution had passed it by, as the abuses of the *ancien régime* were still rife. The nobility still mercilessly exploited serfs, while the development of the *bourgeoisie* was delayed because of numerous official regulations which hampered industrial development.

The collection of nations within the Habsburg domain were bound together, firstly, by the royal house, which had built up the empire since the 13th century by means of a series of marriages, and secondly, by the Roman Catholic church. Metternich's government kept the diverse interest groups in check with centralized control and a policy of suppression. This policy – also known as the Metternich system – succeeded well enough in its point of departure of "divide and rule" in maintaining the status quo and thus keeping the empire intact. Superficially it seemed as if everything was under control, but below the surface the forces of revolution were fast gaining momentum until there was an outburst in 1848. Austro-Hungary, like the other European states, would not succeed in keeping the forces which were unleashed by the French Revolution and the Napoleonic era on a tight rein.

Notwithstanding the government's policy of centralization, the Magyars in Hungary retained their voice in local assemblies, which served as useful outlets for their grievances. Under the pressure of complaints from these bodies against, amongst other matters, unfair taxation, the government agreed to call a meeting of the Hungarian Diet. The last session of this body had taken place in 1812, when it had been dissolved because of its opposition to the government's financial measures. With the meeting of the Diet in 1824, it agitated strongly for the total Magyarization of Hungary, and in particular for the official recognition of the Magyar language in the place of Latin. Although the latter request fell on deaf ears, the language question remained an issue which was only satisfactorily resolved in 1844.

Leaders such as Count Széchényi and Louis Kossuth in due course became the spokesmen of the patriots. It was Kossuth in particular who, during the meeting of the Diet which met at Pressburg from 1832 to 1836, gained extensive support for his aim to replace the obsolete Diet with a democratic, Hungarian Parliament. When the Diet adjourned, Kossuth had to pay for his recalcitrance by serving three years in prison.

After his release in 1840, Kossuth published a newspaper in Magyar which he used as a mouthpiece to insist on judicial reform, freedom of speech and abolition of press censorship, greater independence for Hungary, and parliamentary reforms. Kossuth rapidly gathered a large following, which put him in a strong negotiating position when the Diet met again at Pressburg in 1847.

Meanwhile, national movements had begun to gain momentum in all parts of the empire. The nationalistic aspirations of the Rumanians and the Slavic population, consisting of Czechs, Slovacs, Serbs and Croats, did not have such a strong political component as those of the Magyars, and were almost wholly cultural. The economic conditions, which became ever more oppressive from 1847 onwards, lent nationalism added impetus and paved the way for the stirrings which were to shake the tottering Habsburg empire in 1848.

The news of the February Revolution in France provided the liberals under Kossuth with the opportunity of demanding self-government and a liberal constitution at the Diet which met at Pressburg. In a fiery speech delivered on the 3rd March 1848, Kossuth rejected the Metternich system. The revolutionary sentiments spread rapidly, and there were eruptions in Vienna, Bohemia and Italy. In Vienna the insurrection was led by intellectuals and students who enjoyed the support of the workers. Violent demonstrations close to the palace, and vociferous demands for Metternich's resignation forced the old chancellor to resign his office on the 13th March 1848, disguise himself and flee to England. The terrified emperor gave in to the demands of the insurrectionists, and inter alia, promised press freedom and a liberal constitution.

The fall of Metternich further invigorated revolutionary forces throughout the empire. Spurred on by Kossuth, the Hungarian Diet passed the well-known March laws in March 1848, which were to have a radical effect on the development of Hungary's statehood. The new Hungarian constitution inter alia provided for a substantial extension of the franchise, abolition of press censorship and serfdom, and created an independent Hungarian cabinet. The Viennese government was forced to approve these widespread reforms on the 31st March 1848, which were to make Hungary an autonomous, modern state without blood being shed.

The Czech nationalists in Bohemia were quick to follow Hungary's example. In this province the majority of the population was of Czech descent, but the ruling minority was German. After the two groups had initially joined forces to gain their liberal reforms, self-interest and divergent national sentiments led to the loss of the concessions they had obliged the emperor to extend. The Germans, advocating the idea of a Greater Germany, wanted to join the Frankfurt Parliament, while the Czechs strove for an independent state. These divergent German and Czech interests are a good example of the decisive role which national sentiments played at the time. In Bohemia it was an undoubted factor in both the success and the failure of the insurrection.

The success of the revolutionaries was short-lived. By the end of 1848 the power of the conservatives had revived to such an extent that they could take the offensive. As with most of the thrones of Europe, Austria was saved by a loyal army and bureaucracy. The national separatism which contributed to Metternich's fall also acted as a divisive factor in the rebellious forces, thereby contributing to the restoration of the Habsburgs' supreme authority. Led by military men such as Radetzky, Windischgrätz and Jellacic, the government forces suppressed one revolutionary movement after another. With the victory of the conservative forces, representative government in the Austrian countries was destroyed, and all the heterogeneous territories of the empire were once more combined into a centralized bureaucratic state. Yet the Austrian revolutions did have tangible achievements, as judicial and administrative reforms were made, and serfdom was not reinstituted.

THE ITALIAN STATES, 1815-1848

Metternich aptly summed up Italy's divided condition when he described the country as no more than a geographic expression. The road to unity was blocked by the Habsburgs' dominance of the north, the papal states dividing Italy, and the

Bourbon government of Naples and Sicily in the south. In addition, the Italians had a weakly developed national consciousness.

The advent of Napoleon soon changed the picture. The ousting of the Austrians and Bourbons and the annexation of the papal states, created a unity which made an indelible impression on the Italian patriots. The Congress of Vienna, however, ignored all national aspirations, and Italy was once again subdivided into separate statelets, largely under Austrian authority. The restored rulers, by means of press censorship and arbitrary gaol sentences, exerted every effort to expunge the liberal ideas the people had acquired. Their task was eased considerably by the weak development of national sentiments in a population which had become too accustomed to an authoritarian form of government to offer resistance.

With the effective closure of all the means by which they might have made their grievances known, secret organizations such as the *Carbonari* flourished. The failed insurrections of 1820-1821 in Naples and Piedmont resulted in savagely repressive measures, weakening revolutionary forces to such an extent that there was little resistance to established authority in the years 1820-1830.

The influence of the July Revolution of 1830 in France did not pass Italy by, and the revolutionary tide began to rise once again. In imitation of the French example, and in the hope that Louis Philippe would support the effort, insurrections in Modena, Parma and the papal states followed. The French king was not prepared, however, to become embroiled in a war with Austria. Metternich exploited the opportunities of suppressing the revolutions by force and to restore the rightful rulers to their thrones. Amongst the insurrectionists who had to flee the country was the youthful Louis Napoleon Bonaparte, the subsequent emperor of France.

The defeats of the patriots emphasized the need for better organization and greater co-operation, and the number of secret organizations therefore rapidly increased. In 1831 Guiseppe Mazzini established the society *La Giovine Italia* (Young Italy) which aimed, amongst other matters, at spreading revolutionary ideas and motivating the people to throw off the yoke of Austria. In the years after the failed revolution of 1830, the revolutionary spirit continued to smoulder below the surface, until it burst into flames in 1848.

For the sake of greater clarity, the events of 1848-1849 in Italy can be divided into three phases. First, there was the series of insurrections which began with the revolution in Palermo in Sicily on the 12th January 1848. Some of the most radical elements constituted the leadership, and they were not satisfied with a few mere reforms. They demanded nothing less than the restoration of the constitution of 1812. Ferdinand II, king of Naples and Sicily, fearfully acceded to their demands and governed unwillingly as constitutional monarch. The granting of liberal constitutions in Rome, Tuscany and Piedmont followed. With these victories, it would have seemed as if the storm of the constitutional movement would die down. The February Revolution in France and the consequent fall of Metternich, however, brought renewed unrest, serving as a spur to insurrections in Milan and Venice in March 1848. The Italian people were inspired with fresh courage to drive the Austrian occupation troops from the peninsula. This was the beginning of the second phase in the Italian revolutions which were fast becoming a war of liberation.

King Charles Albert of Sardinia-Piedmont took the lead and appealed to the other rulers to support him in his efforts to drive out the Austrians. Ferdinand of Naples sent a detachment of troops, and volunteers arrived even from the papal states to participate in the struggle for independence. Charles Albert, however, let slip his opportunities by not attacking immediately and dispersing the demoralized Austrian troops. The delay at the beginning of the campaign enabled the eighty year old Radetzky to entrench his troops at strategic positions, which considerably restored their morale. The revolutionary forces furthermore suffered a sensitive blow when Pope Pius IX, despite his enthusiasm for Italian unification, announced on the 29th April 1848 that he did not see his way clear to participating in a war against Roman Catholic Austria. None the less, Charles Albert initially succeeded in achieving some important victories, but the Italians were no match for Radetzky's forces. The ranks of the Austrians were continually swelled by well-equipped and disciplined soldiers, while the Italians began to display corresponding weaknesses. A turning point in the liberation struggle was reached with the defeat of the Italian forces at Custozza on the 23rd July 1848. Weak leadership and mutual differences contributed substantially to Charles Albert's ultimate defeat. His forces were finally defeated at Novara on the 23rd March 1849, and he abdicated in favour of his son, Victor Emmanuel. Charles Albert died in exile in Portugal a few months later.

The heroic "republican" days were the third phase in the Italian struggle. The pope had already fled to Gaeta in November 1848, and the insurrectionists immediately proclaimed a provisional government in Rome. The arrival of Garibaldi and his volunteers reinforced their cause considerably, and on the 9th February 1849 the Roman Republic was established. Mazzini thereupon joined forces with the republicans, and was chosen shortly afterwards to head a triumvirate which was to govern the republic. The pope, however, did not remain inactive, and appealed to the rest of the Roman Catholic world to release him from exile. Louis Napoleon, who was now at the helm in France, reacted quickly in aiding the pope. He was motivated by the realization that Roman Catholic support was essential to his own ideals of establishing a new empire, and that Austria's penetration of Italy was inimical to French interests. Mazzini's Roman republic finally gave way before the French troops in July 1849. In August the Venetian republic under Manin also bent the knee to Austria. This meant that Italy remained divided, without any hope of unification within the foreseeable future.

The defeats of the patriots taught them several valuable lessons for the future. In the first place, they fully realized that, without foreign aid, Italy would never succeed in ousting Austria. It was a lesson which was not to bypass Cavour. Secondly, it was clear that the unification of Italy would not happen under the leadership of the pope. The patriots therefore placed their faith in Victor Emmanuel II of Sardinia, who had refused to revoke the liberal constitution of 1848. Apparently, therefore, the revolutions in Italy had been a failure, but without them, it would have been difficult to find the ultimate direction towards establishing national unity.

GREAT BRITAIN, 1815-1848

In the five years following Waterloo, Britain experienced a period of severe economic recession which had far-reaching social consequences. The restoration of peace exacerbated the problem of unemployment, which in due course manifested itself in riots and demands for reform. The Tory government, under Lord Liverpool, which had led England to victory during the struggle against Napoleon, viewed the riots as the manifestations of a revolutionary spirit rather than as signs of social desperation. Repressive measures, such as the suspension of the *Habeas Corpus* Act, restrictions on public meetings, and heavier fines for incitement did not, however, have the desired effect.

The general dissatisfaction reached a turning point with the Peterloo Massacres in 1819. On this occasion, between 50 000 and 60 000 people had gathered at St Petersfield in Manchester to listen to Henry Hunt who had a gift for inciting the masses with incendiary speeches. The efforts of the authorities to arrest the speakers fanned the sentiments of the crowd. When the situation threatened to get out of hand, there was a cavalry charge. Few people were killed, but there was a large number of wounded, and this quickly increased the resistance and unrest. Parliament passed a number of repressive laws, known as the Six Acts, which curtailed, amongst other matters, the freedom of the press and speech, and restricted public meetings. The revolutionary tendencies were, however, not discouraged by these measures, and demands for reform persisted.

After 1820 the economy showed signs of reviving, and the grievances of the workers diminished. In the political sphere there were also excellent prospects of improvement, as a younger and more liberal element began to appear in the Tory Party. Young Tories such as George Canning, Robert Peel and William Huskisson brought about a series of important reforms which were implemented despite opposition from a reactionary group in the cabinet.

In foreign affairs it was Canning's firm stance against the principle of intervention which contributed to the demise of the Quadruple Alliance, and which ensured the success of the revolutions in Belgium, Greece and Spanish America. It was his firm conviction that it was every nation's privilege to determine its own fate.

Robert Peel set himself the task of improving the penal code and penal procedure. Conditions in gaols were improved, and a permanent police force (named "bobbies" after the popular diminutive of Peel's first name) was established in London. In 1823, Peel succeeded in decreasing the misdemeanours punishable by death from about 200 to less than 100. During the next fifteen years the number of capital crimes were decreased to such an extent that only serious crimes, such as murder and high treason, were punishable by death.

William Huskisson began to destroy the old and obsolete principle of mercantilism by relaxing the navigation acts and promoting free trade.

Reform did not lag in religious matters, either. With the revocation of the Test Act and the Corporation Act in 1828, Protestant dissenters were once again admitted to crown offices. The Catholic Emancipation Act similarly abolished political and official discrimination against Roman Catholics. As far as parliamentary reform was concerned, the Tories refused to budge, as they feared that a redelimitation of constituencies would mean the end of their rule.

The way for the Reform Bill of 1832 was paved by a number of events in 1830, over which the Tories had no control. Firstly, the news of the July Revolution in France reinforced the people's demands for reform. Secondly, the death of King George IV in June was accompanied by the dissolution of Parliament, necessitating a new election. Thirdly, the crop failures of 1830 occasioned large-scale unrest, which had a stimulating influence on political societies.

The Whig government which came into power in 1830 under Lord Grey was committed to parliamentary reform. On the 1st March Lord Russell proposed a bill which exceeded the wildest hopes of the radicals. It did away with representation of the virtually deserted boroughs, each of which had two members in the Lower House. The substantial extension of the franchise gave nearly the whole middle class a voice in government. The bill did not have an easy passage through Parliament. It was voted down on the first reading, and at the second it was passed with a majority of only a single vote.

On Grey's recommendation, the king dissolved Parliament. In the election campaign which ensued, feelings ran high, and it was clear that the Whigs enjoyed widespread support for their reform programme. They also succeeded in considerably increasing their majority. The new Lower House passed the bill by a large majority, but the Upper House rejected it without beating about the bush. The public was outraged. Riots occurred in several cities, which were further inflamed by a weakening of the economy. Lord Grey persuaded the king to enlarge the Upper House in a manner which would ensure the passing of the bill. This threat had the desired effect, and the bill was passed in May 1832. The balance of power in Parliament was thus transferred from the aristocracy and owners of large properties to the prosperous *bourgeoisie,* acknowledging the principle that constitutional change could be wrought without revolution.

The common people still did not have the vote, as is shown by the fact that only 200 000 voters out of a total population of about 16 000 000 were added to the voters' rolls. The law was, none the less, according to the radical leader, William Cobbett, the first step towards further reform.[7] The reform legislation of 1832 already embodied the reforms of 1867 and 1884.

After the passing of the Reform Act, the Whigs and the radicals merged into a single party known as the Liberals. The more moderate wing of the Tories became known as the Conservatives. The Liberal Party had a large majority in the reformed Parliament, and for the next decade, substantial reforms were implemented at all levels of society. Humanitarian considerations were reflected in social legislation such as the abolition of slavery, the regulation of working hours in factories, and aid to the poor. The establishment of penny postage in 1840 improved communications and dramatically increased the country's revenue from postage.

Sir Robert Peel led the reform of the economy. He instituted income tax and lowered the tariffs on a large number of goods in an attempt to stimulate trade. He had to make allowances, however, for the interests of the middle class regarding the revocation of the wheat laws. Wheat, which was cheap and could be imported in large quantities, was subject to high tariffs in terms of these laws, which benefited the British landowner. Agitation for the revocation of the wheat laws began on a more organized basis in 1838 with the establishment of the Anti-Corn Law League. The failure of the Irish potato crop in 1845-1846 forced Peel to take action. Despite the determined opposition of a large faction in his own party, he succeeded in getting the wheat laws revoked in 1846. General free trade was the result. This policy was implemented up to 1932, when protective tariffs were reinstituted.

The disillusionment of the working classes over the Reform Act stimulated the growth of trade unions and contributed to their militant nature. The labour leaders soon realized that no reforms could be gained without the vote. A labour movement, Chartism, was seen as the means to gain this end. In 1838 the London Working Men's Association set out its demands in a document which subsequently became known as the People's Charter. The six points of further reform on which they insisted were: (i) universal male suffrage; (ii) a secret ballot; (iii) equal constituencies; (iv) the abolition of property qualifications for members of Parliament; (v) remuneration of members; and (vi) annual parliamentary elections.

Voteless, the Chartists enjoyed little support in Parliament. They therefore had to make propaganda for their cause outside Parliament by means of mass meetings, petitions, workers' associations and cheap daily newspapers. Petitions with millions of signatures were submitted to Parliament in 1839 and 1842, which rejected them with contempt. The rejections always resulted in strong reaction which took the form of riots and strikes.

The news of the deposition of Louis Philippe in 1848 lent Chartism a last flicker of life. The series of revolutions on the Continent, however, had also put the government on its guard, and a planned mass demonstration of the Chartists was a miserable failure. A monster petition with more than 6 000 000 signatures, which was laid at the door of the Lower House in separate parts because it was so large, was also rejected by Parliament. Forged and fictitious signatures, such as Victoria Rex, the 1st April, the duke of Wellington, Sir Robert Peel, Pugnose and Flatnose made the Chartists look ridiculous. Although the failure of the petition was the death blow of Chartism – to the joy of the wealthy classes – the objectives of the movement were largely to be realized between 1858 and 1918. Only the demand for annual parliamentary elections did not become part of the British election system.

THE FAILURE AND THE MEANING OF THE REVOLUTIONS OF 1848

Although the revolutionaries of 1848 did not all have the same aims, the revolutions still reflect common features in terms of origin, course and end.

One of the most important reasons for the failure of the revolutions was the mutual dissension which characterized the ranks of the rebels. The uprising in Italy is probably the best example of dissension amongst revolutionaries. Because of the divergent aims of King Charles Albert, Pope Pius IX and Mazzini, the opposition to Austria was not effective. In France, Hungary and Germany as well, the revolutionaries could not form a common front. The dissension was further exacerbated by the inexperienced and incompetent leaders drawn from the ranks of journalists, academics, poets· and other intellectuals. As propagandists of certain ideas they were possibly successful, but they fell short in the implementation of practical, responsible politics. The aims of the revolutions were generally only vaguely outlined, thus soon robbing them of the required motivation.

A significant factor which contributed largely to the failures was that the revolutions were almost exclusively limited to the cities. The rural population, whose support was necessary to underpin the movements, remained conservative and was, in reality, not yet ready for the radical social changes which some revolutionaries advocated. In France, for example, the farmers were so dismayed by the socialist onslaught on private property that they supported the government against the revolutionaries. The *bourgeoisie* was equally quick to recognize the dangers of socialism.

The road for counter-revolutionary action was paved by the improvement in the economic situation which, when it had been critical, had been a contributary factor to the unrest. A cholera epidemic which broke out in China in 1844 struck Europe in 1848, considerably weakening resistance.

The power and stability of existing governments further hampered the revolutionaries. With disciplined armies which remained loyal to the respective governments, and with financial and military aid by powers such as Britain and Russia (which escaped the revolutions) ranged against them, the revolutionaries had small hopes of success.

Yet 1848 was not without momentous consequences and significance. It represented the end of an era, a watershed which has been described as the birth pangs of the modern world.[8] The century of Metternich had passed, and in future, reactionism would be on the defence. The revolutionary era had given sufficient proof of the power of nationalism as a force which could determine the unification or dissolution of existing states. The role of the mass of the people in future political dispensations was clearly delineated. The counter-revolutionary forces realized anew the value of a well-organized and disciplined army in achieving political ends. It was a signpost to the blood-and-iron politics of Bismarck.[9]

People's representation and limited kingship became self-evident, despite the temporary setback. Feudalism virtually disappeared from the Continent, and the way was paved for further political development. The Sardinian constitution of 1848 was retained, and later became the constitution of a united Italy. In Hungary the March laws, despite their revocation by imperial decree, were not forgotten by the Magyars, and they served as guidelines to the *Ausgleich* of 1867. Prussia became a constitutional state, while universal suffrage was retained in France.

The dissolution of the Utopian illusions of the revolutionaries led to a more realistic approach concerning the evaluation and achievement of their ideal. As an alternative to violence to bring about change, the new generation employed negotiation, which was marked by greater level-headedness and single-mindedness. The revolutions of 1848 therefore represent a turning point which had a wide response throughout the social, political and military spheres.

NOTES AND SUGGESTIONS FOR SUPPLEMENTARY READING

Chapter 1
NOTES
1. See T. Aston (ed.), *Crisis in Europe 1560-1660*.
2. S. H. Steinberg, *The 'Thirty Years War' and the conflict for European hegemony 1600-1660*, pp. 1-2.
3. C. V. Wedgwood, *The Thirty Years War*, p. 31.
4. D. Maland, *Europe at war 1600-1650*, p. 14.
5. C. V. Wedgwood, *The Thirty Years War*, p. 35.
6. Ibid., p. 70.
7. G. Pagès, *The Thirty Years War 1618-1648*, p. 52.
8. See J. P. Cooper (ed.), *The new Cambridge modern history*, vol. IV: *The decline of Spain and the Thirty Years War 1609-1648/59*, p. 312.
9. S. H. Steinberg, *The 'Thirty Years War' and the conflict for European hegemony 1600-1660*, p. 38.
10. D. Maland, *Europe in the seventeenth century*, pp. 122-123.
11. C. V. Wedgwood, *The Thirty Years War*, p. 246.
12. D. Maland, *Europe at war 1600-1650*, p. 124.
13. Ibid., pp. 126-127; see also T. K. Rabb (ed.), *The Thirty Years War*, pp. 87-106.
14. G. Pagès, *The Thirty Years War 1618-1648*, p. 192.
15. C. V. Wedgwood, *The Thirty Years War*, p. 420.
16. See Chapter 2.
17. D. Maland, *Europe at War 1600-1650*, p. 183.

SUPPLEMENTARY READING
Aston, T. (ed.), *Crisis in Europe 1560-1660* (London, 1965).
Cooper, J. P. (ed.), *The new Cambridge modern history*, vol. IV: *The decline of Spain and the Thirty Years War 1609-1648/59* (Cambridge, 1970).
Cowie, L. W., *Seventeenth-century Europe* (London, 1968).
Koenigsberger, H. G., *The Habsburgs and Europe 1516-1660* (London, 1971).
Maland, D., *Europe at war 1600-1650* (London, 1980).
Maland, D., *Europe in the seventeenth century* (London, 1973).
Pagès, G., *The Thirty Years War 1618-1648* (London, 1970).
Parker, G., *Europe in crisis 1598-1648* (Glasgow, 1979).
Pennington, D. H., *Seventeenth-century Europe* (London, 1970).
Polinsenský, J. V., *The Thirty Years' War* (London, 1971).
Rabb, T. K. (ed.), *The Thirty Years' War* (Boston, 1972).
Steinberg, S. H., *The 'Thirty Years War' and the conflict for European hegemony 1600-1660* (London, 1971).
Wedgwood, C. V., *The Thirty Years War* (London, 1973).

Chapter 2
NOTES
1. R. T. Davies, *The golden century of Spain 1501-1621*, pp. 117 et seq.
2. Ibid., p. 121.
3. A. D. Ortiz, *The golden age of Spain 1516-1659*, pp. 66-67.
4. Ibid., pp. 68 et seq.

5. G. Parker, *Spain and the Netherlands 1559-1659*, pp. 21-22.
6. B. Chudoba, *Spain and the empire 1519-1643*, pp. 125 *et seq.*; see also A. D. Ortiz, *The golden age of Spain* 1516-1659, pp. 80 *et seq.*
7. J. Lynch, *Spain under the Habsburgs*, vol. II, pp. 67 *et seq.*; and D. Maland, *Europe in the seventeenth century*, pp. 216 *et seq.*

SUPPLEMENTARY READING
Chudoba, B., *Spain and the empire 1519-1643* (New York, 1969).
Davies, R. T., *Spain in decline 1621-1700* (London, 1970).
Davies, R. T., *The golden century of Spain 1501-1621* (London, 1954).
Lynch, J., *Spain under the Habsburgs 1516-1598*, vols 1 and 2 (Oxford, 1964).
Maland, D., *Europe in the seventeenth century* (London, 1978).
Ortiz, A. D., *The golden age of Spain 1516-1659* (London, 1971).
Parker, G., *Spain and the Netherlands 1559-1659* (Glasgow, 1979).
Petrie, C., *A short history of Spain* (London, 1975).
Russell, P. E., *Spain, a companion to Spanish studies* (London, 1976).
Stradling, R. A., *Europe and the decline of Spain* (London, 1981).

Chapter 3
NOTES
1. R. T. Davies, *The golden century of Spain 1501-1621*, p. 113.
2. J. H. Shennan, *Government and society in France 1461-1661*, p. 22.
3. J. H. M. Salmon, *Society in crisis: France in the sixteenth century*, p. 117.
4. G. Levet, *Les guerres de religion 1559-1598*, p. 13 (trans.).
5. J. H. M. Salmon, *Society in crisis: France in the sixteenth century*, p. 187.
6. H. O. Wakeman, *The ascendancy of France 1598-1715*, p. 18.
7. C. J. Friedrich, *The age of the baroque 1610-1660*, p. 131.
8. J. Lough, *An introduction to seventeenth-century France*, p. 124.
9. Voltaire, *The age of Louis XIV* (trans. M. P. Pollack), p. 73.
10. F. L. Nussbaum, *The triumph of science and reason 1660-1685*, p. 72.
11. N. Mitford, *The sun king; Louis XIV at Versailles*, p. 17.
12. E. le Roy Ladurie, *Les paysans de Languedoc*, vol. I, p. 611 (trans.).
13. J. B. Wolf, *The emergence of the great powers 1685-1715*, p. 288.
14. P. Hazard, *The European mind 1680-1715* (trans. J. L. May), p. 474.
15. Voltaire, *The age of Louis XIV*, p. 165.
16. P. Gaxotte, *The age of Louis XIV* (trans. M. Shaw), p. 328.
17. G. M. Trevelyan, *England under Queen Anne; the peace and the Protestant succession*, p. 248.
18. P. Roberts, *The quest for security 1715-1740*, p. 1.
19. H. A. L. Fisher, *A history of Europe*, p. 695.

SUPPLEMENTARY READING
Bonney, R., *Political change in France under Richelieu and Mazarin 1624-1661 (Oxford, 1978)*.
Briggs, R., *Early modern France 1560-1715* (Oxford, 1977).
Coveney, P. J., *France in crisis 1620-1675* (London, 1977).
Ekberg, C. J., *The failure of Louis XIV's Dutch War* (Chapel Hill, 1979).
Gaxotte, P., *The age of Louis XIV* (New York, 1970).
Lough, J., *An introduction to seventeenth-century France* (London, 1955).
Maland, D., *Culture and society in seventeenth-century France* (London, 1970).

Mandrou, R., *Introduction to modern France 1500-1640; an essay in historical psychology* (London, 1975).
Nussbaum, F. L., *The triumph of science and reason 1660-1685* (New York & Evanston, 1962).
O'Connell, D. P., *Richelieu* (London, 1968).
Ogg, D., *Louis XIV* (London, 1967).
Roosen, W. J., *The age of Louis XIV; the rise of modern diplomacy* (Cambridge, Mass., 1976).
Rothkrug, L., *Opposition to Louis XIV; the political and social origins of the French Enlightenment* (Princeton, 1965).
Salmon, J. H. M., *Society in crisis; France in the sixteenth century* (London and Tonbridge, 1975).
Tapié, V. L., *France in the age of Louis XIII and Richelieu* (London, 1974).
Treasure, G. R. R., *Cardinal Richelieu and the development of absolutism* (London, 1972).
Treasure, G. R. R., *Seventeenth-century France* (London, 1966).
Wakeman, H. O., *The ascendancy of France 1598-1715* (London, 1963).
Wedgwood, C. V., *Richelieu and the French monarchy* (London, 1949).
Wolf, J. B., *The emergence of the great powers 1685-1715* (New York and Evanston, 1962).

Chapter 4
NOTES
1. G. M. Trevelyan, *History of England*, 3rd ed., p. 323.
2. Ibid., p. 352.
3. The story was different as regards Catholic missionaries, frequently Jesuits, from Europe. Englishmen who returned to their country to revive faltering Catholicism, religiously motivated behaviour which would have had profound political consequences, were hunted down, tortured and executed, for treason, not heresy. About four Catholics died annually under Elizabeth, as against fifty six Protestants annually under her sister, Mary Tudor. Mary reigned for five years, Elizabeth forty five.

SUPPLEMENTARY READING
Aiken, W. A., and Henning, B. D., (eds), *Conflict in Stuart England* (New York, 1960).
Ashley, M. P., *England in the seventeenth century* (London, 1978).
Aylmer, G. E., *The struggle for the constitution, England in the seventeenth century* (London, 1963).
Baxter, S., *William III* (London, 1966).
Black, J. B., *The reign of Elizabeth* (Oxford, 1963).
Clark, G. N., *The later Stuarts* (Oxford, 1947).
Davies, S. G., *The early Stuarts* (Oxford, 1952).
Elton, G. R., *England under the Tudors* (London, 1965).
Firth, C. H., *Oliver Cromwell and the rule of the Puritans in England* (Oxford, 1953).
Gregg, E., *Queen Anne* (London, 1980).
Hill, C., *A century of revolution 1603-1714* (n.p., 1963).
Jones, I. D., *The English revolution 1603-1714* (n.p., 1963).
Lockyer, R., *Tudor and Stuart Britain* (London, 1964).
Manning, B., *Politics and religion in the English revolution* (London, 1973).
Neale, J. E., *Queen Elizabeth* (London, 1950).
Roots, I. (ed.), *Cromwell, a profile* (London, 1973).
Rowse, A. L., *The England of Elizabeth* (London, 1964).
Stone, L., *The causes of the English revolution 1529-1642* (London, 1972).
Tanner, J. E., *English constitutional conflicts of the seventeenth century* (Cambridge, 1952).
Van der Zee, H., and Van der Zee, B., *William and Mary* (London, 1973).

Chapter 5
NOTES
1. S. Haffner, *The rise and fall of Russia*, p. 51.
2. Ibid., p. 52.
3. M. Roberts, *The Swedish imperial experience 1560-1718*, p. 42.
4. Ibid., p. 7.
5. Ibid., p. 127.
6. Ibid., p. 55.
7. Ibid., p. 77.
8. M. T. Florinsky, *Russia. A history and an interpretation*, vol. 1, p. 336.
9. M. S. Anderson, *Peter the Great*, p. 18.
10. D. Maland, *Europe in the seventeenth century*, p. 417.
11. Ibid., p. 421.
12. J. A. R. Marriot and C. G. Robertson, *The evolution of Prussia*, p. 100.
13. D. Ogg, *Europe in the seventeenth century*, p. 469.
14. I. Andersson, *A history of Sweden*, p. 245.
15. M. T. Florinsky, *Russia. A history and an interpretation*, vol. 1, p. 352.
16. B. Pares, *A history of Russia*, p. 197.
17. V. Klyuchevsky, *Peter the Great*, p. 71.
18. M. Roberts, *The Swedish imperial experience . . .*, p. 154.

SUPPLEMENTARY READING
Anderson, M. S., *Peter the Great* (London, 1978).
Andersson, I., *A history of Sweden* (trans. Carolyn Hannay), (London, 1956).
Derry, T. K., *A history of Scandinavia* (London, 1979).
Feuchtwanger, E. J., *Prussia: myth and reality* (London, 1970).
Florinsky, M. T., *Russia. A history and an interpretation*, vol. 1 (New York, 1966).
Gieysztor, A., Kieniewicz, S., Rostworowski, E., Tazbir, J. and Wereszycki, H., *History of Poland* (Warsaw, 1979).
Haffner, S., *The rise and fall of Prussia* (London, 1980).
Klyuchevsky, V. O., *A history of Russia*, vol. 2 (trans. C. J. Hogarth), (New York, 1960).
Klyuchevsky, V. O., *Peter the Great* (trans. L. Archibald), (London, 1963).
Koch, H. W., *A history of Prussia* (London, 1978).
Maland, D., *Europe in the seventeenth century* (London, 1966).
Marriot, J. A. R., and Robertson, C. G., *The evolution of Prussia* (Oxford, 1946).
Oakley, S., *The story of Sweden* (London, 1966).
Ogg, D., *Europe in the seventeenth century* (London, 1976).
Pares, B., *A history of Russia* (New York, 1946).
Reddaway, W. F., Penson, J. H., Halecki, O. and Dyboski, R. (eds), *The Cambridge history of Poland; from Augustus II to Pilsudski 1697-1935* (London, 1951).
Riasonovsky, N. V., *A history of Russia* (New York, 1977).
Roberts, M., *The Swedish imperial experience 1560-1718* (London, 1979).
Scott, F. D., *Sweden. The nation's history* (Minneapolis, 1978).
Vernadsky, G., *A history of Russia* (London, 1969).

Chapter 6
NOTES
1. F. L. Nussbaum, *The triumph of science and reason 1660-1685*, p. x.
2. H. Butterfield, *The origins of modern science 1300-1800*, p. viii.
3. D. Ogg, *Europe in the seventeenth century*, p. 523.
4. G. Clark, *The seventeenth century*, p. ix.
5. H. Butterfield, *The origins of modern science 1300-1800*, p. 169.
6. See L. W. Cowie, *Seventeenth-century Europe*, p. 42.
7. See E. F. Heckscher, *Mercantilism*, vol. 11, p. 17, quoted by D. Ogg, *Europe in the seventeenth century*, p. 520.
8. See L. W. Cowie, *Seventeenth-century Europe*, p. 46.
9. D. Ogg, *Europe in the seventeenth century*, p. 539.

SUPPLEMENTARY READING
Butterfield, H., *The origins of modern science 1300-1800* (London, 1951).
Clark, G., *The seventeenth century* (Oxford, 1972).
Cowie, L. W., *Seventeenth-century Europe* (London, 1975).
Nussbaum, F. L., *The triumph of science and reason 1660-1685* (New York, 1962).
Ogg, D., *Europe in the seventeenth century* (London, 1971).

Chapter 7
NOTES
1. A. Hassall, *The balance of power 1715-1789*, p. 2.
2. D. Ogg, *Europe of the* ancien régime *1715-1783*, p. 128.
3. See M. S. Anderson, *Europe in the eighteenth century 1713-1783*, pp. 167-168.
4. A. Hassall, *The balance of power 1715-1789*, p. 68.
5. W. L. Dorn, *Competition for empire 1740-1763*, p. 154.
6. D. Ogg, *Europe of the* ancien régime *1715-1783*, p. 164.
7. W. L. Dorn, *Competition for empire*, p. 176.
8. J. H. Parry, *Trade and dominion: the European oversea empires in the eighteenth century*, p. 217.
9. W. J. Eccles, *The Canadian frontier 1534-1760*, p. 156.
10. R. Beatson, *Naval and military memoirs of Great Britain from 1727 to 1783*, vol. I, p. 420.
11. In Voltaire's *Candide* (1759).
12. G. Lacour-Gayet, *La marine militaire de la France sous le règne de Louis XV* (trans.), p. 389.
13. L. H. Gipson, *The coming of the revolution 1763-1775*, p. 233.
14. L. Gershoy, *From despotism to revolution 1763-1789*, p. 177.

SUPPLEMENTARY READING
Anderson, M. S., *Europe in the eighteenth century 1713-1783* (London, 1961).
Dorn, W. L., *Competition for empire 1740-1763* (New York, 1963).
Gershoy, L., *From despotism to revolution 1763-1789* (New York, 1963).
Hassall, A., *The balance of power* (London, 1950).
Heater, D. B., *Order and rebellion; a history of Europe in the eighteenth century* (London, 1964).
Horn, D. B., *Great Britain and Europe in the eighteenth century* (Oxford, 1967).
Ogg, D., *Europe of the* ancien régime *1715-1783* (London, 1965).
Parry, J. H., *Trade and dominion; the European oversea empires in the eighteenth century* (London, 1974).
Roberts, P., *The quest for security 1715-1740* (New York, 1963).

Rudé, G., *Europe in the eighteenth century* (London, 1972).
Williams, G., *The expansion of Europe in the eighteenth century* (London, 1966).

Chapter 8
NOTES
1. Phyllis Deane, "The industrial revolution in Great Britain". *The Fontana economic history of Europe* (C. M. Cipolla, ed.), vol. 4: *The emergence of industrial societies*, p. 163.
2. See, for more information on this, David S. Landes, *The unbound Prometheus: technological change and industrial development in Western Europe from 1750 to the present*, pp. 41, 96-99; and C. M. Cipolla, *The economic history of world populations*, pp. 35-37.
3. C. M. Cipolla, *The economic history of world populations*, p. 46.
4. C. M. Cipolla, *Guns, sails and empires: technological innovation and the early phases of European expansion 1400-1700*, p. 64.
5. C. K. Hyde, *Technological change and the British iron industry 1700-1870*, pp. 39-41, 53, 57, 61, 66-67.
6. Ibid., pp. 69, 73-74, 117-119.
7. See notably B. H. Slicher van Bath, "The rise of intensive husbandry in the Low Countries," *Britain and the Netherlands* (J. S. Bromley and E. H. Kossmann, eds), pp. 130-153.
8. Karl Marx, *Capital*, vol. 2 (Everyman's Library ed., 1930). See also J. D. Chambers, "Enclosure and labour supply in the Industrial Revolution". *Agriculture and economic growth in England 1650-1815*, (E. L. Jones, ed.), p. 94.
9. J. D. Chambers and G. E. Mingay, *The agricultural revolution 1750-1880*, p. 93.
10. P. Mathias, *The first industrial nation: an economic history of Britain 1700-1914*, p. 466.
11. P. E. Razell, "Population growth and economic change in eighteenth and early nineteenth century England and Ireland". *Land, labour and population in the industrial revolution*, (E. L. Jones and G. E. Mingay, eds), p. 263.
12. J. D. Chambers, *Population, economy, and society in pre-industrial England*, p. 104.
13. Ibid.
14. P. Mathias, *The first industrial nation: an economic history of Britain 1700-1914*, p. 486.
15. C. K. Hyde, *Technological change and the British iron industry 1700-1870*, pp. 67, 113; P. Deane and W. A. Cole, *British economic growth 1688-1959*, p. 225.
16. P. Mathias, *The first industrial nation: an economic history of Britain 1700-1914*, pp. 466, 468.
17. F. Crouzet, "Angleterre et France au XVIII siècle: essai d'analyse comparée de deux croissances économiques". *Annales* (1966), p. 272.
18. P. O'Brien and C. Keyder, *Economic growth in Britain and France 1780-1914: two paths to the twentieth century*, p. 105
19. Ibid., p. 117.

SUPPLEMENTARY READING
Ashton, T. S., *Iron and steel in the industrial revolution* (Manchester, 1951).
Ashton, T. S., *The industrial revolution 1760-1830* (London, 1948).
Bagwell, P. S., *The transport revolution from 1770* (London, 1974).
Bagwell, P. S., and Mingay, G. E., *Britain and America 1850-1939: a study of economic change* (London, 1970).
Chambers, J. D., and Mingay, G. E., *The agricultural revolution 1750-1880* (London, 1966).
Cipolla, C. M. (ed.), *The Fontana economic history of Europe*, vol. 3: *The industrial revolution* (London, 1973); vol. 4: *The emergence of industrial societies* (London, 1973).

Clapham, J. H., *An economic history of modern Britain*, vol. I: *The early railway age 1820-1850* (Cambridge, 1939).
Clarkson, L. A., *The pre-industrial economy in England 1500-1750* (London, 1971).
Davis, R., *The rise of the Atlantic economies* (London, 1973).
Gourvish, T. R., *Railways and the British economy 1830-1914* (London, 1980).
Hyde, C. K., *Technological change and the British iron industry 1700-1870* (Princeton, 1977).
Jones, E. L. (ed.), "Editor's introduction". *Agriculture and economic growth in England 1650-1815* (London, 1967).
Landes, D. S., *The unbound Prometheus: technological change and industrial development in western Europe from 1750 to the present* (London, 1969).
Lane, P., *The industrial revolution: the birth of the modern age* (London, 1978).
Lilley, S., *Men, machines and history* (London, 1965).
Mathias, P., *The first industrial nation: an economic history of Britain 1700-1914* (London, 1969).
Mitchell, B. R., "The coming of the railway and United Kingdom economic growth". *Journal of economic history*, 1964.
Musson, A. E., *The growth of British industry* (London, 1978).
O'Brien, P., *The new economic history of the railways* (London, 1977).
Pawson, E., *The early industrial revolution: Britain in the eighteenth century* (London, 1979).
Taylor, A. J., "Progress and poverty in Britain, 1780-1850: a reappraisal". *History*, 1960.

Chapter 9
NOTES
1. L. Krieger, *Kings and philosophers 1689-1789*, pp. 153-155.
2. N. Hampson, *The Enlightenment*, p. 157.
3. See J. H. Brumfitt, *The French Enlightenment*, p. 70.
4. Ibid., p. 133.
5. L. Krieger, *Kings and philosophers 1689-1789*, p. 192.
6. R. W. Harris, *Absolutism and Enlightenment*, p. 33.
7. R. Anchor, *The Enlightenment tradition*, p. 117.
8. J. H. Brumfitt, *The French Enlightenment*, p. 160.
9. N. Hampson, *The Enlightenment*, p. 161.
10. Ibid., pp. 139-140.
11. Ibid., pp. 128-129.
12. J. H. Brumfitt, *The French Enlightenment*, pp. 137-138.
13. S. Andrews, *Enlightened despotism*, p. xii.
14. R. J. White, *Europe in the eighteenth century*, p. 191.
15. Ibid., pp. 186-187.
16. Ibid., p. 191.
17. L. Krieger, *Kings and philosophers 1689-1789*, pp. 242-243.
18. R. J. White, *Europe in the eighteenth century*, pp. 191-192.
19. See S. Andrews, *Enlightened despotism*, p. 5.
20. Quoted in R. Wines, *Enlightened despotism: reform or reaction?*, p. 45.

SUPPLEMENTARY READING
Anchor, R., *The Enlightenment tradition* (New York, 1967).
Andrews, S. (ed.), *Enlightened despotism* (London, 1967).
Brumfitt, J. H., *The French Enlightenment* (London, 1972).
Bruun, G., *The Enlightened despots* (New York, 1967).

Gay, P., *Age of Enlightenment* (New York, 1966).
Hampson, N., *The Enlightenment* (Harmondsworth, 1976).
Harris, R. W., *Absolutism and Enlightenment* (London, 1964).
Krieger, L., *Kings and philosophers 1689-1789* (London, 1971).
White, R. J., *Europe in the eighteenth century* (London, 1965).
Wines, R. (ed)., *Enlightened despotism: reform or reaction?* (Boston, 1967).

Chapter 10
NOTES
1. Compare the same author's article "The French Revolution" in *World Spectrum*, vol. 7.
2. G. Lefebvre, *The coming of the French Revolution*, p. 16.
3. S. J. Idzerda, *The background of the French Revolution*, p. 3.
4. Ibid.
5. R. Ergang, *Europe from the Renaissance to Waterloo*, p. 645.
6. S. J. Idzerda, *The background of the French Revolution*, p. 14.
7. C. Breunig, *The age of revolution and reaction 1789-1850*, pp. 1-2.
8. S. J. Idzerda, *The background of the French Revolution*, pp. 15-16.
9. C. Breunig, *The age of revolution and reaction 1789-1850*, p. 2.
10. G. Lefebvre, *The coming of the French Revolution*, p. 23.
11. A. Goodwin, *The French Revolution*, pp. 55-56.
12. G. Lefebvre, *The coming of the French Revolution*, p. 105.
13. L. Gershoy, *The era of the French Revolution 1789-1799*, p. 44.
14. Ibid., p. 59.
15. S. Andrews, *Eighteenth-century Europe*, pp. 315-316.
16. R. Ergang, *Europe from the Renaissance to Waterloo*, p. 693.
17. O. Connelly, *French Revolution. Napoleonic era*, p. 196.

SUPPLEMENTARY READING
Andrews, S., *Eighteenth-century Europe; the 1680s to 1815* (London, 1976).
Breunig, C., *The age of revolution and reaction 1789-1850* (New York, 1970).
Connelly, O., *French Revolution. Napoleonic era* (New York, 1979).
Crawley, C. W. (ed.), *The new Cambridge modern history*, vol. IX: *War and peace in an age of upheaval 1793-1830* (Cambridge, 1965).
Doyle, W., *Origins of the French Revolution* (Oxford, 1980).
Ergang, R., *Europe from the Renaissance to Waterloo* (Lexington, 1967).
Gershoy, L., *The era of the French Revolution 1789-1799* (New York, 1957).
Goodwin, A. (ed.), *The new Cambridge modern history*, vol. VIII: *The American and French Revolutions 1763-93* (Cambridge, 1965).
Goodwin, A., *The French Revolution* (London, 1974).
Hampson, N., *A social history of the French Revolution* (London, 1963).
Hampson, N., *The French Revolution* (London, 1975).
Idzerda, S. J., *The background of the French Revolution* (Baltimore, 1967).
Jones, R. B., *The French Revolution* (London, 1967).
Kafker, F. A., and Laux J. M., *The French Revolution: conflicting interpretations* (New York, 1968).
Lefebvre, G., *The coming of the French Revolution* (Princeton, 1967).
Lefebvre, G., *The French Revolution from its origins to 1793* (London, 1962).
Lefebvre, G., *The French Revolution from 1793 to 1799* (London, 1964).
Lyons, M., *France under the Directory* (Cambridge, 1975).

Roberts, J. M., *The French Revolution* (Oxford, 1978).
Ross, S. T. (ed.), *The French Revolution – conflict or continuity?* (New York, 1971).
Salvemini, G., *The French Revolution 1788-1792* (London, 1954).

Chapter 11
NOTES
1. C. Breunig, *The age of revolution and reaction 1789-1850*, p. 70.
2. J. M. Thompson, *Napoleon Bonaparte*, p. 147.
3. O. Connelly, *The epoch of Napoleon*, pp. 42-43.
4. G. Lefebvre, *Napoleon*, p. 133.
5. J. M. Thompson, *Napoleon Bonaparte*, p. 179.
6. G. Lefebvre, *Napoleon*, pp. 153-154.
7. Compare G. Lefebvre, *Napoleon*, p. 154; O. Connelly, *The epoch of Napoleon*, p. 51; and J. M. Thompson, *Napoleon Bonaparte*, p. 204.
8. R. B. Jones, *Napoleon: man and myth*, p. 115.
9. See, for comparison, the "notables" of the Assembly of Notables in 1787, who were from the aristocracy.
10. C. Breunig, *The age of revolution and reaction 1789-1850*, p. 71.
11. R. B. Jones, *Napoleon: man and myth*, p. 95.
12. G. Lefebvre, *Napoleon*, pp. 73, 75, 89, 151.
13. R. Ergang, *Europe from the Renaissance to Waterloo*, p. 720.
14. C. Breunig, *The age of revolution and reaction 1789-1850*, p. 91.
15. R. B. Jones, *Napoleon: man and myth*, p. 153.
16. F. Markham, *Napoleon and the awakening of Europe*, pp. 24, 31, 100-101.
17. R. B. Jones, *Napoleon: man and myth*, pp. 163-164.
18. O. Connelly, *The epoch of Napoleon*, p. 73.
19. R. Ergang, *Europe from the Renaissance to Waterloo*, p. 736.
20. F. Markham, *Napoleon and the awakening of Europe*, p. 130.

SUPPLEMENTARY READING
Barnett, C., *Bonaparte* (London, 1978).
Bergeron, L., *France under Napoleon* (Princeton, 1981).
Breunig, C., *The age of revolution and reaction 1789-1850* (New York, 1970).
Chandler, D., *Napoleon* (London, 1973).
Connelly, O., *French Revolution. Napoleonic era* (New York, 1979).
Connelly, O., *The epoch of Napoleon* (Huntington, 1978).
Crawley, C. W. (ed.), *The new Cambridge modern history*, vol. IX: *War and peace in an age of upheaval 1793-1830* (Cambridge, 1965).
Geyl, P., *Napoleon, for and against* (London, 1949).
Jones, R. B., *Napoleon: man and myth* (London, 1977).
Lefebvre, G., *Napoleon* (London, 1969).
Markham, F., *Napoleon and the awakening of Europe* (London, 1975).
Thompson, J. M., *Napoleon Bonaparte. His rise and fall* (Oxford, 1969).

Chapter 12
NOTES
1. G. Bruun, *Revolution and reaction*, pp. 13-15.
2. Ibid., pp. 16-17.
3. Ibid.
4. M. B. Garrett and L. Godfrey, *Europe since 1815*, p. 34.
5. See B. Lyon, H. H. Rowen and T. S. Hamerow, *A history of the western world*, pp. 639-640.
6. See J. E. Gillespie, *Europe in perspective*, p. 57.
7. See M. B. Garrett and L. Godfrey, *Europe since 1815*, p. 100.
8. G. Bruun, *Revolution and reaction*, p. 84.
9. D. Thompson, *Europe since Napoleon*, p. 234.

SUPPLEMENTARY READING
Breunig, C., *The age of revolution and reaction 1789-1850* (New York, 1970).
Bruun, G., *Revolution and reaction 1848-1852* (New York, 1958).
Fasel, G., *Europe in upheaval; the revolutions of 1848* (New York, 1970).
Fetjö, F. (ed.), *The opening of an era 1848* (London, 1958).
Garrett, M. B. and Godfrey, L., *Europe since 1815* (New York, 1947).
Gash, N., *Aristocracy and people, Britain 1815-1865* (London, 1979).
Gillespie, J. E., *Europe in perspective, 1815 to the present* (New York, 1968).
Knapton, E. J., *Europe 1815-1914* (London, 1965).
Kranzberg, M. (ed.), *Eighteen-forty eight; a turning point?* (Boston, 1965).
Lyon, B., Rowen, H. H. and Hamerow, T. S., *A history of the western world* (Chicago, 1969).
Maurice, C. E., *The revolutionary movement of 1848-9 in Italy, Austria, Hungary and Germany* (New York, 1969).
Seaman, L. C. B., *From Vienna to Versailles* (New York, 1956).
Talman, J. L., *Romanticism and revolt: Europe 1815-1848* (London, 1967).
Thomson, D., *Europe since Napoleon* (London, 1968).
Whitridge, A., *Men in crisis* (New York, 1949).

INDEX

Abbeville, 85
Abercromby, J. 242
Aboukir Bay, 369
Acadia, 193-4
Aché, A. A. d', 240
Acre, 370
Addington, 386
Addison, 217
Adolphus Frederick of Sweden, 240, 247
Adrianople, Peace of, 165
Aegean Archipelago, 248
Africa, 91, 182-3, 186, 190, 194, 213, 221
Aisne River, 82
Aix-en-Provence, 64
Aix-la-Chapelle, Peace/Treaty of, 59, 89, 231-5, 412
Ajaccio, 367
Alais, Peace of, 22
Aland Isles, 165, 169
Albemarle, Earl of, 243
Alberoni, 218-9, 224
Albert of Austria, 1
Albert Hohenzollern of Ansbach, 142
Alembert, d', 295, 298, 304-5, 319
Alès, 78
Aleth, 87
Alexander I, Tsar, 374, 387-90, 394, 397, 401-4, 409, 412-4
Alexander VII, Pope, 89
Alexander of Parma, 101
Alexis I, Tsar, 148
Alexis Romanov, 167
Algiers, 90
Allen, 111
Almanza, 94
Alps, 54-5, 63, 79, 81, 83, 95, 367, 374, 403
Alsace, 3, 31-2, 37, 80-3, 90, 96
Altmark, Truce of, 22, 29, 146
Altranstadt, Treaty of, 158, 160, 162-3
Alva, Count, 48
Alva, F. A. de Toledo, Duke of, 67-8
Älvsborg, 146
Amazon, 191, 193
Amboina, 191-2
Amboise, 67
America, 41-2, 47, 52-4, 56, 61-2, 181-3, 186, 191, 195, 221, 230-2, 238, 244, 246; *see also* North America, New World and United States of America
Amherst, Baron J., 242
Amiens, 73, 188
Amiens, Treaty of, 374, 383, 386-7
Amsterdam, 49, 89, 176-7, 183, 188-90, 209, 251, 365
Andalusia, 39, 58, 60
Androsovo, Truce of, 149
Angers, 82
Angoulême, 67
Anjou, 82, 202
Anjou, F., Duke of, 70-1
Anjou, P., Duke of, 60
Anne of Austria, 75, 80-1
Anne of England, 93, 95, 122, 130, 133, 136-8, 166
Anne of Russia, 167
Anne Romanov of Russia, 165, 167
Anson, 228
Anson, Lord George, 243
Anspach, 250
Antigua, 192
António, Dom, 71
Antwerp, 48-9, 101, 176-8, 189-90
Antwerp, Peace of, 53
Appalachian Mountains, 235
Aragon, 39, 44, 52, 55, 60, 80
Aranjuez, 233
Arcot, 235, 241
Argenson, d', 303
Argyle, Earl of, 131
Aristotle, 203, 214-6
Arkwright, R., 272, 285
Armentières, 80, 89
Arminius, Jacobus, 107
Arnauld, A., 88
Arnay-le-Duc, 68
Arques, 72
Arras, 82
Arras, Treaty of, 50
Arsac, Ternay d', 243
Artois, 31, 62-3, 68, 83, 186, 202
Artois, Count of, 341
Ashburton, J. Dunning, Lord, 251
Asia, 143, 186, 204

441

Atlantic Ocean, 62, 84-5, 96, 178, 193-4, 206, 234, 244, 254, 283
Atlas Mountains, 54
Audenaarde, 94
Auerstädt, 389
Augereau, Lieutenant, 367
Augsburg, 59, 91-2, 153, 177
Augsburg, Peace of, 8-10, 35, 143
Augustus II of Poland, 92, 154-8, 161-2, 164, 167, 170
Augustus III of Saxony-Poland, 226, 229, 233, 240, 247
Auneau, 71
Aunis, 65
Austerlitz, 388-9
Austria, 2, 13, 16, 28-30, 34, 37, 41, 44-5, 49, 55-61, 75, 79-81, 92-4, 143, 149-51, 157, 167, 171, 176, 218-20, 222-7, 229-34, 237-40, 247-51, 306, 313, 317, 319, 324-5, 327, 352, 355, 360, 364-5, 367-70, 374, 387-90, 397-400, 403, 408-13, 420-1, 428
Austro-Hungary, 406, 421
Auvergne, 72, 83
Avesnes, 83
Avignon, 63, 250
Azores, 71
Azov, 155, 157, 163
Azov, Sea of, 248

Babeuf, 366
Babylon, 98
Bacon, Sir Francis, 111, 173, 179, 203, 206-8, 212, 292, 297, 299
Baden, 380, 387-8
Baden, Treaty of, 96
Baden-Durbach, Margrave of, 37
Bahamas, 192, 246
Baikal, Lake, 144
Bailen, 397
Bakurin, 161
Balearic Islands, 39
Balkans, 163, 390, 401
Baltic, 4-6, 17-20, 23-4, 26, 28, 32, 38, 56, 85, 92, 140-1, 143-6, 148-52, 154-7, 160, 162-6, 168-72, 178, 188, 224-5, 248
Banat, 249
Bancroft, Archbishop, 109
Barbados, 192
Barbara of Braganza, 232
Barcelona, 41, 95

Barcelonnette, 95
Barebone, Praise-God, 126
Barras, 366
Barrière Treaty, 221-3
Barrois, 247
Bart, J., 91
Bärwalda, Treaty of, 24, 27
Basle, 79, 365
Basque Provinces, 58
Bastille, 299, 349
Batavia, 191, 235
Batavian republic, 365, 370, 374, 387-9
Bates, 108-9
Bautzen, 403
Bavaria, 10-1, 15, 17, 22, 24-8, 30, 34, 37, 68, 80, 91-4, 153, 202, 222, 229-30, 233, 250, 380, 387-8, 403
Bavaria, Electress of, 60
Bayle, Pierre, 214, 217, 293, 302
Bayonne, 67
Bayreuth, 250
Beachy Head, 91, 195
Béarn, 76, 86
Beauharnais, Eugene de, 403
Beauharnais, Josephine, 368, 398
Beaujeu, A. de, 62
Beaujeu, D. de, 236
Beaulieu, 70
Belfast Lough, 244
Belgium, 49, 219, 223, 360, 364-5, 369, 374, 380, 387, 410, 426
Belgrade, 248
Belle Ile, 231, 244
Belleisle, Duke of, 229
Bender, 164
Benevento, 250
Benfield, 37
Bengal, 192, 194, 235, 240, 244
Bengal, Bay of, 235
Berezina River, 402
Berg, 10-1
Bergerac, 70
Berkeley, 297
Berlin, 25, 164, 177, 213, 227, 239, 303, 389, 400
Berlin, Treaty of, 230-1
Bernadotte, 403
Bernard of Saxe-Weimar, 28-31, 80
Berwick, 119
Berwick, J., Duke of, 94-5

442

Bessarabia, 248
Bethlen, Gabriel, 14, 16
Bihar, 235
Biscay, Bay of, 63
Bismarck, 429
Black Sea, 155, 163, 249
Blake, 307
Blanc, L., 419
Blekinge, 149
Blénau, 82
Blenheim, 94, 259
Blois, 67-8, 72
Blücher, 403, 405
Bohemia, 1-2, 7, 11-6, 18-20, 22-3, 25-6, 28, 34, 37, 56, 179, 188, 207, 230, 233, 238, 250, 423
Böhuslan, 152
Boileau, 217
Boileau-Despréaux, N., 96
Bolivia, 380
Bologna, 369
Bologna, Concordat of, 65
Bombay, 192, 235
Bonaparte, Jerome, 390, 398
Bonaparte, Joseph, 368, 384, 389, 395, 397-8, 403
Bonaparte, Louis, 389, 392
Bonaparte, Lucien, 371
Bonaparte, Marie-Louise, 398-9, 401
Bonn, 92, 94
Bordeaux, 64, 82, 188, 312, 392
Borneo, 191
Bornholm, 150
Borodino, 402
Boscawen, E., 232, 236, 242-3
Bouchain, 95
Boufflers, L. F., Duke of, 94
Bougainville, L. A. de, 246
Bouillon, H., Duke of, 69, 73
Boulogne, 69, 388
Bourbon, Duke of, 224-5
Bourbon, C. de, 71-2
Bourges, 67
Boyle, Robert, 173, 203, 211, 213, 256
Boyne, 91
Brabant, 89
Braddock, E., 236
Bradstreet, D., 242
Brahé, Tycho, 205
Brandenburg, 80, 87, 89-91, 93, 142, 233, 238, 240
Brandenburg, Margrave and Elector of, 7-8, 10-2, 18, 22, 24-5, 27, 34, 37-8
Brandenburg-Prussia, 140, 143, 146, 148-51, 154, 158, 162, 164, 176, 180, 196, 202, 213; *see also* Prussia
Braunau, 13
Brazil, 59, 62, 93, 182, 191-2
Breda, 31, 127
Breisach, 31, 37, 80-1
Breitenfeld, 25
Bremen, 18, 21, 38, 140, 146-7, 149, 152, 163, 166, 170, 398
Brentford, 124
Breslau, 400
Breslau, Treaty of, 229
Bresse, 75
Brest, 85
Brienne, 367
Brienne, Archbishop de, 343
Brissot, 355, 359
Brissot de Warville, Jacques Pierre, 305, 308
Bristol, 177
Britain, 41, 47, 49-54, 56, 58, 59-61, 86-7, 94-5, 97-139, 163-4, 168-70, 219-46, 248-9, 251-89, 294, 300, 306, 317, 360, 365, 369-70, 374-6, 387-94, 397, 399, 402-6, 408, 410-2, 429; *see also* England
Brittany, 64, 71-3, 84-5, 201-2, 244
British Honduras, 192
Brömsebro, Treaty of, 34, 38, 146, 148-9
Broussel, P., 81
Bruges, 94
Brühe, 82
Brune, 370
Brunswick, 238-9, 357
Brunswick, Duke of, 18-9, 37, 209, 357, 389
Brussels, 3, 10, 15, 30-1, 48, 234, 251
Bucharest, 248
Buckingham, G. Villiers, Duke of, 78, 110, 113-6
Buckinghamshire, 108
Bucquoy, 16
Buenos Aires, 244
Buffon, 303
Bugey, 75
Bukovina, 248
Buonaparte, Carlo, 367
Burgoyne, J., 245
Burgundy, 63-4, 68, 73, 82-3, 86, 196, 201-2
Burke, 307
Burke, E., 245

443

Burkersdorf, 240
Bussy, C. C. de, 235, 241
Bute, Earl of, 240
Byng, Admiral, 224
Byng, John, 240, 242
Byron, J. 246

Cadiz, 41, 51, 102, 183
Cadoudal, 383
Cahors, 70
Cairo, 369-70
Calais, 63, 67, 73, 100
Calas, Jean, 302
Calcutta, 192, 235, 240
Calonne, 339, 342-3
Cambacérès, 373
Cambrai, 73, 82, 88, 90, 224-5
Cambridge, 124, 211-2, 215
Campo Formio, Treaty of, 369, 374
Canada, 85, 93, 193, 231, 234-6, 243-4, 246, 380
Canning, G., 395, 413, 426
Cape Breton Island, 231, 234, 244
Cape Finisterre, 231
Cape of Good Hope, 87, 191, 232, 246, 410
Cape Passaro, 224
Cape Race, 236
Cape St Vincent, 246
Capuchius, 9
Caribbean, 101, 228
Caribbean Sea, 85, 93, 246, 270
Carinthia, 2
Carisbrooke Castle, 125
Carlos, Don, 43, 222, 224-7, 230
Carnatic, 235, 241, 246
Carniola, 2
Carnot, 363, 368
Carolinas, 240
Carpathian Mountains, 143
Carrickfergus, 244
Cartagena, 228
Carteret, 230
Carteret, P., 246
Cartier, J., 62
Carvajal, B., 233
Cas, 143
Casale, 38, 56, 82, 90, 92
Casimir, John, of Poland, 148-50
Cassini, J. D., 96
Castelnaudary, 78

Castile, 39, 41-5, 47, 52, 54-60
Castlereagh, Lord, 409, 411-2
Catalonia, 31, 39, 55, 58, 60, 80-2, 90, 94-5
Cateau-Cambrésis, Peace of, 45, 50, 63, 73
Catherine of Russia, 163
Catherine II, the Great, 225-6, 240, 247-9, 306, 313-4, 317-9, 325-9
Catinat, N. de, 92, 94
Caucasus, 248
Caulet, E. F. de, 87
Cayenne, 90
Cecil, Earl of Salisbury, 108-9
Cecil, William, 98-9, 102
Cerdagne, 82
Cervantes, 52
Cévennes, 77, 86
Ceylon, 191, 246, 374, 410
Chalais, H. de Talleyrand, Marquis of, 78
Chambers, J. D., 268, 273
Chamillart, M. de, 96
Chamlain, 193
Champagne, 66-7, 82
Champlain, Lake, 236, 242
Champlain, S. de, 62
Chandernagar, 194
Chandernagore, 235, 240, 246
Charlemagne, 88, 142, 367, 384, 389
Charleroi, 89-90, 92
Charles IV, Duke of Lorraine, 83
Charles V, Emperor, 41-3, 47, 55, 62
Charles VI, Emperor, 92, 94-6, 142, 169, 222-6, 229
Charles I of England, 78, 107, 110-25, 128, 130
Charles II of England, 82, 89, 127-30, 137, 150, 194, 200, 213
Charles VIII of France, 62
Charles IX of France, 66-9
Charles X of France, 414, 416-7
Charles II of Spain, 58-60, 92-3
Charles III of Spain, 233, 243, 318
Charles IV of Spain, 395
Charles IX of Sweden, 141, 146
Charles X of Sweden, 147-50, 154
Charles XI of Sweden, 90-1, 150, 152-4
Charles XII of Sweden, 152-8, 160-9, 401
Charles Albert, 425, 428
Charles Albert of Bavaria, 229-30
Charles Emmanuel of Savoy, 75, 229
Charles Frederick of Baden, 317

Charles Frederick of Holstein-Gotorp, 165, 167, 169
Charles Gustavus, 147
Charles Louis of Palatine, 37
Charles Theodore, 250
Charlotte of Russia, 167-8
Charolais, 63
Chartres, 67, 72-3
Chatham, W. Pitt, Earl of, 234, 236, 238-40, 242-3, 245
Chaumont, Treaty of, 408, 411
Chauvelin, 226
Cherasco, 79
Cherasco, Treaty of, 57, 369
Cherbourg, 195, 243
Chernigov, 145
Chesapeake Bay, 245
Chesmé, 248
China, 85, 171, 191, 232
Chinon, 72
Choiseul, Duc de, 221
Choiseul, E. F. de, 238-9, 243-4
Christian IV of Denmark, 17-9, 145-6, 154
Christina of Sweden, 26, 35, 147-8, 207
Churchill, A., 94
Cipolla, C., 254
Circars, 235, 242
Cisalpine republic, 369, 374, 386
Clarendon, Earl of, 128-9
Clausewitz, 400
Clement XI, Pope, 88
Clement XIII, Pope, 250
Clement XIV, Pope, 250
Clément, J., 72
Clermont, 83
Cleves, 10-1, 37, 233
Cleves-Jülich, 75
Clive, R., 235, 240
Cobbett, W., 427
Coen, Jan Pieterszoon, 191
Cognac, 68
Cooke, Sir Edward, 110-1, 114, 117, 132
Colbert, 59, 84-5, 95-6, 179-80, 184-7, 189, 192-4, 199, 213, 391
Coldstream, 127
Coligny, G. de, 65-9
Coligny, L. de, 70
Cologne, 82, 89-94, 177
Cologne, Archbishop and Elector of, 7, 9, 12

Columbus, C., 182
Compiègne, 80
Compiègne, Treaty of, 29
Comtat Venaissin, 63
Condé, Prince de, 31
Condé, H. de, 69-71
Condé, L. de, 65-8
Condé, L., Prince of, 80-3, 85, 89
Condillac, 298
Condorcet, 303, 307, 309, 345, 359
Conflans, 82
Conflans, Comte de, 243
Constantinople, 144, 161, 248, 390, 401
Conti, A., Prince of, 82
Conti, L. F., Prince of, 92
Cook, J., 246
Coote, Eyre, 242
Copenhagen, 149, 156, 168
Copenhagen, Treaty of, 150
Copernicus, 204-5, 211
Corbie, 30
Córdoba, Gonzalo de, 41
Corneille, 217
Corneille, P., 96
Cornish, S., 243
Cornwallis, C., 245
Coromandel coast, 91, 244
Corsica, 233, 367-8
Cort, H., 261
Courland, 167, 171, 188, 249
Cour Plénière, 344
Courtrai, 89-90
Coutras, 71
Cracow, 157, 248-9, 398
Cranfield, Lionel, 110-2
Cranmer, 98
Crimea, 248
Crompton, S., 272
Cromwell, Oliver, 82, 123-8, 132
Cromwell, Richard, 127
Crouzet, F., 285
Crown Point, 242
Cuba, 244
Cuddalore, 241
Cumberland, Duke of, 236, 238
Cyprus, 45

Da Gama, Vasco, 182
Dagoe, 177

Danton, 305, 355, 358, 360-1, 363
Danube River, 94-5, 249, 367
Danzig, 5, 177, 248-9, 390
Darby, A., 260-1, 285
Darcy, 111
Darlington, 278
Darnley, 100
Dauphiné, 65, 70-2, 86, 92, 95, 196, 202-2
David, Jean-Luis, 384
Da Vinci, L., 258
Deane, P., 252
Decazes, 416
Deccan, 235, 241
Delaware, 191
Denain, 94-5
Denmark, 4-5, 13, 17-23, 32, 56, 90, 93, 141, 143, 145-6, 148-54, 156, 158, 162, 164-8, 170-1, 176, 196, 225, 232, 237, 245, 247-8, 319, 390, 398
Derubach, Abbot of, 9
Desargues, G., 96
Descartes, René, 96, 173, 175, 203, 207-11, 215, 217, 291-2, 299
Desmarets, N., Marquis of Maillebois, 96
Dessau Bridge, 19
Dettingen, 230
Devonshire, 91
Diderot, Denis, 210, 295, 302-7, 309, 311-4, 327
Dieppe, 72
Digges, Sir Dudley, 114
Dijou, 64
Dinwiddie, R., 236
Dixmude, 90
Djerba, 45
Dnieper River, 149, 160, 162, 248
Dominica, 243, 246
Donauwörth, 10
Dormans, 69
Doullens, 73
Dovai, 95
Dover, 132
Dover, Treaty of, 89, 150
Dowus, 31
Drake, Sir Francis, 51, 102-3
Draper, W., 243
Dresden, 238-9
Dresden, Treaty of, 162, 231
Dreux, 67
Dubois, 224
Du Châtelet, Madame, 303

Ducos, 371
Duelino, Truce of, 145
Duguay-Trouin, R., 93
Dumoriez, 356, 359-61
Duna River, 5
Dunkirk, 58, 80, 82, 85, 94-5, 231, 236, 243-4
Dupleix, J. F., 231, 235
Dupont, 397
Duquesne, A., 90
Duquesne, A. de Menneville de, 235
Durham, 119
Dutch republic, 176
Dvina River, 248

East Anglia, 188, 269
East Indies, 85, 185, 190-1, 194, 232, 234-5, 247
Eastern Galicia, 398
Eastern Pomerania, 37-8, 143
Eastern Prussia, 142, 148-50, 233, 237-8, 249
Edinburgh, 66
Edinburgh, Treaty of, 66
Effingham, Lord Howard of, 102-3
Egmont, Count, 48
Egypt, 369-70, 374, 380, 387
Elba, 80, 82, 404, 415
Elbe River, 17-8, 38, 202
Elbe-Weser, 146
Eliot, Sir John, 110, 114-7
Elizabeth I of England, 44, 50-1, 53, 63, 71, 97-107, 190, 192, 206, 283
Elizabeth of Russia, 238, 240, 328
Elizabeth Farnese, 222, 224-7, 229, 232-3
Elizabeth Romanov, 167
Emden, 232
Engels, F., 274
England, 1, 3-4, 10-1, 15, 17, 19, 62-3, 66-72, 75, 77-8, 81-2, 85, 87-94, 97-139, 146, 150, 153, 155-7, 174-7, 179-85, 187-90, 192, 194-5, 197-8, 200-1, 206-7, 212, 214, 224, 240, 290, 294-6, 299, 301, 309, 311, 319, 331; *see also* Britain
English Channel, 2, 63, 93, 175
Erfurt, 177
Erfurt, Treaty of, 397
Erie canal, 282
Erik of Norway, 141
Erik XIV of Sweden, 141, 145
Essex, 124
Essling-Asperen, 398
Estonia, 5, 140, 145, 150, 158, 162, 165-6, 171

Estrées, J. d', 90
Eugene, Prince, 94
Eylau, 389

Falkland Islands, 244
Farnese, Alexander, 49, 51
Fehrbellin, 151-2
Fénelon, F. de Salignac de la Mothe, 88, 96
Fenestrelle, 95
Ferdinand, Cardinal-Infante, 27, 29-30
Ferdinand I, Emperor, 7, 42, 63
Ferdinand II, Emperor, 12-23, 25-8, 57
Ferdinand III, Emperor, 27-8, 34, 37, 149
Ferdinand of Brunswick, 239
Ferdinand II of Naples, 424-5
Ferdinand of Spain, 39
Ferdinand VI of Spain, 232
Ferdinand VII of Spain, 395
Ferguson, Adám, 291
Fermat, P. de, 96
Fichte, 400
Finland, 4-5, 23, 145, 163, 165, 171, 176, 397
Finland, Gulf of, 145, 158, 165, 171
Flanders, 21, 47-9, 56, 59-60, 63, 82-3, 259, 263, 270, 282-3
Fleix, Peace of, 70
Fleurus, 92
Fleury, 223-9
Florence, 176, 206, 212, 269-70
Florida, 62, 93, 244, 246
Folembray, 73
Fontainebleau, 86-7, 91, 244, 251
Fontainebleau, Treaty of, 26, 393, 404, 408
Fontaine-Française, 73
Fontenelle, Bernard de, 216-7, 293, 314
Fontenelle, B. le Bovier de, 96
Fontenoy, 234
Forbes, J., 242
Formosa, 191-2
Fort Beauséjour, 236
Fort Duquesne, 236, 242
Fortescue, 108
Fort Frontenac, 242
Fort Gaspereau, 236
Fort Niagara, 236, 243
Fort Oswego, 240, 243
Fort St David, 235, 241
Fort St Joseph, 246
Fort William Henry, 240

Fouché, 382
Fouquet, N., 84
Fourth, Firth of, 103
Fox, H., 236
France, 1-4, 10-1, 13, 16-7, 21-4, 27-30, 32, 34-5, 37-9, 41, 44-5, 47-52, 54-60, 62-96, 99, 103, 115, 117, 119, 129-30, 136, 140, 146, 150-5, 158, 163-4, 167, 170, 172, 174-7, 179, 181, 183, 185-9, 192-4, 196, 198, 200-2, 206, 213-5, 217-46, 248-52, 259, 262, 268, 270, 282-90, 292, 294-9, 301-4, 309-12, 318-9, 323-4, 331-405, 408-9, 411-4
Franche-Comté, 2-3, 48, 59, 63, 75, 80, 89-90
Francis I of Austria, 232, 389, 398
Francis II of Austria, 250
Francis II, Emperor, 356, 374, 387-9
Francis I of France, 62, 65
Francis II of France, 66, 100
Francis of Lorraine, 227
Franconia, 25, 27
Frankfurt, 230, 360, 421, 423
Frankfurt-on-Main, 25
Franklin, B., 246
Frederick I, 213
Frederick of Bohemia, 56
Frederick III of Brandenburg-Prussia, 154
Frederick III of Denmark, 149
Frederick IV of Denmark, 154, 156
Frederick of Hohenzollern, Burgrave of Nüremberg, 142
Frederick of Palatine, 110-1, 117
Frederick V of Palatine, 10, 14-8, 37
Frederick I of Prussia, 154, 158, 162, 167
Frederick II, the Great, of Prussia, 218, 229, 231, 233, 238-40, 247-50, 300, 303, 306, 313-4, 317-20, 322-6, 328-9
Frederick I of Sweden, 169-70
Frederick Adolf of Hesse, Prince, 169
Fredericksburg, 170
Frederickshald, 169
Frederick William, 180, 196, 202, 224-5, 227, 317, 320, 323
Frederick William of Brandenburg, 32
Frederick William of Brandenburg-Prussia, 142-3, 148-52, 323
Frederick William I of Prussia, 164-7, 170
Frederick William II of Prussia, 249, 251, 356
Frederick William III of Prussia, 388-90, 399, 403-4, 409, 420-1
Freiburg, 80, 90, 94

447

Fréron, 302
Friedland, 389-90
Friesland, 50
Frontenac, L., de Buade de, 91
Fundy, Bay of, 236
Funen Island, 19
Füssen, 233

Gadebusch, 164
Gaeta, 425
Galicia, 144, 248-9, 410
Galilei, Galileo, 173-4, 203, 205-6, 211-2, 217, 255, 292
Gálvez, B. de, 246
Galway, H. de Massue de Ruvigny, Earl of, 94
Ganges River, 235
Gardie, Magnus de la, 150
Gay, 299
Gelderland, 50
Geneva, 62, 98, 177, 300
Genoa, 21, 90, 233, 269, 410
Genoa, Republic of, 367-9, 387-8, 392
George I of Britain, 95, 166, 168, 170, 222-4, 229
George II of Britain, 225, 229-31, 238
George III of Britain, 245, 387
George, Lake, 240
George William of Brandenburg, 25, 32
Georgia, 235, 245
Germany, 41, 49, 56, 67-9, 71-2, 75, 89-91, 93, 96, 141, 146, 147-8, 150, 164, 167-9, 175-8, 184, 187-8, 206, 209-10, 222, 227, 229, 230-1, 233, 235, 237-9, 255, 283, 287, 290, 295, 306, 308, 406, 410, 412, 419, 428; *see also* Holy Roman empire
Gertruidenberg, 94
Ghent, 90, 94
Ghent, Pacification of, 49
Gibraltar, 61, 93, 95, 222, 225, 226, 232, 246
Girardon, F. 96
Glasgow, 177, 188
Glatz, 231, 240
Gloucester, Duke William of, 136
Gneisenau, 400
Gobi Desert, 144
Godolphin, Lord Treasurer, 138
Goethe, 308, 400
Golitsin, Prince, 160
Golovchina, 160
Goodwin, 108
Gordon, Lord George, 249

Gorée, 243-4
Görtz, Baron George Heinrich, 165, 168-9
Gotland, 146
Gottshed, 320
Goya, 384
Granada, 39, 44, 52
Grasse, F. de, 245-6
Gravelines, 62, 80, 82-3
Great Lakes, 236, 243, 282
Great Meadows, 236
Greece, 173, 413-4, 426
Greenwich, 213
Grenada, 243
Grenoble, 64, 344
Grey, Lord, 427
Grimm, 311
Groningen, 50
Guadeloupe, 93, 193, 243-4, 408
Guastalla, 231
Guericke, O. von, 255-6
Guise, F. de, 62, 65-7
Guise, H. de, 69-72
Guise, L. de, 72
Guise, M. de, 66
Guizot, 418-9
Gustavus I of Sweden, 141
Gustavus III of Sweden, 248, 319
Gustavus Adolphus, 140, 145-7, 153-4
Gustavus Adolphus II of Sweden, 17, 20, 23-7, 31, 38
Guyana, 191
Guyenne, 65, 70, 75-6, 82, 85
Guyon, J., 87-8
Gyllenstierna, Johan, 152

Haarlem, 188
Hague, The, 11, 16, 94
Haiti, 380
Halberstadt, 18, 21, 37, 143
Hales, Sir Edward, 131
Halifax, 236
Halland, 146
Halley, 211, 214
Hamburg, 177, 398
Hamburg, Treaty of, 31
Hamitton, Professor Earl, 178
Hampden, Sir John, 115, 118
Hampton, Court, 107
Hangö-Udd (Hanö), 165

Hanover, 93, 95, 140, 166-70, 209, 219, 222-4, 226-7, 229-31, 234-9, 387-9
Hanover, Convention of, 231
Hanover, Treaty of, 225
Hardenberg, 400, 412
Hardovin-Mansard, J., 96
Härjedalen, 146
Haro, Luis de, 57-8
Harvey, William, 212
Hastings, Warren, 246
Havana, 243
Hawke, Baron E., 243
Hedvig, Sophia, 154, 169
Hein, Piet, 56, 191
Heligoland, 392, 410
Helvétius, 303-4, 307, 309, 311
Helvetian republic, 369-70, 374, 386
Henrietta Maria of England, 78, 113
Henry VII of England, 97, 100, 104, 283
Henry VIII of England, 97-8, 102, 104, 257, 259, 269, 283
Henry II of France, 62-3, 65-6, 99-100
Henry III of France, 51, 69-72
Henry IV of France, 1-2, 10-1, 16, 68-75, 192, 198, 229, 334, 341
Herbert of Cherbury, 296
Herder, 308
Hertfordshire, 124
Hesse-Cassel, 24, 28, 37
Hispaniola, 91
Hobbes, Thomas, 195, 209, 215, 291, 306
Hohenlinden, 374
Hohenlohe, Prince, 389
Holbach, d', 296, 298, 302-4, 307, 309, 311, 319
Holland, 50, 155, 174-5, 178-80, 183-5, 188, 190, 194, 197-8, 200, 206-7, 214, 219-26, 229-30, 295, 311, 319, 389, 392, 398, 403, 410; see also Netherlands
Holstein, 4-5, 17-9
Holstein-Gottorp, 147-8, 153-4, 156, 165, 168-71
Holy Roman empire, 1-28, 31-2, 34-6, 38, 41-3, 57, 140-4, 150-1, 153-4, 158, 162, 167, 169-70, 176, 250, 386-9
Honduras, Gulf of, 244
Hooke, Robert, 213
Hoorn, Count, 48
Hradschin palace, 13
Hubertusburg, Treaty of, 240
Hudson Bay, 95, 194, 222

Hudson River, 282
Humboldt, Wilhelm von, 400
Hume, David, 291, 296, 304
Hungary, 2, 13, 16, 28, 91, 140, 179, 199, 202, 207, 233-4, 237, 248, 251, 326
Hunt, H., 426
Huntingdonshire, 124
Huskisson, W., 426
Huygens, Christiaan, 173, 189, 203, 211, 257
Hyde, C. K., 260
Hyder 'Ali, 246

Iberian Peninsula, 43, 47, 58
Iberville, P. le Moyne d', 91
Ile de France, 73, 194, 202
Ile de Ré, 77-8
Ile d'Oléron, 77
Illinois, 282
Indelnigsverk, 153
India, 53, 85, 191-2, 194-5, 221, 230-2, 234-5, 238, 240-1, 245-6
Indiana, 282
Indian Ocean, 78, 194
Ingria, 5, 140, 145, 150, 156, 166, 171
Innocent IX, Pope, 135
Innocent XI, Pope, 91
Innocent XII, Pope, 87
Inn River, 250
Ionian Islands, 390, 392
Ireland, 50, 53, 87, 91, 121, 124, 135, 176, 244
Isabel Clara Eugenia of Spain, 73
Isabella of Castile, 39
Isle of Wight, 125
Italy, 2-4, 14, 20-2, 29-31, 38, 49, 53, 56-7, 62-3, 65, 75, 79-80, 88, 90, 92-4, 175-8, 184, 205-6, 219, 222, 224, 226-7, 229-4, 237, 270, 290, 367-70, 374, 380, 386-7, 389-91, 398, 403, 406, 410, 423
Ivan III, 144
Ivan IV, 144-5
Ivry, 72

Jaffa, 370
Jamaica, 192
James I of England, 1, 15-6, 53, 105, 107-13, 116, 128, 136, 192
James II of England, 88, 91-4, 128-38, 194, 223
James V of Scotland, 100
James VI of Scotland, 100, 107

James Edward, the Pretender, 223
Jämtland, 146
Jansenius, C., 87-8
Japan, 191, 380
Jarnac, 68
Jassy, Treaty of, 249
Java, 191
Jellacic, 423
Jena, 389-90, 420
Jenkins, Captain, 228
John III of Sweden, 141, 146
John George of Saxony, 15, 25, 37
John Sigismund of Brandenburg, 10, 142
John William of Jülich-Cleves, 10
Joinville, Treaty of, 71
Jones, J. P., 246
Joseph I, Emperor, 95, 157-8, 224, 229
Joseph II of Austria, 240, 250-1, 306, 313-4, 317-9, 323-6
Joseph Ferdinand of Bavaria, 92
Jourdan, 367
Juan, Don, 44-5, 49, 59
Juana of Spain, 41
Jülich, 10-1, 75
Junot, 395, 397
Jutland, 143, 146, 149, 164

Kalisch, Treaty of, 403
Kalmar, 141, 145
Kant, Immanuel, 291, 299, 307-8, 320
Kardis, Peace of, 150, 156
Karelia, 5, 150, 165-6, 171
Karikal, 241
Karlsbad, 420
Kaunitz, W. A., 237-8, 240, 248, 250
Kaunitz, von, 356
Kay, J., 272
Kepler, Johann, 205-6
Keppel, A., 243
Kexholm, 140, 145
Kiev, 143, 155, 160-1
Kievan Russia, 143-4
Kircher, 188
Klein-Schnellendorf, Agreement of, 230
Klissow, 157
Klostergrab, 13
Klosterzeven, Convention of, 238
Knäred, Peace of, 146
Knox, John, 100

Kolin, 238
Königsberg, Treaty of, 148
Kósciwszko, T., 249
Kossuth, L., 422-3
Kotzebue, 420
Krefeld, 239
Künersdorf, 239
Kutshuk-Kainardij, Treaty of, 248
Kutuzov, Field Marshal, 402

Labiau, Treaty of, 149
La Bourdonnais, B. F. Mahé de, 231
La Bruyère, 96, 217
La Charité, 68, 70
La Clue, S. de, 243
Lafayette, 345, 349, 356
La Fère, 70
Laffemas, B., 75
La Fléche, 207
La Fontaine, J. de, 96
La Galissonière, R. M. Barrin de, 235-6
Lagos Bay, 243
La Hire, P., 96
La Hogue, 91, 195
Lally de Tollendal, T. A., 240-2
Lamaignon-Malesherbes, 297
Lamarck, Jean Baptiste, 384
Lamartine, 419
Lambert, General John, 127
La Mettrie, 307, 311
La Motte, Du Bois de, 236
Laudon, G. E., 239
Landrecies, 80, 83
Languedoc, 64-5, 68-70, 72, 84-5, 87, 201-2
Lanson, 300
Laon, 73
La Reynie, N. G. de, 84
La Rochelle, 22, 68-9, 77-9, 114
La Salle, R. C. de, 85, 193
Latvia, 171
Laud, Archbishop William, 111, 114, 117-20
La Vendée, 355, 360, 363, 366, 375, 377
Lawrence, S., 235
Lebrun, 373
Le Brun, C., 96
Lech, 26, 57
Lee, William, 189
Leeds, 287
Leeuwenhoek, Anthonie van, 212

450

Le Havre, 67, 188
Leibnitz, 173, 175, 203, 208-11, 213, 293
Leicester, Earl of, 101
Leipzig, 25, 209, 238, 403, 420
Leith, 100
Le Mas-d'Azil, 77
Le Nôtre, A., 96
Lens, 80
Lenthal, Speaker, 123
Leo X, Pope, 65
Leoben, Peace of, 369
Leon, 39
Leopold, Archduke, 80
Leopold I, Emperor, 60, 89, 91-3, 95, 154
Leopold II, Emperor, 248, 319, 324, 326, 355-6
Lepanto, 45, 47
Lerma, Duke of, 53-6
Le Quesnoy, 95
Lérida, 81
Lesczynski, Maria, 225
Lesczynski, Stanislaus of Poland, 157-8, 160, 162, 226-8, 248
Lesnaia, 160
Lespinasse, de, 297
Lessing, 302, 320
Le Tellier, M., 85
Leuthen, 238
Levant, 85, 221
Le Vau, L., 96
Lévis, F. G. de, 243
Lexington, 245
Leyden, 188, 212
L'Hôpital, M. de, 66-8
Liegnitz, 239
Ligurian republic, 369, 374, 398
Lille, 89, 94
Limburg, 56
Limerick, 91
Lisbon, 47, 51, 176, 395, 397
Lithuania, 141, 148, 171, 248; *see also* Poland-Lithuania
Liverpool, 280, 287
Livonia, 140, 144-6, 148, 150, 155-8, 160, 162, 166-7, 171
Lobkowitz, Count, 12-3
Locke, John, 210, 292-3, 299, 314
Löfo, 169
Loire River, 65, 67-8, 70, 76, 86, 288
Lombardy, 369, 410

London, 103, 124, 127, 170, 176-7, 187-8, 190, 210, 212-3, 235, 243, 250, 270, 273, 288, 308
London, Peace of, 53
Longjumeau, Peace of, 67
Longueville, H. d'Orleans, Duke of, 82
Lorient, 244
Lorraine, 37, 63, 78-9, 83, 89-90, 92, 95, 227-8, 247
Lorraine, Cardinal of, 100
Lorraine, C. de, 66
Louis XIII of France, 27, 30, 75-8, 80
Louis XIV of France, 58-9, 80-96, 129, 131, 137, 150-3, 157, 162, 164, 181, 186, 192, 194-6, 198, 202, 217, 220-1, 227, 254, 285, 288, 293-5, 297-8, 301, 331, 334, 339, 341, 386, 408, 414-6
Louis XV of France, 95, 167, 222-5, 237, 244, 317, 332, 367
Louis XVI of France, 316-7, 238, 250, 340-60, 389
Louis XVII of France, 364
Louisburg, 231, 234, 236, 242
Louisiana, 93, 193, 235, 244, 246, 380
Louis Philippe, 417-9, 424, 428
Louvois, 199
Louvois, M. de Tellier de, 85
Louvre, 384
Löwendal, U. F. W. de, 231
Löwenhaupt, Count, 160, 162
Loyola, Ignatius, 45, 326
Lübeck, 145, 165, 177, 398
Lübeck, Peace of, 19-20
Lublin, 148, 249
Lucca, 410
Lucretius, 217
Lully, J. B., 96
Lund, 152
Lund, Peace of, 152
Lunéville, Peace of, 374, 386
Lusatia, 11, 14-6, 37
Lutter, 19
Lützen, 27, 403
Luxemburg, 50, 90, 380
Luxemburg, F. H., Duke of, 89, 92
Luynes, C. d'Albert, Duke of, 75, 77
Lyons, 67, 177, 183, 188
Lyons, Peace of, 75

Maastricht, 89, 251
Mably, 298, 305, 307
Machault, 299, 303
Machiavelli, 217

Madras, 192, 194, 231, 235, 241; see also Fort St George
Madrid, 11, 111, 113, 177, 287, 395, 397, 401
Magdeburg, 21, 24-5, 37, 143
Magog, 154
Mahé, 242, 246
Mahon, 225
Main River, 367
Maine, 202
Mainz, 92, 360
Mainz, Archbishop and Elector of, 7, 9, 12
Mainz, Elector of, 356
Malabar Coast, 244
Málaga, 45
Malaysia, 191
Malpighi, 212
Malplaquet, 94
Malta, 45, 369, 374, 387, 392, 410
Manchester, 188, 280, 287
Manila, 243
Manin, 425
Mansard, F., 96
Mansfeld, Count Ernst von, 14, 16, 18-9
Mantes, 73
Mantua, 21-2, 38, 56-7, 79, 93-4
Marat, 355, 358
Marengo, 374
Margaret, Queen, 141
Maria of Portugal, 43
Mariana of Austria, 59
Maria Theresa of Austria, 225, 227, 229-30, 232, 234, 238, 240, 248, 250, 314, 317-8, 324-5
Maria Theresa of Spain, 58-9, 83, 89, 93
Marie Antoinette, 238, 340-1, 352, 355-6, 363
Marienburg, Treaty of, 149
Marillac, R. de, 86
Mark, 10-1, 37
Marlborough, J. Churchill, Duke of, 94, 158, 160, 162
Marne River, 69
Marquette, J., 85
Marseilles, 312, 357, 392
Marston Moor, 124
Martignac, 417
Martini, 313
Martinique, 193, 243-4
Martinitz, 12-3
Marx, K., 178, 266, 269
Mary I of England, 62

Mary II of England, 91
Mary of Guise, 100
Mary of Modena, 130
Mary Tudor of England, 50, 97-8
Massachusetts, 235-6, 245
Masséna, 370, 400
Matthias, Emperor, 7, 11-4
Maubeuge, 90
Maurice of Nassau, 16, 75
Mauritius, 408, 410
Maximilian II, Emperor, 7
Maximilian of Bavaria, 10-1, 15-6, 18, 20, 22, 26-7, 37
Maximilian, Joseph, 250
Mayenne, C., Duke of, 72-3, 77
Mazarin, G., Cardinal, 34-5, 37, 80-4, 117, 150, 196, 229
Mazeppa, Ivan, 160-2
Mazzini, G., 425, 428
Meaux, 67-8
Mecklenburg, 18, 20, 24, 38, 167-9, 223
Medina Sidonia, Duke of, 102-3
Mediterranean Sea, 39, 41, 45, 47-9, 54, 63, 73, 84, 90, 94-5, 175, 178, 221-2, 224, 228, 236, 246, 248, 270, 283, 287
Memel, 5
Menshikov, General, 161-2, 165
Mercator, 188
Mesta, 54
Methuen, P., 93
Metternich, Chancellor, 403, 405, 409, 411-3, 422-4
Metz, 37, 63, 81, 352
Meuse River, 63, 80, 251
Mexico, 52, 62, 182
Mexico, Gulf of, 193, 235
Michael Romanov, Tsar, 145, 148
Michigan, 282
Michigan, Lake, 246
Milan, 2-3, 10, 15, 21, 30-1, 42, 48, 56-7, 61, 63, 79, 82, 90, 92, 94, 176, 226, 229, 233-4, 391, 424
Minden, 37, 143, 239
Mingay, G. E., 268
Minorca, 61, 93, 95, 232, 236, 240, 243-4, 246
Mirabeau, 306, 321, 345-6, 348, 351-2
Mir-Ja'far, 240
Mississippi River, 193, 235, 244, 246, 282
Missouri River, 282
Mitchell, 111
Modena, 80, 250, 410, 424

Mogilev, 160
Moldavia, 163, 248, 390, 397
Molière, 96, 217
Moluccas, 191
Mompesson, 111
Moncontour, 68
Monge, Gaspard, 384
Monk, General George, 127
Monmouth, Duke of, 131
Mons, 68, 70, 92, 94
Montaigne, 217
Montauban, 68-9, 77
Montbéliard, 90
Montcalm, L. de, 240, 242-3
Montenegro, 163
Montesquieu, 296, 298, 300-4, 311, 314, 328, 353, 367
Montferrat, 21-2, 38, 56, 79
Montmorency, A. P. A. de, 65-7
Montmorency, H. de, 78
Montmorency-Damville, H. de, 69-70
Montpellier, 67, 77
Montpellier, Treaty of, 77
Montreal, 243
Montserrat, 192
Moore, Sir John, 397
Moravia, 11, 14, 37, 229
Moreau, Field Marshal, 367, 374, 403
Morellet, 306
Morelly, 303, 305, 307
Moscow, 144-5, 160-1, 328, 401-2
Moulins, 67
Mun, Thomas, 184
Munich, 25-6, 177
Münster, 32, 34-5, 38, 80, 89-90
Münster, Peace/Treaty of, 34, 38, 57
Murat, 392, 395, 398
Murillo, 52
Murray, J., 243
Muscovy, 144

Namur, 80, 92, 94
Nancy, 83
Nantes, 73-4, 77-8, 86-7, 91, 131, 152, 244
Naples, 2, 31, 39, 42, 60-2, 81, 94, 176, 212, 222, 225, 227, 250, 318, 360, 369, 374, 389, 392, 395, 398, 413, 424
Napoleon Bonaparte, 102, 157, 366-405, 408-11, 415

Napoleon III, 414, 419, 425
Narva, 144-5, 156-8, 160
Naseby, 125
Navarre, 39, 75, 202
Navarre, Henry of, 50-1
Necker, 297, 341-5, 347, 349, 357
Neerwinden, 92
Nemours, Treaty of, 71
Nelson, Admiral, 369, 388
Nérac, Peace of, 70
Netherlands, 1-4, 10-1, 14-7, 19-22, 24, 27-31, 34-5, 38, 41-2, 45, 47-54, 56-61, 63, 67-8, 70, 72, 77-9, 81, 85, 87-93, 95, 99, 101, 143, 150-3, 156-7, 164, 168, 175, 191-2, 194, 198, 221-2, 228, 231-2, 234-5, 237, 240, 245-6, 251-2, 255, 263-4, 270, 300, 326, 331, 355, 360, 365, 367, 380, 391; *see also* Holland
Netherlands, Austrian, 95, 226, 230-1, 234, 237, 238, 250-1, 360, 369, 410
Netherlands, Spanish, 62, 67, 72, 88-9, 92-4, 150, 177, 187, 219
Neuberg, 10-1
Neuburg, Mary Anne of, 60
Neva River, 158
Nevas, 192
Nevers, Duke of, 38, 56
Newcastle, Duke of, 234
Newcomen, T., 255, 260
New England, 231, 234
Newfoundland, 95, 193-4, 222, 236, 243-4, 246
New France, 193
New Orleans, 235, 244
New South Wales, 246
New Sweden, 191
Newton, Isaac, 173, 203, 205, 210-1, 215-6, 292-3, 299
New World, 182, 186, 193, 196; *see also* America
New York, 240, 280
Nice, 56, 92, 360
Nicole, P., 88
Niemen River, 5, 401-2
Nijmegen, Peace of, 50, 59, 151
Nijstadt, Peace of, 171-2, 224
Nîmes, 69, 78, 188
Nithard, 59
Noailles, A. J. de, 92
Nördlingen, 27-9, 57, 80
Norfolk, 124, 188, 264
Normandy, 65, 67-8, 71-2, 82, 86, 88, 201

453

North, Lord F., 245
North Africa, 47, 52, 54, 204
North America, 78, 85, 87, 91, 93, 95, 191-4, 221-2, 231, 234-6, 240, 242, 245-6, 270, 276, 281-4; *see also* America
North Atlantic, 101
North Sea, 4, 19-20, 23, 38, 56, 168, 264, 391-2, 398
Northumberland, 119, 188, 236
Norway, 4, 141, 146, 168-9, 171, 176, 398, 410
Norwich, 103
Nova Scotia, 93, 95, 222, 236, 246
Novgorod, 143-5
Nuremberg, 177
Nüremberg, Burgrave of, 142
Nymphenburg, Treaty of, 229

Ochakov, 249
Oder River, 38, 151, 170
Oesel, 171
Ohio, 282
Ohio River, 235-6
Oldenbarneveldt, 16
Oleg, 143
Oliva, Peace of, 150
Olivares, Viscount, 55-7
Ontario, Lake, 240, 242
Orbetello, 80
Orissa, 235
Orléannais, 202
Orleans, 66-7
Orleans, Duc d', 222-4
Orleans, Duke of, 341, 349, 363
Orleans, G. d', 78-9
Orleans, Mary of, 60
Öseland, 146
Osnabrück, 18, 32, 34-5, 80
Osnabrück, Peace/Treaty of, 32, 34-5, 155
Ostend, 224-6
Ottoman empire, 155, 370, 374, 390, 397; *see also* Turkey
Overijsel, 50
Oxenstierna, Axel, 26-7, 29-31
Oxenstierna, Bengt, 153, 157
Oxford, 131, 212-3

Pacific, 101, 228, 246
Padua, 205, 212
Palatinate, 7-8, 10, 12-8, 20, 27-8, 37, 56, 91-3, 250

Palermo, 31, 424
Pallisot, 302
Pamiers, 87
Paoli, Governor, 368
Papal States, 45, 176, 374, 388-9, 398
Papin, D., 96, 214, 257
Paris, 11, 30, 60, 63-4, 67-70, 72-5, 77, 80-2, 84, 88, 167, 176-7, 183, 207, 209-10, 213, 270, 287, 297, 308, 311-2, 332, 343, 348-50, 352-3, 355, 357-62, 365, 367, 370, 375-7, 382, 384, 389, 397, 402, 404-5, 418-9
Paris, Treaty of, 29, 77, 244-5, 247, 404, 408
Parma, 29, 224-7, 231, 250, 410, 424
Parma, Duke of, 51, 72, 102, 226
Parma, Marguerite of, 48
Parthenopean republic, 369
Pascal, 88, 96, 211, 217
Patkul, Johann, Baron Wallendorf, 155-8
Paul IV, Pope, 62, 98
Paul, Tsar, 370
Paul, V. de, 87
Pavillon, N., 87
Peel, R., 426-7
Peene River, 165
Pernambuco, 191
Persia, 85
Persia, Shah of, 54
Peru, 182
Peter I, the Great, of Russia, 5, 145, 154-8, 160-3, 165-7, 169-72, 196-7, 199, 203, 213, 221, 223, 317, 328-9
Peter III, 240
Petre, Father, 132
Petty, Sir William, 189
Philadelphia, 236
Philip II of Spain, 42-5, 47-53, 62-3, 70-2, 97, 101-2, 251
Philip III of Spain, 1, 53-5
Philip IV of Spain, 27, 55, 57-9, 83, 89
Philip V of Spain, 60, 93-5, 222-4, 232
Philip, Don, 222, 225, 229, 231-2
Philip Egalité, 341
Philippines, 243-4
Philippsburg, 37, 81
Piacenza, 224-7, 231
Picard, J., 96
Picardy, 30, 63, 70, 73, 85-6, 196
Pichegru, General, 365, 383
Piedmont, 48, 374, 386, 398, 410, 413, 424

Pillau, 5
Pillnitz, 356
Pinerolo, 38, 79, 81, 83, 92
Piombino, 80, 82
Pitt, W., the younger, 245, 251, 387
Pius IV, Pope, 45
Pius VI, Pope, 325, 352
Pius VII, Pope, 377, 384
Pius IX, Pope, 425, 428
Plassey, 240
Plate, River, 62, 244
Plato, 313
Pocock, G., 241, 243
Podolia, 247
Poissy, 66
Poitiers, 67-8, 70
Poitou, 65, 76, 82, 86
Poland, 4-5, 20, 22-4, 29-30, 69, 92-3, 141-6, 148-50, 154-8, 160-5, 167-71, 176, 179, 199, 202, 218, 224-7, 233, 237, 247-9, 356, 388-90, 401-2, 409-10
Poland-Lithuania, 145
Polish Prussia, 23
Poltava, 161-2, 165
Pombal, 319
Pombal, S. de, 243
Pomerania, 20, 23-6, 28-9, 31, 37-8, 90, 140, 143, 147-8, 150-2, 162, 164-6, 170, 238, 240
Pompadour, Madame de, 303
Pondichéry, 85, 91, 194-5, 231, 235, 242, 246
Poniatowski, S., 247
Pontchartrain, L. Phélypeaux de, 96
Pontoise, 66
Ponts-de-Cé, Les, 76
Porta, B. della, 255
Port Mahon, 93
Port Royal, 93, 193, 231
Port-Royal-des-Champs, 88
Portsmouth, 240
Portugal, 1, 31, 47, 50-1, 55, 57-8, 71, 80, 89, 93, 176, 183, 190, 192, 221, 232, 243-4, 247, 250, 319, 360, 390, 395, 397, 399, 413
Potsdam, 319
Pozharski, Prince, 145
Poznan, 249
Prague, 11, 13-6, 27-9, 31-2, 34-6, 205, 230
Prague, Peace of, 27-9, 31-2, 35-6
Pregel River, 5
Pressburg, 422

Pressburg, Peace of, 388-9, 398
Priestley, Joseph, 307
Privas, 78
Provence, 62, 64, 66, 70-2, 86, 94, 201-2, 294
Provence, Count of, 341, 364, 404
Prussia, 141-2, 148-50, 154, 158, 162, 164-72, 176, 188, 196, 202, 218, 220, 224-7, 229-33, 237-40, 247-52, 300, 313, 317-22, 324, 352, 356, 360, 365, 367, 387-91, 393, 398-400, 403-5, 408-9, 411-2, 420-1; *see also* Brandenburg-Prussia
Pruth River, 163
Ptolemy, 204
Pym, John, 110-1, 119, 121
Pyramids, 369
Pyrenees, 62-3, 75-7, 80, 93, 360, 367, 403
Pyrenees, Peace/Treaty of, 32, 58, 82, 150, 183

Quebec, 43, 62, 193, 236
Quesnay, François, 305
Quesnel, P., 88
Quiberon Bay, 243

Racine, 217
Racine, J., 96
Radetzky, 423, 425
Radishev, Alexander, 330
Radom, Confederation of, 247
Ramillies, 94
Ramolini, Letizia, 367
Rastadt, Treaty of, 96, 224
Ratisbon, 32
Ratisbon, Peace of, 90
Ravaillac, F., 75
Ravensberg, 10-1, 37
Raynal, 306, 308, 314
Regensburg, 22-3, 28, 57
Reichenbach, Agreement of, 249
Rennes, 64
Rehtel, 82
Reval, 144-5, 165
Rheinsberg, 314
Rhine, 178, 229
Rhine, Confederation of, 389, 391, 393, 398, 401, 403
Rhineland, 2, 4, 25-6, 31, 239, 262
Rhine River, 4, 10-1, 14, 25, 31, 37, 56-7, 63, 75, 80-1, 88-90, 92, 96, 151, 153, 367, 374, 403-4
Rhône River, 3, 65, 86
Richelieu, A. de, 236, 238

Richelieu, A. J. du Plessis, Cardinal, 2, 16-7, 22-31, 34, 56-7, 77-80, 84, 96, 114, 117-8, 185-6, 193, 196, 229, 319, 334, 415-6
Riga, 5, 165
Rigaud, H., 96
Rijswijk, Treaty/Peace of, 59, 92-3, 153, 194-5
Ripon, 119
Robais, J. van, 85
Robertson, William, 291
Roberval, J. F. de la Rocque de, 62
Robespierre, 305, 351, 355-6, 362-5, 368
Rochambeau, J. B. D. de, 245
Rochefort, 85-6, 180, 243
Rocroi, 31, 57, 80
Rodney, G. B., Baron, 246
Rohan, Duke of, 29-30
Rohan, H. de, 77-8, 80
Rohan-Chabot, de, 299
Rolle, 116
Romagna, 369
Roman republic, 369
Rome, 40, 45, 65, 87, 91, 97-8, 101, 119, 130-1, 144, 177, 206, 212, 287
Rooke, G., 93
Rosetta Stone, 369
Roskilde, Treaty of, 149-50
Rossbach, 238
Rostock, 20
Rouen, 64, 67, 72, 74, 188
Rousseau, Jean-Jacques, 175, 296, 302-9, 311, 313, 337, 351, 353, 363, 367
Roussilon, 80, 82
Rudolf II, Emperor, 7, 11-2
Rueil, Peace of, 82
Rügen, 38
Ruhr, 10, 188
Rupert, Prince, 124
Rurik, 143, 145
Russell, Lord, 427
Russia, 4-5, 23, 93, 96, 143-6, 148-50, 154-8, 160-5, 167-72, 176, 197, 199, 202, 218, 220-1, 223-5, 227, 230, 237-40, 245, 247-50, 306, 313-4, 317, 319, 324, 328, 330, 370, 374, 387-91, 394, 397-8, 401-3, 408-9, 411, 429

Sacramento, 244
Saint-André, J. de Albon de, 66-7
Saint-Antoine, 82
Saint-Cast, 243-4

St Christopher, 192
Saint-Cloud, 72, 370, 392
Saint-Denis, 67, 73
St Domingue, 244
Sainte-Affrigue, 77
Saint-Foy, 243
Saint-Germain, 82, 90-1
Saint-Germain, Peace of, 68-9, 151
St Helena, 191, 380, 394, 404, 418
Saint-Jean-de-Losne (Saint-Jean-Belle-Défense), 30
St Johns, 243
St John's River, 236
St Lawrence, 193
St Lawrence River, 62, 243, 246
St Lucia, 235, 243-4, 246, 408, 410
Saint-Omer, 90
Saintonge, 65, 86
St Petersburg, 158, 160-1, 163, 165, 171, 213, 230, 238, 248, 414
Saint-Pierre, Abbé de, 219
St Pierre and Miquelon, 244
Saint-Quentin, 62
St Vincent, 243
Sales, F. de, 87
Salicetti, 368
Salmasius (Claude de Saumaise), 179
Saltikov, P. 239
Saluzzo, 71, 75
Salzbach, 90
Salzburg, 388, 398
Sancerre, 69
Sancroft, Archbishop, 132
San Domingo, 408
Sans Souci, 314, 319
Saptes, 188
Saratoga, 245
Sardinia, 2, 39, 61, 63, 94, 222, 224, 229-31, 233, 365, 367, 369, 410, 425
Savary, 382
Savery, T., 189, 214, 255, 257
Savoy, 3, 14, 16-7, 29, 38, 55-6, 61, 63, 71-2, 75, 79-80, 91-5, 224, 226-7, 287, 360
Savoy, Duke of, 3, 14, 16, 38
Saxe, Maurice de, 231
Saxony, 12, 15-6, 18, 22, 24-7, 34, 37, 92-3, 154, 156-8, 162, 164, 167, 169, 188, 226, 229, 233, 237-40, 247, 390, 398, 409-10
Saxony, Elector of, 12, 18, 22, 24-7

Scandinavia, 4, 141, 152-3, 163, 167, 170-1, 188
Scania, 146, 149, 152, 163-4
Scharnhorst, 400
Schelde, 177, 189
Scheldt River, 94, 251, 360
Schiller, 308, 400
Schleswig-Holstein, 150, 164, 170
Schomberg, A. F., Duke of, 89
Schönbrunn, Treaty of, 398
Schwarzenberg, 403
Scotland, 44, 50, 66, 70-1, 78, 87, 91, 94-5, 100, 103, 107, 119, 124, 127, 135, 168, 176, 214, 223, 231, 284, 290, 292
Sebastian, Dom, 47
Sedan, 78, 82
Seine River, 254, 384
Seldon, 111
Senegal, 78, 85, 244, 246
Serbia, 163
Sète, 87
Seville, 41-2
Seville, Treaty of, 226
Shaftesbury, 297
Shirley, 107
Shirley, W., 236
Siam, 85
Siberia, 144, 330
Sicily, 2, 39, 42, 58-9, 61, 90, 222, 224-5, 227, 230, 392, 424
Siéyès, Abbot, 345-7, 370-1
Sigismund, Emperor, 142
Sigismund III of Poland and Sweden, 5, 141, 145-6, 148
Silesia, 11, 14, 37, 158, 160, 187-8, 218, 229-30, 231, 233, 237-40, 247, 249, 323-4
Siraj-ud-Daula, 240
Sistova, 248
Slavata, 12-3
Smith, Adam, 180-1, 247, 291, 399
Smolensk, 145, 149, 160, 401-2
Soissons, 224
Sophia, Electress of Hanover, 136
Sorbonne, 302-3, 312
Soubise, B. de Rohan, Prince of, 77-8
Soult, 400
Sound, 4, 17, 23, 32, 146, 149, 154, 156, 170
South America, 213, 244
Southampton, 111
South Carolina, 93

Southwold, 89
Spain, 1-4, 10-1, 13-7, 19-23, 27-31, 34-5, 38-63, 67-73, 75-6, 78-83, 88-96, 97, 99, 101, 110, 113-5, 117, 119, 150-1, 153, 176, 178, 180-1, 183, 188-92, 196, 219-33, 243-6, 250, 259, 270, 283-4, 287, 318, 360, 365, 367, 374, 388, 394-5, 397, 402, 408, 413
Spanish America, 101, 107, 225, 228, 284
Speyer, 360
Spinola brothers, 53
Spinoza, Benedictus de, 173, 195, 203, 208-10, 214, 291, 299
Srirangam, 235
Stael, Madame de, 381
Stair, Lord, 219
Stanhope, James, 169, 219, 222-4
Steenkerke, 92
Stein, Baron von, 399-400, 403
Stenay, 83
Stenbock, General, 164
Stettin, 38, 151, 165, 170
Stockholm, 165-6, 170, 207
Stockton, 278
Stolbova, Peace of, 5, 145
Strafford, Thomas Wentworth, Earl of, 111, 114, 117-8, 120
Stralsund, 20, 22, 24, 38, 151, 166
Strasburg, 37, 81, 90, 92, 96
Struensee, 319
Stuart, Charles Edward, the Young Pretender, 231, 234
Stuart, James, the Old Pretender, 93-5
Stuart, Mary, 50-1
Stuhmsdorf, Treaty of, 30
Styria, 2, 12-3, 19
Suffolk, 89, 124
Suffren-Saint Tropez, P. A. de, 246
Suleiman II, 45
Sully, 75, 187, 192
Sumatra, 191
Svenskund, 248
Swabia, 27, 142
Sweden, 4-5, 13, 17, 20, 22-32, 34-5, 37-8, 56-7, 59, 79-80, 89-91, 93-4, 140-1, 143, 145-57, 161-72, 176, 179, 188, 207, 218, 220-1, 223-5, 229, 232, 237-8, 240, 245, 247-8, 319, 321, 390, 410
Swift, 299
Switzerland, 38, 68, 71, 79, 81, 176-7, 370, 374, 380, 387-8, 410

Syria, 370
Széchényi, Count, 422

Talleyrand, 345, 404, 409, 415
Tannenberg, 142
Targowica, Confederation of, 249
Teignmouth, 91
Teschen, Peace of, 250
Teusina, Treaty of, 145
Theodor of Russia, 145
Thiers, 200, 417-8
Thionville, 83
Thomas Aquinas, 203-4
Thorn, 162, 248-9
Thorn, Perpetual Peace of, 142
Thuringia, 25
Thurot, F., 244
Ticino, 231
Ticonderoga, 243
Tilley, Count, 16, 18-9, 22-3, 25-6
Tilsit, Treaty of, 390-1, 394, 397, 399, 401
Tobago, 90, 235, 246, 408, 410
Toledo, 51
Tönnig, 164
Torbay, 91
Torcy, J. B. Colbert de, 95
Torgau, 239
Torres Vedras, 401
Torricelli, E., 255
Toul, 37, 63, 81
Toulon, 85, 94, 243, 312, 366, 368
Toulouse, 64, 310
Touraine, 202
Tournai, 89
Tours, 67, 188
Tourville, A. de Cotentin de, 91
Trafalgar, 388, 391
Transylvania, 14
Travendal, Treaty of, 156, 158, 163
Trent, 9, 62
Trevithick, R., 255
Trianon, 392-3
Trier, 79
Trier, Archbishop and Elector of, 7, 12, 37, 356
Trinidad, 374, 410
Tripoli, 45, 90
Triptow Heath, 125
Tromp, Admiral, 31
Tromp, van, 191

Trondheim, 150
Troppau, 413
Troyes, 67
Tuileries, 350, 357-8, 375, 386
Turenne, H. de la Tour d' Auvergne de, 31, 80, 82, 85, 89-90
Turgot, 299, 303, 307, 341, 399
Turin, 80, 94
Turin, Treaty of, 92
Turkey, 41, 75, 89, 91, 93, 155-6, 160-5, 167-8, 218, 220, 224, 237, 248-9, 283, 287, 408, 411; *see also* Ottoman empire
Turn, Count Matthias von, 13-14
Tuscany, 80, 82, 227, 233, 319, 398, 410
Two Sicilies, Kingdom of, 63, 233, 243, 250
Tyrol, 2-3, 188

Ukraine, 148, 155, 160-1
Ulm, 388-9
Ulrica Eleonora, 152, 169-70
United States of America, 245-7, 251, 393, 402, 405, 414; *see also* America and North America
Urban VIII, Pope, 21
Usedom, 35, 170
Utrecht, 251
Utrecht, Peace of, 35, 61, 95-6, 163-4, 218-9, 221-3, 227, 231
Utrecht, Union of, 50

Valence, 67
Valencia, 39, 55, 60, 94
Valenciennes, 68, 82, 90
Valmy, 359-60
Valois, E. de, 63
Valois, H. de, 68
Valois, M. de, 68, 75
Valromey, 75
Valtelline, 3-4, 17, 22, 29-31, 48-9, 51, 54-6, 58, 79-80
Vancouver Island, 246
Varennes, 352
Västergotland, 152
Vauban, 85, 196
Vaudreuil-Cavagnal, P. F. de Rigaud de, 243
Vaux, General de, 344
Vega, de, 52
Velasquez, 52
Vendôme, A. de, 65-7
Vendôme, C. de, 78

Vendôme, L. J. de, 94
Venice, 17, 45, 54, 176, 178, 250, 269-70, 369, 374, 392, 410, 424
Verden, 18, 38, 140, 146-7, 163, 166, 170
Verdun, 37, 63, 81, 358-9
Verela, Treaty of, 248
Vergennes, C. Gravier de, 245, 251
Vergt, 67
Vernon, 228
Verona, 177, 270
Versailles, 83, 88, 196, 230, 237-8, 254, 297, 334, 344, 348, 350
Versailles, Treaty of, 171, 238, 246, 411
Vervins, Peace of, 2, 73
Viborg, 145, 165, 171
Victor Emmanuel II, 425
Vienna, 14, 25, 27, 91, 94, 149, 170, 176, 223, 227, 237, 314, 325, 367, 369, 374, 388-9, 398, 404
Vienna, Congress of, 408, 410, 419, 422, 424
Vienna, Peace/Treaties of, 35, 225-7
Vigo, 93
Villars, A. de Brancas de, 73
Villars, C., Duke of, 94-5
Villéle, 416-7
Villeneuvette, 85
Villeroi, F. de, 94
Vimory, 71
Virginia, 236
Vistula, 160
Vivarais, 71, 85-6
Vladimir, 143-4
Voltaire, 42, 175, 210, 240, 242, 296, 299-300, 302-4, 306-7, 309, 311, 313-4, 319-21, 323, 327, 337-8, 367, 381
Vorstka, 161

Wagram, 398
Wales, 176, 284-5
Wallachia, 163, 248, 390, 397
Wallenstein, Albrecht von, 19-21, 23, 25-7
Wallis, John, 213
Walpole, 223, 225-30
Wandiwash, 242
Warburg, 239
Warsaw, 149, 157, 249, 390, 398, 401, 409
Wartburg, 420
Washington, G., 236, 245
Wassy, 66
Waterloo, 252, 284, 404-5, 415

Watt, J., 255, 257, 260-1, 271-2, 277, 282, 285
Weber, Max, 178
Wehlau, Treaty of, 149
Wellington, Duke of, 394-5, 397, 400-1, 403, 405, 413
Wentworth, Peter, 106, 110, 115
Weser River, 17, 38
West Africa, 193, 235, 243-4, 246
Western Galicia, 398, 401
Western Pomerania, 37-8, 150-1, 162, 165, 172
West Indies, 78, 85, 89-91, 93, 95, 183, 190-4, 213, 221, 228, 234-5, 243-4, 246, 283-4
Westminster, 125, 245
Westminster, Convention of, 238
Westphalia, 239, 380, 390, 398
Westphalia, Peace of, 1, 29, 32, 35-8, 57-8, 81, 83, 140, 146-7, 174, 360
West Prussia, 142, 162, 248
Whitehall, 125
Whitehaven, 245-6
White Mountain, 16, 37
White Sea, 144
Wieland, 320
Wilhelmina of the Netherlands, 251
Wilkinson, J., 257
William of Orange, 15, 48-9, 68, 70, 101
William III of Orange and England, 89, 91-2, 95, 132-9, 152, 160, 181, 192
William IV, Stadtholder, 232
William V, Stadtholder, 251-2
Winckelmann, 320
Windischgrätz, 423
Wismar, 20, 38, 140, 166, 168
Wittstock, 31
Wolfe, J., 243
Wolfgang William, Duke of Neuberg, 10-1
Wollin, 38, 170
Worms, 360
Worms, Treaty of, 230
Wren, Sir Christopher, 213
Wright, Edward, 188
Württemberg, 387-8
Württenbach, Duke of, 37
Wüsterhause, Treaty of, 225

Xanten, Treaty of, 11, 37

York, 123
Yorkshire, 187-8, 267

459

Yorktown, 245
Ypres, 90

Zabern, 37
Zealand, 156
Zeeland, 50
Zemski Sobor, 145

Zips, 248
Zollern, 142
Zorndorf, 238
Zurich, 270
Zutphen, 101
Zweibrücken, 90-1